third edition

international business

THE CHALLENGES OF GLOBALIZATION

John J. Wild
UNIVERSITY OF WISCONSIN, MADISON

Kenneth L. Wild
UNIVERSITY OF LONDON, ENGLAND

Jerry C.Y. Han
UNIVERSITY OF HONG KONG

PEARSON

Prentice
Hall

UPPER SADDLE RIVER, NEW JERSEY 07458

Library of Congress Cataloging-in-Publication Data

Wild, John J.
    International business : the challenges of globalization / John J. Wild, Kenneth L. Wild, Jerry
C.Y. Han. –3rd ed.
        p. cm.
    Includes bibliographical references and index.
    ISBN 0-13-143275-3
        1. International business enterprises—Management. 2. International trade. I. Wild, Kenneth L.
II. Han, Jerry C.Y. III. Title.

HD62.4.W586 2005
658'.049—dc22

2004060033

Acquisitions Editor: David Parker
VP/Editorial Director: Jeff Shelstad
Editorial Assistant: Denise Vaughn
Media Project Manager: Jessica Sabloff
Marketing Manager: Anke Braun
Marketing Assistant: Patrick Danzuso
Senior Managing Editor (Production): Judy Leale
Production Editor: Mary Ellen Morrell
Permissions Coordinator: Charles Morris
Associate Director, Manufacturing: Vincent Scelta
Production Manager: Arnold Vila
Manufacturing Buyer: Arnold Vila
Design Director: Maria Lange
Interior Design: Michael Fruhbeis
Cover Design: Michael Fruhbeis
Cover Photo: Grant Symon/The Image Bank/Getty Images, Inc.
Illustrator (Interior): ElectraGraphics
Photo Researcher: Maryann Price
Manager, Print Production: Christy Mahon
Composition/Full-Service Project Management: Pre-Press Company, Inc.
Printer/Binder: Courier-Kendallville

Credits and acknowledgments borrowed from other sources and reproduced, with permission, in
this textbook appear on page 473.

Pearson Education LTD.
Pearson Education Singapore, Pte. Ltd
Pearson Education, Canada, Ltd
Pearson Education–Japan

Pearson Education Australia PTY, Limited
Pearson Education North Asia Ltd
Pearson Educación de Mexico, S.A. de C.V.
Pearson Education Malaysia, Pte. Ltd

10 9 8 7 6 5
ISBN 0-13-143275-3

Wild Wild Han

third edition

international business
THE CHALLENGES OF GLOBALIZATION

Brief Contents

Contents

Preface

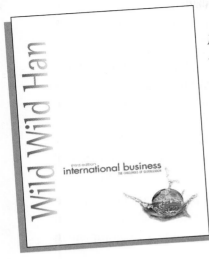

Welcome to the third edition of *International Business: The Challenges of Globalization*. As in the previous two editions, this book is the product of extensive market surveys, chapter reviews, and correspondence with instructors and students. We are delighted that an overwhelming number of instructors, students, and practitioners agree with our approach to understanding and conducting international business. The reception of this book in the United States and across the world has exceeded all expectations.

This best-selling textbook continues to attract instructors and students to international business. We appreciate the valuable comments from both instructors and students on the first two editions that helped make this book a bestseller. This text is successful because it presents international business in a comprehensive, yet concise framework with unrivaled clarity of expression. Recent, real-world examples and engaging features bring the concepts of international business to life. Feedback tells us the reason this book is so popular is that it offers a fresh approach to international business that responds to the needs of both instructors and students. A main goal in this third edition is to continue the tradition of delivering the most *readable, current,* and *concise* international business textbook on the market.

With each passing moment, the world of business changes in important ways. To keep up with this rapid change, many chapter-opening vignettes are either *new* or *updated*, many chapter-closing cases are either *new* or *updated*, and each chapter contains plenty of *new* real-world examples, *new* feature boxes, and *new* exercises. We also know that international business is rich in people, culture, geography, politics, economics, and other human and environmental dynamics—it is not simply about "how to make a profit in other countries." This edition continues to draw upon this richness and go beyond a "U.S.-centric" outlook by taking a global perspective and presenting international business as it genuinely is—a dynamic and rich subject.

What's New in the Third Edition?

New Chapter 1 Titled, "Globalization" **Chapter 1 is completely new and now centers on globalization.** This chapter begins by describing the globalization of markets and production, the drivers behind globalization, and recent attempts to measure how "global" nations are. These topics are followed by detailed coverage of each main argument in the globalization debate. At key points in the debate, we explain which side has the most compelling evidence to date, or declare the debate fairly even at this time. We close the chapter with a unique model that helps students conceptualize the global business environment.

Market Entry Strategy Simulation This *new interactive simulation* asks students to analyze a country in which to introduce a new product. Four activities are available which build on one another:

○ *The Market Intelligence Report (MIR)* is a structured learning experience for students to gather resources and assemble baseline market data to evaluate a prospective national market. This report includes information on the nation's people, economy, government, and technological status.

○ *The Business Environment Analysis Report (BEAR)* gives students the opportunity to analyze a selected country as a potential market. This experiential exercise is designed for groups of students to complete in about 4–6 weeks.

○ *The Report on Opportunities for Market Entry (ROME)* asks students to identify potential import and export prospects for a firm in the chosen national market. This experiential exercise is designed for groups of students to complete in about 6–8 weeks.

○ *The Market Entry Strategy Assignment (MESA)* is a critical and creative thinking exercise for students to develop a "Market Entry Strategy" for launching a new product in a selected country. This group experience is designed for students to complete throughout the course.

Web-based Update To keep this text up-to-date with the rapid changes occurring in international business, we publish a *Web-based Update* one year after this book's initial publication. Organized by chapter, it updates all key maps and tables, as well as important events in the areas of globalization, emerging markets, trade and investment, geopolitical events, currency markets, and much more. ***Look for the "International Business Update" in January 2006!***

Global Challenges Each chapter in Parts I and II of the text contains a *new feature box* titled, "Global Challenges" that presents **topical, high-interest issues on the theme of globalization.** This feature expands on issues addressed in the chapter by identifying obstacles confronting the world that require concerted, global solutions. Matters of culture and ethics are also sometimes addressed in these feature boxes. For example, Chapter 4 presents "Public Health Goes Global," which reports on the human and economic devastation HIV/AIDS, malaria, and tuberculosis cause worldwide and what can be done. This feature includes a *"Want To Know More?"* section containing Web sites *for students to locate further information on the topic.*

Breaking Views Each chapter in Parts I and II of the text contains a *new feature box* titled, "Breaking Views" that **presents ways in which technology is impacting international business.** Some feature boxes discuss how a specific technology is affecting international business activities, while others explain how technology is reshaping the lives of consumers worldwide. For instance, Chapter 1 presents "The E-Biz Surprise," which tells how eBay, Eli Lilly, Expedia, and Dell each used the Internet to create lasting change in their industries. This feature reinforces another of this book's main themes—*technology*.

Bottom Line for Business Chapters 1 through 10 contain *new closing sections* titled, "Bottom Line for Business." These chapters present the national and international business environments, as opposed to international business *management* in Chapters 11 through 16. These new closing sections explain how issues explored in the chapter affect managers and their firms' policies, strategies, and activities abroad. Some of these sections present the latest research by those on the cutting edge of world business.

Quick Study Each chapter contains a *new feature* titled, "Quick Study" that consists of concept checks inserted at appropriate points in the text. These are designed for students to verify they have retained the section's key terms and important concepts. This feature allows students to pause and reflect on what has been learned before going on to the next section of material.

> *Quick Study*
>
> 1. How does *totalitarianism* differ from democracy? Identify its three main features.
> 2. Explain each of the different forms of totalitarianism.
> 3. Identify the economic and social costs of civil war, and potential solutions to such conflicts.
> 4. How might a totalitarian government affect business activities?

Important New and Updated Information for the Third Edition!

In addition to an entirely new Chapter 1, there are several important updates and modifications made to various chapters. They include the following:

○ Chapter 2 contains an expanded discussion of globalization's influence on culture. New topics include how endangered languages are faring in this age of globalization, and how developing and emerging markets are overcoming the global digital divide in material culture.

○ Chapter 3 contains new material on how nations are trying to become business-friendly by implementing e-government, and the economic and human cost of civil strife in poor nations. Updates are provided on how economic and political turmoil in Latin America is undermining support for democracy there, and how terrorism is increasing the cost of international logistics. This chapter also now contains the topics of ethics and social responsibility (moved here from Chapter 1), and closes with a new case study on global counterfeiting.

○ Chapter 4 updates the recent experiences of two big emerging markets—China and Russia—and discusses North Korea's dabbling in market economics. Newly presented are the negative economic impacts of communicable diseases, and how investment in information technology benefits productivity and national economic development.

○ Chapters 5, 6, and 7 present recent data on the volumes and patterns of international trade and investment flows, and discuss the effects of the recent global economic slowdown. Progress of the current "Doha Round" of trade negotiations within the framework of the World Trade Organization is also examined.

○ Chapter 8 discusses opportunities and challenges facing the European Union after its unprecedented expansion in May 2004 when it absorbed 10 new members—yielding a European Union of 25 nations today. Coverage of the European Union single currency, the euro, also is moved here from Chapter 10.

○ Chapter 9 updates the falling value of the dollar on currency markets and tells how this has affected companies' export, import, and production operations across the globe.

○ Chapter 10 examines Argentina's efforts toward economic reform and describes attempts to restructure global institutions such as the IMF and World Bank.

○ Chapters 11 through 16 contain new or updated chapter-opening company profiles, updated case studies, a host of new exercise material, and recent in-text examples where appropriate. This group of chapters also focuses more on strategy than in previous editions and offers readers a more streamlined presentation.

Hallmark Features of *International Business*

Culture Early and Often Culture is a fundamental element of all international business activity. This book's presentation of culture is unrivaled (see graph on inside front cover). Culture appears early (Chapter 2) and is integrated throughout the text, which is partly accomplished by opening each chapter with a culture-rich company profile (see Chapters 1, 2, and 3). Culture is also integrated within each chapter through lively examples of how differences in culture affect international business activities. Feedback tells us covering culture in this way fosters enthusiasm among students for chapter material because it illustrates how concepts relate to the real world.

Accessible A successful book for the first course in international business must be accessible to students. Conceptual material and specialized business activities are described in concrete, straightforward terms and are appropriately illustrated (see Chapters 5, 9, and 10). For instance, we introduce the concepts of absolute and comparative advantage in Chapter 5 with a discussion of whether Tiger Woods should install his own hot tub or let a professional installer perform the job! Our goal—presenting complex material in an accessible manner—is reflected throughout the text. We are convinced that students who use a more readable international business book will better master the material.

Global Perspective Appreciating the dynamic nature of the global marketplace requires an unbiased approach to international business. Feedback on the first two editions shows that this is the only international business book written from a truly global perspective. Rather than take sides in key debates, this book presents the viewpoints of each group or culture involved. This goal was achieved by members of an author team having collective expertise in three major economic regions of the world—Asia, Europe, and North America. Interesting examples

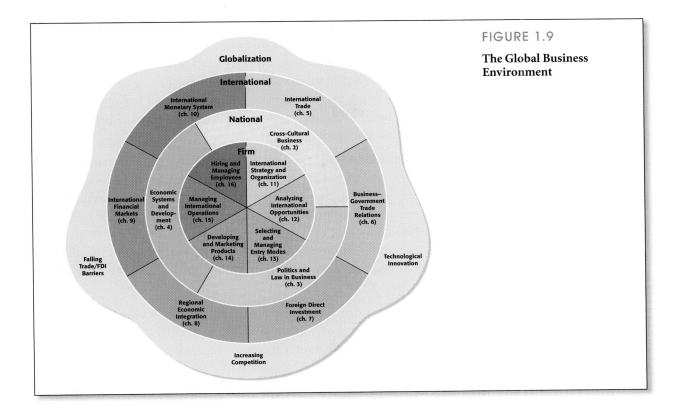

FIGURE 1.9

The Global Business
Environment

from around the world illustrate the experiences of real companies so students see
both what worked and what did not.

Integrative International business is not simply a collection of separate business functions and environmental forces. Instead, it occurs within a dynamic, integrated system that weaves together *national business environments*, the *international business environment*, and *international business management*—all interacting in an age of *globalization*. The model pictured above (and presented in Chapter 1) lays the foundation for an integrated approach to international business. This unique organizing framework helps students understand the complexities of international business and how its elements are related. It also illustrates the forces of globalization (*technological innovation* and *falling trade and investment barriers*) as influencing each element in the model and *increasing competition* for all firms everywhere.

Innovative Pedagogy

Entrepreneur's Survival Kit Each chapter contains a box feature titled, "Entrepreneur's Survival Kit" to underscore the important role entrepreneurs and small businesses play in our global economy. A favorite of instructors and students in previous editions, many of these features provide tips and advice for entrepreneurs and small businesses when expanding abroad. Key Web sites are often included so students can independently learn more about topics presented. Entrepreneurial and small business issues are also woven into the content of each chapter.

Global Manager's Toolbox Each chapter contains a box feature titled, "Global Manager's Toolbox" to expand on issues discussed in the text that pose special problems for today's manager. Popular with readers in earlier editions, many of these contain specific tools and techniques useful to global managers—such as how to cope when experiencing culture shock in an unfamiliar culture. This feature drives home relevant, down-to-earth lessons learned by veterans of international business management.

Full-Color World Atlas Our experience, and that of most international business instructors, tells us many students are inadequately prepared in geography for their first course in international business. In response, this book includes, as a primer and reference, a full-color world atlas as an appendix to Chapter 1. Students are able to test their knowledge of the global landscape by completing 20 questions accompanying the atlas. Important issues regarding world geography and their impact on international business are also integrated throughout the book and its assignment materials.

Beacons Students learn better when provided with a "roadmap" that shows how chapters and topics relate to one another. Therefore, this book contains "Beacons" at the start of each chapter to reinforce the interrelatedness of topics across chapters. Appropriately titled "A Look Back," "A Look at This Chapter," and "A Look Ahead," these signposts provide a structure for students as they advance through the book.

Learning Objectives with Corresponding Summaries Learning objectives are designed to focus on the main lessons students should take away from their study of chapter material. Each chapter also includes summaries that correspond exactly to the chapter's learning objectives.

Chapter-Opening Vignettes Brief, engaging company profiles launch each chapter. These vignettes are designed to pique students' interest, rather than bog them down in fine details. We find students are motivated to turn the page and read on when given short, interesting introductions to subsequent material.

Tools for Active Learning Feedback on previous editions shows that this book has more—and more useful—end-of-chapter assignment material than any other international business book. Well-planned assignment materials span the full range of complexity to test students' knowledge and ability to apply key principles. They are often experiential in nature to help students develop international business skills and make business decisions. Assignment material includes:

❍ "Talk It Over" exercises raise important issues currently confronting entrepreneurs, international managers, policymakers, consumers, and others. They can be used as the basis for in-class discussion or as homework assignments.

❍ "Teaming Up" exercises take students beyond the text and require them to collaborate in teams or proceed through a role-playing exercise. Some of these ask students to engage in an in-class debate or presentation, or conduct an interview with a local business manager.

❍ "Take It to the Web" exercises ask students to conduct brief research assignments using the Internet as a key resource. Students are sometimes sent to specific Web sites to research a single company, or asked to locate information on their own using the Web.

◎ "Ethical Challenges" exercises ask students to consider the ethical dimensions of managerial decisions. Revised by Chris Robertson of Northeastern Univeristy, and now in the new format of "You are the ...", students must assume the role of a manager, government official, or someone else and make a decision based on the facts presented to them.

◎ "Practicing International Management" cases let students analyze the responses of real-world companies to the issues, problems, and opportunities discussed in that chapter.

Dynamic Art and Maps Program Vibrant maps convey and reinforce the location of important places and supplement key concepts with visual learning aids. Colorful charts and figures help students grasp and assimilate important information. Strategically placed color photos add value to the text by providing students with a look at life and work around the world, and are tied to the text with substantive captions. Important terms are boldfaced in the text, defined in the margin, identified as "Key Terms" at the end of each chapter, and assembled in a comprehensive glossary at the end of the book.

The Plan of *International Business*

This book's coverage of international business follows a logical, step-by-step approach to building students' knowledge of the global business environment. In Part I (Chapter 1), we learn how *globalization* is transforming our world—affecting both the national and international business environments and all aspects of international business management. A unique model of the global business environment is presented as an organizing framework for students to grasp the complexities and interrelations of international business.

In Part II (Chapters 2–4), we explore *national business environments*, showing how culture, politics, law, and economics differ from one nation to another. This material is placed early in the text because national differences help frame subsequent topics and discussions—such as how companies modify business practices and strategies when operating across cultures and in differing political, legal, and economic systems.

We investigate major components of the *international business environment* in Part III (Chapters 5–8) and Part IV (Chapters 9–10). Presented are theories of trade and investment and why governments intervene in these two pillars of international business activity. The process of regional economic integration sweeping the globe is examined and its implications for international companies are outlined. We also learn how global financial markets and the international monetary

---

ETHICAL CHALLENGES

1. You are an executive for a U.S. oil firm interested in forming a partnership with an Iranian oil producer. This will be a challenge because of the poor relations between the U.S. and Iran over the years. Since the early 1980s the United States has drawn fire from the business community for imposing economic sanctions (similar to an embargo) against Iran for primarily political reasons. Those sanctions disallow international trade and investment between U.S. and Iranian businesspeople. Business leaders in the United States would like the sanctions removed so they can be included in lucrative Iranian oil and gas deals in which firms from other countries are engaging. Other sanction opponents wonder if a policy of offering "all stick and no carrot" is undermining social and political change in Iran, since the offending regime goes largely unpunished. What arguments do you present to the U.S. government for removing sanctions on Iran? Do you think that one country, acting alone, can bring about reforms through the use of economic sanctions or embargoes?

2. You are the Vice President of a sugar company based in southern Florida. Your firm is struggling lately to meet demand because of poor harvests in the Caribbean Islands where your firm sources much of its raw product. Because of the Helms–Burton Act and the U.S. embargo on Cuba, your firm is not allowed to trade with Cuba. If the embargo were dropped, your firm would have an excellent source of cheap sugar, and profits would improve significantly. A U.S. senator from your state of Florida serves on an influential committee in Washington, D.C., that is reviewing the status of the embargo on Cuba. What arguments would you provide to your senator that could potentially help eliminate this trade barrier?

3. You are a consultant advising the World Trade Organization (WTO) on the U.S. Supreme Court decision regarding the State of Massachusetts and the country of Myanmar. A nonprofit trade and industry group, the National Foreign Trade Council (NFTC), based in Washington, D.C., won a court battle in 2000 against the State of Massachusetts. In a unanimous decision, the U.S. Supreme Court sided with the NFTC and struck down a Massachusetts law that was designed to deny state contracts to any company doing business in Myanmar. The Court ruled that the Massachusetts law intruded on the federal government's authority and was preempted by federal law regarding Myanmar. In fact, the U.S. Constitution states that, "foreign policy is exclusively reserved for the federal government." The NFTC says it shares concern over human rights abuses occurring in Myanmar, but believes that a coordinated, multinational effort would be most effective at instilling change in the nation.
   What advice would you provide the WTO on this issue? Do you think that companies should be penalized in their domestic business dealings because of where they do business abroad? Do you think that the World Trade Organization should get into domestic/international political matters? Why or why not? What do you think would be the effect on domestic firms if every state were allowed to punish firms based on their own foreign policy ideals?

system function, and show how they influence companies' international business activities.

In Part V (Chapters 11–16), ways in which *international business management* differs from managing a purely domestic company are examined. We learn how a firm creates a strategy and organizes itself for international business, how it analyzes and selects markets to enter, and how it chooses an appropriate entry mode. Also described are ways in which specific business activities—developing and marketing products, managing international operations, and managing human resources—differ in the international business environment.

Additional Teaching and Learning Support

⊙ OneKey Online Courses
OneKey offers the best teaching and learning online resources all in one place. OneKey is all instructors need to plan and administer their course. OneKey is all students need for anytime, anywhere access to online course material. Conveniently organized by textbook chapter, these resources save instructors time and help students to reinforce and apply what they have learned. OneKey for convenience, simplicity, and success. *OneKey is available in three course management platforms: Blackboard, CourseCompass, and WebCT.*

For the student:

⊙ Market Entry Strategy Project created by David C. Wyld, of Southeastern Louisiana University. This assignment is an interactive electronic project appropriate for use at both the undergraduate and graduate levels. It stresses the four themes emphasized throughout the text: globalization, technology/e-business, and culture. To be completed by small groups of students, the project has four options based on the time and intensity instructors wish to devote to it.

⊙ Learning Modules that include section reviews, learning activities and pre- and post-tests.

⊙ Student PowerPoints are easy-to-print black and white PowerPoints.

⊙ Research Navigator consists of four exclusive databases of reliable source content to help students understand the research process and complete assignments.

⊙ OneKey is all students need for anytime, anywhere access to online course material. Conveniently organized by textbook chapter, these resources help students to reinforce and apply what they have learned.

For the Instructor:

The Instructor's Resource Center, available on CD, at www.prenhall.com, or in your OneKey online course, provides a variety of presentation and classroom resources. Instructors can collect materials, edit them to create powerful class lectures, and upload them to their preferred online course management system. With the Instructor's Resource Center on CD-ROM, instructors can create custom presentations and export desired files to a hard drive for use in classroom presentations and online courses.

The Instructor's Resource Center contains the following resources:

O PowerPoints

There are two versions of the Instructor's PowerPoints available with this text. The first is a fully developed set of PowerPoints. The second is an essential grab-and-go version of the first set of PowerPoints.

O TestGen Test-generating Software

The test bank contains approximately 100 questions per chapter including multiple-choice, true/false, fill-in, and essay questions. A print version is also available.

O Instructor's Manual

This is a complete instructor's toolkit. Among its many teaching aids, this manual provides a section on cooperative learning, as well as suggested exercise solutions. A print version is also available.

O Test Item File *(Word file)*

Companion Website

The text Web site www.prenhall.com/wild features chapter quizzes and student PowerPoints, which are available for review or can be conveniently printed three-to-a-page for in-class note taking.

Video Cases

Videos are included on topics such as the globalization debate, the impact of culture on business, global business and ethics, foreign direct investment, selected emerging markets, and understanding entry modes.

Financial Times

Financial Times offers student subscriptions for $10.00 when professors adopt a FT/Wild/Wild/Han text value-pack. Participating professors qualify for a complimentary one-year personal subscription to Financial Times ($298 value at regular subscription rates).

ACKNOWLEDGMENTS

We extend a special thank you to the following professors who comprised a special reviewer panel for the third edition. Each of these professors assisted us in developing the design, content, supplements and our new Market Entry Strategy simulation:

Hadi S. Alhorr	Drake University
George Barnes	University of Texas at Dallas
Richard Brisebois	Everglades University
Robert Engle	Quinnipiac University
M. Anaam Hashmi	Minnesota State University at Mankato
Joseph W. Leonard	Miami University (Ohio)

We are grateful for the encouragement, suggestions, and counsel provided by many instructors, professionals, and students in preparing this third edition of *International Business*. We especially thank the following individuals who provided valuable comments and suggestions to improve this and previous editions:

Madan Annavarjula	Northern Illinois University
Wendell Armstrong	Central Virginia Community College
Mernoush Banton	Florida International University
Constance Bates	Florida International University
Marca Marie Bear	University of Tampa
Tope A. Bello	East Carolina University
Martin Calkins	Santa Clara University
Kenichiro Chinen	California State University at Sacramento
Derrick Chong	Royal Holloway, University of London, UK
Randy Cray	University of Wisconsin at Stevens Point
Teck Yong Eng	King's College London, University of London, UK
Herbert B. Epstein	University of Texas at Tyler
Blair Farr	Jarvis Christian College
Stanley Flax	St. Thomas University
Ronelle Genser	Devry University
Carolina Gomez	University of Houston
Jorge A. Gonzalez	University of Wisconsin at Milwaukee
Kenneth R. Gray	Florida A&M University
James Gunn	Berkeley College
James Halteman	Wheaton College
Alan Hamlin	Southern Utah University
Charles Harvey	University of the West of England, UK
Les Jankovich	San Jose State University
R. Sitki Karahan	Montana State University

Ki Hee Kim	William Paterson University
James S. Lawson Jr.	Mississippi State University
Ian Lee	Carleton University
Carol Lopilato	California State University at Dominguez Hills
Donna Weaver McCloskey	Widener University
John L. Moore	Oregon Institute of Technology
Rod Oglesby	Southwest Baptist University
Susan Peterson	Scottsdale Community College
Janis Petronis	Tarleton State University
William Piper	William Piedmont College
Abe Qastin	Lakeland College
C. Richard Scott	Metropolitan State College of Denver
Coral R. Snodgrass	Canisius College
John Stanbury	George Mason University
William A. Stoever	Seton Hall University
Kenneth R. Tillery	Middle Tennessee State University
Paula Weber	St. Cloud State University
James E. Welch	Kentucky Wesleyan College
Steve Werner	University of Houston
David C. Wyld	Southeastern Louisiana University

It takes a dedicated group of individuals to take a textbook from first draft to final manuscript. We would like to thank our partners at Pearson Prentice Hall for their tireless efforts in bringing the third edition of this book to fruition. Special thanks on this project go to Editor, David Parker; Production Editor, Mary Ellen Morrell, and Managing Editor for Production, Judy Leale; Editorial Director, Jeff Shelstad; Director of Marketing, Eric Frank, and Marketing Manager, Anke Braun; Editorial Assistant, Denise Vaughn; and Designer, Mike Fruhbeis.

A Final Word

We believe that international business is a rich and dynamic subject. As instructors, one of our challenges is to instill in our students a passion for international business. Another is to give our students every advantage possible in the global marketplace. As authors, our primary mission in writing *International Business* is to equip today's student with the passion, skills, and knowledge necessary to compete in the global marketplace. We trust that you share our mission. It is our view that quality instructional materials, particularly this textbook, greatly assist us in achieving that shared mission.

John J. Wild
Kenneth L. Wild
Jerry C.Y. Han

About the Authors

As a team, John Wild, Kenneth Wild, and Jerry Han provide a blend of skills uniquely suited to writing an international business textbook. They combine award-winning teaching and research with a global view of business gained through years of living and working in cultures around the world. Together, they make the topic of international business practical, accessible, and enjoyable.

John J. Wild John J. Wild is the Robert and Monica Beyer Distinguished Professor of Business at the University of Wisconsin at Madison. He previously held appointments at the University of Manchester in England and Michigan State University. He received his B.B.A., M.S., and Ph.D. from the University of Wisconsin at Madison.

Teaching business courses at both the undergraduate and graduate levels, Professor Wild has received several teaching honors, including the Mabel W. Chipman Excellence-in-Teaching Award, the Teaching Excellence Award from the 2003 graduation class, and the Beta Alpha Psi Excellence in Teaching Award. He is a prior recipient of national research fellowships from KPMG Peat Marwick and the Ernst and Young Foundation. Professor Wild is also a frequent speaker at universities and at national and international conferences.

The author of more than 50 publications, in addition to four best-selling textbooks, Professor Wild conducts research on a wide range of topics, including corporate governance, capital markets, and financial analysis and forecasting. He is an active member of several national and international organizations, including the Academy of International Business, and has served as Associate Editor or editorial board member for several prestigious journals.

Kenneth L. Wild Kenneth L. Wild is affiliated with the University of London, England. He previously taught at the Pennsylvania State University. He received his Ph.D. from the University of Manchester (UMIST) in England and his B.S. and M.S. degrees from the University of Wisconsin. Dr. Wild also undertook postgraduate work at École des Affairs Internationale in Marseilles, France.

Having taught students of international business, marketing, and management at both the undergraduate and graduate levels, Dr. Wild is a dedicated contributor to international business education. An active member of several national and international organizations, including the Academy of International Business, he has spoken at major universities and at national and international conferences in Austria, Britain, Kuwait, Portugal, and the United States.

Dr. Wild's research, on a range of international business topics including market entry modes, country risk, and international expansion strategies, have taken him to countries spanning the globe. Additionally, he serves as an Associate Editor of the *Middle East Business Review*.

Jerry C.Y. Han Jerry C.Y. Han, who passed away September 26, 2002, was Pong Ding Yuen Professor at the University of Hong Kong School of Business, where he was Director of the School's China Management Programs. He also held appointments at several Chinese Universities, including Beijing University and Renmin University. Professor Han previously held faculty appointments at the University of Buffalo, Hong Kong University of Science and Technology (HKUST), Michigan State University, and National Chung Hsing University. He received his Bachelors degree from National Chung Hsing University, Masters degree from National Chengchi University, and Ph.D. from the University of Buffalo.

Professor Han was a highly recognized teacher, known for his commitment and creativity in business education. He was a prior recipient of research fellowships from the government of Hong Kong, HKUST, Price Waterhouse, and National Chengchi University. Dr. Han was actively involved in several national and international organizations, including serving as President of the North American Chinese Association.

The author of more than 40 publications on various business topics, including international regulatory and disclosure issues, Professor Han served on the editorial boards of several prestigious journals. He also consulted with international companies and government agencies, as well as taught business courses for international companies across several industries.

learning objectives

After studying this chapter, you should be able to

1. Describe the process of *globalization* and how it affects *markets* and *production.*

2. Identify the *two forces* causing globalization to increase.

3. Summarize the evidence for each main argument in the *globalization debate.*

4. Identify the *types of companies* that participate in international business.

5. Describe the *global business environment* and identify its four main elements.

globalization

Part 1   Global Business Environment

1

a look at **this chapter**

This chapter defines the scope of international business and introduces us to some of its most important topics. We begin by presenting globalization—describing its influence on markets and production and the forces behind its growth. Each main argument in the debate over globalization is also analyzed in detail. We then identify the key players in international business today. This chapter closes with a model that depicts international business as occurring within an integrated global business environment.

a look **ahead**

Part II, encompassing CHAPTERS 2, 3, and 4, introduces us to different national business environments. CHAPTER 2 describes important cultural differences among nations. CHAPTER 3 examines different political and legal systems. CHAPTER 4 presents the world's various economic systems and issues surrounding economic development.

Rockin' Globalization

LONDON, England—MTV is American, right? Well, yes, in the United States it is. But in Italy it's Italian, and in China, it's Chinese. Perhaps no company has done a better job of taking its product to the world while absorbing the cultures of other nations. "We've had very little resistance once we explain that we're not in the business of exporting American culture," says Bill Roedy, president of MTV Networks International (*www.mtv.com/mtvinternational*). Roedy (shown here with Jolin Tsai, and Lena and Yulia of "Tatu") even wined and dined Cuban leader Fidel Castro, who wondered if MTV could teach young Cubans the English language.

MTV's policy of airing around 75 percent local programming demonstrates its deep sensitivity to other cultures. By promoting local cultural tastes and musical talent, each international channel remains true to MTV's philosophy to "think globally, act locally." Yet each station benefits from the integrity of the MTV trademark, as well as MTV's overall programming style. MTV Networks International (MTV's London-based, non-U.S. operations) reaches more than 340 million households in 140 countries through 31 localized TV channels and 17 Web sites.

While providing local musicians with the publicity to achieve mass popularity, MTV is increasing the regional and global reach of local music. Producers and veejays keep MTV's offerings fresh by constantly scouring local markets for top talent. Colombian singer, Shakira, was largely unknown outside Latin America until she recorded an MTV

Unplugged program in 1999, and Taiwanese pop star Jolin Tsai gained popularity in mainland China after airplay on MTV. MTV also helped make Indonesia's traditional music, called *Dangdut,* cool with young people.

MTV is a global brand that has gone local, while taking local music to the world. As you read this chapter, consider globalization's effect on the marketing and production of all sorts of products, and how the globalization debate is "rocking" our world.[1]

O ur world is undergoing profound change of unparalleled magnitude. *Globalization* is leading us into uncharted territory, and no aspect of society will remain unaffected. Our cultures are no longer strictly our own, but absorb the traits and practices of others in sometimes distant lands. Our politicians and media have acquired a new vocabulary—sprinkling their speeches and writings with words and terms such as outsourcing, supranational institutions, emerging markets, sustainable development, strategic alliance, and corporate social responsibility. Our nations' economies and standards of living also are being affected—some for the better, some for the worse. Certain nations considered formidable competitors in the global economy appear to have stumbled, while others seem to have just joined the race. The consequence of all this change is the fundamental transformation of our cultures and our political, legal, and economic systems.

Our world of business also is experiencing unprecedented, permanent change. In the past, large companies produced goods mainly in the home market, exported them to the world, and kept much of their wealth at home to enrich the citizens of the home nation. But today, companies approach the decision of where to locate production activities from a global perspective because their markets are also global. Large and small firms alike are relocating or outsourcing production to cost-effective locations as never before. Jobs created in those locations increase the incomes of local people, who themselves become new potential customers. The multinational production and sale of goods and services force international firms to be good citizens wherever they conduct business. Meanwhile, regional and global trade agreements continue to encourage cross-border trade and investment between member nations. All these commercial transformations are causing seismic shifts in the global pattern of trade and investment.

Technology Makes It Happen Perhaps the most remarkable facilitator of these societal and commercial changes is technology, and how people and firms use it in going about their activities. People are using technology to reach out to the world on the Internet—accessing information and purchasing all kinds of goods and services. Companies are using technology to source their materials and products as easily from Ankara, Turkey, as from Anchorage, Alaska. And technology makes these cities equally accessible as markets for the sale of goods and services.

When consumers or firms use technology to conduct transactions they engage in **e-business (e-commerce)**—the purchase, sale, or exchange of goods and services, as well as servicing customers, collaboration with business partners, and transactions within a company via computer networks. Remember those starry-eyed predictions that the value of e-business (business and consumer transactions) would reach $1.4 trillion by 2003? Actually, the value of all e-business activity totaled nearly $2.5 trillion! As one industry analyst put it, "The hype is gone, but the numbers are in."[2] This chapter's Breaking Views feature titled, "The E-Biz Surprise," presents several companies that used the Internet to create lasting change in their industries.

International Business Involves Us All Each of us experiences the result of dozens of international transactions every day. The General Electric alarm clock/radio (*www.ge.com*) that woke you was likely made in *China.* The breaking news buzzing in your ears was produced by *Britain's* BBC radio (*www.bbc.co.uk*). You slip on your Adidas sandals (*www.adidas.com*) made in *Indonesia,* Abercrombie & Fitch T-shirt (*www.abercrombie.com*) made in the *Northern Mariana Islands,* and American Eagle jeans (*www.ae.com*) made in *Mexico.* You pull the charger off your Nokia phone (*www.nokia.com*), which was designed and manufactured in the *United States* with parts from *Taiwan,* and head out the door. You hop into your Toyota

e-business (e-commerce)
Purchase, sale, or exchange of goods and services, as well as servicing customers, collaboration with business partners, and transactions within a company via computer networks.

breaking views

The E-Biz Surprise

A funny thing happened on the way to e-business. After many "dot-coms" crashed and became "dot-bombs," consumers kept filling their online shopping carts, while companies, after a brief pause, kept quietly investing. Today, businesses have a more sober understanding of what the Internet can and cannot do for them. Here are four companies that understand the true power of the Internet:

- **Lollypops to Leer Jets.** Sure, people buy Beanie Babies online. But who would have thought people are willing to buy *never-seen used cars* from *strangers* on the *Internet*? Online auctioneer, eBay, that's who. eBay (*www.ebay.com*) sold around $8 billion in vehicles and parts in 2004, and has featured everything from lollypops to a Leer jet. The idea also is selling in China: eBay's Chinese service is already the biggest e-commerce site in the country. And a growing number of online entrepreneurs (430,000 in the U.S. alone) are earning a significant income from trading on eBay.

- **A Unique Technique.** Eli Lilly & Co. (*www.lilly.com*) had 7,500 employees working in research and development (R&D) in 2001. By 2003, it had three times that number, but none on the payroll. Lilly created an online scientific forum, called InnoCentive (*www.innocentive.com*), where it posts particularly difficult chemical problems. The site is open to anyone, is available in seven languages, and pays cash awards. Solutions can pay up to $100,000 but typical rewards are around $2,000.

- **Numero Uno.** What leisure travel agency is number one on or off the Web? Expedia (*www.expedia.com*), which tallies an impressive 18 million unique visitors a month. Expedia was instrumental in forcing over 13 percent of traditional, offline travel-agency locations to close shop in a single year. As offline firms pull back, the online travel world gets another boost. In mid-2004 the company fired up new Web sites in France and Germany, and is now gobbling up companies that specialize in business travel.

- **The Dell Way.** Dell (*www.dell.com*) rose to dominate its industry by building its manufacturing and sales strategies entirely around the Internet. The message for competitors: adopt Dell's Net-efficient way or exit the business. Dell's approach has forever changed the computer business—the latest Apple and Sony stores are essentially showrooms. Even scarier for rivals is that Dell figures it has so far unlocked only about half the Net's efficiency-boosting potential!

(*www.toyota.com*), which was made in *Kentucky*, and pop in a CD performed by *Canada*'s Avril Lavigne (*www.avril-lavigne.com*). You swing by the local Starbucks (*www.starbucks.com*) to charge your own batteries with coffee brewed from a blend of beans harvested in *Colombia* and *Ethiopia*. Your day is just one hour old but in a way you've already taken a virtual 'round-the-world trip. A quick glance at the "Made in" tags on your jacket, backpack, watch, wallet, or other items with you right now will demonstrate the pervasiveness of international business transactions.

International business is any commercial transaction that crosses the borders of two or more nations. You don't have to set foot outside a small town to find evidence of international business. No matter where you live, you'll be surrounded by **imports**—all goods and services brought into a country that are acquired from organizations located abroad. Your counterparts around the world will undoubtedly spend some part of their day using your nation's **exports**—all goods and services produced or based in one country that are sold abroad. The total value of goods and services (both imports and exports) that cross national borders each year is a staggering $16,263,600,000,000 (over $16.2 trillion). That is nearly 66 times the annual revenue of the world's largest company, Wal-Mart (*www.walmart.com*).[3]

The Global Relay Race But companies don't just sell their products to customers in other countries—they also cross borders to get products made in the first place. This is particularly true in the era of e-commerce. Say you're an IBM (*www.ibm.com*) computer programmer based in Seattle. You may never leave the state of Washington, but you'll be working with colleagues in faraway places such as China, India, and Central and Eastern Europe. A team of computer programmers at Beijing's Tsinghua University (*www.tsinghua.edu.cn*) writes software using Java technology for IBM. At the end of each day, they send their work over the

international business
Any commercial transaction that crosses the borders of two or more nations.

imports
All goods and services brought into a country that are acquired from organizations located abroad.

exports
All goods and services produced or based in one country that are sold abroad.

FIGURE 1.1

Here a Part, There a Part. . .

When Hewlett-Packard (www.hp.com) identified the need for a new low-cost computer server for small businesses, it seized the rewards of globalization. HP designed, manufactured, and assembled the ProLiant ML150 server (priced around $1,100) throughout five Pacific Rim nations and India. The novel approach allowed HP to fulfill the need for a low-cost computer server while constraining costs in a relentlessly competitive industry. Do you know of other products that underwent a similar process?

1 Idea for product hatched in **Singapore**
2 Concept approved in **Houston**
3 Concept design done in **Singapore**
4 Engineering design in **Taiwan,** where many computer components are made; initial manufacture by a Taiwanese contractor.
5 Final assembly in **Singapore, Australia, China,** and **India.** Products made in Australia, China, and India are primarily for those markets; machines made in Singapore go to all of Southeast Asia.

Internet to an IBM facility in Seattle. There, programmers build on it before zapping it 5,000 miles to the Institute of Computer Science in Belarus and the Software House Group in Latvia. From there, the work goes to India's Tata Group (*www.tata.com*), which passes the software back to Tsinghua by the next morning. The process repeats itself until the project is done. IBM's vice president for Internet technology calls this global relay race "Java around the Clock," and it is fast becoming the way things are done.[4]

Development and production of computer hardware also is being spread around the world as never before. Consider how Hewlett-Packard (*www.hp.com*) recently designed and built a new, low-cost computer server aimed at small businesses. HP tries to minimize labor costs, tax burdens, and shipping delays while maximizing the output of its engineers when designing, building, and distributing its products. So, the company dispersed the design and production of the new server throughout an increasingly specialized electronics-manufacturing system (see Figure 1.1). Companies use such innovative production and distribution techniques to squeeze inefficiencies out of their international operations and boost their competitiveness.[5]

Globalization, technology, outsourcing, and competitiveness are just some of the hot-button topics we will come across repeatedly throughout this book. This chapter begins by presenting globalization—we describe its powerful influence on markets and production and explain the forces behind its rapid expansion. Following coverage of each main argument in the debate over globalization, we examine the key players in international business. We then present what makes international business special by explaining the dynamic, integrated global business environment in which it occurs. Finally, the appendix at the end of this chapter contains a world atlas to be used as a primer for this chapter's discussion, and as a reference throughout the remainder of the book.

Globalization

globalization
Trend toward greater economic, cultural, political, and technological interdependence among national institutions and economies.

Although national governments retain much control over the products, people, and capital crossing their borders, the global economy is becoming increasingly intertwined. **Globalization** is the trend toward greater economic, cultural, political, and technological interdependence among national institutions and economies. It is a trend characterized by *denationalization* (in which national boundaries are becoming less relevant), and is different from *internationalization* (which refers to cooperation between national actors). The greater interdependence that globalization causes means an increasingly freer flow of goods, services, money, people, and ideas across national borders.

As the definition above implies, globalization involves much more than the expansion of trade and investment among nations, and is touching each of our lives in new and profound ways. Globalization embraces concepts and theories from political science, sociology, anthropology, and philosophy as well as economics. As such, it is not exclusively reserved for multinational corporations and international financial institutions. Nor is globalization the exclusive domain of those with only altruistic or moral intentions. In fact, globalization has been described as going "well beyond the links that bind corporations, traders, financiers, and central bankers. It provides a conduit not only for ideas but also for processes of coordination and cooperation used by terrorists, politicians, religious leaders, anti-globalization activists, and bureaucrats alike."[6]

Yet our discussion will remain focused on the business implications of globalization. Let's now take a look at two areas of business in which globalization is having profound effects—the globalization of both *markets* and *production*.

Globalization of Markets

Globalization of markets refers to convergence in buyer preferences in markets around the world. This trend is occurring in many product categories, including consumer goods, industrial products, and business services. Clothing retailer L.L.Bean (*www.llbean.com*), shoe producer Nike (*www.nike.com*), and electronics maker Sony (*www.sony.com*) are just a few companies that sell so-called *global products*—products marketed in all countries essentially without any changes. Global products and global competition characterize many industries and markets, including semiconductors (Intel, Philips), aircraft (Airbus, Boeing), construction equipment (Caterpillar, Mitsubishi), autos (Honda, Volkswagen), financial services (Citicorp, HSBC), air travel (Lufthansa, Singapore Airlines), accounting services (Ernst &

"... HERE'S THE SCENARIO FROM MARKETING, ... YOU SCOPE OUT A TERRITORY WHERE WE HAVE NO COMPETITION AND INITIATE OUR GLOBAL STRATEGY, ... ALL YOU NEED IS PROTECTIVE CLOTHING, A MACHETE, INSECT REPELLANT, HAND HELD GLOBAL POSITIONING, A CELLPHONE AND AN INTERPRETER..."

Young, KPMG), consumer goods (Procter & Gamble, Unilever), and fast food (KFC, McDonald's). The globalization of markets is important to international business because it offers companies several important benefits. Let's now look briefly at each of these.

Reduces Marketing Costs
Companies that sell global products can reduce costs by *standardizing* various aspects of their marketing activities. A company selling a global consumer good, such as shampoo, can make an identical shampoo for the global market and then simply design different product packaging to account for the language spoken in each market. Companies can achieve further cost savings by creating the same visual component for all markets, but dubbing its TV ads and translating its print ads into local languages.

Creates New Market Opportunities
A company that sells a global product can explore opportunities abroad if the home market is small or becomes saturated. For example, China holds enormous potential for e-commerce. Although China currently has 80 million Internet users, it is expected to surpass the United States and have 153 million Web surfers by 2006. So, the battle for market share between the top-two online search engines, Yahoo (*www.yahoo.com*) and Google (*www.google.com*), has entered the Middle Kingdom. In 2004, both companies launched or invested in Chinese-language services—Yahoo rolled out Yisou (*www.yisou.com*) and Google took a large financial stake in Baidu (*www.baidu.com*).[7] Seeking sales growth abroad can be absolutely essential for an entrepreneur or small company that sells a global product but has a limited home market.

Levels Uneven Income Streams
A company that sells a global seasonal product can use international sales to level its income stream. By supplementing domestic sales with international sales, the company can reduce or eliminate wide variations in sales between seasons and steady its cash flow. For instance, a firm that produces suntan and sunblock lotions can match product distribution to the summer seasons in the northern and southern hemispheres in alternating fashion—thereby steadying its income from these global, yet highly seasonal, products.

Yet Local Needs Are Important
Despite the potential benefits of global markets, managers must constantly monitor the match between their firms' products and markets to ensure they do not overlook the needs of buyers. The benefit of serving customers with an adapted product may outweigh the benefit of a standardized one. For instance, soft drinks, fast food, and other consumer goods are clearly global products that continue to penetrate markets around the world. But sometimes these products require small modifications so they better suit local tastes. In southern Japan, Coca-Cola (*www.cocacola.com*) sweetens its traditional formula to compete with sweeter-tasting Pepsi (*www.pepsi.com*). In India, where cows are sacred and the consumption of beef is taboo, McDonald's (*www.mcdonalds.com*) markets the "Maharaja Mac"—two all-mutton patties on a sesame-seed bun with all the usual toppings. For further insights into how managers of global companies can succeed in the international marketplace, see the Global Manager's Toolbox titled, "The Keys to International Success."

Globalization of Production

Many production activities are also becoming global. *Globalization of production* refers to the dispersal of production activities to locations that help a company achieve its cost-minimization or quality-maximization objectives for a good or service. This includes the sourcing of key production inputs, such as raw materials or products for assembly, as well as the international outsourcing of services. Like the globalization of markets, globalization of production also offers companies several benefits.

Provides Access to Low-Cost Workers
Global production activities allow companies to reduce overall production costs through access to low-cost labor. For decades, companies located their factories in low-wage nations to churn out all kinds of goods, including toys and stuffed animals, inexpensive electronics, and textiles. Yet whereas relocating production to low-cost locales traditionally meant *production of goods* almost exclusively, it increasingly applies to the *production of services*. For instance, although most services must

The Keys to International Success

Despite the difficulties faced by global managers, many companies prosper when competing beyond their domestic market. Although they work for companies that make everything from 99-cent hamburgers (McDonald's) to $150 million jumbo jets (Boeing), global executives acknowledge certain common threads in their approaches to management and offer the following advice:

- **Know the Customer.** The successful manager has detailed knowledge of what different international customers want and ensures that the company is flexible enough to customize products to meet those needs.

- **Emphasize Global Awareness.** Good global managers ensure that the company designs and builds products and services for export from the beginning, not as an afterthought following the conquest of domestic markets.

- **Develop World-Class Products.** Successful managers know that customers everywhere demand reliability. Top global managers insist on high-quality products and stand behind them with excellent customer service.

- **Market Effectively.** The world cannot beat a path to your door to buy your "better mouse trap" if it does not know about it. A poor global marketing effort can cause products with great sales potential to fade into obscurity.

- **Improve Logistics.** As patterns of global business grow more complex, logistics is becoming critical for large companies. Superior logistics improves a firm's ability to efficiently procure raw materials, supply components to manufacturing, and deliver products to customers in a timely fashion.

- **Know How to Analyze Problems.** Successful managers rarely start out with solutions. Instead, they tackle their international business problems one piece at a time by experimenting and taking carefully calculated risks.

be produced where they are consumed, some services can be performed at remote locations where labor costs are lower. For years, European companies created call centers in Ireland to handle all types of customer service. Now, U.S. and European firms are moving customer service and other nonessential work to places as far away as India. Steve Lanthrope, insurance partner of Accenture (*www.accenture.com*), says, "It will only be a few years before U.K. insurance and pension customers will, as a matter of course, have almost all their business dealt with abroad." As compared with the United Kingdom, a similar call center facility in India leads to cost savings of 40 to 60 percent.[8]

Provides Access to Technical Expertise Companies also produce goods and services abroad to take advantage of technical know-how. For instance, Film Roman (*www.filmroman.com*) produces the TV series, *The Simpsons*, but provides key poses and step-by-step frame directions to AKOM Production Company (*www.akomkorea.com*) in Seoul, South Korea. AKOM then fills in the remaining poses and links them into an animated whole. But there are bumps along the way, says animation director Mark Kirkland. In one middle-of-the-night phone call, Kirkland was explaining to the Koreans how to draw a shooting gun. "They don't allow guns in Korea; it's against the law," says Kirkland. "So they were calling me: 'How does a gun work?' " Kirkland and others put up with such cultural differences and phone calls at odd hours to tap a highly qualified pool of South Korean animators.[9]

Provides Access to Production Inputs Globalization of production allows companies to access resources that are unavailable or more costly at home. The quest for natural resources draws many companies into international markets. Japan, for example, is a small, densely populated island nation with very few natural resources of its own—especially forests. But Japan's largest paper company, Nippon Seishi, does more than simply import wood pulp. The company owns huge forests and corresponding processing facilities in Australia, Canada, and the United States. This gives the firm not only access to an essential resource, but control over earlier stages in the papermaking process. As a result, the company is guaranteed a steady flow of its key ingredient (wood pulp) that is less subject to swings in

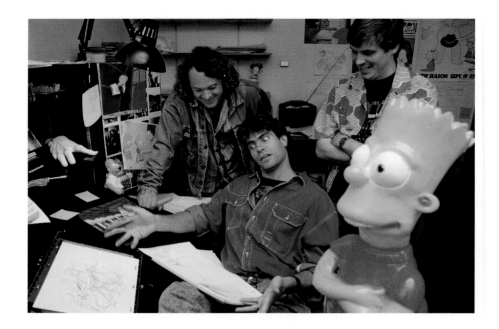

Here, designer Scott Alberts, producer David Silverman, and director Mark Kirkland work on a sketch for The Simpsons. Apart from sometimes being translated into other languages, the show is identical in each market. When the show opens with Bart scribbling his punishment on the blackboard, "Funny noises are not funny," kids around the world get it. U.S.-based Film Roman (**www.filmroman.com**) produces the show, but gets assistance from highly qualified South Korean animators at a good price. Can you think of another product that illustrates the globalization of both production and markets?

prices and supply associated with buying pulp on the open market. Likewise, to access cheaper energy resources used in manufacturing, a variety of Japanese firms are relocating production to China, Mexico, and Vietnam where energy costs are lower.

> ### Quick Study
>
> 1. Give several examples of how companies used the Internet to create lasting change in their industries.
> 2. What do we mean by the term *international business*? Explain how *globalization* and *internationalization* differ.
> 3. List several keys to international success that can help global managers.
> 4. In what ways do companies benefit from: a) the globalization of markets, and b) the globalization of production?

Forces Driving Globalization

Two main forces underlie the globalization of both markets and production: *falling barriers to trade and investment* and *technological innovation*. These two features, more than anything else, are creating an increasingly competitive global economy. As a result of greater competition, companies from around the world are being driven into direct confrontation and cooperation as never before. Local industries previously isolated by time and distance, are increasingly accessible to large international companies based in faraway lands. Many local firms are compelled to cooperate with one another or the large international firms to remain competitive. Others revitalize themselves in a bold attempt to survive the competitive onslaught. And at the global level, consolidation is occurring in many industries as erstwhile competitors are linking up to challenge others on a worldwide basis. Let's now explore the pivotal roles of each of these two driving forces of globalization.

General Agreement on Tariffs and Trade (GATT)
Treaty designed to promote free trade by reducing both tariffs and nontariff barriers to international trade.

Falling Barriers to Trade and Investment

In 1947, political leaders of 23 nations—12 developed and 11 developing economies—made history when they created the **General Agreement on Tariffs and Trade (GATT)**—a treaty designed to promote free trade by reducing both tariffs and nontariff barriers to international trade. *Tariffs* are essentially taxes levied on traded goods, and *nontariff barri-*

ers are limits on the quantity of an imported product. The treaty was quite successful in its early years. In 1988 world merchandise trade was 20 times larger than in 1947 and average tariffs dropped from 40 percent to five percent.

Further progress was made with a 1994 revision of the GATT treaty. Average tariffs on merchandise trade were reduced and subsidies (government financial support) for agricultural products were lowered. The treaty's revision also clearly defined *intellectual property rights*—giving protection to copyrights (including computer programs, databases, sound recordings, and films), trademarks and service marks, and patents (including trade secrets and know-how). A major flaw of the original GATT was that it lacked the power to enforce world trade rules. So, perhaps the greatest accomplishment of the 1994 revision was the creation of an international organization with the power to enforce the rules of international trade—the *World Trade Organization*.

World Trade Organization

The **World Trade Organization (WTO)** is the international organization that regulates trade between nations. The three main goals of the WTO (*www.wto.org*) are: 1) help the free flow of trade, 2) help negotiate the further opening of markets, and 3) settle trade disputes between its members. In fact, it is the power of the WTO to settle trade disputes that really sets it apart from its predecessor, the GATT. The various WTO agreements are essentially contracts between member nations that commit them to maintaining fair and open trade policies. Offenders must realign their trade policies according to WTO guidelines or suffer financial penalties and, perhaps, trade sanctions. Because of its ability to penalize offending member nations, the WTO's dispute settlement system truly is the spine of the global trading system. The WTO replaced the *institution* of GATT but absorbed all of the former GATT *agreements*. Thus the GATT institution no longer officially exists. As of late 2004, the WTO recognized 147 members and over 30 "observer" members.

A new round of negotiations was launched at the WTO meeting in Doha, Qatar, in late 2001 to lower trade barriers further, and to help poor nations in particular. Agricultural subsidies that rich countries pay to their own farmers are worth $1 billion per day—more than six times the value of their combined aid budgets to poor nations. Because 70 percent of poor nations' exports are agricultural products and textiles, wealthy nations intend to open further these and other labor-intensive industries. Poor nations are being encouraged to reduce tariffs among themselves, and are to receive help from rich nations in integrating themselves into the global trading system.[10] Although the Doha round was to conclude by the end of 2004, talks totally collapsed at the September 2003 WTO meeting in Cancun, Mexico. Trade ministers finally agreed on a "negotiating framework" in mid-2004, but by then a completion date for the round was highly uncertain.[11]

Regional Trade Agreements

In addition to the WTO, smaller groups of nations are integrating their economies as never before by fostering trade and boosting cross-border investment. For example, the *North American Free Trade Agreement (NAFTA)* groups three nations (Canada, Mexico, and the United States) into a free-trade bloc. The even more ambitious *European Union (EU)* combines 25 countries. The *Asia Pacific Economic Cooperation (APEC)* consists of 21 nations committed to creating a free-trade zone around the Pacific. The aims of each of these smaller trade pacts are similar to those of the WTO, but are regional in nature. Moreover, because of the difficulties confronting worldwide trade negotiations today (as seen in globalization protests), some nations are placing greater emphasis on such regional pacts.

Trade Agreements and Trade Growth

Together, the WTO agreements and these smaller, regional trade pacts have boosted world trade and cross-border investment significantly. Figure 1.2 illustrates the growth in trade (volume of exports) relative to growth in world output (GDP) over time. The figure shows plainly that international trade has been growing far more rapidly than world output, particularly in the past two decades.

Let's now take a moment in our discussion to clearly define a few terms that we will encounter time and again throughout this book. **Gross domestic product (GDP)** is the value of all goods and services produced by a domestic economy over a 1-year period. GDP excludes a nation's income generated from exports, imports, and the international operations of its companies. We can speak in terms of world GDP (as in Figure 1.2) when we sum

World Trade Organization (WTO)
International organization that regulates trade between nations.

gross domestic product (GDP)
Value of all goods and services produced by a country's domestic economy over a 1-year period.

FIGURE 1.2

World Trade Outpaces World Output

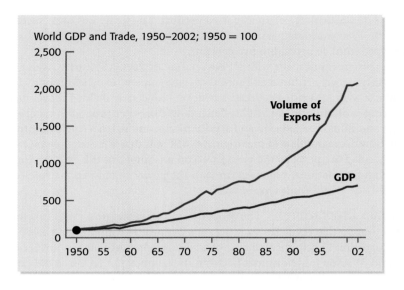

gross national product (GNP)
Value of all goods and services produced by a country during a 1-year period, including income generated by both domestic and international activities.

GDP or GNP per capita
Nation's GDP or GNP divided by its population.

all individual nations' GDP figures. GDP is a somewhat narrower figure than **gross national product (GNP)**—the value of all goods and services produced by a country during a 1-year period, including income generated by both domestic production and the country's international activities. A country's **GDP or GNP per capita** is simply its GDP or GNP divided by its population.

Technological Innovation

While falling barriers to trade and investment encourage globalization, technological innovation is accelerating the process. Significant advancements in information technology and transportation methods are making it easier, faster, and less costly to move data, goods, equipment, and people around the world. Let's now examine several innovations that have had considerable impacts on globalization.

E-mail and Videoconferencing   Operating across borders and time zones can make it more difficult to coordinate and control business activities, such as sourcing raw materials or intermediate products and scheduling production. But technology can speed the flow of information and ease the tasks of coordination and control. Electronic mail (e-mail) is an indispensable tool managers use to stay in contact with international operations and to respond quickly to important matters. Videoconferencing allows managers in different branch offices to meet in virtual face-to-face meetings, and lets engineers view models of new products from remote locations. Primary reasons for the rapid growth (around 20 to 25 percent per year) of videoconferencing include: lower-cost bandwidth (communication channels) used to transmit information; lower-cost equipment; and decreased travel among some businesspeople for cost and safety reasons. By renting facilities from a firm such as V-Span (*www.vspan.com*), a manufacturer in Denver can hold a two-hour video-conference with branch managers in six other nations for about $2,700.[12]

Internet and World Wide Web   Companies use the Internet to quickly and cheaply contact managers in distant locations to, for example, inquire about production runs, revise sales strategies, and check on distribution bottlenecks. Firms are using the Net to sharpen their forecasting, lower their inventories, and improve communication with their suppliers. Further gains arise from the ability of the Internet to cut postproduction costs by decreasing the number of intermediaries through which a product passes on its way to the customer. As a result, the Internet transforms business operations for firms selling products such as books, music, and travel services.

The Web also reduces the cost of reaching an international customer base, which is extremely important for small firms—among the first to use the Web as a global marketing tool. Yet some Internet startups forgot a fundamental rule of running a business—attracting paying customers. Online intermediaries such as Yahoo! (*www.yahoo.com*) funnel surfers to Web sites for a fee. Many companies that did not use an intermediary (or portal) were dissatisfied with traffic in their online stores. As one expert noted, "Launching an e-commerce site without a portal partner is like opening a retail store in the desert. Sure, it's cheap, but does anybody stop there?"[13]

Company Intranets and Extranets   Private networks of internal company Web sites and other information sources (*intranets*) provide access to a company's computer network from distant locations using personal computers. A particularly effective marketing tool on Volvo Car Corporation's (*www.volvocars.com*) intranet is a quarter-by-quarter database of marketing and sales information. The cycle begins when headquarters submits its corporate-wide marketing planning information. In this way, the database acts as a communication tool between headquarters and the national markets because subsidiaries are alerted to the corporate activities that are planned. Marketing managers at the company's subsidiaries around the world then select the items from this menu that apply to their particular markets. After the marketing plan is developed for each market, it is uploaded to the database—allowing each marketing manager to examine the marketing plan of every other market and adapt any relevant aspects to their own plan. In this way, the system acts as a tool for the sharing of best practices and gives managers the ability to develop the most appropriate marketing plan for their particular market.

Also, *extranets* give distributors and suppliers access to a company's database so that they can place orders or restock inventories electronically and automatically. The introduction of new technologies continually permits international companies (along with their suppliers and buyers) to respond to internal and external conditions more quickly, and more appropriately, than ever before.

Advancements in Transportation Technologies   Like advancements in information technology, advances in transportation methods are helping to globalize markets and production activities. Advancements in the shipping industry are facilitating globalization by making shipping more efficient and dependable. Retailers worldwide rely on imports to stock storerooms with bicycles, mobile phones, and backpacks, and to supply factories with needed raw materials and intermediate products. In the past, a cargo ship would sit in port up to 10 days while it was unloaded one pallet at a time. But because cargo today is loaded onto a ship in 20- and 40-foot containers that are quickly unloaded onto railcars or truck chassis at its destination, a 700-foot cargo ship is routinely unloaded in just 15 hours. Also, the operation of cargo ships is being made simpler and safer by computerized charts that pinpoint a ship's movements on the high seas using Global Positioning System (GPS) satellites.[14]

Measuring Globalization

After violent protests against globalization and the terrorist attacks on September 11, 2001, some proclaimed the death of globalization itself. Yet after a brief pause, globalization appears to be marching on. In fact, it is amazing that globalization is continuing so strongly in light of recent events, including: the New York and Washington terror attacks; terrorist bombings in Indonesia, Kenya, the Philippines, Russia, Spain, and elsewhere; wars in both Afghanistan and Iraq; the largest financial (and other corporate) corruption in history in the United States and Europe; more costly logistics because of tighter security at ports; and relatively slower economic growth among rich nations in recent years.

There have been numerous attempts to measure the extent to which individual nations are embracing globalization. One of the most comprehensive indices is that created by A.T. Kearney (*www.atkearney.com*), a management consultancy, and *Foreign Policy* magazine (*www.foreignpolicy.com*).[15] Each nation's ranking in the Index comprises a compilation of over a dozen variables within four categories:

1. *Political engagement*—memberships in international organizations, personnel and financial contributions to U.N. Security Council missions, international treaties ratified, and governmental transfers
2. *Technological connectivity*—Internet users, Internet hosts, and secure servers

3. *Personal contact*—international travel and tourism, international telephone traffic, remittances, and personal transfers (including compensation to employees)

4. *Economic integration*—trade, foreign direct investment, portfolio capital flows, and investment income

By incorporating a wide variety of variables, the index is apt to cut through cycles occurring in any one of the four areas listed above. And by encompassing social factors in addition to economic influences, it tends to capture the broad nature of globalization. Figure 1.3 shows the 20 highest-ranking nations in the 2004 Globalization Index. Europe accounted for 6 of the top 10 spots and the United States made it into the top 10 for the first time—bolstered by having the highest number of both Internet hosts per capita and secure servers. Despite lower levels of *economic integration* (foreign direct investment and portfolio capital flows) in recent years, steady gains in both *personal contact* (travel and telephone traffic) and *technology connectivity* (Internet access) boosted globalization overall.

But it is not only the most global nations that deserve our attention, but the least global as well. The 10 least global nations, according to the index above, account for 50 percent of the world's population, and are found in Africa, East Asia, South Asia, Latin America, and the Middle East. One remarkable commonality among these nations is their low levels of technological connectivity. These nations will likely have a difficult struggle ahead if they are to overcome their lack of global integration. Some are characterized by never-ending political unrest and corruption (Bangladesh, Indonesia, and Venezuela). Other nations with large agricultural sectors face trade barriers in developed countries and are subject to highly volatile prices on commodity markets (Brazil, China, and India). Still others are heavily dependent on oil exports but are plagued by erratic prices in energy markets (Iran and Venezuela). Kenya has suffered from recurring droughts, terrorism, and burdensome visa regulations that hurt tourism. Finally, Turkey and Egypt, along with the entire Middle East, suffer from continued concerns over terrorism, high barriers to trade and investment, and heavy government involvement in the economy. To deepen their global links, each of these nations will need to make great strides in their economic, social, technological, and political environments.

FIGURE 1.3

Globalization's Top 20

This graph shows the world's top 20 nations in terms of their level of globalization. Each nation's ranking reflects its performance on over a dozen variables in four categories: political engagement, technological connectivity, personal contact, and economic integration. The key point in this figure is not absolute levels attained by any individual nation on one or all these variables, but relative globalization. In other words, the extent to which any nation is global is best viewed in the context of how global it is relative to other nations.

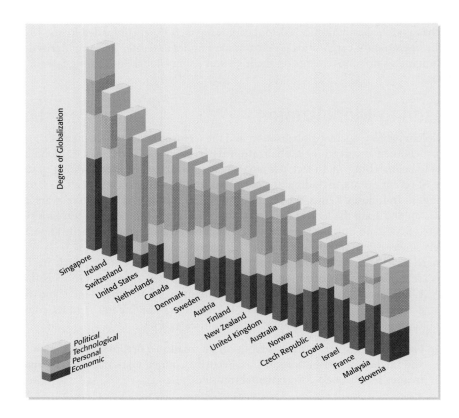

1.   Name the two major forces that underlie the expansion of globalization.

2.   How have global and regional efforts at promoting trade and investment advanced globalization?

3.   How has technological innovation, in all its forms, propelled globalization?

4.   What factors help make some countries more global than others? Identify several highly global nations.

Untangling the Globalization Debate

Globalization means different things to different people. A businessperson may see globalization as an opportunity to source goods and services from lower-cost locations and to pry open new markets. An economist may see it as an opportunity to examine the impact of globalization on jobs and standards of living. An environmentalist may be concerned with how globalization affects our ecology. An anthropologist may wish to examine the influence of globalization on the culture of a group of people. A political scientist may be concerned with the impact of globalization on the power of governments relative to that of multinational companies. And an employee may view globalization either as an opportunity for new work, or as a threat to his or her current job (depending on where he or she lives).

It is because of these different lenses through which each of us views the world and the happenings around us that the debate surrounding globalization is so complex. In the pages that follow we explain the main arguments of those opposed to globalization and the responses of those in favor of it. Opponents of globalization are found in every walk of life. Perhaps you have voiced your concerns over increased globalization by signing a petition on the Web site of an anti-globalization group, attending a teach-in or conference on globalization, donating money to an organization against globalization, or taking part in a protest march even. From entrepreneurs and small business owners to globetrotting managers, all businesspeople must understand not only globalization, but also the arguments of those opposing its continuing expansion. But before we address the intricacies of the globalization debate, it is helpful to put today's globalization into its proper context.

Today's Globalization in Context

Many people forget that there was a first age of globalization that extended from the mid-1800s to the 1920s.[16] Although today's migration levels are high, the world's labor market then was also highly mobile—300,000 people flowed out of Europe each year, reaching 1 million a year after 1900.[17] Other than in wartime, nations did not even require passports for international travel before 1914. And similar to today, workers in wealthy countries during that first age of globalization also feared competition for jobs from other rich nations and low-cost countries alike.

Trade and capital also flowed more freely than ever before during that first age. Huge companies from wealthy nations built facilities in distant lands to extract raw materials and produce all sorts of goods. Large cargo ships plied the seas to deliver their manufactures to distant markets. The transatlantic cable (completed in 1866) allowed news between Europe and the United States to travel faster than ever before. The drivers of that first age of globalization included the steamship, telegraph, railroad, and later, the telephone and airplane.

That first age of globalization was abruptly halted by the arrival of the First World War, the Russian Revolution, and the Great Depression. By encouraging fierce competition in trade and unfettered immigration, globalization may have added to nationalist sentiments and aggravated tensions between countries leading up to the First World War. A "backlash to globalization" in the early 1900s helped usher in high tariffs and barriers to immigration.[18] Between the First and Second World Wars, the great flows of goods, capital, and people became a mere trickle. And for 75 years (from the start of the First World War to the end of the Cold War) the world remained divided. There was a geographic divide between East and West, and an ideological divide between communism and capitalism. Although steady economic gains continued in the West following the Second World War, international flows of goods, capital, and people were confined to their respective capitalist and communist systems and geographies.

Fast-forward to 1989 and the collapse of the Wall separating East and West Berlin. One by one, central and eastern European nations threw off the chains of communism, embraced freedom, and began a march toward democratic institutions and free-market economic systems. The global economy was *reborn*. Yet it was not until the 1990s that international capital flows, in absolute terms, finally recovered to levels seen just prior to the First World War. The drivers of this second age of globalization—communication satellites, fiber optics, microchips, and the Internet—are lowering the cost of telecommunications and binding the world more tightly together.

The Current Globalization Backlash

The rage felt by many bubbled to the surface in Seattle, Washington, in December 1999. The World Trade Organization (WTO) was meeting to discuss further reductions in trade and investment barriers, and groups opposed to globalization showed up in the city determined to disrupt the meetings. A protest staged by a 50,000-strong crowd of activists deteriorated into window smashing and looting of local businesses. The WTO meeting did fail to achieve any substantive accomplishments, but it was disagreement among its members, rather than the protesters, that was the primary cause.

Then in February 2000, the annual meeting of the World Economic Forum (*www.weforum.org*) in Davos, Switzerland, saw protesters completely trash (among other things) a McDonald's restaurant—a potent symbol of globalization. In September 2000, demonstrations at the International Monetary Fund–World Bank joint meeting in Prague, Czech Republic, turned violent and left the city's streets littered with stones and broken glass. Other cities had similar experiences that year as protesters and anarchists seemed to show up at the meetings of practically every possible international organization. Then, in June 2001, a European Union summit in Gothenburg, Sweden, ended with three people shot—the first occasion in modern times that live ammunition was used against groups protesting globalization in the Western world. The low point came in July 2001 in Genoa, Italy, where 150,000 protesters converged on the G8 summit. Two days of rioting left one 23-year-old man shot dead by police and an estimated $45 million in property damage.

Leaving the Anarchists Behind   The protests we witness today are far more orderly by comparison. Those who say they have legitimate protests against globalization argue that for nearly three years anarchists stole the headlines and muddled their messages. For instance, what much of the media did not report on that December day in Seattle was that just blocks away from the carnage was an orderly debate held by the International Forum on Globalization (*www.ifg.org*). So, if we are to truly untangle that complex phenomenon called "globalization," we must leave the anarchists behind at this point and address the complaints put forth by serious individuals. The complaints of opponents to globalization range from the reasonable (simply a greater say in organizations such as the WTO) to the radical (the destruction of capitalism itself). Many groups complain that globalization costs jobs, lowers labor and environmental regulations, destroys ways of life, increases income inequality, and reduces individuals' political say. The breadth of gripes about globalization is evident in a statement by consumer advocate, Ralph Nader: "The essence of globalization is a subordination of human rights, of labor rights, consumer, environmental rights, democracy rights, to the imperatives of global trade and investment."[19] Those in favor of globalization tend to take the opposite (or far less strong) position on all those issues.

There is no denying that many people are apprehensive about the effects of globalization. But while globalization has *coincided* with an increase in the number of man-made and natural disasters, particularly in recent years, it is not necessarily *responsible* for them. Increasing "globaphobia" is at least in part due to the rise of global media, which can quickly broadcast "breaking news" reports from disasters in the world's most

Investing in Security Pays Dividends

The globalization of markets and production creates new challenges for companies around the world. As well as the need to secure lengthier supply lines and distribution channels, companies must pay increased attention to their physical facilities, information systems, and reputations.

○ **A Simple Plan.** Today, not only cargo shipped abroad must be protected from acts of terror, but also facilities at home. Although some executives resist investing in security because of its defensive nature, careful planning and a vulnerability assessment (around $12,000 for a midsize company; $1 million for a large firm) can be well worth it. Despite being located across from the World Trade Center on September 11, 2001, a disaster plan had investment bank Lehman Brothers (*www.lehman.com*) operating the very next day, with employees connecting to the firm's computer system from home, hotel rooms, and rented offices.

○ **Digital Deterrence.** Good online security also is crucial. Computer viruses, software worms, malicious code, and cyber criminals cost the United States $55 billion a year in lost productivity. The usual suspects: disgruntled employees, dishonest competitors, and hackers. Also, fraud accounts for 6 percent of all Internet transactions—the comparable figure in the offline world is 1 percent. And when quitting their jobs, former employees often simply walk away with digital devices containing sensitive employer information, including confidential memos, competitive data, and private e-mails.

○ **Perception Is Reality.** The global reach of today's largest corporations means global dissemination of news regarding their behavior—especially ethical and legal behavior. *Reputational risk* is anything that could harm a firm's image, including accounting irregularities, product recalls, and workers' rights violations. Reputational risk is considered by most firms to be their number-one business hazard because, though typically their most valuable asset, a reputation can be impossible to recover once tarnished. Arthur Andersen and Enron are excellent examples of how rapidly global reputations can implode.

○ **The Challenge.** Like the above risks themselves, the challenges are also varied. Regarding *facility security* management, companies should: 1) identify all the potential risks they face, 2) overcome resistance to investing in security, and 3) plan for business evacuation, continuity, and relocation. To improve *digital security* management, all employees should use and often change passwords, use software patches to guard computers and mobile devices, and return all company-owned digital devices when leaving the firm. To lessen *reputatonal risk*, companies should act ethically and within the law—corporate secrets are increasingly difficult to keep from the probing eyes of governments, non-governmental organizations, and media.

○ **Want to Know More?** Visit leading risk consultancy Kroll (*www.krollworldwide.com*), leading Internet security firm Check Point Software Technologies (*www.checkpoint.com*), and Internet security agency CERT Coordination Center (*www.cert.org*).

remote areas. Yet for companies, globalization does create new risks and accentuate old ones because it exposes firms to new threats as well as to new opportunities. To read about several key risks that globalization heightens and how companies can better manage them, see this chapter's Global Challenges feature titled, "Investing in Security Pays Dividends."

Before We Go On We've already learned about one favorite target of those opposed to globalization, the World Trade Organization. Let's now take a moment to understand the purposes of two other large, supranational institutions commonly in the sights of globalization protesters.

The **World Bank** is an agency created to provide financing for national economic development efforts. The initial purpose of the World Bank (*www.worldbank.org*) was to finance European reconstruction following the Second World War. It later shifted its focus to the general financial needs of developing countries, and today finances many economic development projects in Africa, South America, and Southeast Asia. The **International Monetary Fund (IMF)** is an agency created to regulate fixed exchange rates and enforce the rules of the international monetary system. Today the IMF (*www.imf.org*) has 184 member countries. Some of the purposes of the IMF include: promoting international monetary cooperation; facilitating expansion and balanced growth of international trade; avoiding

World Bank
Agency created to provide financing for national economic development efforts.

International Monetary Fund (IMF)
Agency created to regulate fixed exchange rates and enforce the rules of the international monetary system.

competitive exchange devaluation; and making the resources of the Fund temporarily available to members.

It also is important at this time to note one essential caveat. Each side in the debate over globalization tends to hold up results of social and economic studies they say show "definitive" support for their arguments. Yet many organizations that publish studies on globalization have political agendas, such as decreasing government regulation or expanding government programs. This can make objective consideration of a group's claims and findings difficult. A group's aims may influence the selection of the data to analyze, time period to study, nations to examine, and so forth. It is essential to take into account such factors anytime we hear one or another group presenting findings on the beneficial or harmful effects of globalization.

With the above issues in mind, let us now engage the globalization debate. We address five key arguments, centered on globalization's effect on: *jobs and wages*, *labor and environmental regulation*, *income inequality*, *national sovereignty*, and *cultures*.

Quick Study

1. How does this current period of globalization compare with the first age of globalization?
2. Identify several global challenges that international firms face with regard to security matters.
3. What are the purposes of: a) the *World Bank*, and b) the *International Monetary Fund*?

Globalization's Impact on Jobs and Wages

We open our coverage of the globalization debate with an important topic for both developed and developing countries—the effect of globalization on jobs and wages. We begin with the arguments of those against globalization, and then turn our attention to how supporters of globalization respond.

Globalization Costs Jobs and Lowers Wages
Groups opposed to globalization blame it for eroding standards of living and ruining ways of life in developed nations. Opposition groups make several specific complaints about how globalization and its associated practices affect jobs and wages. It is argued that globalization: *eliminates jobs* and *forces wages lower* in developed nations; and *exploits workers* in developing countries. Let's now take a look at each of these arguments.

Eliminates Jobs in Developed Nations Protesters claim *globalization is responsible for the elimination of manufacturing jobs in developed nations*. Anti-globalization groups criticize the practice of sending good-paying manufacturing jobs abroad to developing countries where wages are a fraction of the cost for international firms.[20] Protesters argue that a label reading "Made in China" translates to "Not Made Here." Although critics admit that importing products from China (or from any other low-wage nation) lowers prices for televisions, sporting goods, and so on, they say this is little consolation for workers who lost their jobs.

To illustrate their argument, globalization critics point to the activities of Wal-Mart (*www.walmart.com*).[21] It is difficult to overstate the power of this retail giant and symbol of globalization. In a recent one-year period, Wal-Mart imported $12 billion worth of merchandise into the United States from China—10 percent of all Chinese imports. Wal-Mart's relentless pursuit of low-cost goods forces its suppliers to move to China and other low-wage nations, it is said. Yet any negative economic impact of Wal-Mart is difficult to estimate precisely. "It's hard to tease out, but Wal-Mart is definitely part of the dynamic, and given its market share and power, probably a significant part," says Jared Bernstein, of the Economic Policy Institute (*www.epinet.org*).[22]

Forces Wages Lower in Developed Countries Opposition groups say *globalization causes worker dislocation that results in a gradual ratcheting-down of wages*. It is alleged that when a manufacturing job is lost in a wealthy nation, the new job (assuming new work is found) pays less than the previous one. Some evidence does suggest that displaced manufacturing workers, and especially older workers, can suffer earnings losses of 30 percent or more in their next job. When this happens, it is said, workers can feel less loyal to employers, employee morale can suffer, and job insecurity increases—causing people to fear globalization and further reductions in trade barriers. One U.S. poll found 78 percent of respondents believed "protecting the jobs of American workers" should have top priority in deciding U.S. policies about trade with other nations.

In this discussion, too, Wal-Mart comes under fire. By contracting with a handful of manufacturers in Southeast Asia, Wal-Mart has driven the retail price of its George brand of jeans it sells in Britain and Germany to just $7.85 from $26.67. As a result of these business policies and practices, critics charge, Wal-Mart has a huge downward impact on wages and working conditions worldwide. Critics are all too happy to point out that Wal-Mart paid its U.S. sales clerks an average yearly salary of $13,861 in 2001, when the U.S. federal poverty line for a family of three was $14,630 (according to documents filed in a lawsuit).[23]

Exploits Workers in Developing Nations Globalization's opponents claim *globalization and international outsourcing exploits workers in low-wage nations.* One notable and vociferous critic of globalization and international outsourcing is Naomi Klein. She vehemently opposes the outsourced call center jobs of western companies, including Victoria's Secret (*www.victoriassecret.com*) and Delta Airlines (*www.delta.com*). Klein says such jobs force young Asians to disguise their nationality, adopt fake Mid-western accents, and work nights (when their customers are awake halfway around the world).

As evidence of the exploitative nature of such work, Klein cites the case of Lubna Baloch, a Pakistani woman hired to transcribe medical files dictated by doctors at a U.S. medical center. Although U.S. transcribers get paid 18 cents per line, Baloch received just 3 cents, and even at that rate her U.S. employer (a contractor's subcontractor's subcontractor) could not afford to make payroll. Claiming hundreds of dollars in back pay and frustrated by her employer, who ignored her e-mails, Baloch threatened to expose the voice files and patient records on the Internet, though she later rescinded the threat. "I feel violated, helpless . . . the most unluckiest person in this world," said Baloch. Klein maintains that free trade policies are "a highly efficient engine of dispossession, pushing small farmers off their land and laying off public-sector workers, making the need all the more desperate for those Victoria's Secret and Delta call center jobs."[24]

Globalization Creates Jobs and Boosts Wages
Globalization supporters credit it with improving standards of living and making possible new ways of life. Pro-globalization groups argue that globalization: *increases wealth and efficiency, generates labor market flexibility,* and *creates jobs* in developed nations; and *advances developing nations' economies.* Let's now take a look at each of these arguments.

Protesters march through the streets of London at the 3rd annual European Social Forum (*www.fse-esf.org*). The Forum brought together anti-globalization campaigners from across the world for days of debates, conferences, and concerts. Represented were trade unions, refugee advocates, peace and anti-imperialist groups, anti-racist movements, and environmental movements, among others. "The atmosphere here is wonderful . . . it shows that a new young left is emerging," declared Stavos Valsamis, a Greek protester.

Increases Wealth and Efficiency   Pro-globalization economists believe *globalization increases wealth and efficiency in both developed and developing nations.* To support this argument, economists point to evidence that openness to international trade raises the overall output of nations. One study found that increasing the ratio of trade to national output by 10 percent over a 20-year period boosts per capita income by 3.3 percent—a highly significant amount. Some economists even predict that the removal of all remaining barriers to free trade would lift worldwide income by $1.9 trillion, with $371 billion going to developing nations alone.[25]

Openness to international trade also allows a nation's businesses to become more efficient and pass the resulting savings on to consumers. By wringing inefficiencies out of the retail supply chain, Wal-Mart saved its U.S. customers alone $20 billion in one recent year. Add the price cuts that competitors must make and total annual savings approach $100 billion. Economists even refer to a "Wal-Mart effect," which has restrained inflation and boosted productivity year after year.[26] In this way, globalization increases consumer spending power by promoting efficiency, it is said.

Generates Labor Market Flexibility   Globalization defenders believe *globalization creates positive benefits by generating labor market flexibility in developed nations.* It is claimed that worker dislocation, or "churning" as it is called when there is widespread job turnover throughout an economy, has benefits. For one thing, flexible labor markets allow workers to be redeployed rapidly to sectors of the economy where they are highly valued and in demand. Also, easy turnover allows employees, particularly young workers, to change jobs easily with few negative effects. For instance, a young person can gain experience and skills with an initial employer, then move to a different job that provides a better match between employee and employer.

Creates Jobs in Developed Nations   Those supporting globalization contend *globalization and international outsourcing creates jobs in developed nations.* Consider the experiences of ClaimPower (*www.claimpower.com*), a small medical-billing service owned and managed by Rajeev Thadani in Fairlawn, New Jersey. Several years ago, with just five employees at the time, Thadani wanted to expand his business. So, he flew to his native Bombay, India, and hired low-wage but highly skilled employees to help file insurance claims on behalf of doctors in New Jersey. This gave ClaimPower a cost advantage over rivals, allowing it to charge clients less yet offer more specialized services. As a result, ClaimPower's client list expanded from 10 to 41 doctors, and revenue grew from $100,000 to $700,000.

Thadani is now rolling out a national expansion strategy and hiring staff in the United States. Although he normally relied on client referrals for new business, he is adding a U.S. sales team and new managers to work with doctors. His goal is to hire a dozen U.S. employees, as well as 30 or more additional people in India, to help him handle claims for 500 doctors nationwide. "This shows that outsourcing is not the one-way street many think it is in the United States," said Joseph Quinlan, chief market strategist at Banc of America Capital Management (*www.bacap.com*). "Outsourcing can also be a catalyst for lowering costs and creating jobs, notably at small and medium-sized companies," added Quinlan.[27]

Advances Developing Nations' Economies   Those in favor of globalization argue *globalization and international outsourcing help to advance developing nations' economies.* India, for one, became attractive as a location for software-writing operations in the 1980s and early 1990s because of its low-cost, well-trained, English-speaking technicians. Particularly booming in recent years are call centers that hire young graduates to sell services for satellite television, remind consumers to pay their overdue credit-card bills, and handle credit card and insurance inquiries. Millions of young Indians, who could not become doctors and lawyers, saw a call center job as a ticket to working for an international firm at a good salary that boosted them into a burgeoning middle class.

Today the relentless march of globalization is making India a base for not only customer service, but also for business process outsourcing—including financial, accounting, payroll, and benefits management. By some estimates, nearly 200,000 jobs in a $2.3 billion back-office industry in India has significantly elevated living standards.[28] As India's economy continues to develop, it will become an even greater attraction for white-collar (professional) occupations. Figure 1.4 illustrates why India is so popular as a location to outsource engineering, for instance. The salary of an electrical engineer in San Jose,

FIGURE 1.4

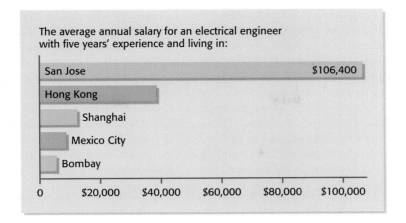

The average annual salary for an electrical engineer with five years' experience and living in:

San Jose — $106,400

California, is about 15 times that of an engineer in Bombay, India. So long as such economic disparities exist, international outsourcing will continue.

Summary of The Jobs and Wages Debate   At the present time, it appears that there is general agreement by all parties that globalization causes dislocation in labor markets. In other words, although globalization eliminates some jobs in a nation, it creates jobs in other sectors of the economy. Yet while some people lose their jobs and find new employment, others may find it difficult to get new work. The real point of difference between the two sides in the debate, then, is whether overall gains that (may or may not) accrue to *national economies* are worth the lost livelihoods that *individuals* (may or may not) suffer. Those in favor of globalization say the individual pain is worth the collective gain; those against say it is not.

Globalization's Impact on Labor and Environmental Regulation

Related to the argument over the impact of globalization on jobs and wages, is its effect on laws designed to guard labor's interests and protect the environment. Those opposed to globalization contend that companies locate operations in nations having the least-strict labor and environmental regulations because they are the lowest-cost sites. Critics argue that this puts downward pressure on labor and environmental protection laws in all countries because nations compete against one another to attract international firms. Let's examine each claim made against globalization and international companies on this topic, and the responses of globalization supporters.

Labor Standards   Trade unions claim that by permitting international firms to continually move to nations with relatively lower labor standards, globalization reduces labor's bargaining power and forces overall labor standards lower.[29] If this were in fact happening, we would expect that international firms would continually relocate to locations having the lowest possible labor standards.

One place to examine the validity of this assertion is in developing nations' *export-processing zones (EPZs)*—special areas in which companies engage in tariff-free importing and exporting (there are more than 850 EPZs employing more than 27 million people worldwide). A study by the International Labor Organization (*www.ilo.org*), hardly a pro-business group, found no evidence to support the claim that nations with a strong trade-union presence suffered any loss of investment in their EPZs. Another study by the World Bank found that the higher occupational safety and health conditions an EPZ had in place, the *greater* foreign investment it attracted.[30] These results fail to support the allegations of globalization protesters that economic openness and foreign investment contribute to lower labor standards.

Environmental Protection   Opponents of globalization contend it causes a "race to the bottom" in environmental conditions and regulations.[31] However, evidence actually shows

that pollution-intensive U.S. firms tend to invest in countries with stricter environmental standards. In fact, many developing nations, including Argentina, Brazil, Malaysia, and Thailand, liberalized their foreign investment environment while simultaneously enacting *stricter* environmental legislation. If large international companies were eager to relocate to nations having the worst environmental protection laws, they would not have invested large sums of money into these countries over decades.

Additional evidence that closed, protectionist economies are far worse than open ones at protecting the environment, includes Mexico before NAFTA, Brazil under military rule, and the Warsaw Pact of communist nations—all of which had extremely poor environmental records.[32] Again, the evidence simply does not support claims of lower environmental standards as a result of economic openness and globalization.

Developing Future Markets   Opponents also allege globalization allows international firms to exploit the local labor and environment to simply export their goods back to the home country. Such claims may not only perpetuate a false image of corporations, but may have no factual basis. Today, when analyzing a country prior to investing, a corporation often searches for a future market for its goods as well as a production base. Under this scenario, what rational management team would enter a market with draconian labor and environmental regulations, depressed local wages, and an awful environment—one where the locals cannot hope to one day afford to purchase the very items they produce?

A study by the U.S. Department of Commerce (*www.commerce.gov*) found that for U.S. affiliates abroad, over 60 percent of their output was sold in the local country and less than 20 percent of output became U.S. imports. Moreover, the scenario in which a U.S. firm invests in a developing country to exploit low-cost resources, then exports the finished product back to the United States, accounts for less than four percent of total U.S. investment abroad.[33] Most international firms today support reasonable labor and environmental laws because, if for no other reason, they want to expand future local markets for their goods and services.

Quick Study

1. What are the claims of those who say globalization costs jobs and lowers wages?
2. Identify the arguments of those who say that globalization creates jobs and boosts wages.
3. How do globalization detractors say it negatively affects labor and environmental regulations?
4. What evidence refutes the claim that globalization negatively affects labor and environmental regulations?

Globalization and Income Inequality

Perhaps no other controversy swirling around globalization is more complex than the debate over its effect on poverty worldwide. Here, we focus on each of the three main branches of the debate over income inequality—inequality *within nations*, inequality *between nations*, and *global inequality*.

Inequality Within Nations   The first inequality debate is whether globalization is increasing income inequality among people *within* nations. Opponents of globalization argue that freer trade and investment allows international companies to close factories in high-cost developed nations and to move to low-wage developing nations, thus increasing income inequality within rich nations. On the other side of this debate are those who argue that more open economies experience more rapid growth and thereby reduce poverty for all of a nation's people.

Two studies of *developed and developing nations* find contradictory evidence on this argument. The first study of 38 countries over nearly 30 years supports the increasing inequality argument: Finding that as a nation increases its openness to trade, income growth among the poorest 40 percent of a nation's population declines, while income growth among other groups increases.[34] The second study of 80 countries over 40 years fails to support the increasing inequality argument: Finding that incomes of the poor rise one-for-one with overall growth—concluding that the poor benefit from international trade along with the rest of the economy.[35] Thus results of studies examining developed *and* developing nations together on this issue (of which these two studies are representative) provide mixed results.

Two studies of *developing nations only* are more consistent in their findings. One study finds that an increase in the ratio of trade to national output of one percent raises average income levels by 0.5 to two percent. Another study shows that incomes of the poor keep pace with growth in average incomes in economies, and periods, of fast trade integration, but that the poor fall behind during periods of declining openness.[36] Thus results of these two studies suggest that by integrating their economies into the global economy, *developing nations* (by far the nations with the most to gain) can boost the incomes of their poorest members of society.

Inequality Between Nations   The second inequality debate is whether globalization is widening the gap in average incomes *between* rich and poor nations. If we compare *average* incomes in rich countries to *average* incomes in poor countries, it appears that the gap between rich and poor nations is increasing. While median income in the richest 10 percent of countries was 77 times greater than median income in the poorest 10 percent in 1980, the income gap had become 122 times greater by 1999.[37] In terms of countries, the 20 richest nations had per capita incomes 16 times greater than in non-oil-producing developing countries in 1960, but had become 35 times higher by 1999.[38] A picture of growing inequality between nations appears to emerge when we separate all the nations of the world into high-income, middle-income, and low-income groups of countries. As shown in Figure 1.5, a gap is clearly present between rich and poor countries and it is clearly widening.

But *averages* conceal many differences among individual nations. On closer inspection, it appears the gap between rich and poor nations is not occurring everywhere: *one group of poor nations is closing the gap with rich economies, while a second group of poor countries is falling further behind.* For example, one study finds that the ratio between U.S. and Chinese GDP per capita levels *fell* from 12.5 in 1980 ($18,300 vs. $1,460) to 6.2 in 1995 ($23,000 vs. $3,700), implying a narrowing gap in incomes between the two nations. Meanwhile, the ratio between U.S. and African GDP per capita levels *rose* from 12.0 in 1960 ($11,200 vs. $930) to 16.9 in 1995 ($23,000 vs. $1,360), implying a widening income gap.[39] There is little, if any, doubt that China's progress is a result of its integration with the world economy and its year-on-year average economic growth rates of around nine percent. Likewise, because of its more recent embrace of globalization, India also is narrowing the income gap relative to the United States.

Supporting those results, a World Bank study finds that by integrating their economies with the global economy, 24 developing countries achieved higher income growth, longer life expectancy, and better schooling. Many of these countries (including China, Hungary,

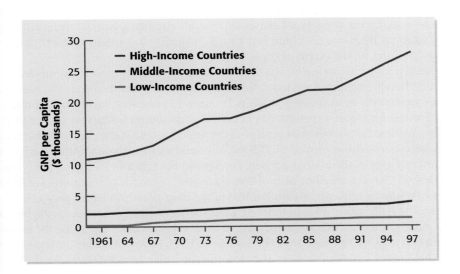

FIGURE 1.5

Income of Rich and Poor Countries

FIGURE 1.6

Benefits of Integration

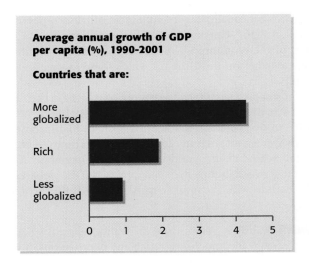

Average annual growth of GDP per capita (%), 1990-2001

Countries that are:

India, and Mexico) adopted pro-globalization policies and institutions, and sharply increased the share of trade in their GDPs. The study also confirms that some 2 billion people in sub-Saharan Africa, the Middle East, and the former Soviet Union are being left behind. Relative to other nations, economies in these regions have shrunk, poverty has risen, and education levels have risen less rapidly.[40]

Figure 1.6 provides additional support for this view and illustrates how different groups of economies fared for a decade following the collapse of communism. Countries that threw open their doors to world trade and investment experienced faster growth rates in GDP per capita than rich nations even. On the other hand, economies that remained relatively closed off from the world economy performed far worse. So, it is clear that some countries have advanced by harnessing the forces of globalization, while others have not.[41]

Global Inequality   The third inequality debate is whether globalization is increasing *global inequality*—widening income inequality between all people of the world, no matter where they live. A recent study by the National Bureau of Economic Research (*www.nber.com*) paints a promising picture of declining poverty. This study finds that the percent of world population living on less than a dollar a day (a common poverty gauge) fell from 17 percent in 1970 to just seven percent in 1998, reducing the number of people in poverty by roughly 200 million.[42] Yet a widely cited study by the World Bank finds that the percent of world population living on less than a dollar a day fell from 33 percent in 1981 to 18 percent in 2001, reducing the number in poverty from 1.5 billion to 1.1 billion.[43] For a variety of reasons, the real picture likely lies somewhere in between these two studies' estimates. One reason is that whereas the second study used population figures for developing countries only, the first study used global population in its analyses—making the poverty estimates smaller, all else being equal.[44] Thus although most studies on this issue conclude that global inequality has fallen in recent decades, they tend to differ on the extent of the fall.

What it must be like to live on less than a dollar a day in abject poverty in sub-Saharan Africa, South Asia, or elsewhere, is too difficult for most of us to comprehend. The continent of Africa presents the most pressing problem. Home to 13 percent of the world's population, Africa accounts for just three percent of world GDP. Rich nations realize they cannot sit idly by while anywhere from seven to 24 percent of the world's people live under such conditions.

So, what can be done? First of all, rich nations could increase the amount of foreign aid they currently give to the poorest nations. Foreign aid has fallen to 0.22 percent of donor countries' GDPs—the smallest proportion since 1947. Second, rich nations are in the process of forgiving some of the debt burdens of the most heavily indebted poor countries (HIPCs). The HIPC initiative is committed to alleviating some 34 countries of roughly $37 billion in debt, and should help the poorest nations to get on track in closing the income gap with rich nations. Reducing the debt burdens of HIPCs also will enable those countries to use that money for social services and to participate more in globalization, rather than simply making interest payments on debts owed to institutions such as the World Bank and the IMF.[45]

Summary of the Income Inequality Debate   First, for the debate over inequality *within nations*, studies suggest that developing nations (by far the nations with the most to gain) can boost incomes of their poorest members of society by integrating themselves into the global economy. This seems to make a strong case for developing nations to embrace globalization. Second, in the debate over inequality *between nations*, it appears that nations that are open to world trade and investment grow even faster than rich nations do. Meanwhile, economies that remain sheltered from the global economy tend to be worse off. This supports the idea that countries can advance their economies by harnessing the forces of globalization. Third, for the debate over *global inequality*, although studies tend to conclude inequality has fallen in recent decades, they differ on the extent of the drop in global poverty. Adopting standard sources and measures for variables would allow better comparisons across studies in this area.

Globalization and National Sovereignty

Today, national sovereignty generally involves the idea that a nation-state: 1) is autonomous; 2) its people can freely select their own government; 3) cannot intervene in the affairs of others; 4) can control movements over its borders; and 5) its political authorities can enter into binding international agreements.[46] Opposition groups allege that globalization erodes national sovereignty and encroaches on the authority of local and state governments. But supporters say globalization has spread democracy to the world and that national sovereignty must be viewed from a long-term perspective.

Globalization: Menace to Democracy
A main argument levied against globalization is that it empowers supranational institutions at the expense of national governments. It is not in dispute that the World Trade Organization, International Monetary Fund, and United Nations are led by appointed, not democratically elected, representatives. What is debatable, however, is whether they unduly impose their will on the citizens of sovereign nations. Critics argue that by undercutting the political and legal authority of national, regional, and local governments, such organizations undercut democracy itself. It is said that the continued activities of these unaccountable institutions will trample, rather than protect, individual liberty.[47]

Opponents of globalization also take issue with the right of national political authorities to enter into binding international agreements on behalf of citizens. Critics charge that such agreements violate the rights of subfederal (local and state) governments. For instance, state and local governments in the United States had no role in creating the North American Free Trade Agreement (NAFTA). Yet WTO rules require the U.S. federal government to take all available actions (including enacting preemptive legislation or withdrawing funding) in order to force subfederal compliance with WTO terms. A potential scenario in which this could happen is a U.S. state's law regarding food safety, for example, that was more restrictive than that permitted under NAFTA terms. Protesters complain that such requirements are a direct attack on the rights and authority of subfederal governments.[48]

Globalization: Guardian of Democracy
Globalization supporters point out that one of the most amazing consequences of globalization has been the spread of democracy worldwide. In 1972 there were 76 nations rated as politically free or partially free, but in 1998 there were 121. People in those nations are better educated, better informed, more assertive, and challenging elites and the old ways of doing things.[49] In other words, globalization has been instrumental in spreading democracy to the world, and has not been used as a tool to send democracy spiraling into decline.

Backers of globalization also contend it is instructive to take a long-term view on the issue of national sovereignty. Witnessing the sovereign state's scope of authority being altered is nothing new, as governments have long given up trying to control issues that they could not resolve. Back in the mid-1600s, governments in Europe surrendered their authority over religion because attempts to control it undermined overall political stability.

Also, governments have long been pressured to treat their subjects or citizens in a certain way. Greece in 1832, Albania in 1913, and former Yugoslavian states in the 1990s had to protect minorities in exchange for international recognition. Today, western forces stand guard over the protectorate of Kosovo within Serbia. Finally, United Nations accords over the past 50 years have made significant progress on genocide, torture, slavery, refugees, women's rights, children's rights, forced labor, and racial discrimination—hardly unimportant matters. Thus some losses of sovereignty are not inherently bad, but enhance the greater good.[50]

Globalization's Influence on Cultures

The effect of globalization on cultures is the final argument in the globalization debate. Let's briefly examine the positions of the globalization opponents and the responses of those who defend globalization.

First, protesters voice their fear that globalization is homogenizing our world and destroying the rich diversity of cultures it contains. Critics say that in some drab, new world we all will wear the same clothes bought at the same brand-name shops, eat the same foods at the same brand-name restaurants, and watch the same movies made by the same production companies.

But globalization supporters counter that globalization allows us all to profit from our differing circumstances and skills.[51] Trade allows a country to specialize in producing those goods and services in which it is most efficient. The nation can then trade those products to other nations in exchange for goods and services it desires but does not produce. In this way, France will still produce the world's finest wines, South Africa will always yield much of the world's diamonds, and the Germans and Japanese will continue to design the finest automobiles. Other nations then trade their goods and services with these countries to enjoy the wines, diamonds, and autos that they do not, or cannot, produce.

Second, those opposed to globalization claim global consumer goods companies, such as McDonald's and Coca-Cola, are destroying cultural diversity (especially in developing nations) because smaller, local companies simply cannot challenge them. Also blamed for reducing diversity are the Internet, global media, increased tourism and business travel into emerging markets, and local marketing by international companies.

But evidence suggests that the cultures of developing nations are thriving and that the influence of their music, art, and literature has grown (not shrunk) throughout the past century, with artists from Picasso to the Beatles drawing on African cultures. As shown in Figure 1.7, the portion of world exports in cultural goods accounted for by developing nations rose from 12 percent to 30 percent over a recent 20-year period.[52]

Finally, some experts on culture argue that although globalization may promote convergence of political and economic ideologies, deeper elements of a people's culture are not

FIGURE 1.7

Global Market for Culture

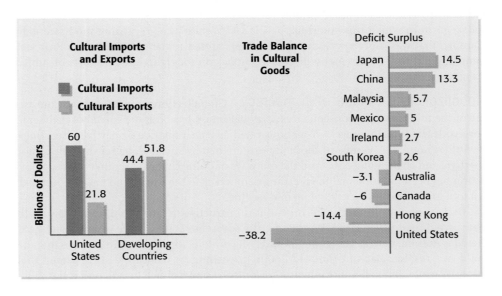

easily altered. Focusing on the consumer goods people buy may examine only the most superficial aspects of culture. In contrast, deeper moral norms that affect how people interact are less affected by globalization of a "consumer culture."[53] We revisit the discussion of globalization's effect on culture in Chapter 2.

Quick Study

1. What does the balance of evidence suggest for each of the three branches of the debate over globalization and income inequality?

2. What are the arguments of each side in the debate over globalization's impact on national sovereignty?

3. Summarize the claims made against globalization regarding its influence on cultures, and the responses of globalization defenders.

Key Players in International Business

Although companies of all types and sizes and in all sorts of industries become involved in international business, they vary in the extent to which they get involved. While a small shop owner might only import supplies from abroad, a large company may have dozens of factories located around the world. And while large companies from the most developed nations still dominate international business, firms from other nations such as China, Indonesia, Brazil, and Mexico are accounting for a larger share of international business activity. Largely because of advances in technology, small and medium-sized companies also are accounting for a greater portion of international business.

Multinational Corporations

A **multinational corporation (MNC)** is a business that has direct investments (in the form of marketing or manufacturing subsidiaries) abroad in multiple countries. Multinational corporations vary widely in size, ranging from the security firm Pinkerton (*www.pinkertons.com*), with about $900 million in annual revenue, to DaimlerChrysler (*www.daimlerchrysler.com*), with revenues of about $134 billion.

multinational corporation (MNC)
Business that has direct investments abroad in multiple countries.

    Why do business headlines focus so sharply on large international companies? First of all, their economic and political muscle makes them highly visible in the eyes of the media. Large companies generate significant jobs, investment, and tax revenue for the regions and nations they enter. Likewise, they can leave many hundreds, perhaps thousands of people out of work when they decide to close or scale back operations. It is because of their large economic impact that the business media focuses so strongly on multinational corporations.

    Second, it is common for large companies' business deals, such as mergers and acquisitions, to be valued in the billions of dollars. Consider the merger between the two global petroleum companies, Exxon and Mobil (*www.exxonmobil.com*). The deal created a merged company that had assets worth nearly $150 billion. Merger-mania peaked in 2000 when the world's largest firms were involved in $1.1 *trillion* worth of cross-border mergers and acquisitions.[54] Nowadays, many mergers are allowed to go through that would have been halted a decade ago. The reason is that the nature of competition today truly is global, not national, and the true size of a market must be measured on that basis. As one indicator of the global nature of mergers today, companies based in emerging markets such as Brazil, China, and India are accounting for a rising portion of these deals.

Profiling the Largest Multinationals
We see the enormous economic clout of multinational corporations when we compare the revenues of the world's largest companies to the value of goods and services generated by various countries. Figure 1.8 shows the top 10 companies (measured in revenue) of the Global 500 inserted into a ranking of

FIGURE 1.8

Comparing the Global 500 with
Selected Countries

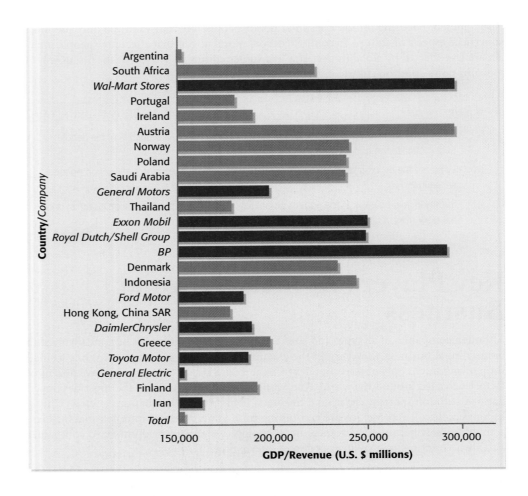

nations according to their national output (GDP). This means that if Wal-Mart (*www.walmart.com*) were a country, it would weigh in as a rich nation and rank ahead of Belgium. Even the 500th largest firm in the world, Kawasaki Heavy Industries of Japan (*www.khi.co.jp*) with over $10 billion in revenues, generates an output larger than that of many countries.[55]

Some companies have more employees than many of the smallest countries and island nations. Wal-Mart has 1,300,000 employees—the most of any company in the Global 500. China National Petroleum (*www.cnpc.com.cn*) is second, with nearly 1,150,000 employees. Finally, all types of industries are represented in the Global 500, ranging from food and beverages to mining and crude oil production. Table 1.1 shows the international distribution of the Global 500.

TABLE 1.1

Distribution of the Global 500

Country	Number of Companies
United States	176
Japan	81
France	39
Germany	37
Britain	37
Canada	13
South Korea	11
China	16
Netherlands	17
Switzerland	11
All others	64

Entrepreneurs and Small Businesses

In this age of globalization, small companies are becoming increasingly active in international trade and investment. As a result, companies are exporting earlier and growing faster, often with help from technology. Whereas traditional distribution channels often gave only large companies access to distant markets, electronic distribution is a cheap and effective alternative for small businesses that sell digitized products. Technology also makes the world market more accessible for companies that sell traditional products by lessening the cost and difficulties associated with global communication.

The age of globalization in which we find ourselves also has given rise to a new international entity, the **born-global firm**—a company that takes a global perspective on its market and engages in international business from or near its inception. Key characteristics of born-global firms tend to include an innovative culture and knowledge-based organizational capabilities. Although these firms first appeared in nations having small domestic markets, today they arise from all major trading nations. Also remarkable is that many of these companies rise to the status of international competitor in less than three-years' time. The arrival of the born-global firm is liberating and encouraging in at least two ways. First, it implies that any firm, regardless of age, experience, and resources, can engage in international business activity. Second, born-global firms inspire optimism for a future of international business characterized by thriving global diversity, not boring homogenization as critics portend.[56]

Perhaps the extreme example of a born-global firm is one that is created and resides exclusively in cyberspace, reaching out to customers around the world solely through the World Wide Web. Alessandro Naldi's *Weekend a Firenze* (Weekend in Florence) Web site (*www.waf.it*) offers global villagers more authentic Florentine products than they'll find in the scores of overpriced tourist shops crowded into downtown Florence. A Florentine himself, Naldi established his site to sell high-quality, authentic Italian merchandise made only in the many small factories of Tuscany. Currently, *Weekend a Firenze* averages 20,000 visitors each month, with 40 percent of its "guests" coming from Japan, 30 percent from the United States, and the remainder from Greece, Australia, Canada, Mexico, Saudi Arabia, and Italy.[57]

Unfortunately, many small businesses that are capable of exporting have not yet begun to do so. By some estimates, only 10 percent of companies in the United States with fewer than 100 employees export—the number is twice as high for companies of all sizes. Although there are certain real obstacles to exporting for small businesses—lack of investment capital, for example—some common myths create artificial obstacles. To explore some of these myths and the facts that dispute them, see the Entrepreneur's Survival Kit titled, "Four Myths Keeping Small Businesses from Export Success."

born-global firm
Company that takes a global perspective on its market and engages in international business from or near its inception.

Why International Business Is Special

As we've already seen in this chapter, international business differs greatly from business in a purely domestic context. The most obvious contrast is that international business takes place between two or more nations, which can have entirely different societies and commercial environments. Let's now take a moment to examine what makes international business special by introducing a model unique to this book—a model we call the *global business environment*.

The Global Business Environment

What makes international business special is that it occurs within a dynamic, integrated system that weaves together four distinct elements:

1. The forces of *globalization*
2. Many *national* business environments
3. The *international* business environment
4. International *firm* management

Four Myths Keeping Small Businesses from Export Success

○ **Myth 1:** Only large companies can export successfully. **Fact:** Exporting increases sales and profitability for small firms and can make both manufacturers and distributors less dependent on the health of the domestic economy. It can also help businesses to avoid seasonal fluctuations in sales. Selling abroad also gives small businesses the advantage of competing with companies from other countries *before* they enter the domestic market.

○ **Myth 2:** Small businesses have no place to turn for export advice. **Fact:** Whether a company is just starting out or is already exporting profitably, the federal government has an assistance program to meet its needs. The U.S. Department of Commerce's Trade Information Center (*www.trade.gov/td/tic*) is a comprehensive resource for information on all federal export-assistance programs. Firms can get advice from international trade specialists on how to locate and use federal, state, local, and private-sector programs. They also receive free information on sources of market research, trade leads, financing, and trade events.

○ **Myth 3:** The licensing requirements needed for exporting are not worth the effort. **Fact:** "Most products,"

according to international trade specialist Linda Jones, "don't need export licenses. Exporters simply write 'NLR' for 'no license required' on their Shipper's Export Declaration. There is no onerous paperwork involved." A license is needed only when exporting certain restricted commodities (such as high-technology or defense-related goods) or when shipping to a country currently under U.S. trade embargo or other restriction. To find out about license requirements, companies can visit the Commerce Department's Bureau of Export Administration Web site at (*www.bxa.doc.gov*).

○ **Myth 4:** There is no export financing available for small businesses. **Fact:** The Small Business Administration (*www.sba.gov*) and the Export-Import Bank (*www.exim.gov*) work together in lending money to small businesses. Whereas the SBA is responsible for loan requests below $750,000, the Ex-Im Bank handles transactions over $750,000. The Overseas Private Investment Corporation (*www.opic.gov*) and the Trade and Development Agency (*www.tda.gov*) also help small and medium-sized firms obtain financing for international projects.

The model in Figure 1.9 identifies each of these main elements and their subparts that together comprise the *global business environment*. Thinking about international business as occurring within this global system helps us understand its complexities and the interrelations between its distinct elements. Let's now preview each of the four main components in the global business environment.

First, *globalization* is a potent force transforming our societies and commercial activities in countless ways. We can envision globalization, and the pressures it creates, as forcing its way through the fault lines between and within each of the four main elements in Figure 1.9. In this way, the drivers of globalization (*technological innovation* and *falling trade and investment barriers*) influence each and every element of the global business environment. The dynamic nature of globalization also creates *increasing competition* for all firms everywhere, as managers begin to see the entire world as an opportunity. At home and abroad, firms must remain vigilant to the fundamental societal and commercial changes that globalization is causing.

Second, each *national business environment* is composed of unique cultural, political, legal, and economic characteristics that define business activity within that nation's borders. This set of national characteristics can differ greatly from country to country. But as nations open up and embrace globalization, their business environments are being transformed. Globalization can cause powerful synergies and enormous tensions to arise within and across various elements of a nation's society. Company managers must be attentive to such nuances, adapting their products and practices as needed.

Third, the *international business environment* influences how firms conduct their operations in both subtle and not-so-subtle ways. No business is entirely immune to events in the international business environment, as evidenced by the long-term trend toward more porous national borders. The drivers of globalization are causing the flows of trade, investment, and capital to grow and become more entwined—often causing firms

FIGURE 1.9

The Global Business Environment

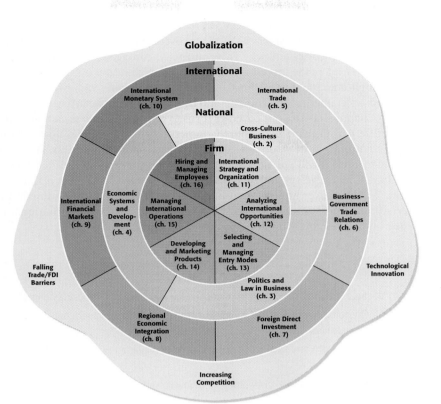

to search simultaneously for production bases *and* new markets. Companies today must keep their finger on the pulse of the international business environment to see how it may affect their business activities.

Fourth, *international firm management* is vastly different from managing a purely domestic business. Companies involved in international business must play by the rules in every market in which they choose to operate. Therefore, the context of international business management is defined by the characteristics of national business environments (the immediate point of contact for firms in Figure 1.9). Because of widely dispersed production and marketing activities today, firms commonly interact with people in distant locations within the international business environment (the second point of contact for firms). Lastly, managers and their firms are compelled to be knowledgeable about the nations in which they operate because of the integrating power of globalization (the third point of contact for firms). By closely monitoring all these elements (globalization, many national business environments, and the international business environment), managers can anticipate events and forces that may affect their firms' activities.

The Road Ahead for International Business

The coverage of international business in this book embraces the model of the global business environment displayed in Figure 1.9. In this chapter, we learned how *globalization* is transforming our world and how elements of the global business environment are becoming increasingly intertwined. As globalization penetrates deeper into the national context, every aspect of international business management is being affected.

In Part II (Chapters 2–4), we explore how *national business environments* differ from one nation to another. How people's attitudes, values, beliefs, and institutions differ from one culture to another and how this affects business will be examined. Also covered in this section is how nations differ in their political, legal, and economic systems. This material is placed early in the text because such differences between countries help frame subsequent topics and discussions—such as how companies modify business practices and strategies when operating in other countries.

We describe major components of the *international business environment* in Part III (Chapters 5–8) and Part IV (Chapters 9–10). Our coverage begins with an examination of trade and investment theories and why governments encourage or discourage trade and investment. We also explore the process of regional economic integration sweeping the globe and outline its implications for international business. Finally, we present how events in global financial markets affect international business and how the global monetary system functions.

In Part V (Chapters 11–16), our coverage turns to ways in which *international business management* differs from managing a purely domestic firm. We explain how a company creates an international strategy, organizes itself for international business, and analyzes and selects the markets it will pursue. Different potential entry modes are then explained, followed by how a firm develops and markets products for specific nations, regions, or the entire world. We then cover how international companies manage their sometimes far-flung international operations. The book closes by discussing how international firms manage their human resources in the global business environment.

Quick Study

1. Why do large *multinational corporations* capture the international business headlines?
2. Explain why small companies and so-called *born-global firms* are increasingly involved in international business.
3. Identify several myths that keep small companies from engaging in exporting. What facts dispel these myths?
4. Describe the global business environment and how its various elements interact.

Bottom Line for Business

The main theme of this chapter is that the world's national economies are becoming increasingly intertwined through the process of globalization. Cultural, political, legal, and economic events in one nation increasingly affect the lives of people in other countries. Companies, too, are discovering that they must remain attentive to how changes within the nations in which they do business and in the international business environment can affect their activities. In this section, we briefly examine several important implications of globalization for international business.

Harnessing the Benefits of Globalization

As the many protests in recent years demonstrate, there is hardly universal praise for globalization. The claims made against globalization are far-reaching, arguing that it negatively impacts wages and environmental protection, reduces political freedom, increases corruption, and inequitably rewards various groups. Yet there is evidence that the most global nations have the strongest records on equality, the most robust protection of natural resources, the most inclusive political systems, and the lowest levels of corruption. It is also in the most global nations that people live the healthiest and longest lives and that women have achieved the most social, educational, and economic progress.[58]

If there is one thing that the debate over globalization has achieved, it is that it has prompted a dialogue on the merits and demerits of globalization. "What is happening now is a recognition that the global marketplace, left to itself, is not going to automatically produce wealth and prosperity in less-developed countries unless there is rule-making and new structures that reduce the potential for destructiveness," says Clyde V. Prestowitz, Jr., president of the Economic Strategy Institute (*www.econstrat.org*).[59]

In fact, what seems to be emerging in recent years is a more sober, less naïve notion of what exactly globalization is for those on each side of the debate. While opponents of globalization are understanding that it can have positive effects on people's lives, globalization defenders are learning that preaching the benefits of greater international linkages does not alleviate the misery of the world's poor.[60] Also altering the nature of the debate is the continued advancement of globalization despite the economic, political, and cultural difficulties of recent years. The debate has gone beyond one side arguing that globalization must be halted versus the other side's belief that globalization is unstoppable, to one of how globalization can be harnessed to make its benefits exceed its costs.[61]

Globalization of Markets and Production

The two forces driving globalization (lower trade and investment barriers and increased technological innovation) are taking companies into previously isolated markets and increasing competitive pressures worldwide. A recent worldwide survey of chief executive officers (CEOs) found that "competition" stood out as the most important issue their companies face. Of the CEOs questioned, 17 percent labeled increased competition a "very substantial" threat, with another 46 percent describing it as a "significant" threat. CEOs are clearly concerned about prevailing in an increasingly competitive global marketplace.[62]

Increasing innovation is hardly likely to slow any time soon. Still holding true today is *Moore's Law*, which states the speed and performance of computer chips doubles every 18 months. If this does not seem very impressive, this translates to a weekly performance improvement of around 1 percent per week! As the cost of computing power continues to fall and new technologies are developed, companies will find it easier and less costly to manage widely dispersed marketing activities and production facilities. Technological developments may even strengthen the case for outsourcing additional white-collar jobs to low-cost locations. Finally, international companies will likely increase their cooperation with suppliers and customers as competition intensifies.

Jobs, Wages, and Inequality

Some labor groups in wealthy nations contend that globalization is forcing companies to join the "race to the bottom" in terms of wages and benefits. But low wages must be accompanied by adequate worker skills that are appropriate to the task. In order to attract investment, a location must offer low-cost, adequately skilled workers in an environment with acceptable levels of social, political, and economic stability.

Yet one occupation in developed nations that is benefiting from globalization is logistics. Because of rapid globalization in both markets and production, delivery has become a complex engineering task. Logistic experts are helping companies untangle lengthy supply chains, monitor shipping lanes, and forecast weather patterns. As companies respond to the pressure to cut costs by outsourcing select activities, more players are added to both supply and distribution channels, making them longer and more complex.

Meanwhile, product demand is becoming less certain and more variable for several reasons. First, product life cycles are becoming shorter because a product introduced in one market can make a competing product obsolete halfway around the world. Second, price competition increases the need for timely deliveries—a 20 percent reduction in prices can raise demand ten-fold. Corporate logistics departments and logistics specialist firms are helping international players respond to such challenges. Jarrett Logistics Systems (*www.jarrettlogistics.com*), is one such firm that is adding new accounts and hiring salespeople as more companies begin outsourcing. High-wage logistics jobs represent the kind of high value-added employment caused by the "churning" in labor markets that is a direct result of globalization.[63]

The Policy Agenda

Countless actions could be taken by both developed and developing nations to lessen any negative effects of globalization. Here are two specific plans that have been put forth. First, the World Bank developed a plan to help developing countries benefit more from globalization. It calls on rich countries to: 1) open their markets to exports from developing countries; 2) slash their agricultural subsidies that hurt poor-country exports; and 3) increase development aid, particularly in education and health. It calls on poor countries to: 1) improve their investment climates, and 2) improve social protection for poor people in a changing economic environment.[64]

Second, the Institute for International Economics (*www.iie.com*) proposed a policy agenda for rich nations on two fronts. On the *domestic front*, it proposes: 1) establishing "trade adjustment assistance" such as on-the-job training to help workers cope; 2) offering "wage insurance" to workers forced to take a lower paying job because a better job was lost due to globalization; 3) subsidizing health insurance costs in case of lost work; and 4) improving primary and secondary education and encouraging lifetime learning among all workers. On the *international front*, it proposes: 1) giving the International Labor Organization (ILO) more resources and political support to enforce labor standards; 2) asking the WTO to clarify the relation between international trade rules and multi-nation environmental agreements; and 3) having governments and the United Nations review the environmental implications of trade agreements.[65]

This chapter has simply introduced you to the study of international business—we hope you enjoy the rest of your journey!

SUMMARY

1. **Describe the process of *globalization* and how it affects *markets* and *production*.** The trend toward greater economic, cultural, political, and technological interdependence among national institutions and economies is called *globalization*. It is marked by "denationalization," in which national borders are becoming somewhat less relevant. It is affecting *markets* in several ways. Companies that sell global products can standardize aspects of their marketing activities to reduce costs. They are also able to explore international markets for their products if the home market is small or becomes saturated. Finally, makers of seasonal products can rely on global markets to level their income streams. Globalization also affects *production*. Firms take advantage of the globalization of production by accessing low-cost labor to make their goods more price-competitive. They can also benefit by gaining access to technical know-how or natural resources that are either nonexistent or too expensive at home.

2. **Identify the *two forces* causing globalization to increase.** The first main force behind increasing globalization is *falling barriers to trade and investment*. The world has made great strides in reducing trade barriers through institutions such as the *General Agreement on Tariffs and Trade* and the *World Trade Organization*—an international organization with the power to enforce the rules of international trade. Smaller groups of nations are also banding together in regional trade agreements to reduce trade barriers. *Technological innovation* is also a main force behind globalization. Companies are more able than ever to monitor their global business activities with the use of e-mail, videoconferencing, intranets, and extranets. These devices increase the speed with which companies can manage their far-flung activities. Innovations in transportation technologies are also making the shipment of goods between nations more efficient and dependable.

3. **Summarize the evidence for each main argument in the *globalization debate*.** Regarding *jobs and wages*, there is agreement that globalization causes dislocation in labor markets. The disagreement lies in that those supporting globalization believe overall gains of national economies are worth potentially lost jobs for individuals. In the debate over *labor and environmental regulation*, labor unions in rich countries argue globalization causes a "race to the bottom" in labor and environmental regulation. Yet evidence tends not to support this argument.

Regarding *income inequality*, it appears developing nations can boost incomes of their poorest members of society by embracing globalization. Also, nations open to world trade and investment tend to grow faster than rich nations. Also, groups tend to agree that global poverty has fallen in recent decades. In terms of *national sovereignty*, globalization has helped to spread democracy worldwide, and has aided progress globally on many important issues. In the debate over *culture*, evidence suggests that the cultures of developing nations are thriving, and that although globalization may promote convergence of political and economic ideologies, deeper elements of culture are not easily abandoned.

4. **Identify the *types of companies* that participate in international business.** Almost any company can participate in international business. Thanks to the Internet and other technologies that permit them to surmount such obstacles as prohibitively high advertising and distribution costs, many small businesses have become increasingly active in international trade and investment. However, large *multinational corporations (MNCs)* conduct most international business transactions. Multinationals dominate the international business news for two reasons: (1) they are highly visible because of their economic and political muscle and (2) their mergers and acquisitions are often valued in the billions of dollars.

Globalization has given rise to a new international entity, the *born-global firm*—a company that takes a global perspective on its market and engages in international business from or near its inception. Born-global firms tend to be innovative and have knowledge-based capabilities.

5. **Describe the *global business environment* and identify its four main elements.** It is helpful to view international business as occurring within an integrated, *global business environment*. Four elements comprise the global business environment. First, *globalization* is the dynamic force transforming our societies and commercial activities and causing increased competition for all firms. Second, separate *national business environments* are composed of unique cultural, political, legal, and economic characteristics that define business activity within that nation's borders. Third, the *international business environment* is where the actions of consumers, workers, companies, financial institutions, and governments from different nations converge. Fourth, *international business management* differs from management of a purely domestic firm in nearly all respects.

TALK IT OVER

1. Today, international businesspeople must think globally about production and sales opportunities. Many global managers will eventually find themselves living and working in cultures altogether different from their own. Many entrepreneurs will find themselves booking flights to places they had never heard of. What do you think companies can do now to prepare their managers for these new markets? What can entrepreneurs and small businesses with limited resources do?

2. In the past, national governments greatly affected the pace of globalization through agreements to lower barriers to international trade and investment. Is the pace of change now outpacing the ability of governments to manage the global economy? Will national governments become more or less important to international business in the future? Explain your answer.

3. Information technologies are developing at a faster rate than ever before. How have these technologies affected globalization? Give specific examples. Do you think globalization will continue until we all live in one "global village"? Why or why not?

4. Consider the following statement: "Globalization and the resulting increase in competition harm people, as international companies play one government against another to get the best deal possible. Meanwhile, governments continually ask for greater concessions from their citizens, demanding that they work harder and longer for less pay." Do you agree? Why or why not?

TEAMING UP

1. Imagine that you and a group of your fellow classmates own a company that manufactures cheap sunglasses. To lower production costs, you want to move your factory from your developed country to a more cost-effective nation. Choose a prospective country to which you will move. What elements of the national business environment will affect your move? Are there any obstacles to overcome in the international business environment? How will managing your company be different when you undertake international activities? What challenges will you face in managing your new employees?

2. With a group of classmates, select a country that interests you. What does its flag look like? What do the various colors and symbols, if any, represent? Identify neighbors with which it shares borders. Give some important facts about the country, including its population, population density, land area, topography, climate, natural resources, and the locations of main industries. What products are produced there? Do any aspects of the natural environment help explain why it produces what it does? Present your findings to the class.

born-global firm (p. 29)

e-business (e-commerce) (p. 4)

exports (p. 5)

GDP or GNP per capita (p. 12)

General Agreement on Tariffs and Trade (GATT) (p. 10)

globalization (p. 6)

gross domestic product (GDP) (p. 11)

gross national product (GNP) (p. 12)

imports (p. 5)

international business (p. 5)

International Monetary Fund (IMF) (p. 17)

multinational corporation (MNC) (p. 27)

World Bank (p. 17)

World Trade Organization (WTO) (p. 11)

TAKE IT TO THE WEB

1. In this chapter, we've seen how globalization is causing fundamental change in our societies and commercial activities. We've also seen how managers can be more effective if they know what drives globalization and are familiar with the debate over globalization's positive and negative effects.

   Select a controversial globalization topic that interests you, and visit the Web sites of two organizations that have opposing views on this topic. (*Hint*: you might begin by visiting the wide range of pro- and anti-globalization organizations mentioned in this chapter.) For the topic you've chosen, report on (1) the specific position(s) of each opposing side in the debate, (2) the evidence each side uses to support its position(s), and (3) the policy agenda, if any, each side promotes.

   Which side of this debate do you agree with most? Have your views on this topic changed as a result of your research? If so, how? In your opinion, which types of firms/industries do you think are most affected by this topic? Explain. Write up a short summary of your research findings, and include key Web sites you found helpful.

ETHICAL CHALLENGES

1. You are a U.S. citizen recently assigned as the manager of distribution in a European country where bribery is relatively accepted. Your job description includes responsibility for accepting shipments as they enter the local port authority. On your first trip down to the docks to sign for a shipment, the customs agent in charge asks for a "tip" to clear the goods for pickup. The value of the incoming shipment is around $150,000. Knowing that the government has recently launched an initiative to reduce corruption, how do you react? If additional information would be helpful to you, what would it be?

2. You are the CEO of Nike. In one widely publicized event, Nike called on civil rights leader Andrew Young to look into labor practices at Asian plants to which Nike outsourced work to determine if practices adhered to the shoemaker's own code of ethical conduct. After a month-long investigation, Young reported no evidence of widespread or systematic mistreatment of workers abroad. Critics charged that the report was shallow because Young admitted to spending only three hours in any factory and was always accompanied by Nike officials. They were also skeptical because Young presented his findings

to Nike's board and senior management a week before making them public. As the CEO of Nike, how do you respond to these criticisms? Are there more effective or objective means of monitoring a company's international activities? If so, what are they?

3. You are the mayor of a mid-size town on the Colorado River between Mexico and Arizona. Contamination from both sides of the border has flowed into your community. The North American Free Trade Agreement (NAFTA) requires the United States to pay for environmental cleanup. But critics accuse the U.S. and Mexican governments of not doing enough to safeguard the environment along the two nations' borders. Among other things, they charge contamination of the dry bed of the Colorado River. As mayor, what can you do to persuade business leaders and government officials to adhere to environmental standards? Which do you think presents your biggest challenge: the Arizona state, U.S. federal, or Mexican federal government? What can business leaders do if governments ignore their environmental responsibilities?

PRACTICING INTERNATIONAL MANAGEMENT CASE

MTV: Going Global with a Local Beat

As goes the Buggles song, did "video kill the radio star"? Well, perhaps not, but no company has been more successful at getting teenagers around the world to tune in to music television than MTV Networks International (*www.mtv.com/mtvinternational*). Applying the maxim "Think globally, act locally," the company beams its irreverent mix of music, news, and entertainment to 340 million homes in over 140 countries—which are as diverse as Brazil, China, India, Russia, and Singapore. Although style and format are largely driven by the U.S. youth culture, content is tailored entirely to local markets. And MTV has never grown old with its audience. Instead, it has remained very true to a specific demographic—young people between the ages of 18 and 24.

In 1987, MTV (*www.mtv.com*) commanded an audience of 61 million in the United States. But because demand was leveling off, the company took the music revolution global by starting MTV Europe (*www.mtv.tv*) and MTV Australia. Through its experiences in Europe, MTV refined its mix of programming to become a "global national brand with local variations." At first, it took a pan-European approach, marketing the same product to all European countries. MTV broadcast primarily British and U.S. music (both of which were topping the charts throughout Europe) and used European "veejays" who spoke English. The European network was a huge overnight success.

Seven years later, however, MTV had become the victim of its own success. Now it had to compete with a new crop of upstart rivals that tailored content to language, culture, and current events in specific countries. One successful competitor was Germany's VIVA (*www.viva.tv*), launched in 1993 and featuring German veejays and more German artists (like Fantastischen 4 and Scooter) than MTV Europe. Managers at MTV Networks were not overly concerned because MTV was still extremely popular. But they did realize they were losing their edge (and some customers) to the new national networks. So, the company's top managers faced a crucial decision—should the company split up MTV Europe into various national stations or continue doing business as it always had?

Because they had spent almost two decades building a global brand identity, MTV executives initially rejected the idea of splitting MTV into national stations. But little by little they changed their collective mind. They decided to move forward because a certain technological innovation made it possible for MTV to think globally and act locally at very little cost. The breakthrough was digital compression technology, which allows suppliers to multiply the number of services offered on a single satellite feed. "Where there were three or four services," explained one MTV official, "now we can broadcast six or eight."

Today, teens all over the world have their MTV cake and eat it, too. German teens see German-language programs that are created and produced there and shown on MTV Germany (*www.mtv.de*)—along with the usual generous helpings of U.S., British, and international music and the ever-popular duo Beavis and Butthead. Today in Europe, those nations that still share an MTV channel are those that have cultural similarities—such as the Nordic nations (*www.mtve.com*)—and the smallest or still-developing markets—such as the eastern European nations that receive MTV Europe (*www.mtv.tv*). Likewise, while much of Latin America receives MTV Latin America (*www.mtvla.com*) Brazilian teens see Portuguese-language programs that are created there and shown on MTV Brazil (*www.mtv.com.br*). An added side benefit for MTV of its national strategy is that national advertisers, who had shunned the channel during its pan-European days, returned to beam more targeted ads to their teenage consumers.

Now, more than 20 years after MTV planted its flag on the pop-culture moon, the beat goes on. "It's the only television entity of any kind that ever had a generation named after it," says Robert Thompson, professor of media and popular culture at Syracuse University. "We don't even have the CNN generation, but we have the MTV generation."

Thinking Globally

1. The past decade has witnessed a growing similarity in the attitudes and spending habits of youthful consumers around the world. As one journalist puts it, "It may still be conventional wisdom to 'think globally and act locally,' but in the youth market, it is increasingly a case of one size fits all." Do you agree or disagree? Why or why not?

2. Some people are concerned that teens exposed to large doses of U.S. youth culture on MTV networks will begin to identify less and less with their own societies. Others worry that teenage consumers in developing countries want more and more Western goods that they can't afford. MTV's response to such criticism: "It's just fun," says one network executive. "It's only TV." What do you think? Are there dangers in broadcasting U.S. programs and ads to both developed and developing countries?

3. Digital compression technology made it possible for MTV to program over a global network. Can you think of any other technological innovations that have helped companies to think globally and act locally?

4. Advances in technology are often accompanied by evolution in the entertainment industry. How do you think new technologies such as the DVD player and Palm Pilot will affect entertainment in the years to come?

As the global marketplace continues to expand into previously isolated business environments, each of us needs a thorough grasp of the global landscape. This atlas presents the world in a series of maps designed to assist your understanding of global business. By knowing the locations of countries and the distances between them, managers in the global marketplace are able to make more informed decisions. Knowing the geography of a place may also give a manager insight into the culture of the people living there.

Because knowing where borders meet is extremely useful in international business, this atlas captures the most recent changes in national political boundaries. Familiarize yourself with each of the maps in this appendix, and then try to answer the following 20 questions. We urge you to return to this atlas frequently in order to refresh your memory of the global landscape, and especially when you encounter the name of an unfamiliar city or country.

Map Exercises

1. Which of the following countries border the Atlantic Ocean?
   a. Bolivia
   b. Australia
   c. South Africa
   d. Japan
   e. United States

2. Which of the following countries are found in Africa?
   a. Guyana
   b. Morocco
   c. Egypt
   d. Pakistan
   e. Niger

3. Which one of the following countries does *not* border the Pacific Ocean?
   a. Australia
   b. Venezuela
   c. Japan
   d. Mexico
   e. Peru

4. Prague is the capital city of:
   a. Uruguay
   b. Czech Republic
   c. Portugal
   d. Tunisia
   e. Hungary

5. If transportation costs for getting your product from your market to Japan are high, which of the following countries might be good places to locate a manufacturing facility?
   a. Thailand
   b. Philippines
   c. South Africa
   d. Indonesia
   e. Portugal

6. Seoul is the capital city of:
   a. Vietnam
   b. Cambodia
   c. Malaysia
   d. China
   e. South Korea

7. Turkey, Romania, Ukraine, and Russia border the body of water called the _____ Sea.

8. Thailand shares borders with:
   a. Cambodia
   b. Pakistan
   c. Singapore
   d. Malaysia
   e. Indonesia

9. Which of the following countries border no major ocean or sea?
   a. Austria
   b. Paraguay
   c. Switzerland
   d. Niger
   e. all of the above

10. Oslo is the capital city of:
    a. Germany
    b. Canada
    c. Brazil
    d. Australia
    e. Norway

11. Chile is located in:
    a. Africa
    b. Asia
    c. the Northern Hemisphere
    d. South America
    e. Central Europe

12. Saudi Arabia shares borders with:
    a. Jordan
    b. Kuwait
    c. Iraq
    d. United Arab Emirates
    e. all of the above

13. The body of water located between Sweden and Estonia is the _____ Sea.

14. Which of the following countries are located on the Mediterranean Sea?
    a. Italy
    b. Croatia
    c. Turkey
    d. France
    e. Portugal

15. The distance between Sydney (Australia) and Tokyo (Japan) is shorter than that between:
    a. Tokyo and Cape Town (South Africa)
    b. Sydney and Hong Kong (China, SAR)
    c. Tokyo and London (England)
    d. Sydney and Jakarta (Indonesia)
    e. all of the above

16. Madrid is the capital city of (capitals are designated with red dots):
    a. Madagascar
    b. Italy
    c. Mexico
    d. Spain
    e. United States

17. Which of the following countries is not located in central Asia?
    a. Afghanistan
    b. Uzbekistan
    c. Turkmenistan
    d. Kazakhstan
    e. Suriname

18. If you were shipping your products from your production facility in Pakistan to market in Australia, they would likely cross the _____ Ocean.

19. Papua New Guinea, Guinea-Bissau, and Guinea are alternative names for the same country.
    a. true
    b. false

20. Which of the following countries are island nations?
    a. New Zealand
    b. Madagascar
    c. Japan
    d. Australia
    e. all of the above

Answers

1. c. South Africa, e. United States; 2. b. Morocco, c. Egypt, e. Niger; 3. b. Venezuela; 4. b. Czech Republic; 5. a. Thailand, b. Philippines, d. Indonesia; 6. e. South Korea; 7. Black; 8. a. Cambodia, d. Malaysia; 9. e. all of the above; 10. e. Norway; 11. d. South America; 12. e. all of the above; 13. Baltic; 14. a. Italy, c. Turkey, d. France; 15. a. Tokyo and Cape Town (South Africa), c. Tokyo and London (England); 16. d. Spain; 17. e. Suriname; 18. Indian; 19. b. false; 20. e. all of the above.

Self-Assessment

If you scored 15 correct answers or more, well done: You are well prepared for your international business journey. If you scored fewer than 8 correct answers, you may wish to review this atlas before moving on to Chapter 2.

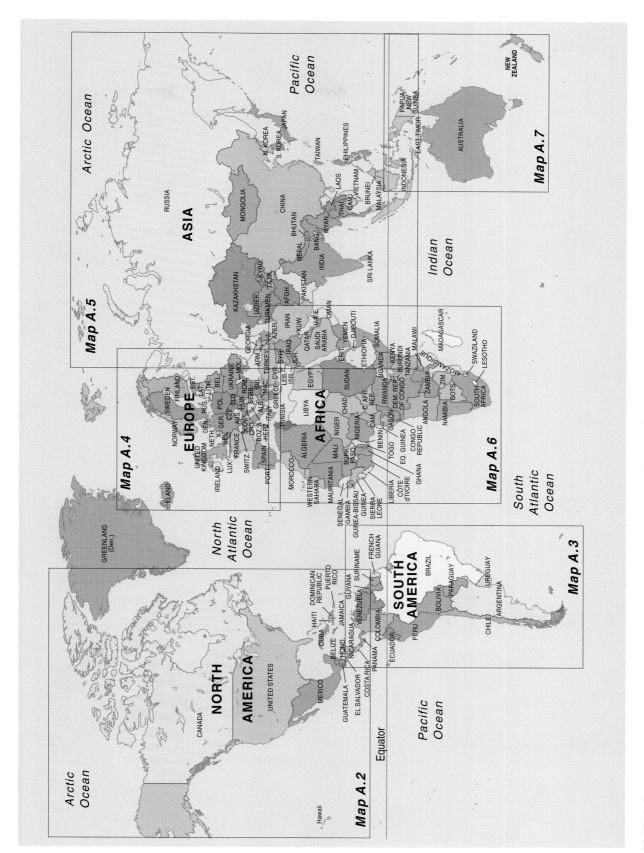

MAP A.1

The World in 2005

This global view identifies each continent and acts as references for the six maps that follow.

MAP A.2

North America

MAP A.3

South America

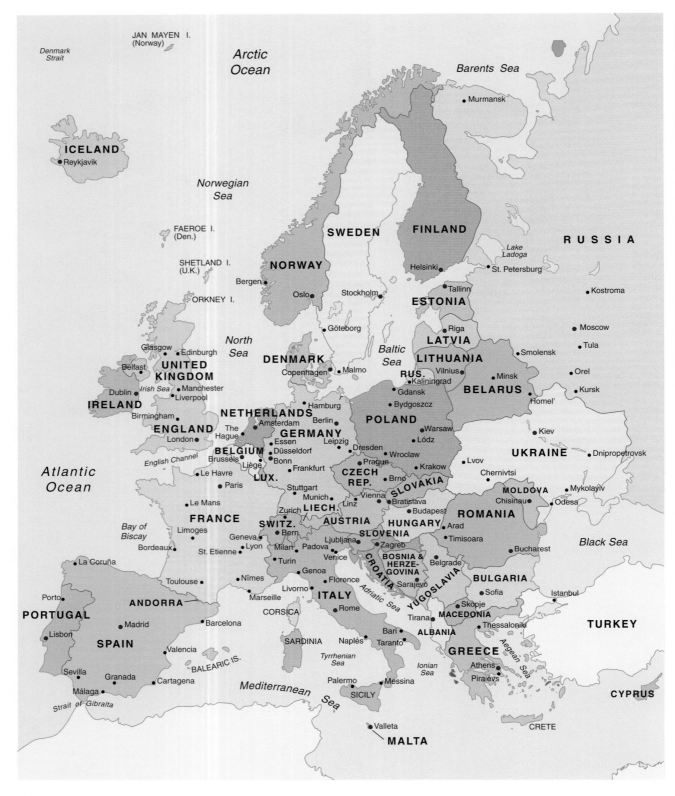

MAP A.4

Europe

MAP A.5

Asia

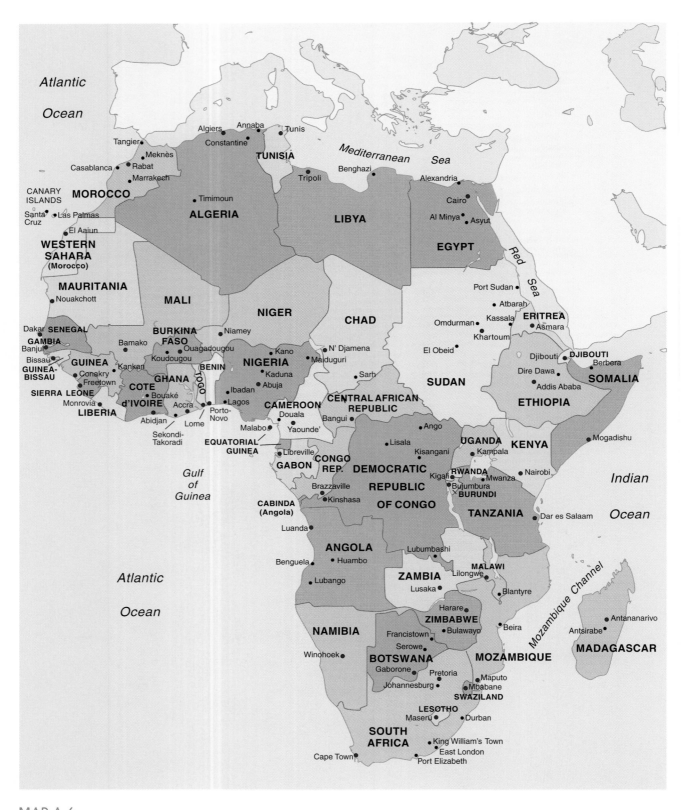

MAP A.6

Africa

MAP A.7

Oceania

Map labels:

Indian Ocean

BORNEO

SULAWESI

I N D O N E S I A

Banjarmasin
Ujung Pandang
Semarang
JAVA
Surabaya
Bandung
Jakarta

Kupang
EAST TIMOR
Dili
Timor Sea
Arafura Sea

Jayapura
PAPUA NEW GUINEA

Port Moresby

SOLOMON ISLANDS
Honiara

Coral Sea

VANUATU
Port-Vila

NEW CALEDONIA (France)
Nouméa

Pacific Ocean

Gulf of Carpentaria

Darwin
Katherine
Tennant Creek

A U S T R A L I A

Alice Springs

Cairns
Townsville
Charters Towers
Mackay
Rockhampton
Bass Strait
Longreach
Bundaberg

Brisbane
Southport
Lismore
Coff's Harbour
Port Macquarie
Newcastle
Ipswich
Toowoomba
Tamworth
Dubbo
Sydney
Wollongong
Shellharbour
Canberra

Broken Hill
Wagga Wagga
Bendigo
Melbourne
Geelong
Ballarat
Elizabeth
Adelaide
Port Augusta
Mount Gambier
Warrnambool

Launceston
TASMANIA
Hobart

Tasman Sea

Great Australian Bight

Kalgoorlie

Geraldton
Perth
Mandurah
Fremantle
Bunbury
Albany

NEW ZEALAND
Auckland
Wellington
Christchurch
Dunedin

learning objectives

After studying this chapter, you should be able to

1. Describe *culture,* and explain the significance of both national culture and *subcultures.*

2. Identify the *components of culture,* and describe their impact on business activities around the world.

3. Describe *cultural change,* and explain how companies and culture affect one another.

4. Explain how the *physical environment* and *technology* influence culture.

5. Describe the two main *frameworks* used to classify cultures and explain their practical use.

cross-cultural

Part 2   N a t i o n a l   B u s i n e s s   E n v i r o n m e n t s

2

business

a look **back**

CHAPTER 1 introduced us to international business. We examined the impact of globalization on markets and production, the forces behind its expansion, and each main argument in the debate over globalization. We also profiled the kinds of companies engaged in international business.

a look **at this chapter**

This chapter introduces us to the important role of culture in international business. We explore the main elements of culture and show how they affect business policies and practices. We learn different methods of classifying cultures and how these methods can be applied to business.

a look **ahead**

CHAPTER 3 describes the political and legal systems of nations. We learn how these systems differ from one country to another and how they influence international business operations. We also discover how managers can reduce the effects of political risk.

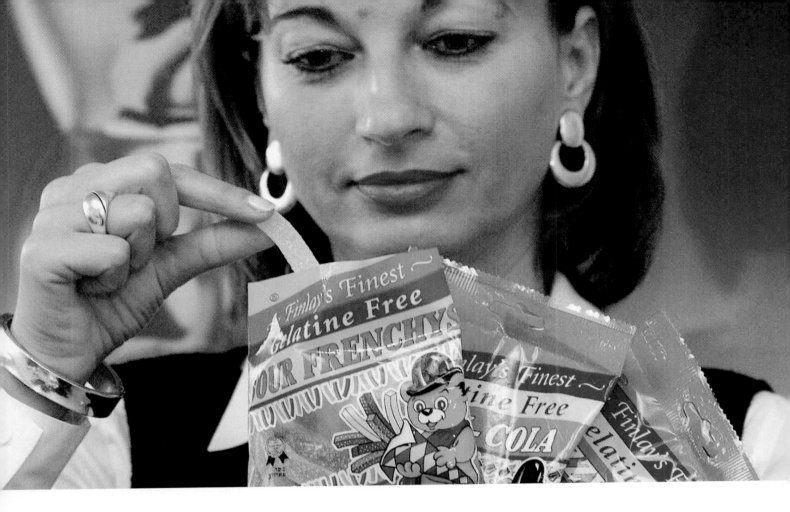

Hold the Pork, Please!

BONN, Germany—"Kids and grownups love it so, the happy world of Haribo!" So goes the phrase that drives global sales of the gummi bear candies made by Germany-based Haribo AG (*www.haribo.com*). These little candies, with names such as Gold Bears and Horror Mix, are available in 46 shapes including Coke bottles and glowworms. Haribo supplies 83 countries from its 17 factories at home and abroad, producing 70 million gummi bears a day. But despite its success, Haribo was not meeting the needs of a globally dispersed subculture potentially worth $2 billion annually. The culprit: the pork-based substance that gives the candy its sticky, rubbery feel makes the candy off-limits to Muslims and Jews who adhere to a strict religious diet.

So the company embarked on a four-year mission to create a candy free of the pork-based gelatin so it conformed to Islamic and Judaic dietary restrictions. "The first time we made it, we got a marmalade you could spread on bread," reported Neville Finlay, the British exporter who ships the new product under his own brand. "And at the other extreme was something you could fill a swimming pool with and drive a truck across," he added. Haribo found success eventually with a bacteria-based compound already common in salad dressings and sauces.

But then a local supplier committed a language blunder—a common occurrence in international business. The printing on the first packages of candies destined for Hebrew communities was backward—Hebrew is read right to left, not left to right like English. But today production is going smoothly. Haribo even has a Jewish rabbi (for *kosher* candies) or a Muslim cleric (for *halal* candies) inspect ingredients and oversee production to ensure that it adheres to religious customs. As you read this chapter, think of the cultural differences you've experienced while traveling abroad or when you've met someone from another culture.[1]

This chapter is the first of three that describe how key aspects of a nation's business environment (culture, politics, law, and economics) affect international business activity. We introduce these topics early because of their strong influence on the way commerce is conducted in different countries. In fact, success in international business can often be traced directly to a deep understanding of some aspect of a people's commercial environment. This chapter (Chapter 2) explores the influence of *culture* on international business activity. Chapter 3 presents the impact of *political and legal systems*, and Chapter 4 examines the role of *economic systems and development* on international business. Together, these three chapters comprise Part II titled, "National Business Environments."

The significance of any nation's commercial environment is apparent in the fact that an assessment of its overall business climate is typically the first step in analyzing its potential as a host for international commercial activity. This means addressing some important questions, such as the following. What language(s) do the people speak? What is the climate like? Are the local people open to new ideas and new ways of doing business? Do government officials and the people want our business? Is the political situation stable enough so that our assets and employees are not placed at unacceptable levels of risk? Answers to these kinds of questions—plus statistical data on items such as income level and labor costs—allow companies to evaluate the attractiveness of a particular location as a place for doing business.

Because of the pivotal role of culture in all international commercial activity, we address it first in our discussion of national business environments. Whether we are discussing an entrepreneur who runs a small import/export business, or a huge global firm directly involved in over 100 countries, *people* are at the center of all business activity. When people from around the world come together to conduct business, they bring with them different backgrounds, assumptions, expectations, and ways of communicating—in other words, *culture*.

We begin this chapter by exploring the influence of nation-states and subcultures on a people's overall cultural image. Next we learn the importance of values, attitudes, manners, and customs in any given culture. We then examine ways in which social institutions, religion, language, and other key elements of culture affect business practices and national competitiveness. We close the chapter with a look at 2 alternative methods of classifying cultures.

What Is Culture?

When traveling in other countries, we often perceive differences in the way people live and work. In the United States dinner is commonly eaten around 6:00 P.M.; in Spain it's not served until 8:00 or 9:00 P.M. In the United States most people shop in large supermarkets once or twice a week; Italians tend to shop in smaller local grocery stores nearly every day. Essentially, we are experiencing differences in culture—the set of values, beliefs, rules, and institutions held by a specific group of people.[2] Culture is a highly complex portrait of a people. It includes everything from high tea in England, to the tropical climate of Barbados, to Mardi Gras in Brazil, to segregation of the sexes in Saudi Arabian schools.

But before we learn about the individual components of culture in detail, let's take a look at two important concepts—one that should be discouraged and one that should be fostered.

Accommodating Culture: Avoiding Ethnocentricity
Ethnocentricity is the belief that one's own ethnic group or culture is superior to that of others. Because ethnocentric-

culture
Set of values, beliefs, rules, and institutions held by a specific group of people.

ethnocentricity
Belief that one's own ethnic group or culture is superior to that of others.

ity causes people to view other cultures in terms of their own and disregard the beneficial characteristics of other cultures, it can seriously undermine international business projects. In fact, ethnocentricity played a role in many stories, some retold in this chapter, of companies that failed dramatically when they tried to implement a new business practice in a subsidiary abroad. The failures occurred because managers ignored a fundamental aspect of the local culture, which provoked a backlash from the local population, their government, or nongovernmental groups.

Globalization demands that businesspeople do away completely with ethnocentric thinking. As new technologies allow suppliers and buyers to treat the world as a single, interconnected marketplace, companies need employees who function without the blinders of ethnocentricity.

Understanding Culture: Developing Cultural Literacy   As globalization continues, people directly involved in international business increasingly benefit from a certain degree of **cultural literacy**—detailed knowledge about a culture that enables a person to function effectively within it. Cultural literacy improves people's ability to manage employees, market products, and conduct negotiations in other countries. For instance, global brands such as GAP (*www.gap.com*) and Starbucks (*www.starbucks.com*) provide a competitive advantage because consumers know and respect these highly recognizable names. Yet cultural differences often dictate alterations in some aspect of a business to suit local tastes and preferences. The culturally literate manager that compensates for local needs and desires brings his or her company closer to customers and improves the firm's competitiveness.

As you read through the concepts and examples in this chapter, try to avoid reacting with *ethnocentricity* while developing your own *cultural literacy*. Because these 2 concepts are central to the discussion of many international business topics, we will encounter them throughout this book. In the final chapter (Chapter 16), we explore specific types of cultural training that companies actually use to develop cultural literacy among their employees.

cultural literacy
Detailed knowledge about a culture that enables a person to function effectively within it.

National Culture and Subcultures

Whether rightly or wrongly, we tend to invoke the concept of the *nation-state* when speaking of culture. In other words, we usually refer to British and Indonesian cultures as if all Britons and all Indonesians were culturally identical. Why? Because we have been conditioned to think in terms of *national culture.* But this is at best a generalization. In Great Britain, campaigns for greater Scottish and Welsh independence continue to make significant progress. Meanwhile, in remote parts of Indonesia, people build homes in the treetops even as other parts of the nation pursue ambitious economic development programs. Because of the diversity that lies beneath the veneer of national culture, let's take a closer look at what a nation's culture often contains.

National Culture   Nation-states *support* and *promote* the concept of a national culture by building museums and monuments to preserve the legacies of important events and people. In so doing, they affirm the importance of national culture to their citizens and organizations. Nation-states also intervene in business to help *preserve* their national cultures. Most nations, for example, regulate culturally sensitive sectors of the economy, such as filmmaking and broadcasting. France continues to voice fears that its language is being tainted with English and its media with U.S. programming. To stem the English invasion, French laws limit the use of English in product packaging and storefront signs. At peak listening times, at least 40 percent of all radio station programming must be reserved for French artists. Similar laws apply to television broadcasting.[3] The French government even fined the local branch of a U.S. university for failing to provide a French translation on its English-language site on the World Wide Web.

Cities, too, get involved in enhancing national cultural attractions, often for economic reasons. Lifestyle enhancements to a city can help it attract companies, which benefit by having an easier task retaining top employees. The Guggenheim museum in Bilbao, Spain (*www.guggenheim-bilbao.es*) designed by Frank Gehry, has revived that old Basque industrial city. Hong Kong's government is enhancing cultural attractions to lure businesses that may otherwise locate elsewhere in the region, such as Singapore and Shanghai, China.[4]

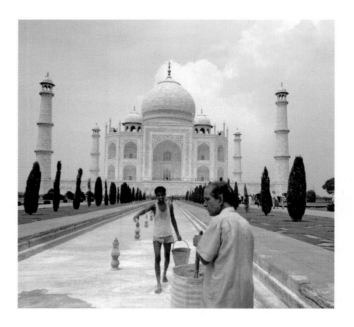

Today, the government of India is facing financial difficulties in properly maintaining India's historic monuments, like the Taj Mahal shown here. So private companies in India are restoring these sites to their original splendor and performing routine maintenance. In return, these companies hope to build goodwill with consumers that will translate into greater sales. Do you know of companies that sponsor the upkeep of historic sites or public places in your city?

subculture

A group of people who share a unique way of life within a larger, dominant culture.

Subcultures   A group of people who share a unique way of life within a larger, dominant culture is called a **subculture**. A subculture can differ from the dominant culture in language, race, lifestyle, values, attitudes, or other characteristics.

Although subcultures exist in all nations, they are often glossed over by our *impressions* of national cultures. But companies must nevertheless be mindful of subcultures when formulating business strategies. For example, the customary portrait of Chinese culture often ignores the fact that the total population of China is comprised of more than 50 distinct ethnic groups. Decisions regarding product design, packaging, and advertising must consider each group's distinct culture. For instance, marketing directed at Tibetans must respect their unique history and ethnic pride, because they would certainly resent any campaign referring to them as Chinese. Marketing campaigns in China must also acknowledge that Chinese dialects in the Shanghai and Canton regions differ from those in the country's interior and that not everyone is fluent in the official Mandarin dialect.

A multitude of subcultures also exist within the United States. The most recent U.S. Census revealed that of slightly more than 280 million U.S. residents, nearly 80 million are black, Hispanic, and Asian. One company that has had success reaching Hispanic consumers, though not initially, is Frito Lay (*www.fritolay.com*). Frito Lay was disheartened that the foreign-born segment of the 46 million U.S. Hispanics was not buying its Latin-flavored versions of Lay's and Doritos chips. The company looked south of the border to its $1 billion Mexican subsidiary, Sabritas, and brought 4 popular brands into the U.S. market, including Sabritones chile and lime puff wheat snacks. The gamble paid off: Frito Lay's Sabritas brand doubled sales to over $100 million between 2002 and 2004.[5]

Yet cultural boundaries do not always correspond to political boundaries—subcultures sometimes exist across national borders. People who live in different nations but who share the same subculture can have more in common with one another than with their fellow nationals. Arab culture, for instance, extends from northwest Africa to the Middle East, with pockets of Arabs in many European countries and the United States. Because Arabs share a common language and tend to share purchasing behaviors related to Islamic religious beliefs, marketing to Arab subcultures can sometimes be accomplished with a single marketing campaign. The company profile at the start of this chapter showed us how Haribo (*www.haribo.com*) worked to make its product acceptable to Muslim (and Jewish) consumers worldwide.

Firms must also take special care when marketing medicines, dangerous chemicals, and other products requiring detailed instructions. If a product's labels and warnings cannot be read and understood by all subcultures, it might inflict physical harm rather than satisfy a need.

Quick Study

1. Define *culture*. How does *ethnocentricity* distort one's view of other cultures?
2. What is *cultural literacy*? Why should businesspeople understand more about other cultures?
3. How do both nation-states and *subcultures* influence a nation's cultural image?

Components of Culture

Both the actions of nation-states and the presence of subcultures help define the culture of a group of people. But a people's culture also includes what they consider beautiful and tasteful, their underlying beliefs, their traditional habits, and the ways in which they relate to one another and their surroundings. Let's now take a detailed look at each main component of culture: *aesthetics, values* and *attitudes, manners* and *customs, social structure, religion, personal communication, education,* and *physical* and *material environments.*

Aesthetics

What a culture considers to be in "good taste" in the arts (including music, painting, dance, drama, and architecture), the imagery evoked by certain expressions, and the symbolism of certain colors is called **aesthetics**.

Aesthetics are important when a firm considers doing business in another culture. The selection of appropriate colors for advertising, product packaging, and even work uniforms can enhance chances of success. For instance, green is a favorable color in Islam and adorns the national flags of most Islamic nations, including Jordan, Pakistan, and Saudi Arabia. That is why product packaging is often green in these countries—companies want to take advantage of the emotional attachment to the color. Across much of Asia, on the other hand, green is associated with sickness. In Europe, Mexico, and the United States, the color of death and mourning is black; in Japan and most of Asia, it's white.

Shoe manufacturer Nike (*www.nike.com*) recently experienced firsthand the importance of imagery and symbolism in international marketing. The company emblazoned a new line of shoes with the word "Air" written to resemble flames or heat rising off blacktop. The shoes were given various names, including *Air Bakin', Air Melt, Air Grill,* and *Air B-Que.* But what Nike did not realize was that the squiggly lines of the "Air" logo resembled Arabic script for "Allah," the Arabic name for God. Under threat of a worldwide boycott by Muslims, who considered it a sacrilege, Nike recalled the shoes and agreed to build several playgrounds in Muslim communities as part of its apology.

The importance of aesthetics is just as great when going international using the Internet. A California-based company called Web of Culture (*www.webofculture.com*) is helping companies cross the cultural divide on the Web. The company is dedicated to educating corporations on how to globalize their Internet presence. The company provides professional guidance on how to adapt Web sites to account for cultural preferences such as color scheme, imagery, and slogans.[6] The advice of specialist firms can be especially helpful for entrepreneurs and small companies because they rarely have in-house employees well-versed in other cultures. To read how entrepreneurs and small companies can readily tailor a Web site to suit local aesthetics and other cultural variables, see the Entrepreneur's Survival Kit titled, "Give Your Web Site a Local Feel."

Finally, music is also deeply embedded in culture and should be considered when developing promotions. When used correctly, music can be a clever and creative addition to a promotion; if used incorrectly, it can be offensive to the local population. The architecture of buildings and other structures should also be researched to avoid making cultural blunders attributable to the symbolism of certain shapes and forms.

aesthetics
What a culture considers to be in "good taste" in the arts, the imagery evoked by certain expressions, and the symbolism of certain colors.

Values and Attitudes

values
Ideas, beliefs, and customs to which people are emotionally attached.

Ideas, beliefs, and customs to which people are emotionally attached are **values.** Values include things like honesty, marital faithfulness, freedom, and responsibility.

Values are important to business because they affect a people's work ethic and desire for material possessions. Whereas certain cultures (say, in Singapore) value hard work and material success, others (in Greece, for instance) value leisure and a modest lifestyle. The United Kingdom and United States value individual freedom, whereas Japan and South Korea value group consensus.

Because values are so important to both individuals and groups, the influx of values from other cultures can be fiercely resisted. Many Muslims believe drugs, alcohol, and certain kinds of music and literature will undermine important values. This is why nations under Islamic law (including Iran and Saudi Arabia) exact severe penalties against anyone possessing items that are illegal, including drugs and alcohol. Deeply held conservative values are why the Arab-world's reality-TV programs tend to be short-lived. In Bahrain, the local version of "Big Brother" was canceled after people objected to the program's format, which involved young unmarried adults of both sexes living under the same roof. The Lebanon-based program "Hawa Sawa," or "On Air Together" was also shut down because its "elimidate" format (in which a young man would gradually eliminate young women to finally select a date) was perceived as too "Western" for many people.[7]

attitudes
Positive or negative evaluations, feelings, and tendencies that individuals harbor toward objects or concepts.

Attitudes are positive or negative evaluations, feelings, and tendencies that individuals harbor toward objects or concepts. Attitudes reflect underlying values. For instance, a Westerner would be expressing an attitude if he or she were to say, "I do not like the Japanese purification ritual because it involves being naked in a communal bath." The Westerner quoted here, for instance, might hold conservative beliefs regarding exposure of the body.

Like values, attitudes are learned from role models, including parents, teachers, and religious leaders. Also, like values, they differ from one country to another because they are formed within a cultural context. But unlike values (which generally concern only important matters), people hold attitudes toward both important and unimportant aspects of life. And whereas values are quite rigid over time, attitudes are more flexible. For instance, young people across Europe are experiencing an unprecedented degree of cultural, political, and economic change as the European Union continues to develop and expand. It seems that a real "European" attitude is sinking into the psyche of young people as companies from different countries merge, industries consolidate, and nations are bound more tightly together. But this shift in attitudes among young Europeans is occurring while their underlying values are tending to remain similar to those of their parents.

Cultural knowledge can help managers decide whether promotions must be adapted to local attitudes in order to maximize the effectiveness of promotional efforts. For instance, it is often believed that people around the world respond similarly toward technological products. So advertising agency Euro RSCG Worldwide (*www.eurorscg.com*) surveyed consumers about their attitudes toward technology and their use of technological products in purchasing situations. Among other things, the survey revealed that consumers in the United Kingdom were far more likely to purchase online than Italian and German consumers. It also found that Web sites were useful in Finland as a source of information on technological products but were considered not at all useful by Italians. Ira Matathia, global director of business development for RSCG, said, "Marketers will have to forfeit the notion of global marketing and look to each country's highly individualized adaptation of technology for clues as to how to build and satisfy consumer desire."[8]

Let's now look at how people's attitudes differ regarding three important aspects of life that directly affect business activities—attitudes toward time, work and achievement, and cultural change.

Attitudes Toward Time
People in many Latin American and Mediterranean cultures are casual about their use of time. They maintain flexible schedules and would rather enjoy their time than sacrifice it to unbending efficiency. Businesspeople, for example, may arrive after the scheduled meeting time and prefer to spend time building personal trust before discussing business. Not surprisingly, it usually takes longer to conduct business in these parts of the world than in the United States or northern Europe.

In contrast, people in Japan and the United States typically arrive promptly for meetings, keep tight schedules, and work long hours. The emphasis on using time efficiently reflects the underlying value of hard work in both these countries. Yet people in Japan and the United States sometimes differ in how they use their time at work. For example, U.S. employees strive toward workplace efficiency and may leave work early if the day's tasks are done, reflecting the value placed on producing individual results. But in Japan, while efficiency is prized, it is equally important to look busy in the eyes of others even when business is slow. Japanese workers wish to demonstrate their dedication to superiors and coworkers—an attitude grounded in values such as the concern for group cohesion, loyalty, and harmony.

Attitudes Toward Work
Whereas some cultures display a strong work ethic, others stress a more balanced pace in juggling work and leisure. People in southern France like to say, "We work to live, while people in the United States live to work." Work, they say, is for them a means to an end. In the United States, they charge, it is an end in itself. Not surprisingly, the lifestyle in southern France is slower-paced. People tend to concentrate on earning enough money to enjoy a relaxed, quality lifestyle. Businesses practically close down during August, when many workers take month-long paid holidays, usually outside the country. In contrast, this attitude is unheard of in many Asian countries, including Japan.

In general, people tend to start their own businesses when capital is available for new business start-ups and when the cultural stigma of entrepreneurial failure is low. In both the United Kingdom and France, start-ups are considered quite risky, and capital for entrepreneurial ventures is relatively scarce. This remains true despite some progress during the dot-com boom, when many Internet companies obtained funding.[9] Moreover, if at some point an entrepreneur's venture in one of those countries goes bust, he or she can find it very hard to obtain financing for future projects because of the stigma of failure. The opposite attitude tends to prevail in the United States. Reference to prior bankruptcy in a business plan is sometimes considered valuable learning experience (assuming, of course, that some lessons were learned). As long as U.S. bankers or venture capitalists see promising business plans, they are generally willing to loan money.[10] Today, many European nations are trying to foster a U.S.-style entrepreneurial spirit to achieve the level of job growth that has occurred in the United States over the past several decades.

Attitudes Toward Cultural Change

cultural trait
Anything that represents a culture's way of life, including gestures, material objects, traditions, and concepts.

A **cultural trait** is anything that represents a culture's way of life, including gestures, material objects, traditions, and concepts. Such traits include bowing to show respect in Japan (gesture), a Buddhist temple in Thailand (material object), relaxing in a tearoom in Kuwait (tradition), and practicing democracy in the United States (concept). Let's look more closely at the role of cultural traits in causing cultural change over time, and the complex relation between international companies and cultural change.

cultural diffusion
Process whereby cultural traits spread from one culture to another.

Cultural Diffusion   The process whereby cultural traits spread from one culture to another is called **cultural diffusion**. As new traits are accepted and absorbed into a culture, *cultural change* occurs naturally and, as a rule, gradually. Globalization and technological advances are increasing the pace of both cultural diffusion and cultural change. Satellite television, videoconferencing, and the Internet are increasing the frequency of international contact and exposing people of different nations to new ideas and practices.

When Companies Change Culture: Charges of Cultural Imperialism   International companies are often agents of cultural change. As trade and investment barriers fall, for example, U.S. consumer-goods and entertainment companies are moving into untapped markets. Critics in some of these places charge that in exporting the products of such firms, the United States is practicing **cultural imperialism**—the replacement of one culture's traditions, folk heroes, and artifacts with substitutes from another.

cultural imperialism
Replacement of one culture's traditions, folk heroes, and artifacts with substitutes from another.

Fears of cultural imperialism are why products from the Walt Disney Company (*www.disney.com*) and its Disneyland Paris theme park continue to be opposed by some French, who see them as harmful to local culture. McDonald's (*www.mcdonalds.com*) is also a frequent target of criticism by antiglobalization protesters. Some consumers across Asia and Europe resent Ronald McDonald and Mickey Mouse because they so quickly dominate their domestic markets. Politicians in Russia have decried the so-called Snickerization of their culture—a snide term that refers to the popularity of the candy bar made by Snickers (*www.snickers.com*). And when the Miss World Pageant was held in India, conservative groups criticized Western corporate sponsors for spreading the message of consumerism and portraying women as sex objects.

Because of the potential charge of cultural imperialism, companies must be sensitive to the needs and desires of people in every culture in which they do business. Firms must focus not only on meeting people's product needs, but also on how their activities and products affect people's traditional ways and habits. Rather than view their influence on culture as the inevitable consequence of doing business, companies can take several steps to soften those effects. For instance, policies and practices that are at odds with deeply held beliefs can be introduced gradually. Also, if new business practices are at odds with local cultural practices, managers could seek the advice of highly respected local individuals (elders play a key role in many developing countries). There are, of course, volatile times in every society, and launching new investment projects or implementing unfamiliar management methods are best reserved for times when a culture is experiencing relative stability. In any case, managers should always make clear to workers the benefits of any proposed changes.

Finally, one area in which U.S. companies may be changing other cultures for the better is fairness in the workplace. Just a few years ago, sexual harassment lawsuits were a peculiar phenomenon of U.S. culture. The spread of this kind of litigation to other nations coincides with the outsourcing of U.S. jobs abroad. As U.S. companies outsource jobs to other nations (and are being held accountable for how these subcontractors treat their employ-

Global companies such as McDonald's, with 28,000 restaurants in 120 countries, must be wary of being charged with cultural imperialism. For example, it has been reported that the average Japanese child thinks that McDonald's was invented in Japan and exported to the United States. And Chinese children, like the one shown here, consider "Uncle" McDonald "funny, gentle, kind, and understanding." Do you think this form of cultural change is harmful over the long term?

ees), it seems they are exporting values of the U.S. workplace, such as what constitutes harassment.[11]

When Cultures Change Companies   Culture often forces companies to adjust their business policies and practices. Managers from the United States, for instance, often encounter cultural differences that force changes in how they motivate Mexican employees. Although it's a time-consuming practice, they sometimes use *situational management*—a system in which a supervisor walks an employee through every step of an assignment or task and monitors the results at each stage. This technique helps employees fully understand the scope of their jobs and clarifies the boundaries of their responsibilities.

Other types of changes might also be needed to suit local culture. Because Vietnam has a traditional, agriculture-based economy, people's concept of time revolves around the seasons. The local "timepiece" is the monsoon, not the clock. Consequently, managers there must modify their approach and take a more patient, long-term view of business. Typically, companies entering Vietnam also need to modify employee evaluation and reward systems. Individual criticism must be delivered privately to save employees from "losing face" among coworkers. Individual praise for good performance can be delivered either in private or in public, if done carefully. Because the Vietnamese place great value on group harmony, an individual can be embarrassed if singled out publicly as being superior to the rest of the work unit.

Is a Global Culture Emerging?   What does the rapid pace of cultural change around the world mean for international business? Are we witnessing the emergence of a new, truly global culture in which all people share similar lifestyles, values, and attitudes? The rapid pace of cultural diffusion and increased interaction among people of different nations are causing cultures to converge to some extent. And it might even be true that people in different cultures are *developing* similar perspectives on the world and *beginning* to think along similar lines.

But it seems that just as often as we see signs of an emerging global culture, we discover some new habit unique to one culture. When that happens, we are reminded of the roles of history and tradition in defining culture. Whereas cultural convergence is certainly taking place in some market segments for some products (say the teenage market for pop music), it seems likely that a broader global culture will take a very long time to develop, if ever. Yes, values and attitudes are under continually greater pressure as globalization continues. But because they are so deeply ingrained in culture, their transformation will continue to be gradual rather than abrupt.

1. What is meant by a culture's *aesthetics*? Give several examples from several different cultures.

2. How can entrepreneurs and others incorporate aesthetics into their Web sites?

3. Compare and contrast *values* and *attitudes*. How do cultures differ in their attitudes toward time, work, and cultural change?

4. Describe the process of *cultural diffusion*. Why should international businesses be sensitive to charges of *cultural imperialism*?

Manners and Customs

When doing business in another culture, it is important to understand a people's manners and customs. At a minimum, understanding manners and customs helps managers to avoid making embarrassing mistakes or offending people. In-depth knowledge, meanwhile, improves the ability to negotiate in other cultures, market products effectively, and manage international operations. Let's explore some important differences in manners and customs from around the world.

manners
Appropriate ways of behaving, speaking, and dressing in a culture.

Manners   Appropriate ways of behaving, speaking, and dressing in a culture are called **manners**. In Arab cultures from the Middle East to northwest Africa, one does not extend a hand to greet an older person unless the elder first offers the greeting. In going first, a younger person would be displaying bad manners. Moreover, because Arab culture considers the left hand the one used for personal hygiene, using it to pour tea or serve a meal is considered very bad manners.

Jack Ma founded Alibaba (*www.alibaba.com*) as a way for suppliers and buyers to increase efficiency by cutting through layers of intermediaries and trading companies. But he realized early that his Chinese clients needed training in business etiquette so they could cross the cultural divide and do business with people from Western cultures. One participant in an Alibaba seminar on business manners, Mr. Chen Xi Guo who owns a machinery factory in Wenzhou city in central China, now promises to spend more time chitchatting with clients. "I will work hard to be nicer," says Mr. Chen. His seminar worksheets instruct him to sprinkle his e-mails with phrases like, "How are you?," "It was great to hear from you," and "Can we work together?"[12]

Conducting business during meals is common practice in the United States. In Mexico, however, it is poor manners to bring up business at mealtime unless the host does so first. Business discussions in Mexico typically begin when coffee and brandy arrive. Likewise, toasts in the United States tend to be casual and sprinkled with lighthearted humor. In Mexico, where a toast should be philosophical and full of passion, a lighthearted toast would be offensive. See the Global Manager's Toolbox titled, "A Globetrotter's Guide to Manners" for some additional pointers on appropriate manners when abroad on business.

customs
Habits or ways of behaving in specific circumstances that are passed down through generations in a culture.

Customs   When habits or ways of behaving in specific circumstances are passed down through generations, they become **customs.** Customs differ from manners in that they define appropriate habits or behaviors in *specific situations*. Sharing food gifts during the Islamic holy month of Ramadan is a custom, as is the Japanese tradition of throwing special parties for young women and men who turn age 20. Let's now examine two types of customs and see how instances of each vary around the world.

folk custom
Behavior, often dating back several generations, that is practiced by a homogeneous group of people.

popular custom
Behavior shared by a heterogeneous group or by several groups.

Folk and Popular Customs   A **folk custom** is behavior, often dating back several generations, that is practiced by a homogeneous group of people. The wearing of turbans by Muslims in southern Asia and the art of belly dancing in Turkey are both folk customs. A **popular custom** is behavior shared by a heterogeneous group or several groups. Popular customs can exist either in just one culture or in two or more cultures at the same time. Wearing blue jeans and playing golf are both popular customs across the globe. Many folk customs that have spread by cultural diffusion to other regions have developed into popular customs.

global manager's TOOLBOX

A Globetrotter's Guide to Manners

Today large multinationals demand top managers who feel comfortable living, working, and traveling around the world. Good manners are just as important internationally as when doing business in the home market. For some additional personal guidelines managers should be aware of when meeting colleagues from other cultures, visit Executive Planet (*www.executiveplanet.com*).

- **Don't Rush Familiarity.** Avoid the temptation to get too familiar too quickly. Use titles such as "doctor" and "mister." Switch to a first-name basis only when invited to do so and do not shorten people's names from, say, Catherine to Cathy.

- **Adapt to Personal Space.** Culture dictates what is considered the appropriate distance between two people. Middle Eastern and Latin American nations close the gap significantly. Expect more touching in Latin America, where the man-to-man embrace occurs regularly.

- **Respect Religious Values.** Be cautious so that your manners do not offend people. Former Secretary of State Madeline Albright briefly acquired the nickname of "the kissing ambassador" because she apparently kissed the Israeli and Palestinian leaders of these profoundly religious peoples.

- **Give and Receive Business Cards Carefully.** In Asia, business cards are considered an extension of the individual. Cards in Japan are typically exchanged after a bow, with two hands extended, and the wording facing the recipient. Leave the card on the table for the entire meeting—don't quickly stuff it in your wallet or toss it into your briefcase.

- **Use Comedy Sparingly.** Use humor cautiously because it often does not translate well. Avoid jokes that rely on wordplay and puns or events in your country, of which local people might have little or no knowledge.

- **Watch Your Body Language.** Do not slouch, or "spread out" by hanging your arms over the backs of chairs. But don't be too stiff either. Look people in the eye lest they deem you untrustworthy, but don't stare too intently in a challenging manner.

We also can distinguish between folk and popular food. Popular Western-style fast food, for instance, is rapidly replacing folk food around the world. In many Asian countries, widespread acceptance of "burgers 'n' fries" (born in the United States), and "fish 'n' chips" (born in Britain) is actually altering deep-seated dietary traditions, especially among young people. They are even becoming part of home-cooked meals in Japan and South Korea. Sadly, many believe the trend toward greater consumption of fast food is at least partly responsible for a rising proportion of overweight people in those nations.

The Business of Gift Giving Although giving token gifts to business and government associates is customary in many countries, the proper type of gift varies. A knife, for example, should not be offered to associates in Russia, France, or Germany, where it signals the severing of a relationship. In Japan, gifts must be wrapped in such a delicate way that it is wise to ask someone trained in the practice to do the honors. It is also Japanese custom not to open a gift in front of the gift giver. Tradition dictates that the giver protest that the gift is something small and unworthy of the recipient. In turn, the recipient waits until later to open the gift. This tradition does not endorse trivial gifts but is simply a custom.

On the other hand, large gifts to business associates sometimes raise suspicion. Cultures differ in their legal and ethical rules against giving or accepting bribes. The U.S. Foreign Corrupt Practices Act, which prohibits companies from giving large gifts to government officials to win business favors, applies to U.S. firms operating at home *and* abroad. In many cultures, however, bribery is woven into a social fabric that has worn well for centuries. In Germany, bribe payments may even qualify for tax deductions. However, gift giving remains controversial. Although governments around the world are adopting stricter measures to control bribery, in some cultures large gifts continue to be an effective means of obtaining contracts, entering markets, and securing protection from competitors.

Social Structure

social structure
A culture's fundamental organization, including its groups and institutions, its system of social positions and their relationships, and the process by which its resources are distributed.

social group
Collection of two or more people who identify and interact with one another.

Social structure embodies a culture's fundamental organization, including its groups and institutions, its system of social positions and their relationships, and the process by which its resources are distributed. Social structure affects business decisions, including production-site selection, advertising methods, and ultimately the costs of doing business in a country. Three important elements of social structure that differ across cultures are *social group associations, social status,* and *social mobility.*

Social Group Associations
People in all cultures associate themselves with a variety of **social groups**—collections of two or more people who identify and interact with one another. Social groups contribute to each individual's identity and self-image. Two groups that play especially important roles in affecting business activity everywhere are family and gender.*

Family   Here are two different types of family groups:

- The *nuclear family* consists of a person's immediate relatives, including parents, brothers, and sisters. This concept of family prevails in Australia, Canada, the United States, and much of Europe.

- The concept of the *extended family* broadens the nuclear family to include grandparents, aunts and uncles, cousins, and relatives through marriage. It is more important as a social group in much of Asia, the Middle East, North Africa, and Latin America.

Extended families can present some interesting situations for businesspeople unfamiliar with the concept. In some cultures, owners and managers in extended families obtain supplies and materials from another company in which someone in the family works before looking elsewhere. Gaining entry into such family arrangements can be difficult because quality and price are not sufficient motives to ignore family ties.

In extended-family cultures, managers and other employees often try to find jobs for relatives inside their own companies. This practice (called "nepotism") can present a challenge to the human resource operations of a Western company, which typically must establish explicit policies on the practice.

Gender   Let's first define *gender.* Gender refers to socially learned traits associated with, and expected of, men or women. It refers to socially learned behaviors and attitudes such as styles of dress and activity preferences. It is not the same thing as sex, which refers to the biological fact that a person is either male or female.

Although many countries have made great strides toward gender equality in the workplace, others have not. For instance, countries operating under Islamic law sometimes segregate women and men in public schools, universities, and social activities, and restrict women to certain professions. Sometimes women are allowed teaching careers, but only in all-female classrooms. At other times they can be physicians, but for female patients only.

In Spain, as in many countries, women have traditionally been denied equal opportunity in the workplace. Although the overall unemployment rate is 14 percent in Spain, the rate for women is 20 percent, more than double that for men and the highest rate in the European Union. It is also true that Spanish women earn 30 to 40 percent less than men in the same occupation. One prominent reason for this situation is the shortage of low-cost day care for children. Many times, salaries are so low and the cost of child care so high that it simply makes more sense for mothers to stay home with their children. Another reason is that caring for children and performing household duties are considered women's work in Spain, rather than the responsibility of the entire family.[13]

Social Status
Another important aspect of social structure is the way a culture divides its population according to *status*—that is, according to positions within the structure.

---

*We put these two "groups" together for the sake of convenience. Strictly speaking, a gender is not a group. Sociologists regard it as a category—people who share some status. A key to group membership is mutual interaction. Individuals in categories know that they are not alone in holding a particular status, but the vast majority remain strangers to one another.

Although some cultures have only a few categories, others have many. The process of ranking people into social layers or classes is called **social stratification**.

Three factors that normally determine social status are family heritage, income, and occupation. In most industrialized countries royalty, government officials, and top business leaders occupy the highest social layer. Scientists, medical doctors, and others with a university education occupy the middle rung. Below are those with vocational training or a secondary-school education, who dominate the manual and clerical occupations. Although rankings are fairly stable, they can and do change over time. For example, because Confucianism (a major Chinese religion) stresses a life of learning, Chinese culture frowned on businesspeople for centuries. In modern China, however, those who have obtained wealth and power through business are now considered important role models for young people.

Social Mobility
Moving to a higher social class is easy in some cultures but difficult or impossible in others. **Social mobility** is the ease with which individuals can move up or down a culture's "social ladder." For much of the world's population today, one of two systems regulates social mobility: a *caste system* or a *class system*.

Caste Systems A **caste system** is a system of social stratification in which people are born into a social ranking, or *caste*, with no opportunity for social mobility. India is the classic example of a caste culture. Although the Indian constitution *officially* bans discrimination by caste, its influence persists. Little social interaction occurs between castes, and marrying out of one's caste is taboo. Opportunities for work and advancement are defined within the system, and certain occupations are reserved for the members of each caste. Because personal clashes would be inevitable, a member of one caste cannot supervise someone of a higher caste.

The caste system forces Western companies to make some hard ethical decisions when entering the Indian marketplace. They must decide whether to adapt to local human resource policies or import their own because they think of them as "more developed." Yet as globalization penetrates deeper into Indian culture, both the nation's social system and international companies will face challenges to be overcome.

Class Systems A **class system** is a system of social stratification in which personal ability and actions determine social status and mobility. It is the most common form of social stratification in the world today. But class systems vary in the amount of mobility they allow. Highly class-conscious cultures offer less mobility and, not surprisingly, experience greater class conflict. Across Western Europe, for instance, wealthy families have retained power for generations by restricting social mobility. As a result, they must sometimes deal with class conflict in the form of labor–management disputes that can increase the cost of doing business there. Strikes (and sometimes even property damage) occur when European companies announce plant closings or layoffs.

Conversely, lower levels of class consciousness encourage mobility and lessen conflict. A more cooperative atmosphere in the workplace tends to prevail when people feel that a higher social standing is within their reach. For instance, most U.S. citizens share the belief that hard work can improve one's standard of living and social status. They attribute higher status to greater income or wealth, but often with little regard for family background. Material well-being is important primarily because it affirms or improves status.

social stratification
Process of ranking people into social layers or classes.

social mobility
Ease with which individuals can move up or down a culture's "social ladder."

caste system
System of social stratification in which people are born into a social ranking, or caste, with no opportunity for social mobility.

class system
System of social stratification in which personal ability and actions determine social status and mobility.

Quick Study

1. How do *manners* and *customs* differ? Give examples of each from several different cultures.

2. What are some manners that managers should keep in mind when doing business in other cultures?

3. What are *folk* and *popular* customs? Describe how a folk custom can become a popular custom.

4. To what does *social structure* refer? Explain how social rank and *social mobility* affect business.

MAP 2.1

Major Religions of the World

*Religion is not confined to national political boundaries but can exist in different regions of the world simultaneously. Different religions can also dominate different regions in a single nation. This map shows where the world's major religions are prominent. The map shows several religions in addition to those discussed in this chapter including: **Taoism**, which began in the 100s B.C. in China. Taoists pray to a mixture of deceased humans who displayed extraordinary powers during their lives, and nonhuman spirits embodying various elements of Tao; **Sikhism,** dating back to 1469, teaches breaking the continuous cycle of reincarnation by waking early, cleansing, meditating, and devoting all activities to God; **Animism** describes all religions involving honoring the souls of deceased humans and worshiping spirits in nature; **Lamaist Buddhism** is a Buddhist sect that emphasizes meditation and has as its spiritual leader, the Dalai Lama; and **Southern Buddhism**, the Buddhist sect that is older than Lamaism and stresses following the teachings of Buddha.*

Religion

Human values often originate from religious beliefs. Different religions take different views of work, savings, and material goods. Understanding why they do so may help us understand why companies from certain cultures are more competitive in the global marketplace than companies from other cultures. It also may help us understand why some countries develop more slowly than others. Knowing how religion affects business practices is especially important in countries with religious governments.

Map 2.1 shows where the world's major religions are practiced. In the following sections, we explore several of these religions—Christianity, Islam, Hinduism, Buddhism, Confucianism, Judaism, and Shinto—to examine their potential effects, both positive and negative, on international business activity.

Christianity   Christianity was born in Palestine around 2,000 years ago among Jews who believed that God sent Jesus of Nazareth to be their savior. Although Christianity boasts more than 300 denominations, most Christians belong to the Roman Catholic, Protestant, or Eastern Orthodox churches. With nearly 2 billion followers, Christianity is the world's single largest religion. The Roman Catholic faith asks its followers to refrain from placing material possessions above God and others. Protestants believe that salvation comes from

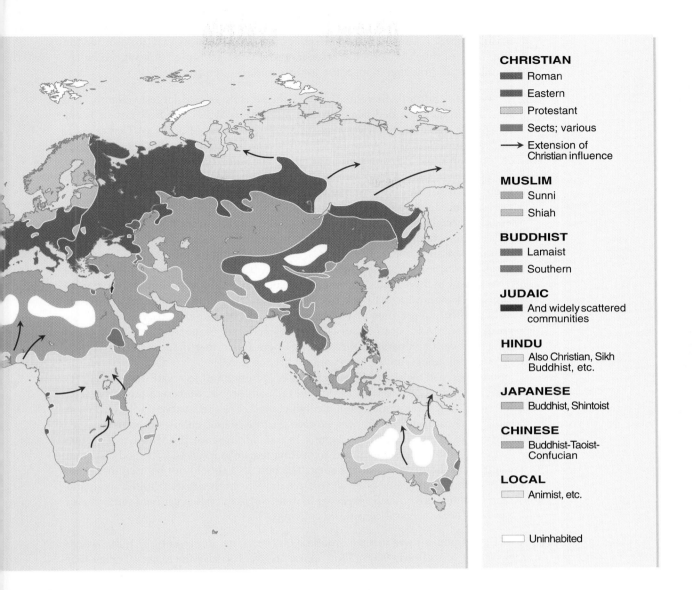

CHRISTIAN
- Roman
- Eastern
- Protestant
- Sects; various
- → Extension of Christian influence

MUSLIM
- Sunni
- Shiah

BUDDHIST
- Lamaist
- Southern

JUDAIC
- And widely scattered communities

HINDU
- Also Christian, Sikh Buddhist, etc.

JAPANESE
- Buddhist, Shintoist

CHINESE
- Buddhist-Taoist-Confucian

LOCAL
- Animist, etc.

- Uninhabited

faith in God and that hard work gives glory to God—a tenet known widely as the "Protestant work ethic." Many historians believe this conviction to be a main factor in the development of capitalism and free enterprise in nineteenth-century Europe.

Christian organizations sometimes get involved in social causes that affect business policy. For example, some conservative Christian groups have boycotted the Walt Disney Company (*www.disney.com*), charging that in portraying young people as rejecting parental guidance, Disney films impede the moral development of young viewers worldwide.

The Church itself became involved in some highly publicized controversies lately. Ireland-based Ryanair (*www.ryanair.com*), Europe's leading low-fare airline, ruffled the feathers of the Roman Catholic Church with a recent ad campaign. The ad depicted the pope (the head of the Church) claiming that the fourth secret of Fatima was Ryanair's low fares. The Church sent out a worldwide press release accusing the airline of blaspheming the pope. But much to the Church's dismay, the press release generated an enormous amount of free publicity for the company.[14]

Several years earlier, the French Bishops' Conference sued Volkswagen-France (*www.volkswagen.fr*). They felt that a billboard ad insulted Christians by parodying the famous image of Leonardo Da Vinci's *The Last Supper*. The conference explained that it was reacting to increasing use of sacred things in advertising throughout Europe.

"Advertising experts," said a conference spokesman, "have told us that ads aim for the sacred in order to shock because using sex does not work anymore." Volkswagen halted the $16 million ad campaign in response to the Church's complaint.[15]

Islam   With 1.3 billion adherents, Islam is the world's second-largest religion. The prophet Muhammad founded Islam around A.D. 600 in Mecca, the holy city of Islam located in Saudi Arabia. Islam thrives in northwestern Africa, the Middle East, Central Asia, Pakistan, and some Southeast Asian nations, including Indonesia. Muslim concentrations are also found in most U.S. and European cities. The word *Islam* means "submission to Allah," and *Muslim* means "one who submits to Allah." Two important religious rites include observance of the holy season of Ramadan and making the pilgrimage (the *Hajj*) to Mecca at least once in one's lifetime.

Religion strongly affects the kinds of goods and services acceptable to Muslim consumers. Islam, for example, prohibits the consumption of alcohol and pork. Popular alcohol substitutes are soda pop, coffee, and tea. Substitutes for pork include lamb, beef, and poultry (all of which must be slaughtered in a prescribed way so as to meet *halal* requirements). As we saw in this chapter's opening company profile, German candy maker Haribo (*www.haribo.com*) produces a pork-free gummi bear that satisfies *halal* requirements. Because hot coffee and tea often play ceremonial roles in Muslim nations, the markets for them are quite large. And because usury (charging interest for money lent) violates the laws of Islam, credit card companies collect management fees rather than interest, and each cardholder's credit line is limited to an amount held on deposit.

Nations governed by Islamic law (see Chapter 3) sometimes segregate the sexes at certain activities and in locations such as schools. In Saudi Arabia, women cannot drive cars. In orthodox Islamic nations, men cannot conduct market research surveys with women at home unless they are family members. Women visiting Islamic cultures need to be especially sensitive to Islamic beliefs and customs. In Iran, for instance, the Ministry of Islamic Guidance and Culture posts a reminder to visiting female journalists: "The body is a tool for the spirit and the spirit is a divine song. The holy tool should not be used for sexual intentions." Although the issue of *hejab* (Islamic dress) is hotly debated, both Iranian and non-Iranian women are officially expected to wear body-concealing garments and scarves over their hair (because hair is considered enticing).[16]

Hinduism   Hinduism was formed around 4,000 years ago in present-day India, where over 90 percent of its nearly 900 million adherents live. It is also the majority religion of Nepal and a secondary religion in Bangladesh, Bhutan, and Sri Lanka. Considered by some to be a way of life rather than a religion, Hinduism recalls no founder and recognizes no central authority or spiritual leader. Integral to the Hindu faith is the caste system described earlier.

Hindus believe in reincarnation—the rebirth of the human soul at the time of death. For many Hindus the highest goal of life is *moksha*—escaping from the cycle of reincarnation and entering a state of eternal happiness called *nirvana*. Strict Hindus do not eat or willfully harm any living creature because it may be a reincarnated human soul. Because Hindus consider cows sacred animals they do not eat beef. However, consuming milk is considered a means of religious purification. Firms like McDonald's (*www.mcdonalds.com*) must work closely with government and religious officials in India to respect Hindu beliefs. In many regions, McDonald's has removed all beef products from its menu and prepares vegetable and fish products in separate kitchen areas. And for those Indians who do eat meat (but not cows because of their sacred status) the company sells the Maharaja Mac, made of lamb, in place of the Big Mac.[17]

In India, there have been attacks on Western consumer-goods companies in the name of preserving Indian culture and Hindu beliefs. Some companies such as Pepsi-Cola (*www.pepsi.com*) have been vandalized, and local officials even shut down a KFC restaurant (*www.kfc.com*) for a time. Although it currently operates in India, Coca-Cola (*www.cocacola.com*) once left the market completely rather than succumb to demands that it reveal its secret formula to authorities. India's investment environment has improved greatly in recent years. Yet labor–management relations sometimes deteriorate to such a degree that strikes cut deeply into productivity.

Buddhism instructs its followers to live a life characterized by simplicity and one void of materialistic ambitions. It also says that one source of human suffering is sense pleasure. But as countries across Asia continue to modernize, the products of Western multinationals are streaming in. Here a young Bhuddist passes in front of an advertisement for Heineken beer. Do you think modernization has to mean "westernization"?

Buddhism   Buddhism was founded about 2,600 years ago in India by a Hindu prince named Siddhartha Gautama. Today, Buddhism has approximately 360 million followers, mostly in Asian nations such as China, Tibet, Korea, Japan, Vietnam, and Thailand. There also are small numbers of Buddhists in Europe and North and South America. Although founded in India, Buddhism has relatively few adherents there, and unlike Hinduism, it rejects the sort of caste system that dominates Indian society. But like Hinduism, Buddhism promotes a life centered on spiritual rather than worldly matters. Buddhists seek *nirvana* (escape from reincarnation) through charity, modesty, compassion for others, restraint from violence, and general self-control.

Although monks at many temples are devoted to lives of solitary meditation and discipline, many other Buddhist priests are dedicated to lessening the burden of human suffering. They finance schools and hospitals across Asia and are active in worldwide peace movements. In Tibet, where most people still acknowledge the exiled Dalai Lama as the spiritual and political head of the Buddhist culture, the Chinese Communist government suppresses allegiance to any outside authority. In the United States, a coalition of religious groups, human rights advocates, and supporters of the Dalai Lama continue to press the U.S. Congress to apply economic sanctions against countries, like China, that are judged to practice religious persecution.

Confucianism   An exiled politician and philosopher named Kung-fu-dz (pronounced *Confucius* in English) began teaching his ideas in China nearly 2,500 years ago. Today, China is home to most of Confucianism's 225 million followers. Confucian thought is also ingrained in the cultures of Japan, South Korea, and nations with large numbers of ethnic Chinese, such as Singapore.

South Korean business practice reflects Confucian thought in its rigid organizational structure and unswerving reverence for authority. Whereas Korean employees do not question strict chains of command, non-Korean managers and workers often feel differently. Efforts to apply Korean-style management in overseas subsidiaries have caused some high-profile disputes with U.S. executives and even physical confrontations with factory workers in Vietnam.

Some observers contend that the Confucian work ethic and educational commitment helped spur east Asia's phenomenal economic growth. But others respond that the link between culture and economic growth is weak. They argue that economic, historical, and international factors are at least as important as culture. They say Chinese leaders distrusted Confucianism for centuries because they believed that it stunted economic growth. Likewise, many Chinese despised merchants and traders because their main objective (earning money) violated Confucian beliefs. As a result, many Chinese businesspeople moved to Indonesia, Malaysia, Singapore, and Thailand, where they launched successful businesses. Today, these countries (along with Taiwan) are financing much of China's economic growth.

Judaism

More than 3,000 years old, Judaism was the first religion to preach belief in a single God. Nowadays, Judaism has roughly 18 million followers worldwide. In Israel, Orthodox (or "fully observant") Jews make up 12 percent of the population and constitute an increasingly important economic segment. In Jerusalem, there is even a modeling agency that specializes in casting Orthodox Jews in ads aimed both inside and outside the Orthodox community. Models include scholars and even one rabbi. In keeping with Orthodox principles, women model only modest clothing and never appear in ads alongside men.[18]

Employers and human resource managers must be aware of important days in the Jewish faith. Because the Sabbath lasts from sundown on Friday to sundown on Saturday, work schedules might need adjustment. Devout Jews want to be home before sundown on Fridays. On the Sabbath itself, they do not work, travel, or carry money. Several other important observances are Rosh Ha-Shanah (the two-day Jewish New Year, in September or October), Yom Kippur (the Day of Atonement, 10 days after New Year), Passover (which celebrates the Exodus from Egypt, in March or April each year), and Hanukkah (which celebrates an ancient victory over the Syrians, usually in December).

Marketers must take into account foods that are banned among strict Jews. Pork and shellfish (such as lobster and crab) are prohibited. Meat is stored and served separately from milk. Other meats must be slaughtered according to a practice called *shehitah*. Meals prepared according to Jewish dietary traditions are called *kosher*. Most airlines offer *kosher* meals and, as we saw earlier, German candy maker Haribo (*www.haribo.com*) makes a special *kosher* gummi bear.

Shinto

Shinto (meaning "way of the gods") arose as the native religion of the Japanese. But today Shinto can claim only about four million strict adherents in Japan. Because modern Shinto preaches patriotism, it is sometimes said that Japan's real religion is nationalism. Shinto teaches sincere and ethical behavior, loyalty and respect toward others, and enjoyment of life.

Shinto beliefs are reflected in the workplace through the traditional practice of lifetime employment (although this is waning today) and through the traditional trust extended between firms and customers. Japanese competitiveness in world markets has benefited from loyal workforces, low employee turnover, and good labor–management cooperation. The success of Japanese companies since the Second World War gave rise to the concept of a Shinto work ethic, certain aspects of which have been emulated by Western managers.

Quick Study

1. What are the main beliefs of each of the seven religions presented above?
2. In what ways does religion affect the international business activities of companies?
3. Identify the dominant religion in each of the following countries: (a) Brazil, (b) China, (c) India, (d) Ireland, (e) Mexico, (f) Russia, and (g) Thailand.

Personal Communication

communication
System of conveying thoughts, feelings, knowledge, and information through speech, actions, and writing.

People in every culture have a **communication** system to convey thoughts, feelings, knowledge, and information through speech, actions, and writing. Understanding a culture's spoken language gives us great insight into why people think and act the way that they do. Understanding a culture's body language helps us avoid sending unintended or embarrassing messages. Let's now examine each of these forms of communication more closely.

Spoken Language

Spoken language is the part of a culture's communication system that is embodied in its spoken and written vocabulary. It is the most obvious difference we notice when traveling in another country. We overhear and engage in a number of conversations, and must read many signs and documents to find our way. Because understanding a people's language is the key to understanding their culture, it often is essential for success in international business.

Linguistically different segments of a population are often culturally, socially, and politically distinct. For instance, Malaysia's population is comprised of Malay (60 percent), Chinese (30 percent), and Indian (10 percent). Although Malay is the official national language, each ethnic group speaks its own language and continues its traditions. The United Kingdom includes England, Northern Ireland, Scotland, and Wales—each of which has its own language and traditions. The native languages of Ireland and Scotland are each dialects of *Gaelic*. In fact, the language of Wales, *Welsh*, long predates the use of English in Britain. Now, after decades of decline, the language is staging a comeback and figures prominently on Welsh radio and television and in school curricula.[19] See the Global Challenges feature titled, "Speaking in Fewer Tongues" for further information on endangered languages and what is being done to help them survive.

The importance of understanding the local language in business is becoming increasingly apparent on the Internet. By 2005 it is estimated that between 70 and 75 percent of the 1 billion Internet users will be nonnative English speakers. But English is the language of roughly two-thirds of all Web pages on the Internet. That is why software solutions providers are assisting companies from English-speaking countries in adapting their Web sites for global e-business. As these software companies are telling their clients, "The 'e' in e-business doesn't stand for English." Web surfers from cultures across the globe bring their own specific tastes, preferences, and buying habits online with them. The company that can provide its customer in Mexico City, Paris, or Tokyo with a quality buying experience in his or her native language will have an edge on the competition.[20]

Language proficiency is also critical in production facilities where nonnative managers are supervising local employees. In the wake of the North American Free Trade Agreement,

global CHALLENGES

Speaking in Fewer Tongues

One day this year, somewhere in the world, an old man or woman will die and with them will go their language. In fact, there are dozens of languages today that have just one native speaker still living. Do you think globalization is placing increased pressure on endangered languages and communities?

Some Are Losing. While it is thought that there are about 6,000 languages in the world, about 90 percent have fewer than 100,000 speakers. By the end of this century over half of the world's languages may be lost, and perhaps under 1,000 will survive. One endangered language is Aramaic, a 2,500 year-old Semitic language that once was the major language in the Middle East, and one of two languages spoken in Mel Gibson's *The Passion of the Christ*.

Some Are Gaining. As minority languages die out, the popularity of three languages continues to grow: Mandarin, Spanish, and English. In fact, English has emerged as the universal language of business, higher education, diplomacy, science, popular music, entertainment, and international travel. Over 70 nations give special status to English (including India, Nigeria, and Singapore) and roughly one quarter of the world's population is fluent or competent in it.

The Consequences. Some argue that the loss of a language means the loss of much of a people's culture, because it is the vehicle of their cultural, spiritual, and intellectual life. That loss can include prayers, myths, humor, poetry, ceremonies, conversational styles, and terms for emotions, behaviors, and habits. When a language is lost, a way must be found to express all of these in the new language with different words, sounds, and grammar. But much can simply vanish.

The Challenge. Linguists are concerned that such a valuable part of human culture could vanish. The impending loss of more languages has linguists creating videotapes, audiotapes, and written records of endangered tongues before they disappear. Communities themselves are also taking action. In New Zealand, Maori communities set up nursery schools called *kohanga reo,* or "language nests," that are staffed by elders and conducted entirely in Maori.

Want to Know More? Visit the Linguistic Society of America (*www.lsadc.org*), European Union's Eurolang (*www.eurolang.net*), and Foundation for Endangered Languages (*www.ogmios.org*).

U.S. corporations continue to expand operations in Mexico. Because Mexican factory workers generally appear relaxed and untroubled at work, one U.S. manager was confused when his workers went on strike at his seemingly happy plant. The problem lay in different cultural perspectives. Mexican workers tend not to take the initiative in matters of problem solving and workplace complaints. In this case, they concluded that the plant manager knew but did not care about their concerns because he did not trouble to question employees about working conditions.

Language Blunders   Advertising slogans and company documents must be translated carefully so that messages are received precisely as intended. There are many stories of companies making terrible language blunders in their international business dealings. General Motors' Chevrolet division (*www.chevrolet.com*) made perhaps the most well-known blunder when it first launched its Chevrolet Nova in Spanish-speaking markets. The company failed to notice beforehand that "No va" means "No go" in Spanish. Chevrolet had far greater success when it renamed the car *Caribe* (piranha)—the voraciously carnivorous freshwater fish native to South America that attacks and destroys living animals! In Sweden, Kellogg (*www.kellogg.com*) had to rename its Bran Buds cereal because the Swedish translation came out roughly as "burned farmer." San Francisco–based start-up Evite (*www.evite.com*) allows visitors to its Web site to send e-mail invitations to special events. But the company's name presents a problem internationally. In the Romance languages, such as French and Spanish, variations of the verb *evite* (*eviter* and *evitar*) mean "to shun or to avoid." Apparently "Avoid My Party" couldn't get European partygoers excited. CEO Josh Silverman concedes, "It's a terrific brand in English, but we're going to have to rebrand for the Romance languages."[21] Several other humorous translation blunders include the following:

- Braniff Airlines' English-language slogan "Fly in Leather" was translated into "Fly Naked" in Spanish.
- A sign in English on a Majorcan storefront read, "English well-talking" and "Here speeching American."
- A sign for non-Japanese-speaking guests in a Tokyo hotel read, "You are respectfully requested to take advantage of the chambermaids."
- An English sign in a Moscow hotel read, "If this is your first visit to the USSR, you are welcome to it."
- A Japanese knife manufacturer labeled its exports to the United States with "Caution: Blade extremely sharp! Keep out of children."

But such blunders are not the exclusive domain of humans. The use of machine translation—computer software used to translate one language into another—is booming along with the explosion in the number of nonnative English speakers using the Internet. Nowhere is this technology hotter than in Asia, although its results are often less than perfect. Singapore-based EWGate (*www.ewgate.com*) allows its users to search the Internet in English and Asian languages, translate Web pages, and compose e-mail in one language and send it in another. Its product, EWSurf, attempted a translation and came up with this meaning in Chinese: "The Chinese Communist Party is debating whether to deny its ban in join the Party is allowed soldier enterprise owners on." The original English sentence: "The Chinese Communist Party is debating whether to drop its ban on private-enterprise owners being allowed to join the party."[22] Various other machine translators turned the French version of "I don't care" ("*Je m'en fou*") into "I myself in crazy," "I of insane," and "Me me in madman."[23]

lingua franca
Third or "link" language that is understood by two parties who speak different native languages.

Lingua Franca   A **lingua franca** is a third or "link" language that is understood by two parties who speak different native languages. Although only five percent of the world population speaks English as a first language, it is the most common *lingua franca* in international business, followed closely by French and Spanish. A recent survey in the European Union confirmed the widespread use of English as a *lingua franca* among different nationalities of Europeans. Seventy percent of those surveyed agreed that "everyone should speak English," although almost as many said their own language needs to be protected.[24]

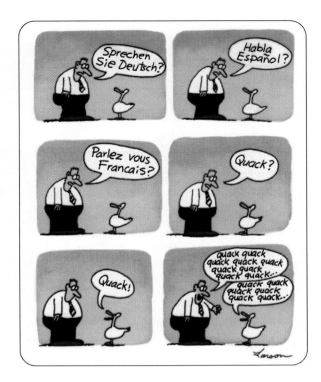

A lingua franca *is a third language that is understood by two parties who speak different native languages. The most common* lingua franca *is English, followed by French and Spanish. Yet knowledge of languages other than these can be invaluable because sometimes there is no alternative but to speak another person's language in order to communicate. The original* lingua franca *arose to support ancient trading activities and contained a mixture of Italian and French, along with Arabic, Greek, and Turkish.*

Source: The Far Side by Gary Larson, © 1983 Far Works Inc.

The Cantonese dialect of Chinese spoken in Hong Kong and the Mandarin dialect spoken in Taiwan and on the Chinese mainland are so different that a *lingua franca* is often preferred. And although India's official language is Hindi, its *lingua franca* among the multitude of dialects is English because it was once a British colony. Yet many young people speak what is referred to as "Hinglish"—a combination of Hindi, Tamil, and English words mixed within a single sentence. Finally, even for the single *lingua franca* of English, differences exist. British-accented English is losing out to North American-accented English in certain locales, particularly in China and South Korea, due to ever-expanding commercial ties with North America.[25]

Because they operate in many nations, each with its own language, multinational corporations sometimes choose a *lingua franca* for official internal communications. Philips (*www.philips.com*) (a Dutch electronics firm), Asea Brown Boveri (*www.abb.com*) (a Swiss industrial giant), and Alcatel (*www.alcatel.com*) (a French telecommunications firm) all use English for internal correspondence. Japan-based Sony and Matsushita also use English abroad, even in some non-English-speaking countries.

Body Language

Body language communicates through unspoken cues, including hand gestures, facial expressions, physical greetings, eye contact, and the manipulation of personal space. Like spoken language, body language communicates both information and feelings and differs greatly from one culture to another. Italians, French, Arabs, and Venezuelans, for example, animate conversations with lively hand gestures and other body motions. Japanese and Koreans, although more reserved, communicate just as much information through their own body languages; a look of the eye can carry as much or more meaning as two flailing arms.

Most body language is subtle and takes time to recognize and interpret. For example, navigating the all-important handshake in international business can be tricky. In the United States it is a firm grip and can include several pumps of the arm. But in the Middle East and Latin America a softer clasp of the hand with little or no arm pump is the custom. And in some countries, like Japan, people do not shake hands at all, but bow to one another. Bows of respect carry different meanings, usually depending on the recipient. Associates of equal standing bow about 15 degrees toward one another. But proper respect for an elder requires a bow of about 30 degrees. Bows of remorse or apology should be about 45 degrees.

body language
Language communicated through unspoken cues, including hand gestures, facial expressions, physical greetings, eye contact, and the manipulation of personal space.

FIGURE 2.1

Some Regional Differences in the Meaning of Gestures

Although Western Europe may be moving toward economic unity, its tapestry of cultures remains diverse. Gestures, for example, continue to reflect centuries of cultural differences. As in the United States, the thumb-and-index circle means "okay" in most of Europe; in Germany, it's an indelicate reference to the receiver's anatomy. In most of Great Britain— England and Scotland—the finger tapping the nose means, "You and I are in on the secret"; in nearby Wales, however, it means, "You're very nosy." If you tap your temple just about anywhere in Western Europe, you're suggesting that someone is "crazy"; in Holland, however, you'll be congratulating someone for being clever.

Proximity is an extremely important element of body language to consider when meeting someone from another culture. If you stand or sit too close to your counterpart (from their perspective), you may invade their personal space and risk appearing aggressive. If you remain too far away, you risk appearing untrustworthy. For North Americans, a distance of about 19 inches is about right between two speakers. For Western Europeans, 14 to 16 inches seems appropriate, but someone from the United Kingdom might prefer about 24 inches. Koreans and Chinese are likely to be comfortable about 36 inches apart, while people from Middle Eastern cultures will close the distance to about eight to 12 inches.[26]

Physical gestures often cause the most misunderstanding between people of different cultures because they can convey very different meanings. The thumbs-up sign is vulgar in Italy and Greece but means "all right" or even "great" in the United States. Figure 2.1 demonstrates how the meaning of other gestures varies across cultures.

Quick Study

1. Define *communication*. Why is knowledge of a culture's *spoken language* important for international business?

2. Describe the threat faced by endangered languages. What is being done to help them survive?

3. What is a *lingua franca*? Describe its implications for conducting international business.

4. Why is *body language* important for international business? Give several examples of how it differs across cultures.

Education

Education is crucial for passing on traditions, customs, and values. Each culture educates its young people through schooling, parenting, religious teachings, and group memberships. Families and other groups provide informal instruction about customs and how to socialize with others. In most cultures, intellectual skills such as reading and mathematics are taught in formal educational settings. Two important topics in education are education level and brain drain.

Education Level
Data provided by governments on the education level of their people must be taken with a grain of salt. Because many nations rely on literacy tests of their own

TABLE 2.1

Illiteracy Rates of Selected
Countries

Country	Adult Illiteracy Rate (Percent of People Age 15 and Up)
Niger	86
Pakistan	51
Morocco	49
Haiti	48
Egypt	43
India	39
Nigeria	33
Cambodia	26
Guatemala	31
Saudi Arabia	22
China	14
Brazil	12
Zimbabwe	10
Jordan	10
Mexico	10
Venezuela	7
Philippines	5
Thailand	4
Argentina	3
Hungary	1

design, they often provide little basis for comparison across countries. Some administer standardized tests, whereas others require only a signature as proof of literacy. But because few other options exist, searching for untapped markets or new factory sites forces managers to rely on such undependable benchmarks. Moreover, as you can see from Table 2.1, some countries have further to go than others in increasing national literacy rates. Nations with excellent programs for basic education tend to attract relatively high-wage industries. Nations that invest in worker training are usually repaid in productivity increases and rising incomes. It is an undisputed fact that whereas nations with skilled, well-educated workforces attract all sorts of high-paying jobs, countries with poorly educated populations attract the lowest-paying manufacturing jobs. By investing in education, a country can attract, and create even, the kind of high-wage industries that are often called "brainpower" industries.[27]

Newly industrialized economies in Asia owe much of their rapid economic development to solid education systems. Hong Kong, South Korea, Singapore, and Taiwan focus on rigorous mathematical training in primary and secondary schooling. University education concentrates on the hard sciences and aims to train engineers, scientists, and managers.

The "Brain Drain" Phenomenon
Just as a country's quality of education affects its economic development, the level and pace of economic development affects its education system. **Brain drain** is the departure of highly educated people from one profession, geographic region, or nation to another.

Political unrest and economic hardship in recent years caused many Indonesians to flee their homeland for the shores of other nations, particularly Hong Kong, Singapore, and the United States. Most of the brain drain that occurred there was among Western-educated professionals in finance and technology (exactly the people Indonesia needs to retain to keep it on the road to development). In Italy, five percent of new college graduates leave the country every year, compared with a European Union average of under one percent. Despite government assistance for their studies, researchers in the sciences are most likely to leave. For the Italian government, "It's like taking an investment and throwing it out," says Giovanni Peri, 34, an Italian expatriate professor at the University of California at Davis.[28]

But one country's brain drain is another's brain gain. Australia reportedly experienced a net gain of more than 155,000 skilled workers over a recent five-year period. According to the Immigration Minister, Australia gained 40,000 managers and administrators, 57,000

brain drain
Departure of highly educated people from one profession, geographic region, or nation to another.

professionals, and 21,000 tradespeople, among others. Many of these gains were made in the all-important information technology sector.[29]

Many countries in Eastern Europe experienced high levels of brain drain early in their transition to market economies. Economists, engineers, scientists, and researchers in all fields fled westward to escape poverty. But as these nations continue their long march away from communism, some are luring professionals back to their homelands—a process known as *reverse brain drain*. In Serbia, economic and legal reforms aimed at remaking the country in the likeness of the Irish Republic (with its young, vibrant, high-tech economy) helped stem a devastating, decade-long brain drain.[30]

Physical and Material Environments

The physical environment and material surroundings of a culture heavily influence its development and pace of change. In this section, we first look at how physical environment and culture are related and then explore the effect of material culture on business.

Physical Environment   Although the physical environment affects a people's culture, it does not directly determine it. Let's take a brief look at two aspects of the physical environment that heavily influence a people's culture: topography and climate.

topography
All the physical features that characterize the surface of a geographic region.

Topography   All the physical features that characterize the surface of a geographic region constitute its **topography**. Some surface features such as navigable rivers and flat plains facilitate travel and contact with others. In contrast, treacherous mountain ranges and large bodies of water can discourage contact and cultural change. Cultures isolated by impassable mountains or large bodies of water will be less exposed to the cultural traits of other peoples. That is why cultural change tends to occur more slowly in isolated cultures than in cultures not isolated in such a manner.

Topography can have an impact on consumers' product needs. For example, there is little market for Honda scooters (*www.honda.com*) in most mountainous regions because their engines are too small. These are better markets for the company's more rugged, maneuverable motorcycles with larger engines. Thinner air at higher elevations might also entail modifications in carburetor design for gasoline-powered vehicles.

Topography and Communication   Topography can have a profound impact on personal communication in a culture. For instance, mountain ranges and the formidable Gobi Desert consume two-thirds of China's land surface. Groups living in the valleys of these mountain ranges continue to hold on to their own ways of life and speak their own languages. Although the Mandarin dialect was decreed the national language many years ago, the mountains, desert, and great land area of China still impair personal communication and, therefore, the proliferation of Mandarin.

climate
Weather conditions of a geographic region.

Climate   The weather conditions of a geographic region are called its **climate**. Climate affects where people settle and helps direct systems of distribution. In Australia, for example, intensely hot and dry conditions in two large deserts, combined with jungle conditions in the northeast, have pushed settlement to coastal areas. As a result—and because water transport is less costly than land transport—coastal waters are still used to distribute products between distant cities.

Climate, Lifestyle, and Work   Climate plays a large role in lifestyle and work habits. The heat of the summer sun grows intense in the early afternoon hours in the countries of southern Europe, northern Africa, and the Middle East. For this reason, people often take afternoon breaks of one or two hours in July and August. People use this time to perform errands, such as shopping, or even take short naps before returning to work until about 7 or 8 P.M. Companies doing business in these regions must adapt to this local tradition. Production schedules, for instance, must be adjusted to allow for hours during which machines stand idle. Shipping and receiving schedules must also reflect afternoon downtime and accommodate shipments made later in the day.

Climate and Customs   Climate also has an impact on customs such as clothing and food. For instance, people in many tropical areas wear little clothing and wear it loosely because of the warm, humid climate. In the desert areas of the Middle East and North Africa, people also wear loose clothing, but they wear long robes to protect themselves from intense sunshine and blowing sand.

A culture's food customs are perhaps more influenced by the physical environment than by any other aspect of culture. But here, too, a people's beliefs can have a major impact on diet. Pigs, for example, are a good source of protein in many parts of the world, including China, Europe, and the Pacific Islands. In the Middle East, however, both Judaism and Islam regard pigs as unclean and prohibit their consumption. The taboo probably originated in environmental factors: Pigs were expensive to feed and produced no materials for clothing. However, because some people were still tempted to squander resources by raising pigs, the prohibition became cultural and was incorporated into both Judaic and Islamic religious texts.[31]

Material Culture   All the technology used in a culture to manufacture goods and provide services is called its **material culture**. Material culture is often used to measure the technological advancement of a nation's markets or industries. Generally, a firm enters a new market under one of two conditions: (1) demand for its products has developed, or (2) the market is capable of supporting its production operations. For example, companies are not flocking to the Southeast Asian nation of Myanmar (formerly Burma) because the nation does not fulfill either of the above conditions. The primary reason is that a wide range of political and social problems under a repressive military government have stalled economic development in Myanmar. In such cases, companies do not consider a market because it simply does not have even the most basic elements of material culture. However, see the Breaking Views feature titled, "Crossing the Digital Divide" for some ways in which technology is eliminating obstacles to nations developing their material culture.

material culture
All the technology used in a culture to manufacture goods and provide services.

breaking **views**

Crossing the Digital Divide

Many regions and nations lack the most basic elements of material culture that exist in a modern society. When used properly, technology can break through old barriers and help those at the bottom of the global economic pyramid improve their lives. In what other ways might technology help the world's poor?

○ **The Hype.**   At the peak of the dot-com bubble, some proclaimed that a personal computer and Internet connection in every home would solve most of the world's ills.

○ **The Reality.**   A dose of pragmatism came from Bill Gates, who told an audience that in the developing world, "Mothers are going to walk right up to that computer and say: 'My children are dying—what can you do?'" As reality sank in, development agencies returned to exploring practical ways to solve the world's social problems.

○ **Solving Basic Problems.**   Some communities facing the most basic social problems found a solution in smart mapping systems—the combination of computer mapping software and global positioning systems. Smart mapping helped stem the mortality rate of a cholera outbreak in South Africa from the usual 10 percent to just 0.2 percent. Health authorities were able to predict where the virus might spread, and warned people there to boil water and milk before consumption.

○ **Making IT Happen Locally.**   Other groups have more advanced needs. Farmers in India typically require copies of deeds to their small plots of land two or three times a year when they request loans from banks to pay for seeds, fertilizer, and crop insurance. But deed fraud by powerful village accountants cost farmers in the state of Karnataka, alone, some $20 million a year. So the state of Karnataka computerized the 20 million deeds of 6.7 million farmers in 30,000 villages. Today, farmers pay just 30 cents for a copy of their deeds, as opposed to between $2 and $22 in the past. But local support is crucial. "These kinds of efforts have to happen locally, and you have to back them up with resources and training on the ground," says Peter Bladin, Director of Grameen Technology Center (*www.grameen-info.org*).

○ **Not a Burden.**   The supranational World Bank (*www.worldbank.org*) and Indian software trade group NASSCOM (*www.nasscom.org*) plan a $1 billion fund to support poverty-reduction efforts. Brazil, Sri Lanka, and others hope to replicate India's most successful projects and apply technology to advance the common good. As management guru C.K. Prahalad says, "If you conceptualize the world's four billion poor as a market, rather than as a burden, they must be considered the biggest source of growth left in the world."

Changes in material culture often cause change in other aspects of a people's culture. Eastern Europe is having a difficult time keeping up with the industrialized nations when it comes to Internet access. One reason is clearly the language gap, as few Web sites are in an eastern European language. Another reason is the technological gap due to underdeveloped telecommunications systems. But as countries in Eastern Europe continue to upgrade their material cultures through economic development programs, people's greater access to information on the Internet will likely affect other aspects of their cultures.

Uneven Material Culture Material culture often displays uneven development across a nation's geography, markets, and industries. For example, much of China's recent economic progress is occurring in coastal cities. Shanghai has long played an important role in China's international trade because of its strategic location and its superb harbor on the East China Sea. Although it is home to only one percent of the total population, Shanghai accounts for about five percent of China's total output—including about 12 percent of both its industrial production and its financial-services output.

Likewise, Bangkok, the capital city of Thailand, houses only 10 percent of the nation's population but accounts for about 40 percent of its economic output. Meanwhile, the northern parts of the country remain rural, consisting mostly of farms, forests, and mountains.

Quick Study

1. Why is the education level of a country's people important to international companies?
2. What is meant by the terms *brain drain* and *reverse brain drain*?
3. How are a people's culture and physical environment related?
4. What is the significance of *material culture* for international business?

Classifying Cultures

Throughout this chapter, you've seen how cultures can differ greatly from one another. People living in broadly different cultures tend to respond differently in similar business situations. There are two widely accepted ways to classify cultures based on differences in characteristics such as values, attitudes, social structure, and so on. Let's now take a detailed look at each of these tools: the Kluckhohn–Strodtbeck and Hofstede frameworks.

Kluckhohn–Strodtbeck Framework

Kluckhohn–Strodtbeck framework
Framework for studying cultural differences along six dimensions, such as focus on past or future events and belief in individual or group responsibility for personal well-being.

The **Kluckhohn–Strodtbeck framework** compares cultures along six dimensions. It studies a given culture by asking each of the following questions:[32]

1. Do people believe that their environment controls them, that they control the environment, or that they are part of nature?
2. Do people focus on past events, on the present, or on the future implications of their actions?
3. Are people easily controlled and not to be trusted, or can they be trusted to act freely and responsibly?
4. Do people desire accomplishments in life, carefree lives, or spiritual and contemplative lives?
5. Do people believe that individuals or groups are responsible for each person's welfare?
6. Do people prefer to conduct most activities in private or in public?

Case: Dimensions of Japanese Culture By providing answers to each of these six questions, we can briefly apply the Kluckhohn–Strodtbeck framework to Japanese culture:

1. *Japanese believe in a delicate balance between people and environment that must be maintained.* Suppose an undetected flaw in a company's product harms

customers using it. In many countries, a high-stakes class-action lawsuit would be filed against the manufacturer on behalf of the victims' families. This scenario is rarely played out in Japan. Japanese culture does not feel that individuals can possibly control every situation but that accidents happen. Japanese victims would receive heartfelt apologies, a promise it won't happen again, and a relatively small damage award.

2. *Japanese culture emphasizes the future.* Because Japanese culture emphasizes strong ties between people and groups, including companies, forming long-term relationships with people is essential when doing business there. Throughout the business relationship, Japanese companies remain in close, continuous contact with buyers to ensure that their needs are being met. This relationship also forms the basis of a communication channel by which suppliers learn about the types of products and services buyers would like to see in the future.

3. *Japanese culture treats people as quite trustworthy.* Business dealings among Japanese companies are based heavily on trust. Once entered into, an agreement to conduct business is difficult to break unless there are extreme uncontrollable factors at work. This is due to the fear of "losing face" if one cannot keep a business commitment. In addition to business applications, society at large reflects the Japanese concern for trustworthiness. Crime rates are quite low and the streets of Japan's largest cities are very safe to walk at night.

4. *Japanese are accomplishment-oriented—not necessarily for themselves, but for their employers and work units.* Japanese children learn the importance of groups early by contributing to the upkeep of their schools. They share duties such as mopping floors, washing windows, cleaning chalkboards, and arranging desks and chairs. They carry such habits learned in school into the adult workplace, where management and labor tend to work together toward company goals—Japanese managers make decisions only after considering input from subordinates. Also, materials buyers, engineers, designers, factory floor supervisors, and marketers cooperate closely throughout each stage of a product's development.

5. *Japanese culture emphasizes individual responsibility to the group and group responsibility to the individual.* This trait has long been a hallmark of Japanese corporations. Traditionally, subordinates promise hard work and loyalty, and top managers provide job security. But a decade of stagnation for the Japanese economy is threatening this tradition. To remain competitive internationally, Japanese companies have eliminated jobs and moved production to low-wage nations like China and Vietnam. As the tradition of job security falls by the wayside, more and more Japanese workers now consider working for non-Japanese companies, whereas others are finding work as temporary employees. Although this trait is diminishing in the business world, it remains a prominent feature in other aspects of Japanese society, especially the family.

6. *The culture of Japan tends to be public.* You will often find top Japanese managers located in the center of a large, open-space office surrounded by the desks of many employees. By comparison, Western executives are often secluded in walled offices located on the perimeter of workspaces in their home countries. This characteristic reaches deep into Japanese society— consider, for example, Japan's continued fondness for public baths.

Hofstede Framework

The **Hofstede framework** grew from a study of more than 110,000 people working in IBM subsidiaries (*www.ibm.com*) in 40 countries.[33] From the study's results, Dutch psychologist Geert Hofstede developed four dimensions for examining cultures.[34] Let's now examine each of these in detail.

Hofstede framework
Framework for studying cultural differences along four dimensions, such as individualism versus collectivism and equality versus inequality.

1. *Individualism versus collectivism.* This dimension identifies the extent to which a culture emphasizes the individual versus the group. Individualist cultures (those scoring high on this dimension) value hard work and promote entrepreneurial risk-taking, thereby fostering invention and innovation. Although people are given freedom to focus on personal goals, they are held responsible for their actions. That is why responsibility for poor business decisions is placed squarely on the shoulders of the individual in charge. At the same time, higher individualism may be responsible for higher rates of employee turnover.

    On the contrary, people in collectivist cultures (those scoring low on this dimension) feel a strong association to groups, including family and work units. The goal of maintaining group harmony is probably most evident in the family structure. People in collectivist cultures tend to work toward collective rather than personal goals and are responsible to the group for their actions. In turn, the group shares responsibility for the well-being of each of its members. Thus, in collectivist cultures success or failure tends to be shared among the work unit, rather than any particular individual receiving all the praise or blame. All social, political, economic, and legal institutions reflect the group's critical role.

2. *Power distance.* This dimension conveys the degree to which a culture accepts social inequality among its people. A culture with large power distance tends to be characterized by much inequality between superiors and subordinates. Organizations tend also to be more hierarchical, with power deriving from prestige, force, and inheritance. This is why executives and upper management in cultures with large power distance often enjoy special recognition and privileges. On the other hand, cultures with small power distance display a greater degree of equality, with prestige and rewards more equally shared between superiors and subordinates. Power in these cultures (relative to cultures with large power distance) is seen to derive more from hard work and entrepreneurial drive and is therefore often considered more legitimate.

    Figure 2.2 shows how the Hofstede study ranked selected countries according to these first two dimensions: power distance and individualism

FIGURE 2.2

Power Distance and Individualism Versus Collectivism

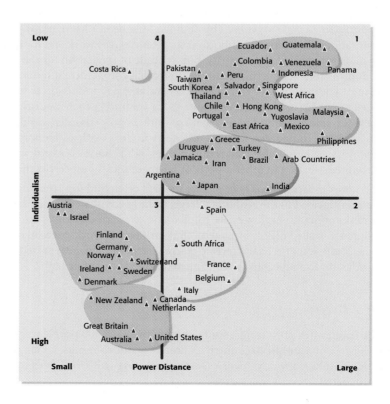

versus collectivism. What is striking about this figure is the tight grouping of nations within the five clusters (plus Costa Rica). You can see the concentration of mostly African, Asian, Central and South American, and Middle Eastern nations in Quadrant 1 (cultures with relatively larger power distance and lower individualism). In contrast, Quadrants 3 and 2 comprise mostly the cultures of Australia and the nations of North America and Western Europe. These nations had the highest individualism scores and many had relatively smaller power distance scores.

3. *Uncertainty avoidance.* This dimension identifies the extent to which a culture avoids uncertainty and ambiguity. A culture with large uncertainty avoidance values security and places its faith in strong systems of rules and procedures in society. It is perhaps not surprising then that cultures with large uncertainty avoidance normally have lower employee turnover, more formal rules for regulating employee behavior, and more difficulty implementing change. Cultures scoring low on uncertainty avoidance tend to be more open to change and new ideas. This helps explain why individuals in this type of culture tend to be entrepreneurial and organizations tend to welcome the best business practices from other cultures. However, because people tend to be less fearful of change, these cultures can also suffer from higher levels of employee turnover.

    Figure 2.3 plots countries according to the second and third dimensions: power distance and uncertainty avoidance. Although the lines of demarcation are somewhat less obvious in this figure, patterns do emerge among the six clusters (plus Jamaica). Quadrant 4 contains nations characterized by small uncertainty avoidance and small power distance, including Australia, Canada, Jamaica, the United States, and many Western European nations. Meanwhile, Quadrant 2 contains many Asian, Central American, South American, and Middle Eastern nations—nations having large power distance and large uncertainty avoidance indexes.

4. *Achievement versus nurturing.* Finally, this dimension captures the extent to which a culture emphasizes personal achievement and materialism versus

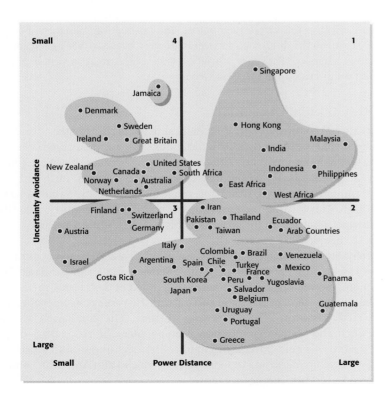

FIGURE 2.3

Power Distance and Uncertainty Avoidance

relationships and quality of life. Cultures scoring high on this index tend to be characterized more by personal assertiveness and the accumulation of wealth, typically translating into an entrepreneurial drive. Cultures scoring low on this dimension generally have more relaxed lifestyles, wherein people are more concerned about caring for others as opposed to material gain.

Locate your country in Figures 2.2 and 2.3. In your personal experience, do you agree with the placement of your nation in these figures? Do you believe managers in your country display the types of behaviors depicted in each of the described dimensions?

Quick Study

1. What are the six dimensions of the *Kluckhohn–Strodtbeck framework* for classifying cultures?
2. What are the four dimensions of the *Hofstede framework* for classifying cultures?
3. Briefly explain how each can be used to analyze a culture.

Bottom Line for Business

This chapter explored how cultural differences between nations affect international business. We saw how problems can erupt from cultural misunderstandings and learned the importance of local cultural knowledge. As globalization continues to draw more and more companies into the international arena, understanding local culture can give a company an advantage over rivals.

The belief that one's own ethnic group or culture is superior to that of others is called ethnocentricity. This way of thinking must be avoided because it causes managers to disregard the positive and beneficial aspects of other cultures. Instead, managers directly involved in international business should develop a certain degree of cultural literacy—detailed knowledge about a culture that enables a person to function effectively within it. Culturally literate managers that compensate for local needs and desires bring their companies closer to customers and, therefore, increase their competitiveness.

Managers should avoid *ethnocentricity* while developing their *cultural literacy* to become more effective marketers, negotiators, and production managers. Being culturally literate can mean the difference between returning home with a signed contract and returning empty-handed. Let's take a brief look at several areas in which culture has a direct impact on international business activity.

Marketing and Cultural Literacy

Many international companies operating in local markets abroad take advantage of the public relations value of supporting national culture. For example, some of India's most precious historical monuments and sites are crumbling because of neglect and the corrosive effect of pollutants. Yet proper upkeep sometimes requires much more than the Indian government can afford. Companies that understand the value of supporting national culture are assisting the government in maintaining some 5,000 sites. As a result, the financial burden on the government is lessened, while companies earn goodwill among the people.[35]

Culturally literate managers also pay attention to significant subcultures within nations. Because minority groups in the United States represent an estimated $1 trillion in total spending power, marketers are keenly interested in their tastes, preferences, and buying habits. One company that's had success with Hispanic consumers because of its marketing tactics is Mott's, Inc. (*www.motts.com*). The company's Mott's Juice, Hawaiian Punch, and Clamato brands have been popular with Hispanics—despite little detailed data on Hispanic purchasing habits. One technique Mott's uses to reach Hispanics is to beef up marketing in those cities in which Latin American bands such as Banda El Recodo and Los Tucanes are touring.[36]

This chapter introduced the Kluckhohn–Strodtbeck and Hofstede frameworks for classifying cultures. A company exploring international markets for its products must consider local cultures. We see the significance of power distance in the export of luxury items. A nation with large power distance accepts greater inequality among its people and tends to have a wealthy upper class that can afford luxury goods. Thus, companies marketing products such as expensive jewelry, high-priced autos, and even yachts could find wealthy market segments within relatively poor nations even.

Work Attitudes and Cultural Literacy

We saw in this chapter the many ways that culture influences people's attitudes toward work. Yet national differences in work attitudes are complex and involve other factors in addition to culture. Perceived opportunity for financial reward is no doubt a strong element in attitudes toward work in any culture. One recent study reported that both U.S. and German employees work longer hours when there is a greater likelihood that good performance will lead to promotion and increased pay. However, it appears that this is relatively less true in Germany, where wages are less variable, and job security and jobless benefits (such as free national health care) are greater. In fact, other aspects of German society that involve tradeoffs made in German politics and economics likely affect work attitudes there. The culturally literate manager understands the complexity of national workplace attitudes and incorporates this knowledge into reward systems, for example. We examine the complexity of national politics and economics further in Chapters 3 and 4.[37]

Expatriates and Cultural Literacy

As stated early in our discussion of classifying cultures, people living in broadly different cultures tend to respond differently in similar business situations. This is why companies that send personnel abroad to unfamiliar cultures must be concerned with cultural differences. An interesting story comes to us from Japan. A Norwegian manager working in Japan for a European car manufacturer, but whose colleagues were mostly Japanese, soon became frustrated with the time needed to make decisions and take action. The main cause for his frustration lay in the fact that the uncertainty avoidance index for Japan is much larger than that in his native Norway (see Figure 2.3). In Japan, the greater aversion to uncertainty led to a greater number of meetings and consultations than would be needed in the home market. The frustrated manager eventually left Japan to return to Europe. We discuss the impact of culture on additional human resource management issues in Chapter 16.

Gender and Cultural Literacy

In Japan, men traditionally hold nearly all positions of responsibility. Women generally serve as office clerks and administrative assistants until their mid- to late twenties, when they are expected to marry and stay at home tending to family needs. Although this is still largely true today, progress is being made in expanding the role of women in Japan's business community. Although women own nearly a quarter of all businesses in Japan, many of these are very small and do not carry a great deal of economic clout. Although greater gender equality prevails in Australia, Canada, Germany, and the United States, women in these countries still tend to earn less money than men in similar positions.

SUMMARY

1. **Describe *culture,* and explain the significance of both national culture and *subcultures*.** Culture is the set of values, beliefs, rules, and institutions held by a specific group of people. Successfully dealing with members of other cultures means avoiding *ethnocentricity* (the tendency to view one's own culture as superior to others) and developing *cultural literacy* (gaining the detailed knowledge necessary to function effectively in another culture).

We are conditioned to think in terms of national culture—that is, to equate a nation-state and its people with a single culture. Nations affirm the importance of national culture by building museums and monuments to preserve national legacies. Nations also intervene in business to help protect the national culture from unwanted influence of other cultures. Most nations are also home to numerous *subcultures*—groups of people who share a unique way of life within a larger, dominant culture. Subcultures contribute greatly to national culture and must be considered in marketing and production decisions.

2. **Identify the *components of culture,* and describe their impact on business activities around the world.** Culture includes a people's beliefs and traditional habits and the ways in which they relate to one another. These factors fall into one or more of the eight major components of culture: (1) aesthetics; (2) values and attitudes; (3) manners and customs; (4) social structure; (5) religion; (6) personal communication; (7) education; and (8) physical and material environments.

   Each of these components affects business activities. *Aesthetics,* for instance, determines which colors and symbols will be effective (or offensive) in advertising. *Values* influence a people's *attitudes* toward time, work and achievement, and cultural change. Knowledge of *manners* and *customs* is necessary for negotiating with people of other cultures, marketing products to them, and managing operations in their country. *Social structure* affects business decisions ranging from production-site selection to advertising methods to the costs of doing business in a country. Different *religions* take different views of work, savings, and material goods. Understanding a people's system of *personal communication* provides insight into their values and behavior. A culture's *education* level affects the quality of the workforce and standard of living. The *physical* and *material environments* influence work habits and preferences regarding products such as clothing and food.

3. **Describe *cultural change,* and explain how companies and culture affect one another.** *Cultural change* occurs when a people integrate into their culture the gestures, material objects, traditions, or concepts of another culture through the process of *cultural diffusion.* Globalization and technology are increasing the pace of cultural change around the world. Companies can influence culture when they import business practices or products into the host country. In order to avoid charges of *cultural imperialism,* they should import new products, policies, and practices during times of stability. Cultures also affect management styles, work scheduling, and reward systems. Adapting to local cultures around the world means heeding the maxim "Think globally, act locally."

4. **Explain how the *physical environment* and *technology* influence culture.** A people's *physical environment* includes *topography* and *climate* and the ways (good and bad) in which they relate to their surroundings. Cultures isolated by topographical barriers, such as mountains or seas, normally change relatively slowly, and their languages are often distinct. Climate affects the hours of the day that people work. For example, people in hot climates normally take siestas when afternoon temperatures soar. Climate also influences customs, such as the type of clothing a people wear and the types of foods they eat.

   Material culture refers to all the technology that people use to manufacture goods and provide services. It is often used to measure the technological advancement of a nation. Businesspeople often use this measure to determine whether a market has developed adequate demand for a company's products and whether it can support production activities. Material culture tends to be uneven across most nations.

5. **Describe the two main *frameworks* used to classify cultures and explain their practical use.** There are two widely accepted frameworks for studying cultural differences: (1) The *Kluckhohn–Strodtbeck framework* compares cultures along six dimensions by seeking answers to certain questions, including: Do people believe that their environment controls them or vice versa? Do people focus on past events or the future? Do they prefer to conduct activities in public or private? (2) The *Hofstede framework* develops four dimensions, such as individualism versus collectivism and equality versus inequality. Understanding a culture's orientation regarding these four dimensions helps companies increase their chances of success. Taken together, these frameworks help companies to understand many aspects of a people's culture including risk-taking, innovation, job mobility, team cooperation, pay levels, and hiring practices.

TALK IT OVER

1. Two students are discussing the various reasons why they are *not* studying international business. "International business doesn't affect me," declares the first student. "I'm going to stay here, not work in some foreign country." "Yeah, me neither," agrees the second. "Besides, some cultures are real strange. The sooner other countries start doing business our way, the better." What counterarguments can you present to these students' perceptions?

2. In this exercise, two groups of four students each will debate the benefits and drawbacks of individualist versus collectivist cultures. After the first student from each side has spoken, the second student questions the opponent's

arguments, looking for holes and inconsistencies. A third student attempts to reply to these counterarguments. Then a fourth student summarizes each side's arguments.

Finally, the class votes on which team presented the more compelling case.

TEAMING UP

1. As a group, select a recent business periodical or news source in print or online—say, the *Economist* (*www.economist.com*), or the *Wall Street Journal* (*www.wsj.com*)—and find three articles discussing the role of culture in international business. Discuss the cultural elements identified by each author and how they pertain to actual business activities in the country being discussed. Write a short summary detailing your findings.

2. Select a company in your city or town that interests you and make an appointment to interview the owner or a senior manager. Your team's goal is to learn how international opportunities and cultural differences affect the decisions of this owner/manager and the activities of his or her company. Be sure to ask your interviewee for specific examples. Present a brief talk on your group's interview findings to the class.

KEY TERMS

aesthetics (p. 53)

attitudes (p. 54)

body language (p. 69)

brain drain (p. 71)

caste system (p. 61)

class system (p. 61)

climate (p. 72)

communication (p. 66)

cultural diffusion (p. 56)

cultural imperialism (p. 56)

cultural literacy (p. 51)

cultural trait (p. 56)

culture (p. 50)

customs (p. 58)

ethnocentricity (p. 50)

folk custom (p. 58)

Hofstede framework (p. 75)

Kluckhohn–Strodtbeck framework (p. 74)

lingua franca (p. 68)

manners (p. 58)

material culture (p. 73)

popular custom (p. 58)

social group (p. 60)

social mobility (p. 61)

social stratification (p. 61)

social structure (p. 60)

subculture (p. 52)

topography (p. 72)

values (p. 54)

TAKE IT TO THE WEB

1. This chapter discussed the many ways in which culture affects the product a company sells in a market or region, how it markets the product, its human resource practices, and so on. It is increasingly important that managers have cultural understanding of their markets in this age of globalization and intensified competition.

   Select a well-known multinational company and visit its Web site. Possible companies include IKEA (*www.ikea.com*), Lands' End (*www.landsend.com*), and Yahoo! (*www.yahoo.com*). Locate the section of the Web site that tells about the company's activities (usually titled "About Our Company"). Report on the (1) main products or services the company offers, (2) extent to which the company pursues international business operations

(often expressed as percentage of sales or assets), (3) ways that the company has adapted to local cultures around the world, and (4) general policies it follows in doing business internationally.

Regarding its Internet presence, how would you rate the user-friendliness of the site on a scale of one to 10? Does it offer its U.S. Web site in another language widely spoken in the United States, such as Spanish or Chinese? Find and click on several of the company's other national Web sites. What kinds of products are advertised on the home page of the different sites? Why do you think the company places these similar/different products up front? Can you identify any other ways the company adapts its Web site to suit cultural preferences?

1. You are the vice president of operations for a U.S.-based software firm. Your firm's board of directors wants you to explore building a software design operation in India. Typically, when international firms enter the Indian market they quickly learn about the various ways in which a rigid caste system can affect business activities. Do you think it will be possible to uphold a U.S. management style in India? Or should your company be prepared to adjust to the local Indian managerial style and human resource practices?

2. You are the vice president of international operations for a large pharmaceutical firm that manufactures an antimalarial drug. Your firm is considering opening up a factory in a small central American nation where malaria is still extremely common. The operation will be a cooperative venture between your firm and the local government. The majority of the people in that country cannot afford the medicine because of the high import tariffs. Yet if your plan goes through, over 200 jobs will be created and the drug's international price will drop by over 50 percent. In a final meeting with a senior government official, the gentleman informs you that if you pay him $500,000 cash, the deal will go through. What issues must you consider? What do you do?

3. You are the public relations director for a company that recently announced its decision to close its factory in the U.S. and outsource the work to manufacturers in Asia and Latin America. Your firm is doing just what many other companies have already done, reducing labor costs by shifting work to low-wage countries such as China, India, Mexico, and central American nations. Yet the media and disgruntled workers are lambasting your firm's decision. Is there a reasonable response to charges that the companies you will hire frequently exploit child labor, force women to work 75-hour weeks, and destroy family units?

PRACTICING INTERNATIONAL MANAGEMENT CASE

Modernization or Westernization? You Make the Call

Many cultures in Asia are in the midst of an identity crisis. In effect, they are being torn between two worlds. Pulling in one direction is a traditional value system derived from agriculture-based communities and extended families—that is, elements of a culture in which relatives take care of one another and state-run welfare systems are unnecessary. Pulling from the opposite direction is a new set of values emerging from manufacturing- and finance-based economies—elements of a culture in which workers must often move to faraway cities to find work, sometimes leaving family members to fend for themselves.

For decades, Western multinationals set up factories across Southeast Asia to take advantage of relatively low-cost labor. Later, local companies sprang up and became competitive global players in their own right. The result was spectacular rates of economic growth in a few short decades that elevated living standards in many Asian countries far beyond what was thought possible. Young people in countries like Malaysia and Thailand felt the lure of "Western" brands. Gucci handbags (*www.gucci.com*), Harley-Davidson motorcycles (*www.h-d.com*), and other global brand names became common symbols of success. Some parents even encouraged brand-consciousness among their teenage children because it signaled family-wide success. But despite the growing consumer society, polls of young people show them holding steadfast to traditional values such as respect for family and group harmony. Youth in Hong Kong, for example, overwhelmingly believe that parents should have much to say about how hard they study, about how they treat family members and elders, and about their choice of friends.

Now globalization is washing over India. The explosion in the number of back-office and call-center jobs is causing a social revolution among the nation's twenty-something graduates of technical colleges and universities. Unlike the high-tech jobs India has traditionally attracted in the service sector, young call center staff are placed in direct contact with Western consumers. They answer calls from people responding to infomercials and taking orders for items such as tummy crunchers, diet pills, and orthopedic insoles. For these young people in India, especially women, the work means money, independence, and freedom—sometimes far away from home in big cities such as Bangalore and Bombay, where the jobs are. But in addition to the training in American accents and geography, they are learning new ideas about family, materialism, and relationships.

The nature of call-center work means that it is often done on night shifts, when consumers in Canada, Europe, or the United States are awake—which fuels the suspicions of parents of the young employees. Binitha Venugopal, a young woman who used to work at a call center quit her job in favor of a "regular" daytime job when her parents objected. Speaking of her former coworkers, she said, "They are materialistic, their values are changing," and that dating and live-in relationships among them are common. Indian tradition dictates that young adults live with their parents at least until they get married (typically to someone their parents choose), and perhaps longer.

Roopa Murthy, who is 24, works for 24/7 Customer (*www.247customer.com*), an Indian company that performs call-center work plus provides back-office services. From her native Mysore, Ms. Murthy moved to Bangalore in 2002 armed with an accounting degree from a woman's college. She now earns $400 per month, which is several times what her father earned before he retired from his government job. Her long hair is now cut short, similar to that of her idol, Dana Scully from the TV show "X-Files," whose name she even adopted for her "telephone name." She has tossed aside her *salwar kameez*, the traditional loose-fitting clothing that she wore back home, in favor of designer-labeled Western attire. Whereas she owned one pair of sandals all through college, she now owns Nike and Adidas sneakers along with half a dozen other pairs of shoes. Although she once shunned drinking and her curfew at home was 9 P.M., she now frequents a pub called Geoffrey's, where she enjoys dry martinis and rum, and The Club, a suburban disco. After sending money home to her parents, she has enough left over to spend on imported cosmetics, jeans, a cell-phone, and dinner at an American chain restaurant. She confesses that she is "seeing someone" but that her parents would disapprove, adding "it is difficult to talk to Indian parents about things like boyfriends." She said she sometimes envies her callers' lives but that she hopes her job will help her succeed. "I may be a small-town girl, but there is no way I'm going back to Mysore after this," she said.

Arundhati Roy, an Indian novelist and activist, argues that call centers strip young Indian workers of their cultural identities, for example, by making them use American names on the phone. She wrote that call centers show "how easily an ancient civilization can be made to abase itself completely." While some blame "Westernization" for a decaying value system and declining morality, many, it seems, want modernization but also want to hold on to traditional beliefs and values.

Thinking Globally

1. If your international firm were doing business in Asia, would you feel partly responsible for these social trends? Is there anything that your company could do to ease the tensions being experienced by these cultures? Be specific.

2. In your opinion, is globalization among the causes of the increasing incidence of divorce, crime, and drug abuse in Asia? Why or why not?

3. Broadly defined, Asia comprises over 60 percent of the world's population—a population that practices Buddhism, Confucianism, Hinduism, Islam, and numerous other religions. Given the fact that there are considerable cultural differences between countries such as China, India, Indonesia, Japan, and Malaysia, is it possible to carry on a valid discussion of "Asian" values? Why or why not?

4. Consider the following statement: "Economic development and capitalism require a certain style of doing *business* in the twenty-first century. The sooner Asian *cultures* adapt, the better." Do you agree or disagree? Explain.

learning objectives

After studying this chapter, you should be able to

1. Describe each main type of *political system*.

2. Identify the origins of *political risk* and how managers can reduce its effects.

3. List the main types of *legal systems*, and explain how they differ.

4. Describe the major *legal* and *ethical issues* facing international companies.

5. Explain how *international relations* affect international business activities.

politics and law

in business

3

a look *back*

CHAPTER 2 explored the main elements of culture and showed how each affects business practices. We learned about different methods used to classify cultures and how these methods can be applied to business.

a look at *this chapter*

This chapter explores the roles of politics and law in international business. We begin by explaining different types of political systems and how managers cope with political risk. Then we examine several kinds of legal systems, ethics and social responsibility, and how international relations affect business.

a look *ahead*

CHAPTER 4 discusses the world's different economic systems. We learn about economic development and explore the challenges facing countries that are transforming their economies into free-market systems.

Taming the Wild, Wild Web

BEIJING, China—"We're not looking to put provocative information up on the site," admits Maury Zeff, regional director of production for Yahoo! Asia. "It's all up to the interpretation of the government." Although the story about human-organ selling in China never appeared on Yahoo's Web site there, it did run on the company's U.S. Web site (*www.yahoo.com*). Yahoo decided it was better to censor itself rather than risk offending Chinese authorities. Many would say that Yahoo censored itself for good reason—China is the world's second largest Internet market after the United States.

But this was not the first time that Yahoo adapted itself to local market constraints; it had already been forced to adapt to laws in Europe. French judge Jean-Jacques Gomez ordered Yahoo to stop offering Nazi artifacts to French consumers on its auction sites because buying Nazi memorabilia is illegal there. But because identifying every French bidder on its auction sites would be impossible, Yahoo withdrew all such items and filtered its Web sites globally to comply with French law.

Around the world, Yahoo helps people communicate, access information, and sell things on the Internet while it remains conscious of political and legal differences. David Filo and Jerry Yang never thought they would one day get caught up in such sensitive global issues when they started Yahoo in 1994 as "Jerry's Guide to the World Wide Web." Wanting a snappier name, the pair liked the general definition of a yahoo: "rude, unsophisticated, uncouth." Today the company has over 237 million users in 25 countries communicating in 13 languages. As you read this chapter, think about the different ways companies adapt to local political and legal conditions around the world.[1]

Chapter 2 explained that an understanding of culture is essential to achieving success in the international marketplace. Yet it is only one element of that success. Another crucial element is political and legal savvy. As Yahoo! (*www.yahoo.com*) learned in our opening company profile, doing business in other countries involves tricky political and legal issues. Yahoo's travails are a striking reminder that although the Internet shrinks the distance between two points, it still matters where those two points are. The Internet community consists of nearly 250 country domains, and as many sets of political and legal environments. This is why just as "bricks and mortar" companies have always adapted to local politics and law in the global marketplace, so too must Internet companies.

But Yahoo is not the first company to censor itself or adapt its policies to local laws. Rupert Murdoch's News Corp. (*www.newscorp.com*) removed BBC news (*www.bbc.co.uk*) from its Asian television broadcasts because it occasionally criticized China.[2] Barnes & Noble (*www.bn.com*) and Amazon (*www.amazon.com*) stopped selling the English-language version of *Mein Kampf* to Germans when the German government complained—although it's illegal only to sell the German-language version. A statement by Barnes & Noble read, "Our policy with regard to censorship remains unchanged. But as responsible corporate citizens, we respect the laws of the countries where we do business."[3]

Understanding the nature of politics and laws in other nations lessens the risks of conducting international business. In this chapter, we present the basic differences between political and legal systems around the world. You will read how disputes grounded in political and legal matters affect business activities and how companies can manage the associated risks. Also presented is how legal issues can sometimes become ethical issues for managers of international companies. This chapter will close with a brief discussion on the interaction of business and international relations.

Political Systems

political system
Structures, processes, and activities by which a nation governs itself.

A **political system** includes the structures, processes, and activities by which a nation governs itself. The Japanese system, for instance, features a prime minister who is chosen by the Japanese Diet (Parliament) to carry out the operations of government with the help of Cabinet ministers. The Diet consists of two houses of elected representatives who enact the nation's laws. These laws affect not only the personal lives of people living in or visiting Japan, but also places demands on the activities of companies doing business there.

Politics and Culture

Politics and *culture* are closely related. A country's political system is rooted in the history and culture of its people. Factors such as population, age and race composition, and per capita income influence a country's political system.

Consider the case of Switzerland, where the political system actively encourages all eligible members of society to vote. By means of *public referendums*, Swiss citizens vote directly on many national issues. Contrast this practice with that of most other democracies, in which representatives of the people, not the people themselves, vote on such issues. The Swiss system works because Switzerland consists of a relatively small population living in a small geographic area.

Political Participation

Political systems can be characterized by *who* participates in them and *to what extent* they participate. *Participation* occurs when people voice their opinions, vote, and show general approval or disapproval of the system.

Participation can be wide or narrow. *Wide participation* occurs when people who are capable of influencing the political system make an effort to do so. For example, most adults in the United States have the right to participate in the political process. Everyone has the right to approve or disapprove of elected representatives and the government in general. *Narrow participation* occurs when few people participate. For instance, in Kuwait participation is restricted to citizens who can prove Kuwaiti ancestry at some time in the past.

But sometimes people eligible to vote don't even bother. For example, turnout in recent national elections ranged from more than 90 percent of the voting-age population in Malta to less than 35 percent in Senegal and Kazakhstan. Prior to 2004, turnout in U.S. Presidential elections had fallen to 54.5 percent of eligible voters, which placed it an embarrassing 139th among 172 nations with democratic elections.[4]

Political Ideologies

We can think of the world's different political systems as falling on a continuum that is defined by three political ideologies:

- At one extreme is *anarchism*—the belief that only individuals and private groups should control a nation's political activities. It views public government as unnecessary and unwanted because it tramples personal liberties.

- At the other extreme is *totalitarianism*—the belief that every aspect of people's lives must be controlled in order for a nation's political system to be effective. Totalitarianism has no concern for individual liberties. In fact, people are often considered slaves of the political system. Institutions such as family, religion, business, and labor are considered subordinate to the state. Totalitarian political systems include authoritarian regimes such as communism and fascism.

- Between anarchism and totalitarianism lies *pluralism*—the belief that both private and public groups play important roles in a nation's political activities. Each of these groups (consisting of people with different ethnic, racial, class, and lifestyle backgrounds) serves to balance the power that can be gained by the other. Pluralistic political systems include democracies, constitutional monarchies, and some aristocracies.

Let's take a look at two prevalent types of political systems—*democracy* and *totalitarianism*—to gain a fuller understanding of the political elements that cause differences in business practices from one country to another.

Democracy   A **democracy** is a political system in which government leaders are elected directly by the wide participation of the people or by their representatives. The foundations of modern democracy go back at least as far as the ancient Greeks.

The Greeks tried to practice a *pure democracy,* one in which all citizens participate freely and actively in the political process. But a "pure" democracy is more an ideal than a workable system, for several reasons. First, some people have neither the time nor the desire to get involved in the political process. Second, as the population expands and the barriers of distance and time increase, each citizen's ability to participate completely and actively is reduced. And third, because direct voting usually results in conflicting popular opinion, leaders in a pure democracy can find it difficult, if not impossible, to form cohesive policies.

Representative Democracy   For practical reasons, most nations have resorted to **representative democracies,** in which citizens elect individuals from their groups to represent their political needs and views. These representatives then help govern the people and pass laws. Representatives performing to the people's satisfaction can be voted back into office. Meanwhile, those who fail to retain a minimum level of popular support are voted out of office.

democracy
Political system in which government leaders are elected directly by the wide participation of the people or by their representatives.

representative democracy
Democracy in which citizens elect individuals from their groups to represent their political needs and views.

To varying degrees, representative democracies strive to provide some or all of the following freedoms:

- *Freedom of expression.* A constitutional right in most democracies, freedom of expression ideally grants the right to voice opinions freely and without fear of punishment.

- *Periodic elections.* Each elected representative serves for a period of time, after which the people (or *electorate*) decide whether or not to retain these representatives. This is why U.S. presidential elections are held every four years, whereas those in France are held every seven.

- *Full civil and property rights.* Civil rights include freedom of speech, freedom to organize political parties, and the right to a fair trial. Property rights are the privileges and responsibilities of owners of property (homes, cars, businesses, and so forth). Map 3.1 illustrates the extent to which people of 192 nations around the world have political rights and civil liberties.

- *Minority rights.* In theory, democracies try to preserve peaceful coexistence among groups of people with diverse cultural, ethnic, and racial backgrounds. Ideally, the same rights and privileges are by law extended to each group, no matter how few members it has.

- *Nonpolitical bureaucracies.* The bureaucracy is the part of government that implements the rules and laws passed by elected representatives. In *politicized bureaucracies,*

MAP 3.1

Political and Civil Liberties Around the World

This map illustrates the level of political rights and civil liberties of the people of each nation and territory. It does not rate national governments, but represents the rights and liberties of individuals. As defined by Freedom House, political rights refer to people's ability to vote and run for public office and, as elected officials, to vote on public policies. Civil liberties include people's freedom to develop views, institutions, and personal autonomy apart from the state. In all, 88 countries (44 percent of the world population) are listed as being free, 55 countries (21 percent of the world population) as partly free, and 49 countries (35 percent of the world population) as not free.

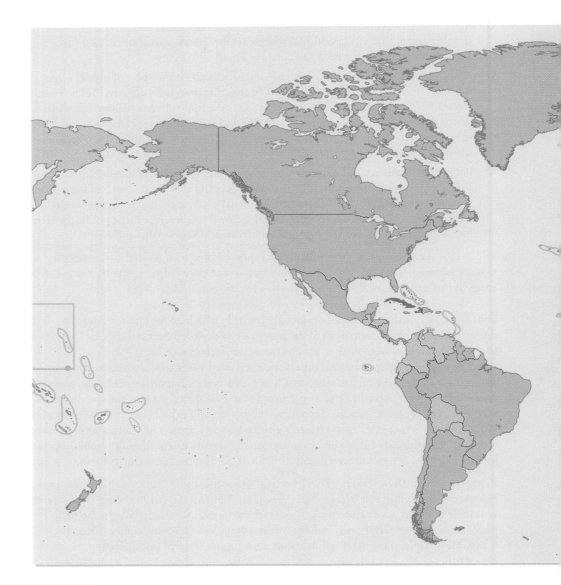

bureaucrats tend to implement decisions according to their own political views rather than those of the people's representatives. This clearly contradicts the purpose of the democratic process.

Despite such shared principles, countries vary greatly in the practice of representative democracy. Britain, for example, practices *parliamentary democracy.* The nation is divided into geographical districts, and people in each district vote for competing *parties* rather than individual candidates. But the party that wins the greatest number of legislative seats in an election does not automatically win the right to run the country. Rather, a party must gain an *absolute majority*—that is, the number of representatives that a party gets elected must exceed the number of representatives that all other parties get elected.

If the party with the largest number of representatives lacks an absolute majority, it can join with one or more other parties to form what is called a coalition government. In a *coalition government,* the strongest political parties share power by dividing government responsibilities among themselves. Coalition governments are often formed in Italy, Israel, and the Netherlands. The large number of political parties in these countries makes it difficult for single parties to gain absolute majorities.

Nations also differ in the relative power possessed by each of their political parties. In some democratic countries, a single political party has effectively controlled the system for extended periods. In Japan, for example, the Liberal Democratic Party (which is actually conservative) has enjoyed nearly uninterrupted control of the government since the

FREEDOM RATING

- Free
- Partly free
- Not free
- No data

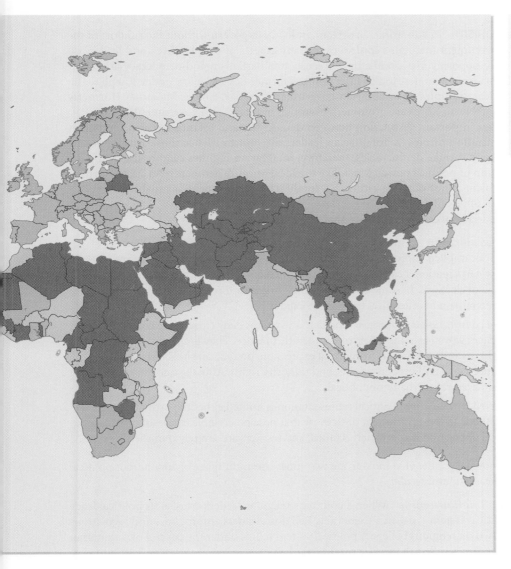

1950s. In Mexico, the Institutional Revolutionary Party (PRI) ran the country for 71 years until Vicente Fox of the conservative National Action Party (PAN) won the presidency in 2000.

Doing Business in Democracies   Democracies maintain stable business environments primarily through laws that protect individual property rights. In theory, commerce prospers when the **private sector** includes independently owned firms that exist to make profits. Bear in mind that although participative democracy, property rights, and free markets tend to encourage economic growth, they do not always do so. For instance, although India is the world's largest democracy, for decades it experienced slow economic growth until recently. Meanwhile, some countries achieved rapid economic growth under nondemocratic political systems. The so-called four tigers of Asia—Hong Kong, Singapore, South Korea, and Taiwan—built strong market economies in the absence of truly democratic practices.

> *private sector*
> Segment of the economic environment comprising independently owned firms that exist to make a profit.

Quick Study

1. What is a *political system*? Explain the relation between political systems and culture.
2. What is *democracy*? Explain the difference between pure and *representative democracy*.
3. Identify several main freedoms a representative democracy strives to provide its people.
4. How might a democratic government affect business activities in a nation?

> *totalitarian system*
> Political system in which individuals govern without the support of the people, government maintains control over many aspects of people's lives, and leaders do not tolerate opposing viewpoints.

Totalitarianism

In a **totalitarian system**, individuals govern without the support of the people, government maintains control over many aspects of people's lives, and leaders do not tolerate opposing viewpoints. In this sense, totalitarianism and democracy are opposites. Nazi Germany under Adolf Hitler and the former Soviet Union under Joseph Stalin are historical examples of totalitarian governments. Today, China, Myanmar (formerly Burma), and North Korea are prominent examples of totalitarian governments.

Another important distinction between democratic and totalitarian governments is the concentration of power. Totalitarian leaders attempt to silence those with opposing political views. Unlike democracies, therefore, totalitarian regimes require the near-total centralization of political power. Much like the ideal of "pure democracy," a "pure" form of totalitarianism is not possible either. No totalitarian government is capable of entirely silencing all of its critics.

Totalitarian governments tend to share three features:

- *Imposed authority.* An individual or group forms the political system without the explicit or implicit approval of the people. Thus, a totalitarian system is marked by narrow participation. Leaders often acquire and retain power by military force or fraudulent elections. In some cases, they come to power through legitimate means but then remain in office after their terms expire.

- *Lack of constitutional guarantees.* Totalitarian systems deny citizens the constitutional guarantees woven into the fabric of democratic practice. They limit, abuse, or reject outright institutions such as freedom of expression, periodically held elections, guaranteed civil and property rights, and minority rights. Also, the bureaucracy may be politicized rather than nonpolitical.

- *Restricted participation.* Political representation is limited either to parties that are sympathetic to the government or to those that pose no credible threat. In most cases, political opposition is completely banned, and resisters are severely punished.

Let's now take a detailed look at the two most common types of totalitarian political systems: *theocratic* and *secular*.

> *theocracy*
> Political system in which a country's political leaders are religious leaders who enforce laws and regulations based on religious beliefs.

> *theocratic totalitarianism*
> Political system in which religious leaders govern without the support of the people and do not tolerate opposing viewpoints.

Theocratic Totalitarianism   When a country's religious leaders are also its political leaders, its political system is called a **theocracy**. Religious leaders enforce laws and regulations that are based on religious beliefs. A political system that is under the control of totalitarian religious leaders is called **theocratic totalitarianism**.

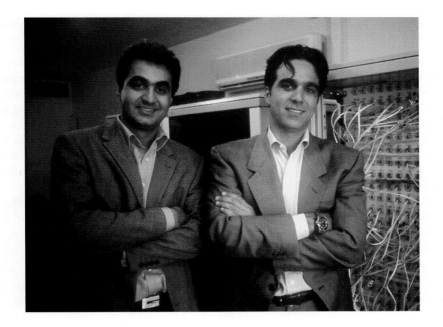

Though political reform has been hindered recently, Iran is arguably more pro-business than at any time in the more than 24 years since the revolution. Two beneficiaries of the change are entrepreneurs Abdollah Fateh, 30, and Madjid Emami, 32, who together started their Internet service provider, Pars Online (**www.parsonline.com**). The pair hope to become the Iranian, or even regional, online company to beat. They certainly have a following. Says a female admirer, "They are the two coolest guys in Tehran."

Iran is a prominent example of a theocratic totalitarian state. Iran has been an Islamic state since the 1979 revolution in which the reigning monarch was overthrown. Today, many young Iranians appear disenchanted with the strict code imposed on many aspects of their public and private lives, including strict laws against products and ideas deemed too "Western." They do not question their religious beliefs but yearn for a more open society. Iranian president Muhammad Khatami pushed through some changes in government policies in recent years despite opposition from conservative religious leaders.

Secular Totalitarianism A political system in which political leaders rely on military and bureaucratic power is called **secular totalitarianism**. It takes three forms: *communist, tribal,* and *right-wing.*

secular totalitarianism
Political system in which leaders rely on military and bureaucratic power.

Communist Totalitarianism Under *communist totalitarianism* (referred to here simply as *communism*), the government has sweeping political and economic powers. The Communist Party controls all aspects of the political system, and opposition parties are given little or no voice. In general, each Party member holding office is required to support all government policies, and dissension is rarely permitted. **Communism** is the belief that social and economic equality can be obtained only by establishing an all-powerful Communist Party and by instituting **socialism**—an economic system in which the government owns and controls all types of economic activity. This includes granting the government ownership of the means of production (such as capital, land, and factories) and the power to decide what the economy will produce and the prices at which goods are sold.

communism
The belief that social and economic equality can be obtained only by establishing an all-powerful Communist Party and by granting the government ownership and control over all types of economic activity.

However, important distinctions separate communism from socialism. Communists follow the teachings of Marx and Lenin; believe that a violent revolution is needed to seize control over resources; and wish to eliminate political opposition. Socialists believe in none of these. Thus, communists are socialists, but socialists are not necessarily communist.

socialism
The belief that social and economic equality is obtained through government ownership and regulation of the means of production.

Communist and socialist beliefs differ markedly from those of **capitalism**—the belief that ownership of the means of production belongs in the hands of individuals and private businesses. Capitalism is also frequently referred to as the *free market.* (The economics of communism and capitalism are covered in detail in Chapter 4.)

capitalism
The belief that ownership of the means of production belongs in the hands of individuals and private businesses.

Communist totalitarianism and economic socialism seem to have lost the battle against capitalism. In the late 1980s, shortly after the former Soviet Union implemented its twin policies of *glasnost* (political openness) and *perestroika* (economic reform), its government began to crumble, as people complained openly about their government. Communist governments in Central and Eastern Europe soon followed suit, and today countries such as the Czech Republic, Hungary, Poland, Romania, and Ukraine have elected republican governments. As a result, there are far fewer communist nations than there were two decades ago. North Korea remains the most prominent, hard-line communist nation today.

Tribal Totalitarianism   Under *tribal totalitarianism,* one tribe (or ethnic group) imposes its will on others with whom it shares a national identity. Although tribal totalitarianism is perhaps the least understood form of totalitarianism, it characterizes the governments of several African nations, including Burundi and Rwanda. With the departure of European colonial powers, many national boundaries in Africa were created with little regard to ethnic differences among inhabitants. Thus, people of different ethnicities live within the same nation, whereas members of the same ethnicity live in different nations. Over time, certain ethnic groups gained political and military power, and animosity among the different groups often erupted in bloody conflict.

Although tribalism plays a role in many of Africa's civil conflicts, it is not always the most significant factor. The Global Challenges feature titled, "From Civil War to Civil Society" explores the economic and social costs of civil wars (particularly in Africa), and what developed nations can do to help put an end to them.

Right-Wing Totalitarianism   Under *right-wing totalitarianism,* the government endorses private ownership of property and a market-based economy but grants few (if any) political freedoms. Leaders generally strive for economic growth while opposing *left-wing* totalitarianism (communism). Argentina, Brazil, Chile, and Paraguay all had right-wing totalitarian governments in the 1980s.

Despite theoretical differences between the two ideologies, the Chinese political system is currently a mix of communist and right-wing totalitarianism. China's leaders are engineering high economic growth by implementing certain characteristics of a capitalist economy while retaining a hard line in the political sphere. The Chinese government is selling off many of its decrepit state-run factories and changing laws to further encourage the

global CHALLENGES

From Civil War to Civil Society

Today, most wars occur *within* nations that were once controlled and stabilized by colonial powers. If these nations are to prosper from globalization, they must break the vicious cycle whereby conflict causes poverty and poverty causes conflict.

○ **War's Root Causes.**   Although tribal or ethnic rivalry is typically blamed for starting civil wars, the most common causes are poverty, low economic growth, and dependency on natural resource exports. In fact, the poorest one-sixth of humanity endures four-fifths of the world's civil wars.

○ **What's at Stake.**   It appears that pitched battles in Bunia, in eastern Congo, are rooted in ethnic conflict. Yet the Hema and the Lendu tribes only began annihilating each other when neighboring Uganda (to control mineral-rich Bunia) started arming rival militias in 1999. In the Darfur region of Sudan, Arab Muslims battle black non-Muslims. Depending on whom you ask, the conflict began as a fight over pastures and livestock, or the oil beneath them.

○ **What Is Lost.**   Apart from the terrible human cost of an average civil conflict, which lasts eight years, there is a financial cost. Health costs are $5 billion per conflict because of collapsed health systems and forced migra-

tions (which worsen and spread disease). GDP falls by 2.2 percent and another 18 percent of income is wasted on arms and militias. Full economic recovery takes a decade, which reduces output by about 105 percent of the nation's pre-war GDP.

○ **The Challenge.**   Recent research offers several solutions to this global challenge. First, because the risk of civil war halves when income per person doubles, conflicts may be *prevented* by funneling more aid to poor nations. Second, war might be *limited* by restricting a nation in conflict (Sierra Leone) from spending the proceeds from its exports (so-called "conflict diamonds") on munitions, or by lowering the world market price of those exports. Finally, to *halt* nations from slipping back into civil war, health and education aid could be increased after war ends, or a foreign power could intervene to keep the peace (as Britain did in Sierra Leone).

○ **Want to Know More?**   Visit the Centre for the Study of African Economies at Oxford University (*www.csae.ox.ac.uk*), the Copenhagen Consensus project (*www.copenhagenconsensus.com*), and the World Bank Conflict Prevention and Reconstruction unit (*www.worldbank.org*).

international investment needed to modernize the country's production technologies. But the government still has little patience for dissidents who demand greater political freedom, and complete freedom of the press does not exist in China.

Doing Business in Totalitarian Countries   What are the costs and benefits of doing business in a totalitarian nation? On the plus side, international companies need not be concerned with political opposition to their activities by non-governmental organizations. On the negative side, they might need to pay bribes and kickbacks to government officials. Refusal to pay could result in loss of market access or even forfeiture of investments in the country.

In any case, doing business in a totalitarian country can be a risky proposition. Many facets of business law pertain to contractual disputes. In a country such as the United States, laws regarding the resolution of such disputes are quite specific. In totalitarian nations, the law can be either vague or nonexistent, and people in powerful government positions can interpret laws largely as they please. For instance, in China it may not matter so much what the law states but how individual bureaucrats interpret the law. The arbitrary nature of totalitarian governments makes it hard for companies to know how laws will be interpreted and applied to their particular business dealings.

Companies that operate in totalitarian nations are sometimes criticized for lacking compassion for people hurt by the oppressive political policies of their hosts. Executives must decide whether to refrain from investing in totalitarian countries—and miss potentially profitable opportunities—or invest and bear the brunt of potentially damaging publicity. The issues are complex, and the controversy remains heated.

Political Systems in Times of Change

People around the world are demanding greater participation in the political process and forcing many nations to abandon totalitarian for democratic systems. But the economic consequences of globalization can cause fundamental changes in people's values and attitudes.

In Latin American nations, while most people believe that a market economy is the only route to prosperity, their attitudes toward democracy are more ambivalent. A recent survey shows mixed support for democracy across the region. In some nations, the number of people who say that an authoritarian government could be preferable under certain circumstances is actually rising. In Paraguay, 44 percent say that an authoritarian government might be preferable to a democratic one. Across Latin America, nearly 55 percent of the people would support authoritarian governments over democracy if that would solve their economic problems.[5]

One of the most closely watched nations in terms of its political change is China. After 1949, when the communists defeated the nationalists in China's civil war, China imprisoned or exiled most of its capitalists. But in 2001 private businesspeople were allowed to join China's Communist Party for the first time ever. The move represented the leadership's struggle to maintain order in the face of increasingly rapid economic and social change. Part of the reason for this move was explained in a government report, which spoke of problems facing the nation. Difficulties reported were the collapse of state-owned industry, a social safety net unable to cope with millions of unemployed, poor relations with the nation's ethnic minorities, an unjust legal system, and a restless peasantry increasingly willing to take up arms against the system.[6] Workers are also being allowed for the first time ever to elect local representatives to the official trade union. Meanwhile, without Beijing's approval, scores of townships in Sichuan, Guangdong, and Shanxi provinces are holding elections for township chiefs, who are normally chosen by Party representatives.[7]

Quick Study

1.   How does *totalitarianism* differ from democracy? Identify its three main features.
2.   Explain each of the different forms of totalitarianism.
3.   Identify the economic and social costs of civil war, and potential solutions to such conflicts.
4.   How might a totalitarian government affect business activities?

Political Risk

political risk
Likelihood that a government or society will undergo political changes that negatively affect local business activity.

All companies doing business internationally confront **political risk**—the likelihood that a government or society will undergo political changes that negatively affect local business activity. Political risk affects different types of companies in different ways. It can threaten the market of an exporter, the production facilities of a manufacturer, or the ability of a company to pull out profits from the country in which they were earned. Map 3.2 shows how the level of political risk varies from nation to nation.

Political risk arises from a variety of sources, including the following:

- Corrupt or poor political leadership
- Frequent changes in the form of government
- Political involvement of religious or military leaders
- An unstable political system
- Conflict among races, religions, or ethnic groups
- Poor relations with other countries

International businesses can unwittingly *increase* their own political risk by stirring up local emotions and sentiments. For example, firms can add to their political risk if they

MAP 3.2

Political Risk Around the World

A nation's political risk is an important factor in a company's decision to do business with or in that country. This map shows how much political risk can vary from one country to another. Some of the factors included in this assessment of political risk levels include government stability, internal and external conflict, military and religion in politics, corruption, law and order, and bureaucracy quality.

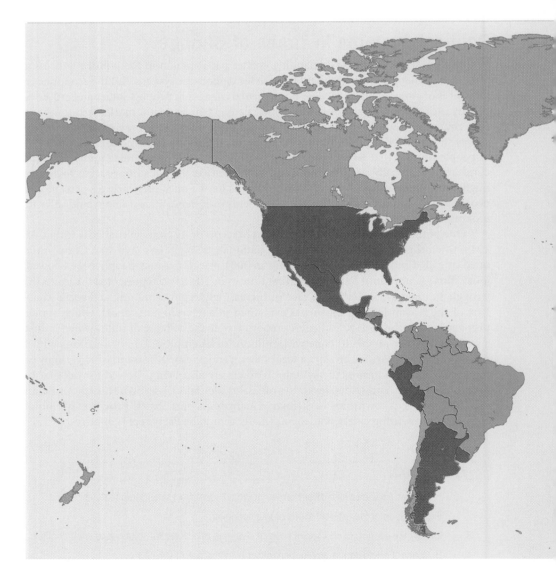

harm the local society in some way or damage the natural environment and fail to provide adequate compensation. If any harm done by an international company in the local market is severe enough, it may even spur legislators to enact laws not in their favor. In order to reduce their companies' exposure to political risk, international managers should have a solid grasp of local values, customs, and traditions.

Types of Political Risk

Managers must be aware of how political risk can affect their companies. In a broad sense, we can categorize political risk according to the range of companies subjected to it. *Macro risk* threatens all companies regardless of industry. For example, every company doing business in Myanmar fears violence against its assets and employees and shares an abiding concern about government corruption. Macro risk affects equally all companies in a country, both domestic and international. *Micro risk* threatens companies within a particular industry or even smaller groups. For instance, steel producers from India, Japan, and Spain complained bitterly after South Korea slapped a punitive tariff of more than 15 percent on steel imports from these nations. The move was in response to charges by South Korean steel makers that these nations were exporting their steel at unfair low prices.[8]

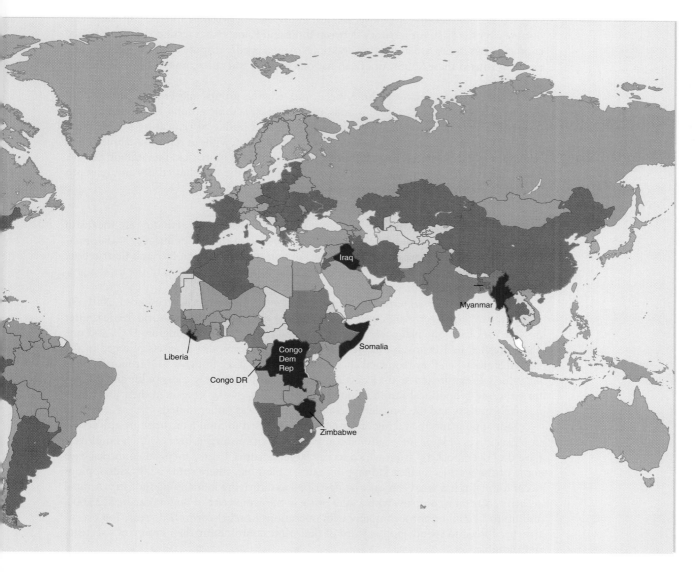

In addition to these two broad categories, we can classify political risk according to the actions that cause it to arise. Let's now examine five different events that can cause political risk:

- Conflict and violence
- Terrorism and kidnapping
- Property seizure
- Policy changes
- Local content requirements

Conflict and Violence Local conflict can strongly discourage investment by international companies. Violent disturbances impair a company's ability to manufacture and distribute products, obtain materials and equipment, and recruit talented personnel. Open conflict also threatens both physical assets (including office buildings, factories, and production equipment) and the lives of employees.

Conflict arises from several sources. First, it may result from people's resentment toward their own government. When peaceful resolution of disputes between people (or factions) and the government fails, violent attempts to change political leadership can ensue. For example, ExxonMobil (*www.exxonmobil.com*) suspended production of liquid natural gas at its facility in Indonesia's Aceh province when separatist rebel forces in the province increasingly made the complex a target of their violence.[9]

Second, conflict may arise over territorial disputes between countries. For example, a dispute over the Kashmir territory between India and Pakistan has resulted in major armed conflict between the two at least several times. And a border dispute between Ecuador and Peru has caused these South American nations to go to war three times—most recently in 1995.

Finally, disputes between ethnic, racial, and religious groups may erupt in violent conflict. Indonesia comprises 13,000 islands, more than 300 ethnic groups, and some 450 languages. Former Indonesian President Suharto had a policy of relocating people from crowded, central islands to remote, less populated ones, but without regard to ethnicity and religion. Violence between these different groups displaced more than one million people. Today, companies doing business in Indonesia still face the risk that ethnic and religious violence will disrupt business operations.[10]

Terrorism and Kidnapping Kidnapping and other terrorist activities are means of making political statements. Small groups dissatisfied with current political or social situations can resort to terrorist tactics aimed at forcing change through fear and destruction. Such groups sometimes have silent approval from a substantial portion of the local population, but just as often they do not.

The world witnessed terrorism on a scale never before seen on September 11, 2001. On that day, two passenger planes were flown into the twin towers of the World Trade Center in New York City, one plane was crashed into the Pentagon in Washington, D.C., and one plane crashed in a Pennsylvania field. Financial and commodity markets plunged in the United States when they reopened after being closed for days. Roughly $1.4 trillion in market value was eliminated in just 5 days of trading.[11] Despite the tragic loss of life and the history-altering geopolitical ramifications of those events, markets regained their lost values relatively quickly and the long-term economic impact was rather muted.

Kidnapping and the taking of hostages may be used to fund a terrorist group's activities. Executives of large international companies are prime targets because their employers have the "deep pockets" from which to pay large ransoms. Latin American countries have some of the world's highest kidnapping rates. Colombia, where some 3,000 kidnappings occur annually, has what can only be described as a thriving kidnapping industry. Annual security costs for a company with a sales office in the capital city of Bogota can be $125,000, and up to $1 million for a company with operations in rebel-controlled areas. Top executives are forced to spend about a third of their time coordinating their company's security in Colombia.[12]

When high-ranking executives are required to enter countries with high kidnapping rates they should enter unannounced, meet with only a few key people in secure locations, and leave just as quickly and quietly. Some companies even purchase kidnap, ransom, and extortion insurance, but most security experts agree that training managers and executives to avoid trouble in the first place is a far better investment. For additional ways managers can stay safe during overseas assignments, see the Global Manager's Toolbox titled, "Your Global Security Checklist."

Property Seizure Governments sometimes seize the assets of companies doing business within their borders. Seizure of assets falls into one of three categories: *confiscation, expropriation,* or *nationalization.*

Confiscation The forced transfer of assets from a company to the government *without compensation* is called **confiscation.** Usually the former owners have no legal basis for requesting compensation or the return of assets. The U.S. 1996 Helms–Burton Law allows U.S. companies to sue companies from other nations that use property confiscated from U.S. companies following Cuba's communist revolution in 1959. But U.S. presidents repeatedly waive the law so that U.S. relations with other countries are not harmed.

confiscation
Forced transfer of assets from a company to the government without compensation.

Expropriation The forced transfer of assets from a company to the government *with compensation* is called **expropriation.** The government doing the expropriating normally determines compensation. There is no framework for legal appeal, and compensation is typically far below market value. Today, governments rarely resort to confiscation or expropriation because by doing so, they jeopardize future investment in their countries. Also, companies already doing business there may leave for fear of losing their valuable assets.

expropriation
Forced transfer of assets from a company to the government with compensation.

Nationalization Whereas expropriation involves one or a small number of companies in an industry, **nationalization** means government takeover of an *entire* industry. Nationalization is more common than confiscation and expropriation. Likely candidates include industries

nationalization
Government takeover of an entire industry.

important to a nation's security and those that generate large revenues. In the 1970s Chile nationalized its vast copper industry and paid international companies a price substantially below market value. Nationalization appeals to governments for four main reasons:

1. Governments may nationalize industries when they believe that international companies are transferring profits to operations in other countries with lower tax rates. Nationalization gives the government control over the cash flow generated by the industry.

2. Governments may nationalize an industry for ideological reasons. The leading political party, for instance, might believe that the government can protect an industry with subsidies. Such was the ideology of the Labor Party that governed Britain for many years after the Second World War.

3. Nationalization is sometimes used as a political tool. Candidates may promise to save local jobs by nationalizing ailing industries.

4. Government ownership may support industries in which private companies are unwilling or unable to invest. For instance, the investment required to build public utilities and train employees is more than most private companies can afford. Governments often approach this problem by controlling utilities industries and subsidizing them with tax revenues.

The extent of nationalization varies widely from country to country. Whereas the governments of Cuba, North Korea, and Vietnam control practically every industry, those of the United States and Canada own very few. Many countries, including France, Brazil, Mexico, Poland, and India, try to strike a balance between government and private ownership.

Policy Changes   Government policy changes are the result of a variety of influences, including the ideals of newly empowered political parties, political pressure from special interests, and civil or social unrest. One common policy tool restricts ownership to domestic companies or limits ownership by nondomestic firms to a minority stake. This is why PepsiCo's (*www.pepsico.com*) ownership of local companies was restricted to 49 percent when it first entered India.

Other policies relate to investments made across borders. Because a global slowdown in the tech sector in 2001 hit Taiwanese companies hard, business leaders and politicians called for a scrapping of the long-held "go slow, be patient" policy. That policy capped investments in mainland China at $50 million and banned investments in infrastructure and those that the Taiwanese government believed were too high-tech (for national security reasons). Taiwan's government responded by announcing a new policy referred to as "active opening, effective management." Although implementing the policy change would take several years, its announcement had an immediate impact on corporate strategies. The general consensus was that the change would have a serious negative impact on Hong Kong's tourism industry and its intermediary role in trade.[13]

Local Content Requirements   Laws stipulating that a specified amount of a good or service be supplied by producers in the domestic market are called **local content requirements**. These requirements can force companies to use locally available raw materials, procure parts from local suppliers, or employ a minimum number of local workers. They ensure that international companies foster local business activity and help ease regional or national unemployment. They also help governments maintain some degree of control over international companies without resorting to extreme measures such as confiscation and expropriation.

But local content requirements can jeopardize an international firm's long-term survival because they pose two potential disadvantages. Specifically, a company may be required to:

1. Hire local personnel, which might force it to take on an inadequately trained workforce or take on excess workers.

2. Obtain raw materials or parts locally, which might increase production costs or reduce quality.

local content requirements
Laws stipulating that a specified amount of a good or service be supplied by producers in the domestic market.

Managing Political Risk

We have already seen that international companies benefit from monitoring and attempting to predict potential political changes that can negatively impact their activities. When an international business opportunity arises in an environment plagued by extremely high risk, simply not investing in the location may very well be the wisest course of action. Yet when risk levels are moderate and the local market is attractive, international companies find other ways to manage political risks that threaten their operations and future earnings. There are three main methods of managing political risk: *adaptation, information gathering*, and *influencing local politics*.

Adaptation *Adaptation* means incorporating risk into business strategies, often with the help of local officials. Companies can incorporate risk by means of five strategies: *local equity and debt, localization, development assistance, partnerships*, and *insurance*.

Local Equity and Debt *Local equity and debt* involves financing local business activities with the help of local firms, trade unions, financial institutions, and government. As partners in local business activities, these groups may help to keep political forces from interrupting operations. If they own shares in local operations (*equity*), the partners get cuts of the profits. If they loan cash (*debt*), they receive interest. The international company's risk exposure is reduced because local partners take an interest in the operation's success and because the company has less of its own capital at risk.

Localization *Localization* entails modifying operations, the product mix, or some other business element—even the company name—to suit local tastes and culture. Consider the global success of MTV (*www.mtv.com*). By customizing the content of certain aspects of MTV programming to regional and sometimes national tastes, the company succeeds in localizing its image. Because MTV is sensitive to local sociocultural and political issues, it is less of a target for nationalists in turbulent times.

Development Assistance Offering local *development assistance* allows an international business to assist the host country or region in developing its distribution and communications networks and improving the quality of life for locals. Because the company and the nation become partners, they both benefit. For example, Anglo-Dutch oil company, Royal Dutch/Shell (*www.shell.com*), operates in many developing nations worldwide. One of the company's current development efforts is a 10-year project to improve the economic opportunities of 100 villages (120,000 people) in Kenya. It has as its goals the doubling of incomes of 60 percent of the poorest households, and increasing the average period of food security from 3 to 9 months.[14] However, critics of the oil giant argue that it could be doing much more to help local peoples where it operates. Canon (*www.canon.com*), the Japanese maker of copiers and printers, goes beyond mere assistance. By practicing *kyosei* ("spirit of cooperation") the firm uses its economic influence to press local governments into making social and political reforms.

Partnerships An increasingly popular way of managing risk, *partnerships* can be excellent for leveraging a company's expansion plans. Such partnerships can be informal arrangements but often include joint ventures, strategic alliances, and cross-holdings of company stock (Chapter 13 discusses these types of arrangements in detail). By partnering with other international firms or local players a company can share the risk of loss, which is often particularly important in developing countries.

Insurance Companies that enter risky national business environments routinely purchase *insurance* against the potential effects of political risk. The *Overseas Private Investment Corporation (OPIC)* (*www.opic.gov*), for example, insures U.S. companies that invest abroad against loss and can provide project financing. Some policies protect companies when local governments restrict the convertibility of local money into home-country currency. Others insure against losses created by violent events, including war and terrorism. Among other services, the *Foreign Credit Insurance Association (FCIA)* (*www.fcia.com*) insures U.S. exporters against losses resulting from a variety of causes.

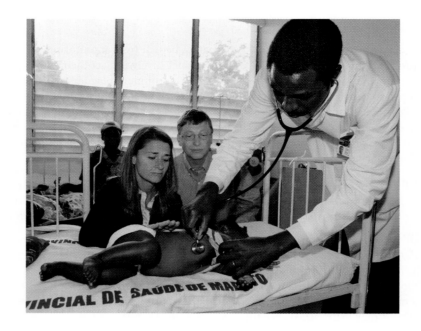

International companies commonly engage in development assistance as a way to demonstrate their concern for the welfare of local people. The same is true for the founders and top executives of these companies, such as Microsoft (www.microsoft.com). Here, Bill and Melinda Gates tour Manhica Health Research Centre (a malaria clinic) north of Maputo, Mozambique. This same day, the Bill and Melinda Gates Foundation (www.glf.org) announced a record $168 million grant to accelerate research into malaria, a disease that kills over a million people each year, most of them young African children. In what other ways do international companies help local peoples?

Information Gathering

International firms often attempt to gather information that will help it predict and manage political risk. There are two sources of data that companies use to conduct accurate political risk forecasting:

1. *Current employees with relevant information.* Employees who have worked in a country long enough to gain insight into local culture and politics are often good sources of information. Individuals who formerly had decision-making authority while on international assignment probably had contact with local politicians and other officials. But because political power can shift rapidly and dramatically, it is important that the employee's international experience be recent.

2. *Agencies specializing in political-risk services.* These include banks, political consultants, news publications, and risk-assessment services that estimate risk using a variety of criteria and methods. Many of these agencies offer reports that detail the levels and sources of political risk for nations. Because these services can be expensive, small companies and entrepreneurs might consider the many free sources of information that are available, notably from their federal governments. Government intelligence agencies are excellent, inexpensive sources to consult.

Influencing Local Politics

Managers must cope with the rules and regulations that apply in each national business environment. Laws in many nations are susceptible to frequent change, with new laws continually being enacted and existing ones modified. To influence local politics in their favor, managers can propose changes that affect their local activities in a positive way.

Influencing local politics always involves dealing with local lawmakers and politicians, either directly or through lobbyists. **Lobbying** is the policy of hiring people to represent a company's views on political matters. Lobbyists meet with local public officials and try to influence their position on issues relevant to the company. The ultimate goal of the lobbyists is to get favorable legislation enacted and unfavorable legislation rejected. Also, lobbyists try to convince local officials that a company benefits the local economy, natural environment, infrastructure, and workforce.

Corruption As we saw in Chapter 2, bribes are one method of gaining political influence. They are routinely used in some countries to get distributors and retailers to push a firm's products through distribution channels. Sometimes they mean the difference between obtaining important contracts and being completely shut out of certain markets.

lobbying
Policy of hiring people to represent a company's views on political matters.

TABLE 3.1

Who Do You Trust?

The Least Corrupt . . .	. . . and the Most Corrupt
1. Finland	133. (*tie*) Indonesia
2. New Zealand	133. (*tie*) Tajikistan
3. (*tie*) Denmark	133. (*tie*) Turkmenistan
3. (*tie*) Iceland	140. (*tie*) Azerbaijan
5. Singapore	140. (*tie*) Paraguay
6. Sweden	142. (*tie*) Chad
7. Switzerland	142. (*tie*) Myanmar
8. Norway	144. Nigeria
9. Australia	145. (*tie*) Bangladesh
10. Netherlands	145. (*tie*) Haiti

In the early 1970s the president of United States–based Lockheed Corp., now Lockheed Martin (*www.lockheedmartin.com*), bribed Japanese officials in order to obtain large sales contracts. Public disclosure of the incident resulted in passage of the 1977 U.S. **Foreign Corrupt Practices Act**, which forbids U.S. companies from bribing government officials or political candidates in other nations (except when a person's life is in danger). A bribe can constitute "anything of value"—money, gifts, and so forth—and cannot be given to any "foreign government official" empowered to make a "discretionary decision" that may be to the payer's benefit. That law also requires firms to keep accounting records that reflect their international activities and assets.

Foreign Corrupt Practices Act
1977 statute forbidding U.S. companies from bribing government officials or political candidates in other nations.

Like many cultural and political elements, the prevalence of corruption varies from one country to another. Corruption is detrimental to society and business for many reasons. Among other things, corruption leads to the misallocation of resources (not always to their most efficient uses), can hurt economic development, distorts public policy, and can damage the integrity of "the system." Table 3.1 shows the least and most corrupt countries according to recent surveys. In addition to the countries shown, Canada, Luxembourg, and the United Kingdom tied for 11th place, Germany ranked 16th, and the United States ranked 18th (tied with Ireland).

In our discussion of political systems and how companies deal with political uncertainty, we touched on several important legal issues. Although there is a good deal of overlap between a nation's political and legal systems, they are distinct. Let's now take a look at several types of legal systems and how they influence the activities of international companies.

Quick Study

1. What are the five main types of *political risk*? How might each affect international business activities?
2. Identify several steps managers can take to stay safe while on an international assignment.
3. Distinguish between *confiscation, expropriation,* and *nationalization.*
4. What three methods can businesses use to manage political risk?

Legal Systems

A country's **legal system** consists of its laws and regulations, including the processes by which its laws are enacted and enforced, and the ways in which its courts hold parties accountable for their actions. A legal system is influenced by many cultural variables, including class barriers, religious beliefs, and whether individualism or group conformity is emphasized. Many laws, rules, and regulations are used to safeguard cultural values and beliefs.

A country's legal system is also influenced by its political system. Totalitarian governments tend to favor public ownership of economic resources and enact laws limiting

legal system
Set of laws and regulations, including the processes by which a country's laws are enacted and enforced and the ways in which its courts hold parties accountable for their actions.

entrepreneurial behavior. In contrast, democracies tend to encourage entrepreneurial activity and to protect small businesses with strong property-rights laws. The rights and responsibilities of parties to business transactions also differ from one nation to another. For all these reasons, business strategies must be flexible enough to adapt to different legal systems.

Therefore, a nation's political and legal systems are naturally interlocked. A country's political system inspires and endorses its legal system, and its legal system legitimizes and supports its political system. It is within the boundaries set by a nation's political and legal frameworks that companies (domestic and nondomestic) must operate. Today, many governments are trying to facilitate better communication and cooperation between themselves and both citizens and businesses. One tool nations are using to accomplish this goal is **e-government**—the use of information technology and e-commerce techniques that allow citizens and businesses to access government information and obtain public services. To read more about governments' experiences with implementing e-government initiatives, see the Breaking Views feature titled, "Governments Take the 'E-nitiative.'"

Legal systems also are affected by political "moods," including upsurges of **nationalism**—the devotion of a people to their nation's interests and advancement. Nationalism typically involves intense national loyalty and cultural pride, and it is often associated with drives toward national independence. In India, for instance, because most business laws originated when the country was struggling for "self-sufficiency," the legal system tended to protect local businesses from international competition. In the 1960s and 1970s India nationalized many industries and intensely scrutinized applicants wanting licenses to start new businesses. Today, however, although nationalism still runs strong in

e-government
Use of information technology and e-commerce techniques that allow citizens and businesses to access government information and obtain public services.

nationalism
Devotion of a people to their nation's interests and advancement.

breaking views

Governments Take the 'E-nitiative'

Governments on the cutting edge are embracing the potential of information technology to transform government as-we-know-it. Yet going from traditional to electronic delivery of government services typically occurs in six, potentially difficult, stages:

- Stage 1: Each governmental department has its own Web site to distribute information.
- Stage 2: People conduct monetary transactions with individual departments.
- Stage 3: People transact with multiple departments through a new, single point of entry (portal).
- Stage 4: Customizable portals give customers more power and the government better understanding of their needs.
- Stage 5: Customers identify with transactions instead of agencies as department divisions blur.
- Stage 6: Walls between services are eliminated and e-government services are fully integrated and personalized.

Here are contrasting stories of how Singapore and Britain implemented their e-government strategies.

- **Cutting Red Tape.** From the get-go, Singapore set the pace in using e-government to boost efficiency. One major initiative was designed to eliminate long waits at government offices and simplify the process of getting

services. Agnes Tan waited in line 90 minutes just to get the floor plan approved for her new sandwich shop. After learning of the new government-to-business (G2B) portal, she did the rest of her tasks—such as getting permits for kitchen equipment and registering employees—from her desktop computer (*www.business.gov.sg*). "Without this, it's a nightmare," said 27-year-old Tan. Singapore also gets kudos for its government-to-citizen (G2C) portal (*www.ecitizen.gov.sg*). Today, the general public can register births, complete school applications, apply to reserve a city park, and much more online.

- **Mind the Gap.** In Britain, at least initially, there seemed to be a large gap between government targets and actual accomplishments. Although a larger percentage of Britons have home Internet access (relative to other nations), a smaller percentage of them use e-government services (*www.direct.gov.uk*). In fact, usage of such services did not grow at all over an early two-year period, and in some cases fell. One reason was the sheer proliferation of government Web sites: Instead of having one point of access, 800 agencies spawned 3,000 sites. Another reason was that some sites initially did not work properly. Citizens will get government services online if it is quicker, easier, or cheaper to do so; many government agencies failed those tests.

India, the government is responding to the pressures of globalization by passing laws that are more pro-business.

With that brief introduction of some key overriding matters, let's now examine each main type of legal system used by countries around the world today.

Types of Legal Systems

There are three main types of legal systems (called legal traditions) in use around the world: *common law, civil law,* and *theocratic law.* This section examines each of these legal traditions and shows how it affects international business activities.

Common Law   The practice of common law originated in England in the eleventh century and was adopted in its territories around the world. Thus, the U.S. legal system, for example, though integrating elements of civil law, is based largely on the common law tradition. A **common law** legal system reflects three factors:

- ❍   *Tradition*: a country's legal history
- ❍   *Precedent*: past cases that have come before the courts
- ❍   *Usage*: the ways in which laws are applied in specific situations

common law
Legal system based on a country's legal history (tradition), past cases that have come before its courts (precedent), and the ways in which laws are applied in specific situations (usage).

Under common law, the justice system decides cases by interpreting the law on the basis of tradition, precedent, and usage. However, each law may be interpreted somewhat differently in each case to which it is applied. In turn, each new interpretation sets a *precedent* that may be followed in future cases. As new precedents arise, laws are altered to clarify vague wording or to accommodate situations not previously considered.

Business *contracts*—legally enforceable agreements between two parties—tend to be lengthy (especially in the United States) because they must consider the many possible contingencies that can arise and the many possible interpretations of the law that may apply in case of a dispute. Companies must devote a good deal of time to devising clear contracts and commit large sums of money to acquiring legal advice. On the positive side, common law systems are flexible. Instead of applying uniformly to all situations, laws take into account particular situations and circumstances. The common law tradition is practiced in Australia, Britain, Canada, Ireland, New Zealand, the United States, and some nations in Asia and Africa.

Civil Law   The civil law tradition can be traced back to Rome in the fifth century B.C. It is the world's oldest and most common legal tradition. A **civil law** system is based on a detailed set of written rules and statutes that constitute a legal *code*. Civil law can be less adversarial than common law because there tends to be less need to interpret laws according to tradition, precedent, and usage. Because all laws are codified and concise, parties to contracts tend to be more concerned only with the explicit wording of the code. All obligations, responsibilities, and privileges follow directly from the relevant code. Therefore, less time and money are typically spent on legal matters. But civil law systems can ignore the unique circumstances of particular cases. The civil law tradition is practiced in Cuba, Puerto Rico, Quebec, all of Central and South America, most of Western Europe, and in many nations in Asia and Africa.

civil law
Legal system based on a detailed set of written rules and statutes that constitute a legal code.

Theocratic Law   A legal tradition based on religious teachings is called **theocratic law**. Three prominent theocratic legal systems are Islamic, Hindu, and Jewish law. Although Hindu law was restricted by India's 1950 constitution, in which the state appropriated most legal functions, it does persist as a cultural and spiritual force. Likewise, after most Jewish communities were stripped of judicial autonomy in the eighteenth century, Jewish law lost much of its influence and today serves few legal functions—although it remains a strong religious force.

theocratic law
Legal system based on religious teachings.

Islamic law is the most widely practiced theocratic legal system today. Islamic law was initially a code governing moral and ethical behavior and was later extended to commercial transactions.[15] It restricts the types of investments that companies can make and sets guidelines for the conduct of business. According to Islamic law, for example, banks cannot charge interest on loans or pay interest on deposits. Instead, borrowers give banks a portion of the profits they earn on their investments, and depositors receive returns based on the profitability of their banks' investments (Islamic banking is discussed further in Chapter 9). Likewise, because the products of alcohol- and tobacco-related businesses violate Islamic beliefs, firms abiding by Islamic law cannot invest in such companies.

Firms operating in countries with theocratic legal systems must be extremely sensitive to local values and beliefs. They should evaluate all business activities, including hiring practices and investment policies, to ensure compliance not only with the law but also with local values and beliefs.

Quick Study

1. What is meant by the term *legal system*? Explain the role of *nationalism* in politics.
2. Identify the stages a government goes through in moving to electronic delivery of its services.
3. What are the main features of each type of legal system (*common, civil,* and *theocratic law*)?
4. List several countries using each type of legal system.

Global Legal and Ethical Issues

Earlier in this chapter, we saw how international companies must work to overcome many kinds of obstacles that an unfamiliar political system presents to them. Likewise, companies must adapt to dissimilar legal systems in global markets. The United States and European Union nations tend to have relatively strong laws related to product quality, product liability, environmental pollution, and the treatment of employees. But such laws are typically far weaker in many countries across Africa, Asia, and Latin America. Therefore, legal differences embodied in national business environments can become ethical issues for managers. Let's now examine several important legal issues facing companies active in international business. Afterward, we look briefly at issues of ethics and social responsibility that confront managers of international companies.

Standardization

Because of differences among legal systems, companies often hire legal experts in each country in which they operate. This can be a very costly practice. Fortunately, standardization of laws across countries is occurring in a few areas. However, *standardization* refers to uniformity in interpreting and applying laws in more than one country, not to the standardizing of entire legal systems.

Although there is no well-defined body of international law, treaties and agreements do exist in several areas, including intellectual property rights, antitrust (antimonopoly) regulation, taxation, contract arbitration, and general matters of trade. In addition, several international organizations promote the standardization process. Among others, the *United Nations (UN)* (*www.un.org*), the *Organization for Economic Cooperation and Development (OECD)* (*www.oecd.org*), and the *International Institute for the Unification of Private Law* (*www.unidroit.org*) work to standardize rules of conduct in international business. In order to remove legal barriers for companies operating in Western Europe, the European Union is also standardizing some areas of its nations' legal systems. Yet some areas of law need further progress across the European Union.

intellectual property
Property that results from people's intellectual talent and abilities.

Intellectual Property

Property that results from people's intellectual talent and abilities is **intellectual property**. It includes graphic designs, novels, computer software, machine-tool designs, and secret formulas, such as that for making Coca-Cola (*www.cocacola.com*). Technically, it results in *industrial property* (in the form of either a *patent* or a *trademark*) or *copyright* and confers a limited monopoly on its holder.

Many legal systems protect **property rights**—the legal rights to resources and any income they generate. Like other types of property, intellectual property can be traded, sold, and licensed in return for fees and/or royalty payments. Intellectual property laws are designed to compensate people whose rights are violated.

But nations vary widely in their intellectual property laws. Business Software Alliance (BSA) (*www.bsa.org*), the trade body for business software makers, participates in an annual study of software piracy rates around the globe. Whereas illegal copies of business software recently made up just 22 percent of the U.S. domestic market (the lowest in the world), pirated software made up a whopping 92 percent of the Chinese and Vietnamese markets. Worldwide, business software piracy averaged 36 percent in 2003 and cost business software makers around $30 billion.[16] Figure 3.1 shows piracy rates for some nations included in the study.

As such figures suggest, the laws in some countries are soft in comparison with those in places such as Canada, Japan, the United States, and across much of Western Europe. European and U.S. software companies continue to lobby their governments to pressure other nations into adopting stronger laws. But, their efforts have had mixed results. In Ireland, BSA implemented a program in which about $5,800 is awarded to members of the public who provide information regarding the illegal use of business software. Shortly after the program began, the BSA took legal action against seven Irish companies on behalf of Adobe (*www.adobe.com*), Microsoft (*www.microsoft.com*), and others.[17]

But when there is software piracy, there is often music and movie piracy as well. According to Le Hong Thanh, director of Saigon Audio Company in Vietnam, up to 95 percent of all compact discs sold in Ho Chi Minh City are pirated. "Our CDs are released in the morning; they already have pirated copies in the afternoon," he lamented. Industry officials blame the problem on the extreme low cost of fakes and technological advances—a fake CD can be made in a few seconds for well under a dollar.[18] In China, peddlers of pirated CDs and DVDs operate openly from sidewalk kiosks and bookstores

FIGURE 3.1

Business Software Piracy

sometimes have sections devoted to pirated movies. In early 2004, Blockbuster (*www.blockbuster.com*) announced it was ending its Hong Kong business and would not enter mainland China, citing piracy as the reason for its decision. A spokesperson explained the company could not earn a viable return competing against pirated movies that sell for around $1.20 each.[19]

Intellectual property can be broadly classified as either *industrial property* or *copyrights*. Let's explore the main issues associated with each category.

Industrial Property

industrial property
Patents and trademarks.

Industrial property includes patents and trademarks—often a firm's most valuable assets. Laws protecting industrial property are designed to reward inventive and creative activity. The purpose of the U.S. Federal Patent Statute is to provide an incentive for inventors to pursue inventions and make them available to consumers. Likewise, trademark law creates incentives for manufacturers to invest in developing new products and also allows consumers to be sure that they are always getting the same product from the same producer. Industrial property is protected internationally under the *Paris Convention for the Protection of Industrial Property* (*www.wipo.int*), to which nearly 100 countries are signatories.

patent
Property right granted to the inventor of a product or process that excludes others from making, using, or selling the invention.

Patents   A **patent** is a right granted to the inventor of a product or process that excludes others from making, using, or selling the invention. Current U.S. patent law went into effect on June 8, 1995, and is in line with the systems of most developed nations. Its provisions are those of the World Trade Organization (WTO), the international organization that regulates trade between nations. The WTO (*www.wto.org*) typically grants patents for a period of 20 years. The 20-year term begins when a patent application is *filed* with a country's patent office, not when it is finally *granted*. Patents can be sought for any invention that is new, useful, and not obvious to any individual of ordinary skill in the relevant technical field.

One field in which patents are drawing special attention is biotechnology. Although gene sequences are commonly included in patents on life and those related to the human body, some question whether a gene sequence is an invention or in fact a discovery.[20] But these patents often include the method used to discover the gene sequences. The argument for awarding patents in such areas is to protect companies' research and development efforts in creating new treatments for all sorts of illnesses.

trademark
Property right in the form of words or symbols that distinguish a product and its manufacturer.

Trademarks   **Trademarks** are words or symbols that distinguish a product and its manufacturer. The Nike (*www.nike.com*) "swoosh" is a trademark, as is the name "Sony" (*www.sony.com*). Consumers benefit from trademarks because they know what to expect when they buy a particular brand. In other words, you would not expect a canned soft drink labeled "Coca-Cola" to taste like one labeled "Sprite."

Trademark protection typically lasts indefinitely, provided the word or symbol continues to be distinctive. Ironically, this stipulation presents a problem for companies such as Coca-Cola and Xerox, whose trademarks "Coke" and "Xerox" (*www.xerox.com*) have evolved into generic terms for all products in their respective categories.

Designers who own trademarks, such as Chanel (*www.chanel.com*), Christian Dior (*www.christiandior.com*), and Gucci (*www.gucci.com*), have long been plagued by shoddily made counterfeit handbags, shoes, shirts, and other products. But recently, pirated products of equal or nearly equal quality are turning up, especially in Italy. Most Italian makers of luxury goods—notably leather and jewelry—outsource production to small manufacturers across the country. Therefore, it is not hard for these same artisans to counterfeit extra copies of a high-quality product. Bootleg copies of a Prada (*www.prada.com*) backpack that costs $500 in New York can be bought for less than $100 in Rome. Jewelry shops in Milan can buy fake Bulgari (*www.bulgari.com*) and Rolex (*www.rolex.com*) watches for $300 and sell them retail for $2,500.

Like trademark laws themselves, enforcement policies differ by country. The maximum penalty for a trademark violation in Italy is three years in prison and a $4,000 fine; in Germany, it is five years and an unlimited fine. But some progress toward standardization is occurring. The European Union, for example, opened a trademark-protection office to police trademark infringement against firms that operate in any EU country.

Copyrights Copyrights give creators of original works the freedom to publish or dispose of them as they choose. The existence of a copyright is typically denoted by inclusion of the well-known symbol ©, a date, and the copyright holder's name. A copyright holder has rights such as the following:

copyright
Property right giving creators of original works the freedom to publish or dispose of them as they choose.

- To reproduce the copyrighted work
- To derive new works from the copyrighted work
- To sell or distribute copies of the copyrighted work
- To perform the copyrighted work
- To display the copyrighted work publicly

Copyright holders include authors and publishers of literary works; composers of musical scores; developers of computer-software programs; and artists, photographers, and painters. Works created after January 1, 1978, are automatically copyrighted for the creator's lifetime plus 50 years. Publishing houses receive copyrights for either 75 years from the date of publication or 100 years after creation, whichever comes first. Copyrights are protected under the **Berne Convention** (*www.wipo.int*)—an international copyright treaty to which the United States is a member—and the 1954 Universal Copyright Convention. More than 50 countries abide by one or both of these treaties.

Berne Convention
International treaty that protects copyrights.

A copyright is granted for the *tangible expression* of an idea, not for the idea itself. For example, no one can copyright the idea of a movie about the sinking of the *Titanic*. However, once the film itself is made to express its creator's treatment of the subject, that film can be copyrighted.

Believe it or not, one of the most well-known songs around the world, "Happy Birthday to You," is actually protected by U.S. copyright law. The song was composed in 1859 and copyrighted in 1935. Although the copyright was set to expire in 2010, on the song's 75th copyright birthday, the U.S. Congress extended it until 2030. Who owns the copyright, and what do they stand to gain from the extension? The media empire Time Warner owns it, and perhaps as much as $20 million.[21]

A major problem for music companies is halting the illegal sharing of digital music files on the Internet. A landmark case of copyright infringement on the Internet was that of Napster (*www.napster.com*). Napster was at the center of the free, unrestricted swapping of digital music files online using so-called peer-to-peer technology. At its peak in 2001, Napster had nearly 1.6 million users logged on worldwide simultaneously swapping music files. Meanwhile, the illegal swapping meant record companies and their artists received no royalties. The world's biggest record labels sued Napster for copyright infringement and won. But it was a rather hollow victory. Music lovers just continued their free swapping of music on the Web sites of Napster alternatives.[22]

Quick Study

1. How does the standardization of laws benefit international companies?
2. What are *property rights*? What is the significance of such rights?
3. What is *industrial property*? Identify its two types and give examples of each.
4. What is a *copyright*? Explain its importance to international business.

Product Safety and Liability

Most countries have product safety laws that lay down standards to be met by manufactured products. **Product liability** holds manufacturers, sellers, and others, including individual company officers, responsible for damage, injury, or death caused by defective products. Injured parties can sue for both monetary compensation through *civil* lawsuits and fines or imprisonment through *criminal* lawsuits. Civil suits are frequently settled before cases go to court.

product liability
Responsibility of manufacturers, sellers, and others for damage, injury, or death caused by defective products.

The United States has the toughest product liability laws in the world, with Europe a close second. Developing and emerging countries have the weakest laws. By the same token, insurance premiums and legal expenses are greater in the nations with strong product liability laws. Damage awards tend to be several times larger in the United States than in other developed countries.

Enforcement of product liability laws differs from nation to nation. In the United States and Canada, for instance, tobacco companies are regularly under attack for their belated warnings about the health effects of tobacco and nicotine and their marketing tactics. But in countries like India and Sri Lanka, tobacco companies are practically free from any scrutiny whatsoever by public-welfare organizations. Because of far less stringent regulation, the biggest market for U.S. cigarette makers is Asia, followed closely by Eastern Europe.

Taxation

National governments use income and sales taxes for many purposes. They use tax revenue to pay government salaries, build military capacity, and shift earnings from people with high incomes to the poor. They also pass indirect taxes, called "consumption taxes," which serve to (1) help pay for the consequences of using a particular product, and (2) make imports more expensive.

Consumption taxes on products such as alcohol and tobacco help pay the health-care costs of treating the illnesses that result from the use of these products. Similarly, gasoline taxes help pay for the road and bridge repairs needed to counteract the effects of traffic and weathering. Taxes on imports give locally made products an advantage among price-sensitive consumers.

value added tax (VAT)
Tax levied on each party that adds value to a product throughout its production and distribution.

Unlike the United States, many countries impose a so-called **value added tax (VAT)**—a tax levied on each party that adds value to a product throughout its production and distribution. Supporters of the VAT system contend that it distributes taxes on retail sales more evenly between producers and consumers. Suppose, for instance, that a shrimper sells the day's catch of shrimp for $1 per kilogram and that the country's VAT is 10 percent (Table 3.2). The shrimper, processor, wholesaler, and retailer pay taxes of $0.10, $0.07, $0.11, and $0.10, respectively, for the value that each adds to the product as it makes its way to consumers. Because the government collects taxes from each party along this path, consumers pay no additional tax at the point of sale. However, because producers and distributors must increase prices to compensate for their tax burdens, consumers end up paying the tax. So that the poor are not overly burdened, many countries exclude the VAT on certain items such as children's clothing.

Antitrust Regulations

antitrust (antimonopoly) laws
Laws designed to prevent companies from fixing prices, sharing markets, and gaining unfair monopoly advantages.

Laws designed to prevent companies from fixing prices, sharing markets, and gaining unfair monopoly advantages are called **antitrust (antimonopoly) laws**. Such laws try to provide consumers with a wide variety of products at fair prices. The United States has the world's strictest antitrust regulation and is its strictest enforcer. The European Union also has rather strict antitrust regulation. In Japan, the Fair Trade Commission enforces

TABLE 3.2

Effect of Value-Added Taxes (VAT)

Production Stage	Selling Price	Value Added	10% VAT	Total VAT
Shrimper	$1.00	$1.00	$0.10	$0.10
Processor	1.70	0.70	0.07	0.17
Wholesaler	2.80	1.10	0.11	0.28
Retailer	3.80	1.00	0.10	0.38

entrepreneur's SURVIVAL KIT

The Long Arm of the Law

Every government has agencies designed to monitor the national business environment and enforce its laws. Here are several important U.S. agencies that entrepreneurs and small business owners can consult for free legal information.

○ **U.S. Patent and Trademark Office (USPTO).** The USPTO is a noncommercial federal bureau within the Department of Commerce. By issuing patents it provides incentives to invent, invest in, and disclose new technologies worldwide. By registering trademarks it protects business investment and safeguards consumers against confusion and deception. By disseminating patent and trademark information it facilitates the development and sharing of new technologies worldwide. To learn more visit the USPTO Web site (*www.uspto.gov*).

○ **U.S. International Trade Commission (USITC).** The USITC is an independent, quasi-judicial federal agency. It provides trade expertise to both the legislative and executive branches of government, determines the impact of imports on U.S. industries, and directs actions against certain unfair trade practices, such as patent, trademark, and copyright infringement. The agency has broad investigative powers on matters of trade and is a national resource where trade data are gathered and analyzed. Visit the USITC Web site (*www.usitc.gov*).

○ **Federal Trade Commission (FTC).** The FTC enforces a variety of federal antitrust and consumer protection laws. It seeks to ensure that the nation's markets function competitively and are vigorous, efficient, and free of undue restrictions. The Commission also works to enhance the smooth operation of the marketplace by eliminating acts or practices that are unfair or deceptive. In general, the Commission's efforts are directed toward stopping actions that threaten consumers' opportunities to exercise informed choice. For more information visit the FTC Web site (*www.ftc.gov*).

○ **U.S. Consumer Product Safety Commission (CPSC).** The CPSC is an independent federal regulatory agency created to protect the public from injury and death associated with some 15,000 types of consumer products, including car seats, bicycles and bike helmets, lawnmowers, toys, and walkers. It also provides information for businesses regarding the export of noncompliant, misbranded, or banned products. Learn more by visiting the CPSC Web site (*www.cpsc.gov*).

---

antitrust laws but is often ineffective because *absolute proof* of wrongdoing is needed to bring charges. To learn about the U.S. agency responsible for antitrust enforcement (and the activities of several other agencies), see the Entrepreneur's Survival Kit titled, "The Long Arm of the Law."

Companies based in strict antitrust countries often argue that they are at a disadvantage against competitors whose home countries condone *market sharing,* whereby competitors agree to serve only designated segments of a certain market. That is why firms in strict antitrust countries often lobby for exemptions in certain international transactions. Small businesses also argue that they could better compete against large international companies if they could join forces without fear of violating antitrust laws.

In the absence of a global antitrust enforcement agency, international companies must concern themselves with the antitrust laws of each nation in which they do a significant amount of business. In fact, a nation (or group of nations) can block a merger or acquisition between two nondomestic companies if those companies do a good deal of business within it. This is exactly what happened to the proposed $43 billion merger between General Electric (GE) (*www.ge.com*) and Honeywell (*www.honeywell.com*). GE wanted to marry their manufacture of airplane engines to Honeywell's production of advanced electronics for the aviation industry. Although both companies are based in the United States, together they employ 100,000 Europeans. GE alone earned $25 billion in Europe the year before the proposed merger's collapse. The European Union blocked the merger because it believed that the result would be higher prices for customers, particularly airlines.[23]

Ethics and Social Responsibility

Although all nations have legal systems that set boundaries for the lawful behavior of individuals and actions of corporations, no legal system can anticipate nor address every conceivable situation in which a person or firm may find themselves. Sadly, some international companies and their managers exploit differences in national legal standards. For example, a firm might sell products abroad that are banned in its home country or set up operations abroad to take advantage of less stringent pollution regulations. Thus, *legal differences* can develop into *ethical issues* for international businesspeople.

When companies venture into the global business environment, managers are exposed to different cultures. This means that they are exposed to different conceptions of ethical behavior, and different guidelines for socially responsible behavior. Confronting unfamiliar practices presents companies with both tremendous opportunities and potential pitfalls. Child labor, human rights, the environment, and plant closings are at the heart of many debates on the actions of international companies. Today, managers must monitor their own behavior, that of all the firm's employees, and even the behavior of those with whom the firm does business abroad.

ethical behavior
Personal behavior that is in accordance with rules or standards for right conduct or morality.

Ethical Behavior   **Ethical behavior** is personal behavior that is in accordance with rules or standards for right conduct or morality. Ethical dilemmas are not legal questions. When a law exists to guide a manager toward a legally correct action, the legally correct path must necessarily be followed. In ethical dilemmas there are no right or wrong decisions, but there are alternatives, each of which may be equally valid, depending on one's perspective.

Ethical questions often arise when managers attempt to either abide by local management practices or import practices from their home country. One viewpoint believes that home-country policies should be implemented wherever a company operates. Another viewpoint agrees with the old saying, "When in Rome, do as the Romans do." However, this philosophy often runs into trouble when large international companies from developed nations do business in developing nations. Consider one case publicized by human rights and labor groups investigating charges of worker abuse at the factory of one of Nike's Vietnamese suppliers. Twelve of 56 female employees reportedly fainted when a supervisor forced them to run around the factory as punishment for not wearing regulation shoes. Nike confirmed the report and, in suspending the supervisor, took steps to implement practices more in keeping with the company's home-country ethics.[24]

On November 8, 2001, Enron acknowledged in a federal filing that it had overstated earnings by nearly $600 million since 1997. The company said that about two-thirds of that was because two partnerships had improperly been treated as separate entities. The disclosure sent a signal that Enron hadn't been forthcoming about its true financial condition and sent investors fleeing in droves.[25] The company's stock price, which hit a high of $90 in August 2000, was trading at $1.01 per share within a month of the disclosure—when Enron sought bankruptcy-law protection. Although Enron executives earned millions over the years in salaries and bonuses, the company's rank and file saw their retirement savings disappear as the firm met its demise.

Enron's failure sent a shock wave around the world, as investors feared the effect that "Enronitis" would have on their markets. Banks across Europe would never see the roughly $2 billion that they had lent to Enron and its subsidiaries. At its peak, Enron accounted for about 20 percent of the total volume traded on European energy exchanges, and its collapse threw energy trading markets into chaos. The futures of people at energy operations in which Enron had a stake in Brazil, England, Germany, India, and other markets were suddenly uncertain.[26] The U.S. Congress opened hearings into the Enron debacle, and then came the criminal charges against senior executives, including chairman of the board Kenneth Lay, chief executive officer Jeffrey Skilling, chief financial officer Andrew Fastow, and chief accounting officer, Richard Causey.[27] After the U.S. Justice Department filed a criminal indictment against the firm's auditor, Arthur Andersen, on obstruction of justice charges for the shredding of important documents related to its

A fresh coat of bright yellow paint is applied to the ends of these logs as they sit on the banks of the Madeira River deep in Brazil's Amazon forest. The logs belong to Gethal Amazonas (**www.gethalamazonas.com.br**), the first tropical plywood maker in the world to be certified by the Forest Stewardship Council (FSC). The goal of the FSC—a nonprofit initiative between environmentalists, logging companies, and wood merchants and retailers—is to convert the world's timber companies to sustainable forest management. Do you think international firms do enough to help protect the environment?

work for Enron, the company could not endure the damage to its reputation and collapsed. In 2002, the U.S. Congress passed the *Sarbanes-Oxley Act* on corporate governance, which established new, stringent accounting standards and reporting practices for firms. Around the world, governments, accounting standards boards, and other regulators and interest groups called for higher standards and more transparent financial reporting by companies.

Social Responsibility   In addition to individual managers behaving ethically, corporations are expected to exercise **social responsibility**—the practice of going beyond legal obligations to actively balance commitments to investors, customers, other companies, and communities. In recent years governments, labor unions, consumer groups, and human rights activists have combined to force apparel companies from developed nations to implement codes of conduct and monitoring principles in their international production activities. Pertinent issues include trade initiatives with developing nations (a government issue), the relocation of home-country factories to locations abroad (a labor issue), and the treatment of workers by local contractors abroad (a human rights issue).

social responsibility
Practice of companies going beyond legal obligations to actively balance commitments to investors, customers, other companies, and communities.

Today, companies often don't wait for governments to pressure them before undertaking policy changes. Most business leaders realize that the future of their companies rests on healthy workforces and environments worldwide. Levi-Strauss (**www.levistrauss.com**) is a pioneer in using a set of practical codes both to control working conditions at contractors' facilities and to assess countries as potential locations for doing business. A global staff then monitors working conditions in the factories of Levi's contractors abroad. The company does business only with partners that meet its so-called Terms of Engagement, which involve meeting demands on matters of ethical standards, legal requirements, environmental requirements, employment standards, and community involvement.[28]

Another company that is working hard to operate in a socially responsible manner is Starbucks (**www.starbucks.com**). The company tries to help ease the plight of citizens in poor coffee-producing countries. Starbucks does this by building schools, health clinics, and coffee-processing facilities to improve the well-being of families in coffee-farming communities. Also, the company sells what it calls "fair trade coffee." Fair trade products are those that involve companies working with suppliers in more equitable, meaningful, and sustainable ways. For Starbucks, this is coffee bearing the fair trade logo, which indicates its certification by TransFair USA (*www.transfairusa.org*), a nonprofit organization that provides independent certification of fair trade products. In part, the alliance between Starbucks and TransFair USA is designed to ensure that coffee farmers earn a fair price for their coffee crop and to help coffee growers farm in environmentally friendly ways.[29]

Quick Study

1. What are *product liability* laws? Describe how they can differ from country to country.
2. Identify the ramifications of taxation and *antitrust (antimonopoly) laws* for international businesses.
3. List several agencies small business owners can consult for free legal information.
4. What is meant by *ethical behavior* and *social responsibility*? Give examples of how they might arise in international business.

Business and International Relations

The political relations between a company's home country and nations in which it does business affect its international business activities. Favorable political relationships foster stable business environments and increase international cooperation in many areas, including the development of international communications and distribution infrastructures. In turn, a stable environment requires a strong legal system through which disputes can be resolved quickly and fairly. In general, favorable political relations lead to increased business opportunities and lower risk.

To generate stable business environments, some countries have turned to *multilateral agreements*—treaties concluded among several nations, each of whom agrees to abide by treaty terms even if tensions develop. According to the European Union's founding treaty, goods, services, and citizens of member nations are free to move across members' borders. Every nation must continue to abide by such terms even if it has a conflict with another member. For instance, although Britain and France disagree on many issues, neither can treat goods, services, and citizens coming and going between their two nations any differently than it treats any other EU nation's goods, services, and citizens. See Chapter 8 for a detailed presentation of the European Union.

The United Nations

United Nations (UN)
International organization formed after World War II to provide leadership in fostering peace and stability around the world.

Although individual nations sometimes have the power to influence the course of events in certain parts of the world, they cannot monitor political activities everywhere at once. The **United Nations (UN)** (*www.un.org*) was formed after the Second World War to provide leadership in fostering peace and stability around the world. The UN and its many agencies provide food and medical supplies, educational supplies and training, and financial resources to poorer member nations. The UN receives its funding from member contributions based primarily on gross national product (GNP). Practically all nations in the world are UN members—except for several small countries and territories that have observer status.

Figure 3.2 gives an overview of the UN system. A Secretary General who is elected by all members and serves for a five-year term heads the UN. The UN system consists of six main bodies:

- ⊙ All members have an equal vote in the *General Assembly,* which discusses and recommends action on any matter that falls within the UN Charter. It approves the UN budget and the makeup of the other bodies.

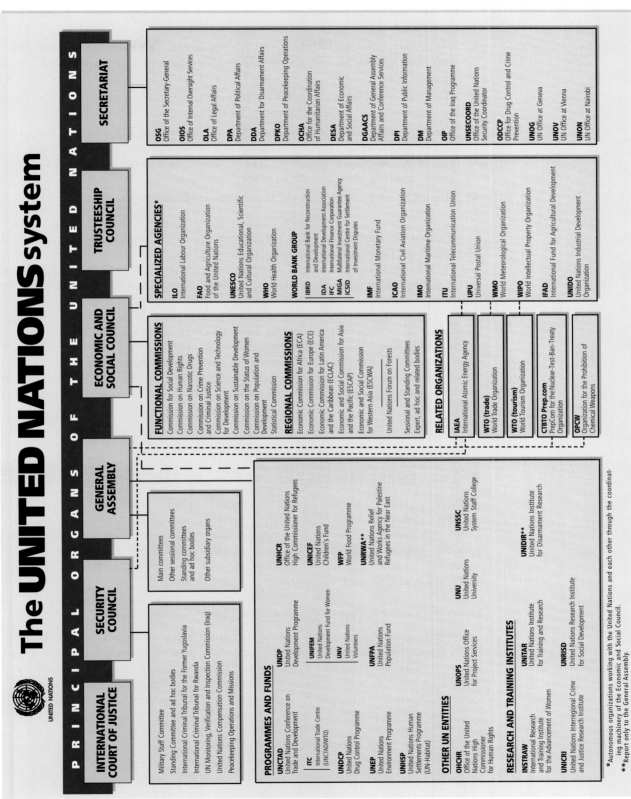

The UNITED NATIONS system

PRINCIPAL ORGANS OF THE UNITED NATIONS

INTERNATIONAL COURT OF JUSTICE
SECURITY COUNCIL
GENERAL ASSEMBLY
ECONOMIC AND SOCIAL COUNCIL
TRUSTEESHIP COUNCIL
SECRETARIAT

Military Staff Committee
Standing Committee and ad hoc bodies
International Criminal Tribunal for the Former Yugoslavia
International Criminal Tribunal for Rwanda
UN Monitoring, Verification and Inspection Commission (Iraq)
United Nations Compensation Commission
Peacekeeping Operations and Missions

Main committees
Other sessional committees
Standing committees and ad hoc bodies
Other subsidiary organs

PROGRAMMES AND FUNDS

UNCTAD United Nations Conference on Trade and Development
  ITC International Trade Centre (UNCTAD/WTO)
UNDCP United Nations Drug Control Programme
UNEP United Nations Environment Programme
UNHSP United Nations Human Settlements Programme (UN-Habitat)

UNDP United Nations Development Programme
  UNIFEM United Nations Development Fund for Women
  UNV United Nations Volunteers
UNFPA United Nations Population Fund

UNHCR Office of the United Nations High Commissioner for Refugees
UNICEF United Nations Children's Fund
WFP World Food Programme
UNRWA** United Nations Relief and Works Agency for Palestine Refugees in the Near East

OTHER UN ENTITIES

OHCHR Office of the United Nations High Commissioner for Human Rights

UNOPS United Nations Office for Project Services

UNU United Nations University

UNSSC United Nations System Staff College

RESEARCH AND TRAINING INSTITUTES

INSTRAW International Research and Training Institute for the Advancement of Women
UNICRI United Nations Interregional Crime and Justice Research Institute

UNITAR United Nations Institute for Training and Research
UNRISD United Nations Research Institute for Social Development

UNIDIR** United Nations Institute for Disarmament Research

FUNCTIONAL COMMISSIONS

Commission for Social Development
Commission on Human Rights
Commission on Narcotic Drugs
Commission on Crime Prevention and Criminal Justice
Commission on Science and Technology for Development
Commission on Sustainable Development
Commission on the Status of Women
Commission on Population and Development
Statistical Commission

REGIONAL COMMISSIONS

Economic Commission for Africa (ECA)
Economic Commission for Europe (ECE)
Economic Commission for Latin America and the Caribbean (ECLAC)
Economic and Social Commission for Asia and the Pacific (ESCAP)
Economic and Social Commission for Western Asia (ESCWA)

United Nations Forum on Forests

Sessional and Standing Committees
Expert, ad hoc and related bodies

RELATED ORGANIZATIONS

IAEA International Atomic Energy Agency
WTO (trade) World Trade Organization
WTO (tourism) World Tourism Organization
CTBTO Prep.com PrepCom for the Nuclear-Test-Ban-Treaty Organization
OPCW Organization for the Prohibition of Chemical Weapons

SPECIALIZED AGENCIES*

ILO International Labour Organization
FAO Food and Agriculture Organization of the United Nations
UNESCO United Nations Educational, Scientific and Cultural Organization
WHO World Health Organization

WORLD BANK GROUP
  IBRD International Bank for Reconstruction and Development
  IDA International Development Association
  IFC International Finance Corporation
  MIGA Multilateral Investment Guarantee Agency
  ICSID International Centre for Settlement of Investment Disputes

IMF International Monetary Fund
ICAO International Civil Aviation Organization
IMO International Maritime Organization
ITU International Telecommunication Union
UPU Universal Postal Union
WMO World Meteorological Organization
WIPO World Intellectual Property Organization
IFAD International Fund for Agricultural Development
UNIDO United Nations Industrial Development Organization

OSG Office of the Secretary-General
OIOS Office of Internal Oversight Services
OLA Office of Legal Affairs
DPA Department of Political Affairs
DDA Department for Disarmament Affairs
DPKO Department of Peacekeeping Operations
OCHA Office for the Coordination of Humanitarian Affairs
DESA Department of Economic and Social Affairs
DGAACS Department of General Assembly Affairs and Conference Services
DPI Department of Public Information
DM Department of Management
OIP Office of the Iraq Programme
UNSECOORD Office of the United Nations Security Coordinator
ODCCP Office for Drug Control and Crime Prevention
UNOG UN Office at Geneva
UNOV UN Office at Vienna
UNON UN Office at Nairobi

*Autonomous organizations working with the United Nations and each other through the coordinating machinery of the Economic and Social Council.
**Report only to the General Assembly.

FIGURE 3.2

The United Nations System

- The *Security Council* consists of 15 members. Five (China, France, the United Kingdom, Russia, and the United States) are permanent. Ten others are elected by the General Assembly for two-year terms. The Council is responsible for ensuring international peace and security, and all UN members are supposed to be bound by its decisions.

- The *Economic and Social Council,* which is responsible for economics, human rights, and social matters, administers a host of smaller organizations and specialized agencies.

- The *Trusteeship Council* consists of the five permanent members of the Security Council and administers all trustee territories under UN custody.

- The *International Court of Justice* consists of 15 judges elected by the General Assembly and Security Council. It can hear disputes only between nations, not cases brought against individuals or corporations. It has no compulsory jurisdiction, and its decisions can be, and have been, disregarded by specific nations.

- Headed by the Secretary General, the *Secretariat* administers the operations of the UN.

An important body within the UN Economic and Social Council is the United Nations Conference on Trade and Development (UNCTAD) (*www.unctad.org*). The organization has a broad mandate in the areas of international trade and economic development. One recent conference focused on how developing nations' musical traditions can alert young people worldwide to pressing development issues, including AIDS, poverty, and national debt. The conference proposed a new initiative designed to develop the business management skills of individuals in developing nations so they can profit from the rich cultural assets they behold. One success story is that of an artist/entrepreneur named Youssou N'Dour. He set up his own music company to record musicians from all over Africa and export the music directly from Dakar, Senegal. As a result, people across the world experienced the musical component of many of Africa's rich cultures thanks to this enterprising young man.[30]

Bottom Line for Business

Differences in political and legal systems present both opportunities and risks for international companies. Because of the intricate connections among politics, law, and culture, gaining complete control over events is extremely difficult in even the most stable national business environment. Nevertheless, understanding differences in culture, politics, and law is the first step for any company that hopes to manage the risks of doing business in an unfamiliar environment.

Implications for Doing Business in Democracies

Democracies tend to provide stable business environments for business activity through laws that protect individual property rights. Commerce should prosper when the private sector includes independently owned firms that exist to make profits. But although participative democracy, property rights, and free markets tend to encourage economic growth, they do not always do so. India is the world's largest democracy, yet experienced slow economic growth for decades. Meanwhile, some countries achieved rapid economic growth under nondemocratic political systems. The so-called four tigers of Asia—Hong Kong, Singapore, South Korea, and Taiwan—built strong market economies in the absence of truly democratic practices.

Implications for Doing Business in Totalitarian Nations

Although it is extremely unlikely that an international company will face any sort of political opposition to their activities by non-governmental organizations, bribery and payment of kickbacks to government officials will likely be prevalent. Refusal to pay is not an option because loss of markets or property in the country would be a real possibility. As such, business activities in totalitarian nations are inherently risky. Also, business law in totalitarian nations is either vague or nonexistent and interpretation of the law is highly subjective, which makes it difficult to know how laws will be applied to a particular business arrangement. Yet companies that do business in, or with, totalitarian nations are criticized by some groups for helping to sustain oppressive political regimes. Executives must decide whether investing and bearing the brunt of potentially damaging publicity is worth the business activity in the nation.

So, Which Government Is Best for Business?

Do democratic governments provide more "stable" national business environments than totalitarianism? This question is not easily answered. Democracies, for example, pass laws to protect individual civil liberties and property rights. But totalitarian governments could also grant such rights. What would be the difference? Whereas democracies strive to *guarantee* such rights, totalitarian governments retain the power to repeal them whenever they wish.

What about prospects for a nation's rate of economic growth—the increase in the amount of goods and services produced by a nation? We can say with certainty only that a democracy does not guarantee high rates of economic growth and that totalitarianism does not doom a nation to slow economic growth. The rate of growth is influenced by many variables other than political and civil liberty, including a country's tax system, its encouragement or discouragement of investment, the availability of capital, and the trade and investment barriers that it erects or guards against.

Implications of Legal Issues for Companies

One area in which political and legal environments have important implications is copyright law. For example, Napster (*www.napster.com*) suddenly gave people the power to share digital music files for free and directly with one another through the Internet. Meanwhile, record companies and artists were stripped of compensation from royalties. Yet with the recording industry on their tails, individuals turned to *darknets*—password-protected, members-only networks on the Internet. Data flowing through darknets is typically encrypted and readable only by a group's members. The introduction of a new digital technology, such as Napster, can be devastating because it can spread worldwide in a matter of days.[31] Managers of international companies also need to understand how other global legal issues, including product safety and antitrust laws, affect operations and strategy.

In the next chapter, we will continue our discussion of national business environments by examining the different ways in which *economic systems* function.

SUMMARY

1. **Describe each main type of *political system.*** A *political system* consists of the structures, processes, and activities by which a nation governs itself. In a *democratic system,* leaders are elected directly by the wide participation of the people or the people's representatives. Most democracies take the form of a *representative democracy,* in which citizens nominate individuals from their groups to represent them.

In a *totalitarian system,* individuals govern without the people's support, maintain control over most aspects of people's lives, and do not tolerate opposing viewpoints. Under *theocratic totalitarianism,* a country's religious leaders enforce laws and regulations based on religious and totalitarian beliefs. Under *secular totalitarianism,* political leaders rely on military and bureaucratic power. Secular totalitarianism takes 3 forms. Under *communist totalitarianism,* the government aims for social equality by planning economic activity. Under *tribal totalitarianism,* one tribe imposes its will on others in the country. *Right-wing totalitarianism* is capitalist economics without political freedom.

2. **Identify the origins of *political risk* and how managers can reduce its effects.** *Political risk* is the likelihood that a government or society will undergo political changes that negatively affect business activity. Political risk arises from: (1) corrupt or poor political leadership; (2) frequent changes in the form of government; (3) political involvement of religious or military leaders; (4) unstable political system; (5) conflict among races, religions, or ethnic groups; and (6) poor relations with other countries. *Macro risk* threatens all companies in a nation regardless of industry. *Micro risk* threatens firms in a particular industry or smaller groups.

There are five main forms of political risk: (1) conflict and violence; (2) terrorism and kidnapping; (3) property seizure; (4) policy changes; and (5) local content requirements. *Property seizure*—the taking of a company's assets by a local government—may take one of three forms: *confiscation* (forced transfer of assets without compensation); *expropriation* (forced transfer with compensation); or *nationalization* (forced takeover of an entire industry). The main strategies used to manage political risk are: (1) *adaptation* (incorporating risk into business strategy); (2) *information gathering* (monitoring local political events); and (3) *political influence* (such as by *lobbying* local political leaders).

3. **List the main types of *legal systems,* and explain how they differ.** A *legal system* is a country's set of laws and regulations, including the processes by which its laws are enacted and enforced and the ways in which its courts hold parties accountable for their actions. There are three categories of legal systems. Under *common law*, the justice system decides cases by interpreting the law on the basis of *tradition* (legal history), *precedent* (past cases), and *usage* (application of laws in specific situations). *Civil law* is based on a detailed set of written rules and statutes that constitute a legal *code*. All obligations, responsibilities, and privileges follow directly from the written code. *Theocratic law* is based on religious teachings.

4. **Describe the major *legal* and *ethical issues* facing international companies.** Although there is no well-defined body of international law, some efforts are being made to achieve *standardization*—uniformity in interpreting and applying laws in more than one country.

Chief legal issues facing international businesses are: (1) protection of *property rights* (legal rights to resources and any income they generate); (2) protection of *intellectual property* (including *patents*, *trademarks*, and *copyrights*); (3) *product liability* standards (holding firms responsible for damage, injury, or death); (4) *taxation* policies (which can discourage product use or increase prices of imports); (5) *antitrust regulations* (preventing companies from fixing prices, sharing markets, and gaining unfair monopoly); and (6) *ethical dilemmas* and *social responsibility* (which can present special challenges for international firms).

5. **Explain how *international relations* affect international business activities.** Political relations between a company's home country and those with which it does business strongly affect its international activities. In general, favorable political relations lead to increased opportunity and stable business environments. The mission of the *United Nations (UN)* is to provide leadership in fostering peace and stability around the world. Although its global peacekeeping efforts have had mixed results, its many agencies continue to aid poorer nations by providing food and medical supplies, educational supplies and training, and financial resources.

TALK IT OVER

1. The Internet and the rise of "e-government" are forcing politicians to change their methods of governing. How might the Internet change totalitarian political systems, such as China and North Korea? What might the Net's future expansion mean for nations with theocratic systems (for example, Iran)? What changes might technology bring to the way that democracies function?

2. Under a totalitarian political system, the Indonesian economy grew strongly for 30 years. In India, meanwhile, the economic system of the world's largest functioning democracy was relatively poor for decades until recently. Relying on what you learned in this chapter, do you think the Indonesian economy grew despite or because of a totalitarian regime? What might explain India's relatively poor performance under a democratic political system?

3. Consider the following statement: "Democratic political systems, as opposed to totalitarian ones, provide international companies with more stable environments in which to do business." Do you agree? Why or why not? Support your argument with specific country examples.

1. Two groups of four students each will debate the ethics of doing business in countries with totalitarian governments. After the first student from each side has spoken, the second student will question the opposing side's arguments, looking for holes and inconsistencies. The third student will attempt to answer these arguments. A fourth student will present a summary of each side's arguments. Finally, the class will vote to determine which team has offered the more compelling argument.

2. As a team, select one article per team member from business magazines (in print or on the Web). One or more articles should discuss the political element of a country's business environment, and one or more a legal element of the same environment. Potential topics include corruption and pending legislation relevant to international companies. Summarize the articles and explain what businesses can do to prepare for, or respond to, any special problems the articles discuss.

3. Select a country that interests all the members of your group. What type of political and legal systems does the country have? Do free elections take place? Is the government heavily involved in the economy? Is the legal system effective and impartial? Do political and legal conditions suggest that it could be further considered as a potential market? If so, for what kinds of goods or services might the market be appealing? Present your findings to the class.

KEY TERMS

antitrust (antimonopoly) laws (p. 108)

Berne Convention (p. 107)

capitalism (p. 91)

civil law (p. 103)

common law (p. 103)

communism (p. 91)

confiscation (p. 97)

copyright (p. 107)

democracy (p. 87)

e-government (p. 102)

ethical behavior (p. 110)

expropriation (p. 97)

Foreign Corrupt Practices Act (p. 101)

industrial property (p. 106)

intellectual property (p. 104)

legal system (p. 101)

lobbying (p. 100)

local content requirements (p. 98)

nationalism (p. 102)

nationalization (p. 97)

patent (p. 106)

political risk (p. 94)

political system (p. 86)

private sector (p. 90)

product liability (p. 107)

property rights (p. 105)

representative democracy (p. 87)

secular totalitarianism (p. 91)

social responsibility (p. 111)

socialism (p. 91)

theocracy (p. 90)

theocratic law (p. 103)

theocratic totalitarianism (p. 90)

totalitarian system (p. 90)

trademark (p. 106)

United Nations (UN) (p. 112)

value added tax (VAT) (p. 108)

TAKE IT TO THE WEB

1. To attract investment by domestic and foreign companies, nations compete against each other to provide top-notch services. This chapter's Breaking Views feature presented the steps nations are taking to implement e-government services.

   The government of Hong Kong, SAR (Special Administrative Region of China), is at the forefront of providing e-government services to citizens and businesses. Visit the main government portal of Hong Kong (*www.gov.hk*) and select your preferred language. Can you identify several sections of the site that are government-to-business (G2B) and government-to-citizen (G2C)? Visit the "E-Business" section and read about Hong Kong's e-government strategy. What are some of the key milestones it has achieved? Identify several main planks of its "roadmap" for future e-government initiatives.

   Return to the main e-government portal and explore the available services. List the types of services that would be available to you 1) as a citizen of Hong Kong, 2) as a tourist going to visit Hong Kong, 3) as an individual thinking of starting a business in Hong Kong, and 4) as a company currently operating in Hong Kong. Can you think of additional services that the government does not currently provide but should offer?

ETHICAL CHALLENGES

1. You are the president of a firm that publishes textbooks for medical students in over 30 languages. On a recent trip to a university in a developing country (with a GDP per capita of under $1,000 per year) you discover that students are using bound photocopies of your best-selling medical textbook. Speaking with several students, they inform you that if they were required to pay for the actual books, they could not afford medical school. Witnessing the clear copyright violation firsthand, how do you react? What possible courses of action might you take? If additional information would be helpful to you, what would it be?

2. You are the proprietor of a fledging computer graphics company in Shanghai, China. The sophisticated business application software you need for your business normally sells for 2,900 renminbi (around $350) at computer stores in Shanghai. But with an income of just over $5,000 a year, you cannot afford to buy the original graphics software for your business. But a friend has told you she can get you all the software you need, and more, at a nearby street market for only $40. Because very few people buy official software, you know the authorities will not punish you if you are caught. Is it unethical for you to purchase the pirated software? Do you believe you are justified in doing so?

3. You are the CEO of a major pharmaceutical firm that holds worldwide patents on several highly successful drugs. Your company invests heavily to develop its drugs because patents allow it to recoup its investment. But your firm has come under pressure from competitors selling cheaper alternatives, and from politicians and nongovernmental groups to supply drugs to people in poor nations at reduced prices. Several senior executives in your company feel the firm is unfairly being asked to discount its drugs that treat diseases afflicting people of poor nations. Some executives suggested that the firm focus on drugs to treat diseases (such as heart disease and cancer) that occur mostly in wealthy nations, but you are uneasy with such a move. Would such a course of action be ethical? Diseases such as AIDS, cancer, and heart disease all kill their patients. Should drugs for only certain diseases be exempt from patent protection?

PRACTICING INTERNATIONAL MANAGEMENT CASE

Caveat Emptor—*Who Said Latin Was Dead?*

As we saw in this chapter, the piracy of intellectual property—computer software, films, books, music CDs, and pharmaceutical drugs—is a common problem. By churning out high-quality fakes of well-known brand name goods, increasingly sophisticated pirates routinely violate the patents, trademarks, and copyrights of companies worldwide. The cost of global trademark counterfeiting amounts to between five and seven percent of world trade, or around $500 billion a year! Traditionally peddled by sidewalk vendors and in back-street markets, counterfeiters are adding the Internet to its usual channels of distribution. Just as the Internet drastically reduces the cost and hassles of starting a business for honest folks, it has the same effect for counterfeiters.

Tiffany & Company (*www.tiffany.com*), the New York retailer renowned for its expensive jewelry, filed a lawsuit against online auctioneer eBay (*www.ebay.com*) in mid-2004. Tiffany's suit alleges that eBay contributed directly to infringement of the Tiffany trademark because of the "substantial volume" of counterfeit Tiffany jewelry sold through eBay's Web site. In the complaint, Tiffany said that of the 186 jewelry pieces bearing the Tiffany name that it randomly purchased on eBay, 73 percent were phony. Tiffany argues that because eBay profits significantly from the sale of the fake merchandise, provides a forum for such sales, and promotes it, that the company "should bear responsibility for the sale of counterfeit merchandise on its site." Others say that the impracticality of requiring online auctioneers to verify the authenticity of products they sell would deliver a severe blow to the efficiency and popularity of e-commerce. They compare it to ordering newspapers to verify the authenticity of everything sold through their classified-ads section.

The market for automotive parts is another industry experiencing rampant pirating, which costs it an estimated $12 billion a year. Seemingly, nothing is off-limits to counterfeiters, including brakes, fluids, fuel and oil filters, spark plugs, batteries, and windshields. Worries that the problem is causing are twofold—fears of liability lawsuits because of malfunctioning counterfeits, and concerns of lost revenue for producers of the genuine articles. For example, if someone winds up getting in an accident because of a counterfeit product, legitimate manufacturers would need to prove the product is not their own. Car manufacturers list potentially harmful fakes such as brake linings made of compressed sawdust, and transmission fluid that is nothing more than cheap oil with added dye. Boxes bearing legitimate-looking labels make it difficult for consumers to tell the difference between a fake and the real deal. Tony Bol of General Motors (*www.gm.com*) says the carmaker is "finding more [fake] products coming into North America" in recent years, but that "the Middle East is the larger market for consumption."

So, which nations are havens for people creating much of the world's phony goods? It is no secret that China, India, South Korea, Malaysia, Taiwan, and Thailand are all leading sources of counterfeit products. In China and India, because of a combination of lax anti-piracy regulations and booming economies, the problem is expected to persist and perhaps grow worse. Many potential traps related to intellectual property await companies that want to do business in the big emerging markets of China and India. For instance, Indian law gives international pharmaceutical firms five- to seven-year patents on *processes used to manufacture drugs*—but *not on the drugs themselves*. Thus local companies pirate the property of international pharmaceutical companies by slightly modifying the patented production processes in order to arrive at the finished drugs.

China presents a special problem in the area of counterfeiting. Political protection for pirates of intellectual property remains fairly common in China. In fact, government officials, people working for the government, and even the People's Liberation Army (China's national army) operate many factories churning out pirated products. Many others operate on government-owned land. Often, criminals are connected to political leaders and receive legal protection from prosecution. As a result, international companies find themselves in a difficult position when fighting piracy in China because filing a lawsuit can severely damage its business relations there.

Yet international opinion appears divided on the root causes of rampant intellectual-property violations in China. The European Union Chamber of Commerce in China studied piracy there and lauded China's intellectual-property laws and regulations. The Chamber blamed poor enforcement for prevailing rates of piracy, adding that sometimes Beijing's regulatory body allows "the counterfeiter to remove the infringing trademarks and re-use the substandard goods." Others point out that the relevant Chinese legislation is vaguely worded and difficult to enforce. "It has been half measures," says Joseph Simone of Baker & McKenzie (*www.bakerandmckenzie.com*) in Hong Kong. Among technology companies that claim they've been harmed by China's weak protection of intellectual property are Microsoft (*www.microsoft.com*), which claims that its software is widely pirated, and Cisco Systems (*www.cisco.com*), which sued a Chinese hardware maker for allegedly copying and using Cisco networking software.

Designer Giorgio Armani (*www.giorgioarmani.com*), which has not had much of a presence in China except for a small Beijing shop since 1998, also finds fake goods across the country emblazoned with his logo. Yet Armani is not put off by China, opening both an Armani boutique and an Emporio Armani store on Shanghai's historic Bund in 2004. And despite ambitious plans to launch as many as 36 more units by 2008, Armani understands the challenges that counterfeiting presents his company. Although Armani says he feels pirating is flattering "because it means you are doing the right thing," he concedes that the problem requires action. So, you just may want to remember that old Latin phrase, *caveat emptor*, "let the buyer beware."

Thinking Globally

1. What actions can companies and governments take to ensure that products cannot be easily pirated? Be specific.

2. Do you think that the international business community is being too lax about the abuse of intellectual property rights? Are international companies simply afraid to speak out for fear of jeopardizing access to attractive markets?

3. Increased digital communication may pose a threat to intellectual property because technology allows people to create perfect clones of original works. How do you think the Internet might affect intellectual-property laws?

4. Update the Tiffany vs. eBay lawsuit mentioned in the case. Identify each main argument of both the plaintiff and the defendant. If there has been a settlement, what were the terms? If the case has been tried in the courts, what was the verdict? What have been the implications of the lawsuit for counterfeits sold on online auctions?

learning objectives

After studying this chapter, you should be able to

1. Describe what is meant by a *centrally planned economy* and explain why its use is declining.

2. Identify the main characteristics of a *mixed economy* and explain the emphasis on *privatization*.

3. Explain how a *market economy* functions and identify its distinguishing features.

4. Describe the different ways to measure a nation's *level of development*.

5. Discuss the process of *economic transition* and identify the remaining obstacles for businesses.

economic systems

and development

4

a look **back**

CHAPTER 3 presented the ways in which different political and legal systems affect international business activities. We also explored some of the ways managers can cope with the risks that political and legal uncertainties create.

a look at **this chapter**

This chapter explains different types of economic systems and examines the effect that economics has on international business. We also describe economic development and the difficulties facing countries undergoing transition to market economies.

a look **ahead**

CHAPTER 5 introduces us to a major form of international business activity—international trade. We examine the patterns of international trade and outline several theories that attempt to explain why nations conduct trade.

India's Tech King

BANGALORE, India—When Wipro (*www.wipro.com*) was founded in 1945 its main product was cooking oil. Today the company is one of India's top providers of information technology services with blue-chip customers, heavyweight rivals, 23,000 employees, and nearly $1 billion in revenue. Wipro and other Indian firms supply high-quality software and consulting services while undercutting rivals' prices by a third or more. Just as China drove down worldwide prices in manufacturing, India seems set to do the same in services.

But China and India are following two distinct paths to development. While China developed its economy by throwing open its doors to foreign direct investment, international companies were for a long time unsure of India's commitment to free-market reform. So, India underwent organic growth and spawned some powerful, homegrown firms such as Wipro in cutting-edge, knowledge-based industries. Despite its reputation for high taxes and burdensome regulations, India long had some of the most basic foundations of a market economy—including private enterprise, democratic government, and Western accounting practices. Its capital markets are also more efficient and transparent than China's, and its legal system is more advanced. And the fact that China is following a top-down approach to development while India pursues a bottom-up approach reflects their opposing political systems: India is a democracy, and China is not.

If India were to become a fast-growth economy, it would be the first developing nation to advance economically by relying on the brainpower of its people. By contrast, China is relying on its natural resources and inexpensive factory labor to develop economically. The growth strategy that is best—the organic-led path of India versus the investment-led path of China—depends on a nation's circumstances. Yet some are already asking the question: "Can India surpass China?" As you read this chapter, consider the importance of a nation's business environment to economic development, and how companies can work with nations to improve standards of living.[1]

Like culture and systems of politics and law, economic systems differ from one country to another. In Chapter 2, we saw that one defining element of a culture is its tendency toward *individualism* or *collectivism*. In Chapter 3 we also saw how a people's history and culture affect the development of their political and legal systems. In this chapter, we learn about the interconnectedness of culture and economic systems.

Economic systems in individualist cultures tend to provide incentives and rewards for individual business initiative. Collectivist cultures tend to offer fewer such incentives and rewards. For example, in individualist cultures *entrepreneurs*—businesspeople who accept the risks and opportunities involved in creating and operating new business ventures—tend to be rewarded with relatively low tax rates that encourage their activities. Furthermore, national culture can have a strong impact on a nation's economic development. In turn, the development of a country's economy can dramatically affect many aspects of its culture.

In this chapter, we introduce the world's different economic systems and examine the link between culture and economics. We begin by explaining each main type of economic system. Then we explore economic development and ways of classifying nations using several indicators of development. We conclude by looking at how countries are implementing market-based economic reforms and the challenges they face.

Economic Systems

economic system
Structure and processes that a country uses to allocate its resources and conduct its commercial activities.

A country's **economic system** consists of the structure and processes that it uses to allocate its resources and conduct its commercial activities. No nation is either completely individualist or completely collectivist in its cultural orientation. Likewise, no economic system reflects a completely individual or group orientation. The economies of all nations display a blend of individual and group values (the latter of which are often reflected in government involvement in business activities). In other words, no economy is entirely focused on individual reward at the expense of social well-being. Nor is any economy so completely focused on social well-being that it places no value on individual incentive and enterprise.

Yet every economy displays a *tendency* toward individualist or collectivist economic values. This allows us to organize systems along a continuum that characterizes them as *centrally planned*, *mixed*, or *market economies* (see Figure 4.1). Let's now take a look at each of these three types of economic systems.

FIGURE 4.1

Continuum of Economic Systems

Centrally Planned Economy

A **centrally planned economy** is a system in which a nation's land, factories, and other economic resources are owned by the government. The government makes nearly all economy-related decisions—including who produces what and the prices of products, labor, and capital. Central planning agencies specify production goals for factories and other production units and even decide prices. In the former Soviet Union, for instance, communist officials set prices for staples such as milk, bread, eggs, and other essential goods. The ultimate goal of central planning is to achieve a wide range of political, social, and economic objectives by taking complete control over production and distribution of a nation's resources.

centrally planned economy
Economic system in which a nation's land, factories, and other economic resources are owned by the government, which plans nearly all economic activity.

Origins of the Centrally Planned Economy
Central planning is rooted in the ideology that the welfare of the group is more important than individual well-being. Just as collectivist cultures emphasize group over individual goals, a centrally planned economy strives to achieve economic and social equality.

German philosopher Karl Marx popularized the idea of central economic planning in the nineteenth century. Marx formulated his ideas while witnessing the hardship endured by working people in Europe during and after the Industrial Revolution. Marx argued that the economy could not be reformed, but that it must be overthrown and replaced with a more equitable "communist" system.

Different versions of Marx's ideas were implemented in the twentieth century by means of violent upheaval. Revolutions installed totalitarian economic and political systems in Russia in 1917, China and North Korea in the late 1940s, and Cuba in 1959. By the 1970s, central planning was the economic law in lands stretching across Central and Eastern Europe (Albania, Bulgaria, Czechoslovakia, East Germany, Hungary, Poland, Romania, and Yugoslavia), Asia (Cambodia, China, North Korea, and Vietnam), Africa (Angola and Mozambique), and Latin America (Cuba and Nicaragua).

Decline of Central Planning
In the late 1980s, nation after nation began to dismantle communist central planning in favor of market-based economies. Economists, historians, and political scientists attribute the decline of centrally planned economies to a combination of several factors.

Failure to Create Economic Value Central planners paid little attention to the task of producing quality goods and services at the lowest possible cost. In other words, they failed to see that commercial activities succeed when they create economic value for customers. Along the way, scarce resources were wasted in the pursuit of commercial activities that were not self-sustaining.

Failure to Provide Incentives Government ownership of economic resources drastically reduced incentives for people and organizations to maximize the benefits obtained from those resources. There were few incentives to create new technologies, new products, and new production methods (except in the areas of aerospace, nuclear power, and other sciences, in which government scientists excelled). The result was little or no economic growth and consistently low standards of living. Government policies that eliminate incentives to create wealth and develop effective production techniques impair development.

Even today, for example, North Korea remains arguably the most closed economy in the world. For the most part, the policy of *juche* (self-reliance) is causing extreme hardship for its people. The combination of recurring floods and droughts, a shortage of fertilizers, and a lack of farm machinery pose a continual roadblock to the nation reaching its peak food production potential—reasons why North Korea often must rely on aid from abroad to feed its people.[2]

Failure to Achieve Rapid Growth Leaders in communist nations took note of the high rates of economic growth in countries like Hong Kong, Singapore, South Korea, and Taiwan—the so-called four tigers. The realization that a once-poor region of the world had achieved such growth awakened central planners. They realized that an economic system based on private ownership fosters growth much better than one hampered by central planning.

While farming in other nations today is a highly mechanized and even computerized endeavor, it is labor-intensive and inefficient in North Korea. The government's failed communist economic policies hamper development and are at the root of its inability to afford fertilizers and modern machinery that could boost food production. Famine and general economic collapse throughout the 1990s cut the life expectancy by more than six years. The nation is only now taking its first tentative steps toward free-market economics.

North Korea, once again, provides us a good example. Each year for a decade until 1999, the North Korean economy did not grow but in fact contracted. Out of desperation, the country's leaders began to tinker quietly, very quietly, with free market reforms. Leader Kim Jong Il has since allowed the opening of small businesses, including restaurants and bakeries. Also dotting the countryside are some 300 small bazaars where licensed individuals and companies can trade goods. And in 2003 the government raised $265 million for infrastructure through the sale of bonds—the first such sale since 1950. Says Jo Dong Ho, of the Korea Development Institute, "The economic changes that have taken place in the past couple of years are much greater than those witnessed in the previous 50 years." What has resulted from these and other reforms? After a decade of economic contraction, the North Korean economy likely grew an estimated 1.8 percent in 2003—small gains, yes, but gains nonetheless.[3]

Failure to Satisfy Consumer Needs Would-be consumers in many centrally planned economies were tired of standards of living that had slipped far below those of their counterparts in predominantly market economies. Ironically, although central planning was conceived as a means for creating a more equitable system for distributing wealth, too many central planners failed to provide even basic necessities such as adequate food, housing, and medical care. Underground economies (black markets) for all kinds of goods and services flourished and in some cases even outgrew "official" economies. Prices on the black markets were much higher than the official prices set by governments.

Focus on China
China began its experiment with central planning in 1949, when communists defeated the nationalists in a long and bloody civil war. Today, the country's leaders describe its economic philosophy as "socialism with Chinese characteristics." There is possibly no country on earth that has done more for its people economically over the past two decades than China. Glistening skyscrapers dominate the Shanghai and Beijing cityscapes. Although rural China continues to look and function much as it has for centuries, today many people in large cities have good job prospects. The country's immense population, rising incomes, and expanding opportunities are attracting new business ventures like never before.

The Early Years From 1949 until reforms were initiated in the late 1970s, China had a unique economic system. Agricultural production was organized into groups of people who formed production "brigades" and production "units." Communes were larger entities responsible for planning agricultural production quotas and industrial production schedules. Rural families owned their own homes and parcels of land on which to produce particular crops. Production surpluses could be consumed by the family or sold at a profit on the open market. In 1979 the government initiated agricultural reforms that strengthened work incentives in this sector. Family units could then grow whatever crops they chose and sell the produce at market prices.

At about the same time, township and village enterprises (TVEs) began to appear. Each TVE relied on the open market for materials, labor, and capital and used a non-governmental distribution system. Each TVE employed managers who were directly responsible for profits and losses. Although the government initially regarded TVEs as illegal operations unrelated to the officially sanctioned communes, they were legalized in 1984, further laying the groundwork for a market economy.

***Patience and* Guanxi**   If there is one trait that is needed by all private companies in China, it's patience. Despite obvious ideological differences between itself and the private sector, China's Communist Party is trying very hard to appear well suited to running the country. Karl Marx once summed up Communism as the "abolition of private property," and the name of China's Communist Party (in Chinese characters) literally means "common property party." But after the Communist Party allowed businesspeople to become party members for the first time in 2002, businesses and citizens alike demanded a constitutional amendment to make private property rights "inviolable." But change does not come fast or easy in China. Despite all the economic reforms swirling around them, party scholars refuse to repudiate Marxist political ideology. One scholar actually wrote in a recent article that "Developing the private and other non-state sectors is aimed at the eventual elimination of the system of private ownership." With scholarly writings like that, it is little wonder why patience is needed in China.[4]

A personal touch is another necessary ingredient for success in China. Initially, and in line with communist ideology, non-Chinese companies were restricted from participating in China's economy. Ever since the mid-1980s, though, outsiders have continually enjoyed ever-greater opportunities to create joint ventures with local partners. Nevertheless, one of the most important factors in forming a successful venture in China is *guanxi*—the Chinese term for "personal relationships." To learn more about the secrets of *guanxi*, see this chapter's Global Manager's Toolbox titled, "Guidelines for Good *Guanxi*."

Challenges Ahead   Economic reforms are moving along very well in China, and the country continues to experience strong growth. However, *political and social problems* pose threats to China's future economic performance. Unrest continues in China in the form of skirmishes between secular and Muslim Chinese in western provinces and occasional terrorist attacks in Beijing. Meanwhile, for the most part political leaders continue to restrict democratic reforms.

Another potential problem is *unemployment*. Intensified competition and the entry of international companies into China are placing greater emphasis on efficiency and the cutting of payrolls in some industries. But the biggest contributor to the unemployed sector seems to be migrant workers. Hundreds of thousands of workers have left their farms and now go from city to city searching for better-paying factory work or construction jobs. Unhappiness with economic progress in the countryside and the misery of migrant workers are serious potential sources of social unrest for the Chinese government.

Another key issue today is *reunification* of "greater China." In 1997 China regained control of Hong Kong after 99 years under British rule. For the most part, China has kept its promise of "one country, two systems." While the economic (and to a lesser extent political) freedoms of people in Hong Kong would remain largely intact, the rest of China would continue along the lines drawn by the communist leadership. The southern coastal territory of Macao also returned to Chinese control in 1999. Only a 1-hour ferry ride from Hong Kong, Macao was under Portuguese administration since it was founded in 1557. Although Macao's main function used to be that of trading post, today it serves mainly as a gambling outpost. In fact, it is commonly referred to as "Asia's Vegas."

It is important for China to manage its one country, two systems policy well to preserve order in China, Hong Kong, and Macao. The island of Taiwan is watching very closely. Any chance of its eventual reunification with the Chinese mainland depends on the successful integration of Hong Kong and Macao. For now at least, things appear to be

Guidelines for Good Guanxi

⊙ **The Importance of Contacts, Not Contracts.** In China, face-to-face communication and personal relationships take priority over written contracts. Mu Dan Ping, a partner in the Chinese Business Group at Ernst & Young's (*www.ey.com*) Los Angeles office, offers the following diagram to show the different priorities:

> **United States:** Reason → Law → Relationship
> **China:** Relationship → Reason → Law

Managers from the United States look for the rationale or reason first, says Mu. Is there a market with profit potential? If so, they want a legal contract before they spend time on a business relationship. Conversely, explains Mu, Chinese need to establish a trust relationship first. Then they look for common goals as a reason for doing business. In a way, the legal contract is just a formality, serving to ensure mutual understanding.

⊙ **Pleasure before Business.** It seems impossible not to talk business when you've come to China for the express purpose of conducting business. But experts advise that you leave your sales pitches on the back burner and follow the lead of your Chinese hosts. Many companies seeking partnerships in China overlook the importance of personal relationships. They send their top performers to wow Chinese businesspeople with savvy sales pitches. But companies that send their salesperson of the year can return empty-handed—friendship comes before business.

⊙ **Business Partners Are Family Members Too.** In China, family is extremely important. Visiting businesspeople should never turn down invitations to partake in a Chinese executive's family life. When Lauren Hsu was market analyst for Kohler Company (*www.kohler.com*), a manufacturer of plumbing fixtures, she was responsible for researching the Chinese market and identifying potential joint venture partners. Once, in the midst of negotiations, Hsu was invited to go bowling with the partner's daughter and then to a piano concert with the entire family. Such activities had little to do with promoting Kohler plumbing fixtures, but two years of meetings and visits to get acquainted eventually resulted in a joint venture deal.

⊙ **Research, Research, Research.** China is not a single market, but many different regional markets with different cultures and even different languages. No one knows the importance of research more than Bob Wilner, director of international human resources for McDonald's Corporation (*www.mcdonalds.com*). Wilner went to China to learn as much as possible about the market, how people were managed, and the country's employment systems. "Unlike the way we cook our hamburgers exactly the same in all 101 countries," says Wilner, "the way we manage, motivate, reward and discipline is more sensitive to the culture." Wilner and other McDonald's managers were able to develop that sensitivity only through repeated visits.

going smoothly. Reunification seems more likely as economic ties between China and Taiwan grow steadily. Taiwan recently scrapped a 50-year ban that capped the size of investments in China and eased restrictions on direct financial flows between Taiwan businesses and the mainland.[5] Also, China's entry into the World Trade Organization (*www.wto.org*) in 2001 and Taiwan's entry in 2002 are encouraging further integration of their two economies.[6]

Finally, some say that *China's rise to rule the global economy is overstated*. It is argued that China's culture today does not foster two key characteristics to propel it to true world power status—western-style entrepreneurship and management practices. For example, it is argued that China stifles a true entrepreneurial spirit because it still regards enterprises as "work units" within a central plan, as opposed to "firms" in a market economy. It is also said that Chinese enterprises do not take a marketing orientation even, but build factories to crank out inexpensive products designed elsewhere. Finally, individuals who run many enterprises are there not because of their professional credentials, but because of their political connections, it is said. Whether these are traits of most Chinese businesses is debatable. What is not open to debate is that (barring any cataclysmic event) China will continue to develop its economy toward a free market, ever so slowly. Once again, patience will reveal whether the rise of China is overstated.[7]

1. What is meant by *economic system*? Explain the relation between culture and economics.

2. What is a *centrally planned economy*? Describe the link between central planning and communism.

3. Identify several factors that contributed to the decline of centrally planned economies.

4. Describe China's experience with central planning, and the challenges it faces. What are some guidelines for good *guanxi*?

Mixed Economy

A **mixed economy** is a system in which land, factories, and other economic resources are rather equally split between private and government ownership. In a mixed economy, the government owns fewer economic resources than does the government in a centrally planned economy. Yet in a mixed economy, the government tends to control the economic sectors that it considers important to national security and long-term stability. Such sectors usually include iron and steel manufacturing (for building military equipment), oil and gas production (to guarantee continued manufacturing and availability), and automobile manufacturing (to guarantee employment for a large portion of the workforce). Many mixed economies also maintain generous welfare systems to support the unemployed and provide health care for the general population.

mixed economy
Economic system in which land, factories, and other economic resources are rather equally split between private and government ownership.

Mixed economies are found all around the world: Denmark, France, Germany, Norway, Spain, and Sweden in Western Europe; India, Indonesia, Malaysia, Pakistan, and South Korea in Asia; Argentina in Latin America; and South Africa. Although all governments of these nations do not centrally plan their economies, they all influence economic activity by means of special incentives, including hefty subsidies to key industries, and significant government involvement in the economy.

Origins of the Mixed Economy
Proponents of mixed economies contend that a successful economic system must be not only efficient and innovative, but also should protect society from the excesses of unchecked individualism and organizational greed. The goal is to achieve low unemployment, low poverty, steady economic growth, and an equitable distribution of wealth by means of the most effective policies.

Proponents point out that European and U.S. rates of productivity and growth were almost identical for decades after the Second World War. Although the United States has created more jobs, it has done so at the cost of widening social inequality, proponents say. They argue that nations with mixed economies should not dismantle their social-welfare institutions but modernize them so they contribute to national competitiveness. Austria, the Netherlands, and Sweden are taking this route. In The Netherlands, labor unions and the government agreed to an epic deal involving wage restraint, shorter working hours, budget discipline, new tolerance for part-time and temporary work, and the trimming of social benefits. As a result, Dutch unemployment today tends to hover between five and six percent. By comparison, unemployment in next-door Belgium is around twelve percent and the average jobless rate for all European Union nations is around nine percent.[8]

Decline of Mixed Economies
Many mixed economies are remaking themselves to resemble more market-based systems. When assets are owned by the government there seems to be less incentive to eliminate waste or to practice innovation. Extensive government ownership tends to result in a lack of responsibility and accountability, rising costs, defective products, and slow economic growth. Many government-owned businesses in mixed economies needed large infusions of taxpayers' money to survive as world-class competitors. That is why taxes and prices were higher and standards of living lower. Underpinning the move toward more market-based systems is large-scale *privatization*.

Move Toward Privatization As discussed earlier, people in many European nations prefer a combination of rich benefits and higher unemployment to the low jobless rates and smaller social safety net of the United States. In France, for instance, the French electorate continues to hold fast to a deeply embedded tradition of social welfare and job security in government-owned firms. "Here," reports Ernest Antoine-Seilliere, president of the French conglomerate CGIP (*www.cgip.fr*), "social security and social solidarity weigh more than efficiency."[9]

Yet such attitudes are costly in terms of economic efficiency. The selling of government-owned economic resources to private operators is called **privatization**. The main goal of privatization is to increase economic efficiency and labor productivity. It also removes many of the subsidies formerly paid to government-owned companies and curtails the practice of appointing managers for political reasons rather than for their professional expertise. Because privatized companies compete in open markets for material, labor, and capital, they are subject to market forces and under greater pressure to produce competitive products at fair prices.

To improve competitiveness, governments across Europe have privatized companies worth many billions of dollars. Electric utilities in Britain, Italy, and Spain that already are in private hands are applying pressure on the French government to do the same to its state-owned utility, Electricité de France (EDF). In fact, EDF (*www.edf.fr*) is the last major European utility to enjoy protected monopoly status. Driving the resistance to privatization of EDF are the utility's unionized employees—who can retire at age 55 with pensions totaling 75 percent of their salaries. So, despite obvious benefits, it appears that some government-owned companies in certain nations are not quite ready to submit to the efficiency inspiring forces of the free market.[10]

Market Economy

In a **market economy**, the majority of a nation's land, factories, and other economic resources are privately owned, either by individuals or businesses. Nearly all economy-related decisions—including who produces what and the prices of products, labor, and capital—are determined by the interplay of two forces:

- **Supply**—the quantity of a good or service that producers are willing to provide at a specific selling price.
- **Demand**—the quantity of a good or service that buyers are willing to purchase at a specific selling price.

As supply and demand change for a good or service, so does its selling price. The lower the price, the more people will demand the product; the higher the price, the less people will demand it. Likewise, the lower the price, the smaller the quantity that producers will supply; the higher the price, the more they will supply. In this respect, what is called the "price mechanism" (or "market mechanism") dictates supply and demand.

Margin glossary

privatization
Policy of selling government-owned economic resources to private companies and individuals.

market economy
Economic system in which the majority of a nation's land, factories, and other economic resources are privately owned, either by individuals or businesses.

supply
Quantity of a good or service that producers are willing to provide at a specific selling price.

demand
Quantity of a good or service that buyers are willing to purchase at a specific selling price.

Piccadilly Circus in central London buzzes with activity on a sunny spring afternoon. The U.K. government began selling off state-owned companies in the 1980s in an effort to improve efficiency. Today, the U.K. economy lies somewhere between the more collectivist economies of continental Europe and the more individualist one of the United States. What is your personal view regarding the balance between individualist and collectivist government policies?

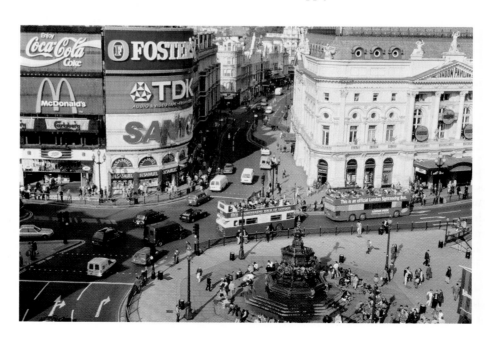

Market forces and uncontrollable natural forces can affect prices for many products, particularly commodities. Chocolate lovers, for example, should consider how the interplay of several forces affects the price of cocoa, the principal ingredient in chocolate. Suppose that consumption suddenly rises in large cocoa-consuming nations such as Britain, Japan, and the United States. Suppose further that disease and pests plague crops in cocoa-producing countries such as Brazil, Ghana, and the Ivory Coast. As worldwide consumption of cocoa begins to outstrip production, market pressure is felt on both the demand side (consumers) and the supply side (producers). Falling worldwide reserves of cocoa then force the price of cocoa higher.

Origins of the Market Economy
Market economics is rooted in the belief that individual concerns should be placed above group concerns. In this view, the group benefits when individuals receive incentives and rewards to act in certain ways. If people are allowed to own their homes, it is argued, they are likely to take better care of the property. Conversely, under a system of publicly owned property, individuals may have fewer incentives to care for property.

Laissez-Faire Economics For many centuries the world's dominant economic philosophy supported government control of a significant portion of a society's assets and government involvement in its international trade. But in the mid-1700s a new approach to national economics called for less government interference in commerce and greater individual economic freedom. This approach became known as a *laissez-faire* system, loosely translated from French as "allow them to do [without interference]."

Canada and the United States are examples of contemporary market economies. It is no accident that both these countries have individualist cultures (although to a somewhat lesser extent in Canada). As much as an emphasis on individualism fosters a democratic form of government, it also supports a market economy.

Features of a Market Economy
To function smoothly and properly, a market economy requires three things: *free choice*, *free enterprise*, and *price flexibility*.

- *Free choice* gives individuals access to alternative purchase options. In a market economy, few restrictions are placed on consumers' ability to make their own decisions and exercise free choice. For example, a consumer shopping for a new car is guaranteed a variety from which to choose. The consumer can choose among dealers, models, sizes, styles, colors, and mechanical specifications such as engine size and transmission type.

- *Free enterprise* gives companies the ability to decide which goods and services to produce and the markets in which to compete. Companies are free to enter new and different lines of business, select geographic markets and customer segments to pursue, hire workers, and advertise their products. They are, therefore, guaranteed the right to pursue interests profitable to them.

- *Price flexibility* allows most prices to rise and fall to reflect the forces of supply and demand. In contrast, nonmarket economies often set and maintain prices at stipulated levels. Interfering with the price mechanism violates a fundamental principle of the market economy.

Government's Role in a Market Economy
In a market economy, the government has relatively little direct involvement in business activities. Even so, it usually plays four important roles: *enforcing antitrust laws, preserving property rights, providing a stable fiscal and monetary environment*, and *preserving political stability*. Let's look briefly at each of these activities.

Enforcing Antitrust Laws When one company is able to control a product's supply—and, therefore, its price—it is considered a monopoly. The goal of *antitrust* (or *antimonopoly*) *laws* is to encourage the development of industries with as many competing businesses as the market will sustain. (These laws are explained fully in Chapter 3.) In competitive industries, prices are kept low by the forces of competition. By enforcing antitrust laws, governments prevent trade-restraining monopolies and business combinations that exploit consumers and constrain the growth of commerce.

The Federal Trade Commission (FTC) of the U.S. government seeks to ensure the competitive and efficient functioning of the nation's markets. But the FTC (*www.ftc.gov*) can also evaluate proposed deals outside the United States when the U.S. market is likely to be affected. For instance, the FTC reviewed a proposed acquisition of Sweden's Svedala Industri (*www.svedala.com*) by Finland's Metso Oyj (*www.metsocorporation.com*) for about $1.6 billion. Metso and Svedala were the world's two largest suppliers of rock-processing equipment at the time. In response to FTC concerns over potential anticompetitive effects in the global market for rock-processing equipment, the two companies agreed to sell parts of their businesses to third parties.[11]

Preserving Property Rights A smoothly functioning market economy rests on a legal system that safeguards individual property rights. By preserving and protecting individual property rights, governments encourage individuals and companies to take risks such as investing in technology, inventing new products, and starting new businesses. Strong protection of property rights ensures entrepreneurs that their claims to assets and future earnings are legally safeguarded. This protection also supports a healthy business climate in which a market economy can flourish.

Providing a Stable Fiscal and Monetary Environment Unstable economies are often characterized by high inflation and unemployment. These forces create general uncertainty about a nation's suitability as a place to do business. Governments can help control inflation through effective *fiscal policies* (policies regarding taxation and government spending)

MAP 4.1

Economic Freedom Around the World

This map classifies countries according to their levels of economic freedom. Only 16 countries and territories are considered completely "free," whereas 55 nations are "mostly free." But the scale tips in favor of a lack of economic freedom: There are 72 nations labeled "mostly unfree" and 12 nations labeled "repressed."

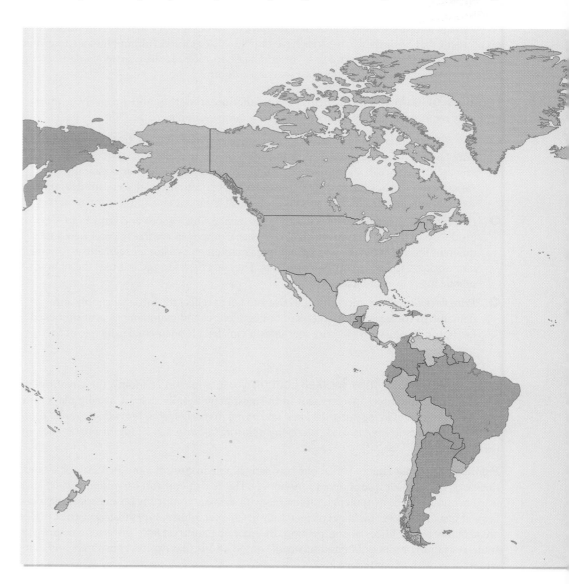

and *monetary policies* (policies controlling money supply and interest rates). A stable economic environment helps companies make better forecasts of costs, revenues, and the future of the business in general. Such conditions reduce the risks associated with future investments, such as new product development and business expansion.

Preserving Political Stability   A market economy depends on a stable government for its smooth operation and, indeed, for its future existence. Political stability helps businesses engage in activities without worrying about terrorism, kidnappings, and other political threats to their operations. (See Chapter 3 for extensive coverage of political risk and stability.)

Economic Freedom   So far we have discussed the essence of market economies as being grounded in freedom: free choice, free enterprise, free prices, and freedom from direct intervention by government. Map 4.1 shows how countries rank according to their levels of economic freedom. Some of the factors involved in the rankings include trade policy, government intervention in the economy, property rights, black markets, and wage and price controls. Of the 155 countries ranked, 71 are either "free" or "mostly free," whereas 84 are "mostly unfree" or "repressed."

Recall that in Chapter 3 we said the connection between political freedom and economic growth is not at all certain. Likewise, we can say only that countries with the greatest economic freedom *tend to have* the highest standards of living, whereas those with the lowest freedom *tend to have* the lowest standards of living. Figure 4.2 shows that the greater a people's economic freedom, the higher their per capita income. It also demonstrates that economic freedom does not *guarantee* a high per capita income. You can see that some countries rank very low on

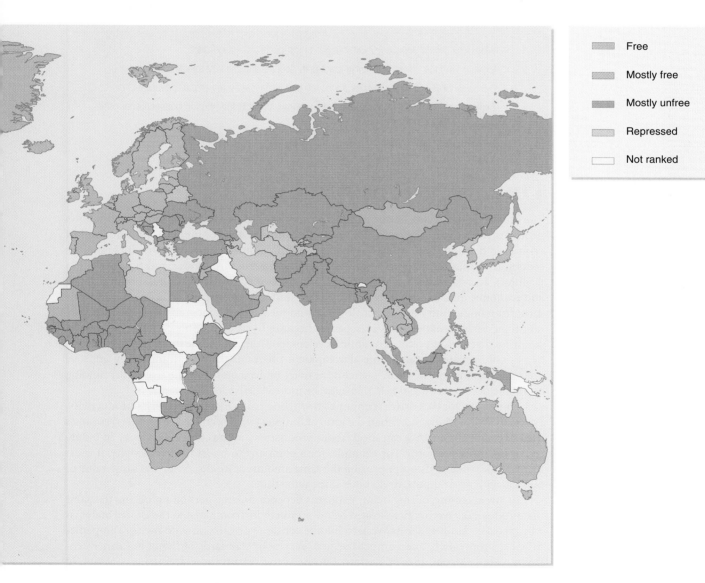

Free
Mostly free
Mostly unfree
Repressed
Not ranked

FIGURE 4.2

Economic Freedom and Wealth

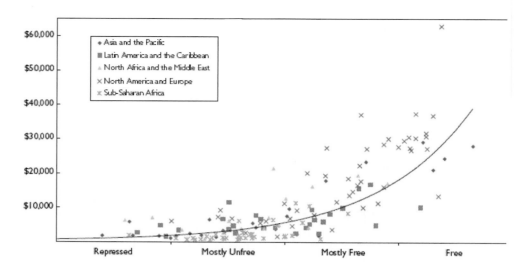

economic freedom yet have higher per capita incomes than some countries with far greater freedom. But, on average, once an economy moves from the "mostly unfree" category to the "mostly free" category, per capita income increases nearly four times.[12]

Quick Study

1. What is a *mixed economy*? Explain the origin of mixed economies.
2. Explain why the mixed-economy ideal is in decline and the key role of *privatization*.
3. Define what is meant by *market economy* and identify its three required features.
4. Explain government's role in a market economy. What is the relation between economic freedom and standards of living?

Development of Nations

economic development
Measure for gauging the economic well-being of one nation's people as compared with that of another nation's people.

The economic well-being of one nation's people as compared with that of another nation's people is reflected in the country's level of **economic development**. A nation's level of economic development reflects several economic and human indicators, including its economic output (agricultural and industrial), infrastructure (power and transportation facilities), and its people's physical health and level of education. Cultural, political, legal, and economic differences between nations can cause great differences in economic development from one country to another. Today, economic development is an increasingly important topic for international businesspeople because firms commonly conduct business in countries that are low on the economic-development scale. But while these countries tend to be poor, they may have ambitious development programs that can dramatically improve their attractiveness as markets. Therefore, a fuller understanding of the issues surrounding economic development can help managers be more effective in their work.

One key factor that drives economic growth and rising living standards is productivity. *Productivity* is nothing more than the ratio of outputs (what is created) to inputs (resources used to create output). We can speak about productivity in the context of a firm, an industry, or an entire economy. For example, for a company to boost its productivity, it must increase the value of its outputs using the same amount of inputs, create the same value of outputs with fewer inputs, or do both at the same time.

In any economy, raising living standards depends in large part on unlocking the gains that productivity has to offer. Relatively low productivity (compared to the United States) is why mixed economies across Western Europe continue privatizing state-owned companies to boost productivity and competitiveness. Very poor standards of living in former centrally planned economies of Eastern Europe is the reason those countries continue to

The debate over whether investment in information technology (IT) boosts productivity has been controversial. Some proclaim IT the savior of their company or industry even, while others complain bitterly about its promises never fulfilled. But the fact is, IT investment directed toward the drivers of productivity in an industry pays dividends.

○ **The Productivity Paradox.** Robert Solow, Nobel laureate in economics, once observed, "You can see the computer age everywhere but in the productivity statistics." This was the case throughout the 1980s and early 1990s—productivity actually slowed as U.S. companies invested heavily in computers and telecommunications. But now the U.S. economy is racking up impressive productivity growth rates. After posting respectable annual growth rates of 2.5 percent between 1995 and 2000, labor productivity grew a phenomenal 3.4 percent a year from 2000 to 2003, and looks set to grow 3.3 percent in 2004.

○ **Solving the Paradox.** There is good reason why productivity does not shoot higher the moment a computer is plugged in. Gains in productivity arise only after companies reorganize their business practices around new technologies. Some areas of IT investment now paying off include servicing customers online, buying materials and parts online, and outsourcing operations. For example, it costs FedEx (*www.fedex.com*)

$2.40 to track a package for a customer on the telephone, but just four cents online. Sometimes, simply ditching the old ways of doing things and embracing new technologies can boost productivity handsomely.

○ **Targeting Productivity Levers.** Just pouring money into IT does not automatically boost a firm's competitiveness. In fact, companies most successful in their IT investments follow three practices. First, such firms target IT investments at crucial areas—called productivity levers—that contribute most to success in their industries and themselves. Second, the firms think carefully through the timing and sequence of their investments. And third, they develop their managerial innovations along with (not in isolation from) their technological ones.

○ **To Be Continued . . .** Optimistic economists are predicting IT will drive productivity growth rates of between three and four percent for the next five to 10 years. By comparison, the steam age of the 1800s boosted productivity growth an average of just one percent a year in Britain. And at the peak of the electricity revolution in the 1920s, U.S. productivity growth averaged 2.3 percent a year. If the optimistic forecasts for IT actually come to pass, IT will have had a far greater impact than *any* previous technological revolution.

implement free market reforms. And a decade-long economic contraction in North Korea (which has one of the lowest standards of living in the world outside Africa) finally impelled that nation's leadership to begin taking its baby steps toward reform. Yet while the world's poorest nations are revamping the most basic drivers of productivity growth (such as creating basic infrastructure), companies in the world's richest nations are benefiting from the latest advancements in information technology (IT). To read how information technology is helping drive productivity gains for companies, industries, and nations, see this chapter's Breaking Views feature titled, "IT Matters to Productivity."

There are a variety of measures that businesspeople can use to estimate a country's level of economic development. But because each measure has its advantages and disadvantages, it can be wise to consider a combination of measures when analyzing potential markets. Let's now take a look at a few of the main gauges of economic development.

National Production

Recall from Chapter 1 that the broadest measure of economic development is *gross national product (GNP)*, which is the value of all goods and services produced by a country during a one-year period. This figure includes income generated both by domestic production and by the country's international activities. *Gross domestic product (GDP)* is the value of all goods and services produced by the domestic economy over a 1-year period. GDP is a narrower figure that excludes a nation's income generated from exports, imports, and the international operations of its companies. A country's *GDP per capita* is simply its GDP divided by its population. GNP per capita is calculated similarly. Both GDP per capita and GNP per capita measure a nation's income per person. Map 4.2 shows how the World Bank

MAP 4.2

Country Classification by Gross National Income per Capita

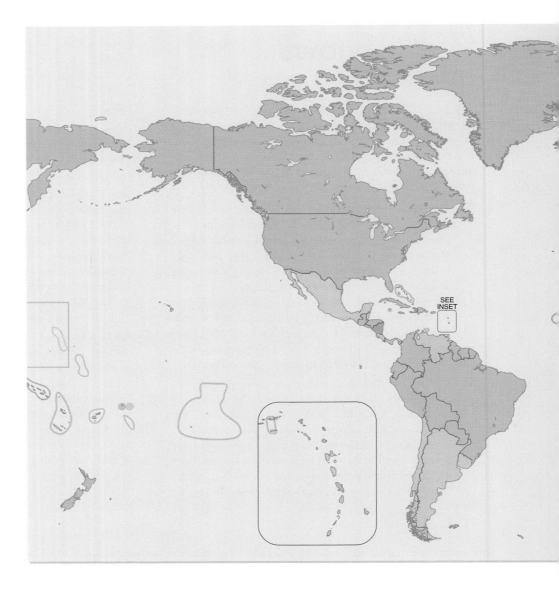

(*www.worldbank.org*) classifies countries according to their Gross National Income per Capita (a term it uses).

Marketers often use GDP or GNP per capita figures to determine whether a country's population is wealthy enough to begin purchasing its products. For instance, the Asian nation of Myanmar, with a GDP per capita of about $120 per year, is very poor. Here, you won't find computer companies marketing laptops or designer-apparel firms selling expensive clothing. Yet several large makers of personal-care products are staking out territory in Myanmar. Companies like Colgate-Palmolive (*www.colgate.com*) and Unilever (*www.unilever.com*) are traditional explorers of uncertain but promising markets in which they can offer relatively inexpensive, everyday items such as soap and shampoo.

Although GDP and GNP are the most popular indicators of economic development, they have several important drawbacks. In the following sections, we discuss each of these in some detail.

Uncounted Transactions For a variety of reasons, many of a nation's transactions do not get counted in either GDP or GNP. Some of the activities not included are:

- ➲ Volunteer work
- ➲ Unpaid household work
- ➲ Illegal activities such as gambling and black market (underground) transactions
- ➲ Unreported transactions conducted in cash

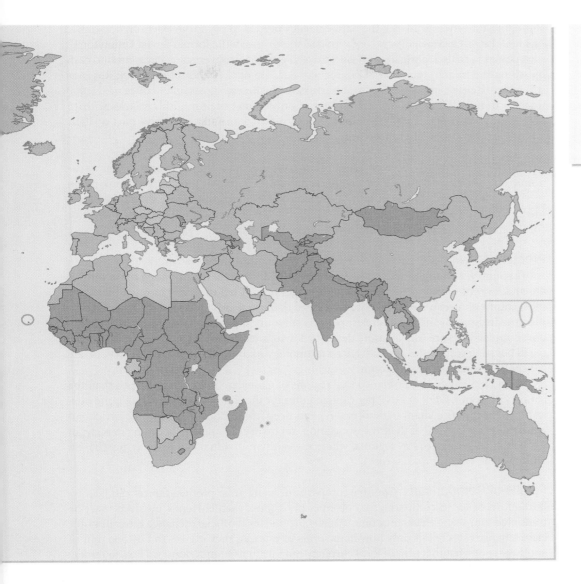

■	High income ($9,076 or more)
■	Upper-middle income ($2,936–$9,075)
■	Lower-middle income ($736–$2,935)
■	Low income ($735 or less)

In some cases, the underground economy is so large and prosperous that official statistics such as GDP per capita are almost meaningless. In the case of Myanmar, for instance, economists report that official numbers mask a thriving underground economy spurred by differences between official and black-market currency exchange rates. Across all developing nations, the informal economy accounts for 41 percent of official GDPs. In Zimbabwe, the figure is 60 percent and in Turkey and Brazil around half of national output comes from their informal economies. By contrast, the figure for wealthy nations is around 18 percent.[13]

The unofficial economy accounts for a large percentage of overall GDP in several central and eastern European countries as well. In Ukraine, according to official statistics, GDP has *shrunk* by more than 60 percent since the break from Moscow in 1991.[14] Why, then, do kids in Reeboks (*www.reebok.com*) dash through Kiev streets snarled with Jeeps (*www.jeep.com*) and shiny Mercedes-Benzes (*www.mercedes.com*)? The answer is that roughly half of the GDP flows through the country in unreported cash. Who generates this cash? Well, there's little incentive for a small Kiev manufacturer to go the official route when faced with a gauntlet of regulatory and permit steps just to export a batch of shorts to neighboring Poland, for example. It is much simpler for the company to do business in the underground economy.

In addition, *barter* (the exchange of goods and services for other goods and services instead of money) regularly occurs in many developing countries. Barter is a popular alternative for buyers who lack the hard currency needed to pay for imports. In one classic incident, Pepsi-Cola (*www.pepsi.com*) traded soft drinks in the former Soviet Union for 17 submarines, a cruiser, a frigate, and a destroyer. Pepsi then converted its payment into cash by selling the military goods as scrap metal.[15] Because of their lack of currency, Russians still make extensive use of barter. In a bizarre case, the Russian government once paid 8,000 teachers in the Altai republic (1,850 miles east of Moscow) their monthly salaries with 15 bottles of vodka each. Teachers had previously refused an offer to receive part of their salaries in toilet paper and funeral accessories.[16]

Question of Growth   Because gross product figures are a snapshot of one year's economic output, they do not tell us whether a nation's economy is growing or shrinking. In predicting a country's future output, its expected economic growth rate should be examined. Thus, even a nation with moderate GDP or GNP figures will inspire greater investor confidence and international investment if growth rates are high.

Problem of Averages   Remember that per capita numbers give an average figure for an entire country. Although these numbers can be broadly helpful in estimating the quality of life and level of economic development, averages do not tell the story in much detail. In most countries, urban areas are more developed than rural areas and have higher per capita income. In less-advanced countries, regions surrounding good harbors or other transportation facilities are usually more developed than interior regions. Sometimes industrial parks boasting companies with advanced technology in production or design can generate a disproportionate share of a country's earnings.

Because Shanghai and other coastal regions of China are far more developed than the country's interior, GDP or GNP per capita figures for the country as a whole are quite misleading. For instance, many agricultural regions deep inside China still rely on bicycles and animals for a good deal of their transportation. Yet luxury car sales are booming in many of China's cities along coastal regions, where a wealthy individual can actually purchase a Hummer H2 (*www.hummer.com*).[17]

Pitfalls of Comparison   Country comparisons using gross product figures can be misleading. In order to compare gross product per capita, each currency involved must be translated into a single currency unit (usually the dollar) at official exchange rates. But official exchange rates tell us only how many units of one currency it takes to buy one unit of another—not what that unit of local currency can buy in its home country. Thus, to understand the true value of a currency in its home country, we must apply the concept of *purchasing power parity*.

Purchasing Power Parity

purchasing power
Value of goods and services that can be purchased with one unit of a country's currency.

purchasing power parity (PPP)
Relative ability of two countries' currencies to buy the same "basket" of goods in those two countries.

Using gross product figures to compare production across countries does not account for the different cost of living in each country. **Purchasing power** is the value of goods and services that can be purchased with one unit of a country's currency. **Purchasing power parity (PPP)** is the relative ability of two countries' currencies to buy the same "basket" of goods in those two countries. This basket of goods is representative of ordinary, daily-use items such as apples, rice, soap, toothpaste, and so forth. Estimates of gross product per capita at PPP allow us to see what a currency can actually buy in real terms.

Using purchasing power parity to compare the wealth of nations produces some interesting results. Table 4.1 shows how several countries compare to the United States when their respective GDPs per capita are adjusted to reflect PPP. Thus, if we convert Swiss francs to dollars at official exchange rates, we estimate Swiss GDP per capita at $37,400. However, if we estimate Switzerland's GDP per capita at PPP, we realize that it is actually lower than that of the United States—$30,500, as compared with $36,100. Why the difference? GDP per capita at PPP is lower in Switzerland because of that nation's higher cost of living. This means that it costs more to buy the same basket of goods in Switzerland than it does in the United States. The opposite phenomenon occurs in the case of the Czech Republic. Because

TABLE 4.1

Estimates of GDP per Capita at PPP (Selected Countries)

Country	GDP per Capita (U.S.$)	PPP Estimate of GDP per Capita (U.S. = 100)
United States	37,600	37,600
Switzerland	43,500	32,600
Canada	27,000	30,400
Australia	26,400	30,100
United Kingdom	30,300	30,100
Japan	33,600	28,000
Czech Republic	8,900	17,300
Hungary	8,100	15,100
Mexico	6,200	9,600
Turkey	3,400	7,000

the cost of living there is lower than in the United States, the Czech Republic's GDP per capita rises from $6,800 to $15,100 when PPP is considered. We discuss PPP in far greater detail in Chapter 10.

Quick Study

1. What is meant by *economic development*? Explain how productivity (and information technology) helps improve standards of living.

2. Describe three measures of economic development and list their advantages and disadvantages.

3. Explain the concept of *purchasing power parity*. What are its implications for a nation's *relative* income per capita?

Human Development

The purchasing power parity concept does a fairly good job of revealing differences between nations' levels of economic development. Unfortunately, it leaves much to be desired *as an indicator of a people's total well-being*.

Table 4.2 shows how selected countries rank according to the United Nations' **human development index (HDI)**—the measure of the extent to which a people's needs are satisfied and the degree to which these needs are addressed equally across a nation's entire population. As such, the HDI goes beyond calculations of a country's financial wealth. It measures the satisfaction of a people's needs along three dimensions: (1) a long and healthy life, (2) an education, and (3) a decent standard of living. The three factors the HDI incorporates to evaluate success along these dimensions are life expectancy, educational attainment, and income.

Table 4.2 also illustrates the disparity that can be present between wealth and the HDI. For example, we see that the United States ranks 2nd in terms of GDP per capita but ranks 7th in providing health care, education, and a decent standard of living. A conspicuous example in the table is the entry for Botswana. The country ranks 125th in terms of HDI but ranks 60th in terms of GDP per capita. Perhaps most striking in Table 4.2 is the column showing each nation's life expectancy at birth. We see that the people of first-ranked Norway have a life expectancy that is more than twice that of last-ranked Sierra Leone.

Unlike the other measures we have discussed, the HDI looks beyond financial wealth. By stressing the human aspects of economic development, the HDI demonstrates that high national income alone does not guarantee human progress. However, the importance of national income should not be underestimated. Countries need money to build good schools, provide quality health care, support environmentally friendly industries, and underwrite other programs designed to improve the quality of life.

human development index (HDI)
Measure of the extent to which a people's needs are satisfied and the degree to which these needs are addressed equally across a nation's entire population.

TABLE 4.2

Human Development Index (HDI)

HDI Rank	Country	HDI Value	GDP per Capita Rank	Life Expectancy at Birth (Years)
High Human Development				
1	Norway	0.963	3	79.4
5	Canada	0.949	7	80.0
7	Switzerland	0.947	8	80.5
10	United States	0.944	4	77.4
11	Japan	0.943	13	82.0
15	United Kingdom	0.939	18	78.4
20	Germany	0.930	14	78.7
22	Hong Kong, China (SAR)	0.916	17	81.6
31	Czech Republic	0.874	38	75.6
53	Mexico	0.814	60	75.1
Medium Human Development				
62	Russia	0.795	59	65.3
63	Brazil	0.792	64	70.5
85	China	0.755	96	71.6
120	South Africa	0.658	52	48.4
131	Botswana	0.565	61	36.3
Low Human Development				
151	Yemen	0.489	166	60.6
164	Tanzania	0.418	175	46.0
177	Niger	0.281	169	44.4

Of special concern today regarding human and economic development is the spread of communicable diseases that cause economic loss, social disintegration, and political instability in the world's poorest nations. Such diseases decimate local human capital (due to adult deaths), cause social decay, blunt productivity growth, and divert funds away from more productive investments. The additional health care costs required of nations combating such diseases can significantly hamper their economic development. To read how three particularly lethal diseases are devastating human and economic development, see the Global Challenges feature titled, "Public Health Goes Global."

Classifying Countries

Nations are commonly classified as being *developed, newly industrialized,* or *developing.* These classifications are based on national indicators such as GDP per capita, portion of the economy devoted to agriculture, amount of exports in the form of industrial goods, and overall economic structure. However, there are no consensus lists of countries in any category, and borderline countries are often classified differently in different listings. Let's take a closer look at each of these classifications.

Developed Countries
Countries that are highly industrialized, highly efficient, and whose people enjoy a high quality of life are developed countries. People in developed countries usually receive the finest health care and benefit from the best educational systems in the world. Most developed nations also support aid programs for helping poorer nations to improve their economies and standards of living. Countries in this category include Australia, Canada, Japan, New Zealand, the United States, all western European nations, and Greece.

Newly Industrialized Countries
Countries that recently increased the portion of their national production and exports derived from industrial operations are newly industrialized countries (NICs). The NICs are located primarily in Asia and Latin America. Most listings of NICs include Asia's "four tigers" (Hong Kong, South Korea, Singapore, and Taiwan), Brazil, China, India, Malaysia, Mexico, South Africa, and Thailand. Depending on the pivotal criteria that we use for classification, a number of other countries could be

developed country
Country that is highly industrialized, highly efficient, and whose people enjoy a high quality of life.

newly industrialized country (NIC)
Country that has recently increased the portion of its national production and exports derived from industrial operations.

Public Health Goes Global

As they hitch rides with refugees, vacationers, and business-people, three communicable diseases (HIV/AIDS, tuberculosis, and malaria) are presenting the world with a serious global challenge. Beyond the dreadful human suffering, these diseases dim hopes for economic development in poor nations and put a drag on the global economy.

- **HIV/AIDS.** This disease has killed nearly as many people as the Plague that struck 14th century Europe. AIDS has already killed at least 22 million worldwide, and at least 40 million are infected with HIV/AIDS. In Africa alone, 20 million are dead and 30 million are infected. The disease has cut GDP growth by 2.6 percent in some African countries, and could *decrease* South Africa's average household income 8 percent by 2013. Having overrun Africa, the epidemic is now spreading to Asia and Eastern Europe (where between 700,000 and 1.5 million Russians are infected).

- **Tuberculosis.** Each year, tuberculosis (TB) kills about two million people and sickens another eight million. More than 90 percent of TB cases occur in low- and lower-middle-income countries across Southeast Asia, Eastern Europe, and sub-Saharan Africa. TB is on the rise because of economic hardship, broken health systems, the emergence of drug-resistant TB, and a linkage between TB and HIV/AIDS whereby each speeds the other's progress. TB depletes the incomes of the world's poorest nations by about $12 billion.

- **Malaria.** Each year, malaria kills one million people and indirectly causes the deaths of up to three million.

Malaria is prevalent from Vietnam's Mekong Delta to central Africa to Brazil's Amazon Basin. But it is in central and sub-Saharan Africa where 90 percent of the world's malaria deaths occur (mostly young children and pregnant women), and where malaria kills roughly 20 percent of all children that die before the age of five. In the worst affected African nations, malaria costs about 1.3 percent of GDP.

- **The Challenge.** To combat *HIV/AIDS*, rich nations could donate money for training new doctors and nurses in poor nations to replace those either dying of the disease or emigrating to richer countries. To battle *tuberculosis*, more aid money could purchase drugs that cost just $10 per person for the full six-to-eight-month TB treatment. To fight *malaria*, distribution of insecticide-treated bed nets must be improved as only two percent of children in Africa sleep under such nets. More companies also could follow the lead of Swiss drug-maker Novartis (*www.novartis.com*), which sells its anti-malaria drug to poor countries under cost, but sells the exact same drug to (richer) European travelers at a far higher price to recoup development costs.

- **Want to Know More?** Visit the Global Business Coalition on HIV/AIDS (*www.businessfightsaids.org*); Global Fund for AIDS, Tuberculosis, and Malaria (*www.theglobalfund.org*); Malaria Foundation International (*www.malaria.org*); and World Health Organization TB site (*www.who.int/gtb*).

---

placed in this category, including Argentina, Brunei, Chile, the Czech Republic, Hungary, Indonesia, the Philippines, Poland, Russia, Slovakia, Turkey, and Vietnam.

When we combine newly industrialized countries with countries that have the potential to become newly industrialized, we arrive at a category often called **emerging markets**. Generally, emerging markets have developed some (but not all) of the operations and export capabilities associated with NICs. However, debate continues over the defining characteristics of such classifications as *newly industrialized country* and *emerging market*.

emerging markets
Newly industrialized countries plus those with the potential to become newly industrialized.

Developing Countries Nations with the poorest infrastructures and lowest personal incomes are called **developing countries** (also called *less-developed countries*). These countries often rely heavily on one or a few sectors of production, such as agriculture, mineral mining, or oil drilling. They might show potential for becoming newly industrialized countries, but typically lack the necessary resources and skills to do so. Most lists of developing countries include many nations in Africa, the Middle East, and the poorest formerly communist nations in Eastern Europe and Asia.

developing country (also called less-developed country)
Nation that has a poor infrastructure and extremely low personal incomes.

Developed countries use the latest technological advances in their manufacturing sectors. However, developing countries (and NICs as well) are sometimes characterized by a high degree of **technological dualism**—use of the latest technologies in some sectors of the economy coupled with the use of outdated technologies in others.

technological dualism
Use of the latest technologies in some sectors of the economy coupled with the use of outdated technologies in other sectors.

1. Explain the value of the *Human Development Index (HDI)* in measuring a nation's level of development.

2. How are communicable diseases devastating human and economic development in some poor nations?

3. Identify the main characteristics of: a) *developed countries,* b) *newly industrialized countries,* and c) *developing countries.*

4. Name three countries that fall into each of the three country classifications.

Economic Transition

economic transition
Process by which a nation changes its fundamental economic organization and creates new free-market institutions.

Over the past two decades, countries with centrally planned economies have been remaking themselves in the image of stronger market economies. This process, called economic transition, involves changing a nation's fundamental economic organization and creating entirely new free-market institutions. Some nations take transition further than others do, but the process typically involves five reform measures:[18]

1. Macroeconomic stabilization to reduce budget deficits and expand credit availability

2. Liberalization of economic activity that is decided by prices reflecting supply and demand

3. Legalization of private enterprises and privatization of state-owned enterprises in accord with an effective system of individual property rights

4. Removal of trade and investment barriers in goods and services, and removal of controls on convertibility of the nation's currency

5. Development of a social-welfare system designed to ease the transition process

Obstacles to Transition

There is little doubt that transition from central planning to free-market economics is generating tremendous international business opportunities. But difficulties arising from years of socialist economic principles have hampered progress from the start. Some countries that emerged from behind the iron curtain of the former Soviet Union still endure high unemployment rates. In many nations undergoing transition, worries over employment affect children as well as adults, troubling social experts. Surveys find that when children in transition countries are asked what kind of country they want to live in, employment and the economy are primary concerns.

Let's now take a look at the key remaining obstacles that are hindering former socialist and communist countries in their transition to free-market economies: *lack of managerial expertise, shortage of capital, cultural differences*, and *environmental degradation*.

Lack of Managerial Expertise
One challenge facing companies in transitional economies is a lack of managers qualified to conduct operations in a highly competitive global economy. Because central planners formerly decided nearly every aspect of the nation's commercial activities, there was little need for production, distribution, and marketing plans or strategies—or for trained individuals to devise them.

Likewise, because the types of goods and services to be offered were decided by central planning committees, there was little need to investigate consumer wants and needs—or for specialists who were capable of conducting such research. Because central planners set prices, very little thought was given to strategies for delivering competitively priced products—or to the need for experts in operations, inventory, distribution, or logistics. Because all products were basically the same, there was no need for marketers with advertising skills.

Factory managers at government-owned firms had only to meet production requirements already set by central planners. In fact, some products rolled off assembly lines merely to be stacked outside the doors of the factory. After all, knowing where they went after that—and who took them there—was not the factory manager's job.

Signs of Progress Although managers in transitional countries tend to lack expertise in some areas of business management, the situation is improving. "The gap in education and experience between managers from advanced countries and those of the former socialist bloc has narrowed dramatically," says Thomas Allgäuer, managing partner at Egon Zehnder International (*www.zehnder.com*), an executive search company. The reasons he cites for this trend are improved education, opportunities to study and work abroad, and changes in work habits caused by companies investing locally.[19]

Some managers from former communist nations are even finding managerial opportunities in Western Europe and the United States with some of the largest multinationals. One success story is that of 30-year-old Vanda Wolfová. She is employed by Ogilvy EMEA marketing agency (*www.ogilvy.com*) in Paris, France. This journalist with a bachelor's degree in mass communication became Ogilvy & Mather's first employee in Prague. After establishing and running O&M Focus, a subsidiary specializing in public relations, she took an offer to work on global projects in Paris. "Of course, they looked at me differently from the way they would had I been from England," she admits. "I had to prove that I could do it."[20]

Shortage of Capital

Not surprisingly, transition is very expensive. To facilitate the process and ease the pain, governments must usually spend a great deal of money in three areas:

1. Developing a telecommunications and infrastructure system, including highways, bridges, rail networks, and sometimes subways

2. Setting up financial institutions, including stock markets and a banking system

3. Educating people in the ways of market economics

Unfortunately, governments of transition economies still cannot afford all the required investment. Usually they lack capital because of the same financial management practices that they are trying to replace. However, outside sources of capital are available, including national and international companies, other governments, and international financial institutions, such as the World Bank, the International Monetary Fund (IMF), and the Asian Development Bank. But another problem facing many transition countries is that they already owe substantial amounts of money to international lenders.

Cultural Differences

Economic transition and reform make deep cultural impressions on a nation's people. As we saw in Chapter 2, cultures differ greatly, with some more open to change than others. Likewise, certain cultures welcome economic change more easily than others do. Transition often replaces dependence on the government with greater emphasis on individual responsibility, incentives, and rights. In some cultures such changes can be traumatic. Deep cuts in welfare payments, unemployment benefits, and guaranteed government jobs can present a major shock to a nation's people. Importing modern management practices without tailoring them to the local culture can also have serious consequences.

South Korea's Daewoo Motors (*www.dm.co.kr*) faced a culture clash when it entered Central Europe. Korea's management system is based on a rigid hierarchical structure and an obsessive work ethic. Managers at Daewoo's domestic car plant in Pupyong-Gu were expected to arrive an hour early for work to stand at the company gates and greet workers—who arrive singing the company anthem. But implementing the Korean work ethic in its central and eastern European factories proved tricky. Korean managers could not understand why employees wanted holidays that coincide with their children's school breaks or why European managers so frequently switched companies. So Daewoo tried to bridge the cultural and workplace gaps. At any one time, 500 Romanians, Poles, and Uzbeks were studying their Korean colleagues' work habits and methods by staffing assembly lines at

Daewoo Motors' plant in Korea for 6-month stretches. Traveling in the other direction were Korean managers and technicians who specialized in assembly-line efficiency.[21]

Environmental Degradation

The economic and social policies of former communist governments in Central and Eastern Europe were disastrous for the natural environment. The direct effects of environmental destruction are evident in increased levels of sickness and disease, including asthma, blood deficiencies, and cancer—the result of which is lower productivity in the workplace. Countries in transition often suffer periods during which the negative effects of a market economy seem to outweigh its benefits—it's hard to enjoy a larger paycheck when the streets are choked with smog and the parks and rivers are polluted. Commuters can suffer carbon monoxide poisoning, children can get lead poisoning from flaking house paint, smokestacks pollute the air, and toxic chemicals can flow down the rivers.

Focus on Russia

Russia's experience with communism dates back to 1917. For the next 75 years, factories, distribution, and all other facets of operations, as well as the prices of labor, capital, and products, were controlled by the government. While China was experimenting with private farm ownership and a limited market-price system, the Soviet Union remained staunchly communist under a system of complete government ownership. The total absence of market institutions meant that, unlike China, Russia endured massive political change along with economic reform when it embarked on its transition.

Rough Transition

In the 1980s the former Soviet Union entered a new era of freedom of thought, freedom of expression, and economic restructuring. For the first time since the communist takeover, people were allowed to speak freely about their lives under economic socialism. And speak freely they did—venting their frustrations over a general lack of consumer goods, poor-quality products, and long lines at banks and grocery stores.

But the transition from government ownership and central planning has been challenging for ordinary Russians. Except for criminals and wealthy businesspeople, whom the Russians refer to as "oligarchs," people are having difficulty maintaining their standard of living and affording many basic items such as food and clothing. Today, some Russians are doing rather well financially because they were factory managers under the old system and retained their jobs in the new system. Others have turned to the black market, creating organized-crime syndicates and relying on extortion payments to amass personal wealth. Still others are working hard to build legitimate companies but find themselves forced into making "protection" payments to organized crime. Despite the difficulties of doing business in Russia, ambitious businesspeople with an entrepreneurial spirit are not deterred. For some insights on doing business in today's Russia, see the Entrepreneur's Survival Kit titled, "The Rules of the Game."

Challenges Ahead for Russia

Several challenges lie ahead for Russia. As in so many other transitional economies, managerial talent needs to be fostered. Years of central planning hampered development of the managerial skills needed to operate companies in a market-based economy. Russian managers must improve their skills in every facet of management practice, including financial control, research and development, employee hiring and training, marketing, and pricing. Yet Russian managers are very adept at playing by their own rules of business. With an opaque legal system and many law enforcement officials on the take, Russia can be a place where non-Russian businesspeople must always operate cautiously.[22]

Political instability, especially in the form of intensified nationalist sentiment, is another potential threat to further progress toward transition. Some experts also worry about the future disposition of Russia's nuclear weapons stockpiles. Almost everyone in Russia is badly in need of currency, and sales of such stockpiles can earn large sums of hard currency. Although the temptation to sell weapons to other nations is particularly great, in the hands of terrorists they can threaten global security, even that of Russia itself. After all, Russia must continue to deal with its own terrorist problems in the troubled republic of Chechnya.

entrepreneur's
SURVIVAL KIT

The Rules of the Game

The business scene in Russia can be tough, brutal even, at times. Yet some go-getting entrepreneurs and small business owners are venturing into this rugged land. If you are one of them, or just an interested observer, here are a few pointers on doing business in Russia.

➲ **Hit the Ground Running.** A visit to your country's local chamber of commerce in Russia should be high on your list. The best organized and managed of these hold regularly scheduled luncheons at which you can make contacts with Russians and others wanting to do business. They might also offer programs on getting acquainted with the business climate in Russia. Many businesses get started in Moscow, St. Petersburg, or Vladivostok, depending in part on their line of business.

➲ **Wanted: Adventurous Manager.** The kind of person who will succeed in Russia thrives on adventure and enjoys a good challenge. He or she also should not demand predictability in their day-to-day activities—Russia is anything but predictable. Initially, knowledge of Russian is helpful though not essential, but eventual proficiency will be necessary. Prior experience working and living in Eastern Europe would be a big plus.

➲ **Office Space for Rent.** Doing business in Russia demands a personal touch. Locating an office in Russia is crucial if you eventually want to receive income from your operations. Your office does not need to be a suite off Red Square. Almost any local address will do and a nice flat can double as an office at the start. For business services, upscale hotels commonly have business centers in them. Eventually, renting an average Russian-style office would be more than adequate.

➲ **Let's Make a Deal.** Business in Russia takes time and patience. The Russian negotiating style, like the country itself, is tough and ever changing. During negotiations emotional outbursts, walkouts, or threats to walk out should not be unexpected from your Russian counterparts. Finally, signed contracts in Russia are not always followed to the letter, as your Russian associate may view new circumstances as a chance to renegotiate terms. All in all, the personalities of individuals involved in business dealings counts for much in Russia.

One Bright Spot Russia needs tax revenue to establish the institutions that are essential to the functioning of a market economy, such as well-running stock markets, a strong central bank, and an effective tax system. But without being able to collect taxes from individuals and corporations, the government cannot afford to establish these institutions or to pay coal miners, teachers, and the pensions of the elderly and to invest in education and infrastructure. Payment for goods and services through barter, not cash, exacerbates this problem because such transactions are not taxed.

Before the Russian currency (the ruble) collapsed in 1998, large sums of international aid covered up the hole in the budget caused by the lack of tax revenues, which resulted in part from extensive barter. But afterward, a lack of international aid forced the government to crack down. The government and energy suppliers began demanding that companies pay their energy bills in cash. Faced with a threat of disconnection, and sometimes bankruptcy, firms suddenly found the cash to pay up. The move caused a ripple effect throughout the economy as firms began demanding cash payments from their customers. So, although barter remains a problem in Russia, it accounts for much less of the nation's economic activity than it has in the past.[23]

For the most part, foreign investors who took flight in 1998 after the Russian government defaulted on its international loans and the economy tanked, have returned. Yet an uneasy truce appears to have fallen over the relationship between Russia's government and its business community. The uneasiness stems from the government's decision in October 2003 to arrest Mikhail Khodorkovsky, then head of oil giant Yukos (*www.yukos.ru*) and Russia's richest man. His trial on charges of fraud, embezzlement, and tax evasion began in June 2004. Many see Khordorkovsky's arrest as payback for his outspoken support of the political opposition in the run-up to the presidential elections in March 2004. Although President Vladimir Putin won reelection easily, doubts over whether it was a truly democratic process were inflamed by his tightening of state controls over the press prior to the polling. To explain Khodorkovsky's arrest, others point to Yukos' aggressive opposition to planned changes in the tax laws aimed at taming the oil barons who had grown tremendously wealthy in the early years of economic transition. They say the arrest of the head of Yukos was designed as a signal to the business community that the government's economic reforms would go forward, spreading prosperity more widely throughout Russian society. So, it just might be that the Yukos affair was, in finance minister Alexei Kudrin's words, "inevitable, not in the political sense, but in the sense of a clarification of the rules of the game."[24]

Quick Study

1. What are several of the reform measures involved in undergoing *economic transition* to a market economy?

2. Describe some of the remaining obstacles to businesses in transitional economies.

3. Explain Russia's experience with economic transition. What are some tips for people wishing to do business in Russia?

Bottom Line for Business

This chapter completes our three-chapter coverage of national business environments. We've seen in this section, Part II of the text, the importance of culture, politics, laws, and economics for international business activities. In this chapter, we saw that although economic freedom *tends to generate* the highest standards of living, it does not *guarantee* a high per capita income. Yet this is enough to cause leaders of mixed economies to free their businesses from unnecessary regulation and their economies from government interference. One-time centrally planned economies are also continuing their free-market reforms to drive domestic entrepreneurial activity and attract international investors. These general trends are changing the face of global capitalism.

In economic development circles around the world, much will likely be discussed in coming years, if not decades, about what can be done for Africa. These discussions are important and necessary. It is an awful reality, indeed, that such abject poverty and rampant famine, disease, and war can coexist with a wider world in which people are continually on the lookout for the latest technological gadget or advancement. Yet apart from Africa's continuing struggle, two main topics are likely to dominate conversations on development—the race between China and India, and the productivity disparity between the United States and Europe. Let's now take a look at each of these because of their enormous implications for international business.

Economic Development in China vs. India

As stated in this chapter's opening company profile, China and India are following two different development models. China is attracting far more foreign investment than India, yet India has more, and more competitive, native multinationals than China does. One major reason for these differences between China and India lies in the help they get from overseas Chinese and Indians, respectively. Much of China's foreign investment over decades came from an ethnic Chinese population that scattered widely during the country's civil war and the eventual communist takeover. These ethnic Chinese were eager to help the motherland when it began to reacquaint itself with capitalism. But the investment turning China into the world's factory still comes mainly from foreign companies. This has done little to help China create powerful multinationals of its own that can rival giant U.S. and European multinationals.

India, meanwhile, was highly suspicious of ethnic Indians who had settled abroad to make a better life. These individuals likewise felt less responsibility to help India become a major world power and did not invest like overseas Chinese did. The result was that India's growth became organic, in which native entrepreneurs developed highly competitive firms in cutting-edge, knowledge-based industries. Large Indian multinationals include Infosys (*www.infosys.com*) in software and consulting, and Ranbaxy (*www.ranbaxy.com*) in pharmaceuticals and biotechnology. In fact, a recent *Forbes 200* ranking of the world's best small companies included 13 Indian firms, but only four from China.[25]

Another key difference between China and India that is affecting their chosen paths of development is their institutional infrastructures. Although India long had a reputation for high taxes and burdensome regulations, it also has had in place the foundations of a market economy, such as private enterprise, democratic government, and Western accounting practices. Also, India's capital markets are more efficient and its legal system is more advanced than China's. And China's top-down approach to development and India's bottom-up approach are reflective of their political systems: India is a democracy, and China is not.[26]

Every nation on earth has so far followed a path to development that relied on its natural resources and/or its relatively cheap labor—this is the model China is following. If India can achieve sustained economic growth similar to China's, it will become the first developing nation to advance economically by relying on the brainpower of its people. We must wait and see what the future holds for both these nations. Although China is growing very rapidly, some wonder if it lacks the skills needed to take it to the next level of competitiveness—homegrown entrepreneurs that create new products and processes, and western-style managerial skills that increase productivity. India, on the other hand, is blessed with large numbers of entrepreneurs possessing such talents. But India will need to prove that its economy can support such creativity and produce more world-class companies that can compete with the best of the West.[27]

So, for the development contest between China and India, one event seems certain, and the other less so. First, international companies are keenly aware that both China and India have immense potential for growth. It is certainly only a matter of time before China and India have burgeoning middle classes of their own—each will boast more middle-class consumers (over 300 million each) than the United States has people. Second, it is less certain if the contest between China and India will help us determine which growth strategy is best for other nations to follow: the organic-led path of India, or the investment-led path of China. The appropriate strategy is likely to depend on a nation's unique circumstances. For now, it is a big enough exercise to try to answer the question, "Can India surpass China?"

Productivity in the United States vs. Europe

We saw in this chapter that productivity growth is a key driver of living standards in any nation. Although productivity growth in Europe kept pace with that in the United States for decades following the Second World War, it has fallen behind for nearly a decade since 1995. In fact, while U.S. productivity growth was around 3.3 percent in 2004, the rate in France and Germany was a little more than half that. Even in Britain, whose productivity growth rates are normally closer to U.S. rates than those of continental Europe, productivity growth is slowing.

So why is there a gap at all? First, despite the benefits of implementing information technology (IT), European companies spend less on IT than U.S. firms. In fact, while U.S. spending on IT is around 4.4 percent of GDP, outlays on IT in France are below two percent of GDP. Second, stronger labor laws in Europe make it more difficult and costly to shed workers there, relative to the United States. So, even if European companies invest in IT to increase labor productivity, they may be unable to lower labor costs because it is more difficult to rid themselves of excess workers. Thus Europeans are discouraged from spending on IT for systemic reasons. Third, while the U.S. tech sector is a big driver behind higher U.S. productivity growth, the tech sector in Europe is far smaller by comparison. Fourth, although spending on R&D is a big boost to productivity growth, Europe spends far less overall on R&D as well as IT. In fact, some of the biggest European R&D spenders are shifting more of their R&D work to the U.S. market to be closer to their most important customers. For these reasons, and others, many economists are calling for further deregulation in Europe to help it achieve U.S. levels of productivity and living standards.

It is a fact that strong productivity growth means higher profits, better living standards, and stable prices. So, many European officials are calling for an even greater shift toward free-market reform there to try and match the consistently higher U.S. productivity growth rates over the past 10 years. And European officials appear to be finally taking the challenge seriously, knowing that robust productivity growth is the only way for their citizens to close the considerable gap with their U.S. counterparts. "Future economic growth will require a substantial increase in our productivity," said European Union Economic Affairs Minister, Jan Brinkhorst.[28]

SUMMARY

1. **Describe what is meant by a *centrally planned economy* and explain why its use is declining.** An *economic system* consists of the structure and processes that a country uses to allocate its resources and conduct its commercial activities. In a *centrally planned economy*, the government owns land, factories, and other economic resources, and plans nearly all economic-related activities. The philosophy of central planning stresses the group over individual well-being and strives for economic and social equality.

   The use of central planning is declining for several reasons. First, scarce resources were wasted because central planners paid little attention to product quality and buyers' needs. Second, a lack of incentives to innovate resulted in little or no economic growth and consistently low standards of living. Third, central planners realized that other economic systems were achieving far higher growth rates for other countries. Fourth, consumers became fed up with a lack of basic necessities such as adequate food, housing, and health care.

2. **Identify the main characteristics of a *mixed economy* and explain the emphasis on *privatization*.** In a *mixed economy*, land, factories, and other economic resources are split between private and government ownership, with governments tending to control the economic sectors crucial to national security and long-term stability. Proponents of mixed economies contend that a successful economic system must be not only efficient and innovative, but also should protect society from the excesses of unchecked individualism and organizational greed. However, attempting to become more efficient in their use of scarce resources, many mixed economies are engaging in *privatization*—the sale of government-owned economic resources to private operators.

3. **Explain how a *market economy* functions and identify its distinguishing features.** In a *market economy*, private individuals or businesses own the majority of land, factories, and other economic resources. Economic decisions are influenced by the interplay of *supply* (the quantity of a product that producers are willing to provide at a specific selling price) and *demand* (the quantity of a product that buyers are willing to purchase at a specific selling price). Market economics is rooted in the belief that individual concerns are paramount and that the group benefits when individuals receive proper incentives and rewards.

   To function smoothly, the market economy requires (1) free choice (in buyers' purchasing options), (2) free enterprise (in producers' competitive decisions), and (3) price flexibility (reflecting supply and demand). The government's role in a market economy centers on (1) enforcing antitrust laws, (2) preserving property rights, (3) providing a stable fiscal and monetary environment, and (4) preserving political stability.

4. **Describe the different ways to measure a nation's *level of development*.** *Economic development* refers to the economic well-being of one nation's people compared with that of another nation's people. There are three methods for gauging economic development: (1) *National production*, which includes measures such as *gross national product (GNP)* (the value of all goods and services produced in one year by a country) and *gross domestic product (GDP)* (the value of all goods and services produced in one year by the domestic economy). (2) *Purchasing power parity (PPP)*, which refers to the relative ability of two countries' currencies to buy the same "basket" of goods in those two countries and is used to correct comparisons made at official exchange rates. (3) The United Nations' *human development index (HDI)*, which measures the extent to which a people's needs are satisfied and addressed equally across the population.

5. **Discuss the process of *economic transition* and identify the remaining obstacles to businesses.** The process whereby a nation changes its fundamental economic organization in order to create free-market institutions is called *economic transition*. Typically, five reform measures are involved: (1) macroeconomic stabilization, (2) liberalization of economic activity, (3) legalization of private enterprises and privatization of state-owned enterprises, (4) removal of barriers to free trade, investment, and currency flows, and (5) development of a social welfare system.

   There are four major obstacles to successful economic transition. First, there is a *lack of managerial expertise* because central planners made virtually all operations, pricing, and sales decisions. Second, there is a *shortage of capital* to pay for new communications and infrastructure, new financial institutions, and the education of people about the working of a market economy. Third, *cultural differences* between transition economies and the West can make it difficult to introduce modern management practices. Fourth, *environmental degradation* has caused lower workforce productivity due to substandard health conditions.

TALK IT OVER

1. The Internet has penetrated many aspects of business and culture in developed countries, but it is barely available in many poor countries. Do you think that this technology is going to widen the economic development gap between rich and poor countries? Why or why not? Is there a way that developing countries can use such technologies as a tool for economic development?

2. Imagine that you are the director of a major international lending institution supported by funds from member countries. What one area in newly industrialized and developing economies would be your priority for receiving development aid? Do you suspect that any member countries will be politically opposed to aid in this area? Why or why not?

3. Two students are discussing the pros and cons of different measures of economic development. "GDP per capita," declares the first, "is the only true measure of how developed a country's economy is." The second student counters: "I disagree. The only true measure of a country's economic development is its people's quality of life, regardless of its GDP." Why is each of these students incorrect?

TEAMING UP

1. In this project, two groups of four students debate the benefits and drawbacks of both market and mixed economies. After the first student from each side has spoken, the second student questions the opponent's arguments, looking for holes and inconsistencies. The third student attempts to answer these arguments. The fourth student presents a summary of each side's arguments. Finally, the class will vote on which team has offered the more compelling argument.

2. Select several (one for each team member) recent articles from business magazines in print or online discussing economic issues in a particular country. Potential topics include privatization of state-owned companies, the influence of a capital shortage on transition, and investment in advancing human development such as public health programs, and so forth. Have each team member summarize their article and explain how local and international companies will be affected by, and respond to, the issue. As a group, what sort of economic picture emerges for the country when you pull all the articles together?

3. Select a country that interests the members of your group. What type of economic system does it have? Has it always had this type of economic system? Is it developed, newly industrializing, or developing? How does it rank on the various measures of economic development? Has it undergone any form of economic transition within the past 15 years? If so, what have been the effects of that transition on the culture and the country's political, legal, and economic systems? Write up your findings in a brief report.

KEY TERMS

centrally planned economy (p. 123)

demand (p. 128)

developed country (p. 138)

developing country (also called *less-developed country*) (p. 139)

economic development (p. 132)

economic system (p. 122)

economic transition (p. 140)

emerging markets (p. 139)

human development index (HDI) (p. 137)

market economy (p. 128)

mixed economy (p. 127)

newly industrialized country (NIC) (p. 138)

privatization (p. 128)

purchasing power (p. 136)

purchasing power parity (PPP) (p. 136)

supply (p. 128)

technological dualism (p. 139)

1. In this chapter, we learned how governments across Western Europe are privatizing state-owned companies, and how nations in Eastern Europe are in transition toward market-based economies. For the most part, these changes are designed to boost Europe's competitiveness in the global economy by increasing productivity and efficiency.

   Go the European Union (EU) Web site (*www.europa.eu.int*) and search for information regarding its progress on issues presented in this chapter. Possible topics include privatization, economic and social development, global competition, and nations' infrastructures. For the topic(s) of your choice, what are the EU's goals? What specific policies does the EU have in place to help it achieve those goals? Does the EU directly address the challenges (such as increased competition) that globalization presents to firms based there?

   Some countries (such as Estonia, Hungary, and Poland) outperformed others (such as Bulgaria and Romania) during their post-communist transitions. As the European Union marches continually eastward, it is absorbing many formerly communist nations. For your topic(s), what specific policies does the EU have in place to help nations in transition develop? Identify as many economic and social/cultural efforts as you can.

ETHICAL CHALLENGES

1. You are the CEO of a Canadian–Chinese joint venture that operates in China. Your Chinese partner is the People's Liberation Army (PLA). The PLA has built a sprawling network of businesses enterprises that do everything from raise pigs to run airlines and hospitals, mine coal, manage hotels, and operate paging and cellular networks. As a business conglomerate, of course, the PLA partners with international investors. Some argue that a large portion of foreign investment going to China is with companies and cartels controlled by the Chinese military. Others argue that it's easy to read too much into the PLA's foray into business. They point out that there is little centralized coordination among the thousands of businesses with military affiliations, and that some companies are run by retired officers, others by civilians. As the CEO of the joint organization do you have any ethical concerns about partnering with the PLA? If so, what are they? Suppose a clash between pro-democracy demonstrators and the PLA turns bloody. How would this turn of events affect business relations with your PLA partner? Are the ethical issues of partnering with the Chinese military any different from those that arise from exporting to China? Why or why not?

2. You are the managing director of your U.S. firm's subsidiary in southern France. The social-welfare states of Western Europe were founded after the Second World War with specific ethical considerations in mind: reduce social and economic inequality; improve living standards for the poor; and provide nearly free health care for all. Now many of these countries have trimmed social-welfare provisions and increased their reliance on market forces. Do you think that the ethical concerns of half a century ago are a thing of the past? Or do you feel that market reforms will simply recreate the conditions that motivated the development of the welfare state in the first place? What can you do as a manager to alleviate workers' fears that a more open economy will reduce their social safety net?

Talkin' Bout a Revolution

When the Soviet Union still existed, Cuba would barter sugar with its communist allies in return for oil and other goods. But when the Soviet Union crumbled in 1989, Cuba had to kiss its preferential barter rates and Soviet subsidies good-bye. The only option left to Cuba's leader, Fidel Castro, was to sell the nation's sugar on the open market. But whereas sugar exports earned Cuba $5 billion in 1990, a recent year's harvest earned just $430 million. Also, production has fallen from a peak of 8.1 million tons in 1989 to around 3.6 million tons. With decreasing revenues on world markets, falling production, and inefficient sugar mills that guzzle expensive oil, Castro had no choice but to shutter about half the island nation's mills.

With the remaining state-owned industrial dinosaurs wheezing away and the economy under immense strain, Castro opened up key state industries to non-Cuban investment. As a result, joint ventures became a key plank in the effort to prop up Cuba through limited economic reforms. The money came chiefly from Canada, Mexico, and Europe—all of whom benefited from the absence of Cuba's neighbor and nemesis, the United States, which has maintained a trade embargo against Cuba since 1960. Much of the investment occurred in another commodity that Cuba has to offer the world—nickel. Cuba holds 30 percent of the world's reserves of nickel, which is used in stainless steel and other alloys, and exports 75 percent of its nickel to Europe. One of the biggest mining firms active in Cuba today is Canada's Sherritt International Corporation (*www.sherritt.com*). Sherritt's flag flutters outside the island's biggest nickel mine, and Sherritt rigs are reviving output from old oil fields. After turning around the ailing nickel mine at Moa, Sherritt received Castro's go-ahead to develop beach resorts and beef up communications and transport networks.

Although international concerns like Sherritt are free to invest in Cuba, they face some harsh realities and restrictions. Although Castro allowed a bit of capitalism into his communist haven, he burdens it with complex and contradictory rules and regulations. And once foreigners begin to figure out the rules, the government changes them. "There are times when the Cubans seem to go out of their way to create obstacles," complained one European businessman. "They need us, we can do business here, so I don't understand what the problem is." By the remarks of Cuba's minister of foreign investment, Marta Lomas, it became clear the government was going to do little to help. "You know the rules when you get here," she said.

Ricardo Elizondo came to Cuba from Mexico to help manage his company's stake in ETECSA, Cuba's national telecommunications firm. Elizondo reports that anyone who wants to do business in Cuba must accept the reality of partnership with a socialist state. Cuba lacks a legal system to enforce commercial contracts; it lacks a banking system to offer credit; and there are no private-property

rights. One thing the governm[...] laws—and these are onerous. N[...] or even pay workers directly. Th[...] vide laborers who, in turn, ar[...] ments. For instance, Sherritt p[...] year per worker, according to human r[...] (*www.freedomhouse.org*). Yet the government then pays [...] only $120 to $144 per year.

Why do companies investing in Cuba put up with such restrictions? For one thing, they are getting a great return on their investment. "Cuba's assets are incredibly cheap, and the potential return is huge," says Frank Mersch, VP at Toronto's Altamira Management (*www.altamira.com*), which holds 11 percent of Sherritt. Castro, say analysts, is offering outsiders deals with rates of return up to 80 percent a year. Moreover, international investors tend to agree with the widespread belief that the Castro regime won't last very long. Once Castro loses his hold on Cuba, whether through capitulation, exile, or death, the United States will likely end its embargo. In that case, property prices will soar. Companies like Sherritt and ETECSA, who stepped in first, will have gained a valuable toehold in what could be a vibrant market economy.

Thinking Globally

1. Why do you think the Cuban government requires non-Cuban businesses to hire and pay workers only through the government? Do you think it is ethical for non-Cuban businesses to enter into partnerships with the Cuban government? Why or why not?

2. "See Cuba before Castro dies," is the chant of some young travelers reacting to reports that 75-year-old Fidel Castro is in poor health. Do some research on Cuba, and describe a scenario for economic transition in the event that the Castro regime collapses. How do you think that the transition to a market economy in Cuba would be the same as, or different from, the transitions now taking place in Russia and China?

3. Besides its trade embargo against Cuba, the United States also has enacted a law that permits U.S. companies to sue companies from other nations that traffic in the property of U.S. firms nationalized by Castro when he took over. The law also empowers the U.S. government to deny entry visas to the executives of such firms as well as their families. Why do you think the United States maintains such a hard line against doing business with Cuba? Do you think this embargo is in the United States' best interests? Why or why not?

learning objectives

After studying this chapter, you should be able to

1. Describe the relation between *international trade volume* and *world output*, and identify overall *trade patterns.*

2. Describe *mercantilism,* and explain its impact on the world powers and their colonies.

3. Explain *absolute advantage* and *comparative advantage* and identify their differences.

4. Explain the *factor proportions* and *international product life cycle* theories.

5. Explain the *new trade* and *national competitive advantage* theories.

international trade

Part 3 International Trade and Investment

5

a look **back**

CHAPTERS 2, 3, AND 4 examined cultural, political, legal, and economic differences between countries. We covered these differences early because of their important influence on international business activities.

a look at **this chapter**

This chapter begins our study of the international trade and investment environment. We explore the oldest form of international business activity—international trade. We discuss the benefits and volume of international trade and explore the major theories that attempt to explain why trade occurs.

a look **ahead**

CHAPTER 6 explains business–government trade relations. We explore both the motives and methods of government intervention in trade relations, and how the global trading system works to promote free trade.

A Zero-Sum Game?

BENTONVILLE, Arkansas — Wal-Mart (*www.walmart.com*) first became an international company in 1991 when it built a new store near Mexico City, Mexico. Today Wal-Mart has more than 1,300 stores in nine countries outside the United States. With more than $246 billion in sales globally, Wal-Mart is the world's largest company—yet based in a state in which chickens outnumber people.

Aggressive global expansion by Wal-Mart (and similar firms) is helping boost international trade. As it extends its reach around the world, Wal-Mart relies on its signature "Everyday Low Prices" policy to win over local customers everywhere. To fulfill its promise to deliver the lowest priced goods, the retail discounter sources inexpensive merchandise from low-cost production locations such as China. Wal-Mart accounts for 10 percent ($12 billion) of all Chinese goods entering the United States annually, and has played a big part in the tripling of Chinese imports to the U.S. over the past decade. The actions of Wal-Mart and other global firms have propelled world exports of goods and services to around $7.6 trillion.

Expanding international trade and globalization are causing growing interdependence between China and the rest of the world. Wal-Mart and other firms facing stiff price competition are quickly transforming China into the world's factory. Illustrating China's growing importance in international trade is a rate of trade growth that is around two to three times faster than trade growth for the rest of the world. In fact, 18 percent of Japan's imports come from China and about 12 percent of all goods imported by the United States are Chinese-made. Yet China today also buys more goods from other nations. From the United States, China imports everything from steel that feeds its booming construction industry to x-ray machines and other devices to improve its health care.

As you read this chapter, think about why nations trade in the first place, and how the ambitions of firms such as Wal-Mart are continuing to drive growing world trade.[1]

Today, people around the world are accustomed to purchasing goods and services from companies in other countries. In fact, many consumers get their first taste of another country's culture through merchandise purchased from that country. Chanel No. 5 (*www.chanel.com*) perfume evokes the romanticism of France. The fine artwork on Imari porcelain conveys the Japanese attention to detail and quality. And American Eagle jeans (*www.ae.com*) portray the casual lifestyle of people in the United States.

In this chapter, we explore international trade in goods and services. We begin by examining the benefits, volume, and patterns of international trade. We then explore a number of important theories that attempt to explain why nations trade with one another.

Overview of International Trade

international trade
Purchase, sale, or exchange of goods and services across national borders.

The purchase, sale, or exchange of goods and services across national borders is called **international trade**. This is in contrast to domestic trade, which occurs between different states, regions, or cities within a country.

Over the past decade, a majority of the world's economies have seen an increase in the importance of trade. One way to measure the importance of trade to a nation is to examine

MAP 5.1

The Importance of Trade

This map shows each nation's trade volume as a share of its gross domestic product (GDP). Trade as a share of GDP is defined as follows: The sum of exports and imports (of both goods and services) measured as a share of GDP. (Reminder: GDP is the value of all goods and services produced by a domestic economy over a one-year period.)

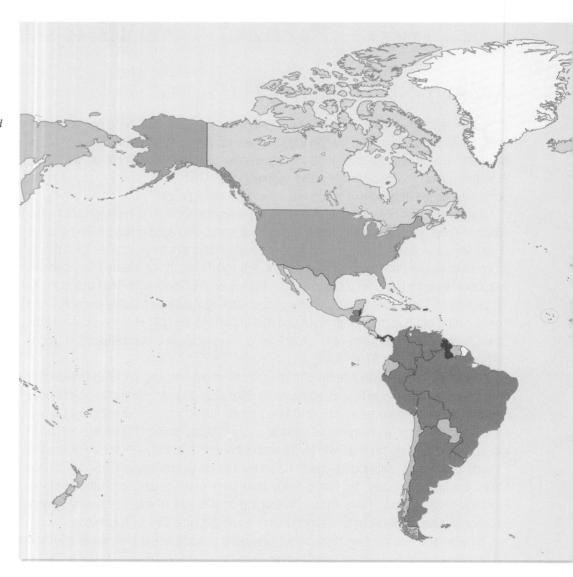

the volume of an economy's trade relative to its total output. As Map 5.1 demonstrates, the value of trade passing through some nations' borders actually exceeds the amount of goods and services that they produce (the "100.1% and up" category).

Benefits of International Trade

International trade is opening doors to new entrepreneurial opportunity across the globe. It also provides a country's people with a greater choice of goods and services. For example, because Finland has a cool climate, it cannot be expected to grow cotton. But it can sell paper and other products made from lumber (which it has in abundance) to the United States. Finland can then use the proceeds from the sale of products derived from lumber to buy Pima cotton from the United States. Thus, people in Finland get cotton they would otherwise not have. Likewise, although the United States has vast forests, the wood-based products from Finland might be of a certain quality that fills a gap in the U.S. marketplace.

International trade is an important engine for job creation in many countries. The Department of Commerce of the United States (*www.doc.gov*) estimates that for every $1 billion increase in exports, 22,800 jobs are created in the country.[2] Moreover, it is estimated that 12 million U.S. jobs depend on exports and that these jobs pay on average from 13 to

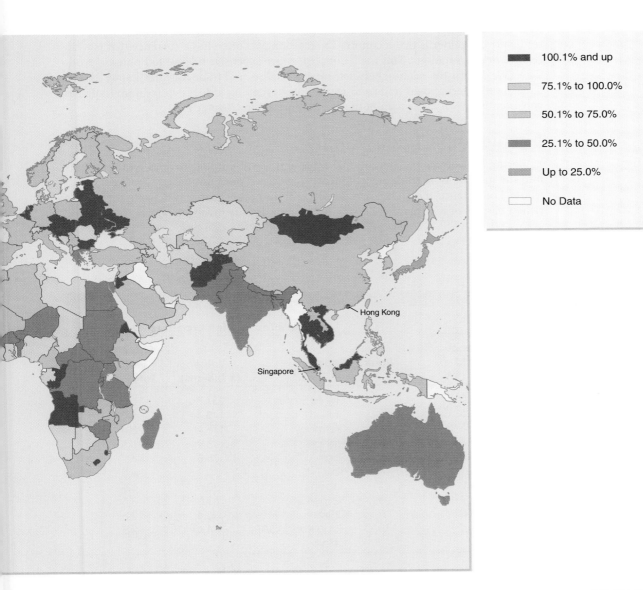

■	100.1% and up
	75.1% to 100.0%
	50.1% to 75.0%
■	25.1% to 50.0%
	Up to 25.0%
☐	No Data

18 percent more than those not related to international trade.[3] Expanded trade often benefits other countries similarly.

Volume of International Trade

The value and volume of international trade continues to increase. Today, world merchandise exports are roughly $6.1 trillion and service exports are approaching the $1.5 trillion mark. Table 5.1 shows the world's largest exporters of merchandise and services. Perhaps not surprisingly, the United States dominates the rest of the world in the export of both merchandise and commercial services.

Most of world merchandise trade is comprised of trade in manufactured goods. The dominance of manufactured goods in the trade of merchandise has persisted over time and will likely continue to do so. The reason is its growth is much faster than trade in the two other classifications of merchandise—mining and agricultural products. Although the importance of trade in services is growing for many nations, it tends to be relatively more important for the world's richest countries. Trade in services accounts for around 20 percent of total world trade.

Trade and World Output The level of world output in any given year influences the level of international trade in that year. Slower world economic output slows the volume of international trade, and higher output propels greater trade. Trade slows in times of economic recession because when people are less certain about their own financial futures they buy fewer domestic and imported products. Another reason output and trade move together is that a country in recession also often has a currency that is weak relative to other nations. This makes imports more expensive relative to domestic products. (We discuss the relation between currency values and trade fully in Chapter 10.) In addition to international trade and world output moving in lockstep fashion, trade has consistently grown faster than output (see Figure 1.2 in Chapter 1).

International Trade Patterns

Exploring the volume of international trade and world output provides useful insights into the international trade environment. However, it does not tell us who trades with whom. For instance, it does not reveal whether trade occurs primarily between the world's richest nations or whether there is significant trade activity involving poorer nations.

TABLE 5.1

World's Top Exporters

World's Top Merchandise Exporters				World's Top Service Exporters			
Rank	Exporter	Value ($ billions)	Share of World Total (%)	Rank	Exporter	Value ($ billions)	Share of World Total (%)
1	Germany	748.3	10.0	1	United States	287.7	16.0
2	United States	723.8	9.6	2	United Kingdom	143.4	8.0
3	Japan	471.8	6.3	3	Germany	115.6	6.4
4	China	437.9	5.8	4	France	98.9	5.5
5	France	386.7	5.2	5	Spain	76.3	4.2
6	United Kingdom	304.6	4.1	6	Italy	72.7	4.0
7	Netherlands	294.1	3.9	7	Japan	70.6	3.9
8	Italy	292.1	3.9	8	Netherlands	63.0	3.5
9	Canada	272.7	3.6	9	China	46.4	2.6
10	Belgium	255.3	3.4	10	Hong Kong, (SAR) China	44.6	2.5

Customs agencies in most countries record the destination of exports, the source of imports, and the physical quantities and values of goods crossing their borders. Although this type of data is revealing, it is sometimes misleading. For example, governments sometimes deliberately distort the reporting of trade in military equipment or other sensitive goods. In other cases, extensive trade in underground economies (black markets) can distort the real picture of trade between nations. Nevertheless, customs data tend to reflect general trade patterns among nations rather well.

Large ocean-going cargo vessels are needed to support these patterns in international trade and deliver merchandise from one shore to another. In fact, Greek and Japanese merchant ships own over 30 percent of the world's total capacity (measured in tons shipped, or tonnage) of merchant ships. As a whole, the developing countries' share of the total is rising and today stands at nearly 20 percent.[4] Figure 5.1 lists the top 10 countries that own the greatest share of the world's shipping capacity (and the portion of each national fleet that sails under the flags of other nations).

Who Trades with Whom?

Not surprisingly, a broad pattern of merchandise trade among the world's nations tends to persist. Trade between the world's high-income economies accounts for roughly 60 percent of total world merchandise trade. Two-way trade between high-income countries and low- and middle-income nations accounts for about 34 percent of world merchandise trade. Meanwhile, merchandise trade between low- and middle-income nations accounts for only about 6 percent of total world trade. These figures reveal the low purchasing power of the world's poorest nations and indicate their general lack of economic development.

Table 5.2 shows trade data for the major regions of the world economy. The number representing intraregional exports for Western Europe (which is at the intersection of the row and column titled "Western Europe") immediately stands out. This number tells us that nearly $1.8 trillion (over 67 percent) of Western Europe's exports are destined for other nations in Western Europe. In contrast, intraregional exports account for 49 percent of all exports in Asia and 40 percent of exports in North America. These data underscore the rationale behind, and results of, efforts toward European regional integration called the European Union—discussed fully in Chapter 8.

Data in the table also reveal why headlines in the United States often complain that Asia's markets are not open to goods from North America. The value of North American exports to Asia, $204 billion, is only slightly more than half the value of Asian exports to North America, $394 billion. But as economies across Asia develop, these figures should

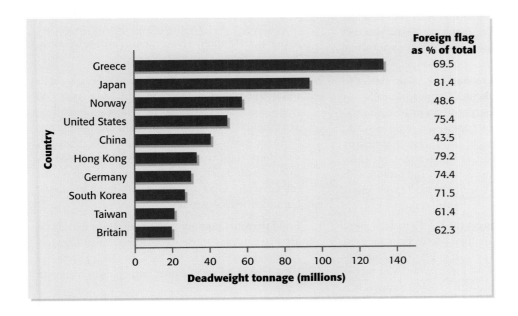

FIGURE 5.1

Who Owns the High Seas?

World trade requires large merchant fleets of ships to deliver merchandise from one shore to another. The top 10 countries that own the greatest share of the world total shipping capacity are shown.

	Destination							
Origin	North America	Latin America	Western Europe	C.E./Europe/ Baltic States/CIS	Africa	Middle East	Asia	World
North America	404	153	180	8	12	20	219	997
Latin America	218	59	51	4	5	4	29	378
Western Europe	298	57	2,130	214	80	83	248	3,145
C./E. Europe/ Baltic States/CIS	19	7	228	98	4	9	30	401
Africa	33	4	84	1	18	3	31	173
Middle East	46	3	48	2	10	22	145	299
Asia	428	41	319	32	31	56	949	1,901
World	1,446	324	3,041	360	161	198	1,651	7,294

TABLE 5.2

Intra- and Inter-Regional Merchandise Trade (U.S. $ billions)

adjust to reflect their greater purchasing power. Some economists call this century the "Pacific century," referring to the expected future growth of Asian economies and the resulting shift in trade flows from the Atlantic Ocean to the Pacific. As these nations' economies grow, it will become increasingly important for managers to fully understand how to do business in Asia. See this chapter's Global Manager's Toolbox titled, "Building

global manager's TOOLBOX

Building Good Relations in the Pacific Rim

To do business in Pacific Rim countries (those that rim the Pacific Ocean in Asia), start by recognizing two facts: (1) Asian customers can be as diverse as their individual cultures, and (2) aggressive salesmanship doesn't work in the land of the "four tigers." Cultural nuances and business etiquette demand a little homework before you visit these countries. Some general rules apply, however. Here are five:

1. **Count on third-party contacts.** Asians prefer to do business with people they know. Cold calls—in which you call a company with no prior contact—and other direct-contact methods seldom work. Meeting the right people in an Asian company almost always depends on having the right introduction. Use a proper intermediary. If the person with whom you hope to do business respects your intermediary, chances are he or she will respect you.

2. **Carry a bilingual business card.** To make a good first impression, have bilingual cards printed, even though many Asians speak English—the international language of business. It shows both respect for the language and commitment to doing business in a particular country. It also translates your title into

the local language. Asians generally are not comfortable until they know your position and whom you represent.

3. **Leave the hard sell at home.** Asian businesspeople are tough negotiators, but they dislike argumentative exchanges. Harmony and consensus are the bywords. Be prepared to be patient but firm.

4. **Go easy with legalese.** Legal documents are not as important as personal relationships. Most Asians do not like detailed contracts and will often insist that agreements be left flexible so that adjustments can be made easily to fit changing circumstances. It's very important to foster good relations based on mutual trust and benefit. The importance of a contract in many Asian societies is not what it stipulates, but rather who signed it.

5. **Build personal rapport.** Social ease and friendship are prerequisites to doing business. Accept invitations and be sure to reciprocate. As much business is transacted in informal dinner settings as in corporate settings.

Good Relations in the Pacific Rim" for some pointers on doing business in Pacific Rim nations.

Trade Dependence and Independence

All countries fall on a continuum of trade interdependencies, with total dependence on another country at one end, and total independence from other countries at the other. Complete independence was considered desirable from the sixteenth century through much of the eighteenth. Some remote island nations were completely independent simply because they lacked methods of transportation to engage in trade. However, today this is far less common, and isolationism is generally considered undesirable.

Effect on Developing and Transition Nations
Developing and transition nations that share borders with developed countries are often dependent on their wealthier neighbors. Trade dependency has been a blessing for many central and eastern European nations. A large number of joint ventures now bridge the borders between Germany and its neighbors—Germany has more than 6,000 joint ventures in Hungary alone. Germany also is the single-most important trading partner of the central and eastern European nations that in 2004 joined the European Union (*www.europa.eu.int*). To gain an advantage over the competition, German firms are combining German technology with relatively low-cost labor in Central and Eastern Europe. For instance, Opel (*www.opel.com*), the German arm of General Motors Corporation (*www.gm.com*), built a $440 million plant in Szentgotthard, Hungary, to make parts for and assemble its Astra hatchbacks destined for export.

Dangers of Trade Dependency
Trade dependency can be dangerous. If the nation that is depended on experiences economic recession or political turmoil, the dependent nation can experience serious economic problems. Trade dependency is causing concern today in Mexico. For the past 25 years, Mexico has seen rising investment by U.S. companies, assembling products such as refrigerators, calculators, laptop computers, and mobile phones. Since the free trade agreement (NAFTA) between Canada, Mexico, and the United States came into effect in 1994, Mexico's exports have tripled and inward investment has totaled $85 billion. But poor education, rampant corruption, red tape, relatively high taxes compared to similar markets, and an outdated infrastructure are forcing some companies to abandon Mexico for locations in Asia and Europe—leaving many unemployed in their wake. Mexico's garment industry recently lost 22,000 jobs,

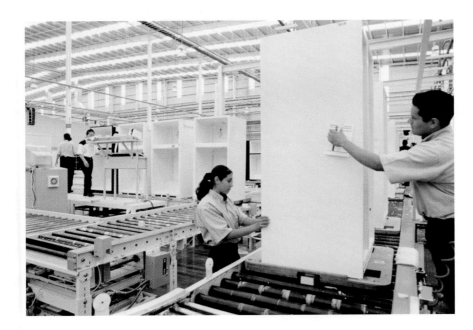

Shown here, employees in Mexico churn out all of General Electric's gas ranges and most of its electric stoves sold in the United States. For over 25 years, companies flocked to Mexico to set up assembly plants that brought jobs to ordinary Mexicans. But today some companies are moving production of price-sensitive goods to cheaper locations, such as China. As a result, Mexico is experiencing some negative aspects of its dependence on U.S. trade. Do you know of specific companies that are moving out of Mexico for cost reasons?

many of them going to China and the Caribbean. Thus, although trade dependency was a blessing for Mexico for many years, it may now feel the pain as some companies shift jobs out of the country.[5]

Balance Between Dependence and Independence   Today trade between most nations is characterized by a certain degree of interdependency. Companies in the developed countries do a great deal of business with those in other developed nations. In addition, the level of interdependency between certain pairs of countries often reflects the amount of trade that occurs between a company's subsidiaries in the two nations. For example, transactions between subsidiaries of international companies account for about one-third of U.S. exports and about two-fifths of U.S. imports. The Mercedes-Benz (*www.mercedes.com*) plant in Tuscaloosa, Alabama, imports most of its components for production of its Mercedes-Benz sport utility vehicle from Germany. The completed vehicle is then sent back to Germany or to affiliates in other countries.

Quick Study

1. What portion of world trade occurs in: a) merchandise, and b) services?
2. What is the relation between trade and world output?
3. Describe the broad pattern of *international trade*.
4. Why is a nation's level of trade dependence or independence important?

Theories of International Trade

Trade between different groups of people has occurred for many thousands of years. But it was not until the fifteenth century that people tried to explain why trade occurs and how trade can benefit both parties to an exchange. Figure 5.2 shows a timeline of when the main theories of international trade were proposed. Today, efforts to refine existing trade theories and to develop new ones continue. Let's now discuss the first theory that attempts to explain why nations should engage in international trade—*mercantilism*.

mercantilism
Trade theory that nations should accumulate financial wealth, usually in the form of gold, by encouraging exports and discouraging imports.

Mercantilism

The trade theory that nations should accumulate financial wealth, usually in the form of gold, by encouraging exports and discouraging imports is called **mercantilism**. It states

FIGURE 5.2

Trade Theory Timeline

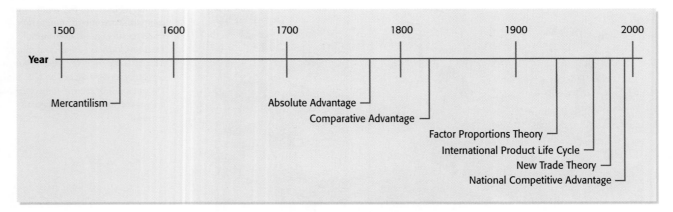

that other measures of a nation's well-being, such as living standards or human development, are irrelevant. Nation-states in Europe followed this economic philosophy from about 1500 to the late 1700s. The most prominent mercantilist nations included Britain, France, The Netherlands, Portugal, and Spain.

How Mercantilism Worked
When navigation was a fairly new science, Europeans explored the world by sea, claiming the lands they encountered in the name of the European monarchy that was financing their voyage. Early exploration led them to Africa, Asia, and North, South, and Central America, where they established colonies. Colonial trade was conducted for the benefit of mother countries, and colonies were generally treated as exploitable resources.

In recent times, former colonies have struggled to diminish their reliance on the former colonial powers. For example, in an effort to decrease their dependence on their former colonial powers, African nations are welcoming trade relationships with partners from Asia and North America. But because of geographic proximity, the European Union is still often preferred as a trading partner.

Just how did countries implement mercantilism? The practice of mercantilism rested upon three essential pillars: *trade surpluses*, *government intervention*, and *colonization*. Let's take a brief look at each of these.

Trade Surpluses   Nations believed they could increase their wealth by maintaining a **trade surplus**—the condition that results when the value of a nation's exports is greater than the value of its imports. In mercantilism, a trade surplus meant that a country was taking in more gold on the sale of its exports than it was paying out for its imports. A **trade deficit** is the opposite condition—one that results when the value of a country's imports is greater than the value of its exports. In mercantilism, trade deficits were to be avoided at all costs. (We discuss the importance of national trade balance more fully in Chapter 7.)

Government Intervention   National governments actively intervened in international trade to maintain a trade surplus. According to mercantilism, the accumulation of wealth depended on increasing a nation's trade surplus, not necessarily expanding its total value or volume of trade. The governments of mercantilist nations did this by either banning certain imports or imposing various restrictions on them, such as tariffs or quotas. At the same time, they subsidized home-based industries to expand exports. Governments also typically outlawed the removal of their gold and silver to other nations.

Colonization   Mercantilist nations acquired less-developed territories (colonies) around the world to serve as sources of inexpensive raw materials and as markets for higher-priced finished goods. Colonies were the source of many essential raw materials, including tea, sugar, tobacco, rubber, and cotton. These resources would be shipped to the mercantilist nation, where they were incorporated into finished goods such as clothing, cigars, and other products. These finished goods would then be sold to the colonies. Trade between mercantilist countries and their colonies were a huge source of profits for the mercantilist powers. The colonies received low prices for basic raw materials but paid high prices for finished goods.

The mercantilist and colonial policies greatly expanded the wealth of the nations using them. This wealth allowed nations to build armies and navies to control their far-flung colonial empires and to protect their shipping lanes from attack by other nations. It was a source of a nation's economic power that in turn increased its political power relative to other countries. Today, countries seen by others as trying to maintain a trade surplus and expanding their national treasuries at the expense of other nations are accused of practicing *neo-mercantilism* or *economic nationalism*. Fairly or not, Japan has often been accused of practicing neo-mercantilism because of its consistently high trade surplus with several industrial nations—particularly the United States. Also, France's trading partners have labeled it neo-mercantilist for trying to export its way out of past economic difficulties.

trade surplus
Condition that results when the value of a nation's exports is greater than the value of its imports.

trade deficit
Condition that results when the value of a country's imports is greater than the value of its exports.

Flaws of Mercantilism   Despite its seemingly positive benefits for any nation implementing it, mercantilism is inherently flawed. Mercantilist nations believed that the world's wealth was limited and that a nation could increase its share of the pie only at the expense of its neighbors—called a *zero-sum game*. The main problem with mercantilism is that if all nations were to barricade their markets from imports and push their exports onto others, international trade would be severely restricted. In fact, trade in all nonessential goods would likely cease altogether.

In addition, paying colonies little for their exports but charging them high prices for their imports impaired their economic development. Thus, their appeal as markets for goods was less than it would have been if they were allowed to accumulate greater wealth. These negative aspects of mercantilism were made apparent by a trade theory developed in the late 1700s—*absolute advantage*.

Quick Study

1. How did *mercantilism* work? Identify its three essential pillars.

2. What types of policies might a country have in place to be called neo-mercantilist?

3. Describe the main flaws of mercantilism. What is meant by the term *zero-sum game*?

Absolute Advantage

absolute advantage
Ability of a nation to produce a good more efficiently than any other nation.

Scottish economist Adam Smith first put forth the trade theory of absolute advantage in 1776.[6] The ability of a nation to produce a good more efficiently than any other nation is called an **absolute advantage**. In other words, a nation with an absolute advantage can produce a greater output of a good or service than other nations using the same amount of, or fewer, resources.

Among other things, Smith reasoned that international trade should not be banned or restricted by tariffs and quotas, but allowed to flow according to market forces. If people in different countries were able to trade as they saw fit, no country would need to produce all the goods it consumed. Instead, a country could concentrate on producing the goods in which it holds an absolute advantage. It could then trade with other nations to obtain the goods it needed but did not produce.

Suppose professional golfer Tiger Woods needs to install a hot tub in his family's home during the PGA Tour season. Should he do the job himself or hire a professional installer to do it for him? Suppose Woods (who has never installed a hot tub before) would have to take 1 month off from playing golf and forgo roughly $800,000 in salary to complete the job. On the other hand, the professional installer (who does not play professional golf) can complete the job for $10,000 and do it in two weeks. Whereas Woods has an absolute advantage in playing professional golf, the installer has an absolute advantage in installing hot tubs. It takes Woods 1 month to do the job the installer can do in two weeks. Thus, Woods should hire the professional to install the hot tub to save himself both time and money resources.

Let's now apply the absolute advantage concept to an example of two trading countries to see how trade can increase production and consumption in both nations.

Case: Riceland and Tealand

Suppose that we live in a world of just two countries (Riceland and Tealand), two products (rice and tea), and transporting goods between these two countries costs nothing. Riceland and Tealand currently produce and consume their own rice and tea. The table below shows the number of units of resources (labor) each country expends in creating rice and tea. In Riceland, just one resource unit is needed to produce a ton of rice, but five units of resources are needed to produce a ton of tea. In Tealand, six units of resources are needed to produce a ton of rice, whereas three units are needed to produce a ton of tea.

	Rice	Tea
Riceland	1	5
Tealand	6	3

Another way of stating each nation's efficiency in the production of rice and tea is:

- In Riceland, 1 unit of resources = 1 ton of rice *or* 1/5 ton of tea
- In Tealand, 1 unit of resources = 1/6 ton of rice *or* 1/3 ton of tea

These numbers also tell us one other thing about rice and tea production in these two countries. Because one unit of resources produces 1 ton of rice in Riceland compared with Tealand's output of only 1/6 ton of rice, Riceland has an absolute advantage in rice production—it is the more efficient rice producer. However, because one resource unit produces 1/3 ton of tea in Tealand compared to Riceland's output of just 1/5 ton, Tealand has an absolute advantage in tea production.

Gains from Specialization and Trade   Suppose now that Riceland specializes in rice production to maximize the output of rice in our two-country world. Likewise, Tealand specializes in tea production to maximize world output of tea. Although each country now specializes and world output increases, both countries face a problem. Riceland can consume only its rice production and Tealand can consume only its tea production. The problem can be solved if the two countries trade with each other to obtain the good that it needs but does not produce.

Suppose that Riceland and Tealand agree to trade rice and tea on a one-to-one basis—a ton of rice costs a ton of tea and vice versa. Thus, Riceland can produce 1 extra ton of rice with an additional resource unit and trade with Tealand to get 1 ton of tea. This is a lot better than the 1/5 ton of tea that Riceland would have gotten by investing that additional resource unit in making tea for itself. Thus, Riceland definitely benefits from the trade. Likewise, Tealand can produce 1/3 extra ton of tea with an additional resource unit and trade with Riceland to get 1/3 ton of rice. This is twice as much as the 1/6 ton of rice it could have produced using that additional resource unit to make its own rice. Thus, Tealand also benefits from the trade. The gains resulting from this simple trade are shown in Figure 5.3.

Although Tealand does not gain as much as Riceland does from the trade, it does get more rice than it would without trade. The gains from trade for actual countries would depend on the total number of resources each country had at its disposal. Another important determinant of the actual benefits from trade is the demand for each good in each country.

As this example shows, the theory of absolute advantage destroys the mercantilist idea that international trade is a zero-sum game. Instead, because there are gains to be had by both

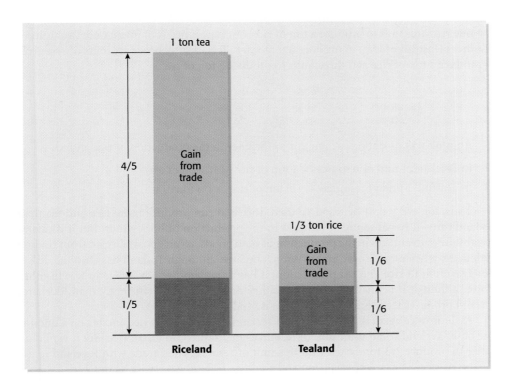

FIGURE 5.3

Gains from Specialization and Trade: Absolute Advantage

countries party to an exchange, international trade is a *positive-sum game*. The theory also calls into question the objective of national governments to acquire wealth through restrictive trade policies. It argues that nations should instead open their doors to trade so their people can obtain a greater quantity of goods more cheaply. Thus, the theory does not measure a nation's wealth by how much gold and silver it has on reserve, but by the living standards of its people.

Despite the power of the theory of absolute advantage in showing the gains from trade, there is one potential problem. What happens if one country does not hold an absolute advantage in the production of any product? Are there still benefits to trade, and will trade even occur? To answer these questions, let's take a look at an extension of absolute advantage, the theory of *comparative advantage.*

Comparative Advantage

An English economist named David Ricardo developed the theory of comparative advantage in 1817.[7] He proposed that if one country (in our example of a two-country world) held absolute advantages in the production of both products, specialization and trade could still benefit both countries. A country has a **comparative advantage** when it is unable to produce a good more efficiently than other nations, but produces the good more efficiently than it does any other good. In other words, *trade is still beneficial even if one country is less efficient in the production of two goods, as long as it is less inefficient in the production of one of the goods.*

Let's return to our hot-tub example. Now suppose that Tiger Woods has previously installed many hot tubs and can do the job in one week—twice as fast as the hot tub installer. Thus, Tiger Woods now holds absolute advantages in both golf and hot tub installation. Although the professional installer is at an absolute disadvantage in both hot tub installation and golf, he is less inefficient in hot tub installation. However, despite his absolute advantage in both areas, Woods would still have to give up $200,000 to take time off from playing golf to complete the work. Is this a wise decision? No. Woods should hire the professional installer. The installer earns money he would not earn if Woods did the job himself, and Woods earns more money continuing to play golf than he would save if he installed the hot tub himself.

Gains from Specialization and Trade   To see how the theory of comparative advantage works with international trade, let's return to our example of Riceland and Tealand. In our earlier discussion, Riceland had an absolute advantage in rice production and Tealand had an absolute advantage in tea production. Suppose that Riceland now holds absolute advantages in the production of both rice *and* tea. The table below shows the number of units of resources each country now expends in creating rice and tea. Riceland still needs to expend just one resource unit to produce a ton of rice, but now it needs to invest only two units of resources (instead of five) to produce a ton of tea. Tealand still needs six units of resources to produce a ton of rice and three units to produce a ton of tea.

	Rice	Tea
Riceland	1	2
Tealand	6	3

Another way of stating each nation's efficiency in the production of rice and tea is:

- ❍ In Riceland, 1 unit of resources = 1 ton of rice *or* 1/2 ton of tea
- ❍ In Tealand, 1 unit of resources = 1/6 ton of rice *or* 1/3 ton of tea

Thus, for every unit of resource used, Riceland can produce more rice and tea than Tealand can—it has absolute advantages in the production of both goods. But if Riceland has absolute advantages in the production of both goods, it can't possibly gain from trading with a less-efficient producer, right? Wrong, because although Tealand has absolute disadvantages in both rice and tea production, it has a *comparative* advantage in tea. In other words, although it is unable to produce either rice or tea more efficiently than Riceland, Tealand produces tea more efficiently than it produces rice.

Assume once again that Riceland and Tealand decide to trade rice and tea on a one-to-one basis. Tealand could use 1 unit of resources to produce 1/6 ton of rice. But it would do better to produce 1/3 ton of tea with this unit of resources and trade with Riceland to get 1/3 ton of rice. Thus, by specializing and trading, Tealand gets twice as much rice than it

comparative advantage
Inability of a nation to produce a good more efficiently than other nations, but an ability to produce that good more efficiently than it does any other good.

FIGURE 5.4

Gains from Specialization and Trade: Comparative Advantage

could if it were to produce the rice itself. There are also gains from trade for Riceland despite its dual absolute advantages. Riceland could invest one unit of resources in the production of 1/2 ton of tea. However, it would do better to produce one ton of rice with the one unit of resources and trade that rice for one ton of tea. Thus, Riceland gets twice as much tea through trade than if it were to produce the tea itself. This is in spite of the fact that it is a more efficient producer of tea than Tealand.

The benefits for each country from this simple trade are shown in Figure 5.4. Again, the benefits from trade for actual countries depends on the amount of resources at their disposal and each market's desired level of consumption of each product.

Assumptions and Limitations Throughout the discussion of absolute and comparative advantage, we made several important assumptions that limit the real-world application of the theories. First, we assumed that countries are driven only by the maximization of production and consumption. This is often not the case. In fact, governments of most nations involve themselves in international trade issues out of a concern for workers or consumers. (The role of government in international trade is discussed in detail in Chapter 6.)

Second, the theories assume that there are only two countries engaged in the production and consumption of just two goods. This is obviously not the situation that exists in the real world. There currently are more than 180 countries and literally a countless number of products being produced, traded, and consumed worldwide.

Third, it is assumed that there are no costs for transporting traded goods from one country to another. In reality, transportation costs are a major expense of international trade for some products. If transportation costs for a good are higher than the savings generated through specialization, trade will not occur.

Fourth, the theories consider labor the only kind of resource for the production process because labor accounted for a very large portion of the total production cost of most goods at the time the theories were developed. Moreover, it is assumed that resources are mobile within each nation but cannot be transferred between them. Labor, and especially natural resources, can be difficult and costly to transfer between nations. However, this is definitely changing. For example, people from a nation that belongs to the European Union are allowed to live and work in any other member nation.

Finally, it is assumed that specialization in the production of one particular good does not result in gains in efficiency. But we know that specialization results in increased knowledge of a task and perhaps even future improvements in how that task is performed. Thus, the amount of resources needed to produce a specific amount of a good should decrease over time.

Despite the assumptions made in the theory of comparative advantage, research reveals that it appears to be supported by a substantial body of evidence.[8] Nevertheless, economic researchers continue to develop and test new theories to explain the international purchase and sale of products. Let's now examine one of these, the theory of *factor proportions*.

Quick Study

1. What is meant by the term *absolute advantage*? Describe how it works using a numerical example.
2. What is meant by the term *comparative advantage*? How does it differ from an absolute advantage?
3. Explain why countries can gain from trade even without having an absolute advantage.

Factor Proportions Theory

In the early 1900s, an international trade theory emerged that focused attention on the proportion (supply) of resources in a nation. The cost of any resource is simply the result of supply and demand: Factors in great supply relative to demand will be less costly than factors in short supply relative to demand. **Factor proportions theory** states that countries produce and export goods that require resources (factors) that are abundant and import goods that require resources in short supply.[9] The theory resulted from the research of two economists, Eli Heckscher and Bertil Ohlin, and is therefore sometimes called the Heckscher–Ohlin theory.

factor proportions theory
Trade theory holding that countries produce and export goods that require resources (factors) that are abundant and import goods that require resources in short supply.

Factor proportions theory differs considerably from the theory of comparative advantage. Recall that the theory of comparative advantage states that a country specializes in producing the good that it can produce more efficiently than any other good. Thus, the focus of the theory (and absolute advantage as well) is on the *productivity* of the production process for a particular good. In contrast, factor proportions theory says that a country specializes in producing and exporting goods using the factors of production that are most *abundant*, and thus *cheapest*—not the goods in which it is most productive.

Labor Versus Land and Capital Equipment
Factor proportions theory breaks a nation's resources into two categories: labor on the one hand, land and capital equipment on the other. It predicts that a country will specialize in products that require labor if the cost of labor is low relative to the cost of land and capital. Alternatively, a country will specialize in products that require land and capital equipment if their cost is low relative to the cost of labor.

Factor proportions theory is conceptually appealing. For example, Australia has a great deal of land (nearly 60 percent of which is meadows and pastures) and a small population relative to its size. Australia's exports consist largely of mined minerals, grain, beef, lamb, and dairy products—products that require a great deal of land and natural resources. Australia's imports, on the other hand, consist mostly of manufactured raw materials, capital equipment, and consumer goods—things needed in capital-intensive mining and modern agriculture. But instead of looking only at anecdotal evidence, let's see how well factor proportions theory stands up to scientific testing.

Evidence on Factor Proportions Theory: The Leontief Paradox
Despite its conceptual appeal, factor proportions theory is not supported by studies that examine the trade flows of nations. The first large-scale study to document such evidence was performed by a researcher named Wassily Leontief in the early 1950s.[10] Leontief tested whether the United States, which uses an abundance of capital equipment, exports goods requiring capital-intensive production and imports goods requiring labor-intensive production. Contrary to the predictions of the factor proportions theory, his research found that U.S. exports require more labor-intensive production than its imports. This apparent paradox between the predictions using the theory and the actual trade flows is called the *Leontief*

paradox. Leontief's findings are supported by more recent research on the trade data of a large number of countries.

What might account for the paradox? One possible explanation is that factor proportions theory considers a country's production factors to be homogeneous—particularly labor. But we know that labor skills vary greatly within a country—more highly skilled workers emerge from training and development programs. When expenditures on improving the skills of labor are taken into account, the theory seems to be supported by actual trade data. Further studies examining international trade data will help us better understand what reasons actually account for the Leontief paradox.

Because of the drawbacks of each of the international trade theories mentioned so far, researchers continue to propose new ones. Let's now examine a theory that attempts to explain international trade on the basis of the life cycle of products.

International Product Life Cycle

Raymond Vernon put forth an international trade theory for manufactured goods in the mid-1960s. His **international product life cycle theory** says that a company will begin by exporting its product and later undertake foreign direct investment as the product moves through its life cycle. The theory also says that for a number of reasons a country's export eventually becomes its import.[11]

Although Vernon developed his model around the United States, we can generalize it today to apply to any of the developed and innovative markets of the world, such as Australia, the European Union, Japan, and North America. Let's now examine how his theory attempts to explain international trade flows.

Stages of the Product Life Cycle   International product life cycle theory follows the path of a good through its life cycle (from new to maturing to standardized product) to determine where it will be produced (see Figure 5.5). In the *new product stage*, stage 1, the high purchasing power and demand of buyers in an industrialized country spur a company to design and introduce a new product concept. Because the exact level of demand in the domestic market is highly uncertain at this point, the company keeps its production volume low and based in the home country. Keeping production where initial research and development occurred and staying in contact with customers allows managers to monitor buyer preferences and to modify the product as needed. Although initially there is virtually no export market, exports do begin to pick up late in the new product stage.

In the *maturing product stage,* stage 2, the domestic market and markets abroad become fully aware of the existence of the product and its benefits. Demand rises and is sustained over a fairly lengthy period of time. As exports begin to account for an increasingly greater share of total product sales, the innovating company introduces production facilities in the countries with the highest demand. Near the end of the maturity stage, the

international product life cycle theory
Theory holding that a company will begin by exporting its product and later undertake foreign direct investment as the product moves through its life cycle.

FIGURE 5.5

International Product Life Cycle

product begins generating sales in developing nations, and perhaps some manufacturing presence is established there.

In the *standardized product stage,* stage 3, competition from other companies selling similar products pressures companies to lower prices in order to maintain sales levels. As the market becomes more price-sensitive, the company begins searching aggressively for low-cost production bases in developing nations to supply a growing worldwide market. Furthermore, as most production now takes place outside the innovating country, demand in the innovating country is supplied with imports from developing countries and other industrialized nations. Late in this stage, domestic production might even cease altogether.

Limitations of the Theory
Vernon developed his theory at a time when most of the new products being developed in the world were originating and being sold first in the United States. One reason U.S. companies were strong globally in the 1960s was that their domestic production bases were not destroyed during the Second World War, as was the case in Europe (and to some extent Japan). In addition, during the war the production of many durable goods in the United States, including automobiles, was shifted to the production of military transportation and weaponry. This laid the foundation for an enormous post-war demand for new capital-intensive consumer goods, such as autos and home appliances. Furthermore, advances in technology that were originally developed with military purposes in mind were integrated into consumer goods. A wide range of new and innovative products like televisions, photocopiers, and computers, met the seemingly insatiable appetite of consumers in the United States.

Thus, the theory seemed to explain world trade patterns quite well when the United States dominated world trade. But today its ability to depict the trade flows of nations accurately is weak. The United States is no longer the sole innovator of products in the world. New products seem to be springing up everywhere as the research and development activities of companies continue to globalize.

Furthermore, companies today design new products and make product modifications at a very quick pace. The result is quicker product obsolescence and a situation in which companies "cannibalize" their existing products with new product introductions. This is forcing companies to introduce products in many markets simultaneously to recoup a product's research and development costs before its sales decline and it is dropped from the product line. The theory has a difficult time explaining the resulting trade patterns.

In fact, older theories might better explain today's global trade patterns. Much production in the world today more closely resembles what is predicted by the theory of comparative advantage. Boeing's (*www.boeing.com*) assembly plant in Everett, Washington, constructs its wide-body aircraft—the 747, 767, and 777. The shop floor has wooden crates marked "Belfast, Ireland" containing nose landing-gear doors. On a metal rack, there is a stack of outboard wing flaps from Italy. The entire fuselage of the 777 has traveled in quarter sections from Japan. Its wing tip assembly comes from Korea, its rudders from Australia, and so on.[12] This pattern resembles the theory of comparative advantage in that a product's components are made in the country that can produce them at a high level of productivity. Components are later assembled in a chosen location.

Finally, the theory is challenged by the fact that more companies are operating in international markets from their inception.[13] Many small companies are teaming up with companies in other markets to develop new products or production technologies. This strategy is particularly effective for small companies that would otherwise be unable to participate in international production or sales. Ingenico of France (*www.ingenico.com*) is now the number one world supplier of secure transaction systems, including terminals and their associated software. But the company began small and worked with a global network of entrepreneurs scattered around the world, who acted as Ingenico's agents by giving the company a local face and helping it to conquer local markets. Managing Director Gerard Compain explained the usefulness of its global network, "These people know their countries better than we do. And they know how to design and sell products for those markets."[14] The Internet also makes it easier for a small company to reach a global audience from its inception. For a discussion of several pitfalls small companies can avoid in fulfilling their international orders taken on the Internet, see the Entrepreneur's Survival Kit titled, "Five Common Fulfillment Mistakes."

The international product life cycle theory does retain some explanatory power when applied to technology-based products that are eventually mass-produced. However, other more powerful international trade theories continue to emerge.

Quick Study

1. What does the *factor proportions theory* have to say about a nation's imports and exports?
2. Identify the two categories of national resources in factor proportions theory. What is the *Leontief paradox*?
3. What are the three stages of the *international product life cycle theory*? Identify its limitations.

New Trade Theory

During the 1970s and 1980s, a new theory emerged to explain trade patterns.[15] The **new trade theory** states that (1) there are gains to be made from specialization and increasing economies of scale, (2) the companies first to enter a market can create barriers to entry, and (3) government may play a role in assisting its home-based companies. Because the theory emphasizes productivity rather than a nation's resources, it is in line with the theory of comparative advantage but at odds with factor proportions theory.

First-Mover Advantage

According to the new trade theory, as a company increases the extent to which it specializes in the production of a particular good, output rises because of gains in efficiency. Regardless of the amount of a company's output, it has fixed production costs such as the cost of research and development, and the plant and equipment needed to produce the product. The theory states that as specialization and output increase, companies can realize economies of scale, thereby pushing the unit costs of production lower.

new trade theory
Trade theory holding that (1) there are gains to be made from specialization and increasing economies of scale, (2) the companies first to market can create barriers to entry, and (3) government may play a role in assisting its home companies.

That is why as many companies expand, they lower prices to buyers and force potential new competitors to produce at a similar level of output if they want to be competitive in their pricing. Thus, the presence of large economies of scale can create an industry that supports only a few large firms.

A **first-mover advantage** is the economic and strategic advantage gained by being the first company to enter an industry. This first-mover advantage can create a formidable barrier to entry for potential rivals. The new trade theory also states that a country may dominate in the export of a certain product because it has a firm that has acquired a first-mover advantage.[16]

Because of the potential benefits of being the first company to enter an industry, some businesspeople and researchers make a case for government assistance. They say that by working together to target potential new industries, a government and its home-based companies can take advantage of the benefits of being the first mover in an industry. Government involvement has always been widely accepted in undertakings such as space exploration, for national security reasons, but less so in purely commercial ventures. But the fear that governments of other countries might participate with industry to gain first-mover advantages spurs many governments into action.

The theory is still too fresh, and not enough evidence is yet available to judge its accuracy or value. Let's now look at the last major theory of international trade—*national competitive advantage.*

National Competitive Advantage

Michael Porter put forth a theory in 1990 to explain why certain countries are leaders in the production of certain products.[17] His **national competitive advantage theory** states that a nation's competitiveness in an industry depends on the capacity of the industry to innovate and upgrade. Porter's work incorporates certain elements of previous international trade theories but also makes some important new discoveries.

Porter is not preoccupied with explaining the export and import patterns of nations, but with explaining why some nations are more competitive in certain industries. He identifies four elements, present to varying degrees in every nation, that form the basis of national competitiveness. Figure 5.6 shows the *Porter diamond,* which consists of: (1) factor conditions; (2) demand conditions; (3) related and supporting industries; and (4) firm strategy, structure, and rivalry. Let's take a look at each of these elements and see how they all interact to support national competitiveness.

Factor Conditions
Factor proportions theory considers a nation's resources, such as a large labor force, natural resources, climate, or surface features, as paramount factors in what products a country will produce and export. Porter acknowledges the value of such resources, which he terms *basic* factors, but also discusses the significance of what he calls *advanced* factors.

Advanced Factors Advanced factors include things such as the skill levels of different segments of the workforce and the quality of the technological infrastructure in a nation. Advanced factors are the result of investments in education and innovation such as worker training and technological research and development. Whereas the basic factors can be the initial spark for why an economy begins producing a certain product, advanced factors account for the sustained competitive advantage a country enjoys in that product.

Today for example, Japan has an advantage in auto production and the United States in the manufacture of airplanes. In the manufacture of computer components, Taiwan reigns supreme, although China is an increasingly important competitor. These countries did not attain their status in their respective areas because of basic factors. For example, Japan did not acquire its advantage in autos because of its natural resources of iron ore—it has virtually none and must import most of the iron it needs. These countries developed their productivity and advantages in producing these products through deliberate efforts, including worker training and development, and improvements in technology and work processes.

Demand Conditions
Sophisticated buyers in the home market are also important to national competitive advantage in a product area. A sophisticated domestic market drives companies to modify existing products to include new design features and develop entirely

---

first-mover advantage
Economic and strategic advantage gained by being the first company to enter an industry.

national competitive advantage theory
Trade theory holding that a nation's competitiveness in an industry depends on the capacity of the industry to innovate and upgrade.

FIGURE 5.6

new products and technologies. Companies in markets with sophisticated buyers should see the competitiveness of the entire group improve. For example, the sophisticated U.S. market for computer software has helped give companies based in the United States an edge in developing new software products.

Related and Supporting Industries
Companies that belong to a nation's internationally competitive industries do not exist in isolation. Rather, supporting industries spring up to provide the inputs required by the industry. How does this happen? Companies that can benefit from the product or process technologies of an internationally competitive industry begin to form clusters of related economic activities in the same geographic area. The presence of these clusters serves to reinforce the productivity, and therefore competitiveness, of each industry within the cluster. For example, Italy is home to a successful cluster in the footwear industry that greatly benefits from the country's closely related leather-tanning and fashion-design industries. Map 5.2 shows the locations of some important clusters in the United States. Looking at the cluster in Colorado, we see that mining and the exploration of oil and gas depend heavily on the provision of engineering services, which in turn require advanced computer hardware and software.

A relatively small number of clusters usually account for a major share of regional economic activity. They also often account for an overwhelming share of the economic activity that is "exported" to other locations. *Exporting clusters*—those that export products or make investments to compete outside the local area—are the primary source of an area's long-term prosperity. Although the demand for a local industry is inherently limited by the size of the local market, an exporting cluster can grow far beyond that limit.[18]

Firm Strategy, Structure, and Rivalry
The strategic decisions of firms have lasting effects on their future competitiveness. Managers committed to producing quality products that are valued by buyers while maximizing the firm's market share and/or financial returns are essential. But highly skilled managers are not all that are needed. Equally as important is the industry structure and rivalry between a nation's companies. The more intense the struggle is to survive between a nation's domestic companies, the greater will be their

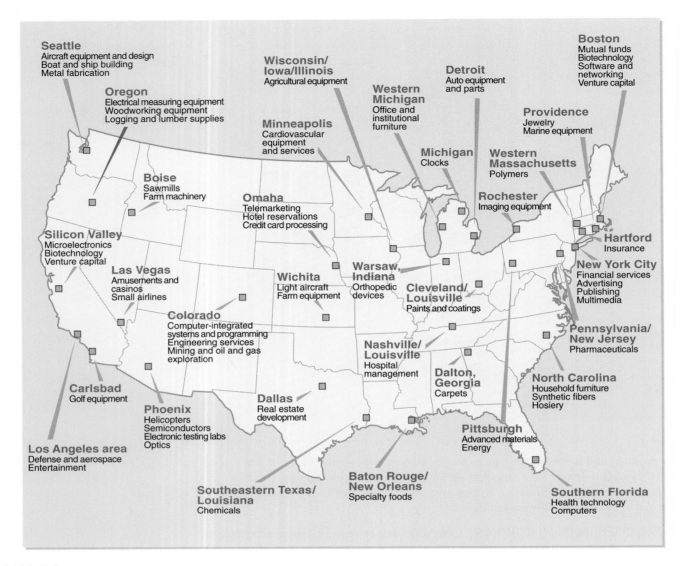

MAP 5.2

Mapping Selected U.S. Clusters

Labels on map:

Seattle — Aircraft equipment and design, Boat and ship building, Metal fabrication

Oregon — Electrical measuring equipment, Woodworking equipment, Logging and lumber supplies

Wisconsin/Iowa/Illinois — Agricultural equipment

Minneapolis — Cardiovascular equipment and services

Western Michigan — Office and institutional furniture

Detroit — Auto equipment and parts

Boston — Mutual funds, Biotechnology, Software and networking, Venture capital

Providence — Jewelry, Marine equipment

Boise — Sawmills, Farm machinery

Michigan — Clocks

Western Massachusetts — Polymers

Omaha — Telemarketing, Hotel reservations, Credit card processing

Rochester — Imaging equipment

Silicon Valley — Microelectronics, Biotechnology, Venture capital

Las Vegas — Amusements and casinos, Small airlines

Wichita — Light aircraft, Farm equipment

Warsaw, Indiana — Orthopedic devices

Cleveland/Louisville — Paints and coatings

Hartford — Insurance

New York City — Financial services, Advertising, Publishing, Multimedia

Colorado — Computer-integrated systems and programming, Engineering services, Mining and oil and gas exploration

Nashville/Louisville — Hospital management

Dalton, Georgia — Carpets

Pennsylvania/New Jersey — Pharmaceuticals

Carlsbad — Golf equipment

Dallas — Real estate development

North Carolina — Household furniture, Synthetic fibers, Hosiery

Phoenix — Helicopters, Semiconductors, Electronic testing labs, Optics

Pittsburgh — Advanced materials, Energy

Los Angeles area — Defense and aerospace, Entertainment

Southeastern Texas/Louisiana — Chemicals

Baton Rouge/New Orleans — Specialty foods

Southern Florida — Health technology, Computers

competitiveness. This heightened competitiveness helps them to compete against imports and against companies that might develop a production presence in the home market.

Government and Chance   Apart from the four factors identified as part of the diamond, Porter identifies the roles of government and chance in fostering the national competitiveness of industries.

First, governments, by their actions, can often increase the competitiveness of firms and perhaps even entire industries. For example, a report by McKinsey & Company (*www.mckinsey.com*), an international consultancy, discussed how the Indian government could increase GDP growth from 6 percent per year to 10 percent. Among other things, it placed the blame on the government's slow pace of privatization. The report argues that the government should reduce its sky-high ownership of 43 percent of India's capital stock to boost productivity. In a dozen "modern sectors" of the economy, labor productivity is, on average, 15 percent of U.S. productivity levels. Although productivity is 44 percent of the U.S. average in software, it is as low as 1 percent in electricity distribution. Privatization of government-owned companies would force them to become more competitive in world markets if they are to survive.[19]

Second, although chance events can help the competitiveness of a firm or an industry, it can also threaten it. McDonald's (*www.mcdonalds.com*) holds a clear competitive advantage worldwide in the fast-food industry. But its overwhelming dominance was threatened by the discovery of Mad Cow Disease. To keep customers from flocking to the non-beef substitute products of competitors, McDonald's introduced the McPork sandwich.

Porter's theory holds promise but has just begun to be subjected to research using actual data on each of the factors involved and national competitiveness. There are important implications for companies and governments if the theory accurately identifies the important drivers of national competitiveness. For instance, government policies should not be designed to protect national industries that are not internationally competitive, but develop the components of the diamond that contribute to increased competitiveness. Support for or against this latest and influential theory will accumulate over time as research into its value continues.

Quick Study

1. What is the *new trade theory*? Explain what is meant by the term *first-mover advantage*.
2. Describe the *national competitive advantage theory*. What is meant by an "advanced" factor?
3. What are the four elements and two influential factors of the Porter diamond?

Bottom Line For Business

This chapter introduced and explained a number of concepts regarding international trade. We explored the benefits of international trade and its volume and pattern in the world today. Trade can liberate the entrepreneurial spirit and bring economic development to a nation and its people. As the value and volume of trade continue to expand worldwide, new theories will likely emerge to explain why countries trade and why they have advantages in producing certain products.

Globalization and Trade

A main underlying theme of this book is how companies are adapting to the era of globalization. Globalization, and the increased competition it causes, are forcing companies to locate particular operations to those places where they can be performed most efficiently. Firms are doing this either by relocating their own production facilities to other nations, or by outsourcing certain activities to companies in other countries. The reason companies are undertaking such action is to boost competitiveness.

The relocation and outsourcing of business activities are altering international trade in both goods and services. In this chapter's opening company profile we saw that Wal-Mart relies on the sourcing of products from low-cost production locations (such as China) to deliver on its promise of "Everyday Low Prices." Hewlett-Packard also makes use of globalization and international trade to minimize costs while maximizing output. The company dispersed the design and production of a new computer server throughout an increasingly specialized electronics-manufacturing system. HP conceptualized and designed the computer in Singapore, engineered and manufactured many parts for it in Taiwan, and assembled it in Australia, China, India, and Singapore. Companies are using such production and distribution techniques to maximize efficiency.

But today, not only is goods production being sent to distant locations, but so too is the delivery of business services, such as financial accounting, data processing, and the handling of credit card and insurance inquiries. Even jobs requiring higher-level skills such as engineering, computer programming, and scientific research are migrating to distant locations. The motivation for companies is the same as when they send manufacturing jobs to more cost-effective locations—remaining viable in the face of increasing competitive pressures.

Supporting Free Trade

International trade theory is fundamentally no different when it comes to the relocation of services production as compared with the production of goods. As we've seen in this chapter, trade theory tells us that if a refrigerator bound for a Western market can be made more cheaply in China, it should be. The same reasoned logic tells us that if a credit card inquiry from a Western market can be more cheaply processed in India, it should be. In both cases, the importing country benefits from a less-expensive product, and the exporting country benefits from inward-flowing investment and more numerous and better-paying jobs.

Finally, there are policy implications for governments. Although employment in developed countries should not be negatively affected in the aggregate, job dislocation is a concern. Many governments are encouraging lifelong education among workers to guard against the possibility that an individual may become "obsolete" in terms of lacking marketable skills relative to workers in other nations. And no matter how loud the calls for protectionism in the service sector become, governments will do well to resist such temptations. Experience tells us that erecting barriers to competition results in less competitive firms and industries, greater job losses, and lower standards of living than would be the case under free trade. The next chapter discusses business-government trade relations and the policy agenda in depth.

SUMMARY

1. **Describe the relation between *international trade volume* and *world output*, and identify overall *trade patterns*.** *International trade* is the purchase, sale, or exchange of goods and services across national borders. International trade provides a country's people with a greater choice of goods and services and is an important engine for job creation in many countries. Most of world merchandise trade is comprised of trade in manufactured goods. Service exports make up roughly 20 percent of total world trade annually. Slower world economic output slows the volume of international trade, and higher output spurs greater trade. Also, trade has consistently grown faster than output.

The pattern of international trade in merchandise is dominated by flows among the high-income economies of the world (60 percent), followed by trade among high-income countries and low- and middle-income nations (34 percent). Trade among the low- and middle-income nations is just 6 percent of the total. A large amount of trade in Western Europe is intraregional, meaning that it largely occurs between Western European nations.

2. **Describe *mercantilism*, and explain its impact on the world powers and their colonies.** The trade theory that nations should accumulate financial wealth, usually in the form of gold, by encouraging exports and discouraging imports is called *mercantilism*. Nation-states in Europe followed this economic philosophy from about 1500 to the late 1700s.

Countries implemented mercantilism by doing three things. First, they increased their wealth by maintaining a *trade surplus*—the condition that results when the value of a nation's exports is greater than the value of its imports. Second, national governments actively intervened in international trade to maintain a trade surplus. Third, mercantilist nations acquired less-developed territories (colonies) around the world to serve as sources of inexpensive raw materials and as markets for higher-priced finished goods. Mercantilism assumes that a nation increases its wealth only at the expense of other nations—a *zero-sum game*.

3. **Explain *absolute advantage* and *comparative advantage* and identify their differences.** The ability of a nation to produce a good more efficiently than any other nation is

called an *absolute advantage*. According to this theory, international trade should be allowed to flow according to market forces. A country can concentrate on producing the goods in which it holds an absolute advantage and then trade with other nations to obtain the goods it needs but does not produce. Because there are gains to be had by both countries party to an exchange, international trade is shown to be a *positive-sum game*. The theory measures a nation's wealth by the living standards of its people.

A nation holds a *comparative advantage* in the production of a good when it is unable to produce the good more efficiently than other nations, but can produce it more efficiently than it can any other good. As a result, trade is still beneficial even if one country is less efficient in the production of two goods, so long as it is less inefficient in the production of one of the goods.

4. **Explain the *factor proportions* and *international product life cycle* theories.** The *factor proportions theory* states that countries produce and export goods that require resources (factors) that are abundant and import goods that require resources that are in short supply. The factor proportions theory predicts that a country will specialize in products that require labor if its cost is low relative to the cost of land and capital. Alternatively, a country will specialize in products that require land and capital equipment if their cost is low relative to the cost of labor. The apparent paradox between predictions of the theory and actual trade flows is called the *Leontief paradox*.

The *international product life cycle theory* says that a company will begin exporting its product and later undertake foreign direct investment as the product moves through its life cycle. In the *new product stage* production volume is low and remains based in the home country. In the *maturing product stage* the company introduces production facilities in the countries with the highest demand. In the *standardized product stage* competition forces an aggressive search for low-cost production bases in developing nations to supply a worldwide market.

5. **Explain the *new trade* and *national competitive advantage* theories.** The *new trade theory* argues that as a company increases the extent to which it specializes in the

production of a particular good, output rises because of gains in efficiency. As specialization and output increase, companies can realize economies of scale, thereby pushing the unit costs of production lower. The presence of large economies of scale can allow a firm to gain a *first-mover advantage*—the economic and strategic advantage gained by being the first company to enter an industry.

National competitive advantage theory states that a nation's competitiveness in an industry (and, therefore, trade flows) depends on the capacity of the industry to innovate and upgrade. The *Porter diamond* identifies four elements that form the basis of national competitiveness: (1) *Factor conditions*, including the skill levels of different segments of the workforce and the quality of the technological infrastructure; (2) *demand conditions*, such as a sophisticated domestic market; (3) *related and supporting industries* that spring up and form clusters of related economic activities; and (4) *firm strategy, structure, and rivalry* conditions that are present in an industry. Finally, the actions of *governments* and the occurrence of *chance events* can also affect the competitiveness of a nation's companies.

TALK IT OVER

1. If the nations of the world were to suddenly cut off all trade with one another, what products might you no longer be able to obtain in your country? Choose one other country and identify the products it would need to do without.

2. Many economists predict the eventual rise of China as a "superpower" because of economic reform, along with the work ethic and high education of its population. How do you think trade between Asia, Europe, and North America will be affected by China's continued development?

3. Because of its abundance of natural resources, Brazil was once considered a nation certain to attain advanced economic status quickly. Yet over the past two decades Brazil has sometimes been referred to as an economic "basket case." What forces do you think are preventing Brazil's economic progress?

TEAMING UP

1. In this project, two groups of four students debate the advantages and disadvantages of completely free international trade. After the first student from each side has spoken, the second student questions the opponent's arguments, looking for holes and inconsistencies. The third student attempts to answer these arguments. The fourth student presents a summary of each side's arguments. Finally, the class will vote on which team has offered the more compelling argument.

2. Locate the annual report (or other publicly available information) of a multinational firm in your library or on the Internet. To what extent does the company rely on imports to supply its production facilities in various countries? How much of the company's total sales are outside its home country? Does the company import from and export to mostly high-income countries only, or low- and middle-income countries as well? Are the company's export revenues increasing or decreasing, and at what rate? Supply any other relevant information and present your group's findings to the class.

3. As a team, select a recent business periodical and find an article that discusses the deteriorating export situation of a country. Has it tried to export its way out of slow economic growth? If so, what forces led it to resort to increasing exports to stimulate its economy? If not, why hasn't it? What is the forecast for the recovery of its export sector in the near term? Write a short report on your findings.

KEY TERMS

absolute advantage (p. 160)

comparative advantage (p. 162)

factor proportions theory (p. 164)

first-mover advantage (p. 168)

international product life cycle theory (p. 165)

international trade (p. 152)

mercantilism (p. 158)

national competitive advantage theory (p. 168)

new trade theory (p. 167)

trade deficit (p. 159)

trade surplus (p. 159)

1. According to the theory of national competitive advantage, a country gains a competitive advantage in an industry when its home-based companies form a cluster of activities that support one another. New trade theory and the theory of national competitive advantage emphasize a role for governments in helping their firms become strong internationally.

   The government of France has invested heavily in a rather unique public-private venture in Europe called Genopole. Located in a specially designated area within France, the genetic research and development project is designed to thrust France to the forefront of life sciences research. Visit the Web site of Genopole (*www.genopole.com*). Report on the 1) various participants (public and private) involved in the venture, 2) specific types of research (genetics, biotechnology, etc.) the organization carries out, and 3) several specific scientific achievements of the project.

   Regarding the aims of Genopole, what do you think each group has to offer the cluster to encourage the cross-fertilization of ideas and innovations? Why do you think governments today often try to create clusters around groundbreaking research in high-technology products and processes? Do you think governments should undertake such efforts or let markets, on their own, decide who should succeed or fail? Can you identify a cluster that exists in your hometown or city, or that of your college or university? If so, identify its members and the contribution of each to the cluster.

1. You are a research fellow for a Washington, D.C.-based research institute investigating the ethics of restrictions on the international movement of labor. In the practice of international trade, both physical resources and capital cross international borders rather freely, whereas labor is heavily restricted. In fact, it can be extremely difficult for individuals to obtain a permit that allows them to be gainfully employed within many countries. Thus, while companies are free to set up production in markets where labor is cheap, labor cannot move to markets where wages are higher. Some argue this locks poor people to their poor geographies and gives them little hope for advancement. Why do you think this situation prevails? Is it ethical that of all the components of production, labor is the one most subject to restrictions on its international mobility? Explain.

2. You are the production manager for a European-based firm that is considering outsourcing its manufacturing to a producer in China. You are asked by your firm's CEO to prepare a report that outlines the benefits and drawbacks of this potential change. During your research, you consider the fact that international trade theories propose that protectionist actions that restrict imports harm a nation's standard of living—an argument for free trade. Yet, you know that free trade and global competition is driving firms like your own to move production to cheaper locations abroad, thereby eliminating jobs in their home countries. Clearly, the gains and losses of free trade are not always distributed evenly across the population. As part of your report to the CEO, argue either for or against the need for measures that protect domestic production and, therefore, jobs at home.

3. You are a member of a World Trade Organization task force that is reviewing the recent banana conflict between the United States and the European Union. The European Union and the United States recently ended a 9-year battle over trade in bananas. The European Union was giving preferential treatment to banana exporters from Africa, the Caribbean, and the Pacific island nations. But the United States challenged what it saw as unfair trading practices, and the World Trade Organization agreed. Large global fruit companies such as Dole, Chiquita, and Del Monte—which alone account for nearly two-thirds of the fruit traded worldwide—supported the U.S. action. The European Union argued it was trying to support struggling economies, for which bananas make up a large portion of their income. Create a report that discusses the ethics of managing trade in the interests of countries that are seen as vulnerable in the global economy. Would you have argued on behalf of the United States or the European Union? Why? What are the pros and cons of each side's arguments?

PRACTICING INTERNATIONAL MANAGEMENT CASE

DHL Worldwide Express Is First in Asia and the World

What company is the leading international express carrier? If you answered Federal Express (*www.fedex.com*) or UPS (*www.ups.com*) you're wrong. Try DHL Worldwide Express (*www.dhl.com*). This company, today based in Brussels, Belgium, actually carved out the niche for international express service in 1969 when it began shipping bills of lading and other documents from San Francisco to Honolulu. Soon the company got requests to deliver and pick up in Japan and other Asian countries, and the whole business of international express delivery was born.

Today the company delivers and picks up from 120,000 destinations in over 220 countries and territories and employs more than 160,000 employees worldwide, many of them based in Asia, the company's first and most important international market. Customer service and reliability are what DHL prides itself on most. The company hires DHL personnel in the countries in which it operates and sees this practice as key to forging relationships with customers in its overseas markets. "Unlike many of our competitors," says one DHL executive, "we don't take a package and hand it off to an agent. We ensure that our deliveries and pick-ups are made by DHL personnel and that we can manage business locally by using local people who know local customs." Because relationships are the name of the game in service businesses, DHL is currently cultivating relationships with customs agents. The archaic customs clearance procedures in many countries are the biggest obstacle to speedy international deliveries.

Express air delivery is now a huge business in Asia, but DHL has several formidable competitors snapping at its heels. These include Federal Express, which offers competitive rates, and local players like Hong Kong Delivery, whose small size makes it highly flexible. DHL cannot simply rest on its number-one position or boast of its long years of experience to stay ahead. The dangers of complacency were brought home to the company in the mid-1980s, when its DHL Japan office faced customer resistance to a price hike. DHL employees had simply assumed that the firm would always be number one and had grown lax on service. In fact, an objective "shipment test" revealed that DHL Japan provided the worst service at what were already the highest prices. Japanese customers had simply continued to use DHL because it was the first in the business and because loyalty was important. Yet, the proposed price hike might have been the decisive factor in convincing formerly compliant customers to defect. Fortunately, DHL Japan's then-president, Shinichi Momose, was able to get the affiliate back on track through aggressive initiatives.

Today DHL's customer service record is winning repeated kudos in Asia and around the world. For example, a DHL division called DHL Logistics earned a gold medal for excellence in 2001 for the second consecutive year in the eighteenth annual Quest for Quality survey conducted by the industry's Logistics Management and Distribution Report. It is also often voted the "Best Express Service" at the annual Asian Freight Industry Awards. "We operate in an increasingly competitive business," explains DHL Far East Regional Managing Director John A. Kerr, "and our customers are demanding both increased levels of services and sophisticated logistics solutions. . . . We cannot afford to be so complacent in the years ahead. We will continue to listen to our customers, understand their needs, and work to meet their requirements."

Demonstrating its commitment to remaining the best in its class, in 2003 DHL orchestrated a successful merger with Airborne Express that continued into 2004. The merger, designed to restructure the business and slash overhead expenses, integrated the two companies' ground and courier networks—offering customers a seamless global network. As a result, DHL could then offer its U.S. customers with the best of both worlds: the world-class international services of DHL combined with the strong domestic service offerings of Airborne. John Fellows, CEO of DHL Holdings (USA), Inc. said of the successful merger, "Customers of the new DHL are empowered with more choices in their shipping options than ever before, as they reap the benefits of the most extensive global transportation network in the industry."

Thinking Globally

1. As the first to set up an international air express business in 1969, DHL had the first-mover advantage over other companies. Is being a first mover as advantageous for a service company, such as DHL Worldwide Express, as it is for a manufacturing company, such as Boeing? Explain.

2. When it comes to global expansion and setting up affiliates abroad, how is a service company's focus different from that of a manufacturing company? What elements do you think are necessary for a service company to achieve global success? What are the obstacles to global expansion?

3. DHL prides itself on having its own full-time staff of more than 160,000 people spread across the globe instead of relying on local agents. Discuss the merits and drawbacks of this international staffing approach.

4. After reading the above case, what do you think are the dangers, if any, of being a first mover?

learning objectives

After studying this chapter, you should be able to

1. Describe the *political, economic,* and *cultural motives* behind governmental intervention in trade.

2. List and explain the methods governments use to *promote* international trade.

3. List and explain the methods governments use to *restrict* international trade.

4. Discuss the importance of the *World Trade Organization* in promoting free trade.

business–government

6

trade relations

a look *back*

CHAPTER 5 explored theories that have been developed to explain the pattern that international trade should take. We examined the important concept of comparative advantage and the conceptual basis for how international trade benefits nations.

a look *at this chapter*

This chapter discusses the active role of national governments in international trade. We examine the motives for government intervention and the tools that nations use to accomplish their goals. We then explore the global trading system and show how it promotes free trade.

a look *ahead*

CHAPTER 7 continues our discussion of the international business environment. We explore recent patterns of foreign direct investment, theories that try to explain why it occurs, and the role of governments in influencing investment flows.

Ringing Up Success

HOLLYWOOD, California — Time Warner (*www.timewarner.com*) is the world's leading media and entertainment company, whose businesses include television networks (HBO, Turner Broadcasting), publishing (*Time, Sports Illustrated*), music (Warner Music Group), Interactive services (America Online), and film entertainment (New Line Cinema, Warner Bros.). The company's annual revenue from all its business units is around $44 billion.

New Line Cinema's *The Lord of the Rings* trilogy (based on the tale by J.R.R. Tolkien) is the most successful film franchise in history. The final installment in the trilogy, *The Lord of the Rings: The Return of the King*, earned more than $1 billion at the worldwide box office, and the entire trilogy earned more than $2.8 billion. *The Lord of the Rings: The Return of the King* won 11 Academy Awards—altogether the trilogy won 17. Pictured above, special effects artist, Richard Taylor, signs an autograph in the presence of a lifelike Gollum.

Warner Bros.' ongoing series of *Harry Potter* films, based on the novels of former British schoolteacher J.K. Rowling, has also been magically successful. After first snatching up the books in every major language, kids from Tampa to Tokyo pour into cinemas to be awed by young Harry on the silver screen. As the Time Warner group of companies literally marches across the globe, people in practically every nation on the planet view its media creations.

Yet Time Warner (and other media companies) must tread carefully as they expand their reach around the world. Some governments fear that their own nations' writers, actors, directors, and producers will be drowned out by big-budget Hollywood productions such as *The Lord of the Rings* and *Harry Potter*. Others fear the replacement of their traditional values with those depicted in the imported entertainment. As you read this chapter, think about the nature of different products and the reasons governments get involved in international trade.[1]

Chapter 5 presented theories that describe what the patterns of international trade *should* look like. The theory of comparative advantage states that the country having a comparative advantage in the production of a certain good will produce that good when barriers to trade do not exist. However, this ideal does not accurately characterize trade in today's global marketplace. Despite efforts by organizations such as the World Trade Organization (*www.wto.org*) and smaller groups of countries, nations still retain many barriers to trade.

In this chapter, we look in detail at business–government trade relations. We first explain why nations erect barriers to trade, exploring the cultural, political, and economic motives for such barriers. We then examine the instruments countries use to restrict both imports and exports. Efforts of the global trading system to promote trade by reducing trade barriers are then presented. In Chapter 8 we cover how smaller groups of countries are eliminating barriers to both trade and investment.

Why Do Governments Intervene in Trade?

free trade
Pattern of imports and exports that would result in the absence of trade barriers.

The pattern of imports and exports that would result in the absence of trade barriers is called **free trade**. Despite the advantages of free trade that we discussed in Chapter 5, national governments have long intervened in the trade of goods and services. Why do governments impose restrictions on free trade? In general, they do so for reasons that are political, economic, or cultural—or some combination of the three. Countries often intervene in trade by strongly supporting their domestic companies' exporting activities. But the more emotionally charged trade intervention occurs when a nation's economy is underperforming. In tough economic times businesses and workers will often lobby their governments to protect them from imports that are reducing work and eliminating jobs in the domestic market. Let's now take a closer look at government involvement in trade by examining the political, economic, and cultural motives for intervention.

Political Motives

Government officials often make trade-related decisions based on political motives. Why? Because a politician's very survival might depend on pleasing voters and getting reelected. However, a trade policy based purely on political motives is seldom the wisest policy in the long run. The main political motives behind government intervention in trade include protecting jobs, preserving national security, responding to other nations' unfair trade practices, and gaining influence over other nations.

To Protect Jobs   Short of an unpopular war, nothing will oust a government faster than high rates of unemployment. Thus, practically all governments become involved when trade threatens jobs at home. For example, the president of Guyana, in South America, urged her fellow citizens to buy local goods instead of imports saying, "A foreign product does not mean it's better. Local goods are quite good. I use them all the time." Making her case on her weekly radio talk show, she went so far as to ask importers to act "as patriots and not bring things that are not needed into the country to crowd locally made products off the shelves."[2]

But efforts to protect jobs can receive far less publicity. Fuji (*www.fujifilm.com*) of Japan and Kodak (*www.kodak.com*) of the United States control large shares of the market for photographic film in China. This caused Chinese nationalists to urge the government to support China Lucky Film, the struggling state-owned company whose market share recently plunged to seven percent. Fearing the death of yet another major Chinese brand, the government considered whether to prohibit a proposed joint venture between Kodak and Lucky. China's National Association of Light Industry urged the government to provide $240 million in cash and low-interest loans to rescue Lucky while maintaining a ban on joint ventures in film manufacturing.[3]

To Preserve National Security   Industries considered essential to national security often receive government-sponsored protection. This is true for both imports and exports.

National Security and Imports   Preserving national security by restricting certain imports is supported by the argument that a government must have access to a domestic supply of certain items—such as weapons, fuel, and air, land, and sea transportation—in the event that war could restrict their availability. For example, many nations (particularly the United States) continue to search for oil within their borders in case war disrupts the flow of oil from outside sources. Legitimate national security reasons for intervention can be difficult to argue against, particularly when they have the support of most of a country's people.

Some countries fiercely protect their agricultural sector for national security reasons because a nation that imports its food supplies could face starvation in times of war. France has come under attack by other European nations as well as countries outside Europe for protecting its agricultural sector. French agricultural subsidies are intended to provide a fair financial return for French farmers, who traditionally operate on a small scale and therefore have high production costs and low profit margins. But many developed nations are exposing agribusiness to market forces, prompting farms to increase their efficiency. As a result, farmers are discovering new ways to manage risk and improve efficiency. Other farmers are experimenting with alternating crops, more intensive land management, high-tech "precision farming," and greater use of biotechnology.

However, protection from import competition does have its drawbacks. Perhaps the main one is the added cost of continuing to produce a good or provide a service that could be supplied more efficiently by an international supplier. Also, once a policy of protection is adopted it may remain in place much longer than necessary. Thus, policy makers should consider whether the trade policy decision is truly a matter of national security before intervening.

Demonstrators march through the streets of Montreal, Quebec, during a protest against genetically modified organisms (GMOs) in food. Many crops today, including corn, soybeans, and wheat are grown with genetically enhanced seed technology to resist insects and disease. Even more than Canada, European nations fiercely resist U.S. efforts to export GM crops to their markets. Do you believe the Europeans are right to refuse the importation of genetically modified crops?

National Security and Exports   Governments also have national security motives for banning certain defense-related goods from export to other nations. Most industrialized nations have agencies that review requests to export technologies or products that are said to have *dual uses*—meaning they have both industrial and military applications. Products designated as dual use are classified as such and require special governmental approval before export can take place. Bans on the export of dual-use products were strictly enforced during the years of the Cold War between the Western powers and the former Soviet Union. Some countries have relaxed enforcement of these controls since the early 1990s. However, because of the continued presence of terrorist threats and rogue nations that badly want weapons of mass destruction, such bans are receiving renewed support.

For example, several years ago it was revealed that technology transfers to China fell into the dual-use category. It was alleged that two U.S. firms—Hughes Electronics Corporation (*www. hughes.com*) and Loral Space and Communications (*www.loral.com*) —helped China improve its long-range ballistic missile capabilities. The companies used Chinese rockets to launch satellites and helped Chinese scientists improve their rocket technology after the failure of some launches. Both companies denied wrongdoing and acted only after receiving approval from the government for the technology transfers. Loral responded to the charges in a written statement, saying "We believe we demonstrated that any material exchanged with the Chinese was from open sources, readily available in standard engineering textbooks."[4] This situation worries officials, who fear that China (as it has in the past) might sell the missile technology to India's longtime foe Pakistan, thus disrupting the balance of power in the region.

To Respond to "Unfair" Trade

Many observers argue that it makes no sense for one nation to allow free trade if other nations actively protect their own industries. Governments often threaten to close their ports to another nation's ships or to impose extremely high tariffs on its goods if the other nation does not concede on some trade issue that is seen as being unfair. In other words, if one government thinks another nation is not "playing fair," it will often threaten to play unfairly unless certain concessions are agreed.

To Gain Influence

Governments of the world's largest nations may become involved in trade to gain influence over smaller nations. For example, Japan has a good deal of influence in Asia. Japan accounts for a large portion of the imports and exports of many countries throughout Asia and Southeast Asia, and lent the region a large amount of money to help it recover from recent financial crises. No doubt the Japanese government expects to generate goodwill among its neighbors through such deals.

Similarly, the United States goes to great lengths to gain and maintain control over events in all of Central, North, and South America as well as the Caribbean basin. This is one reason behind the free-trade initiatives in the Americas that are strongly supported by the United States. The potential to exert influence on internal politics is also a primary reason that the United States is maintaining its embargo on communist Cuba.

Economic Motives

Although governments intervene in trade for highly charged cultural and political reasons, they also have economic motives for their intervention. The most common economic reasons given for nations' attempts to influence international trade are the protection of young industries from competition and the promotion of a strategic trade policy.

To Protect Infant Industries

According to the *infant industry argument*, a country's emerging industries need protection from international competition during their development phase until they become sufficiently competitive internationally. This argument is based on the idea that infant industries need protection because of a steep learning curve. In other words, only as an industry grows and matures does it gain the knowledge it needs to become more innovative, efficient, and competitive.

Although this argument is conceptually appealing, it does have several problems. First, the argument requires governments to distinguish between industries that are worth protecting and those that are not. This is very difficult, if not impossible, to do. For years, Japan has targeted infant industries for protection, low-interest loans, and other

The United States has maintained a trade embargo on Cuba since 1961 in the hope of exerting political influence against Fidel Castro's communist regime. Although some observers believe the embargo is punishing ordinary Cubans, the Cuban government claims it is having minimal effect on daily life. Meanwhile, dangerous, illegal migration to the United States using homemade rafts, human smugglers, or fake visas continues. How do you feel about the embargo: Is it working or should it be lifted?

benefits. Its performance on assisting these industries was very good from the 1950s to the early 1980s but has been less successful since then. Until the government achieves future success in identifying and targeting industries, supporting this type of policy remains questionable.

Second, protection from international competition can cause domestic companies to become complacent toward innovation. This can limit a company's incentives to obtain the knowledge it needs to become more competitive. The most extreme examples of complacency are industries within formerly communist nations. When their communist protections collapsed in the late 1980s and early 1990s, practically all the state-run companies were decades behind their international competitors. Indeed, many required financial assistance in the form of infusions of capital or outright purchase to survive.

Third, protection can do more economic harm than good. Consumers often end up paying more for products because a lack of competition typically creates fewer incentives to cut production costs or improve quality. Meanwhile, companies become more reliant on protection. For example, protection of domestic industries in Japan has caused a two-tier economy to emerge. In one tier are protected and noncompetitive domestic industries; in the other are highly competitive multinationals. In the flagging domestic industries of banking, property, construction, retailing, and local manufacturing, higher costs are the result of protected markets, high wages, overregulation, and barriers to imports. In contrast, the large multinationals enjoy low-cost advantages because of their efficient production facilities in East Asia, Europe, Latin America, and the United States. Because these multinationals regularly face rivals in overseas markets, they've learned to be strong competitors in order to survive.[5]

Fourth, the infant industry argument also holds that it is not always possible for small, promising companies to obtain funding in capital markets, and thus they need financial support from their government. However, international capital markets today are far more sophisticated than in the past, and promising business ventures can normally obtain funding from private sources.

To Pursue Strategic Trade Policy   Recall from our discussion in Chapter 5 that new trade theorists believe government intervention can help companies take advantage of economies of scale and be the first movers in their industries. First-mover advantages result because economies of scale in production limit the number of companies that an industry can sustain.

Benefits of Strategic Trade Policy   Supporters of strategic trade policy argue that it results in increased national income. Companies should earn a good profit if they obtain first-mover advantages and solidify positions in their markets around the world. They also claim that strategic trade policies helped South Korea build global conglomerates (called *chaebol*) that dwarf the competition. For example, Korean shipbuilders over many years received a variety of government subsidies, including low-cost financing. The *chaebol* made it possible for companies to survive poor economic times because of the wide range of industries in which they competed. Such policies also had spin-off effects on related industries such as transportation. By the mid-1990s one of the country's largest shipping firms, Hanjing Shipping, had become the largest cargo transporter between Asia and the United States.[6]

Drawbacks of Strategic Trade Policy   Although it sounds as if strategic trade policy has only benefits, there can be drawbacks as well. Lavish government assistance to domestic companies caused inefficiency and high costs for both South Korean and Japanese companies in the late 1990s. For example, because of high wages at home attributable to large government concessions to local labor unions, Korea's *chaebol* were operating under very low profit margins. When the Asian currency crisis hit in the summer of 1997, the *chaebol* were not prepared for the consequences. The government realized it had given away too much in the good times and pulled back some of its support by, for one thing, passing a law to make it easier for companies to fire employees.[7]

In addition, when governments decide to support specific industries, their choice is often subject to political lobbying by the groups seeking government assistance. It is possible that special-interest groups could capture all the gains from assistance with no benefit for consumers. If this were to occur, consumers could end up paying more for lower-quality goods than they could otherwise obtain.

Cultural Motives

Nations often restrict trade in goods and services to achieve cultural objectives, the most common being protection of national identity. In Chapter 2 we saw how culture and trade are intertwined and significantly affect one another. The cultures of countries are slowly altered by exposure to the people and products of other cultures. Unwanted cultural influence in a nation can cause great distress and cause governments to block imports that it believes are harmful—recall our discussion of *cultural imperialism* in Chapter 2.

The French try to keep their language free of alien English words such as *jeans* and *hamburger*. French law bans foreign-language words from virtually all business and government communications, radio and TV broadcasts, public announcements, and advertising messages—at least whenever a suitable French alternative is available. You can't advertise a *best-seller;* it has to be a *succès de librairie.* You can't sell *popcorn* at *le cinéma;* French movie-goers must snack on *maïs soufflé.* A select group of individuals comprising the Higher Council on French Language works against the inclusion of such so-called "Franglais" phrases as *le marketing, le cash flow,* and *le brainstorming* into commerce and other areas of French culture.

Canada is another country making headlines for its attempts to mitigate the cultural influence of entertainment products imported from the United States. Canada requires at least 35 percent of music played over Canadian radio to be by Canadian artists. In fact, many countries are considering laws to protect their media programming for cultural reasons. The problem with such restrictions is that they reduce the selection of products available to consumers.

Cultural Influence of the United States   Certainly, the United States, more than any other nation, is seen as a threat to national cultures around the world. Why is this? The reason is the global strength of the United States in entertainment and media (such as movies, magazines, and music) and consumer goods. Such products are highly visible to all consumers and cause groups of various kinds to lobby government officials for protection from their cultural influence. Because the rhetoric of protectionism tends to receive widespread public support, domestic producers of competing products find it easy to join in the calls for protection.

How does the English language so easily infiltrate the cultures of other nations? Despite the grand conspiracy theories put forth by some individuals and groups, it is the natural result of international trade. International trade in all sorts of goods and services is exposing people around the world to new words, ideas, products, and ways of life. But as international trade continues to expand, many governments try to limit potential adverse effects on their cultures and economies. This is where the theory of international trade meets the reality of international business today.

Quick Study

1. What are some political reasons governments intervene in trade? Explain the role of national security concerns.
2. Identify the main economic motives for government trade intervention. What are the drawbacks of each approach?
3. What cultural motives do nations give for intervening in *free trade*?

Methods of Promoting Trade

In the previous discussion we alluded to the types of instruments available to governments in their efforts to promote or restrict trade with other nations. The most common instruments that governments use are shown in Table 6.1. In this section we examine each specific method of trade promotion. We cover methods of trade restriction in the next section.

Subsidies

Financial assistance to domestic producers in the form of cash payments, low-interest loans, tax breaks, product price supports, or some other form is called a **subsidy**. Regardless of the form a subsidy takes, it is intended to assist domestic companies in fending off international competitors. This can mean becoming more competitive in the home market or increasing competitiveness in international markets through exports. Because of the many forms a subsidy can take, it is virtually impossible to calculate the amount of subsidies any country offers its producers. In fact, the World Trade Organization is often called on to settle arguments over charges of unfair subsidies, doing so only after a long and arduous investigation. Even then, the losing party generally disagrees with the verdict but is bound to accept the organization's ruling (the World Trade Organization is discussed in detail below).

subsidy
Financial assistance to domestic producers in the form of cash payments, low-interest loans, tax breaks, product price supports, or some other form.

Subsidies in Media and Entertainment
As mentioned earlier, media and entertainment are commonly subsidized in many nations. However, France does stand out as being very generous with its subsidies to entertainment. The French film authority, *Le Centre National de la Cinématographie* (*www.cnc.fr*), subsidizes many films each year. In one recent year, some French films received "automatic" subsidies to the tune of

TABLE 6.1

Methods of Promoting and Restricting Trade

Trade Promotion	Trade Restriction
Subsidies	Tariffs
Export financing	Quotas
Foreign trade zones	Embargoes
Special government agencies	Local content requirements
	Administrative delays
	Currency controls

about $54 million while others benefited from about $20 million a year in advances against box-office receipts. The French government argues that such subsidies are necessary to counteract the influence of Hollywood films and TV programs. Whereas Hollywood films are privately financed and driven by market demand, critics contend that France's films are less competitive because they have to satisfy bureaucratic agendas for funding.[8] However, the fact that many French films are critically acclaimed worldwide might present one argument against removing subsidies that apparently stoke artistic inspiration.

Drawbacks of Subsidies Critics charge that subsidies cover costs that truly competitive industries should be able to absorb on their own. In this sense, it is argued, subsidies simply encourage inefficiency and complacency. Because governments generally pay for subsidies with funds obtained from income and sales taxes, it is widely believed that subsidies benefit companies and industries that receive them but harm consumers. Thus, although subsidies provide short-term relief to companies and industries, the idea that government subsidies help the nation's citizens in the long term is highly questionable.

One fact that has recently caught the attention of policy makers concerned with the environmental consequences of government policies is that subsidies lead to an overuse of resources. For example, subsidies in developing nations to cover the high cost of energy total more than $230 billion a year—more than four times the total amount of financial assistance to developing countries. Such wasteful spending deprives developing countries of resources that could be invested in other more productive ways, including the transition to more sustainable forms of energy.[9]

Export Financing

Governments often promote exports by helping companies finance their export activities. They can offer loans that a company could otherwise not obtain or charge them an interest rate that is lower than the market rate. Another option is for a government to guarantee that it will repay the loan of a company if the company should default on repayment; this is called a *loan guarantee.*

Many nations have special agencies dedicated to helping their domestic companies gain export financing. For example, a very well known institution is called the *Export-Import Bank of the United States*—or *Ex-Im Bank* for short. The Ex-Im Bank (*www.exim.gov*) finances the export activities of companies in the United States and offers insurance on foreign accounts receivable. Another U.S. government agency, the *Overseas Private Investment Corporation (OPIC)*, also provides insurance services, but for investors. Through OPIC (*www.opic.gov*), companies that invest abroad can insure against losses due to three factors: (1) expropriation, (2) currency inconvertibility, and (3) war, revolution, and insurrection.

Receiving financing from government agencies is often crucial to the success of small businesses that are just beginning to export. In fact, taken together, the "little guys" account for over 80 percent of all transactions handled by the Ex-Im Bank. According to Lalitha Swart, senior vice president at Silicon Valley Bank (*www.svb.com*) in Santa Clara, California, most of the customers that her bank links up with the Ex-Im Bank are small to medium-sized exporters. "I would describe them as emerging high-growth companies," says Swart. "They tend to be in industries such as telecommunications, life sciences, software, computer peripherals, [and] managed healthcare."[10]

In recent years, the Ex-Im Bank has launched several programs to fuel growth in small business exporting. For instance, a revolving loan to Lynch Machinery of Bainbridge, Georgia, allowed the firm to hire 60 new employees and fill orders for $50 million in glass presses for computers and high-definition TVs for export to China and other Asian markets. The Bank's future changes include creating a new system that makes it easier for the Ex-Im Bank to approve requests for small loans. Another new program is designed to reach small businesses that are owned by minorities and women, are in depressed urban and rural areas, and that produce environmentally beneficial products. For a survey of ways in which the Ex-Im Bank helps businesses gain export financing, see the Entrepreneur's Survival Kit titled, "Ex-Im Bank: Experts in Export Financing."

Ex-Im Bank: Experts in Export Financing

What follows are some of the ways that the Ex-Im Bank helps businesses. For more information, visit (*www.exim.gov*).

City/State Program. This program brings the Ex-Im Bank's financing services to small and medium-size U.S. companies that are ready to export. These partnership programs currently exist with 38 state and local government offices and private-sector organizations.

Working Capital Guarantee Program. This program helps small and medium-sized businesses that have exporting potential but lack the needed funds by encouraging commercial lenders to loan them money. The bank guarantee covers 90 percent of the loan's principal and accrued interest. The exporter may use the guaranteed financing to purchase finished products for export or pay for raw materials, for example.

Credit Information Services. The bank's repayment records provide credit information to U.S. exporters and commercial lenders. The bank can provide information on a specific country or individual company abroad. But the bank does not divulge confidential financial data on non-U.S. buyers to whom it has extended credit, or confidential information regarding particular credits or conditions in other countries.

Export Credit Insurance. This program helps U.S. exporters develop and expand their overseas sales by protecting them against loss should a non-U.S. buyer or other non-U.S. debtor default for political or commercial reasons. The insurance policy can make obtaining export financing easier because, with approval by the bank, the proceeds of the policy can be used as collateral.

Guarantee Program. This program provides repayment protection for private-sector loans made to creditworthy buyers of U.S. capital equipment, projects, and services. The bank guarantees that, in the event of default, it will repay the principal and interest on the loan. The non-U.S. buyer must make a cash payment of at least 15 percent. Most guarantees provide comprehensive coverage against political and commercial risks.

Loan Program. The bank makes loans directly to non-U.S. buyers of U.S. exports and intermediary loans to creditworthy parties that provide loans to non-U.S. buyers. The program provides fixed-interest-rate financing for export sales of U.S. capital equipment and related services.

However, export-financing programs are not immune to controversy. In general, few criticize government support of small business exporting activities. But support for large multinational corporations is often controversial. The Ex-Im Bank's financing of large companies has angered critics, who contend that subsidizing large private companies at taxpayer expense amounts to corporate welfare. Furthermore, the Ex-Im Bank's original mandate was to support domestic employment; it thus offered low-cost financing only for exports whose content was 100 percent domestic. But companies pressured the Ex-Im Bank to relax this restriction, and now it will finance exports with at least 50 percent domestic content.

Foreign Trade Zones

Most countries promote trade with other nations by creating what is called a **foreign trade zone (FTZ)**—a designated geographic region in which merchandise is allowed to pass through with lower customs duties (taxes) and/or fewer customs procedures. Often, the intended purpose of foreign trade zones is increased employment, with increased trade a by-product. A good example of a foreign trade zone is Turkey's Aegean Free Zone, in which the Turkish government allows companies to conduct manufacturing operations free from taxes.

Customs duties increase the total amount of a good's production cost and increase the time it takes to get it to market. Companies can reduce such costs and time by establishing a facility inside a foreign trade zone. A common purpose of many companies' facilities in such zones is final product assembly. For example, Japanese car plants in Indiana, Kentucky, Ohio, and Tennessee are designated as foreign trade zones that are administered

foreign trade zone (FTZ)
Designated geographic region in which merchandise is allowed to pass through with lower customs duties (taxes) and/or fewer customs procedures.

by the U.S. Department of Commerce (*www.doc.gov*). The car companies are allowed to import parts from other production facilities around the world at 50 percent of the normal duty charged on such parts. After assembly the vehicles are sold within the United States market with no further duties being charged. Thus, state governments offer lower customs duties in return for the jobs created by having the assembly take place in the United States.

China has established a number of large foreign trade zones to reap the employment advantages they offer. Goods imported into these zones do not require import licenses or other documents, nor are they subject to import duties. International companies can also store goods in these zones before shipping them on to other countries without incurring taxes in China. Moreover, five of these zones are located within specially designated economic zones in which local governments can offer additional opportunities and tax breaks to international investors.

Another country that has enjoyed the beneficial effects of foreign trade zones is Mexico. As early as the 1960s, Mexico established such a zone along its northern border with the United States. Creation of the zone caused development of companies called *maquiladoras* along the border inside Mexico. The *maquiladoras* import materials or parts from the United States without duties, perform some processing on them, and export them back to the United States, which charges duties only on the value added to the product in Mexico. The program has expanded rapidly over the four decades since its inception, employing hundreds of thousands of people from all across Mexico who come north looking for work.

Special Government Agencies

The governments of most nations have special agencies responsible for promoting exports. Such agencies can be particularly helpful to small and midsize businesses that have limited financial resources. Government trade-promotion agencies often organize trips for trade officials and businesspeople to visit other countries to meet potential business partners and generate contacts for new business. They also typically open trade offices in other countries. These offices are designed to promote the home country's exports and introduce businesses to potential business partners in the host nation. Government trade-promotion agencies typically do a great deal of advertising in other countries to promote the nation's exports. For instance, the government of Chile's Trade Commission, ProChile, has 35 commercial offices worldwide and a Web site (*www.chileinfo.com*).

Governments not only promote trade by encouraging exports but also can encourage imports that the nation does not or cannot produce. For example, the Japan External Trade Organization (JETRO) (*www.jetro.go.jp*) is a trade-promotion agency of the government. The agency coaches small and midsize overseas businesses on the protocols of Japanese deal making, arranges meetings with suitable Japanese distributors and partners, and even assists in finding temporary office space for first-time visitors.

Town & Country (T&C) Cedar Homes (*www.cedarhomes.com*), based in Petoskey, Michigan, manufactures prefabricated homes. The company credits JETRO for making Japan indispensable to its livelihood. Says T&C president Stephan Biggs: "JETRO's office in Michigan received requests from Japan, searched their database, and put our hand in theirs. And that was it. It has to do with relationships, and we couldn't have done it without JETRO." By linking with the Intercontinental Trading Corporation, a Japanese distributor, T&C has introduced a new style of home to affluent Japanese. Now sales to Japan comprise 20 percent of T&C's total sales.[11]

For all companies, and particularly small ones with fewer resources, just finding out about the wealth of government regulations in other countries is a daunting task. What are the tariffs charged on a product? Are quotas placed on certain products? Fortunately, it is now possible to get answers to questions like these through the Internet. For a list of some very informative Web sites, see the Global Manager's Toolbox titled, "Surfing the Regulatory Seas."

U.S. Department of Commerce

○ The International Trade Administration (ITA) Web site (*www.ita.doc.gov*) offers trade data by country, region, and industry sector. It also has information on export assistance centers around the United States, a national export directory, and detailed background information on each trading partner of the United States.

○ The FedWorld Web site (*www.fedworld.gov*) is a comprehensive central access point for locating and acquiring information on U.S. government activities and trade regulations.

○ The Stat-USA Web site (*www.stat-usa.gov*) lists databases on trade regulations and documentation requirements on a country-by-country basis.

U.S. Chamber of Commerce

Dun & Bradstreet's (*www.dnb.com*) 2,000-page Exporter's Encyclopedia has been called the "bible of exporting," and it's now available online on the U.S. Chamber of Commerce's International Business Exchange Web site (*www.uschamber.org/international*). Access to the encyclopedia is offered as part of a chamber membership package, which also includes information on a variety of international trade topics.

United States Trade Representative

The Office of the United States Trade Representative Web site (*www.ustr.gov*) has a wealth of free information on trade policy issues. Up-to-date reports on the site list important barriers that affect U.S. exports to other countries. It also is a source for information on trade negotiations, including a wide range of documents on all subjects relating to trade talk agendas, as well as a helpful section on acronyms to help you get through the entries.

Trade Compass Inc.

By paying a monthly fee to Trade Compass (*www. tradecompass.com*) you can search full-text articles from the *Federal Register*, Congressional Bills dataset, and the U.S. Code of Federal Regulations, as well as information on tariff actions, rules of origin, free trade issues, and more.

Quick Study

1. How do governments use *subsidies* to promote trade? Identify the drawbacks of subsidies.

2. How does export financing promote trade? Explain its importance to small and medium-sized firms.

3. Define what is meant by the term *foreign trade zone*. How can it promote trade?

4. How can special government agencies help promote trade?

Methods of Restricting Trade

We saw earlier in this chapter some of the political, economic, and cultural reasons why governments intervene in trade. In this section we discuss the methods governments can use to restrict unwanted trade. There are two general categories of trade barrier available to governments: *tariffs* and *nontariff barriers*. A **tariff** is a government tax levied on a product as it enters or leaves a country. Tariffs add to the cost of imported products and therefore tend to lower the quantity sold of the products levied with a tariff. Nontariff barriers limit the quantity of an imported product. In turn, the lower quantity of the product available in the market tends to increase its price and thus decrease sales. Let's now take a closer look at tariffs and the various types of nontariff barriers.

tariff
Government tax levied on a product as it enters or leaves a country.

Tariffs

We can classify tariffs into three categories according to the country that levies the tariff. First, a tariff levied by the government of a country that is exporting a product is called an *export tariff*. Countries can use export tariffs when they think that the price of an export is lower than it should be. Developing nations whose exports consist mostly of low-priced natural resources often levy export tariffs. Second, a tariff levied by the government of a country that a product is passing through on its way to its final destination is called a *transit tariff*. Transit tariffs have been almost entirely eliminated worldwide through international trade agreements. Third, a tariff levied by the government in a country that is importing a product is called an *import tariff*. The import tariff is by far the most common tariff used by governments today.

We can further break down the import tariff into three subcategories based on the manner in which it is calculated. First, an **ad valorem tariff** is levied as a percentage of the stated price of an imported product. Second, a **specific tariff** is levied as a specific fee for each unit (measured by number, weight, etc.) of an imported product. Third, a **compound tariff** is levied on an imported product and calculated partly as a percentage of its stated price and partly as a specific fee for each unit. Let's now discuss the two main reasons why countries levy tariffs.

To Protect Domestic Producers
First, tariffs are a way of protecting domestic producers of a product. Because import tariffs raise the effective cost of an imported good, domestically produced goods can appear more attractive to buyers. In this way, domestic producers gain a protective barrier against imports. Although producers that receive tariff protection can gain a price advantage, in the long run protection can keep them from increasing efficiency. A protected industry can be devastated if protection encourages complacency and inefficiency and it is later thrown into the lion's den of international competition. For example, Mexico began reducing tariff protection in the mid-1980s as a prelude to NAFTA negotiations. Although Mexican producers struggled to become more efficient, many were forced into bankruptcy.

To Generate Revenue
Second, tariffs are a source of government revenue. Using tariffs to generate government revenue is most common among relatively less developed nations. The main reason is that less-developed nations tend to have less formal domestic economies that lack the capability to record domestic transactions accurately. The lack of accurate record keeping makes collection of sales taxes within the country extremely difficult. Nations solve the problem by simply raising their needed revenue through import and export tariffs. As countries develop, however, they tend to generate a greater portion of their revenues from taxes on income, capital gains, and other economic activity.

The discussion so far leads us to question: "Who benefits from tariffs?" We've already mentioned the two principle reasons for tariff barriers—protecting domestic producers and raising government revenue. Thus, on the surface it appears that governments and domestic producers benefit. We also discussed that tariffs raise the effective price of a product because importers typically must charge buyers a higher price to recover the cost of this additional tax. Thus, it appears on the surface that consumers do not benefit. As we also mentioned earlier, there is the danger that tariffs will create inefficient domestic producers that may go out of business once protective import tariffs are removed. Analysis of the total cost to a country is far more complicated and goes beyond the scope of our discussion. Suffice it to say that tariffs tend to exact a cost on countries as a whole because they lessen the gains that a nation's people obtain from trade.

Quotas

A restriction on the amount (measured in units or weight) of a good that can enter or leave a country during a certain period of time is called a **quota.** After tariffs, a quota is the second most common type of trade barrier. Governments typically administer their quota systems by granting quota licenses to the companies or governments of other nations (in the case of import quotas) and domestic producers (in the case of export quotas). Governments normally grant such licenses on a year-by-year basis.

Reason for Import Quotas
A government may impose an *import quota* to protect its domestic producers by placing a limit on the amount of goods allowed to enter the country. This helps domestic producers maintain their market shares and prices because competitive forces are restrained. In this case, domestic producers win because of the protection

---

ad valorem tariff
Tariff levied as a percentage of the stated price of an imported product.

specific tariff
Tariff levied as a specific fee for each unit (measured by number, weight, etc.) of an imported product.

compound tariff
Tariff levied on an imported product and calculated partly as a percentage of its stated price and partly as a specific fee for each unit.

quota
Restriction on the amount (measured in units or weight) of a good that can enter or leave a country during a certain period of time.

of their markets. Consumers lose because of higher prices and limited selection attributable to lower competition. Other losers include domestic producers whose own production requires the import subjected to a quota. Companies relying on the importation of so-called intermediate goods will find the final cost of their own products increase.

A few years ago, China had in place an import quota system in its filmmaking industry. One year, state-run China Film Corporation imported just 10 blockbuster movies—all through revenue-sharing agreements with international distributors. The agreement resulted in Buena Vista International (*www.bvimovies.co.uk*) earning a mere $500,000 in China on its immensely popular Disney film *The Lion King*, although the film grossed more than $1.3 million in Shanghai alone. "[Chinese] taxes are unlike [those] anywhere else in the world," reports Buena Vista executive Larry Kaplan. "A hit there brings in less than in a small central European country." Under international pressure China later abolished its quota system.[12]

Historically, countries have placed import quotas on the textiles and apparel products of other countries under what is called the Multi-Fiber Arrangement. Countries affected by this arrangement account for over 80 percent of world trade in textiles and clothing each year. Although the 1974 arrangement was originally planned to last just four years, it has since been continually revised and extended. However, it is expected that all quotas on textiles will be completely phased out by 2005.

Reasons for Export Quotas
There are at least two reasons why a country imposes *export quotas* on its domestic producers. First, it may wish to maintain adequate supplies of a product in the home market. This motive is most common among countries that export natural resources that are essential to domestic business or the long-term survival of a nation.

Second, a country may limit the export of a good to restrict its supply on world markets, thereby increasing the international price of the good. This is the motive behind the formation and activities of the Organization of Petroleum Exporting Countries (OPEC) (*www.opec.org*). This group of nations from the Middle East and Latin America attempts to restrict the world's supply of crude oil to earn greater profits. Although OPEC was quite successful in its early years, the 1970s, it has been finding it difficult in recent years to get a consensus among its members to restrict oil production.

Voluntary Export Restraints
A unique version of the export quota is called a **voluntary export restraint (VER)**—a quota that a nation imposes on its own exports, usually at the request of another nation. Countries normally self-impose a voluntary export restraint in response to the threat of an import quota or total ban on the product by an importing nation. The classic example of the use of a voluntary export restraint is the automobile

voluntary export restraint (VER)
Unique version of export quota that a nation imposes on its exports, usually at the request of an importing nation.

International pressure forced China to abandon its import quota system in the filmmaking industry. In the mid 1990s, when the system was still in effect, Buena Vista International earned a mere $500,000 from the showing of the popular Disney film, The Lion King, *although the film grossed more than $1.3 million in Shanghai alone. Under what circumstances, if any, do you think nations should be allowed to impose import quotas?*

industry in the 1980s. Japanese carmakers were making significant market share gains in the U.S. market. The closing of U.S. carmakers' production facilities in the United States was creating a volatile anti-Japan sentiment among the population and the U.S. Congress. Fearing punitive legislation in Congress if Japan did not limit its automobile exports to the United States, the Japanese government and its carmakers self-imposed a voluntary export restraint on cars headed for the United States.

If domestic producers do not curtail production, consumers in the country that imposes an export quota benefit from lower prices due to a greater supply. Producers in an importing country benefit because the goods of producers from the exporting country are restrained, which may allow them to increase prices. Export quotas hurt consumers in the importing nation because of reduced selection and perhaps higher prices. However, export quotas might allow these same consumers to retain their jobs if imports were threatening to put domestic producers out of business. Again, detailed economic studies are needed to determine the winners and losers in any particular export quota case.

Tariff-Quotas A hybrid form of trade restriction is called a **tariff-quota**—a lower tariff rate for a certain quantity of imports and a higher rate for quantities that exceed the quota. Figure 6.1 shows how a tariff-quota actually works. Imports entering a nation under a quota limit of, say, 1,000 tons are charged a 10 percent tariff. But subsequent imports that do not make it under the quota limit of 1,000 tons are charged a tariff of 80 percent. Tariff-quotas are used extensively in the trade of agricultural products. Many countries implemented tariff-quotas in 1995 after their use was permitted by the international trade agency known as the GATT (now part of the World Trade Organization).

Embargoes

A complete ban on trade (imports and exports) in one or more products with a particular country is called an **embargo**. An embargo may be placed on one or a few goods or it may completely ban trade in all goods. It is the most restrictive nontariff trade barrier available, and it is typically applied to accomplish political goals. Embargoes can be decreed by individual nations or by supranational organizations such as the United Nations. Because they can be very difficult to enforce, embargoes are used less today than they have been in the past. One example of a total ban on trade with another country is the United States' embargo on trade with Cuba. In fact, U.S. tourists are not legally able to vacation in Cuba.

After a military coup ousted elected President Aristide of Haiti in the early 1990s, restraints were applied to force the military junta either to reinstate Aristide or to hold new elections. One restraint was an embargo by the Organization of American States. Because of difficulties in actually enforcing the embargo and after two years of fruitless United Nations diplomacy, the embargo failed. Then the United Nations stepped in with a ban on

tariff-quota
Lower tariff rate for a certain quantity of imports and a higher rate for quantities that exceed the quota.

embargo
Complete ban on trade (imports and exports) in one or more products with a particular country.

FIGURE 6.1

How a Tariff-Quota Works

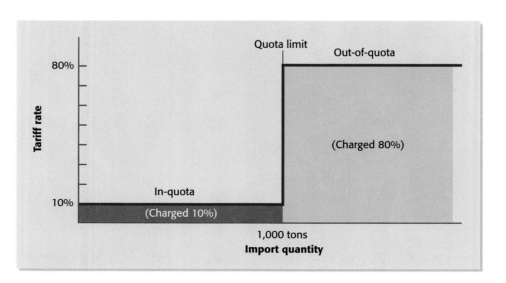

trade in oil and weapons. Despite some smuggling through the Dominican Republic, which shares the island of Hispaniola with Haiti, the embargo was generally effective, and Aristide was eventually reinstated.

Local Content Requirements

Recall from Chapter 3 that *local content requirements* are laws stipulating that producers in the domestic market must supply a specified amount of a good or service. These requirements can state that a certain portion of the end product consists of domestically produced goods or that a certain portion of the final cost of a product has domestic sources.

The purpose of local content requirements is to force companies from other nations to use local resources in their production processes—particularly labor. Similar to other restraints on imports, such requirements help protect domestic producers from the price advantage of companies based in other, low-wage, countries. Today, many developing countries use local content requirements as a strategy to boost industrialization. Companies often respond to local content requirements by locating production facilities inside the nation that stipulates such restrictions.

Although many people consider music the universal language, not all cultures are equally open to the world's diverse musical influences. To prevent Anglo-Saxon music from "corrupting" French culture, French law requires radio programs to include at least 40 percent French content. Such local content requirements are intended to protect both the French cultural identity and the jobs of French artists against other nations' pop culture that regularly washes up on French shores.

Administrative Delays

Regulatory controls or bureaucratic rules designed to impair the rapid flow of imports into a country are called **administrative delays**. This nontariff barrier includes a wide range of government actions, such as requiring international air carriers to land at inconvenient airports, requiring product inspections that damage the product itself, purposely understaffing customs offices to cause unusual time delays, and requiring special licenses that take a long time to obtain. The objective of all such administrative delays for a country is to discriminate against imported products—it is, in a word, protectionism.

Although Japan has removed some of its trade barriers, many subtle obstacles to imports remain. Products ranging from cold pills and vitamins to farm products and building materials find it hard to penetrate the Japanese market. One journalist visiting Japan reports that because her cold tablets contained more pseudoephedrine sulfate than Japanese law allows, she had to hand them over to customs agents—they were considered narcotics![13]

Saudi Arabia opened its markets further to imports when it simplified its customs clearance process. Government agencies eliminated the annual review of product registration and lowered registration fees that they charge importers. They also began allowing 60 product-testing facilities and more than 180 laboratories located outside Saudi Arabia to provide certification testing services for conformity to Saudi laws. Some of the products covered by the changes include children's toys and playground equipment.[14]

Currency Controls

Restrictions on the convertibility of a currency into other currencies are called **currency controls.** A company that wishes to import goods generally must pay for those goods in a common, internationally acceptable currency such as the U.S. dollar, European Union euro, or Japanese yen. Generally, it must also obtain the currency from its nation's domestic banking system. Governments can require companies that desire such a currency to apply for a license to obtain it. Thus, a country's government can discourage imports by restricting who is allowed to convert the nation's currency into the internationally acceptable currency.

Another way governments apply currency controls to reduce imports is by stipulating an exchange rate that is unfavorable to potential importers. Because the unfavorable

administrative delays
Regulatory controls or bureaucratic rules designed to impair the rapid flow of imports into a country.

currency controls
Restrictions on the convertibility of a currency into other currencies.

exchange rate can force the cost of imported goods to an impractical level, many potential importers simply give up on the idea. Meanwhile, the country will often allow exporters to exchange the home currency for an international currency at favorable rates to encourage exports.

Quick Study

1.   How do *tariffs* and *quotas* differ from one another? Identify the different forms each can take.
2.   Describe how a *voluntary export restraint* works, and how it differs from a quota.
3.   What is an *embargo*? Explain why it is seldom used today.
4.   Explain how *local content requirements, administrative delays,* and *currency controls* restrict trade.

Global Trading System

The global trading system certainly has seen its ups and downs. World trade volume reached a peak in the late 1800s, only to be devastated when the United States passed the Smoot–Hawley Act in 1930. The act represented a major shift in U.S. trade policy from one of free trade to one of protectionism. The act set off round after round of competitive tariff increases among the major trading nations. Other nations felt that if the United States was going to restrict its imports, they were not going to give exports from the United States free access to their domestic markets. The Smoot–Hawley Act, and the global trade wars that it helped to usher in, crippled the economies of the industrialized nations and helped spark the Great Depression. Living standards around the world were devastated throughout most of the 1930s.

We begin this section by looking at early attempts to develop a global trading system, the *General Agreement on Tariffs and Trade*, and then examine its successor, the *World Trade Organization*.

General Agreement on Tariffs and Trade (GATT)

Attitudes toward free trade changed markedly in the late 1940s. In the previous 50 years, extreme economic competition among nations and national quests to increase their resources for production helped create two world wars and the worst global economic recession ever. As a result, economists and policy makers proposed that the world band together and agree on a trading system that would help to avoid similar calamities in the future. A system of multilateral agreements was developed that became known as the *General Agreement on Tariffs and Trade (GATT)*—a treaty designed to promote free trade by reducing both tariff and nontariff barriers to international trade. The GATT was formed in 1947 by 23 nations—12 developed and 11 developing economies—and came into force in January 1948.[15]

The GATT was highly successful throughout its early years. Between 1947 and 1988, it helped to reduce average tariffs from 40 percent to 5 percent and multiply the volume of international trade by 20 times. But by the middle to late 1980s, rising nationalism worldwide and trade conflicts led to a nearly 50 percent increase in nontariff barriers to trade. Also, services (not covered by the original GATT) had become increasingly important—accounting for between 25 and 30 percent of total world trade. It was clear that a revision of the treaty was necessary, and in 1986 a new round of trade talks began.

Uruguay Round of Negotiations
The ground rules of the GATT resulted from periodic "rounds" of negotiations between its members. Though relatively short and straightforward in the early years, negotiations became protracted later as issues grew more complex. Table 6.2 shows the eight completed negotiating rounds that occurred under the auspices of the GATT. Note that whereas tariffs were the only topic of the first

TABLE 6.2

The Rounds of GATT

Year	Site	Number of Countries Involved	Topics Covered
1947	Geneva, Switzerland	23	Tariffs
1949	Annecy, France	13	Tariffs
1951	Torquay, England	38	Tariffs
1956	Geneva	26	Tariffs
1960–1961	Geneva (Dillon Round)	26	Tariffs
1964–1967	Geneva (Kennedy Round)	62	Tariffs, antidumping measures
1973–1979	Geneva (Tokyo Round)	102	Tariffs, nontariff measures, "framework agreements"
1986–1994	Geneva (Uruguay Round)	123	Tariffs, nontariff measures, rules, services, intellectual property, dispute settlement, investment measures, agriculture, textiles and clothing, natural resources, creation of the WTO

five rounds of negotiations, other topics were added in subsequent rounds (we discuss the yet-to-be completed Doha negotiations below).

The Uruguay Round of GATT negotiations, begun in 1986 in Punta del Este, Uruguay (hence its name), was the largest trade negotiation in history. It was the eighth round of GATT talks within a span of 40 years and took more than 7 years to complete. The Uruguay Round made significant progress in reducing trade barriers by revising and updating the 1947 GATT. In addition to developing plans to further reduce barriers to merchandise trade, the negotiations modified the original GATT treaty in several important ways.

Agreement on Services   Because of the ever-increasing importance of services to the total volume of world trade, nations wanted to include GATT provisions for trade in services. The General Agreement on Trade in Services (GATS) extended the principle of nondiscrimination to cover international trade in all services, although talks regarding some sectors were more successful than were others. The problem is that although trade in goods is a straightforward concept—goods are exported from one country and imported to another—it can be difficult to define exactly what a service is. Nevertheless, the GATS created during the Uruguay Round identifies four different forms that international trade in services can take:

1. *Cross-border supply.* Services supplied from one country to another (for example, international telephone calls).

2. *Consumption abroad.* Consumers or companies using a service while in another country (for example, tourism).

3. *Commercial presence.* A company establishing a subsidiary in another country to provide a service (for example, banking operations).

4. *Presence of natural persons.* Individuals traveling to another country to supply a service (for example, business consultants).

Agreement on Intellectual Property   Like services, products consisting entirely or largely of intellectual property are accounting for an increasingly large portion of international trade. Recall from Chapter 3 that *intellectual property* refers to property that results from people's intellectual talent and abilities. Products classified as intellectual property are supposed to be legally protected by copyrights, patents, and trademarks.

Although international piracy continues, the Uruguay Round took an important step toward getting it under control. It created the Agreement on Trade-Related Aspects of Intellectual Property (TRIPS) to help standardize intellectual-property rules around the world. The TRIPS Agreement concurs that protection of intellectual-property rights benefits society because it encourages the development of new technologies and other creations. It supports the articles of both the Paris Convention and the Berne Convention (see Chapter 3) and in certain instances takes a stronger stand on intellectual-property protection.

Agreement on Agricultural Subsidies Trade in agricultural products has long been a bone of contention for most of the world's trading partners at one time or another. Some of the more popular barriers countries use to protect their agricultural sectors include import quotas and subsidies paid directly to farmers. The Uruguay Round addressed the main issues of agricultural tariffs and nontariff barriers in its Agreement on Agriculture. The result is increased exposure of national agricultural sectors to market forces and increased predictability in international agricultural trade. The agreement forces countries to convert all nontariff barriers to tariffs—a process called "tariffication." It then calls on developed and developing nations to cut agricultural tariffs significantly, but places no requirements on the least-developed economies.

World Trade Organization (WTO)

Perhaps the greatest achievement of the Uruguay Round was the creation on January 1, 1995, of the *World Trade Organization (WTO)*—the international organization that regulates trade between nations. The three main goals of the WTO (*www.wto.org*) are to help the free flow of trade, to help negotiate further opening of markets, and to settle trade disputes between its members. One key component of the WTO that was carried over from GATT is the principle of nondiscrimination called **normal trade relations** (formerly called "most favored nation status")—a requirement that WTO members extend the same favorable terms of trade to all members that they extend to any single member. For example, if Japan were to reduce its import tariff on German automobiles to 5 percent, it must reduce the tariff it levies against auto imports from all other WTO nations to 5 percent.

The WTO replaced the *institution* of GATT but absorbed the GATT *agreements* (such as on services, intellectual property, and agriculture) into its own agreements. Thus, the GATT institution no longer officially exists. As of mid-2004, the WTO recognized 147 members and over 30 "observer" members.

Dispute Settlement in the WTO The power of the WTO to settle trade disputes is what really sets it apart from the GATT. Under the GATT, nations could file a complaint against another member and a committee would investigate the matter. If appropriate, the GATT would identify the unfair trade practices and member countries would pressure the offender to change its ways. But in reality, GATT rulings (usually given only after very long investigative phases that sometimes lasted years) were likely to be ignored.

In contrast, the various WTO agreements are essentially contracts between member nations that commit them to maintaining fair and open trade policies. When one WTO member files a complaint against another, the Dispute Settlement Body of the WTO moves into action swiftly. Decisions are to be rendered in less than 1 year—9 months if the case is urgent, 15 months if the case is appealed. The WTO dispute settlement system is not only faster and automatic, but its rulings cannot be ignored or blocked by members. Offenders must realign their trade policies according to WTO guidelines or suffer financial penalties and perhaps trade sanctions. Because of its ability to penalize offending member nations, the WTO's dispute settlement system is the spine of the global trading system.

Dumping and the WTO The WTO also gets involved in settling disputes that involve "dumping" and the granting of subsidies. When a company exports a product at a price that is either lower than the price normally charged in its domestic market, or lower than the cost of production, it is said to be **dumping**. Charges of dumping are made (fairly or otherwise) against almost every nation at one time or another and can occur in any type of industry. For example, Western European plastic producers considered retaliating against Asian competitors whose prices were substantially lower in European markets than at home. More recently, U.S. steel producers and their powerful union charged that steelmakers in Brazil, Japan, and Russia were dumping steel on the U.S. market at low prices. The

---

normal trade relations (formerly "most favored nation status")
Requirement that WTO members extend the same favorable terms of trade to all members that they extend to any single member.

dumping
Practice of exporting a product at a price either lower than the price that the product normally commands in its domestic market or lower than the cost of production.

problem arose as nations tried to improve their economies (through exporting) in the wake of continued reverberations from the Asian financial crisis.

Because dumping is an act by a company, not a country, the WTO cannot punish the country in which the company accused of dumping is based. Rather, it can only respond to the steps taken by the country that retaliates against the company. The WTO allows a nation to retaliate against dumping if it can show that dumping is actually occurring, can calculate the damage to its own companies, and can show that the damage is significant. The normal way a country retaliates is to charge an **antidumping duty**—an additional tariff placed on an imported product that a nation believes is being dumped on its market. But such measures must expire within five years of the time they are initiated unless a country can show that circumstances warrant their continued existence. A large number of antidumping cases have been brought before the WTO in recent years. Gary Horlick, an antidumping lawyer in Washington, D.C., remarked that the reliance on antidumping investigations looks like "Smoot–Hawley in slow motion" (referring to the destructive U.S. tariff-raising law of 1930).[16]

antidumping duty
Additional tariff placed on an imported product that a nation believes is being dumped on its market.

Subsidies and the WTO

Governments often retaliate when the competitiveness of their companies is threatened by a subsidy that another country pays its own domestic producers. Like antidumping measures, nations can retaliate against product(s) that receive an unfair subsidy by charging a **countervailing duty**—an additional tariff placed on an imported product that a nation believes is receiving an unfair subsidy. Unlike dumping, because payment of a subsidy is an action by a country, the WTO regulates the actions of the government that reacts to the subsidy as well as those of the government that originally paid the subsidy.

countervailing duty
Additional tariff placed on an imported product that a nation believes is receiving an unfair subsidy.

New Round of Negotiations

A new round of negotiations to lower trade barriers even further was agreed to at the WTO meeting in Doha, Qatar, in late 2001. The new round of negotiations could bring particular benefits for developing nations. Agricultural subsidies in the world's rich countries are worth $1 billion per day—more than six times the value of their combined aid budgets. Poor countries should also obtain greater access to rich countries' textile markets and other markets that are labor-intensive. The potential benefits are enormous considering that over 70 percent of poor nations' exports are agriculture and textiles. The Doha round also will prompt poor nations to reduce tariffs among themselves. Finally, poor nations are to receive help from rich nations in integrating themselves into the global trading system.[17]

The WTO and the Environment

Steady gains in global trade and rapid industrialization in many developing and emerging economies have generated environmental concerns among both governments and special-interest groups. Of concern to many people are levels of carbon dioxide emissions—the principal greenhouse gas, believed to contribute to global warming. Most carbon dioxide emissions are created from the burning of fossil fuels and the manufacture of cement.

The World Trade Organization has no separate agreement that deals with environmental issues. The WTO explicitly states that it is not to become a global environmental agency responsible for setting environmental standards. It leaves such tasks to national governments and the many intergovernmental organizations that already exist for such purposes. The WTO works alongside the roughly 200 international agreements on the environment. Some of these include the Montreal Protocol for protection of the ozone layer, the Basel Convention on international trade or transport of hazardous waste, and the Convention on International Trade in Endangered Species.

Nevertheless, the preamble to the agreement that established the WTO does mention the objectives of environmental protection and sustainable development. The WTO also has an internal committee called the Committee on Trade and Environment. The committee's responsibility is to study the relationship between trade and the environment and to recommend possible changes in the WTO trade agreements.

In addition, the WTO does take explicit positions on some environmental issues related to trade. First, although the WTO supports national efforts at labeling "environmentally friendly" products as such, it states that labeling requirements or policies cannot discriminate against the products of other WTO members. Second, the WTO supports policies of the least-developed countries that require full disclosure of potentially hazardous products entering their markets for reasons of public health and environmental damage.

Quick Study

1. What was the General Agreement on Tariffs and Trade (GATT)? List its main accomplishments.
2. What is the World Trade Organization (WTO)? Describe how the WTO settles trade disputes.
3. Explain the difference between an *antidumping duty* and a *countervailing duty*.
4. What efforts have been made to protect the environment from trade and rapid industrialization?

Bottom Line for Business

Despite the theoretical benefits of free trade that we discussed in Chapter 5, nations do not simply throw open their doors to trade and force their domestic businesses to sink or swim. This chapter presented the reasons governments continue to protect all or some of their industries and how they go about it. The global trading system, through the World Trade Organization, tries to strike a balance between national desires for protection and international desires for free trade.

Implications of Protection

Theoretically, globalization and the protection of free trade allow firms to relocate the production of goods and the delivery of services to locations that maximize efficiency. Yet in this chapter we've seen how the theory of free trade stands up when confronted with government interference. The involvement of governments in the flow of trade in goods and services has important implications for production efficiency and, therefore, firm strategy.

Subsidies often encourage complacency on the part of companies receiving them because they discourage competition. Subsidies can be thought of as a redistribution of wealth in society. International firms will be at a disadvantage competing against companies whose governments award subsidies. These unsubsidized firms must either reduce costs of producing and delivering their product, or differentiate it in some way to justify a higher selling price.

Because *import tariffs* raise the cost of an imported good they make domestically produced goods more attractive to consumers. This protects domestic producers and gives them a price advantage over imports. But again, because a tariff can create inefficient domestic producers that are endangered once protective tariffs are removed, deteriorating competitiveness may offset its benefits. The usual strategy for firms trying to enter markets having high import tariffs is to produce within the nation or region imposing them.

An *import quota* helps a domestic producer maintain market share and prices because competitive forces are restrained. Here, the domestic producer protected by the quota wins because its market is protected. Yet other producers lose if their production processes require the import that is subjected to a quota. These companies will likely need to pay more for their intermediate products (if available), or relocate production facilities outside the nation imposing the quota.

Similar to other restraints on imports, *local content requirements* protect domestic producers from the price advantage of companies based in low-cost countries. A firm trying to sell to a market imposing local content requirements may have no alternative strategy but to create a local production facility there. The objective of *administrative delays* for a country is to discriminate against imported products. This form of protectionism also may discourage efficiency.

A government imposing *currency controls* can require that firms apply for a license to obtain an internationally acceptable currency. In this way, a nation discourages imports by restricting who is allowed to obtain a currency that is accepted by international firms as payment for goods. A government may also block imports by stipulating an exchange rate that is unfavorable to potential importers. The unfavorable exchange rate can force the cost of imported goods to an impractical level, causing many potential importers to simply give up on the idea. On the other hand, the same country often allows exporters to exchange the home currency for an international currency at favorable rates to encourage exports.

Government subsidies for specific industries are typically paid for with the income earned from levying taxes across the economy. Whether subsidies help a nation's citizens long term is questionable at best, and they may actually harm a nation overall. Consumers may also not benefit from import tariffs because imports are more costly and domestic firms receiving protection may also raise the price of domestically produced goods. Consumers lose from import quotas because of higher prices and limited selection attributable to lower competition. In the end, these forms of protection tend to lessen the long-term gains that a nation's people obtain from free trade.

Implications of the Global Trading System

Development of the global trading system has benefited international companies greatly by promoting free trade through the reduction of both tariffs and nontariff barriers to international trade. The GATT treaty was successful in its early years, and its revision significantly improved the climate for trade. Average tariffs on merchandise trade were reduced and subsidies for agricultural products were lowered. Firms also benefited from an agreement that extended the principle of nondiscrimination to cover trade in services. The revision of GATT also clearly defined intellectual property rights—giving protection to copyrights, trademarks and service marks, and patents. This encourages firms to develop new products and processes because they know their rights to the property will be protected.

The creation of the WTO is also good for international firms because the various WTO agreements commit member nations to maintaining fair and open trade policies. Both domestic and international firms based in relatively poor nations should benefit most from a new round of negotiations launched in Doha, Qatar, in 2001. Because poor nations tend to export agricultural products and textiles, their firms in these industries will benefit from wealthy nations reducing barriers to imports in these sectors. Companies based in poor countries should also benefit from better cooperation among poor countries and their further integration into the global trading system.

SUMMARY

1. **Describe the *political, economic,* and *cultural motives* behind governmental intervention in trade.** Despite the advantages of *free trade,* government intervention is common. The main *political* motives behind government intervention in trade include (a) protecting jobs, (b) preserving national security, (c) responding to other nations' unfair trade practices, and (d) gaining influence over other nations.

The most common *economic* reasons given for nations' attempts to influence international trade are (a) protection of young industries from competition and (b) promotion of a strategic trade policy. According to the *infant industry argument,* a country's emerging industries need protection from international competition during their development phase until they become sufficiently competitive internationally. Although conceptually appealing, this argument can cause domestic companies to become noncompetitive, and inflate prices. Believers in *strategic trade policy* argue that government intervention can help companies take advantage of economies of scale and be first movers in their industries. But government assistance to domestic companies can result in inefficiency, higher costs, and even trade wars between nations.

Perhaps the most common *cultural* motive for trade intervention is protection of national identity. Unwanted cultural influence can cause a government to block imports that it believes are harmful.

2. **List and explain the methods governments use to *promote* international trade.** A *subsidy* is financial assistance to domestic producers in the form of cash payments, low-interest loans, tax breaks, product price supports, or some other form. It is intended to assist domestic companies in fending off international competitors. Critics charge that subsidies amount to corporate welfare and are detrimental in the long term.

Governments also can offer *export financing*—loans to exporters that they would not otherwise receive or loans at below-market interest rates. Another option is to guarantee that the government will repay a company's loan if the company should default on repayment—called a *loan guarantee*.

Most countries promote trade with other nations by creating what is called a *foreign trade zone (FTZ)*—a designated geographic region in which merchandise is allowed to pass through with lower customs duties (taxes) and/or fewer customs procedures. Finally, most nations have *special government agencies* responsible for promoting exports. These agencies organize trips abroad for trade officials and businesspeople and open offices abroad to promote home country exports.

3. **List and explain the methods governments use to *restrict* international trade.** A *tariff* is a government tax levied on a product as it enters or leaves a country. An *export tariff* is one that is levied by the government of a country that is exporting a product. A tariff levied by the government of a country that a product is passing through on its way to its final destination is called a *transit tariff*. An *import tariff* is one that is levied by the government of a country that is importing a product. Three categories of import tariff are *ad valorem tariffs*, *specific tariffs*, and *compound tariffs*.

A restriction on the amount (measured in units or weight) of a good that can enter or leave a country during a certain period of time is called a *quota*. Governments may impose *import quotas* to protect domestic producers or *export quotas* to maintain adequate supplies in the home market or increase prices of a product on world markets.

A complete ban on trade (imports and exports) in one or more products with a particular country is called an *embargo*. Laws stipulating that a specified amount of a good or service be supplied by producers in the domestic market are called *local content requirements*. Governments can also discourage imports by causing *administrative delays* (regulatory controls or bureaucratic rules to impair imports) or *currency controls* (restrictions on the convertibility of a currency).

4. **Discuss the importance of the *World Trade Organization* in promoting free trade.** The *General Agreement on Tariffs and Trade (GATT)* was a treaty designed to promote free trade by reducing both tariff and nontariff barriers to international trade. The *Uruguay Round* of GATT negotiations that ended in 1994 made significant progress in several areas: (1) International trade in services was included for the first time; (2) intellectual property rights were clearly defined; (3) tariff and nontariff barriers in agricultural trade were reduced significantly; and (4) the *World Trade Organization (WTO)*—an international organization to regulate trade—was created.

The three main goals of the WTO are to help the free flow of trade, to help negotiate further opening of markets, and to settle trade disputes between its members. A key component of the WTO is the principle of nondiscrimination called *normal trade relations* that requires WTO members to treat all members equally.

When a company exports a product at a price either lower than the price it normally charges in its domestic market or lower than the cost of production, it is said to be *dumping*. The WTO allows a nation to retaliate against dumping under certain conditions.

TALK IT OVER

1. Imagine that the people in your nation are convinced that international trade is harmful to their wages and jobs and that your task is to change their minds. What kinds of programs would you implement to educate your people about the benefits of trade? Describe how each would help change people's attitudes.

2. Most countries create a list of "hostile" countries and require potential exporters to those nations to apply for special permission before they are allowed to proceed. Which countries and products would you place on such a list for your nation, and why?

3. Two students are discussing efforts within the global trading system to reduce trade's negative effects on the environment. One student says, "Sure, there may be pollution effects, but they're a small price to pay for a higher standard of living." The other student agrees saying, "Yeah, those 'tree-huggers' are always exaggerating those effects anyway. Who cares if some little toad in the Amazon goes extinct? I sure don't." What counterarguments can you offer to these students?

1. As a group, select a recent business periodical in print or online and find an article that discusses government intervention in promoting or restricting trade. Write a short summary (about 800 words) of what motivated the action, which industries or individual companies are affected, and the reaction of other nations or the World Trade Organization.

2. With several of your classmates, select a company in your city or town that is involved in importing or exporting. Make an appointment to interview the owner or a manager. Your goal is to understand how government involvement in international trade has helped or harmed the company's business activities. Be sure to inquire about specific past examples and the future potential impacts of government intervention. Present the findings of your interview and other research to the class.

3. In this project, two groups of four students each will debate the case for and against protectionism surrounding a recent dramatic rise in the import of coffee into your country. One team represents businesspeople in your country who welcome the imports because they benefit their livelihood. The other group represents businesspeople who oppose the imports because they hurt their livelihood. The goal is to convince your government to introduce or not introduce protection for domestic coffee growers. After the first student from each side has spoken, the second student questions the opponent's arguments, looking for holes and inconsistencies. The third student attempts to answer these arguments. The fourth student presents a summary of each side's arguments. Finally, the class will vote on which team has offered the more compelling argument.

ad valorem tariff (p. 188)

administrative delays (p. 191)

antidumping duty (p. 195)

compound tariff (p. 188)

countervailing duty (p. 195)

currency controls (p. 191)

dumping (p. 194)

embargo (p. 190)

foreign trade zone (FTZ) (p. 185)

free trade (p. 178)

normal trade relations (p. 194)

quota (p. 188)

specific tariff (p. 188)

subsidy (p. 183)

tariff (p. 187)

tariff-quota (p. 190)

voluntary export restraint (VER) (p. 189)

1. The WTO recently ruled against a U.S. law that gave tax breaks to the nation's exporters. The WTO ordered the United States to repeal $4 billion of tax breaks for U.S. exporters who operate through offshore subsidiaries, or face possible sanction. Although the case was brought by the European Union, many European companies were ambivalent about the tax breaks because they have U.S. subsidiaries that benefit from them.

   Visit the Web site of the WTO (*www.wto.org*) and the Web sites of business periodicals on the Internet. Identify a case on which the WTO has recently ruled. What countries are involved? What cultural, political, or economic reasons do you think motivated the country to bring the case? List as many as you can. Do you think it was a fair charge and do you think the ruling was correct? Explain your answer.

   Do you think the WTO should have the power to dictate the trade policies of individual nations and punish them if they do not comply? Why or why not? Do you think countries experiencing economic difficulties should be allowed to erect temporary tariff and non-tariff barriers? Why or why not? What effect do you think such an allowance would have on the future of the global trading system?

ETHICAL CHALLENGES

1. You are an executive for a U.S. oil firm interested in forming a partnership with an Iranian oil producer. This will be a challenge because of the poor relations between the U.S. and Iran over the years. Since the early 1980s the United States has drawn fire from the business community for imposing economic sanctions (similar to an embargo) against Iran for primarily political reasons. Those sanctions disallow international trade and investment between U.S. and Iranian businesspeople. Business leaders in the United States would like the sanctions removed so they can be included in lucrative Iranian oil and gas deals in which firms from other countries are engaging. Other sanction opponents wonder if a policy of offering "all stick and no carrot" is undermining social and political change in Iran, since the offending regime goes largely unpunished. What arguments do you present to the U.S. government for removing sanctions on Iran? Do you think that one country, acting alone, can bring about reforms through the use of economic sanctions or embargoes?

2. You are the Vice President of a sugar company based in southern Florida. Your firm is struggling lately to meet demand because of poor harvests in the Caribbean Islands where your firm sources much of its raw product. Because of the Helms–Burton Act and the U.S. embargo on Cuba, your firm is not allowed to trade with Cuba. If the embargo were dropped, your firm would have an excellent source of cheap sugar, and profits would improve significantly. A U.S. senator from your state of Florida serves on an influential committee in Washington, D.C., that is reviewing the status of the embargo on Cuba. What arguments would you provide to your senator that could potentially help eliminate this trade barrier?

3. You are a consultant advising the World Trade Organization (WTO) on the U.S. Supreme Court decision regarding the State of Massachusetts and the country of Myanmar. A nonprofit trade and industry group, the National Foreign Trade Council (NFTC), based in Washington, D.C., won a court battle in 2000 against the State of Massachusetts. In a unanimous decision, the U.S. Supreme Court sided with the NFTC and struck down a Massachusetts law that was designed to deny state contracts to any company doing business in Myanmar. The Court ruled that the Massachusetts law intruded on the federal government's authority and was preempted by federal law regarding Myanmar. In fact, the U.S. Constitution states that, "foreign policy is exclusively reserved for the federal government." The NFTC says it shares concern over human rights abuses occurring in Myanmar, but believes that a coordinated, multinational effort would be most effective at instilling change in the nation.

   What advice would you provide the WTO on this issue? Do you think that companies should be penalized in their domestic business dealings because of where they do business abroad? Do you think that the World Trade Organization should get into domestic/international political matters? Why or why not? What do you think would be the effect on domestic firms if every state were allowed to punish firms based on their own foreign policy ideals?

PRACTICING INTERNATIONAL MANAGEMENT CASE

Unfair Protection or Valid Defense?

"Canada Launches WTO Challenge to U.S.... Mexico Widens Anti-dumping Measure... China to Begin Probe of Synthetic Rubber Imports... Steel Dispute Raises Issue of Free-Trade Credibility.... It Must Be Stopped," are just a sampling of headlines around the world.

International trade theories argue that nations should open their doors to trade. Conventional free-trade wisdom says that by trading with others, a country can offer its citizens a greater quantity and selection of goods at cheaper prices than it could in the absence of trade. Nevertheless, truly free trade still does not exist because national governments intervene. Despite the efforts of the World Trade Organization (WTO) and smaller groups of nations, governments still cry foul in the trade game. Worldwide, the number of antidumping cases initiated averaged 234 per year over the past 7 years, with cases at an all-time-high of 356 in 1999.

In the past, the world's richest nations would typically charge a developing nation with dumping. But today, emerging markets, too, are jumping into the fray. China recently launched an inquiry to determine whether synthetic rubber imports (used in auto tires and footwear) from Japan, South Korea, and Russia are being dumped in the country. Mexico expanded coverage of its Automatic Import Advice System. The system requires importers (from a select list of countries) to notify Mexican officials of the amount and price of a shipment 10 days prior to its expected arrival in Mexico. The 10-day notice gives domestic producers advanced warning of low-priced products so they can report dumping before the products clear customs and enter the marketplace. India set up a new government agency to handle antidumping cases. Even Argentina, Indonesia, South Africa, South Korea, and Thailand are using this recently popular tool of protectionism.

Why is dumping so popular? Oddly enough, the WTO allows it. The WTO has made major inroads on the use of tariffs, slashing them across almost every product category in recent years. But it does not have authority to punish companies, only governments. Thus, the WTO cannot make judgments against individual companies that are dumping products in other markets. It can only pass rulings against the government of the country that imposes an antidumping duty. But the WTO allows countries to retaliate against nations whose producers are suspected of dumping when it can be shown that (1) the alleged offenders are significantly hurting domestic producers, and (2) the export price is lower than the cost of production or lower than the home-market price.

Alternatives to bringing antidumping cases before the WTO do exist. U.S. President George W. Bush relied on a Section 201 or "global safeguard" investigation under U.S. trade law in 2002 to slap tariffs of up to 30 percent on steel imports. The U.S. steel industry had been suffering under an onslaught of steel imports from many nations, including Brazil, the European Union, Japan, and South Korea. Yet, nations still brought complaints about the action before the WTO. Similarly, in 2004 the U.S. government slapped around 100 percent tariffs on shrimp imported from China and Vietnam, charging those nations with dumping the crustaceans on U.S. shores.

Supporters of antidumping tariffs claim that they prevent dumpers from undercutting the prices charged by producers in a target market, driving them out of business. Another claim in support of antidumping is that it is an excellent way of retaining some protection against the potential dangers of totally free trade. Detractors of antidumping tariffs charge that once such tariffs are imposed they are rarely removed. They also claim that it costs companies and governments a great deal of time and money to file and argue their cases. It is also argued that the fear of being charged with dumping causes international competitors to keep their prices higher in a target market than would otherwise be the case. This would allow domestic companies to charge higher prices and not lose market share—forcing consumers to pay more for their goods.

Thinking Globally

1. "You can't tell consumers that the low price they are paying for that fax machine or automobile is somehow unfair. They're not concerned with the profits of some company. To them, it's just a great bargain and they want it to continue." Do you agree with this statement? Do you think that people from different cultures would respond differently to this statement? Explain your answers.

2. As we have seen, currently the WTO cannot get involved in punishing individual companies—its actions can only be directed toward governments of countries. Do you think this is a wise policy? Why or why not? Why do you think the WTO was not given authority to charge individual companies with dumping? Explain.

3. Identify a recent antidumping case that was brought before the WTO. Locate as many articles in the press as you can that discuss the case. Identify the nations, product(s), and potential punitive measures involved. Supposing you were part of the WTO's Dispute Settlement Body, would you vote in favor of the measures taken by the retaliating nation? Why or why not? *Hint*: A good Web site to visit is that of the World Trade Organization (*www.wto.org*).

learning objectives

After studying this chapter, you should be able to

1. Describe the worldwide patterns of *foreign direct investment (FDI)* and the reasons for these patterns.

2. Describe each of the *theories* that attempt to explain why foreign direct investment occurs.

3. Discuss the important *management issues* in the foreign direct investment decision.

4. Explain why *governments* intervene in the free flow of foreign direct investment.

5. Discuss the *policy instruments* that governments use to promote and restrict foreign direct investment.

foreign direct

investment

7

a look *back*

CHAPTER 6 explained business–government relations in the context of world trade in goods and services. We explored the motives and methods of government intervention. We also examined the global trading system and how it promotes free trade.

a look *at this chapter*

This chapter examines another significant form of international business, foreign direct investment (FDI). Again, we are concerned with the patterns of FDI and the theories on which it is based. We also explore why and how governments intervene in FDI activity.

a look *ahead*

CHAPTER 8 explores the trend toward greater regional integration of national economies. We explore the benefits of closer economic cooperation and examine prominent regional trading blocs that exist around the world.

VW: Untouchable

FRANKFURT, Germany—The Volkswagen Group (*www.vw.com*) owns some of the most prestigious and best-known automotive brands in the world, including Audi, Bentley, Bugatti, Lamborghini, Rolls-Royce, Seat, Skoda, and Volkswagen. From its 43 production facilities worldwide it produces 5 million cars annually. The company has sales in more than 150 countries and currently holds a 12 percent share of the world market.

But Volkswagen, like companies everywhere, is not doing it entirely on its own. Governments around the world zealously defend their biggest firms because of the fruits of business success. German Chancellor Gerhard Schröder is heavily involved in promoting Volkswagen abroad. In fact, Mr. Schröder once served on Volkswagen's supervisory board when he was governor of the state of Lower Saxony. Mr. Schröder recently opened a new assembly line at the Volkswagen plant in Anchieta, near São Paulo, Brazil, and drove Volkswagen's new Phaeton in the first public use of the new luxury model.

Volkswagen is special in Germany. The carmaker remains protected by its own law known as "Lex VW," which allows the government to block a takeover using special voting rights. Germany single-handedly killed a takeover reform proposal of the European Union (EU), partly over concern about the effect on Volkswagen. Chancellor Schröder recently told a crowd of cheering autoworkers in central Germany, "Any efforts by the commission in Brussels to smash the VW culture will meet the resistance of the federal government as long as we are in power."

Volkswagen's special treatment is rooted in the carmaker's importance to jobs in the domestic economy and in the close ties between government and management. Volkswagen employs tens of thousands of people and symbolizes the resurgence of the German economy over the past 60 years. While reading this chapter, think about the foreign direct investments of companies worldwide, and the relations between businesses and local, regional, and national governments everywhere.[1]

M any early trade theories were created at a time when most production factors (such as labor, financial capital, capital equipment, and land or natural resources) either could not be moved or could not be moved easily across national borders. But today, all of the above except land are internationally mobile. In fact, inequities in the distribution of these factors among countries often propel resources toward those countries where scarcity exists. Companies can easily finance expansion from international financial institutions, and whole factories can be picked up and moved to another country. Even labor is more mobile than in years past, although many barriers restrict the complete mobility of labor.

Foreign direct investment (FDI) is the purchase of physical assets or a significant amount of the ownership (stock) of a company in another country to gain a measure of management control. Thus, at the core of foreign direct investment are international flows of capital. But there is wide disagreement on what exactly constitutes foreign direct investment. Nations set different thresholds at which they classify an international capital flow as FDI. Most governments set the threshold at anywhere from 10 to 25 percent of stock ownership in a company abroad—the U.S. Commerce Department sets it at 10 percent. In contrast, an investment that does not involve obtaining a degree of control in a company is called a **portfolio investment**.

In this chapter, we examine the importance of foreign direct investment to the operations of international companies. We begin by exploring the growth of FDI in recent years and investigating its sources and destinations. We then take a look at several theories that attempt to explain foreign direct investment flows. Next, we turn our attention to several important management issues that arise in most decisions about whether a company should undertake FDI. This chapter closes by discussing the reasons why governments encourage or restrict foreign direct investment and the methods they use to accomplish these goals.

foreign direct investment
The purchase of physical assets or a significant amount of the ownership (stock) of a company in another country to gain a measure of management control.

portfolio investment
Investment that does not involve obtaining a degree of control in a company.

Patterns of Foreign Direct Investment

Just as international trade displays distinct patterns (see Chapter 5), so too does foreign direct investment. In this section we first take a look at the factors that have propelled growth in FDI over the past decade. We then turn our attention to the destinations and sources of foreign direct investment.

Ups and Downs of Foreign Direct Investment

Flows of foreign direct investment (FDI) expanded rapidly throughout the 1990s. After growing about 20 percent per year in the first half of the 1990s, *FDI inflows* grew by about 40 percent per year in the second half of the decade. FDI inflows then jumped 57 percent in 1999, and grew another 29 percent in 2000 to peak at around $1.4 trillion. A contraction of

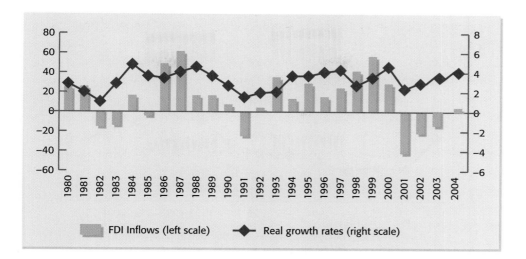

FIGURE 7.1

Growth Rate of FDI Versus GDP

FDI Inflows (left scale)   Real growth rates (right scale)

41 percent in 2001 and another 21 percent in 2002 brought down FDI inflows to around $651 billion. This pattern is illustrated in Figure 7.1, which also shows changes in FDI flows are far more erratic than changes in overall world GDP.[2]

Main causes of the recent downturn in FDI are slower economic growth in many developed nations since 2000, tumbling stock market valuations, and fewer privatizations of state-owned firms than in the past. But despite the ebb and flow in FDI flows we see in Figure 7.1, the long-term trend points toward greater FDI inflows worldwide. It appears the downturn in FDI bottomed out in 2003, and a new emphasis on "off-shoring" activity in services is driving renewed activity in FDI flows. Two main reasons account for the rising tide of FDI flows over the past decade or so, and will continue to propel it in the future—*globalization* and *mergers and acquisitions.*

Globalization   Recall from Chapter 6 that in the 1980s old barriers to trade were not being reduced and new, creative barriers seemed to be popping up in many nations. This presented a problem for companies that were trying to export their products to markets around the world. This resulted in a wave of FDI, as many companies entered promising markets to get around growing trade barriers. But then the Uruguay Round of GATT negotiations created renewed determination to further reduce barriers to trade. As countries lowered their trade barriers, companies realized that they could now produce in the most efficient and productive locations around the world, and simply export to their markets worldwide. This set off another wave of FDI flows into low-cost newly industrialized and emerging nations worldwide. Therefore, the forces that are causing globalization to occur are part of the reason for long-term growth in foreign direct investment.

Increasing globalization is also causing a growing number of international companies from emerging markets to undertake FDI. For example, companies from Taiwan began investing heavily in other nations in the mid-1980s. Acer (*www.acer.com*), headquartered in Singapore but founded in Taiwan, manufactures personal computers and computer components. Just 20 years after it opened for business, Acer had spawned 10 subsidiaries worldwide and became the dominant industry player in many emerging markets.

Mergers and Acquisitions   The number of *mergers and acquisitions (M&A)* and their exploding values also underlie long-term growth in foreign direct investment. In fact, cross-border M&As are the main vehicle through which companies undertake foreign direct investment. Throughout the 1980s and 1990s, all M&A activity (domestic and international) grew at 42 percent annually, numbering more than 26,000 per year at the end of the 1990s. Over that period, the value of all M&A activity as a share of GDP rose from 0.3 percent to 8 percent. Cross-border M&As peaked in 2000 at around

FIGURE 7.2

Value of Cross-Border M&As

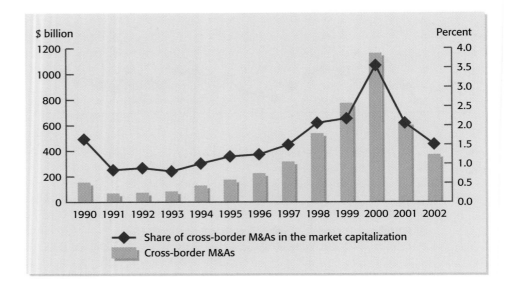

$1.15 trillion, accounting for about 3.7 percent of the market capitalization of stock exchanges worldwide (see Figure 7.2). Although the reasons mentioned above for lower FDI inflows also caused less cross-border M&A activity, indicators point to a coming rebound in such activity.[3]

The power of the largest multinationals seems to be multiplying every year. The largest deal ever was the $203 billion takeover of Mannesmann of Germany by Vodafone Group (*www.vodafone.com*) of Britain. Their growing confidence is apparent in the comments of an executive during a meeting over the merger of Travelers Group (*www.travelers.com*) and Citicorp (*www.citicorp.com*). At one point in the merger talks, a director apparently asked the question: "Can anyone stop us?" After a brief silence, someone replied, "NATO" (the military alliance between the United States, Canada, and nations across Europe). Such confidence is fueling the continuation of mergers worldwide.[4]

Many cross-border M&A deals are driven by the desire of companies to do any or all of the following:

- Get a foothold in a new geographic market
- Increase a firm's global competitiveness
- Fill gaps in companies' product lines in a global industry
- Reduce costs in areas such as research and development, production, or distribution

But large global companies and the mergers and buyouts occurring among them do not comprise all foreign direct investment. Entrepreneurs and small businesses also play important roles in the expansion of FDI flows.

Role of Entrepreneurs and Small Businesses
Data do not exist that specifically state the portion of worldwide FDI that is contributed by entrepreneurs and small businesses. Nevertheless, we know from anecdotal evidence that these companies are engaged in FDI.

Consider the case of Brian Bowen and a few adventurous buddies from Perry, Georgia. When Uzbekistan (a former Soviet Union republic) opened its borders to investment in the 1990s, Bowen and five fellow entrepreneurial friends took their savings and went in to set up cellular phone service in Tashkent, Uzbekistan. Tashkent was almost entirely leveled by an earthquake in 1966 and the surviving landline telephone service dated from the 1920s. But today, the country would shut down without the cellular service provided by Bowen's company, International Communication Group (ICG). Bowen and his friends share ownership of the company with the Uzbekistan government. Bowen admits that the arrangement did present some difficulties: "I don't have any experience dealing with the KGB, the mafia, or the family connections in the bureaucracy here." In addition to learning the ins and outs of the government bureaucracy, Bowen has learned to eat horsemeat, drink vodka toasts, and enjoy *plov*—a dish of pilaf rice and mutton. The company has 7,000 subscribers, 240 employees, and could be worth as much as $100 million by some industry estimates.[5]

Unhindered by many of the constraints of a large company, entrepreneurs investing in other markets often demonstrate an inspiring can-do spirit mixed with ingenuity and bravado. For a day-in-the-life look at a young entrepreneur who is realizing his dreams in China, see the Entrepreneur's Survival Kit titled, "Cowboy Candy Rides into Manchuria."

Worldwide Flows of FDI

More than 64,000 multinational companies with over 870,000 affiliates abroad are driving the FDI flows.[6] Developed countries remain the prime destination for FDI because cross-border M&As are concentrated in developed nations. Developed countries account for around 70 percent ($460 billion) of global FDI inflows, which were a little over $650 billion in 2002. In comparison, FDI inflows to developing countries were valued at $162 billion—about 30 percent of world FDI inflows and down from a peak of a little more than 40 percent in 1994. Countries in Central and Eastern Europe accounted for nearly 4.5 percent of global FDI, or almost $29 billion in 2002.

Among developed countries, European Union (EU) nations, the United States, and Japan accounted for the vast majority of world inflows. The EU was the world's largest FDI recipient (more than 57 percent of the world total), with inflows of more than $374 billion in 2002. The driving force behind this figure is increased consolidation in Europe among large national competitors, which is being encouraged by further efforts at EU regional integration.

Developing nations had varying experiences in 2002. FDI inflows to developing nations in Asia were just over $95 billion in 2002, with China itself attracting nearly $53 billion. Meanwhile, Hong Kong came in second with nearly $14 billion. More FDI into China is sure to come following its entry into the World Trade Organization in 2002. India, the largest recipient on the Asian subcontinent, had inflows of nearly $3.5 billion. Outward FDI from developing nations in Asia is also on the rise, coinciding with the rise of these nations' own global competitors.

Elsewhere, FDI inflows to all of Africa accounted for about 1.7 percent of total world FDI inflows in 2002. FDI to Africa declined from about $19 billion in 2001 to just over $11 billion. After tripling during the second half of the 1990s, FDI flows into Latin America and the Caribbean also fell in 2002, despite privatization efforts there. Finally, FDI inflows to Central and Eastern Europe held fairly steady and hit nearly $29 billion in 2002.

Quick Study

1. What is the difference between *foreign direct investment* and *portfolio investment?*
2. What factors influence global flows of foreign direct investment?
3. Identify the main destinations of foreign direct investment. Is a shift in the pattern taking place?

Explanations for Foreign Direct Investment

So far we have examined the flows of foreign direct investment but have not investigated explanations for why FDI occurs. There are four main theories that attempt to explain why companies engage in foreign direct investment: *international product life cycle, market imperfections (internalization), eclectic theory,* and *market power.* Let's now look at each of these in detail.

International Product Life Cycle

international product life cycle Theory stating that a company will begin by exporting its product and later undertake foreign direct investment as a product moves through its life cycle.

Although we introduced the international product life cycle in Chapter 5 in the context of international trade, it also has been used to explain foreign direct investment.[7] The theory of the **international product life cycle** states that a company will begin by exporting its product and later undertake foreign direct investment as a product moves through its life cycle. In the *new product stage,* a good is produced in the home country because of uncertain domestic demand and to keep production close to the research department that developed the product. In the *maturing product stage,* the company directly invests in production facilities in countries where demand is great enough to warrant its own production facilities. In the final *standardized product stage,* increased competition creates pressures to reduce production costs. In response, a company builds production capacity in low-cost developing nations to serve its markets around the world.

Despite its conceptual appeal, the international product life cycle theory is limited in its power to explain why companies choose FDI over other forms of market entry. A local firm in the target market could pay for the right (license) to use the special assets needed to manufacture a particular product. In this way, a company could avoid the additional risks associated with direct investments in the market. The theory also fails to explain why firms choose FDI over exporting activities. It might be less expensive to serve a market abroad by increasing output at the home-country factory rather than by building additional capacity within the target market.

The theory explains why the FDI of some firms follows the international product life cycle of their products. But it does not explain why other market entry modes are inferior or less advantageous options. Let's now look at a more recently developed theory—*market imperfections (internalization) theory.*

Market Imperfections (Internalization)

A market that is said to operate at peak efficiency (prices are as low as they can possibly be) and where goods are readily and easily available is said to be a *perfect market.* However, perfect markets are rarely, if ever, seen in business because of factors that cause a breakdown in the efficient operation of an industry—called *market imperfections.* **Market imperfections** theory states that when an imperfection in the market makes a transaction less efficient than it could be, a company will undertake foreign direct investment to internalize the transaction and thereby remove the imperfection. There are two market imperfections that are relevant to this discussion—trade barriers and specialized knowledge.

Trade Barriers
One common market imperfection in international business is trade barriers, such as tariffs. For example, the North American Free Trade Agreement stipulates that a sufficient portion of a product's content must originate within Canada, Mexico, or the United States in order for the product to escape tariff charges when it is imported to any of these three markets. That is why a large number of Korean manufacturers of videocassette recorders (VCRs) invested in production facilities in Tijuana, Mexico, just south of Mexico's border with California. By investing in production facilities in Mexico, the Korean companies were able to skirt the North American tariffs that would have been levied if they were to export VCRs from Korean factories. The presence of a market imperfection (tariffs) caused those companies to undertake foreign direct investment.

Specialized Knowledge
The unique competitive advantage of a company sometimes consists of specialized knowledge. This knowledge could be the technical expertise of engineers or the special marketing abilities of managers. When the knowledge is technical expertise, companies can charge a fee to companies in other countries for use of the knowledge in producing the same or a similar product. But when a company's specialized knowledge is embodied in its employees, the only way to exploit a market opportunity in another nation may be to undertake FDI.

The possibility that a company will create a future competitor by charging another company for access to its knowledge is another market imperfection that can encourage FDI. Rather than trade a short-term gain (the fee charged another company) for a long-term loss (lost competitiveness), a company will prefer to undertake investment. For example, as Japan rebuilt its industries in the 1950s following the Second World War, many Japanese companies paid Western firms for access to the special technical knowledge embodied in their products. Those Japanese companies became adept at revising and improving many of these technologies and became leaders in their industries, such as electronics and automobiles.

Eclectic Theory

The **eclectic theory** states that firms undertake foreign direct investment when the features of a particular location combine with ownership and internalization advantages to make a location appealing for investment.[8] A *location advantage* is the advantage of locating a particular economic activity in a specific location because of the characteristics (natural or acquired) of that location.[9] These advantages have historically been natural resources such as oil in the Middle East, timber in Canada, and copper in Chile. However, they can also be acquired advantages, such as a productive workforce. An *ownership advantage* is the advantage that a company has because of its ownership of some special asset, such as brand recognition, technical knowledge, or management ability. An *internalization advantage* is the advantage that arises from internalizing a business activity rather than leaving it to a relatively inefficient market. This theory states that when all these advantages are present, a company will undertake FDI.

market imperfections
Theory stating that when an imperfection in the market makes a transaction less efficient than it could be, a company will undertake foreign direct investment to internalize the transaction and thereby remove the imperfection.

eclectic theory
Theory stating that firms undertake foreign direct investment when the features of a particular location combine with ownership and internalization advantages to make a location appealing for investment.

Market Power

market power
Theory stating that a firm tries to establish a dominant market presence in an industry by undertaking foreign direct investment.

vertical integration
Extension of company activities into stages of production that provide a firm's inputs (backward integration) or absorb its output (forward integration).

Firms often seek the greatest amount of power possible in their industries relative to rivals. The **market power** theory states that a firm tries to establish a dominant market presence in an industry by undertaking foreign direct investment. The benefit of market power is greater profit because the firm is far better able to dictate the cost of its inputs and/or the price of its output.

One way a company can achieve market power (or dominance) is through **vertical integration**—the extension of company activities into stages of production that provide a firm's inputs (*backward integration*) or absorb its output (*forward integration*). Sometimes a company can effectively control the world supply of an input needed by its industry if it has the resources or ability to integrate backward into supplying that input. Companies may also be able to achieve a great deal of market power if they can integrate forward to increase control over output. For example, they could perhaps make investments in distribution to leapfrog channels of distribution that are tightly controlled by competitors.

Quick Study

1. Explain the *international product life cycle theory* of foreign direct investment (FDI).
2. How does the theory of *market imperfections* (internalization) explain FDI?
3. Explain the *eclectic theory,* and identify the three advantages necessary for FDI to occur.
4. How does the theory of *market power* explain the occurrence of FDI?

Management Issues in the FDI Decision

Decisions about whether to engage in foreign direct investment involve several important issues regarding management of the company and its market. Some of these issues are grounded in the inner workings of firms that undertake FDI, such as the control desired over operations abroad or the firm's cost of production. Others are related to the market and industry in which a firm competes, such as the preferences of customers or the actions of rivals. Let's now examine each of these important issues.

Control

Many companies investing abroad are greatly concerned with controlling the activities that occur in the local market, for a variety of reasons. Perhaps the company wants to be certain that its product is being marketed in the same way in the local market as it is at home. Or maybe it wants to ensure that the selling price remains the same in both markets. Some companies try to maintain ownership of a large portion of the local operations, say even up to 100 percent, in the belief that greater ownership gives them greater control.

However, for a variety of reasons even complete ownership does not *guarantee* control. For example, the local government might intervene and require a company to hire some local managers rather than bringing them all in from the home office. Companies may need to prove a scarcity of skilled local managerial talent before the government will let them bring managers in from the home country. Governments might also require that all goods produced in the local facility be exported so they do not compete with products of the country's domestic firms.

Partnership Requirements Because of the importance of control, many companies have strict policies regarding how much ownership they will take in firms in other nations. In fact, prior to the 1990s IBM (*www.ibm.com*) had the strict policy that international

At one time, Boeing aircraft were made entirely in the United States. But today Boeing can source its landing-gear doors from Northern Ireland, outboard wing flaps from Italy, wing tip assemblies from Korea, rudders from Australia, and fuselages from Japan. Sometimes, Boeing buys a large portion of their international suppliers' physical assets or traded stock (called foreign direct investment) to gain some decision making power in supplier organizations. Can you think of other companies that control suppliers through a large percentage of ownership?

subsidiaries needed to be 100 percent owned by the home office. However, companies must sometimes abandon such policies when a country demands shared ownership in return for access to its market.

Governments saw such requirements as a way to shield their workers and industries from what they perceived as exploitation or domination by large international firms. Companies would sometimes sacrifice control to pursue a market opportunity, but frequently they did not. By the 1980s, most countries retreated from such a hard-line stance and began to open their doors to investment by multinationals. For example, in the 1980s Mexico was making its decisions on investment by multinationals on a case-by-case basis. IBM was trying to negotiate for 100 percent ownership of a facility in Guadalajara and got the go-ahead after the company made numerous concessions in other areas.

Benefits of Cooperation
Recent years have seen greater harmony between governments and international companies, though the business press still tends to highlight the controversies. The reason is that governments of many developing and newly industrialized countries have come to realize the benefits of investment by multinationals, including decreased unemployment, increased tax revenues, training to create a more highly skilled workforce, and the transfer of technology. A country with a reputation for overly restricting the operations of multinational enterprises can see its inward investment flow dry up. Indeed, restrictive policies of India's government continue to deny the nation the foreign direct investment flows in the proportions that neighboring Southeast Asian nations are receiving.

Cooperation also frequently opens important communication channels that help firms to maintain positive relationships in the host country. Both parties tend to walk a fine line—cooperating most of the time, but holding fast on occasions when the stakes are especially high.

Cooperation with a local partner and respect for national pride in Central Europe contributed to the successful acquisition of Hungary's Borsodi brewery (formerly a state-owned enterprise) by Belgium's Interbrew (*www.interbrew.com*). From the start, Interbrew wisely insisted it would move ahead provided (1) the local brand would receive total backing, (2) local management would be in charge, and (3) Interbrew would assist local management with technical, marketing, sales, distribution, and general management training. Borsodi eventually became one of the parent company's key subsidiaries and is now run entirely by Hungarian managers.

Purchase-or-Build Decision

Another important matter for managers is whether to purchase an existing business or to build a subsidiary abroad from the ground up—called a *greenfield investment.* An acquisition generally provides the investor with an existing plant and equipment as well as personnel. The acquiring firm may also benefit from the goodwill the existing company has built up over the years and, perhaps, brand recognition of the existing firm. The purchase of an existing business may also allow for alternative methods of financing the purchase, such as an exchange of stock ownership between the companies. Factors that can reduce the appeal of purchasing existing facilities include obsolete equipment, poor relations with workers, and an unsuitable location.

Mexico's Cemex, S.A. (*www.cemex.com*), is a multinational company that made a fortune by buying struggling, inefficient plants around the world and reengineering them. Chairman Lorenzo Zambrano has long figured that it was "Buy big globally, or be bought." The success of Cemex in using FDI has confounded, even rankled, its competitors in developed nations. An example is when Cemex borrowed money and carried out a $1.8 billion purchase of Spain's two largest cement companies, Valenciana and Sanson. Of the company's $8 billion in assets at the time, nearly half of the total was international.

But adequate facilities are sometimes simply unavailable and a company must go ahead with a greenfield investment. Because Poland is a source of skilled and inexpensive labor, it is an appealing location for car manufacturers. But the country had little in the way of advanced car-production facilities when General Motors (*www.gm.com*) was considering investing there. So, GM built a $320 million facility in Poland's Silesian region. The factory has the potential to produce 200,000 units annually—some of which are designated for export to profitable markets in Western Europe. However, greenfield investments can have their share of headaches—obtaining the necessary permits and financing and hiring local personnel can be a real problem in some markets.

We have only addressed some of the issues important to managers when considering purchasing or building in a market abroad. We will have more to say on this topic in Chapter 15, where we will see how companies actually take on such an ambitious goal. In the meantime, for additional insight into the concerns of managers in this situation see the Global Manager's Toolbox titled, "Investing Abroad? Be Prepared for Surprises."

Production Costs

There are many factors that affect the cost of production in any national market. For example, labor regulations can increase the hourly cost of production severalfold. Companies may be required to provide benefits packages for their employees that are over and above hourly wages. More time than was planned for might be required to train workers adequately to bring productivity up to an acceptable standard. Although the cost of land and the tax rate on profits can be lower in the local market (or purposely lowered to attract multinationals), it cannot be assumed that they will remain constant. Companies from around the world using Taiwan as a production base have witnessed rising wages and land prices that erode profits as the economy continues to industrialize. Companies are instead finding that China is their low-cost location of choice.

rationalized production
System of production in which each of a product's components is produced where the cost of producing that component is lowest.

Rationalized Production   One approach companies use to contain production costs is **rationalized production**—a system of production in which each of a product's components is produced where the cost of producing that component is lowest. All the components are then brought together at one central location for assembly into the final product. Consider the typical stuffed animal made in China whose components are all imported to China (with the exception of the polycore thread with which it's sewn). The stuffed animal's eyes are molded in Japan. Its outfit is imported from France. The polyester-fiber stuffing comes from either Germany or the United States, and the pile-fabric "fur" is produced in Korea. Only final assembly of these components occurs in China.

global manager's TOOLBOX

Investing Abroad? Be Prepared for Surprises

The decision of whether to build facilities in a market abroad or to purchase the existing operations of a company already in the local market can be a difficult task. Managers can minimize their risk by preparing themselves and their company for any number of surprises that their firms might face, including the following:

- **Human Resource Policies.** This aspect of FDI often holds the biggest surprise. Many managers erroneously assume the policies they use at home can simply be imported into the local culture with minimal revision. Unfortunately, these policies seldom address local customs and abide by local regulations. For example, many European countries require government approval for a plant to run a continuous operation in several shifts and have regulations governing shift work for women in certain manufacturing operations.

- **Labor Costs.** This factor of production is often higher than expected. For instance, Denmark has a minimum wage of about $13 an hour—more than twice as high as that of the United States. Mexico has a minimum daily rate of only $3. But the effective rate is nearly double because of government-mandated benefits and employment practices.

- **Mandated Benefits.** These often cover elements totally alien to managers and can include things such as company-supplied clothing and meals, required profit sharing, guaranteed employment contracts, and generous dismissal policies. Costs of these programs can top 100 percent of an employee's wages. Such programs are typically nonnegotiable and strictly enforced. Violations can result in government seizure of company property,

assessment of large fines, and even prison terms for executives.

- **Unions.** These differ a great deal from country to country. In some countries organized labor is present at almost every company, although relations can be more or less hostile than in the home market and strikes at individual plants can be frequent or seldom. In Scandinavia, rather than dealing with a single union at its plant, an employer may have to negotiate with five or six—each representing a different skill or profession.

- **Economic-Development Incentives.** Existing in most countries these can be substantial and can change constantly. For example, the European Union is trying to standardize incentives based on unemployment levels. But some member countries continually stretch the rules, and several have been penalized for exceeding guidelines.

- **Information.** Comprehensive and comparable data on vital factors such as the availability of labor, utility services, and plant sites simply do not exist in some countries. Such information, although varying in quality and availability, is generally good in developed countries; in undeveloped countries it is suspect at best. Therefore, any firm considering international expansion must perform careful research early in the decision process.

- **Personal and Political Contacts.** These types of contacts can be extremely important—especially in developing and emerging nations—and are sometimes the only way to get operations established. But using them can be difficult. Moreover, complying with practices that are common in the local market can create ethical dilemmas for managers.

Although highly efficient, a potential problem with this production model is that a work stoppage in one country can bring the entire production process to a standstill. For example, production of automobiles is highly rationalized, with parts coming in from a multitude of countries for assembly. When the United Auto Workers (*www.uaw.com*) union held a strike for many weeks against General Motors (*www.gm.com*) several years ago, many of GM's international assembly plants were threatened. The plant at which the UAW chose to launch their strike supplied brake pads to virtually all of GM's plants throughout North America.

Focus on the Mexican *Maquiladora* Stretching 2,000 miles from the Pacific Ocean to the Gulf of Mexico, the 130-mile-wide strip along the U.S.–Mexican border may well be North America's fastest-growing region. With 11 million people and $150 billion in output, the region's economy is larger than that of Poland's and close to the size of Thailand's. The combination of a low-wage regional economy nestled next to a prosperous giant is now becoming a model for other regions that are split by wage or technology gaps. Some analysts compare the U.S.–Mexican border region to that between Hong Kong and its manufacturing realm, China's Guangdong Province. Officials from cities along the border between Germany and Poland are also studying the U.S.–Mexican experience. Yet, ethical dilemmas have arisen over the wide gap between Mexican and U.S. wages and over the loss of U.S. union jobs to *maquiladora* nonunion jobs. *Maquiladoras* also do not operate under the same stringent environmental regulations to which companies across the border must adhere.

Cost of Research and Development   As the role of technology as a powerful competitive factor continues to grow, the soaring cost of developing subsequent stages of technology has led multinationals to engage in cross-border alliances and acquisitions. For instance, huge multinational pharmaceutical companies are intensely interested in the pioneering biotechnology work done by smaller, entrepreneurial start-ups. Cadus Pharmaceutical Corporation of New York used yeast to determine the function of 400 genes that are related to so-called receptor molecules. Many disorders are associated with the improper functioning of these receptors—making them good targets for drug development. Britain's SmithKline Beecham then invested around $68 million with Cadus in order to access Cadus' yeast work [SmithKline Beecham has since merged with pharmaceutical firm Glaxo, visit the combined firm at (*www.gsk.com*).][10]

One indicator of the significance of technology in foreign direct investment is the amount of R&D being conducted by affiliates of parent companies in other countries. The globalization of innovation and the phenomenon of foreign direct investment in R&D are not necessarily motivated by demand factors such as the size of local markets. Instead, foreign direct investment in R&D appears more likely to be spurred by supply factors such as gaining access to high-quality scientific and technical human capital.[11]

Customer Knowledge

The behavior of buyers is frequently an important issue in the decision of whether to undertake foreign direct investment. A local presence can help companies gain valuable knowledge about customers that could not be obtained in the home market. For example, when customer preferences for a product differ a great deal from country to country, a local presence might help companies to better understand such preferences and tailor their products accordingly.

Some countries have quality reputations in certain product categories. German automotive engineering, Italian shoes, French perfume, and Swiss watches impress customers as being of superior quality. Because of these perceptions, it can be profitable for a firm to produce its product in the country with the quality reputation, although the company is based in another country. For example, a cologne or perfume producer might want to bottle its fragrance in France and give it a French name. Such image appeal can be strong enough to encourage foreign direct investment.

Following Clients

Firms commonly engage in foreign direct investment when doing so puts them close to firms for which they act as a supplier. This practice of "following clients" can be expected in industries in which many component parts are obtained from suppliers with whom a manufacturer has a close working relationship. It also tends to result in clusters in which companies that supply one another's inputs congregate in a certain geographic region (see Chapter 5). For example, when Mercedes (*www.mercedes.com*) opened its first international plant just outside Tuscaloosa, Alabama, as many as nine automobile-parts suppliers also moved to the area from Germany—bringing with them additional investment in the millions of dollars.

Following Rivals

FDI decisions frequently resemble a "follow the leader" scenario in industries with a limited number of large firms. In other words, many of these firms believe that choosing not to make a move parallel to that of the "first mover" might result in being shut out of a potentially lucrative market. For example, when firms based in industrial countries moved back into South Africa after the end of apartheid, their competitors followed. Of course, each market can sustain only a certain number of rivals. Firms that cannot compete will choose the "least damaging option." This seems to have been the case for Pepsi (*www.pepsi.com*), which went back into South Africa in 1994, but withdrew in 1997 after being crushed there by Coke (*www.cocacola.com*).

Quick Study

1. Why is control important to companies considering the FDI decision?
2. What is the role of production costs in the FDI decision? Define *rationalized production*.
3. Explain the need for customer knowledge, following clients, and following rivals in the FDI decision.

Government Intervention in Foreign Direct Investment

Nations often intervene in the flow of FDI to protect their cultural heritages, domestic companies, and, of course, jobs. For instance, the French government, wanting to preserve its national culture, provides financial backing to promote French culture. Asterix and Obelix, the Gallic warriors loved by comic fans worldwide, came to life in the most expensive film in French history: $48.2 million. Also receiving foreign investment from Germany and Italy, the film provided an "image of resistance to American cinematographic imperialism," as French newspaper, *Le Monde*, put it, referring to the importation of Hollywood movies.

Nations can enact laws, create regulations, or construct administrative hurdles with which companies from other nations must deal if they wish to invest in the nation. Yet with FDI flows down from earlier years, nations are competing against one another to attract investment by multinational companies. The result of increased national competition for investment is seen in the regulatory changes governments enact to encourage or discourage investment. As Table 7.1 demonstrates, the number of regulatory changes governments have introduced in recent years has climbed significantly, the vast majority of which are *more favorable* to FDI.

TABLE 7.1

National Regulations and FDI

	1993	1994	1995	1996	1997	1998	1999	2000	2001	2002
Number of countries that changed their investment regimes	57	49	64	65	76	60	63	69	71	70
Number of changes that were:	102	110	112	114	151	145	140	150	208	248
More favorable to FDI	101	108	106	98	135	136	131	147	194	236
Less favorable to FDI	1	2	6	16	16	9	9	3	14	12

In a general sense, a bias toward protectionism or openness is rooted in a nation's culture, history, and politics. Values, attitudes, and beliefs form the basis for much of a government's position regarding foreign direct investment. For example, South American nations with strong cultural ties to a European heritage (such as Argentina) are generally enthusiastic about investment received from European nations. South American nations with stronger indigenous influences (such as Ecuador) are generally less enthusiastic.

Opinions vary widely on the appropriate amount of foreign direct investment a country should allow. At one extreme are those who favor complete economic self-sufficiency and oppose any form of FDI. At the other extreme are those who favor free markets with no government intervention at all. However, most countries believe that a certain amount of FDI is desirable to raise national output and enhance the standard of living for their peoples. Thus, in between the two extremes are those who believe that the decision of whether to allow investment depends on the particular situation. Besides philosophical ideals, countries intervene in FDI for a host of far more practical reasons. But before we take a look at those reasons, we must understand what is meant by a country's *balance of payments*.

Balance of Payments

balance of payments
A national accounting system that records all payments to entities in other countries and all receipts coming into the nation.

A country's **balance of payments** is a national accounting system that records all payments to entities in other countries and all receipts coming into the nation. International transactions that result in payments (outflows) to entities in other nations are reductions in the balance of payments accounts, and are therefore recorded with a minus sign. International transactions that result in receipts (inflows) from other nations are additions to the balance of payments accounts, and thus are recorded with a plus sign. For example, when a U.S. company buys 40 percent of the publicly traded stock of a Mexican company on Mexico's stock market, the U.S. balance of payments records the transaction as an outflow of capital and it is recorded with a minus sign. Table 7.2 shows the recent balance of payments accounts for the United States. As shown in the table, any nation's balance of payments consists of two major components—the *current account* and *capital account*. Let's now describe each of these accounts and discuss how to read Table 7.2.

TABLE 7.2

U.S. Balance of Payments Accounts, (U.S. $ millions)

Current Account		
Exports of goods and services and income receipts	1,418,568	
Merchandise	772,210	
Services	293,492	
Income receipts on U.S. assets abroad	352,866	
Imports of goods and services and income payments		−1,809,099
Merchandise		−1,224,417
Services		−217,024
Income payments on foreign assets in U.S.		−367,658
Unilateral transfers		−54,136
Current account balance		−444,667
Capital Account		
Increase in U.S. assets abroad (capital outflow)		−580,952
U.S. official reserve assets		−290
Other U.S. government assets		−944
U.S. private assets		−579,718
Foreign assets in the U.S. (capital inflow)	1,024,218	
Foreign official assets	37,619	
Other foreign assets	986,599	
Capital account balance	443,266	
Statistical discrepancy	55,537	

Current Account The **current account** is a national account that records transactions involving the import and export of goods and services, income receipts on assets abroad, and income payments on foreign assets inside the country. The *merchandise* account in Table 7.2 includes exports and imports of tangible goods such as computer software, electronic components, and apparel. The *services* account includes exports and imports of services such as tourism, business consulting, and banking services. Suppose a company in the United States receives payment for consulting services provided to a company in another country. The receipt is recorded as an "export of services" and assigned a plus sign in the services account in the balance of payments.

The *income receipts* account includes income earned on U.S. assets held abroad. When a U.S. company's subsidiary in another country remits profits back to the parent in the United States, the receipt is recorded in the income receipts account and given a plus sign. The *income payments* account includes income paid to entities in other nations that is earned on assets they hold in the United States. For instance, when a French company's U.S. subsidiary sends profits earned in the United States back to the parent company in France, the transaction is recorded in the income payments account as an outflow and given a minus sign.

A **current account surplus** occurs when a country exports more goods and services and receives more income from abroad than it imports and pays abroad. Conversely, a **current account deficit** occurs when a country imports more goods and services and pays more abroad than it exports and receives from abroad. Table 7.2 shows that the United States had a current account deficit in that particular year.

Capital Account The **capital account** is a national account that records transactions involving the purchase or sale of *assets*. Suppose a U.S. citizen buys shares of stock in a Mexican company on Mexico's stock market. The transaction would show up on the capital accounts of both the United States and Mexico—as an outflow of assets from the United States and an inflow of assets to Mexico. Conversely, suppose a Mexican investor buys real estate in the United States. That transaction also shows up on the capital accounts of both nations—as an inflow of assets to the United States and as an outflow of assets from Mexico. Although the balances of the current and capital accounts should be the same, there commonly is error caused by recording methods. This figure is recorded in Table 7.2 as a *statistical discrepancy*.

Reasons for Intervention by the Host Country

A number of reasons underlie a government's decisions regarding foreign direct investment by international companies. Let's now look at the two main reasons countries intervene in FDI flows—the *balance-of-payments* and *to obtain resources and benefits*.

Balance of Payments Many governments see intervention as the only way to keep their balance of payments under control. First, because foreign direct investment inflows are recorded as additions to the balance of payments, a nation gets a balance-of-payments boost from an initial FDI inflow. Second, as we saw in Chapter 6, countries can impose local content requirements on investors from other nations coming in for the purpose of local production. This gives local companies the chance to become suppliers to the production operation. This can help to reduce the nation's imports and thereby improve its balance of payments. Third, exports (if any) generated by the new production operation can have a favorable impact on the host country's balance of payments.

But when companies repatriate profits back to their home countries, they deplete the foreign exchange reserves of their host countries. These capital outflows decrease the balance of payments of the host country. To shore up its balance of payments, the host nation may prohibit or restrict the nondomestic company from removing profits to its home country.

Alternatively, host countries conserve their foreign exchange reserves when international companies reinvest their earnings. Reinvesting in local manufacturing facilities can also improve the competitiveness of local producers and boost a host nation's exports—thus improving its balance-of-payments position.

current account
A national account that records transactions involving the import and export of goods and services, income receipts on assets abroad, and income payments on foreign assets inside the country.

current account surplus
When a country exports more goods and services and receives more income from abroad than it imports and pays abroad.

current account deficit
When a country imports more goods and services and pays more abroad than it exports and receives from abroad.

capital account
A national account that records transactions involving the purchase or sale of assets.

Obtain Resources and Benefits   Beyond balance-of-payments reasons, governments might intervene in FDI flows to acquire resources and benefits such as *technology* and *management skills and employment*.

Access to Technology   Investment in technology, whether in products or processes, tends to increase the productivity and competitiveness of individual nations. That is why host nations have a strong incentive to encourage the importation of technology. For years, developing countries in Asia were introduced to expertise in industrial processes as multinationals set up factories within their borders. But today some of them are trying to acquire and develop their own technological expertise. Singapore has been particularly successful in gaining access to high technology. German industrial giant Siemens (*www.siemens.com*) chose Singapore as the site for an Asia-Pacific microelectronics design center employing 60 people. Singapore has also gained valuable semiconductor technology by joining with U.S.-based Texas Instruments (*www.ti.com*) and others to set up the country's first wafer-fabrication plant.

Management Skills and Employment   As we saw in Chapter 4, many once-communist nations suffer from a lack of the management skills needed to succeed in the global economy. By encouraging FDI, these nations can allow talented managers to come in who can train locals so that, over time, the international competitiveness of their domestic companies will improve. Furthermore, locals who are trained in modern management techniques may eventually leave the firm to start their own local businesses—further expanding employment opportunities. However, detractors argue that although FDI may create jobs, it may also destroy jobs because less competitive local firms may be forced out of business.

Reasons for Intervention by the Home Country

Home nations (those from which international companies launch their investments) may also seek to encourage or discourage *outflows* of FDI for a variety of reasons. However, there generally tend to be fewer concerns among home nations because they tend to be prosperous, industrialized nations. For these countries, an outward investment seldom has a national impact—unlike the impact on developing or emerging nations that receive the FDI. Nevertheless, among the most common reasons for discouraging outward FDI are the following:

❍   *Investing in other nations sends resources out of the home country.* As a result, fewer resources are used for development and economic growth at home. On the other hand, profits on assets abroad that are returned home increase both a home country's balance of payments and its available resources.

❍   *Outgoing FDI may ultimately damage a nation's balance of payments by taking the place of its exports.* This can occur when a company creates a production facility in a market abroad, the output of which replaces exports that used to be sent there from the home country. For example, if a Volkswagen (*www.vw.com*) plant in the United States fills a demand that U.S. buyers would otherwise satisfy with purchases of German-made autos, Germany's balance of payments is correspondingly decreased. But although the investment has an initial negative balance-of-payments effect, the nation's balance of payments is positively affected when companies repatriate profits earned abroad. Thus, despite the initial negative impact, an international investment might make a positive contribution to the balance-of-payments position of the country in the long term.

❍   *Jobs resulting from outgoing investments may replace jobs at home.* This is often the most contentious issue for home countries. The relocation of production to a low-wage nation can have a strong impact on a locale or region. However, the impact is rarely national, and its effects are often muted by other job opportunities in the economy. In addition, there may be an offsetting improvement in home-country employment if additional exports are needed to support the activity represented by the outgoing FDI. For example, if Hyundai (*www.hyundai.com*) of South Korea builds an automobile manufacturing plant in Brazil, Korean employment may increase in order to supply the Brazilian plant with parts.

But foreign direct investment is not always a negative influence on home nations. In fact, under certain circumstances they actually might encourage it. Specifically, countries promote outgoing FDI for the following reasons:

● *Outward FDI can increase long-term competitiveness.* Today, businesses frequently compete on a global scale. The most competitive firms tend to be those that conduct business in the most favorable location anywhere in the world, continuously improve their performance relative to competitors, and derive technological advantages from alliances formed with other companies. Japanese companies have become masterful at benefiting from FDI and cooperative arrangements with companies from other nations. The key to their success is that Japanese companies see every cooperative venture as a learning opportunity.

● *Nations may encourage FDI in industries that they have determined to be "sunset" industries.* Sunset industries are those that use outdated and obsolete technologies or employ low-wage workers with few skills. These jobs are not greatly appealing to countries having industries that pay skilled workers high wages. By allowing some of these jobs to go abroad and retraining workers in higher-paying skilled work, they can upgrade their economies toward "sunrise" industries. This represents a trade-off for governments between a short-term loss of jobs and the long-term benefit of developing workers' skills.

Quick Study

1. What is a country's *balance of payments*? Briefly explain its usefulness.
2. Explain the difference between the *current account* and the *capital account*.
3. For what reasons do *host* countries intervene in FDI?
4. For what reasons do *home* countries intervene in FDI?

Government Policy Instruments and FDI

Over time, both host and home nations have developed a range of methods to either promote or restrict FDI (see Table 7.3). Governments use these tools for many reasons, including improving balance-of-payments positions, acquiring resources, and, in the case of outward investment, keeping jobs at home. Let's now take a look at these methods.

Host Countries: Restriction

Host countries have a variety of methods to restrict incoming FDI. These take two general forms—*ownership restrictions* and *performance demands*.

TABLE 7.3

Methods of Promoting and Restricting FDI

	FDI Promotion	**FDI Restriction**
Host Countries	Tax incentives Low-interest loans Infrastructure improvements	Ownership restrictions Performance demands
Home Countries	Insurance Loans Tax breaks Political pressure	Differential tax rates Sanctions

Ownership Restrictions Governments can impose *ownership restrictions* that prohibit nondomestic companies from investing in certain industries or from owning certain types of businesses. Such prohibitions typically apply to businesses in cultural industries and companies vital to national security. For instance, as India and some Islamic countries in the Middle East try to protect traditional values, accepting investment by Western companies is a controversial issue between purists and moderates. Also, most nations do not allow FDI in their domestic weapons or national defense firms.

Another ownership restriction is a requirement that nondomestic investors hold less than a 50 percent stake in local firms when they undertake foreign direct investment. This requirement was popular in earlier times, when host countries thought that 51 percent local ownership gave them control over a local subsidiary.

But nations are eliminating such restrictions because companies today often can choose another location that has no such restriction in place. For example, when GM was deciding whether to invest in an aging automobile plant in Jakarta, Indonesia, the Indonesian government scrapped its ownership restriction of an eventual forced sale to Indonesians. Indonesia's action was no doubt prompted by the fact that China and Vietnam were also courting GM for its financial investment.

Performance Demands More common than ownership requirements are *performance demands* that influence how international companies operate in the host nation. Although typically viewed as intrusive, most international companies allow for them in the same way they allow for home-country regulations. Performance demands include ensuring that a portion of the product's content originates locally, stipulating the portion of output that must be exported, or requiring that certain technologies be transferred to local businesses.

Host Countries: Promotion

Host countries also offer a variety of incentives to encourage inflows of FDI. Again, these take two general forms—*financial incentives* and *infrastructure improvements*.

Financial Incentives Host governments of all nations grant companies financial incentives if they will invest within their borders. One method includes *tax incentives,* such as lower tax rates or offers to waive taxes on local profits for a period of time—extending as far out as five years or more. A country may also offer *low-interest loans* to investors.

However, the downside of incentives such as these is that they can allow multinationals to create bidding wars between locations that are vying for the investment. In such cases, the company eventually invests in the most appealing region after the locations endure rounds of escalating incentives. Companies have even been accused of engaging other governments in negotiations so as to force concessions from locations already selected for investment. The cost to taxpayers of snaring FDI can be several times what the actual jobs themselves pay—especially in the case of a bidding war.

Infrastructure Improvements Because of the problems associated with financial incentives, some governments are taking an alternative route to luring investment. Lasting benefits for communities surrounding the investment location can result from making local *infrastructure improvements*—better seaports suitable for containerized shipping, improved roads, and increased telecommunications systems. For instance, Malaysia is carving a $40 billion Multimedia Super Corridor (MSC) into a region's forested surroundings. The region has planned a paperless government, an intelligent city called Cyberjaya, two telesuburbs, a technology park, a multimedia university, and an intellectual-property-protection park. The MSC is dedicated to creating the most advanced technologies in telecommunications, medicine, distance learning, and remote manufacturing.

Home Countries: Restriction

To limit the effects of outbound FDI on the national economy, home governments may exercise either of the following two options:

⦿ Impose *differential tax rates* that charge income from earnings abroad at a higher rate than domestic earnings.

⦿ Impose outright *sanctions* that prohibit domestic firms from making investments in certain nations.

Home Countries: Promotion

On the other hand, to encourage outbound FDI, home-country governments can do any of the following:

⦿ Offer *insurance* to cover the risks of investments abroad, including, among others, insurance against expropriation of assets, losses from armed conflict, kidnappings, and terrorist attacks.

⦿ Grant *loans* to firms wishing to increase their investments abroad. A home-country government may also guarantee the loans that a company takes from financial institutions.

⦿ Offer *tax breaks* on profits earned abroad or negotiate special tax treaties. For example, several multinational agreements reduce or eliminate the practice of double taxation—profits earned abroad being taxed both in the home and host countries.

⦿ Apply *political pressure* on other nations to get them to relax their restrictions on inbound investments. Non-Japanese companies often find it very difficult to invest inside Japan. The United States, for one, repeatedly pressures the Japanese government to open its market further to FDI. But because such pressure has achieved little success, many U.S. companies cooperate with local Japanese businesses.

Quick Study

1. Identify the main methods host countries use to restrict and promote FDI.
2. What methods do home countries use to restrict and promote FDI?

Bottom Line for Business

In this chapter, we learned about foreign direct investment (FDI)—the second major way companies engage in international business, in addition to trade. Companies ranging from massive global corporations to adventurous entrepreneurs all contribute to FDI flows. The flow of foreign direct investment fell off in recent years because of recent slower economic growth in developed nations, tumbling stock market valuations, and fewer privatizations of state-owned firms than in the past. Yet the long-term trend in FDI is pointing toward greater FDI worldwide.

This chapter discussed many factors that influence a company's decision about where to invest abroad. Here we briefly discuss the influence of nations on FDI flows, and FDI in two important regions for international business activity: Asia and Europe.

National Governments and FDI

The actions of national governments have important implications for business. Companies can either be thwarted in their efforts or be encouraged to invest in a nation, depending on the philosophies of home and host governments. The balance-of-payments positions of both home and host countries are also important because FDI flows affect the economic health of nations. To attract investment, a nation must provide a climate conducive to business operations, including essential elements such as pro-growth economic policies, a stable regulatory environment, and a sound infrastructure, to name just a few.

The downturn in FDI flows in recent years has increased competition among governments to attract foreign investment by multinationals. This increased competition has resulted in regulatory changes more favorable to FDI. Moreover, just as nations around the world are creating free trade agreements (covered in Chapter 8), they are also embracing bilateral investment treaties. These bilateral investment treaties are becoming prominent tools used to attract investment. Investment provisions within free trade agreements are also receiving greater attention than in the past. These efforts at attracting investment have direct implications for the strategies of multinational companies, particularly when it comes to deciding where to locate production, logistics, and back-office service activities.

Foreign Direct Investment in Europe

Developing nations in Africa, Latin America, and much of Southeast Asia were hit especially hard by the recent downturn in FDI flows. But developing (transition) nations of Central and Eastern Europe faired well through recent lean years in FDI flows, and attracted significant investment from multinationals. Those countries that in May 2004 entered the European trading bloc called the European Union did particularly well. They saw less investment in areas supporting low-wage, unskilled occupations, and greater investment in higher value-added activities that take advantage of a well-educated workforce.

Yet the main reason for the fast pace at which foreign direct investment is occurring in Western Europe is regional economic integration (see Chapter 8). The European Union expanded in May 2004 to include 25 members today. Some of the foreign investment reported by this region certainly went to the relatively less developed markets of the new central and eastern European members. But much of the activity occurring among western European companies is industry consolidation brought on by the opening of markets and the tearing down of barriers to free trade and investment. This change in the economic landscape across Europe is creating a more competitive business climate there.

Foreign Direct Investment in Asia

The global downturn in foreign direct investment flows was barely noticed in China. In fact, China is attracting the majority of Asia's FDI, luring companies with a low-wage workforce and access to an enormous domestic market. Many companies already active in China are upping their investment further, and companies not yet there are developing strategies for how to include China in their future plans. It also appears that a new emphasis on "off-shoring" activity in services will propel renewed FDI activity in coming years. India is the primary destination for the vast majority of new foreign direct investment in call center work and other back-office jobs, including payroll accounting and all sorts of information processing. The main attraction of India is a well-educated, low-cost workforce having impeccable English-language skills.

Finally, one aspect of national business environments that has implications for future business activity is the natural environment. By their actions, businesses are laying the foundation for people's attitudes toward FDI by multinationals, particularly among developing Asian nations. Take China, for instance. The World Bank claims that 16 of the world's 20 most polluted cities are in China, and that it costs the nation up to $170 billion per year. Greater decentralization in China's political system means local Communist Party bosses and bureaucrats are less concerned about the environmental implications of business deals than they are interested in the short-term payoff of deals. But better late than never seems to be a fitting motto. The courts are being granted more power to punish polluters, the government is increasing spending on protecting the environment, and multinationals are being asked to help in the cleanup.[12]

1. **Describe the worldwide patterns of *foreign direct investment (FDI)* and the reasons for these patterns.** *Foreign direct investment (FDI)* expanded rapidly throughout the 1990s. After growing about 20 percent per year in the first half of the 1990s, FDI inflows grew by about 40 percent per year in the second half of the decade. FDI inflows peaked in 2000 at around $1.4 trillion. FDI also continues to grow faster than both world production and trade. Developed countries account for around 70 percent of global FDI inflows. In comparison, developing countries' share of world FDI flows is 30 percent.

    Among developed countries, European Union nations, the United States, and Japan account for the majority of world inflows. The EU was the world's largest FDI recipient (more than 57 percent of the world total), with inflows of more than $374 billion in 2002. FDI inflows to developing Asian nations were just over $95 billion in 2002, with China attracting nearly $53 billion and India attracting nearly $3.5 billion. FDI inflows to all of Africa accounted for about 1.7 percent of total world FDI inflows in 2002.

    Globalization and a growing number of *mergers and acquisitions* account for the rising tide of FDI flows over the past decade or so, and will continue to propel it in the future.

2. **Describe each of the *theories* that attempt to explain why foreign direct investment occurs.** The *international product life cycle* states a company will begin by exporting its product and later undertake foreign direct investment as a product moves through its life cycle. A product passes through three stages: new product stage, maturing product stage, and standardized product stage.

    Market imperfections theory states when an imperfection in the market makes a transaction less efficient than it could be, a company will undertake foreign direct investment to internalize the transaction and thereby remove the imperfection.

    The *eclectic theory* states firms undertake foreign direct investment when the features of a particular location combine with ownership and internalization advantages to make a location appealing for investment. The *market power* theory states that a firm tries to establish a dominant market presence in an industry by undertaking foreign direct investment.

3. **Discuss the important *management issues* in the foreign direct investment decision.** Companies investing abroad are often concerned with *controlling* activities in the local market. But local governments might require a company to hire local managers or require that all goods produced locally be exported.

    A key concern is whether to *purchase an existing business or to build an international subsidiary from the ground up*. Acquisition generally provides an investor with an existing plant and equipment and personnel. Factors reducing the appeal of purchasing existing facilities include obsolete equipment, poor relations with workers, and an unsuitable location. Adequate facilities are sometimes simply unavailable and a company must go ahead with a *greenfield investment*.

    Labor regulations can increase the hourly *cost of production* several times. An approach companies may use to contain production costs is *rationalized production*—in which a product's components are produced in the lowest-cost location.

    A local market presence might help companies gain valuable knowledge about the *behavior of buyers* that it could not obtain from the home market. Firms commonly engage in foreign direct investment when doing so puts them close to both *client* firms and *rival* firms.

4. **Explain why *governments* intervene in the free flow of foreign direct investment.** Both host and home countries interfere in the free flow of FDI for a variety of reasons. One reason that governments of *host countries* intervene in foreign direct investment flows is to protect their *balance of payments*. Allowing FDI to come in gives a nation a balance-of-payments boost. Countries also improve their balance-of-payments position from the exports of local production operations created by FDI. But when direct investors send profits made locally back to the parent company in the home country, the balance of payments decreases. Local investment in *technology* also tends to increase the productivity and competitiveness of the nation. Encouraging FDI also brings in people with *management skills* who can train locals and improve the competitiveness of local firms. Furthermore, many local *jobs* are also created as a result of incoming FDI.

    Home countries also intervene in FDI flows. For one thing, investing in other nations sends resources out of the home country—lowering the balance of payments. Yet profits on assets abroad that are returned home increase a home country's balance of payments. Also, outgoing FDI may ultimately damage a nation's balance of payments by taking the place of its exports.

And jobs that result from outgoing investments may replace jobs at home that were based on exports to the host country.

5. **Discuss the *policy instruments* that governments use to promote and restrict foreign direct investment.** Host-country governments can impose *ownership restrictions* that prohibit nondomestic companies from investing in businesses in cultural industries and those vital to national security. They can also create *performance demands* that influence how international companies operate in the host nation.

They can also grant companies *tax incentives* such as lower tax rates or offer to waive taxes on local profits for a period of time. A country may also offer *low-interest loans* to investors. Some governments prefer to lure investment by making local *infrastructure improvements*—better seaports suitable for container-

ized shipping, improved roads, and increased telecommunications systems.

To limit the effects of outbound FDI on the national economy, home governments may impose *differential tax rates* that charge income from earnings abroad at a higher rate than domestic earnings. Or they can impose outright *sanctions* that prohibit domestic firms from making investments in certain nations. But to encourage outbound FDI home-country governments can offer *insurance* to cover investment risks abroad. They can also grant *loans* to firms that wish to increase their investments abroad. A home-country government may guarantee loans that a company takes from financial institutions. They might also offer *tax breaks* on profits earned abroad or negotiate special tax treaties. Finally, they may apply *political pressure* on other nations to get them to relax restrictions on inbound investments.

TALK IT OVER

1. You overhear your superior tell another manager in the company: "I'm fed up with our nation's companies sending manufacturing jobs abroad and off-shoring service work to lower-wage nations. Don't any of them have any national pride?" The other manager responds, "I disagree. It is every company's duty to make as much profit as possible for its owners. If that means going abroad to reduce costs, so be it." Do you agree with either of these managers? Why or why not? Now step into the conversation and explain where you stand on this issue.

2. The global carmaker you work for is investing in an automobile assembly facility in Costa Rica with a local part-

ner. Explain the potential reasons for this investment. Will your company want to exercise a great deal of control over this operation? Why or why not? Over what areas might your company want to exercise control, and what areas might it cede control to the partner?

3. This chapter presented several theories that attempt to explain why firms undertake foreign direct investment. Which of these theories seems most appealing to you? Why is it appealing? Can you think of one or more companies that seem to fit the pattern described by the theory? In your opinion, what faults do the alternative theories have?

TEAMING UP

1. In a small group, locate several articles in the business press that discuss a cross-border merger or acquisition that has taken place within the past year. What reasons did each company give for the merger or acquisition? Was it a marriage of equals or did a larger partner absorb a far smaller one? Do the articles identify any internal issues with which managers had to deal following the merger or acquisition? What is the performance of the new company? Write a one- to two-page report of your group's findings.

2. Select a country that interests you and several classmates. Using the most recent data you can find, what is the nation's balance-of-payments position? What is its cur-

rent account balance? What is its capital account balance? What are some possible causes for the surplus or deficit you see? What are some of the effects on the nation of this surplus or deficit? Prepare a brief report and present it to the class.

3. As a team, visit your city's chamber of commerce office and/or its economic development office. Does the city have a practice of offering incentives to lure companies into the area? Does it try to attract international companies and, if so, how? Does it try to persuade companies in certain industries to invest in the region? Ask other questions you feel are pertinent. Present your findings to the class.

TAKE IT TO THE WEB

1. In this chapter, we've seen many reasons why companies directly invest in other nations, and the factors involved in the decision of whether and where to invest abroad. We also saw the important role that governments have in influencing global flows and patterns of foreign direct investment.

   Research the economy of the Philippines and its neighbors on the Internet. In what economic sectors is each country strong? Do the strengths of each country really complement one another, or do they compete directly with one another? If you were considering investing in the Philippines, what management issues would concern you? Be specific in your answer. (*Hint*: A good place to begin your research is the CIA's World Factbook (*www.odci.gov/cia/publications/ factbook*).

   Many Southeast Asian governments fear they are losing ground to China in the race to attract investment from multinational corporations. What do you think those governments could do to increase the attractiveness of their homelands for multinationals?

   We live in an era of intense national competition to attract investment from abroad to create jobs and raise living standards. Find a recent article on the Web that describes a company's decision to relocate some or all of its business operations (production or services). What reasons are stated for the relocation? Has any consideration been given to the plight of the employees being put out of work?

ETHICAL CHALLENGES

1. You are a sales manager working in international sales for a major U.S. beef distributor. Your firm is attempting to sell a large quantity of beef to a developing market in northern Africa where U.S. beef is a rarity. The vice president for new business development has instructed you to sell the beef well below market price quickly. Standing at the coffee machine, you overhear two quality assurance managers discussing "the potentially tainted beef heading for Africa." You are aware that in the past your firm has come across small traces of typhoid in some of its products. What do you do? Do you go through with the northern Africa deal? Do you first contact someone inside or outside the company? If additional information would be helpful to you, what would it be?

2. You are the U.S. senator deciding whether to vote up or down on a new piece of legislation. The potential new law places restrictions on the practice of outsourcing work to low-wage countries and is designed to protect U.S. workers' jobs. These days it is increasingly common for companies to promise manufacturing contracts to overseas suppliers in exchange for entry into that country's market. Labor union representatives argue that these kinds of deals are made at the expense of jobs at home. After all, if a company can have parts made in China at lower wages, why keep factories going at home? They also are concerned that the transfer of technology will breed strong competitors in other nations and thereby threaten even more domestic jobs in the future. But others argue that increased sales abroad actually helps create more jobs at home. Discuss the ethics of companies contracting out production to factories abroad in exchange for sales contracts. How would you vote on the pending legislation? What other issues must you consider?

3. You are the U.S. Ambassador to Malaysia. In order to become a major export platform for the semiconductor industry, Malaysia's government not only offered tax breaks but also guaranteed that electronics workers would be prohibited from organizing independent labor unions. The government decreed that the goal of national development required a "union-free" environment for the "pioneers" of semiconductors. Under pressure from U.S. labor unions, the Malaysian government offered a weak alternative to industry unions—company-by-company "in-house" unions. Yet, as soon as workers organized one at a Harris Electronics plant, the 21 union leaders were fired and the new union was disbanded. In another instance, when French-owned Thomson Electronics inherited a Malaysian factory with a union of 3,000, it closed the plant and moved the work to Vietnam. Newly industrialized nations such as Malaysia feel that their futures depend on investment by multinationals. Yet their governments are acutely aware that in the absence of incentives such as a "union-free" workforce, international companies can easily take their investment money elsewhere. Discuss the problems that these governments face in balancing the needs of their citizens with the long-term quest for economic development. As the Ambassador, what advice do you give Malaysian business and government leaders? Can you think of examples from other nations that can help you make the case for local unions?

PRACTICING INTERNATIONAL MANAGEMENT CASE

Mercedes-Benz: Footloose in Tuscaloosa

"Aloof." "Serious." "Not youthful." Definitely "not fun." These were the unfortunate epithets applied to Mercedes-Benz by a market research firm that assesses product personalities. Research among American dealers also revealed that consumers felt so intimidated by Mercedes that they wouldn't sit in the cars at the showroom. In order to increase sales and broaden the market to a more youthful and value-conscious consumer, Mercedes-Benz (*www.mercedes.com*) of North America came up with a series of inventive, free-spirited ads featuring stampeding rhinos and bobbing aliens. Although the new ads boosted sales, the company needed more than a new marketing message to ensure its future growth. What it needed was an all-new Mercedes. Enter the Mercedes M-Class, a sports utility vehicle (SUV). With a base price of $35,000 and a luxury lineage, Mercedes placed its M-Class to compete squarely against the Ford Explorer and Jeep Grand Cherokee.

Not only was the M-Class Mercedes' first SUV, but it was also the first car that Mercedes had manufactured outside of Germany—in the heart of Dixie, no less. The rough-hewn town of Vance, Alabama (population 400), where people hang out at the local barbecue joint, is the last place you'd expect to find button-down engineers from Stuttgart, Germany. But this small town outside of Tuscaloosa appealed to Mercedes for several reasons. Labor costs in the U.S. Deep South are 50 percent lower than in Germany. Also, Alabama offered an attractive $250 million in tax refunds and other incentives to win the much-needed Mercedes jobs. Mercedes also wanted to be closer to the crucial U.S. market and to create a plant from the ground up, one that would be a model for its future international operations.

The gleaming, E-shaped Mercedes plant is the brainchild of engineer-turned-CEO, Andreas Renschler. When Japanese carmakers entered the U.S. market in the 1980s, they reproduced their car-building philosophies, cultures, production practices, and management styles in the United States. But Mercedes started with the proverbial blank sheet of paper. In order to appeal to U.S. workers, Mercedes knew it had to abandon the rigid hierarchy of the typical Mercedes production line and create a more egalitarian shop floor. Thus, administrative offices in the Vance plant run through the middle of the manufacturing area, and although it is all glassed in, team members still have easy access to administrators. The plant is also designed so that workers can unilaterally stop the assembly line to correct manufacturing problems. So far, the system has been a catalyst to communication among the Alabama plant's 1,500 U.S. workers, German trainers, and diverse management team that includes executives from both Detroit and Japan. Even so, Mercedes spent an enormous amount of time and effort to train its U.S. workforce. Explains Sven Schoolman, a 31-year-old trainer from Sindelfingen, "In Germany, we don't say we build a car. We say we build a Mercedes. We had to teach that."

So far the Mercedes' M-class is competing very well against the entrenched competition. The company is also gaining valuable experience in how to set up and operate a plant in another country. "It was once sacrosanct to talk about our cars being 'Made in Germany,'" said Jurgen E. Schrempp, CEO of Mercedes' parent, DaimlerChrysler (*www.daimlerchrysler.com*). "We have to change that to 'Made by Mercedes,' and never mind where they are assembled."

Thinking Globally

1. What do you think were the chief factors involved in Mercedes' decision to undertake FDI in the United States rather than build the M-Class in Germany?

2. Why do you think Mercedes decided to build the plant from the ground up in Alabama rather than buying an existing plant in, say, Detroit? List as many reasons as you can, and explain your answer.

3. Do you think Mercedes risks diluting its "Made in Germany" reputation for engineering quality by building its M-class in Alabama? Why or why not?

4. What do you see as the pros and cons of Mercedes' approach to managing FDI—abandoning the culture and some of the practices of its home country? What are the pros and cons of the approach of the Japanese carmakers—trying to duplicate the culture and production practices of the home country?

1. | Define *regional economic integration,* and identify its five levels.

2. | Discuss the *benefits* and *drawbacks* associated with regional economic integration.

3. | Describe regional integration in *Europe,* and its pattern of enlargement.

4. | Discuss regional integration in the *Americas,* and analyze its future prospects.

5. | Characterize regional integration in *Asia,* and discuss how it differs from integration elsewhere.

6. | Describe regional integration in the *Middle East* and *Africa,* and explain why progress there has been slow.

regional economic
integration

8

a look **back**

CHAPTER 7 examined recent patterns of foreign direct investment. We explored the theories that try to explain why it occurs and saw how governments influence investment flows.

a look **at this chapter**

This chapter explores the trend toward greater integration of national economies. We first examine the reasons why nations are making significant efforts at regional integration. We then study the most prominent regional trading blocs in place around the world today.

a look **ahead**

CHAPTER 9 begins our inquiry into the international financial system. We describe the structure of the international capital market and explain how the foreign exchange market operates.

Think Global, Act Regional?

VEVEY, Switzerland—The products of Switzerland-based Nestlé (*www.nestle.com*) are available in nearly every country on the planet, even in North Korea. The company brilliantly turns humdrum products like bottled water and pet food into well-known global brands.

Nestlé, as the world's largest food company, does business across cultural borders 24 hours a day—earning just two percent of its sales at home. Yet food is an integral part of the social fabric of every nation. That is why Nestlé tries to respect the cultural and political traditions of countries in which its products are produced and sold. Years ago, Nestlé was blamed for the deaths of infants in Africa because mothers were inadequately instructed and used impure water to mix Nestlé's infant formulas. Pictured above, a couple purchases Nestlé's Nescafe coffee in a nation that had banned Nestlé products after the infant-formula incident. When it markets infant foods today, Nestlé tries to be more sensitive to the traditional ways in which babies are fed. Nestlé must also watch for changes in attitudes that result from greater cross-cultural contact caused by regional integration.

The laws of regional trading blocs also affect the business activities of Nestlé. When Nestlé and Coca-Cola (*www.cocacola.com*) announced a joint venture to develop coffee and tea drinks, they first had to show the European Union (EU) Commission that they would not stifle competition across the region. Firms operating within the EU also have to abide by EU environmental protection laws. In this regard, Nestlé minimizes the amount of packaging waste that results from use of its products. The firm also works closely with Germany, for example, to develop and manage waste-recovery programs. As you read this chapter, think of all the ways business activities are affected when groups of nations band together in regional trading blocs.[1]

R egional trade agreements are changing the landscape of the global marketplace. Companies like Nestlé of Switzerland are finding that these agreements are lowering trade barriers and opening up new markets for goods and services. Markets otherwise off-limits because tariffs made imported products too expensive can become quite attractive once tariffs are lifted. But trade agreements can be double-edged swords for many companies. Not only do they allow domestic companies to seek new markets abroad, but they also let competitors from other nations enter the domestic market. Such mobility increases competition in every market that takes part in an agreement.

Trade agreements can allow companies to alter their strategies, sometimes radically. Nations in the Americas are working to create a free-trade area that runs from the northern tip of Alaska to the southern tip of South America. Some U.S. companies doing business in Latin America are pushing strongly for completion of this so-called Free Trade Area of the Americas (FTAA). United States–based Eastman Kodak (*www.kodak.com*) manufactures cameras, film, photographic paper, and chemicals in Brazil, Canada, Mexico, and the United States. The company estimates that it could save $25 million annually on import duties under the agreement. "If you've got tariff-free trade, you can use your factories in new and different ways," says Christopher Padilla, Eastman's director for international trade relations. In the absence of tariffs, multinationals can save money by supplying entire regions from just a few plants, rather than plants in each nation.[2]

We began Part Three of this book by discussing the gains resulting from specialization and trade. We now close by showing how groups of countries are cooperating to dismantle barriers that threaten these potential gains. In this chapter, we focus on regional efforts to encourage freer trade and investment. We begin by defining *regional economic integration* and describing its five different levels. Then we examine the benefits and drawbacks of regional trade agreements. Finally, we explore in detail several long-established trade agreements and several agreements that are in the earliest stages of development.

What Is Regional Economic Integration?

The process whereby countries in a geographic region cooperate with one another to reduce or eliminate barriers to the international flow of products, people, or capital is called **regional economic integration (regionalism)**. A group of nations in a geographic region undergoing economic integration is called a *regional trading bloc.*

regional economic integration (regionalism)
Process whereby countries in a geographic region cooperate with one another to reduce or eliminate barriers to the international flow of products, people, or capital.

The goal of nations undergoing economic integration is not only to increase cross-border trade and investment but also to raise living standards for their people. We saw in Chapter 5, for instance, how specialization and trade create real gains in terms of greater choice, lower prices, and increased productivity. Regional trade agreements are designed to help nations accomplish these objectives. Regional economic integration sometimes has additional goals, such as protection of intellectual property rights or the environment, or even eventual political union.

Levels of Regional Integration

Since the development of theories demonstrating the potential gains available through international trade, nations have tried to reap these benefits in a variety of ways. Figure 8.1

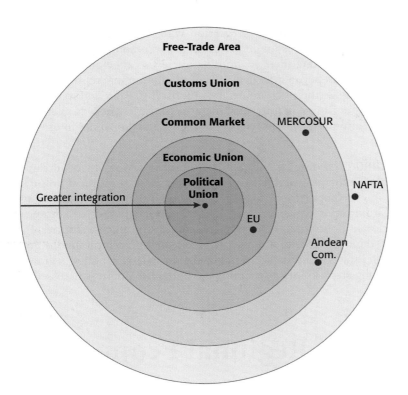

FIGURE 8.1

Levels of Regional Integration

shows five potential levels (or degrees) of economic and political integration for regional trading blocs. A *free-trade area* is the lowest extent of national integration, *political union* the greatest. Each level of integration incorporates the properties of those levels that precede it.

Free-Trade Area

Economic integration whereby countries seek to remove all barriers to trade between themselves, but each country determines its own barriers against nonmembers is called a **free-trade area**. A free-trade area is the lowest level of economic integration that is possible between two or more countries. Countries belonging to the free-trade area strive to remove all tariffs and nontariff barriers, such as quotas and subsidies, on international trade in goods and services. However, each country is able to maintain whatever policy it sees fit against nonmember countries. These policies can differ widely from country to country. Countries belonging to a free-trade area also typically establish a process by which trade disputes can be resolved.

Customs Union

Economic integration whereby countries remove all barriers to trade among themselves, but erect a common trade policy against nonmembers is called a **customs union**. Thus, the main difference between a free-trade area and a customs union is that the members of a customs union agree to treat trade with all nonmember nations in a similar manner. Countries belonging to a customs union might also negotiate as a single entity with other supranational organizations, such as the World Trade Organization.

Common Market

Economic integration whereby countries remove all barriers to trade and the movement of labor and capital between themselves but erect a common trade policy against nonmembers is called a **common market**. Thus, a common market integrates the elements of free-trade areas and customs unions and adds the free movement of important factors of production—people and cross-border investment. Because it requires at least some cooperation in economic and labor policy, this level of integration is very difficult to attain. Furthermore, the benefits to individual countries can be uneven because skilled labor may move to countries where wages are higher, and investment capital may flow to where returns are greater.

free-trade area
Economic integration whereby countries seek to remove all barriers to trade between themselves, but each country determines its own barriers against nonmembers.

customs union
Economic integration whereby countries remove all barriers to trade between themselves but erect a common trade policy against nonmembers.

common market
Economic integration whereby countries remove all barriers to trade and the movement of labor and capital between themselves but erect a common trade policy against nonmembers.

Economic Union Economic integration whereby countries remove barriers to trade and the movement of labor and capital, erect a common trade policy against nonmembers, and coordinate their economic policies is called an **economic union**. An economic union goes beyond the demands of a common market by requiring member nations to harmonize their tax, monetary, and fiscal policies and to create a common currency. Economic union requires that member countries concede a certain amount of their national autonomy (or sovereignty) to the supranational union of which they are a part.

Political Union Economic and political integration whereby countries coordinate aspects of their economic *and* political systems is called a **political union**. A political union requires member nations to accept a common stance on economic and political policies regarding nonmember nations. However, nations are allowed a degree of freedom in setting certain political and economic policies within their territories. Individually, Canada and the United States provide early examples of political unions. In both these nations smaller states and provinces combined to form larger entities. A group of nations currently taking steps in this direction is the European Union—discussed later in this chapter.

Effects of Regional Economic Integration

Few topics in international business are as hotly contested and involve as many groups as the effects of regional trade agreements on people, jobs, companies, cultures, and living standards. The topic often spurs debate over the merits and demerits of such agreements. On one side of the debate are people who see the bad that regional trade agreements cause—on the other, those who see the good. Each party to the debate cites data on trade and jobs that bolster their position. They point to companies that have picked up and moved to another country where wages are lower after a new agreement was signed or companies that have stayed at home and kept jobs there. The only thing made clear as a result of such debates is that both sides are right some of the time.

Then there is the cultural aspect of such agreements: Some people argue that they will lose their unique cultural identity if their nation cooperates too much with other nations. As we saw in this chapter's opening company profile, Nestlé tries to be as sensitive as possible to cultural differences across markets. But such large global companies are often lightning rods for those warning of cultural homogenization. Let's now take a closer look at the main benefits and drawbacks of regional integration.

Benefits of Regional Integration

Recall from Chapter 5 that nations engage in specialization and trade because of the gains in output and consumption. Greater specialization, increased efficiency, greater consumption, and higher standards of living all should result from higher levels of trade between nations.

Trade Creation As we have seen, economic integration removes barriers to trade and/or investment for nations belonging to a trading bloc. The increase in the level of trade between nations that results from regional economic integration is called **trade creation**. One result of trade creation is that consumers and industrial buyers in member nations are faced with a wider selection of goods and services not available before. For example, the United States has many popular brands of bottled water, including Coke's Dasani (*www.dasani.com*) and Pepsi's (*www.pepsi.com*) Aquafina (the number-one best-seller). But grocery and convenience stores inside the United States stock a wide variety of lesser-known brands of bottled water imported from Canada, including Stonepoint's Classic

economic union
Economic integration whereby countries remove barriers to trade and the movement of labor and capital, erect a common trade policy against nonmembers, and coordinate their economic policies.

political union
Economic and political integration whereby countries coordinate aspects of their economic and political systems.

trade creation
Increase in the level of trade between nations that results from regional economic integration.

Selection Spring Water (*www.mystonepoint.com*). No doubt, the free-trade agreement between Canada, Mexico, and the United States (discussed below) created export opportunities for these Canadian brands.

Another result of trade creation is that buyers can acquire goods and services at lower cost after trade barriers such as tariffs are lowered. Furthermore, lower costs tend to lead to higher demand for goods because people have more money left over after a purchase to buy other products.

Greater Consensus

In Chapter 6 we saw how the World Trade Organization (WTO) works to lower barriers on a global scale. Efforts at regional economic integration differ in that they comprise smaller groups of nations—ranging from several countries to as many as 30 or more. The benefit of trying to eliminate trade barriers in smaller groups of countries is that it can be easier to gain consensus from fewer members as opposed to, say, the 147 countries that comprise the WTO.

Political Cooperation

There can also be *political* benefits from efforts toward regional economic integration. A group of nations can have significantly greater political weight than each nation has individually. Thus, the group, as a whole, can have more say when negotiating with other countries in forums such as the WTO or perhaps even the United Nations. Moreover, integration involving political cooperation can reduce the potential for military conflict between member nations. In fact, peace was at the center of early efforts at integration in Europe in the 1950s. The devastation of two world wars in the first half of the twentieth century caused Europe to see integration as one way of preventing further armed conflicts.

Employment Opportunities

Regional integration can also expand employment opportunities by enabling people to move from one country to another to find work, or simply to earn a higher wage. Regional integration has opened doors for young people in Europe. Vincent Wauters is a 26-year-old Belgian who has a degree in history and speaks three languages. His willingness to pick up and move made him a good catch for French catalog retailer La Redoute (*www.laredoute.fr*). "I have a vision that is clearly European," says Wauters. "I have a sense of our common history, our cultural diversity, and I'm used to the kind of flexibility that's needed for people to adapt to one another." Anne-Marie Ronayne, a consultant with the international recruiting firm EMDS (*www.emdsnet.com*), agrees. "Companies," she says, "are looking for their future leaders. That means finding people with good attitudes, who can think across borders."[3] In this way regional integration can help improve the quality of life and living standards for a nation's people.

Drawbacks of Regional Integration

Although regional integration tends to benefit countries, it can also have substantial negative effects. Let's now examine the more important of these.

Trade Diversion

The flip side of trade creation is **trade diversion**—the diversion of trade away from nations not belonging to a trading bloc and toward member nations. Trade diversion can occur after formation of a trading bloc because of the lower tariffs charged between member nations. It can actually result in increased trade with a less-efficient producer within the trading bloc and reduced trade with a more-efficient non-member producer. In this sense, economic integration can unintentionally reward a less-efficient producer within the trading bloc. Unless there is other internal competition for the producer's good or service, buyers will likely pay more after trade diversion because of the inefficient production methods of the producer.

A World Bank report caused a stir over the results of the free-trade bloc between Latin America's largest countries, MERCOSUR (discussed later in this chapter). The report suggested that the bloc's formation only encouraged free trade in the lowest-value products of local origin, while deterring competition for more sophisticated goods manufactured outside the market. Closer analysis showed that while imports

trade diversion
Diversion of trade away from nations not belonging to a trading bloc and toward member nations.

from one member state to another tripled during the period studied, imports from the rest of the world also tripled. Thus, the net effect of the agreement was trade creation, not trade diversion as critics had charged.[4] Also, the Australian Department of Foreign Affairs and Trade released results of a study that examined the impact of the North American Free Trade Agreement on Australia's trade with and investment in North America. The study found no evidence of trade diversion in the five years following the agreement's formation.[5]

Shifts in Employment   Perhaps the most controversial aspect of regional economic integration is how people's jobs are affected. Because the formation of trading blocs significantly reduces or eliminates barriers to trade among members, the producer of a particular good or service is likely to be the most productive producer. Industries requiring mostly unskilled labor, for example, will tend to shift production to low-wage nations within a trading bloc. But figures on the numbers of jobs lost or gained vary depending on the source.

The U.S. government contends that rising U.S. exports to Mexico and Canada have created a minimum of 900,000 jobs.[6] But the AFL-CIO (*www.aflcio.org*), the federation of U.S. unions, disputes these figures and claims a loss of jobs due to NAFTA. Trade agreements do cause dislocations in labor markets—some jobs are lost while others are gained. For instance, some jobs were no doubt gained as a result of expanding transportation and warehousing industries on the U.S. side of the border. But U.S. jobs also were lost in some manufacturing sectors.

It is highly likely that once trade and investment barriers are removed, countries protecting low-wage domestic industries from competition will see these jobs move to the country where wages are lower. But this is also an opportunity for workers to upgrade their skills and gain more advanced job training. This can help nations increase their competitiveness, because a more educated and skilled workforce attracts higher-paying jobs than does a less skilled workforce. However, an opportunity for a nation to improve some abstract "factors of production" is little consolation to people finding themselves suddenly out of work.

Loss of National Sovereignty   Successive levels of integration require that nations surrender more of their national sovereignty. The least amount of sovereignty that must be surrendered to the trading bloc occurs in a free-trade area. Countries are allowed to set their own barriers to trade against all nonmember nations. However, a political union requires nations to give up a high degree of sovereignty in foreign policy. This is why a political union is so hard to achieve. Long histories of cooperation or animosity between nations do not disappear when a group of countries forms a union. Because one member nation may have very delicate ties with a nonmember nation with which another member may have very strong ties, the setting of a common foreign policy can be extremely tricky.

Because of the benefits and despite the drawbacks of regional trade agreements, economic integration is taking place throughout the world. Europe, the Americas, Asia, the Middle East, and Africa are all undergoing integration to some degree. Table 8.1 summarizes the members of each regional trading bloc presented in this chapter. Let's now begin our coverage of specific efforts toward economic integration by exploring the region having the longest history and highest level of integration—Europe.

Quick Study

1.   What is the ultimate goal of *regional economic integration*?

2.   What are the five levels, or degrees, of regional integration? Briefly describe each one.

3.   Identify several potential benefits and several potential drawbacks of regional integration.

4.   What is meant by the terms *trade creation* and *trade diversion*? Why are these concepts important?

TABLE 8.1

The World's Main Regional Trading Blocs

EU	**European Union**	
	Austria, Belgium, Britain, Czech Republic, Denmark, Estonia, Finland, France, Germany, Greece, Greek Cyprus (southern portion), Hungary, Ireland, Italy, Latvia, Lithuania, Luxembourg, Malta, Netherlands, Poland, Portugal, Slovakia, Slovenia, Spain, Sweden	
EFTA	**European Free Trade Association**	
	Iceland, Liechtenstein, Norway, Switzerland	
NAFTA	**North American Free Trade Agreement**	
	Canada, Mexico, United States	
Andean	**Andean Community**	
	Bolivia, Colombia, Ecuador, Peru, Venezuela	
ALADI	**Latin American Integration Association**	
	Argentina, Bolivia, Brazil, Chile, Colombia, Ecuador, Mexico, Paraguay, Peru, Uruguay, Venezuela	
MERCOSUR	**Southern Common Market**	
	Argentina, Brazil, Paraguay, Uruguay (Bolivia and Chile are associate members)	
CARICOM	**Caribbean Community and Common Market**	
	Antigua and Barbuda, Bahamas, Barbados, Belize, Dominica, Grenada, Guyana, Haiti, Jamaica, Montserrat, St. Kitts and Nevis, St. Lucia, St. Vincent and the Grenadines, Suriname, Trinidad and Tobago	
CACM	**Central American Common Market**	
	Costa Rica, El Salvador, Guatemala, Honduras, Nicaragua	
FTAA	**Free Trade Area of the Americas**	
	Caribbean, Central America, North America, South America	
TEP	**Transatlantic Economic Partnership**	
	European Union (25 countries), United States	
ASEAN	**Association of Southeast Asian Nations**	
	Brunei, Cambodia, Indonesia, Laos, Malaysia, Myanmar, Philippines, Singapore, Thailand, Vietnam	
APEC	**Asia Pacific Economic Cooperation**	
	Australia, Brunei, Canada, Chile, China, Hong Kong, Indonesia, Japan, South Korea, Malaysia, Mexico, New Zealand, Papua New Guinea, Peru, Philippines, Russia, Singapore, Taiwan, Thailand, United States, Vietnam	
GCC	**Gulf Cooperation Council**	
	Bahrain, Kuwait, Oman, Qatar, Saudi Arabia, United Arab Emirates	
ECOWAS	**Economic Community of West African States**	
	Benin, Burkina Faso, Cape Verde, Gambia, Ghana, Guinea, Guinea-Bissau, Ivory Coast, Liberia, Mali, Niger, Nigeria, Senegal, Sierra Leone, Togo	

Integration in Europe

The most sophisticated and advanced example of regional integration that we can point to today is occurring in Europe. European efforts at integration began shortly after the Second World War as a cooperative endeavor among a small group of countries and involved a few select industries. Regional integration now encompasses practically all of Western Europe and all industries. Let's now explore integration in Europe, beginning with its earliest attempts at cooperation.

European Union

In the middle of the twentieth century, many would have scoffed at the idea that the European countries, which had spent so many years at war with one another, could present a relatively unified whole by the close of the century. How did Europe come so far in such a relatively short time?

The Early Years A war-torn Europe emerged from the Second World War in 1945 facing two challenges. First, it needed to rebuild itself and avoid further armed conflict. Second, it needed to increase its industrial strength to stay competitive with an increasingly powerful United States. Cooperation seemed to be the only way of facing these challenges. Belgium, France, West Germany, Italy, Luxembourg, and the Netherlands signed the Treaty of Paris in 1951, creating the *European Coal and Steel Community*. These nations were determined to remove barriers to trade in coal, iron, steel, and scrap metal so as to coordinate coal and steel production among themselves, thereby controlling the postwar arms industry.

The members of the European Coal and Steel Community signed the Treaty of Rome in 1957, creating the *European Economic Community* (see Map 8.1). The Treaty of Rome outlined a future common market for these nations. It also aimed at establishing common transportation and agricultural policies among members. In 1967 the Community's scope was broadened to include additional industries, notably atomic energy, and changed its name to the *European Community*. As the goals of integration continued to expand, so too did the bloc's membership. Waves of enlargement occurred in 1973, 1981, 1986, 1995, and 2004. In 1994 the bloc once again changed its name, to the *European Union (EU)*. Today the 25-member European Union (*www.europa.eu.int*) has a population of about 455 million people and a GDP of $9.3 trillion.

MAP 8.1

Regional Integration in Europe

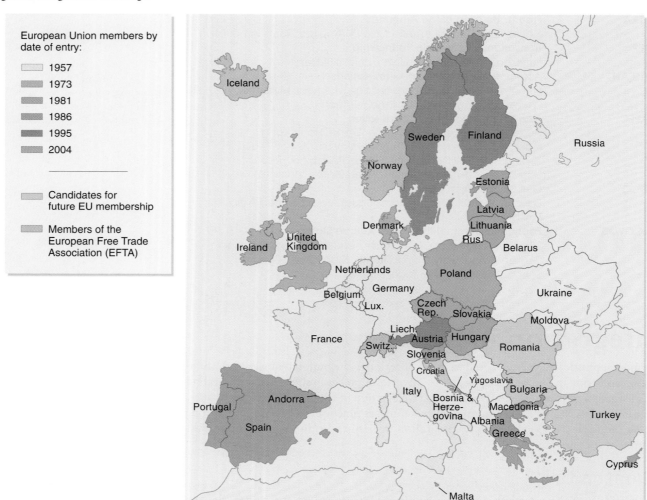

European Union members by date of entry:

- ☐ 1957
- ☐ 1973
- ☐ 1981
- ☐ 1986
- ☐ 1995
- ☐ 2004

- ☐ Candidates for future EU membership
- ☐ Members of the European Free Trade Association (EFTA)

Over the past two decades two important milestones contributed to the EU's continued progress: the *Single European Act* and the *Maastricht Treaty*.

Single European Act   By the mid-1980s, EU member nations were frustrated by remaining trade barriers and a lack of harmony on several important matters, including taxation, law, and regulations. The important objective of harmonizing laws and policies was beginning to appear unachievable. A commission that was formed to analyze the potential for a common market by the end of 1992 put forth several proposals. The goal was to remove remaining barriers, increase harmonization, and thereby enhance the competitiveness of European companies. The proposals became the *Single European Act (SEA)* and went into effect in 1987.

As companies positioned themselves to take advantage of the opportunities that the SEA offered, a wave of mergers and acquisitions swept across Europe. Large firms combined their special understanding of European needs, capabilities, and cultures with their advantage of economies of scale. Small and medium-sized companies were encouraged through EU institutions to engage in networking with one another to offset any negative consequences resulting from, for example, changing product standards.

Maastricht Treaty   Some members of the EU wanted to take European integration further still. A 1991 summit meeting of EU member nations took place in Maastricht, Netherlands. The meeting resulted in the *Maastricht Treaty*, which went into effect in 1993.

The Maastricht Treaty had three aims. First, it called for banking in a single, common currency after January 1, 1999, and circulation of coins and paper currency on January 1, 2002. Second, the treaty set up monetary and fiscal targets for countries that wished to take part in monetary union. Third, the treaty called for political union of the member nations—including development of a common foreign and defense policy and common citizenship. Progress on political integration will wait until the countries gauge the success of the final stages of economic and monetary union. Let's now take a closer look at monetary union in Europe.

European Monetary Union   As stated above, EU leaders were determined to create a single, common currency. **European monetary union** is the European Union plan that established its own central bank and currency in January 1999. The Maastricht Treaty stated the economic criteria with which member nations must comply in order to partake in the single currency, the *euro*. First, consumer price inflation must be below 3.2 percent and must not exceed that of the three best-performing countries by more than 1.5 percent. Second, the debt of government must be 60 percent of GDP or lower. An exception is made if the ratio is diminishing and approaching the 60 percent mark.

European monetary union
The European Union plan that established its own central bank and currency.

Third, the general government deficit must be at or below three percent of GDP. An exception is made if the deficit is close to three percent, or if the deviation is temporary and unusual. Fourth, interest rates on long-term government securities must not exceed, by more than two percent, those of the three countries with the lowest inflation rates. Meeting these criteria better aligned countries' economies and paved the way for smoother policy making under a single European Central Bank. The EU member nations that adopted the single currency are Austria, Belgium, Finland, France, Germany, Greece, Ireland, Italy, Luxembourg, the Netherlands, Portugal, and Spain.

Management Implications of the Euro   The move to a single currency influences all the activities of companies within the European Union. First, the euro completely eliminates exchange-rate risk for business deals between member nations using the euro. It reduces transaction costs by eliminating the cost of converting from one currency to another. In fact, the EU leadership estimates the financial gains to Europe could eventually be 0.5 percent of GDP. The efficiency of trade between participating members resembles that of interstate trade in the United States because only a single currency is involved.

Second, the euro makes prices between markets more transparent, making it more difficult to charge different prices in different markets. This should help end the need for shoppers to flock to other countries to save on high-ticket items. For instance, shortly before monetary union a Mercedes-Benz S320 (*www.mercedes.com*) cost $72,614 in Germany but only $66,920 in Italy. A Renault Twingo (*www.renault.com*) that sold for

$13,265 in France cost $11,120 in Spain. Car brokers and shopping agencies even sprang up specifically to help European consumers reap such savings.

Enlargement of the European Union

One of the most historic events across Europe in recent memory was EU enlargement from 15 to 25 members in May 2004. Countries admitted in 2004 included Cyprus (southern portion), the Czech Republic, Estonia, Hungary, Latvia, Lithuania, Malta, Poland, Slovakia, and Slovenia. Candidates for EU membership include Bulgaria, Croatia, Romania, and Turkey (see Map 8.1). These countries are to become members after they meet certain demands laid down by the EU. These so-called *Copenhagen Criteria* require each country to demonstrate that it:

- Has stable institutions, which guarantee democracy, the rule of law, human rights, and respect for and protection of minorities.

- Has a functioning market economy, capable of coping with competitive pressures and market forces within the European Union.

- Is able to assume the obligations of membership, including adherence to the aims of economic, monetary, and political union.

- Has the ability to adopt the rules and regulations of the Community, the rulings of the European Court of Justice, and the Treaties.

Although it has applied for membership, membership negotiations have not yet begun with Turkey. One reason for the failure of Turkey to win support in the EU is charges (fair or not) by member nations of human rights abuses with regard to its Kurdish minority. Another reason is intense opposition by Greece, Turkey's longtime foe. However, Turkey does have a customs union with the EU, and this is increasing trade between the two. Despite disappointment for some countries that are EU hopefuls and despite intermittent setbacks in the enlargement process, integration is going forward. To learn a bit more about how entrepreneurs can do business in one country recently admitted to the EU, see the Entrepreneur's Survival Kit titled, "Czech List."

entrepreneur's SURVIVAL KIT

Czech List

The demise of communism in Eastern Europe means more opportunity. Those opportunities were apparent to Howard Woffinden and Greg Gold soon after filming a series of Claudia Schiffer fitness videos in Prague, Czech Republic. They joined Prague partner Tomas Krejci in 1996 and formed Los Angeles–based Milk & Honey Films (*www.milkandhoneyfilms.com*) to support U.S. filmmakers who were shooting abroad and overseas shops who were shooting in the United States. Yet they admit that working in the Czech Republic can be challenging. Here's their advice:

- **Don't rush familiarity.** Czech society is very formal. "Unless you know people well, use a formal manner of speaking," says Woffinden. This includes using titles like "doctor" and "mister." It's rarely appropriate to use first names unless you're close friends.

- **Build relationships.** What matters most isn't money, says Gold, but "being referred by someone you've done business with, building personal relationships or [cashing in] favors owed."

- **Find a Czech partner.** Because the Republic was communist for 40 years before becoming a capitalist democ-

racy, Woffinden says, "The method for getting things done is different from ours." You'll need a local to deal with the still-prevalent communist attitudes.

- **Expect limited resources.** Woffinden points out that the country's infrastructure, though improving, is still underdeveloped. "When we arrived five years ago, the phone system was archaic. Often, you can't call someone—you have to physically locate them." The Internet also facilitates communication in the absence of personal phones.

- **Hire local professionals.** Milk & Honey Films uses a Czech accountant to handle the paperwork required by Czech taxes (including a VAT tax of 17 to 22 percent) and red tape. It also employs a bilingual attorney to interpret differences between Czech and U.S. law.

- **Establish who's in charge.** Companies must have a "responsible person" (*jednatel*), who is in charge of all aspects of the business. Woffinden notes that Czechs often want to work directly with this *jednatel* rather than company reps.

FIGURE 8.2

Institutions of the European Union

Structure of the European Union

Five EU institutions play particularly important roles in monitoring and enforcing economic and political integration (see Figure 8.2). Let's now examine each of these institutions to see how they support the work of the EU.

European Parliament   The European Parliament consists of more than 700 members elected by popular vote within each member nation every five years. As such, they are expected to voice their particular political views on EU matters. The European Parliament fulfills its role of adopting EU law by debating and amending legislation proposed by the European Commission. It exercises political supervision over all EU institutions—giving it the power to supervise commissioner appointments and to censure the commission. It also has veto power over some laws (including the annual budget of the EU). There is a call for increased democratization within the EU, and some believe this could be achieved by strengthening the powers of the Parliament. The Parliament conducts its activities in Belgium (in the city Brussels), France (in the city Strasbourg), and Luxembourg.

Council of the European Union   The Council is the legislative body of the EU. When it meets it brings together representatives of member states at the ministerial level. The makeup of the Council changes depending on the topic under discussion. For instance, when the topic is agriculture, the Council comprises the ministers of agriculture of each member nation. No proposed legislation becomes EU law unless the Council votes it into law. Although passage into law for sensitive issues such as immigration and taxation still requires a unanimous vote, some legislation today requires only a simple majority to win approval. The Council also concludes, on behalf of the EU, international agreements with other nations or international organizations. The Council is headquartered in Brussels, Belgium.

European Commission   The Commission is the executive body of the EU. It comprises commissioners appointed by each member country—larger nations get two commissioners, smaller countries get one. Member nations appoint the president and commissioners after being approved by the European Parliament. It has the right to draft legislation, is responsible for managing and implementing policy, and monitors member nations' implementation of, and compliance with, EU law. Each commissioner is assigned a specific policy area, such as competitive policy or agricultural policy. Although commissioners are appointed by their national governments, they are expected to behave in the best interest of the EU as a whole, not in the interest of their own country. The European Commission is headquartered in Brussels, Belgium.

Court of Justice   The Court of Justice is the court of appeals of the EU and is composed of one justice from each member country. One type of case that the Court of Justice hears is one in which a member nation is accused of not meeting its treaty obligations. Another type is one in which the commission or council is charged with failing to live up to their responsibilities under the terms of a treaty. Like the commissioners, justices are required to act in the interest of the EU as a whole, not in the interest of their own countries. The Court of Justice is located in Luxembourg.

Court of Auditors   The Court of Auditors comprises 25 members (one from each member nation) appointed for 6-year terms. The Court is assigned the duty of auditing the EU accounts and implementing its budget. It also aims to improve financial management in the EU and report to member nations' citizens on the use of public funds. As such, it issues annual reports and statements on implementation of the EU budget. The Court has roughly 250 auditors and 300 additional staff to assist it in carrying out its functions. The Court of Auditors is based in Luxembourg.

European Free Trade Association (EFTA)

Certain European nations were reluctant to join in the ambitious goals of the EU, fearing destructive rivalries and a loss of national sovereignty. Some of these nations did not want to be part of a common market but instead wanted the benefits of a free-trade area. That is why in 1960 several countries banded together and formed the *European Free Trade Association (EFTA)* to focus on trade in industrial, not consumer, goods. Because some of the original members joined the EU and some new members joined EFTA (*www.efta.int*), today the group consists of only Iceland, Liechtenstein, Norway, and Switzerland (see Map 8.1).

The population of EFTA is slightly less than 12 million, and it has a combined GDP of around $410 billion. Despite its relatively small size, members remain committed to free-trade principles and raising standards of living for their people. The EFTA and EU created the *European Economic Area (EEA)* to cooperate on matters such as the free movement of goods, persons, services, and capital among member nations. The two groups also cooperate in other areas, including the environment, social policy, and education.

Quick Study

1. Why did Europe initially desire to form a regional trading bloc?
2. Describe the evolution of the European Union (EU). What are its five primary institutions?
3. What is *European monetary union*? Explain its importance to business in Europe.
4. Briefly describe the European Free Trade Association (EFTA).

The European Union (EU) began as a grouping of just 6 member nations, had 15 members for years, and expanded to include 25 members today. To balance what are sometimes divergent national interests, the EU (www.europa.eu.int) designed a one-of-kind system of government. It also designed the role of each EU institution to reflect this balancing act. But some question whether the EU will function effectively following the enlargement from 15 to 25 members in 2004. What potential disagreements could you foresee developing in such a large organization?

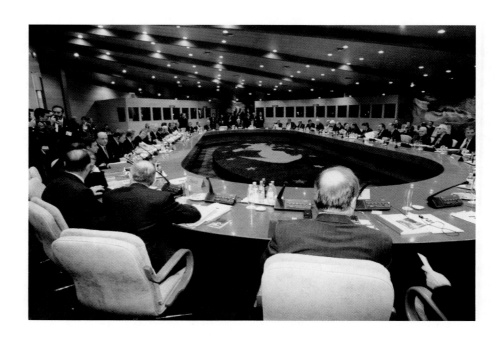

Integration in the Americas

Europe's success at economic integration caused other regions to consider the benefits of forming their own regional trading blocs. Latin American countries began forming regional trading arrangements in the early 1960s but made substantial progress only in the 1980s and 1990s. North America was about three decades behind Europe in taking major steps toward economic integration. Let's now explore the major efforts toward economic integration in North, South, and Central America, beginning with North America.

North American Free Trade Agreement (NAFTA)

There has always been a good deal of trade between Canada and the United States. In fact, the two nations are each other's largest trading partners. Canada and the United States had in the past established trade agreements in several industrial sectors of their economies, including automotive products. In January 1989 the *U.S.–Canada Free Trade Agreement* went into effect. The goal was to eliminate all tariffs on bilateral trade between Canada and the United States by 1998.

But accelerating progress in Europe in the late 1980s and early 1990s caused new urgency in the task of creating a North American trading bloc that included Mexico. Mexico joined what is now the World Trade Organization in 1987 and began privatizing state-owned enterprises in 1988. Talks between Canada, Mexico, and the United States in 1991 eventually resulted in the formation of the *North American Free Trade Agreement (NAFTA)*. NAFTA (*www.nafta-sec-alena.org*) became effective in January 1994 and superseded the U.S.–Canada Free Trade Agreement. Today NAFTA comprises a market with 420 million consumers and a GDP of around $12 trillion (see Map 8.2).

As a free-trade agreement, NAFTA seeks to eliminate most tariffs and nontariff trade barriers on most goods originating from within North America by 2008. The agreement also calls for liberalized rules regarding government procurement practices, the granting of subsidies, and the imposition of countervailing duties (see Chapter 6). Other provisions deal with issues such as trade in services, intellectual property rights, and standards of health, safety, and the environment.

Local Content Requirements and Rules of Origin
Manufacturers and distributors are finding that while NAFTA encourages free trade between Canada, Mexico, and the United States, the resulting trade is anything but hassle-free. Local content requirements and rules of origin are among the agreement's most complex criteria. These rules create special problems for producers and distributors. Although they rarely know the precise origin of every part or component in a piece of industrial equipment, they are responsible for determining whether a product has sufficient North American content to qualify for tariff-free status. The producer or distributor must also provide a NAFTA "certificate of origin" to an importer to claim an exemption from tariffs. Four criteria determine whether a good meets NAFTA rules of origin:[7]

- Goods wholly produced or obtained in the NAFTA region
- Goods containing nonoriginating inputs but meeting Annex 401 origin rules (which covers regional input)
- Goods produced in the NAFTA region wholly from originating materials
- Unassembled goods and goods classified in the same harmonized system category as their parts that do not meet Annex 401 rules but have sufficient North American regional value content

Effects of NAFTA
Since NAFTA went into effect, trade among the three nations has increased markedly, with the greatest gains occurring between Mexico and the United States. Today the United States exports more to Mexico than it does to Britain, France, Germany, and Italy combined. In fact, in 1997 Mexico became the second largest export market for the United States for the first time ever. Mexico was also staying just ahead of

MAP 8.2

**Regional Integration
in North America**

U.S.–Canada
Free Trade Agreement

North American
Free Trade
Agreement (NAFTA)

Central American
Free Trade
Agreement (CAFTA)

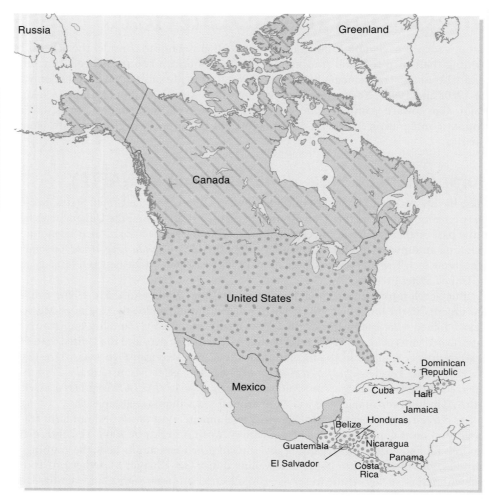

China in terms of exports to the United States, until 2003 that is, when it finally lost out to China.

Nevertheless, since the start of NAFTA Mexico's exports to the United States jumped an astonishing 240 percent, from almost $40 billion to nearly $136 billion (an average annual rate of 34 percent). Meanwhile, U.S. exports to Mexico grew nearly 170 percent, from a little over $41 billion to more than $111 billion.[8] Over the same period, Canada's exports to the United States more than doubled, from almost $117 billion to $242 billion, while U.S. exports to Canada grew 76 percent, from $100 billion to $176 billion. Canada exported very little to Mexico before NAFTA, but afterward exports grew 114 percent from $640 million to nearly $1.4 billion.[9]

The agreement's effect on employment and wages is not as easy to determine. The U.S. Trade Representative Office claims that exports to Mexico and Canada support 2.9 million U.S. jobs (900,000 more than in 1993), which pay 13 to 18 percent more than national averages for production workers.[10] But the AFL-CIO group of unions dispute this claim; they argue that since its formation NAFTA has cost the United States 750,000 jobs and job opportunities.[11]

Despite the disparity in the numbers referenced by different groups, it is certainly true that some U.S. companies headed for the border after NAFTA came into being. One U.S. firm that made a massive manufacturing commitment to Mexico is Delphi Automotive Systems (*www.delphiauto.com*). Delphi has 70,000 employees in its 45 facilities in

Mexico—many along the border with the United States. Delphi manufactures a variety of lighting, electric, and steering assemblies for many of the world's automotive companies. The company cemented its commitment to Mexico by opening a Tech Center in Ciudad Juarez, its first major engineering effort outside the United States. By locating this center closer to manufacturing facilities, the company benefits from reduced lead times and start-up costs.[12]

In addition to claims of job losses, opponents claim that NAFTA has damaged the environment, particularly along the United States–Mexico border. Although the agreement included provisions for environmental protection, Mexico is finding it difficult to deal with the environmental impact of greater economic activity. But Mexico's *Instituto Nacional de Ecologia* (*www.ine.gob.mx*) has developed an industrial-waste-management program, including an incentive system to encourage waste reduction and recycling.

Expansion of NAFTA

Continued ambivalence among some regarding the long-term effects of NAFTA, including the concerns of union leaders and environmental watchdogs, is delaying its expansion. Chile's significant economic progress in the past two decades caused business leaders to argue for its integration into NAFTA. The slender nation of 14 million people is no economic giant, but it might be a model for economic reform in other South American nations. Chile began its market reforms about 15 years ahead of Brazil (the largest economy in South America), and today is largely open to trade and investment.[13]

The pace at which NAFTA expands will depend to a large extent on whether the U.S. Congress grants successive U.S. presidents trade-promotion ("fast-track") authority. Trade-promotion authority allows a U.S. administration to engage in all necessary talks surrounding a trade deal without the official involvement of Congress. After the deal's details are decided, Congress then simply votes yes or no on the deal and cannot revise the treaty's provisions.

But there is little doubt that future integration will occur among nations in the Americas. In fact, it is even possible that the North American economies will one day adopt a single currency. As the former deputy managing director of the International Monetary Fund, Stanley Fischer, said, "As trade relations between Mexico and the U.S. strengthen and as the economies open up to each other, I think having two currencies won't make a great deal of sense." Fischer noted that although this could be difficult for both Canada and Mexico to stomach politically, in the long run he expects to see one currency for all of North America.[14] Ecuador has already "dollarized" its economy.

Andean Community

Attempts at integration among Latin American countries had a rocky beginning. The first try, the *Latin American Free Trade Association (LAFTA)*, was formed in 1961. The agreement first called for the creation of a free-trade area by 1971 but then extended that date to 1980. Yet because of a crippling debt crisis in South America and a reluctance of member nations to do away with protectionism, the agreement was doomed to an early demise. Disappointment with LAFTA led to the creation of two other regional trading blocs—the Andean Community and the Latin American Integration Association.

Formed in 1969, the *Andean Community* (originally the Andean Pact) today includes five South American countries located in the Andes mountain range—Bolivia, Colombia, Ecuador, Peru, and Venezuela (see Map 8.3). The group comprises a market of more than 105 million consumers and a combined GDP of about $500 billion. The main objectives of the group included tariff reduction for trade among member nations, a common external tariff, and common policies in both transportation and certain industries. But political ideology was somewhat hostile to the concept of free markets and favored a good deal of government involvement in business affairs. Also, inherent distrust among members made lower tariffs and more open trade hard to achieve.

MAP 8.3

Regional Integration in Latin America

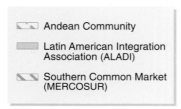

- Andean Community
- Latin American Integration Association (ALADI)
- Southern Common Market (MERCOSUR)

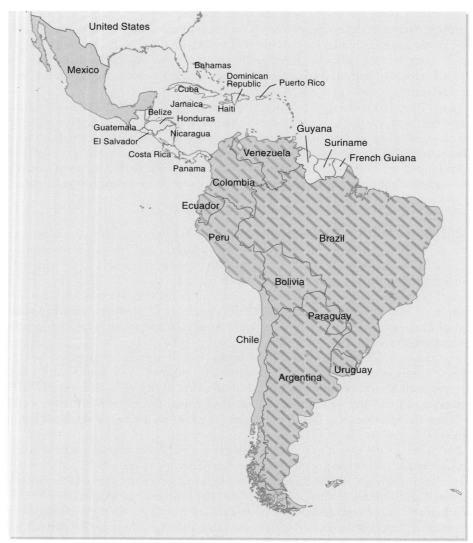

The Andean Community had the ambitious goal of establishing a common market by 1995, but delays mean that it remains a somewhat incomplete customs union. The group now hopes to have the common market in place by 2005. The Andean countries posted nearly 30 percent annual gains in trade from 1990 to 1997 but experienced recession in the late 1990s. Furthermore, political violence in Colombia continues to threaten the stability of its government, and the nation's economy is experiencing its worst problems in decades. According to official estimates, meanwhile, as much as 80 percent of Venezuelans have fallen below the poverty line.

The common market will be difficult to implement within the framework of the Andean Community. One reason is that each country has been given significant exceptions in the tariff structure that they have in place for trade with nonmember nations. Another reason is that countries continue to sign agreements with just one or two countries outside the Andean Community framework. Such independent action impairs progress internally and hurts the credibility of the Andean Community with the rest of the world. Furthermore, Bolivia and Chile have gained associate membership in the trading bloc known as MERCOSUR (discussed below), which indicates a lack of confidence in the future success of the Andean Community.

1. What was the impetus for the formation of the North American Free Trade Agreement (NAFTA)?

2. What effect has NAFTA had on trade between its member nations?

3. What is the Andean Community? Identify why it is behind schedule.

Latin American Integration Association (ALADI)

The *Latin American Integration Association (ALADI)* was formed in 1980. Map 8.3 shows the countries that belong to the ALADI trading bloc. Because of the failure of the first attempt at integration (LAFTA), the objectives of ALADI were scaled back significantly. The ALADI agreement calls for preferential tariff agreements to be made between pairs of member nations (called *bilateral* agreements) that reflect the economic development of each nation. Although the agreement resulted in roughly 24 bilateral agreements and five subregional pacts, the agreements did not accomplish a great deal of cross-border trade. Dissatisfaction with progress once again caused certain nations to form a trading bloc of their own—MERCOSUR.

Southern Common Market (MERCOSUR)

The *Southern Common Market (MERCOSUR)* was established in 1988 between just Argentina and Brazil, but it expanded to include Paraguay and Uruguay in 1991. In 1996 MERCOSUR (*www.mercosur.org.uy*) underwent another expansion when Bolivia and Chile became associate, but not full, members of the bloc (see Map 8.3). Peru and Venezuela are also showing interest in MERCOSUR.

Today MERCOSUR acts as a customs union and boasts a market of more than 220 million consumers (nearly half of Latin America's total population) and 60 percent of its total economic output. Its first years of existence were very successful—trade between members grew nearly fourfold during the 1990s. MERCOSUR is progressing on trade and investment liberalization and is emerging as the most powerful trading bloc in all of Latin America. It may even incorporate all the countries of South America into a South American Free Trade Agreement, after which it would link up with NAFTA to form a Free Trade Area of the Americas (discussed below). But the bloc's pace of integration has been hampered by (1) differing trade agendas and macroeconomic policy frameworks and (2) the economic problems being experienced by Argentina and Brazil.[15]

Regional economic integration in Latin America has certainly caught the eye of European businesses as well. Some notable European companies in Latin America include Germany's Volkswagen (*www.vw.com*) and Italy's Fiat (*www.fiat.com*) in autos, France's supermarket chain Carrefour (*www.carrefour.com*), and the British/Dutch personal-care products group Unilever (*www.unilever.com*). As European companies continue making inroads into Latin America, U.S. companies are pressuring their government to move more quickly in integrating Chile into NAFTA and accelerating the creation of the Free Trade Area of the Americas. Latin America's large consumer base and its potential as a low-cost production platform for worldwide export appeal to both the European Union and the United States.[16]

Central America and the Caribbean

Attempts at economic integration in Central American countries and throughout the Caribbean basin have been much more modest than efforts elsewhere in the Americas. Nevertheless, let's look at two efforts at integration in these two regions—CARICOM and CACM.

Caribbean Community and Common Market (CARICOM)   The *Caribbean Community and Common Market (CARICOM)* trading bloc was formed in 1973. Map 8.4

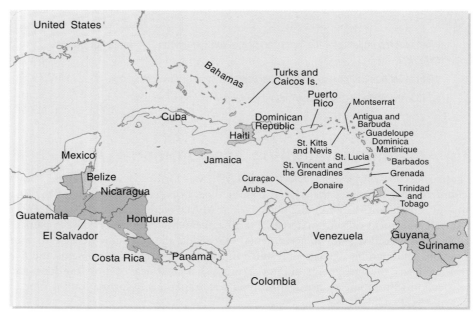

MAP 8.4

Regional Integration in Central America and the Caribbean

- Caribbean Community and Common Market (CARICOM)
- Central American Common Market (CACM)

shows the members of CARICOM (*www.caricom.org*). Although the Bahamas is a member of the Community it does not belong to the Common Market. As a whole, CARICOM has a combined GDP of nearly $30 billion and a market of almost 6 million people.

In early 2000, CARICOM members signed an agreement calling for the establishment of the CARICOM Single Market, which calls for the free movement of factors of production including goods, services, capital, and labor. However, several members have yet to ratify the agreement.[17] The main difficulty CARICOM will continue to face is that most members trade more with nonmembers than they do with one another simply because members do not have the imports each other needs.

Central American Common Market (CACM)

The *Central American Common Market (CACM)* was formed in 1961 to create a common market between Costa Rica, El Salvador, Guatemala, Honduras, and Nicaragua (see Map 8.4). Together, the members of CACM (*www.sieca.org.gt*) comprise a market of 33 million consumers and have a combined GDP of about $120 billion. However, the common market was never realized because of a long and bloody war between El Salvador and Honduras and guerrilla conflicts in several countries. But renewed peace is creating more business confidence and optimism, which is driving double-digit growth in trade between members.

Furthermore, the group has not yet created a customs union. External tariffs among members range anywhere from 4 percent to 12 percent. And the tentative nature of cooperation was obvious in 2000 when Honduras and Nicaragua slapped punitive tariffs on each other's goods during a dispute over a patch of water. But officials remain positive, saying that their ultimate goal is European-style integration, closer political ties, and adoption of a single currency—probably the dollar. In fact, El Salvador adopted the U.S. dollar as its official currency in 2000, and Guatemala already uses the dollar alongside its quetzal.[18]

Free Trade Area of the Americas (FTAA)

Sure to dominate future discussion of regional trading blocs in the Americas is creation of a *Free Trade Area of the Americas (FTAA)*. The objective of the FTAA (*www.alca-ftaa.org*)

is to create the largest free-trade area on the planet, stretching from the northern tip of Alaska to the southern tip of Tierra del Fuego, in South America. The FTAA would comprise 34 nations and 800 million consumers and have a collective GDP of more than $12 trillion. The only Western Hemisphere nation that would not be part of the FTAA is Cuba. The FTAA would work alongside the different trading blocs such as NAFTA, MERCOSUR, the Andean Community, and CACM. After going into effect, the FTAA would remove tariffs and nontariff barriers between all member countries over the course of a decade or more.

The first official meeting, the 1994 Summit of the Americas, created the broad blueprint for the agreement. Government representatives reaffirmed their commitment to the FTAA at the Second Summit of the Americas in April 1998. Actual negotiations began in September 1998 and are scheduled to finish no later than 2005. The Third Summit of the Americas was held in April 2001 and met with protests by labor organizations, environmentalists, and others protesting increased globalization. In an effort to placate the concerns of some of these groups, leaders attending the summit declared that they would halve the number of people living in extreme poverty by 2015.[19]

The reasons for a renewed U.S. quest for completing the FTAA are apparent when we consider the fact that the United States participates in just two free-trade agreements out of 130 worldwide. In the Western Hemisphere, it participates in just one of 30.[20] One businessperson supporting the FTAA is William Weiller, chairman and CEO of Purafil, Inc. (*www.purafil.com*) of Atlanta, Georgia. In 2000, this maker of air-purification systems exported just 15 percent of its $22 million in sales to Latin America because of the cost added to the products by existing tariffs. Weiller believes that removing tariffs could cause his exports south of the border to leap to 25 percent of sales. Says Weiller, "If there's a level playing field, we'll be more aggressive."[21]

Corruption in Latin America is an area of contention for Canada and the United States, who fear that closer cooperation could mean more piracy and lost sales to counterfeit goods. Latin America has long been identified as a market for pirated merchandise, particularly music on CD-ROMs and computer software. Some music is even produced in Macao, China, and sent for sale in Latin America.[22] If the FTAA is going to be a success (or if it comes to pass even), corruption will have to be rooted out.

Transatlantic Economic Partnership (TEP)

The *Transatlantic Economic Partnership (TEP)* between the United States and the European Union surfaced in May 1998 at the EU–United States summit meeting. In addition to the goal of forging closer economic ties between the EU and the United States, the partnership aims to contribute to stability, democracy, and development worldwide. Although the EU and the United States differ in important ways, the partnership is one of equals in terms of the size of their economies.

There is good reason for partnership. Together, the United States and the European Union have a combined population of 740 million, account for over half the world's GDP, and have trade and investment flows that amount to nearly $1 billion every day! Moreover, each is the other's largest single trading partner (considering all the EU countries as a whole) and most important source of, and destination for, foreign investment.[23]

Quick Study

1. Identify the members of the Southern Common Market (MERCOSUR). How has it performed?

2. What is the objective of the Free Trade Area of the Americas (FTAA)? What are its current prospects for success?

3. What is the Transatlantic Economic Partnership (TEP)? Identify its main goals.

Integration in Asia

Efforts outside Europe and the Americas at economic and political integration have tended to be looser arrangements. Let's take a look at two important coalitions in Asia and among Pacific Rim nations—the Association of Southeast Asian Nations and the organization for Asia Pacific Economic Cooperation.

Association of Southeast Asian Nations (ASEAN)

Indonesia, Malaysia, the Philippines, Singapore, and Thailand formed the *Association of Southeast Asian Nations (ASEAN)* in 1967. Brunei joined in 1984, Vietnam in 1995, Laos and Myanmar in 1997, and Cambodia in 1998 (see Map 8.5). Together, the ASEAN (*www.aseansec.org*) countries comprise a market of about 500 million consumers and a GDP of more than $800 billion. The three main objectives of the alliance are to (1) promote economic, cultural, and social development in the region; (2) safeguard the region's economic and political stability; and (3) serve as a forum in which differences can be resolved fairly and peacefully.

The intention to admit Cambodia, Laos, and Myanmar (formerly Burma) was met with criticism from some Western nations. The concern regarding Laos and Cambodia being admitted stems from their roles in supporting the communists during the Vietnam War. The

MAP 8.5

Regional Integration in Asia

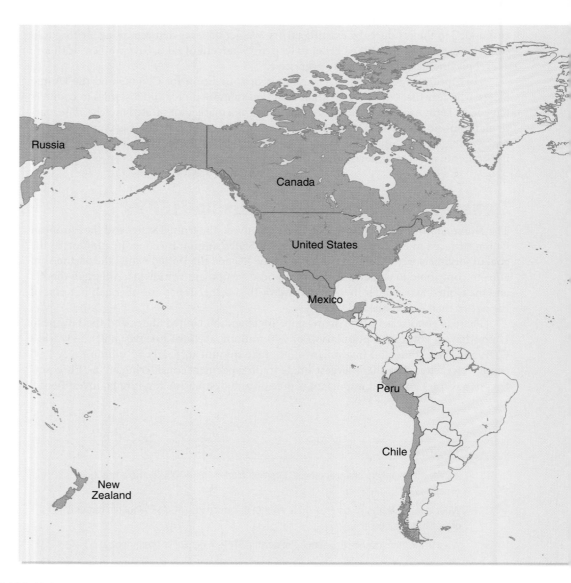

quarrel with Myanmar centers on evidence cited by the West of its continued human rights violations. Nevertheless, ASEAN felt that by adding these countries to the coalition, it could counter China's rising strength and its resources of cheap labor and abundant raw materials.[24]

Companies involved in Asia's developing economies are likely to be doing business with an ASEAN member. This is even a more likely prospect as China, Japan, and South Korea speed up their efforts at joining ASEAN as soon as 2008. The new arrangement would allow China to act "as a bridge between the less advanced and more advanced economies," said Supachai Panitchpakdi, deputy prime minister of Thailand.[25] Some key facts about ASEAN that companies must consider are contained in the Global Manager's Toolbox titled, "The Ins and Outs of ASEAN."

Asia Pacific Economic Cooperation (APEC)

The organization for *Asia Pacific Economic Cooperation (APEC)* was formed in 1989. Begun as an informal forum among 12 trading partners, APEC (*www.apecsec.org.sg*) now has 21 members (see Map 8.5). Together, the APEC nations account for more than half of world trade and a combined GDP of more than $16 trillion.

The stated aim of APEC is not to build another trading bloc. Instead, it desires to strengthen the multilateral trading system and expand the global economy by simplifying

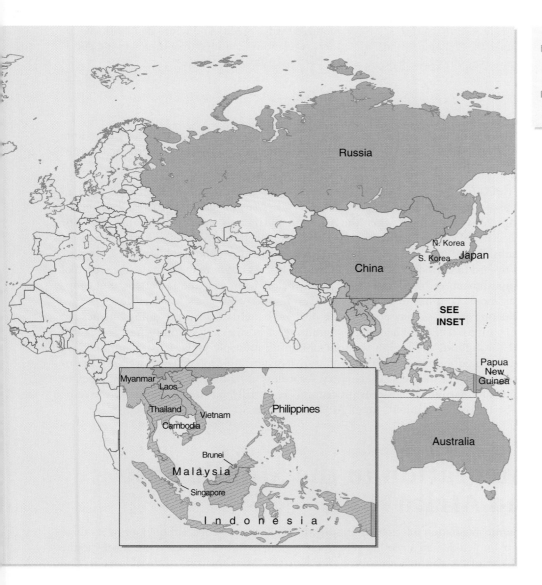

Association of Southeast Asian Nations (ASEAN)

Asia Pacific Economic Cooperation (APEC)

The Ins and Outs of ASEAN

Businesses that are unfamiliar with operating in ASEAN do need to exercise caution in their dealings. Some inescapable facts about ASEAN that warrant consideration are the following:

◆ **Diverse cultures and politics.** The Philippines is a representative democracy, Brunei is an oil-rich sultanate, and Vietnam is a state-controlled communist country. Business policies and protocol must be adapted to each country.

◆ **Economic competition.** Many ASEAN nations are feeling the effects of China's power to attract investment from multinationals worldwide. Whereas ASEAN members used to attract around 30 percent of foreign direct investment into Asia's developing economies, it now attracts about half that.

◆ **Corruption and black markets.** Bribery and black markets are common in many ASEAN countries, including Indonesia, Myanmar, the Philippines, and Vietnam. Corruption studies typically place these countries at or very near the bottom of nations surveyed.

◆ **Political change and turmoil.** Several nations in the region recently elected new leaders. Indonesia in particular has gone through presidents at a fast clip recently. Companies must remain alert to shifting political winds and laws regarding trade and investment.

◆ **Border disputes.** Parts of Thailand's borders with Cambodia and Laos are tested frequently. Hostilities break out sporadically between Thailand and Myanmar over border alignment and ethnic Shan rebels operating along the border.

◆ **Lack of common tariffs and standards.** Doing business in ASEAN nations can be costly. Harmonized tariffs, quality and safety standards, customs regulations, and investment rules would cut transaction costs significantly.

and liberalizing trade and investment procedures among member nations. In the long term, APEC hopes to have free trade and investment throughout the region by 2010 for developed nations and 2020 for developing ones.

The Record of APEC APEC has succeeded in halving members' tariff rates from an average of 15 percent to 7.5 percent. The early years saw the greatest progress, but liberalization received a setback when the Asian financial crisis struck in the late 1990s. For instance, members have not yet specified complete timetables for eliminating trade barriers and subsidies by 2010 and 2020.[26] APEC is at least as much a political body as it is a movement toward freer trade. After all, APEC certainly does not have the focus or the record of accomplishments of NAFTA or the EU. Nonetheless, open dialogue and attempts at cooperation should continue to encourage progress toward APEC goals, however slow.

Further progress may create some positive benefits for people doing business in APEC nations. APEC is changing the granting of business visas so businesspeople can travel throughout the region without obtaining multiple visas. It is recommending mutual recognition agreements on professional qualifications so that engineers, for example, could practice in any APEC country, regardless of nationality. And APEC is ready to simplify and harmonize customs procedures. Eventually, businesses could use the same customs forms and manifests for all APEC economies.

Integration in the Middle East and Africa

Economic integration has not left out the Middle East and Africa, although progress there is more limited than in any other geographic region. Its limited success is due mostly to the small size of the countries involved and their relatively low level of development. The largest of these coalitions are the Gulf Cooperation Council and the Economic Community of West African States.

Gulf Cooperation Council (GCC)

Several Middle Eastern nations formed the *Gulf Cooperation Council (GCC)* in 1980. Members of the GCC are Bahrain, Kuwait, Oman, Qatar, Saudi Arabia, and the United Arab Emirates (see Map 8.6). The primary purpose of the GCC at its formation was to cooperate with the increasingly powerful trading blocs in Europe at the time—the EU and EFTA. However, as it has evolved the GCC has become as much a political as an economic entity. Its cooperative thrust allows citizens of member countries to travel freely in the GCC without visas. It also permits citizens of one member nation to own land, property, and businesses in any other member nation without the need for local sponsors or partners.

Economic Community of West African States (ECOWAS)

The *Economic Community of West African States (ECOWAS)* was formed in 1975 but relaunched its efforts at economic integration in 1992 because of a lack of early progress (see Map 8.6). One of the most important goals of ECOWAS (*www.ecowas.int*) is the formation of a customs union and eventual common market and monetary union. Together, the ECOWAS nations comprise a large portion of the economic activity in sub-Saharan Africa.

Progress on market integration is almost nonexistent. In fact, the value of trade occurring among ECOWAS nations is just 11 percent of the value of the trade members undertake

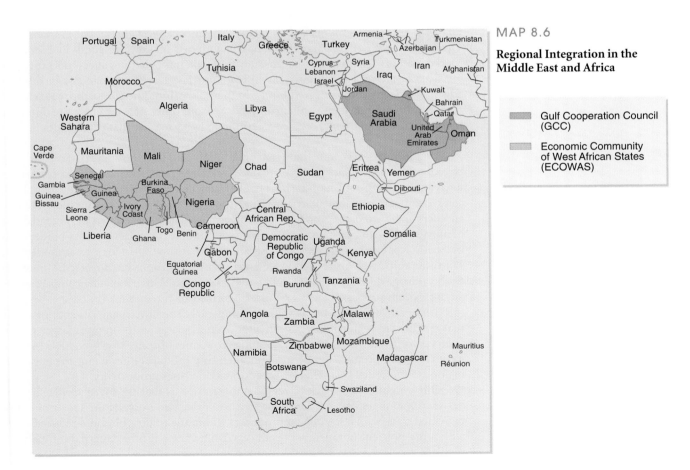

MAP 8.6

Regional Integration in the Middle East and Africa

- Gulf Cooperation Council (GCC)
- Economic Community of West African States (ECOWAS)

with third parties. But ECOWAS has made progress in the free movement of people, construction of international roads, and development of international telecommunication links. Some of the main problems ECOWAS has encountered arise because of political instability, poor governance, weak national economies, poor infrastructure, and poor economic policies.

Quick Study

1. Identify the three main objectives of the Association of Southeast Asian Nations (ASEAN).
2. How do the goals of the Asia Pacific Economic Cooperation (APEC) forum differ from those of other regional blocs?
3. What is the Gulf Cooperation Council (GCC)? Identify its members.
4. What is the Economic Community of West African States (ECOWAS)? Explain why it has had limited success.

Bottom Line for Business

This chapter described the main regional integration efforts throughout the world today. Such efforts are occurring despite debate over their merits and demerits. Regional economic integration can provide consumers and industrial buyers with greater choice at lower prices, improve firm productivity, and boost national competitiveness. We also learned about some of the ethical elements of such agreements and the actions of governments and independent organizations to counter the negative effects of integration. Here, we focus on only the main issues regarding regional integration—business operations and employment.

Regional Integration and Business Operations

Regional trade agreements are changing the landscape of the global marketplace. They are lowering trade barriers and opening up new markets for goods and services. Markets otherwise off-limits because tariffs made imported products too expensive can become attractive once tariffs are lifted. But trade agreements can also be double-edged swords for companies. Not only do they allow domestic companies to seek new markets abroad, but they also let competitors from other nations enter the domestic market. Such mobility increases competition in every market that participates in such an agreement.

Despite increased competition that often accompanies regional integration, there can be economic benefits, such as those provided by a single currency. For example, companies today in the European Union clearly benefit from the common currency, the euro. First, costs (commissions) inherent in converting from one member nation's currency to that of another can be avoided. Second, business owners need not worry about the potential loss of money due to shifting exchange rates between national currencies on cross-border deals in the EU. Not having to cover such costs and risks frees up capital for greater investment. Third, the euro makes prices between markets more transparent, causing it to be more difficult to charge different prices in different markets. This helps companies compare prices among various suppliers of a raw material, intermediate product, or service.

There are other benefits as well for companies. The lowering or absence of tariffs that result from regional integration allows a multinational to supply a larger region from one or fewer factories, thus exploiting economies of scale. This is possible because a company can produce in one location, then ship products throughout the low-tariff region at little added cost. This lowers costs and increases productivity.

One potential drawback of regional integration is that the lower tariffs charged between members of a trading bloc can result in trade diversion. This can cause increased trade with less-efficient producers within the trading bloc and reduced trade with more-efficient nonmember producers. Unless there is other internal competition

1. It is likely that the proliferation and growth of regional trading blocs will continue into the foreseeable future. At what point do you think the integration process will stop (if ever)? Explain your answer.

2. Some people believe that the rise of regional trading blocs threatens free-trade progress made by the World Trade Organization (WTO). Do you agree? Why or why not?

3. Certain groups of countries, particularly in Africa, are far less economically developed than other regions, such as Europe and North America. What sort of integration arrangement do you think developed countries could create with less-developed nations to improve living standards? Be as specific as you can.

1. Some analysts believe that NAFTA can extend its current arrangement to more advanced levels of economic integration. In small groups of several students or more, discuss the obstacles that NAFTA nations might face as they seek to bring other nations into their fold. Discuss whether political integration is a possibility.

2. As a team, go to your library or link to a business information service on the Internet. Locate articles that describe how a large international company is coping with regional economic integration. Write a 3-page report on how the company is responding to the integration. Are the company's strategies paying off, or are there problems? Describe the factors behind the company's success or problems.

3. In this project, two groups of four students debate the advantages and disadvantages of regional economic integration. After the first student from each side has spoken, the second student questions the opponent's arguments, looking for holes and inconsistencies. The third student attempts to answer these arguments. The fourth student presents a summary of each side's arguments. Finally, the class votes on which team offered the more compelling argument.

common market (p. 231)

customs union (p. 231)

economic union (p. 232)

European monetary union (p. 237)

free-trade area (p. 231)

political union (p. 232)

regional economic integration (regionalism) (p. 230)

trade creation (p. 232)

trade diversion (p. 233)

1. In this chapter, we explored the trend toward greater integration of national economies, understanding the potential benefits and drawbacks of regional integration. One proposed regional agreement we covered was the Free Trade Area of the Americas (FTAA).

   Visit the official Web site of the FTAA (*www.alca-ftaa.org*). What are the stated reasons why governments across the Americas are pushing for the free trade area? Now visit the Web site of a group determined to derail the FTAA (*www.stopftaa.org*). What are the reasons why the anti-FTAA group is protesting its implementation? Do you think that the FTAA would help lift the living standards for people in the smallest countries (such as Ecuador or Nicaragua)? Or would the FTAA only be a boon for the largest nations such as Brazil, Canada, and the United States?

   Small companies typically have difficulty competing against large multinationals when their governments take part in regional trading blocs. What could governments do to help their small companies compete after the formation of such blocs? Do you think that by forming sub-regional trading blocs *small nations* can really strengthen their negotiating positions against large nations? Do you think that very small nations should even participate in regional trade agreements with very large nations? Why or why not?

Do you think that subregional or regional trade agreements cause instability on a subregional, regional, or global scale, or do you believe they foster cooperation? Explain your answer. After all you've read in this chapter about regional trade agreements, what is your assessment of their value? Should their progress continue or be rolled back?

ETHICAL CHALLENGES

1. You are a member of the U.S. Congress from the state of Florida. Many constituents in your district have complained NAFTA is unfair to the economies of the Caribbean islands where they have family. Some experts argue that the term "free-trade agreement" in describing NAFTA or the European Union is misleading. They say these agreements are really "preferential trade agreements" that offer free trade only to members and relative protection against nonmembers. You worry that this is the case for Caribbean nations excluded from NAFTA. Some argue that from apparel factories in Jamaica to sugar cane fields in Trinidad, NAFTA has cost jobs, market share, and income for the vulnerable island nations of the region as jobs have migrated to Mexico. Given the impact on nonmember nations, do you think such trade agreements are ethical? Why do you think islands in the Caribbean basin were not invited to be part of NAFTA? As a member of the U.S. Congress, what arguments do you make for including the Caribbean in the expansion of NAFTA?

2. You are a world-renowned economist hired by Ecuador's government to advise it on its current involvement with the Andean Community. The Andean Community is a customs union that consists of five nations in South America: Venezuela, Colombia, Ecuador, Peru, and Bolivia. Member nations are permitted free access to one another's markets, with nonmember nations required to negotiate tariffs with community members. Because Ecuador recently adopted the U.S. dollar as its currency, some believe that the other Andean members are perhaps holding Ecuador back from more rapid development. As the consultant, what pros and cons do you present to the Ecuadorian government for breaking free from the Andean Community?

3. You are the economic adviser to the President of Mexico. Labor unions and environmentalists in the United States aren't the only ones speaking out against NAFTA. There continues to be opposition in Mexico by those complaining of a loss of national sovereignty and who feel that the income gap between the two countries will never be narrowed. Average hourly wages on the U.S. side of the border can be six times that on the Mexican side. Mexican critics fear that their entire country will be subsumed by companies from the United States, which do not contribute to Mexico's higher standard of living, but who instead use Mexico as a low-cost assembly site while keeping high-paying, high-skilled jobs at home. Do you think that there is a way for trade agreements to help close the economic gap between poor and wealthy partners? Or will the interests of poorer nations always be subordinate to wealthier countries within regional trading blocs? As the economic adviser, how do you suggest the president protect Mexico's workforce?

PRACTICING INTERNATIONAL MANAGEMENT CASE

Tainted Trade: Increasing Imports Brings Increase in Illness

Today, U.S. citizens in the dead of a Minnesota winter can indulge their cravings for summer-fresh raspberries. Europeans who are thousands of miles away from North America can put Mexican mangoes in their breakfast cereal. Japanese shoppers can buy radishes that were grown from seeds cultivated in Oregon. Eating fresh and natural produce is a growing consumer trend, and globalization of the food industry, falling barriers to trade, and formation of regional trading blocs make it possible for people to choose from produce grown all over the world. Unfortunately, these forces have also made it more likely that these same consumers will get debilitating—and even deadly—illnesses from foodborne pathogens.

In the United States several outbreaks linked to the burgeoning global trade in produce have made headlines in recent years. One very serious case occurred several years ago when 2,300 people were victims of a parasite called cyclospora that had hitched a ride on raspberries grown in Guatemala. Outbreaks of hepatitis A and salmonella from tainted strawberries and alfalfa sprouts, respectively, have also alarmed consumers. Although health officials say there is no evidence that imports are inherently more dangerous, they do cite some real reasons for worry. For one thing, imported produce often comes from countries where food hygiene and basic sanitation are less advanced. For another, some microbes that cause no damage in their home country are deadly when introduced on foreign soil. Finally, the longer the journey from farm to table, the greater is the chance of contamination. Just consider the journey taken by the salmonella-ridden alfalfa sprouts: The seeds for the sprouts were bought from Uganda and Pakistan, among other nations, shipped through the Netherlands, flown into New York, and trucked all around the United States.

Incidences of food contamination show no signs of abating. Since the passage of NAFTA, cross-border trade in food among Canada, Mexico, and the United States has skyrocketed. Meanwhile, federal inspections of U.S. imports by the Food and Drug Administration have dropped significantly. The increase in imports has clearly strained the U.S. food-safety system, which

was built 100 years ago for a country contained within its own borders. Although it isn't feasible for the United States to plant FDA inspectors in every country, options are available. The U.S. Congress could tighten further the ban on importing fruit and vegetables from countries that do not meet expanded U.S. food-safety standards. More money could be given to the FDA to enable it to hire investigators to inspect more fully not just produce but also farming methods and government safety systems in other countries. Countries that blocked the new inspections would be forbidden to sell fruit and vegetables in the United States. Although such measures would irk trading partners of the United States, it most certainly would fuel the worldwide debate on food safety and trade.

Thinking Globally

1. How do you think countries with a high volume of exports to the United States, such as Mexico, would respond to stricter food-safety rules? Do you think such measures are a good way to stem the tide of food-related illnesses? Why or why not?

2. Sue Doneth of Marshall, Michigan, is a mother of one of the schoolchildren who was exposed to the hepatitis A virus after eating tainted frozen strawberry desserts. Speaking before Congress she said, "We are forcing consumers to trade the health and safety of their families for free trade. That is not fair trade. NAFTA is not a trade issue: it is a safety issue." Do you think food-safety regulations should be built into an extension of NAFTA? Why or why not? What are the benefits and drawbacks of putting food-safety regulations into international trade pacts?

3. The lack of harmonized food-safety practices and standards is just one of the challenges faced by the food industry as it becomes more global. What other challenges face the food industry in an era of economic integration and opening markets?

learning objectives

After studying this chapter, you should be able to

1. Discuss the purposes, development, and financial centers of the *international capital market.*

2. Describe the *international bond, international equity,* and *Eurocurrency markets.*

3. Discuss the four primary functions of the *foreign exchange market.*

4. Explain how currencies are *quoted* and the different *rates* given.

5. Identify the main *instruments* and *institutions* of the foreign exchange market.

6. Explain why and how governments restrict *currency convertibility.*

international financial

Part 4 The International Financial System

markets

a look **back**

CHAPTER 8 introduced the most prominent efforts at regional economic integration occurring around the world. We saw how international companies are responding to the challenges and opportunities that regional integration is creating.

a look **at this chapter**

This chapter introduces us to the international financial system by describing the structure of international financial markets. We learn first about the international capital market and its main components. We then turn to the foreign exchange market, explaining how it works and outlining its structure.

a look **ahead**

CHAPTER 10 concludes our study of the international financial system. We discuss the factors that influence exchange rates and explain why and how governments and other institutions try to manage exchange rates. In so doing, we focus on recent monetary problems in emerging markets worldwide.

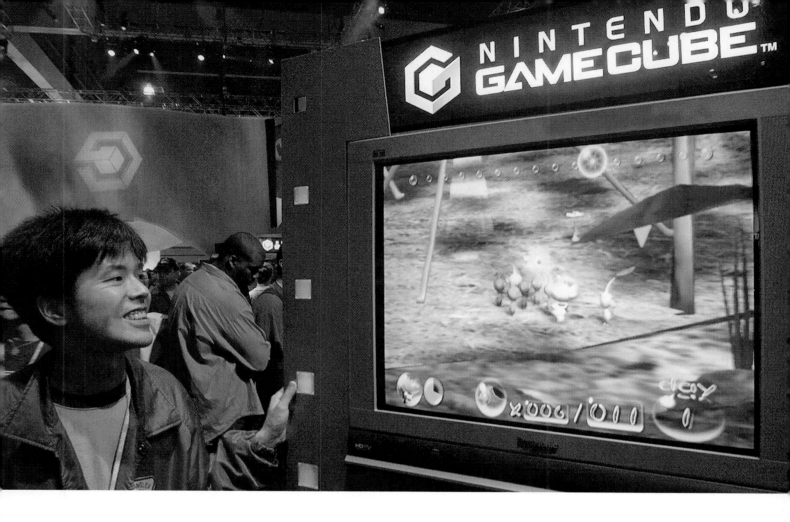

A Yen for Nintendo

KYOTO, Japan—In a *New Yorker* cartoon, a boy recites his latest book report before his classmates. The caption below: "Game Boy: A Memoir of Addiction, by Ronald Markowitz." Since 1989, the Nintendo Company, (*www.nintendo.com*) has been feeding the addiction of Game Boy fanatics worldwide.

Nintendo traces its roots to 1889 when Fusajiro Yamauchi began manufacturing *Hanafuda* Japanese playing cards in Kyoto, Japan. Today, Nintendo produces and sells video game systems, including Nintendo 64, Game Boy Advance, and GameCube. To date, the company has sold more than 1 billion video games worldwide, and more than 40 percent of U.S. households own a Nintendo game system. The company created such icons as Mario, Donkey Kong, and Pokémon, which pop up in cultures worldwide. Practically everywhere Nintendo characters adorn licensed merchandise, including children's furniture, backpacks, coloring books, mugs, T-shirts, potato chip bags, and canned soda.

But Nintendo's game-design and marketing talents are not all that affect its performance—so do exchange rates between the Japanese yen (¥) and other currencies. The earnings of Nintendo's 40 subsidiaries and affiliates worldwide are integrated into the consolidated financial statements at the end of the year. Translating subsidiaries' earnings from other currencies into yen when it is relatively strong decreases Nintendo's stated earnings in yen. The firm reported net income in 2003 of ¥ 67.3 billion

($561 million), but also reported that income was greater prior to a foreign exchange loss of ¥ 22.6 billion ($189 million). The loss resulted from a rise in the yen against foreign currencies prior to the translation of subsidiaries' earnings into Japanese yen. As you read this chapter, keep in mind how shifting currency values affect company performance, and what companies can do to shield themselves from adverse changes.[1]

Well-functioning financial markets are an essential element of the international business environment. They funnel money from organizations and economies with excess funds to those with shortages. International financial markets also allow companies to exchange one currency for another. Such exchanges, as well as the rates at which currencies are exchanged, are critical to international business.

For example, suppose you purchase a CD player imported from a company based in the Philippines. Whether you realize it or not, the price you paid for that CD player was affected by the *exchange rate* between your country's currency and the Philippine peso. Ultimately, the Filipino company that sold you the CD player must convert the purchase made in your currency into Philippine pesos. Thus, the profit earned by the Filipino company is also influenced by the exchange rate between your currency and the peso. Managers must understand how changes in currency values—and thus in exchange rates—affect the profitability of their international business activities. Among other things, managers at our hypothetical company in the Philippines must know how much to charge you for their CD player.

In this chapter, we launch our study of the international financial system by exploring the structure of the international financial markets. The two interrelated systems that comprise the international financial markets are the (1) international capital market and (2) foreign exchange market. We start by examining the purposes of the international capital market and tracing its recent development. We then take a detailed look at the international bond, equity, and Eurocurrency markets, each of which helps companies to borrow and lend money internationally. Following that, we take a look at the functioning of the foreign exchange market—an international market for currencies that facilitates international business transactions. Finally, we explore how currency convertibility affects international transactions.

International Capital Market

capital market
System that allocates financial resources in the form of debt and equity according to their most efficient uses.

A **capital market** is a system that allocates financial resources in the form of debt and equity according to their most efficient uses. Its main purpose is to provide a mechanism through which those who wish to borrow or invest money can do so efficiently. Individuals, companies, governments, mutual funds, pension funds, and all types of nonprofit organizations participate in capital markets. For example, an individual might want to buy her first home; a midsize company might want to add production capacity; and a government might want to develop a new fiber optic telecommunications system. Sometimes these individuals and organizations have excess cash to lend; at other times, they need funds.

Purposes of National Capital Markets

There are two primary means by which companies obtain external financing: *debt* and *equity*. Capital markets function to help them obtain both types of financing. However, to understand the international capital market fully we need to review the purposes of capital markets in domestic economies. Quite simply, national capital markets help individuals and institutions borrow the money that other individuals and institutions want to lend. Although in theory borrowers could search individually for various parties who are willing to lend or invest, this would be a time-consuming process. Consequently, intermediaries of

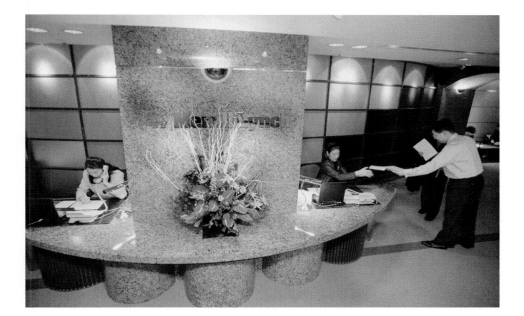

Large financial institutions benefit borrowers and lenders worldwide in many ways. As investment banks, they underwrite debt and equity securities and advise corporations, governments, and institutions. As asset managers, they are caretakers of the personal financial savings of individuals. In fact, Merrill Lynch (**www.ml.com**) has a truly global reach, with offices in 35 countries and total client assets of around $1.5 trillion. Pictured here is the head office of Merrill Lynch in Tokyo, Japan.

all kinds exist to facilitate financial exchanges. Most of us are familiar with the most common capital-market intermediaries:

- *Commercial banks* lend borrowers their investors' deposits at a specific rate of interest. They provide loans for new investment projects and may help to finance a firm's import or export activities.

- *Investment banks* help clients to invest excess capital and to borrow needed capital. They act as *agents,* introducing clients to organizations that provide either investment or borrowing opportunities.

Role of Debt

Debt consists of loans, for which the borrower promises to repay the borrowed amount (the *principal*) plus a predetermined rate of *interest.* Company debt normally takes the form of **bonds**—instruments that specify the timing of principal and interest payments. The holder of a bond (the *lender*) can force the borrower into bankruptcy if the borrower fails to pay on a timely basis. Bonds issued for the purpose of funding investments are commonly issued by private-sector companies and by municipal, regional, and national governments.

Role of Equity

Equity is part ownership of a company, in which the equity holder participates with other part owners in the company's financial gains and losses. Equity normally takes the form of **stock**—shares of ownership in a company's assets that give *shareholders (stockholders)* a claim on the company's future cash flows. Shareholders may be rewarded with *dividends*—payments made out of surplus funds—or by increases in the value of their shares. Of course, they may also suffer losses due to poor company performance—and thus decreases in the value of their shares. Dividend payments are not guaranteed, but are determined by the company's board of directors and based on financial performance. In capital markets, shareholders can either sell one company's stock for that of another or *liquidate* them—exchange them for cash. **Liquidity**, which is a feature of both debt and equity markets, refers to the ease with which bondholders and shareholders may convert their investments into cash.

Purposes of the International Capital Market

The **international capital market** is a network of individuals, companies, financial institutions, and governments that invest and borrow across national boundaries. It consists of both formal exchanges (in which buyers and sellers meet to trade financial instruments) and electronic networks (in which trading occurs anonymously). This market makes use of

debt
Loans in which the borrower promises to repay the borrowed amount (the principal) plus a predetermined rate of interest.

bond
Debt instrument that specifies the timing of principal and interest payments.

equity
Part ownership of a company in which the equity holder participates with other part owners in the company's financial gains and losses.

stock
Shares of ownership in a company's assets that give shareholders a claim on the company's future cash flows.

liquidity
Ease with which bondholders and shareholders may convert their investments into cash.

international capital market
Network of individuals, companies, financial institutions, and governments that invest and borrow across national boundaries.

unique and innovative financial instruments specially designed to fit the needs of investors and borrowers located in different countries that are doing business with one another. Large international banks play a central role in the international capital market. They gather the excess cash of investors and savers around the world and then channel this cash to borrowers across the globe.

Expanding the Money Supply for Borrowers   The international capital market is a conduit for joining borrowers and lenders in different national capital markets. Thus, a company that is unable to obtain funds from investors in its own nation can seek financing from investors elsewhere, making it possible for the company to undertake an otherwise impossible project. The option of going outside the home nation is particularly important to firms in countries with small or developing capital markets of their own—particularly those with emerging stock markets. An expanded supply of money also benefits small but promising companies that might not otherwise get financing if there is intense competition for capital.

Reducing the Cost of Money for Borrowers   An expanded money supply reduces the cost of borrowing. Like the prices of potatoes, wheat, and other commodities, the "price" of money is determined by supply and demand. If its supply increases, its price—in the form of interest rates—falls. That is why excess supply creates a buyer's (borrower's) market, forcing down interest rates and the cost of borrowing. Projects regarded as infeasible because of low expected returns might be viable at a lower financing cost.

Reducing Risk for Lenders   The international capital market expands the available set of lending opportunities. In turn, an expanded set of opportunities helps reduce risk for lenders (investors) in two ways:

1.   *Investors enjoy a greater set of opportunities from which to choose.* They can thus reduce overall portfolio risk by spreading their money over a greater number of debt and equity instruments. In other words, if one investment loses money, the loss can be offset by gains elsewhere.

2.   *Investing in international securities benefits investors because some economies are growing while others are in decline.* For example, the prices of bonds in Thailand do not follow bond-price fluctuations in the United States, which are independent of prices in Hungary. In short, investors reduce risk by holding international securities whose prices move independently.

Unfortunately, small would-be borrowers still face some serious problems in trying to secure loans. In particular, interest rates are often high, and many entrepreneurs have nothing to put up as collateral. But as you can see from the Entrepreneur's Survival Kit titled, "Where Microcredit Is Due," some unique methods are available for getting capital into the hands of small businesspeople—particularly in developing nations.

Forces Expanding the International Capital Market

Around 40 years ago, national capital markets functioned largely as independent markets. But since that time, the amount of debt, equity, and currencies traded internationally has increased dramatically. This rapid growth can be traced to three main factors:

◗   *Information Technology.* Information is the lifeblood of every nation's capital market because investors need information about investment opportunities and their corresponding risk levels. Large investments in information technology over the past two decades have drastically reduced the costs, in both time and money, of communicating around the globe. Investors and borrowers can now respond in record time to breaking news in the international capital market. The introduction of electronic trading after the daily close of formal exchanges also facilitates faster response times.

◗   *Deregulation.* Deregulation of national capital markets has been instrumental in the expansion of the international capital market. The need for deregulation became apparent in the early 1970s, when heavily regulated markets in the largest countries

entrepreneur's SURVIVAL KIT
Where Microcredit Is Due

Obtaining capital challenges the entrepreneurial spirit in many developing countries. If a person is lucky enough to obtain a loan, it is typically from a loan shark, whose inordinate interest rates devour most of the entrepreneur's profits. However, an alternative money-lending practice is growing in popularity. In obtaining microcredit, small groups of low-income entrepreneurs borrow money at competitive rates without having to put up collateral. Besides being collateral-free, microcredit offers the following advantages:

⮕ **Borrowers Sink or Swim Together.** For better or worse, group members are joined at the economic hip: If a member fails to pay off a loan, everyone may lose future credit. Often, however, peer pressure and support help to defend against this contingency. In addition, strong family ties in developing countries tend to furnish important support networks.

⮕ **Most Loans Go to Women.** Although the outreach to male borrowers is increasing, most microcredit bor-

rowers are women. Women tend to be better at funneling profits into family nutrition, clothing, and education, as well as into business expansion. The successful use of microcredit in Bangladesh has increased wages, community income, and the status of women. One local bank that has already loaned $450 million to 2.1 million borrowers enjoys a 98 percent on-time payback record.

⮕ **It Might Work Even in Developed Countries.** The microcredit concept was pioneered in developed countries as a way for developing countries to create the foundation for a market economy. Nowadays, the use of microcredit within developed nations might be a way to spur economic growth in depressed geographic areas, such as inner cities. But whereas microcredit loans in developing countries typically average less than $100, those in developed nations average a minimum of $500.

were facing fierce competition from less regulated markets in smaller nations. Deregulation increased competition, lowered the cost of financial transactions, and opened many national markets to global investing and borrowing. Continued growth in the international capital market depends on further deregulation. For instance, although Japan opened its banking industry somewhat to outsiders in the late 1990s, more needs to be done to spur greater competition there.

⮕ *Financial Instruments.* Greater competition in the financial industry is creating the need to develop innovative financial instruments. One result of the need for new types of financial instruments is securitization—the unbundling and repackaging of hard-to-trade financial assets into more liquid, negotiable, and marketable financial instruments (or *securities*). For instance, a mortgage loan from a bank is not liquid or negotiable because it is a customized contract between the bank and the borrower: Banks cannot sell loans and thus raise capital for further investment because each loan differs from every other loan. But agencies of the U.S. government, such as the Federal National Mortgage Association (*www.fanniemae.com*), guarantee mortgages against default and thus accumulate them as pools of assets. They then sell securities in capital markets that are backed by these mortgage pools. When mortgage bankers participate in this process, they are able to raise capital for further investment.[2]

securitization
Unbundling and repackaging of hard-to-trade financial assets into more liquid, negotiable, and marketable financial instruments (or securities).

World Financial Centers

The world's three most important financial centers are London, New York, and Tokyo. But officials at traditional exchanges worry that information technology may make formal stock exchanges obsolete. Indeed, unless they continue to modernize, cut costs, and provide new customer services, they might be rendered obsolete by trading on the Internet and other new electronic systems.

Offshore Financial Centers
An **offshore financial center** is a country or territory whose financial sector features very few regulations and few, if any, taxes. These centers tend to be characterized by economic and political stability and usually provide access to

offshore financial center
Country or territory whose financial sector features very few regulations and few, if any, taxes.

Japan's capital market got a boost when the government removed some stifling regulations in its financial services industry. Yet, experts warn that much more needs to be done to pull the world's second largest economy out of a recession lasting more than a decade. Many Japanese, like this couple, remain leery of teetering banks and interest rates less than 0.1 percent. So, they opt instead for the relative security offered by at-home safes. For an update on the Japanese economy, see the Bank of Japan's Web site at (www.boj.or.jp/en).

the international capital market through an excellent telecommunications infrastructure. As we will see in Chapter 10, most governments protect their own currencies by restricting the amount of activity that domestic companies can conduct in foreign currencies. That is why companies often find it hard to borrow funds in foreign currencies and so turn to offshore centers, which offer large amounts of funding in currencies other than their own. In short, offshore centers are sources of (usually cheaper) funding for companies with multinational operations.

Offshore financial centers fall into two categories:

- *Operational centers* see a great deal of financial activity. Prominent operational centers include London (which does a good deal of currency trading) and Switzerland (which supplies a great deal of investment capital to other nations).

- *Booking centers* are usually located on small island nations or territories with favorable tax and/or secrecy laws. Little financial activity takes place here. Rather, funds simply pass through on their way to large operational centers. In fact, booking centers are typically home to offshore branches of domestic banks that use them merely as book-keeping facilities to record tax and currency-exchange information.[3] Some important booking centers are the Cayman Islands and the Bahamas in the Caribbean; Gibraltar, Monaco, and the Channel Islands in Europe; Bahrain in the Middle East; and Singapore in Southeast Asia.

Increasingly, offshore centers are attracting attention in the rapidly expanding world of electronic commerce. Anguilla, a small Caribbean island that belongs to the United Kingdom, is attempting to become a center for Internet-based companies. How? In Anguilla, such firms are allowed to do all the electronic commerce they want via the Internet and pay no taxes on their profits. To meet one "Webpreneur" who is working to attract business to Anguilla, see his Web site at (*www.offshore.com.ai*).

Quick Study

1. What are the three main purposes of the *international capital market*? Explain each briefly.
2. Identify the factors expanding the international capital market. What is meant by the term *securitization*?
3. What is an *offshore financial center*? Explain its appeal to businesses.

Main Components of the International Capital Market

Now that we have covered the basic features of the international capital market, let's take a closer look at its main components: the international bond, international equity, and Eurocurrency markets.

International Bond Market

The **international bond market** consists of all bonds sold by issuing companies, governments, or other organizations *outside their own countries*. Issuing bonds internationally is an increasingly popular way to raise needed funding. Typical buyers include medium-sized to large banks, pension funds, mutual funds, and governments with excess financial reserves. Large international investment banks, such as Morgan Stanley (*www.ms.com*) and JPMorgan Chase (*www.jpmorganchase.com*), typically manage the sales of new international bond issues for corporate and government clients.

international bond market
Market consisting of all bonds sold by issuing companies, governments, or other organizations outside their own countries.

Types of International Bonds
One instrument used by companies to access the international bond market is called a **Eurobond**—a bond issued outside the country in whose currency it is denominated. In other words, a bond issued by a Venezuelan company, denominated in U.S. dollars, and sold in Britain, France, Germany, and the Netherlands (but not available in the United States or to its residents) is a Eurobond. Because this Eurobond is denominated in U.S. dollars, the Venezuelan borrower both receives the loan and makes its interest payments in dollars.

Eurobond
Bond issued outside the country in whose currency it is denominated.

Eurobonds are popular (accounting for 75 to 80 percent of all international bonds) because the governments of countries in which they are sold do not regulate them. The absence of regulation substantially reduces the cost of issuing a bond. Unfortunately, it increases its risk level—a fact that may discourage some potential investors. The traditional markets for Eurobonds are Europe and North America.

Companies also obtain financial resources by issuing so-called **foreign bonds**—bonds sold outside the borrower's country and denominated in the currency of the country in which they are sold. For instance, a yen-denominated bond issued by the German carmaker BMW in Japan's domestic bond market is a foreign bond. Foreign bonds account for about 20 to 25 percent of all international bonds.

foreign bond
Bond sold outside the borrower's country and denominated in the currency of the country in which it is sold.

Foreign bonds are subject to the same rules and regulations as the domestic bonds of the country in which they are issued. Countries typically require issuers to meet certain regulatory requirements and to disclose details about company activities, owners, and upper management. Thus BMW's *samurai bonds* (the name for foreign bonds issued in Japan) would need to meet the same disclosure and other regulatory requirements that Toyota's bonds in Japan must meet. Foreign bonds in the United States are called *yankee bonds,* and those in the United Kingdom *bulldog bonds.* Foreign bonds issued and traded in Asia outside Japan (and normally denominated in dollars) are called *dragon bonds.*

Interest Rates: A Driving Force
Today, low interest rates (the cost of borrowing) are fueling growth in the international bond market. Low interest rates in developed nations are resulting from low levels of inflation but also mean that investors earn little interest on bonds issued by governments and companies in domestic markets. Thus, banks, pension funds, and mutual funds are seeking higher returns in the newly industrialized and developing nations, where higher interest payments reflect the greater risk of the bonds. At the same time, corporate and government borrowers in developing countries badly need capital to invest in corporate expansion plans and public works projects. As the demand for money outstrips the supply, interest rates in these markets might go even higher.

This situation raises an interesting question: How can investors who are seeking higher returns and borrowers who are seeking to pay lower interest rates both come out ahead? The answer, at least in part, lies in the international bond market:

⊙ By issuing bonds in the international bond market, borrowers from newly industrialized and developing countries can borrow money from other nations where interest rates are lower.

⊙ By the same token, investors in developed countries buy bonds in newly industrialized and developing nations in order to obtain higher returns on their investments (although they also accept greater risk).

Despite the attraction of the international bond market, many emerging countries see the need to develop their own national markets. Volatility in the global currency market—such as the drop in value of several major Southeast Asian currencies in the late 1990s—can wreak havoc when projects that earn funds in Indonesian rupiahs or Filipino pesos must pay off debts in dollars. Why? A drop in a country's currency forces borrowers to shell out more local currency to pay off the interest owed on bonds denominated in an unaffected currency.

International Equity Market

international equity market
Market consisting of all stocks bought and sold outside the issuer's home country.

The **international equity market** consists of all stocks bought and sold outside the issuer's home country. Both companies and governments frequently sell shares in the international equity market. Buyers include other companies, banks, mutual funds, pension funds, and individual investors. The stock exchanges that list the greatest number of companies from outside their own borders are Frankfurt, London, and New York. Large international companies frequently list their stocks on several national exchanges simultaneously and sometimes offer new stock issues only outside their country's borders. Four factors are responsible for much of the past growth in the international equity market.

Spread of Privatization
With many countries continuing to abandon central planning and socialist-style economics, the pace of privatization is accelerating worldwide. A single privatization often places billions of dollars of new equity on stock markets. When the government of Peru sold its 26 percent share of the national telephone company, Telefonica del Peru (*www.telefonica.com.pe*), it raised $1.2 billion. Of the total value of the sale, 48 percent was sold in the United States, 26 percent to other international investors, and another 26 percent to domestic retail and institutional investors in Peru.

Increased privatization in Europe is also expanding worldwide equity. Although historically Europe has been more devoted to debt as a means of financing, an "equity culture" is taking root. As the European Union becomes more thoroughly integrated, investors will become more willing to invest in the stocks of companies from other European nations.

Economic Growth in Developing Countries
Continued economic growth in newly industrialized and developing countries is also contributing to growth in the international equity market. As companies based in emerging economies succeed and grow, they require greater investment. Because only a limited supply of funds is available in these nations, the international equity market is a major source of funding.

Activity of Investment Banks
Investment banks facilitate the sale of a company's stock worldwide by bringing together sellers and large potential buyers. Increasingly, investment banks are searching for investors outside the national market in which a company is headquartered. In fact, this method of raising funds is becoming more common than listing a company's shares on another country's stock exchange.

Advent of Cybermarkets
The automation of stock exchanges is encouraging growth in the international equity market. The term *cybermarkets* denotes stock markets that have no central geographic locations. Rather, they consist of global trading activities conducted on the Internet. Cybermarkets (consisting of supercomputers, high-speed data lines, satellite uplinks, and individual personal computers) match buyers and sellers in nanoseconds. They allow companies to list their stocks worldwide through an electronic medium in which trading takes place 24 hours a day.[4]

Eurocurrency Market

All the world's currencies that are banked outside their countries of origin are referred to as *Eurocurrency* and traded on the **Eurocurrency market**. Thus, U.S. dollars deposited in a bank in Tokyo are called *Eurodollars* and British pounds deposited in New York are called *Europounds.* Japanese yen deposited in Frankfurt are called *Euroyen,* and so forth.

Because the Eurocurrency market is characterized by very large transactions, only the very largest companies, banks, and governments are typically involved. Deposits originate primarily from four sources:

❍ Governments with excess funds generated by a prolonged trade surplus

❍ Commercial banks with large deposits of excess currency

❍ International companies with large amounts of excess cash

❍ Extremely wealthy individuals

Eurocurrency originated in Europe during the 1950s—hence the "Euro" prefix. Communist governments of eastern European nations feared that they might forfeit dollar deposits made in U.S. banks if claims were filed against them by U.S. citizens. To protect their dollar reserves, they deposited them in banks across Europe. Banks in the United Kingdom began lending these dollars to finance international trade deals, and banks in other countries (including Canada and Japan) followed suit. The Eurocurrency market is valued at around $6 trillion, with London accounting for about 20 percent of all deposits. Other important markets include Canada, the Caribbean, Hong Kong, and Singapore.

Appeal of the Eurocurrency Market Typically, governments strictly regulate commercial banking activities in their own currencies within their borders. For example, they often force banks to pay deposit insurance to a central bank, where they must keep a certain portion of all deposits "on reserve" in non-interest-bearing accounts. Although such restrictions protect investors, they add costs to banking operations.

The main appeal of the Eurocurrency market is the complete absence of regulation. The absence of regulation and its resulting lower costs mean that banks can charge borrowers less, pay investors more, and still earn healthy profits. In addition, extremely large transactions considerably reduce transaction costs. Moreover, **interbank interest rates**—rates that the world's largest banks charge one another for loans—are determined by the free market. The most commonly quoted rate in the Eurocurrency market is the *London Interbank Offer Rate (LIBOR)*—the interest rate that London banks charge other large banks that borrow Eurocurrency. The *London Interbank Bid Rate (LIBID)* is the interest rate offered by London banks to large investors for Eurocurrency deposits.

An unappealing feature of the Eurocurrency market is greater risk: Government regulations that protect depositors in national markets are nonexistent. However, despite the greater risk of default, Eurocurrency transactions are fairly safe because of the size of the banks involved.

Eurocurrency market
Market consisting of all the world's currencies (referred to as "Eurocurrency") that are banked outside their countries of origin.

interbank interest rates
Interest rates that the world's largest banks charge one another for loans.

Foreign Exchange Market

Unlike domestic transactions, international transactions involve the currencies of two or more nations. To exchange one currency for another in international transactions, companies rely on a mechanism called the **foreign exchange market**—a market in which currencies are bought and sold and their prices determined. Financial institutions convert one currency into another at a specific **exchange rate**—the rate at which one currency is exchanged for another. Rates depend on the size of the transaction, the trader conducting it, general economic conditions, and sometimes, government mandate.

In many ways, the foreign exchange market is like the markets for commodities such as cotton, wheat, and copper. The forces of supply and demand determine currency prices, and transactions are conducted through a process of *bid* and *ask quotes*. If someone asks for the current exchange rate of a certain currency, the bank does not know whether it is dealing with a prospective buyer or seller. Thus, it quotes two rates: The *bid quote* is the price at which it

foreign exchange market
Market in which currencies are bought and sold and their prices determined.

exchange rate
Rate at which one currency is exchanged for another.

will buy, the *ask quote* is the price that it will pay. For example, say that the British pound is quoted in U.S. dollars at $1.6296. The bank may then bid $1.6294 to *buy* British pounds and offer to *sell* them at $1.6298. The difference between the two rates is the *bid–ask spread*. Naturally, banks always buy low and sell high, earning their profits from the bid–ask spread.

Functions of the Foreign Exchange Market

The foreign exchange market is not really a source of corporate finance. Rather, it facilitates corporate financial activities and international transactions. Investors use the foreign exchange market for four main reasons.

Currency Conversion
Companies use the foreign exchange market to convert one currency into another. Suppose a Malaysian company sells a large number of computers to a customer in France. The French customer wishes to pay for the computers in euros, the European Union currency, whereas the Malaysian company wants to be paid in its own ringgit. How do the two parties resolve this dilemma? They turn to banks to exchange the currencies for them.

Companies also must convert to local currencies when they undertake foreign direct investment. Later, when a firm's international subsidiary earns a profit and the company wishes to return some of it to the home country, it must convert the local money into the home currency.

currency hedging
Practice of insuring against potential losses that result from adverse changes in exchange rates.

Currency Hedging
The practice of insuring against potential losses that result from adverse changes in exchange rates is called **currency hedging**. International companies commonly use hedging for one of two purposes:

1. To lessen the risk associated with international transfers of funds
2. To protect themselves in credit transactions in which there is a time lag between billing and receipt of payment.

Suppose a South Korean carmaker has a subsidiary in Britain. The parent company in Korea knows that in 30 days—say, on February 1—its British subsidiary will be sending it a payment in British pounds. Because the parent company is concerned about the value of that payment in South Korean won 1 month in the future, it wants to insure against the possibility that the pound's value will fall over that period—meaning, of course, that it will receive less money. Therefore, on January 2 the parent company contracts with a financial institution, such as a bank, to exchange the payment in 1 month at an agreed-upon exchange rate specified on January 2. In this way, as of January 2 the Korean company knows exactly how many won the payment will be worth on February 1.

currency arbitrage
Instantaneous purchase and sale of a currency in different markets for profit.

Currency Arbitrage
Currency arbitrage is the instantaneous purchase and sale of a currency in different markets for profit. For instance, assume that a currency trader in New York notices that the value of the European Union euro is lower in Tokyo than in New York. Therefore, the trader can buy euros in Tokyo, sell them in New York, and earn a profit on the difference. High-tech communication and trading systems allow the entire transaction to occur within seconds. However, if the difference between the value of the euro in Tokyo and the value of the euro in New York is not greater than the cost of conducting the transaction, it is not worth making.

Currency arbitrage is a common activity among experienced traders of foreign exchange, very large investors, and companies in the arbitrage business. Firms whose profits are generated primarily by another economic activity, such as retailing or manufacturing, take part in currency arbitrage only if they have very large sums of cash on hand.

interest arbitrage
Profit-motivated purchase and sale of interest-paying securities denominated in different currencies.

Interest Arbitrage **Interest arbitrage** is the profit-motivated purchase and sale of interest-paying securities denominated in different currencies. Companies use interest arbitrage to find better interest rates abroad than those that are available in their home countries. The securities involved in such transactions include government treasury bills, corporate and government bonds, and even bank deposits. Suppose a trader notices that the interest rates paid on bank deposits in Mexico are higher than those paid in Sydney, Australia (after adjusting for exchange rates). He can convert Australian dollars to Mexican pesos and deposit the money in a Mexican bank account for, say, 1 year. At the

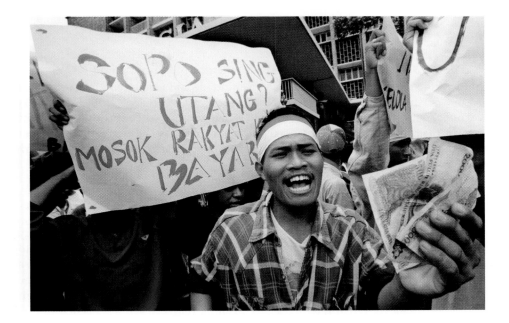

Ordinary citizens across Southeast Asia suffered badly after the values of their nations' currencies collapsed in the late 1990s. An Indonesian protester with a fist full of rupiah banknotes shouts during a demonstration in front of the central bank as riot police look on in Jakarta. He was one of a group of people protesting rising food prices as Indonesia battled its worst economic crisis in three decades. The sign behind the man reads "The country's debt—why should the people pay?"

end of the year, he converts the pesos back into Australian dollars and earns more in interest than the same money would have earned had it remained on deposit in an Australian bank.

Currency Speculation

Currency speculation is the purchase or sale of a currency with the expectation that its value will change and generate a profit. The shift in value might be expected to occur suddenly or over a longer period. The foreign exchange trader may bet that a currency's price will go either up or down in the future. Suppose a trader in London believes that the value of the Japanese yen will increase over the next three months. Therefore, today she buys yen with pounds at the current price, intending to sell them in 90 days. If the price of yen rises in that time, she earns a profit; if it falls, she takes a loss. Speculation is much riskier than arbitrage because the value, or price, of currencies is quite volatile and is affected by many factors. Like arbitrage, currency speculation is commonly the realm of foreign exchange specialists rather than the managers of firms engaged in other endeavors.

currency speculation
Purchase or sale of a currency with the expectation that its value will change and generate a profit.

A classic example of currency speculation unfolded in Southeast Asia in 1997. After news emerged in May about Thailand's slowing economy and political instability, currency traders sprang into action. They responded to poor economic growth prospects and an overvalued currency, the Thai baht, by dumping the baht on the foreign exchange market. When the supply glutted the market, the value of the baht plunged. Meanwhile, traders began speculating that other Asian economies were also vulnerable. From the time the crisis first hit until the end of 1997, the value of the Indonesian rupiah fell by 87 percent, the South Korean won by 85 percent, the Thai baht by 63 percent, the Philippine peso by 34 percent, and the Malaysian ringgit by 32 percent.[5] Although many currency speculators made a great deal of money, the resulting hardship experienced by these nations' citizens caused some to question the ethics of currency speculation on such a scale. (We cover the Asian crisis and currency speculation in detail in Chapter 10.)

Quick Study

1. Describe the *international bond market*. What one factor is most fueling its growth?
2. What is the *international equity market*? Identify the factors responsible for its expansion.
3. Describe the *Eurocurrency market*. What is its main appeal?
4. For what four reasons do investors use the foreign exchange market?

How the Foreign Exchange Market Works

Because of the importance of foreign exchange to trade and investment, businesspeople must understand how currencies are quoted in the foreign exchange market. Managers must understand the financial instruments available to help them protect the profits earned by their international business activities. They must also be aware of government restrictions that may be imposed on the convertibility of currencies and know how to work around these and other obstacles.

Quoting Currencies

quoted currency
In a quoted exchange rate, the currency with which another currency is to be purchased.

base currency
In a quoted exchange rate, the currency that is to be purchased with another currency.

There are two components to every quoted exchange rate: the quoted currency and the base currency. If an exchange rate quotes the number of Japanese yen needed to buy one U.S. dollar (¥/$), the yen is the **quoted currency** and the dollar the **base currency**. When you designate any exchange rate, the quoted currency is always the *numerator* and the base currency the *denominator*. For example, if you were given a yen/dollar exchange rate quote of 120/1 (meaning that 120 yen are needed to buy 1 dollar), the numerator is 120 and the denominator 1. We can also designate this rate as ¥ 120/$.

Direct and Indirect Rate Quotes

Table 9.1 lists exchange rates between the U.S. dollar and a number of other currencies as reported by the *Wall Street Journal* on May 13, 2004. There is one important note to make about this table. As we learned in Chapter 8, the currencies of nations participating in the single currency (euro) of the European Union are already out of circulation. Therefore, to look up exchange rates for these nations, we examine the line reading "Euro" at the end of Table 9.1.

The second column of numbers in Table 9.1, under the heading "Currency per U.S. $," tells us *how many units of each listed currency can be purchased with one U.S. dollar.* For example, find the row labeled "Japan (Yen)." The number 114.50 in the second column tells us that 114.50 Japanese yen can be bought with one U.S. dollar. We state this exchange rate as ¥ 114.50/$. Because the yen is the quoted currency, we say that this is a *direct quote* on the yen and an *indirect quote* on the dollar. This method of quoting exchange rates is called *European terms* because it is typically used outside the United States.

The first column of numbers in Table 9.1, under the heading "U.S. $ equivalent," tells us how many U.S. dollars it costs to buy one unit of each listed currency. The first column following the words "Japan (Yen)," tells us that it costs $0.008734 to purchase 1 yen (¥)—less than one U.S. cent. We state this exchange rate as $0.008734/¥. In this case, because the dollar is the quoted currency, we have a *direct quote* on the dollar and an *indirect quote* on the yen. The practice of quoting the U.S. dollar in direct terms is called *U.S. terms* because it is used mainly in the United States.

Whether we use a direct or an indirect quote, it is easy to find the other: simply divide the quote into the numeral 1. The following formula is used to derive a direct quote from an indirect quote:

$$\text{Direct quote} = \frac{1}{\text{Indirect quote}}$$

And for deriving an indirect quote from a direct quote:

$$\text{Indirect quote} = \frac{1}{\text{Direct quote}}$$

For example, suppose we are given an indirect quote on the U.S. dollar of ¥ 114.50/$. To find the direct quote, we simply divide ¥ 114.50 into $1:

$$\$1 \div ¥\,114.50 = \$0.008734/¥$$

Country	U.S. $ Equivalent	Currency per U.S. $	Country	U.S. $ Equivalent	Currency per U.S. $
Argentina (peso)	0.3336	2.9976	Mexico (peso)	0.09169	10.906
Australia (dollar)	0.7546	1.3252	New Zealand (dollar)	0.7022	1.4241
Bahrain (dinar)	2.6525	0.3770	Norway (krone)	0.1545	6.4725
Brazil (real)	0.4376	2.2852	Pakistan (rupee)	0.01674	59.737
Canada (dollar)	0.8542	1.1707	Peru (new sol)	0.2953	3.3864
1 Month Forward	0.8549	1.1697	Philippines (peso)	0.01817	55.036
3 Months Forward	0.8564	1.1677	Poland (zloty)	0.3033	3.2971
6 Months Forward	0.8585	1.1648	Russia (ruble)	0.03508	28.506
Chile (peso)	0.001832	545.85	Saudi Arabia (riyal)	0.2666	3.7509
China (renminbi)	0.1236	8.0901	Singapore (dollar)	0.5909	1.6923
Colombia (peso)	0.0004367	2,289.9	Slovak Republic (koruna)	0.03084	32.425
Czech Republic (koruna)	0.04058	24.643	South Africa (rand)	0.1494	6.6934
Commercial Rate			South Korea (won)	0.0009565	1,045.5
Denmark (krone)	0.1618	6.1805	Sweden (krona)	0.1268	7.8864
Ecuador (U.S. dollar)	1.0000	1.0000	Switzerland (franc)	0.7795	1.2829
Egypt (pound)	0.1735	5.7630	1 Month Forward	0.7817	1.2793
Hong Kong (dollar)	0.1290	7.7539	3 Months Forward	0.7864	1.2716
Hungary (forint)	0.004789	208.81	6 Months Forward	0.7932	1.2607
India (rupee)	0.02220	45.045	Taiwan (dollar)	0.02971	33.659
Indonesia (rupiah)	0.0001001	9,990.0	Thailand (baht)	0.02448	40.850
Israel (shekel)	0.2161	4.6275	Turkish (lira)	0.7375	1.3560
Japan (yen)	0.008632	115.85	U.K. (pound)	1.7742	0.5636
1 Month Forward	0.008662	115.45	1 Month Forward	1.7735	0.5639
3 Months Forward	0.008726	114.60	3 Months Forward	1.7728	0.5641
6 Months Forward	0.008823	113.34	6 Months Forward	1.7734	0.5639
Jordan (dinar)	1.4100	0.7092	United Arab (dirham)	0.2723	3.6724
Kuwait (dinar)	3.4238	0.2921	Uruguay (peso) Financial	0.04290	23.310
Lebanon (pound)	0.0006653	1,503.1	Venezuela (bolivar)	0.0004660	2,145.9
Malaysia (ringitt)	0.2649	3.7750	Special Drawing Rights*	1.4479	0.6907
Malta (lira)	2.8116	0.3557	Euro	1.2069	0.8286

*Special Drawing Rights (SDR) are based on exchange rates for the U.S., British, and Japanese currencies.

TABLE 9.1

Exchange Rates, Thursday, May 13, 2004

Note that our solution matches the number in the first column of numbers in Table 9.1 following the words "Japan (Yen)." Conversely, to find the indirect quote, we divide the direct quote into 1. In our example, we divide $0.008734 into ¥ 1:

$$¥\,1 \div \$0.008734 = ¥\,114.50/\$$$

This solution matches the number in the second column of numbers in Table 9.1 following the words "Japan (Yen)."

Calculating Percent Change   Why are businesspeople and foreign exchange traders interested in tracking currency values over time as measured by exchange rates? Because changes in currency values can benefit or harm current and future international transactions. **Exchange-rate risk (foreign exchange risk)** is the risk of adverse changes in exchange rates. Managers develop strategies to minimize this risk by tracking percent changes in exchange rates. For example, take P_N as the exchange rate at the end of a period (the currency's *new* price), and P_O as the exchange rate at the beginning of that period (the currency's *old* price). Now we can calculate percent change in the value of a currency with the following formula:

exchange-rate risk (foreign exchange risk)
Risk of adverse changes in exchange rates.

$$\text{Percent change (\%)} = \frac{P_n - P_o}{P_o} \times 100$$

Note: This equation yields the percent change in the base currency, not in the quoted currency.

Let's illustrate the usefulness of this calculation with a simple example. Suppose that on February 1 of the current year, the exchange rate between the Polish zloty (PLZ) and the U.S. dollar was PLZ 5/$. On March 1 of the current year, the exchange rate stood at PLZ 4/$. What is the change in the value of the base currency—the dollar? If we plug these numbers into our formula, we arrive at the following change in the value of the dollar:

$$\text{Percent change (\%)} = \frac{4-5}{5} \times 100 = -20\%$$

Thus, the value of the dollar has fallen 20 percent. In other words, one U.S. dollar buys 20 percent fewer Polish zloty on March 1 than it did on February 1.

To calculate the change in the value of the Polish zloty, we must first calculate the indirect exchange rate on the zloty; this is necessary because we want to make the zloty our base currency. Using the formula presented earlier, we obtain an exchange rate of \$.20/PLZ (1 ÷ PLZ 5) on February 1 and an exchange rate of \$.25/PLZ (1 ÷ PLZ 4) on March 1. Plugging these rates into our percent-change formula, we get:

$$\text{Percent change (\%)} = \frac{.25-.20}{.20} \times 100 = 25\%$$

Thus, the value of the Polish zloty has risen 25 percent. One Polish zloty buys 25 percent more U.S. dollars on March 1 than it did on February 1.

How important is this difference to businesspeople and exchange traders? Consider the fact that the typical trading unit in the foreign exchange market (called a *round lot*) is \$5 million. Therefore, a \$5 million purchase of zlotys on February 1 would yield PLZ 25 million. But because the dollar has lost 20 percent of its buying power by March 1, a \$5 million purchase would get us only 20 million Polish zloty—5 million fewer zloty than a month earlier.

Cross Rates International transactions between two currencies other than the U.S. dollar often use the dollar as a vehicle currency. For instance, a retail buyer of merchandise in the Netherlands might convert its euros (recall that the Netherlands now uses the EU currency) to U.S. dollars and then pay its Japanese supplier in U.S. dollars. The Japanese supplier may then take those U.S. dollars and convert them to Japanese yen. This process was more common years ago, when fewer currencies were freely convertible and when the United States greatly dominated world trade. Today, a Japanese supplier may want payment in euros. In this case, both the Japanese and the Dutch companies need to know the exchange rate between their respective currencies. To find this rate using their respective exchange rates with the U.S. dollar, we calculate what is called their **cross rate**—an exchange rate calculated using two other exchange rates.

Cross rates between two currencies can be calculated using either currency's indirect or direct exchange rates with another currency. For example, suppose we want to know the cross rate between the currencies of the Netherlands and Japan. If we return to Table 9.1 we see that the *direct* quote on the euro is € 0.8461/\$. The *direct* quote on the Japanese yen is ¥ 114.50/\$. To find the cross rate between the euro and the yen, with the yen as the base currency, we simply divide € 0.8461/\$ by ¥ 114.50/\$:

$$€\,0.8461/\$ \div ¥\,114.50/\$ = €\,0.0074/¥$$

Thus, it costs 0.0074 euros to buy 1 yen.

We can also calculate the cross rate between the euro and the yen by using the indirect quotes for each currency against the U.S. dollar. Again, we see in Table 9.1 that the *indirect* quote on the euro to the dollar is \$1.1819/€. The *indirect* quote on the yen to the dollar is \$0.008734/¥. To find the cross rate between the euro and the yen, again with the yen as the base currency, we divide \$1.1819/€ by \$0.008734/¥:

$$\$1.1819/€ \div \$0.008734/¥ = €\,135.32/¥$$

We must then perform an additional step to arrive at the same answer as we did earlier. Because *indirect* quotes were used in our calculation, we must divide our answer into 1:

$$1 \div €\,135.32/¥ = €\,0.0074/¥$$

cross rate
Exchange rate calculated using two other exchange rates.

TABLE 9.2

Key Currency Cross Rates

	Dollar	Euro	Pound	SFranc	Peso	Yen	CdnDlr
Canada	1.1707	1.4129	2.0770	0.9125	0.1073	0.0101	—
Japan	115.85	139.82	205.84	90.304	10.622	—	98.957
Mexico	10.906	13.163	19.350	8.5015		0.0941	9.3162
Switzerland	1.2829	1.5483	2.2761	—	0.1176	0.0111	1.0958
United Kingdom	0.5636	0.6803	—	0.4394	0.0517	0.0049	0.4815
Euro	0.8286	—	1.4700	0.6459	0.0760	0.0072	0.7078
United States	—	1.2069	1.7742	0.7795	0.00917	0.0086	0.8542

Again (as in our earlier solution), we see that it costs 0.0074 euros to buy 1 yen.

Table 9.2 shows the cross rates for major world currencies. When finding cross rates using direct quotes, currencies down the left-hand side represent quoted currencies; those across the top represent base currencies. Conversely, when finding cross rates using indirect quotes, currencies down the left-hand side represent base currencies; those across the top represent quoted currencies. Look at the intersection of the "Euro" row (the quoted currency in our example) and the "Yen" column (our base currency). Note that our solutions for the cross rate between euro and yen match the listed rate of 0.0074 euros to the yen.

Naturally, the exchange rate between the euro and the yen is quite important to both the Japanese supplier and Dutch retailer we mentioned earlier. If the value of the euro falls relative to the yen, the Dutch company must pay more in euros for its Japanese products. This situation will force the Dutch company to take one of two steps: either increase the price at which it resells the Japanese product (perhaps reducing sales), or keep prices at current levels (thus reducing its profit margin). Ironically, the Japanese supplier will suffer if the yen rises too much. Why? Under such circumstances, the Japanese supplier can do one of two things: allow the exchange rate to force its euro prices higher (thus maintaining profits) or reduce its yen prices to offset the decline of the euro (thus reducing its profit margin). Both the Japanese supplier and the Dutch buyer can absorb exchange rate changes by squeezing profits—but only to a point. Once that point is passed, they will no longer be able to trade. The Dutch buyer will be forced to look for a supplier in a country with a more favorable exchange rate or for a supplier in its own country (or another European country that uses the euro).

Spot Rates

All the exchange rates we've discussed so far are called **spot rates**—exchange rates that require delivery of the traded currency within two business days. Exchange of the two currencies is said to occur "on the spot," and the **spot market** is the market for currency transactions at spot rates. The spot market assists companies in performing any one of three functions:

1. Converting income generated from sales in another country into their home-country currency
2. Converting funds into the currency of an international supplier
3. Converting funds into the currency of a country in which they wish to invest

spot rate
Exchange rate requiring delivery of the traded currency within 2 business days.

spot market
Market for currency transactions at spot rates.

Buy and Sell Rates
The spot rate is available only for trades worth millions of dollars. That is why it is available only to banks and foreign exchange brokers. If you are traveling to another country and want to exchange currencies at your bank before departing, you will not be quoted the spot rate. Rather, banks and other institutions will give you a *buy rate* (the exchange rate at which the bank will buy a currency) and an *ask rate* (the rate at which it will sell a currency). In other words, you will receive what we described when introducing the foreign exchange market as *bid* and *ask quotes*. These rates reflect the amounts that large currency traders are charging, plus a markup.

For example, suppose that you are leaving Mexico for a business trip to Canada and need to buy some Canadian dollars (C$). The bank will quote you exchange rate terms, such as peso 7.6785/95 per C$. In other words, the bank will buy Canadian dollars at the rate of peso 7.6785/C$ and sell them at the rate of peso 7.6795/C$.

Forward Rates

When a company knows that it will need a certain amount of foreign currency on a certain future date, it can exchange currencies using a **forward rate**—an exchange rate at which two parties agree to exchange currencies on a specified future date. Forward rates represent the expectations of currency traders and bankers regarding a currency's future spot rate. Reflected in these expectations are a country's present and future economic conditions (including inflation rate, national debt, taxes, trade balance, and economic growth rate) as well as its social and political situation. The **forward market** is the market for currency transactions at forward rates.

Companies commonly use the forward market to insure themselves against unfavorable exchange-rate changes. It can be used for all types of transactions that require future payment in other currencies, including credit sales or purchases, interest receipts or payments on investments or loans, and dividend payments to stockholders in other countries. However, not all currencies are traded in the forward market. In particular, these include the currencies of countries with high inflation rates or currencies that generate little demand on international financial markets.

Forward Contracts   Suppose a Brazilian bicycle maker imports parts from a Japanese supplier. Under the terms of their contract, the Brazilian importer must pay 100 million Japanese yen in 90 days. The Brazilian firm can wait until one or two days before payment is due, buy yen in the spot market, and pay the Japanese supplier. Unfortunately, in the 90 days between the contract and the due date, the exchange rate will probably change. What if the value of the Brazilian real goes down? In that case, the Brazilian importer will have to pay more reals to get the same 100 million Japanese yen. Therefore, our importer may want to pay off the debt before the 90-day term. But what if it does not have the cash on hand? What if it needs those 90 days to collect accounts receivable from its own customers?

To decrease its exchange-rate risk, our Brazilian importer can enter into a **forward contract**—a contract that requires the exchange of an agreed-upon amount of a currency on an agreed-upon date at a specific exchange rate. Forward contracts are commonly signed for 30, 90, and 180 days into the future, but customized contracts (say, for 76 days) are possible. Note that a forward contract *requires* exchange of an agreed-upon amount of a currency on an agreed-upon date at a specific exchange rate: The bank must deliver the yen, and the Brazilian importer must buy them at the prearranged price. Forward contracts belong to a family of financial instruments called **derivatives**—instruments whose values *derive* from other commodities or financial instruments. These include not only forward contracts, but also currency swaps, options, and futures (which we discuss below).

In our example, the Brazilian importer can use a forward contract to pay yen to its Japanese supplier in 90 days. It is always possible, of course, that in 90 days, the value of the real will be lower than its current value. But by locking in at the forward rate, the Brazilian firm protects itself against the less favorable spot rate at which it would have to buy yen in 90 days. In this case, the Brazilian company protects itself from paying more to the supplier at the end of 90 days than if it were to pay at the spot rate in 90 days. Thus, it protects its profit from further erosion if the spot rate becomes even more unfavorable over the next 3 months. Remember, too, that such a contract prevents the Brazilian importer from taking advantage of any increase in the value of the real in 90 days that would reduce what the company owed its Japanese supplier.

Premiums and Discounts   As we have already seen, a currency's forward exchange rate can be higher or lower than its current spot rate. If its forward rate is higher than its spot rate, the currency is trading at a *premium*. If its forward rate is lower, it is trading at a *discount*. Return once again to Table 9.1. Locate the row under "U.K. (Pound)" labeled "1 Month Forward." This is the 30-day forward exchange rate for the British pound (GBP). Note that the rate of $1.7580/GBP is *less* than the spot rate of $1.7630/GBP (the spot rate quoted in the previous row of Table 9.1). The pound, therefore, is trading at a *discount* on the 1-month forward contract. We know, then, that a contract to deliver British pounds in 30 days costs $0.005 less per pound in 30 days than it does today. Likewise, the 3- and 6-month forward rates tell us that pounds cost $0.0142 and $0.0272 less in 90 and 180 days, respectively. Clearly, the pound is also trading at a discount on 3- and 6-month forward contracts.

Swaps, Options, and Futures

In addition to forward contracts, three other types of currency instruments are used in the forward market: currency swaps, options, and futures.

Currency Swaps

A **currency swap** is the simultaneous purchase and sale of foreign exchange for two different dates. Currency swaps are an increasingly important component of the foreign exchange market. Suppose a Swedish carmaker imports parts from a subsidiary in Turkey. The Swedish company must pay the Turkish subsidiary in Turkish lira for the parts when they are delivered tomorrow. It also expects to receive Turkish liras for cars sold in Turkey in 90 days. Our Swedish company exchanges krona for lira in the spot market today to pay its subsidiary. At the same time, it agrees to a forward contract to sell Turkish lira (and buy Swedish krona) in 90 days at the quoted 90-day forward rate for lira. In this way, the Swedish company uses a swap both to reduce its exchange-rate risk and to lock in the future exchange rate. In this sense, we can think of a currency swap as a more complex forward contract.

> **currency swap**
> Simultaneous purchase and sale of foreign exchange for two different dates.

Currency Options

Recall that a forward contract *requires* exchange of an agreed-upon amount of a currency on an agreed-upon date at a specific exchange rate. In contrast, a **currency option** is a right, or *option*, to exchange a specific amount of a currency on a specific date at a specific rate. In other words, whereas forward contracts require parties to follow through on currency exchanges, currency options do not.

Suppose a company buys an option to purchase Swiss francs at SF 1.27/$ in 30 days. If, at the end of the 30 days, the exchange rate is SF 1.30/$, the company would *not* exercise its currency option. Why? It could get 0.03 more Swiss francs for every dollar by exchanging at the spot rate in the currency market rather than at the stated rate of the option. Companies often use currency options to hedge against exchange rate risk or to obtain foreign currency.

> **currency option**
> Right, or option, to exchange a specific amount of a currency on a specific date at a specific rate.

Currency Futures Contracts

Similar to a currency forward contract is a **currency futures contract**—a contract requiring the exchange of a specific amount of currency on a specific date at a specific exchange rate. All of these conditions are fixed and not adjustable.

> **currency futures contract**
> Contract requiring the exchange of a specific amount of currency on a specific date at a specific exchange rate, with all conditions fixed and not adjustable.

Quick Study

1. What is meant by: a) *quoted currency*, and b) *base currency*?
2. Explain how to calculate percent change in currency prices. Why is *exchange-rate risk* important to companies?
3. What is meant by the term *cross rate*? Explain how it is useful to businesses.
4. Explain how a *spot rate* and *forward rate* are used in the foreign exchange market.
5. What are the main differences between *currency swaps, options,* and *futures*?

Foreign Exchange Market Today

The foreign exchange market is actually an electronic network that connects the world's major financial centers. In turn, each of these centers is a network of foreign exchange traders, currency trading banks, and investment firms. In a single day, the volume of trading on the foreign exchange market (comprising currency swaps and spot and forward contracts) totals more than $1.2 trillion—roughly the yearly gross domestic product of Italy.[6] Several major trading centers and several currencies dominate the foreign exchange market.

Trading Centers

Most of the world's major cities participate in trading on the foreign exchange market. However, in recent years, just three countries have come to account for slightly more than half of all global currency trading: the United Kingdom, the United States, and Japan. Accordingly, most of this trading takes place in the financial capitals of London, New York, and Tokyo.

London dominates the foreign exchange market for historic and geographic reasons. The United Kingdom was once the world's largest trading nation. British merchants needed to exchange currencies of different nations, and London naturally assumed the role of financial trading center. London quickly came to dominate the market and still does so because of its location halfway between North America and Asia. A key factor is its time zone. Because of differences in time zones, London is opening for business as markets in Asia close trading for the day. When New York opens for trading in the morning, trading continues in London for several hours.

Map 9.1 shows why it is possible to trade foreign exchange 24 hours a day (except weekends and major holidays). At least one of the three major centers (London, New York, and Tokyo) keeps the market open for 21 hours each day. Moreover, trading does not stop during the three hours they are closed because other trading centers (including San Francisco and Sydney, Australia) remain open. Also, most large banks that are active in foreign exchange ensure continuous trading by employing overnight traders.

Important Currencies

vehicle currency
Currency used as an intermediary to convert funds between two other currencies.

Although the United Kingdom is the major location of foreign exchange trading, the U.S. dollar is the currency that dominates the foreign exchange market. Because the U.S. dollar is so widely used in world trade, it is considered a **vehicle currency**—a currency used as an intermediary to convert funds between two other currencies. The currencies most often involved in currency transactions are the U.S. dollar, British pound, Japanese yen, and European Union euro.

MAP 9.1

Financial Trading Centers, by Time Zone

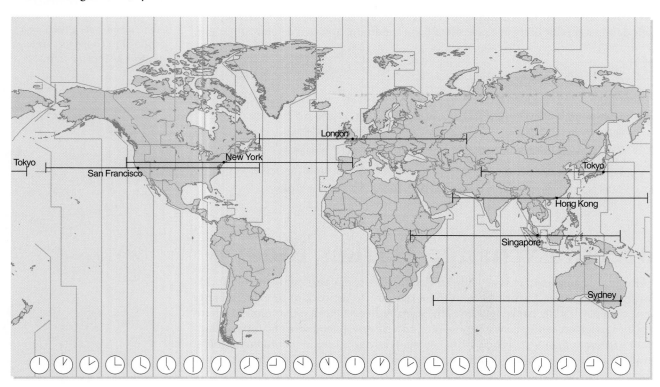

The U.S. dollar is a vehicle currency for two main reasons. First, the United States is the world's largest trading nation. Because the United States is so heavily involved in international trade, many international companies and banks maintain dollar deposits, making it easy to exchange other currencies with dollars. Second, following World War II, all of the world's major currencies were tied indirectly to the dollar because it was the most stable currency. In turn, the dollar's value was tied to a specific value of gold—a policy that held wild currency swings in check. Although world currencies are no longer linked to the value of gold (see Chapter 10), the stability of the dollar, along with its resistance to inflation, helps people and organizations maintain their purchasing power better than their own national currencies. Even today, people in many countries convert extra cash from national currencies into dollars.

Institutions of the Foreign Exchange Market

So far, we have discussed the foreign exchange market only in general terms. We now look at the three main components of the foreign exchange market: the *interbank market, securities exchanges,* and the *over-the-counter market.*

Interbank Market

It is in the **interbank market** that the world's largest banks exchange currencies at spot and forward rates. Many companies receive their foreign exchange services from the banks with which they do most of their business. Each bank satisfies client requests for exchange quotes by obtaining them from other banks in the interbank market. For transactions that involve commonly exchanged currencies, the largest banks often have sufficient currency on hand. But rarely exchanged currencies are not typically kept on hand and may in fact not be obtainable from another bank. In such cases, banks turn to *foreign exchange brokers,* who maintain vast networks through which to obtain seldom traded currencies.

In the interbank market, then, banks act as agents for client companies. In addition to locating and exchanging currencies, banks commonly offer advice on trading strategy, supply a variety of currency instruments, and provide other risk-management services. They also help clients manage exchange-rate risk by providing information on rules and regulations around the world.

Large banks in the interbank market have significant power in currency markets and use their influence to get better rates than smaller players. Of course, clients benefit when banks pass on savings in the form of lower fees. However, small firms often find it difficult to get favorable bank rates because they deal only in small volumes of currencies and do so rather infrequently. For this reason, a small company might choose a discount international payment service to provide it with better quotes.

interbank market
Market in which the world's largest banks exchange currencies at spot and forward rates.

Clearing Mechanisms   Clearing mechanisms are an important element of the interbank market. Banks continuously perform foreign exchange transactions with other banks and foreign exchange brokers. These accounts are not settled after each individual trade in a single currency. Rather, they are settled after a number of transactions have been processed. The process of aggregating the currencies that one bank owes another and then carrying out that transaction is called **clearing**. In the past, clearing was normally done each day or once every two days and involved the actual transportation of currencies from one bank to another. But nowadays clearing is performed more frequently and handled through computerized clearing mechanisms.

clearing
Process of aggregating the currencies that one bank owes another and then carrying out the transaction.

Securities Exchanges

Securities exchanges specialize in currency futures and options transactions. Buying and selling currencies on these exchanges entails the use of securities *brokers,* who facilitate transactions by transmitting and executing clients' orders. Transactions on securities exchanges are much smaller than those in the interbank market and vary with each currency. The world's largest futures and options exchange is the Chicago Board of Trade (*www.cbt.com*). The exchange has 3,600 members trading in 50 different futures and options products.[7] The second-largest futures exchange is the Chicago Mercantile Exchange (*www.cme.com*), a company with 2,725 members—mostly banks, investment firms, brokers, and independent traders. That exchange deals in a variety of financial futures, including futures for most major currencies.[8]

securities exchange
Exchange specializing in currency futures and options transactions.

The third-largest exchange is the London International Financial Futures Exchange (*www.liffe.com*), which trades futures and options for major currencies. In the United States, trading in currency *options* occurs only on the Philadelphia Stock Exchange (*www.phlx.com*), the leading currency options exchange in the world. It deals in both standardized options and customized options, allowing investors flexibility in designing currency option contracts.[9]

Over-the-Counter Market The **over-the-counter (OTC) market** is an exchange with no central trading location: It consists of a global computer network of foreign exchange traders and other market participants. All foreign exchange transactions can be performed in the OTC market. The major players are large financial institutions and investment banks, including Goldman Sachs (*www.gs.com*) and Merrill Lynch (*www.ml.com*).

The over-the-counter market has grown rapidly because it offers several benefits for business. First, it allows businesspeople to search freely for the institution that provides the best (lowest) price for conducting a transaction. Second, it offers greater opportunities for designing customized transactions. See the Global Manager's Toolbox titled, "Five Strategies for More Effective Foreign Exchange Management" for other ways that companies can become more adept in their foreign exchange activities.

over-the-counter (OTC) market
Exchange consisting of a global computer network of foreign exchange traders and other market participants.

global manager's TOOLBOX

Five Strategies for More Effective Foreign Exchange Management

1. **Analyze your foreign exchange activities and choose service providers who best fit your needs.** Analyze your needs. What is the nature of your foreign exchange activity? What types of transactions do you undertake and in which currencies? How frequent and how large are your wire transfers? Could repetitive transfers be consolidated? Next, take a close look at the range of service providers available to you. Many businesspeople automatically turn to local bankers when they need to transfer funds abroad, but this may not be the best choice. In some cases, a mix of service providers might offer the best solution.

2. **Trade with major players in the foreign exchange market.** In terms of cost and service, money-center banks—those located in financial centers—who participate directly in the foreign exchange market may have some advantages over local banks. Often, dealing directly with a large trading institution is more cost effective than dealing with a local bank because it avoids the additional markup that the local bank charges for its services.

3. **Consolidate transactions to boost your buying power and realize economies of scale.** Depending on your circumstances, you may want to time international payments in order to consolidate multiple transfers into one large transaction. If you find yourself making multiple smaller payments in the same currency, consider opening a local-currency account abroad against which you can write drafts. Likewise, allowing foreign receivables to accumulate in an interest-bearing local account until they can be repatriated in a lump sum may prove more advantageous than exchanging each payment individually.

4. **Encourage competition between providers, and be an aggressive negotiator.** If your foreign exchange activity is substantial, work to develop relationships with at least two money-center banks. Then you can play one against the other to get the best rates. You should also monitor the rates you're getting over time. Some institutions raise rates gradually, especially if they sense you're not shopping around. To monitor your exchange rates accurately, you'll need access to real-time market rates provided by firms like Reuters, Telerate, and Bloomberg. A word of caution: Beware of less expensive, time-delayed services that delay data by 15 minutes or more—an eternity in the foreign exchange market where rates can change by the second.

5. **Automate your operations for greater accuracy and efficiency.** Every phone call, fax, or transmittal opens the door to human error and delays in getting funds where and when you need them. That is why it makes sense to harness the power of computers to your international wire transfers and drafts. Widely available from banks and specialized service providers, automated software programs greatly reduce the potential for errors and miscommunication while speeding the execution of transfers.

Currency Convertibility

Our discussion of the foreign exchange market so far assumes that all currencies can be readily converted to another in the foreign exchange market. A **convertible (hard) currency** is traded freely in the foreign exchange market, with its price determined by the forces of supply and demand. Countries that allow full convertibility are those that are in strong financial positions and have adequate reserves of foreign currencies. Such countries have no reason to fear that people will sell their own currency for that of another. However, many newly industrialized and developing countries do not permit the free convertibility of their currencies. Let's now take a look at why governments place restrictions on the convertibility of currencies and how they do it.

convertible (hard) currency
Currency that trades freely in the foreign exchange market, with its price determined by the forces of supply and demand.

Goals of Currency Restriction

Governments impose currency restrictions to achieve several goals. One goal is to preserve a country's reserve of hard currencies with which to repay debts owed to other nations. Developed nations, emerging markets, and some countries that export natural resources tend to have the greatest amounts of foreign exchange. Without sufficient reserves (liquidity), a country could default on its loans and thereby discourage future investment flows. This is precisely what happened to Argentina in January 2002, when the country defaulted on its international public debt.

A second goal of currency restriction is to preserve hard currencies to pay for imports and to finance trade deficits. Recall from Chapter 5 that a country runs a *trade deficit* when the value of its imports exceeds the value of its exports. Currency restrictions help governments maintain inventories of foreign currencies with which to pay for such trade imbalances. They also make importing more difficult because local companies cannot obtain foreign currency to pay for imports. The resulting reduction in imports directly improves the country's trade balance.

A third goal is to protect a currency from speculators. For instance, in the wake of the 1997–1998 Asian financial crisis, some Southeast Asian nations considered the control of their currencies as an option to limit the damage done by economic downturns. For example, Malaysia stemmed the outflow of foreign money by preventing local investors from converting their Malaysian holdings into other currencies. The move also curtailed currency speculation but, in the process, effectively cut off Malaysia from investors elsewhere in the world.

A fourth (less common) goal is to keep resident individuals and businesses from investing in other nations. These policies are designed to generate more rapid economic growth by forcing investment in the home country. Unfortunately, although this might work in the short term, it normally slows long-term economic growth. The reason is that there is no guarantee that domestic funds held in the home country will be invested there. Instead, they might be saved or even spent on consumption. Ironically, increased consumption can mean further increases in imports, making the balance-of-trade deficit even worse.

Policies for Restricting Currencies

Certain government policies are frequently used to restrict currency convertibility. Governments can require that all foreign exchange transactions be performed at or approved by the country's central bank. They can also require import licenses for some or all import transactions. These licenses help the government control the amount of foreign currency leaving the country.

Some governments implement systems of *multiple exchange rates,* specifying a higher exchange rate on the importation of certain goods or on imports from certain countries. The government can thus reduce importation while ensuring that important goods still enter the country. It also can use such a policy to target the goods of countries with which it is running a trade deficit.

Other governments issue *import deposit requirements* that require businesses to deposit certain percentages of their foreign exchange funds in special accounts before being granted import licenses. In addition, *quantity restrictions* limit the amount of foreign currency that residents can take out of the home country when traveling to other countries as tourists, students, or medical patients.

countertrade
Practice of selling goods or services that are paid for, in whole or part, with other goods or services.

Countertrade   Finally, one way to get around national restrictions on currency convertibility is **countertrade**—the practice of selling goods or services that are paid for, in whole or part, with other goods or services. One simple form of countertrade is a *barter* transaction, in which goods are exchanged for others of equal value. Parties exchange goods and then sell them in world markets for hard currency. For instance, Cuba once exchanged $60 million worth of sugar for cereals, pasta, and vegetable oils from the Italian firm Italgrani, and Boeing (*www.boeing.com*) has sold aircraft to Saudi Arabia in return for oil. The many different forms of countertrade are covered in detail in Chapter 13.

Quick Study

1. What are the world's main foreign-exchange trading centers? Identify the currencies most used in the foreign exchange market.
2. Describe the three main institutions of the foreign exchange market.
3. What are the reasons for restrictions on currency conversion? Identify policies governments use to restrict currency conversion.

Bottom Line for Business

This chapter surveyed the most important components of international financial markets. We learned about the international bond, equity, and Eurocurrency markets. We also learned the fundamentals of exchange rates and saw how the foreign exchange market is structured. Well-functioning financial markets are essential to conducting international business. International financial markets supply companies with the mechanism they require to exchange currencies, and more. Here we focus only on the main implications of these markets for international companies.

The International Capital Market and Firms

The international capital market joins borrowers and lenders in different national capital markets. A company unable to obtain funds in its own nation may use the international capital market to obtain financing elsewhere—allowing the firm to undertake an otherwise impossible project. This option can be especially important for firms in countries with small or emerging capital markets.

Like the prices of any other commodity, the "price" of money is determined by supply and demand. If its supply increases, its price—in the form of interest rates—falls. The international capital market opens up additional sources of financing for companies, possibly financing projects previously regarded as infeasible. The international capital market also expands lending opportunities, which reduces risk for lenders by allowing them to spread their money over a greater number of debt and equity instruments, and benefiting from the fact that securities markets do not move up and down in tandem.

The International Financial Market and Firms

Companies must convert to local currencies when they undertake foreign direct investment. Later, when a firm's international subsidiary earns a profit and the company wishes to return profits to the home country, it must convert the local money into the home currency. The prevailing exchange rate at the time profits are exchanged influences the amount of the ultimate profit or loss.

This raises an important aspect of international financial markets—fluctuation. International companies can use hedging in foreign exchange markets to lessen the risk associated with international transfers of funds, and to protect themselves in credit transactions in which there is a time lag between billing and receipt of payment. Some firms also take part in currency arbitrage if there are times during which they have very large sums of cash on hand. Companies can also use interest arbitrage to find better interest rates abroad than those that are available in their home countries.

Businesspeople are also interested in tracking currency values over time because changes in currency values affect their international transactions. Profits earned by companies that import products for resale are influenced by the exchange rate between their currency and that of the nation from which they import. Managers who understand that changes in these currencies' values affect the profitability of their international business activities can develop strategies to minimize risk.

In the next chapter, we extend our coverage of the international financial system to see how market forces (including interest rates and inflation) have an impact on exchange rates. We also conclude our study of the international financial system by looking at the roles of government and international institutions in managing movements in exchange rates.

SUMMARY

1. **Discuss the purposes, development, and financial centers of the *international capital market*.** The international capital market has three main purposes. First, it provides an expanded supply of capital for borrowers because it joins together borrowers and lenders in different nations. Second, it lowers the cost of money for borrowers because a greater supply of money lowers the cost of borrowing (interest rates). Third, it lowers risk for lenders because it makes available a greater number of investments.

   Growth in the international capital market is due mainly to three factors. First, advances in *information technology* allow borrowers and lenders to do business more quickly and cheaply. Second, the *deregulation* of capital markets is opening the international capital market to increased competition. Third, innovation in *financial instruments* is increasing the appeal of the international capital market.

   The world's most important financial centers are London, New York, and Tokyo. These cities conduct a large number of financial transactions daily. Other locations, called *offshore financial centers*, handle less business but have few regulations and few, if any, taxes.

2. **Describe the *international bond, international equity,* and *Eurocurrency markets*.** The *international bond market* consists of all bonds sold by issuers outside their own countries. It is experiencing growth primarily because investors in developed markets are searching for higher rates from borrowers in emerging markets and vice versa. The *international equity market* consists of all stocks bought and sold outside the home country of the issuing company. The four factors primarily responsible for the growth in international equity are privatization, greater issuance of stock by companies in newly industrialized and developing nations, greater international reach of investment banks, and global electronic trading. The

Eurocurrency market consists of all the world's currencies that are banked outside their countries of origin. The appeal of the Eurocurrency market is its lack of government regulation and, therefore, lower cost of borrowing.

3. **Discuss the four primary functions of the *foreign exchange market*.** The foreign exchange market is the market in which currencies are bought and sold and in which currency prices are determined. It has four primary functions. First, individuals, companies, and governments use it, directly or indirectly, to *convert* one currency into another. Second, it offers tools with which investors can *insure against* adverse changes in exchange rates. Third, it is used to *earn a profit* from the instantaneous purchase and sale of a currency, or other interest-paying security, in different markets. Finally, it is used to *speculate* about a change in the value of a currency.

4. **Explain how currencies are *quoted* and the different *rates* given.** Currencies are quoted in a number of different ways. An *exchange-rate quote* between currency A and currency B (A/B) of 10/1 means that it takes 10 units of currency A to buy 1 unit of currency B. This example reflects a *direct quote* of currency A and an *indirect quote* of currency B. The exchange rate in this example is calculated using their actual values. We can also calculate an exchange rate between two currencies by using their respective exchange rates with a common currency; the resulting rate is called a *cross rate*. A *spot rate* is an exchange rate that requires delivery of the traded currency within two business days. This rate is normally obtainable only by large banks and foreign exchange brokers. The *forward rate* is the rate at which two parties agree to exchange currencies on a specified future date. Forward exchange rates represent the market's expectation of what the value of a currency will be at some point in the future.

5. **Identify the main *instruments* and *institutions* of the foreign exchange market.** Companies involved in international business make extensive use of certain financial instruments in order to reduce exchange-rate risk. A *forward contract* requires the exchange of an agreed-upon amount of a currency on an agreed-upon date at a specific exchange rate. A *currency swap* is the simultaneous purchase and sale of foreign exchange for two different dates. A *currency option* is the right to exchange a specific amount of a currency on a specific date at a specific rate. It is sometimes used to acquire a needed currency. Finally, a currency *futures contract* requires the exchange of a specific amount of currency on a specific date at a specific exchange rate. It is similar to a forward contract except that none of the terms is negotiable.

   The world's largest banks exchange currencies in the *interbank market*. These banks locate and exchange currencies for companies and sometimes provide additional services. *Securities exchanges* are physical locations at which currency futures and options are bought and sold (in smaller amounts than those traded in the interbank market). The *over-the-counter (OTC) market* is an exchange that exists as a global computer network linking traders to one another.

6. **Explain why and how governments restrict *currency convertibility.*** There are four main goals of currency restriction. First, a government may be attempting to preserve the country's hard currency reserves for repaying debts owed to other nations. Second, convertibility might be restricted to preserve hard currency to pay for needed imports or to finance a trade deficit. Third, restrictions might be used to protect a currency from speculators. Finally, such restrictions can be an attempt to keep badly needed currency from being invested abroad. Policies used to enforce currency restrictions include government approval for currency exchange, imposed import licenses, a system of multiple exchange rates, and imposed quantity restrictions.

TALK IT OVER

1. What factors do you think are holding back the creation of a truly *global* capital market? How might a global capital market function differently from the present-day international market? (*Hint:* Some factors to consider are interest rates, currencies, regulations, and financial crises for some countries.)

2. The use of different national currencies creates a barrier to further growth in international business activity. What are the pros and cons, among companies *and* governments, of replacing national currencies with regional currencies? Do you think a global currency would be possible someday? Why or why not?

3. Governments dislike the fact that offshore financial centers facilitate money laundering. Do you think that electronic commerce makes it easier or harder to launder money and camouflage other illegal activities? Do you think offshore financial centers should be allowed to operate as freely as they do now, or do you favor regulation? Explain your answers.

TEAMING UP

1. This chapter taught us that information technology, deregulation, and innovative financial instruments are behind the growth in the international capital market. Write a group report (about 800 words) on the ways in which recent advances in one of these three areas is helping to grow the international capital market. Your team might want to focus on a specific technology, nation (other than your own), international organization, or new financial instrument. Report your group's findings to the class in a brief presentation.

2. With several of your classmates, select a country that interests you. Does the country have a city that is an important financial center? What volume of bonds is traded on the country's bond market? What is the total value of stocks traded on its stock exchange(s)? Does it have an emerging stock market? How has its stock market performed over the past year? What is the exchange rate between its currency and that of your own country? What factors are responsible for the stability or volatility in that exchange rate? Are there any restrictions on the exchange of the nation's currency? How is the forecast for the country's currency likely to influence business activity in its major industries? Present a brief summary of your findings to the class. (*Hint:* Two good sources to begin your research are the monthly *International Financial Statistics* and the annual *Exchange Arrangements and Exchange Restrictions*, both published by the International Monetary Fund (*www.imf.org*).)

3. Form a team with several of your classmates, and suppose you work for a firm that has $10 million in excess cash to invest for one month. Your group's task is to invest this

money in the foreign exchange market to earn a profit— holding dollars is not an option. Select the currencies you wish to buy at today's spot rate, but do not buy less than $2.5 million of any single currency. Track the spot rate for each currency over the next month in the business press.

On the last day of the month, exchange your currencies at the day's spot rate. Calculate your team's gain or loss over the 1-month period. (Your instructor will determine whether, and how often, currencies may be traded throughout the month.)

KEY TERMS

base currency (p. 270)

bond (p. 261)

capital market (p. 260)

clearing (p. 277)

convertible (hard) currency (p. 279)

countertrade (p. 280)

cross rate (p. 272)

currency arbitrage (p. 268)

currency futures contract (p. 275)

currency hedging (p. 268)

currency option (p. 275)

currency speculation (p. 269)

currency swap (p. 275)

debt (p. 261)

derivative (p. 274)

equity (p. 261)

Eurobond (p. 265)

Eurocurrency market (p. 267)

exchange rate (p. 267)

exchange-rate risk (foreign exchange risk) (p. 271)

foreign bond (p. 265)

foreign exchange market (p. 267)

forward contract (p. 274)

forward market (p. 274)

forward rate (p. 274)

interbank interest rates (p. 267)

interbank market (p. 277)

interest arbitrage (p. 268)

international bond market (p. 265)

international capital market (p. 261)

international equity market (p. 266)

liquidity (p. 261)

offshore financial center (p. 263)

over-the-counter (OTC) market (p. 278)

quoted currency (p. 270)

securities exchange (p. 277)

securitization (p. 263)

spot market (p. 273)

spot rate (p. 273)

stock (p. 261)

vehicle currency (p. 276)

TAKE IT TO THE WEB

1. In this chapter, we learned how the international capital market works and came to understand how essential the foreign exchange market is to international business. Visit the Web site of a financial institution or business periodical that publishes exchange rates among the world's currencies. Possibilities include the *Wall Street Journal* (*www.wsj.com*) or even CNN (*www.cnn.com*). Compare the performance of the U.S. dollar against the European Union euro since May 13, 2004—the date of the information contained in Table 9.1.

Between that date and now, has the dollar fallen or risen in value against the euro? What is the exchange rate

between the dollar and euro using: a) an indirect quote on the dollar, and b) a direct quote on the dollar? What percentage change has occurred in the *value of the dollar* against the euro? (Remember to mind your quoted and base currencies!)

Now, conducting Web-based research, what reasons lie behind the exchange-rate movement between the dollar and euro? Is the shift in the exchange rate due more to movement in the value of the dollar or the euro? Explain your answer. How has the exchange-rate change affected international business activity between the U.S. and European nations using the euro? Be specific.

1. You are a U.S. senator serving on a subcommittee with the task of developing new regulations for U.S. firms doing business through offshore financial centers (OFCs). Bank deposits in offshore financial centers grew from the tens of billions of dollars a few decades ago to more than $1 trillion today. "Dirty money" obtained through drug trafficking, gambling, and other illicit activities use offshore financial centers to escape the same thing as respectable "clean capital": national taxation and government regulations. Some experts argue that institutions such as international currency markets and offshore tax havens reduce stability and are hostile to the public interest. They say people use such institutions to get beyond the reach of the law and undermine what they consider to be inefficient and bureaucratic attempts to impose a certain morality on people. As senator, what form of regulations do you support? What rationale do you give business leaders in your constituency who do business with OFCs? Do you think corporate use of OFCs to avoid home-country bureaucracies and taxes is ethical? Why or why not?

2. You are a member of the board of directors for one of the nation's largest banks. Although recent banking deregulation is fostering greater competition in the industry, you are concerned about the direction in which banking is headed. The top management team of your bank is to meet soon with government officials to discuss the situation. The goal of government *regulation* of financial-services industries is to maintain the integrity and stability of financial systems, thereby protecting both depositors and investors. Regulations include prohibitions against insider trading, against lending by management to itself or to closely related entities (a practice called "self-dealing"), and against other transactions in which there is a conflict of interest. Yet in less than two decades *deregulation* has transformed the world's financial markets. It spurred competition and growth in financial sectors and allowed capital to flow freely across borders, which boosted the economies of developing countries. What advice do you give your bank's executives prior to meeting with the government? What do you see as the "dark side" of deregulation, in terms of business ethics? What do you think Adam Smith, one of the first philosophers of capitalism, meant when he warned against the dangers of "colluding producers"? Do you think this warning applies to the financial-services sector today?

PRACTICING INTERNATIONAL MANAGEMENT CASE

Argentina: Back from the Abyss?

Argentina's past President, Eduardo Duhalde, had summed it up perfectly. "Argentina is bust. It's bankrupt. Business is halted, the chain of payments is broken, there is no currency to get the economy moving and we don't have a peso to pay Christmas bonuses, wages, or pensions," said Mr. Duhalde in a speech to Argentina's Congress.

Although it was the star of Latin America in the 1990s, Argentina defaulted on its $155 billion of public debt in early 2002, the largest default by any country ever. After taking office in January 2002, President Duhalde implemented many measures to keep the country's fragile economy from complete collapse after four years of recession. For 10 years the Argentine peso was fixed at parity to the dollar through a currency board. The president cut those strings immediately. But when it was allowed to float freely on currency markets, Argentina's peso quickly lost two-thirds of its value and was trading at 3 pesos to the dollar. Then, strapped for cash, the government seized the savings accounts of its citizens and restricted how much they could withdraw at a time. When street protesters turned violent they beat up several politicians and attacked dozens of banks. Michael Smith, manager of HSBC's Argentine subsidiary (*www.hsbc.com.ar*), addressed people's feelings of distrust. "We're somewhat less popular than serial killers," said Smith.

Local companies were having an equally difficult time. Many companies blamed their defaults on the requirement that they get authorization from the central bank to send money abroad. Stiff restrictions on foreign-currency exchange forced importers to wait several months or more while the government authorized payments in dollars. Companies also struggled with new rules that raised taxes on exporters and other cash-rich firms to help the government pay for social services. Local firms also had a hard time obtaining funds to pay their debts to foreign suppliers. But the loss of confidence among non-Argentine businesses was more difficult to quantify. Many entered Argentina during a wave of free-market changes and privatizations in the 1990s. "If the government can just arbitrarily change contracts," said a foreign diplomat in Buenos Aires, "how can you feel safe about any business relationship here in the coming months?"

The declining peso intensified problems for U.S. companies that fought to manage soaring debts and mounting losses from their Argentine operations. Argentine units of U.S. companies, which tend to collect revenues in pesos, had an increasingly difficult time repaying their dollar-denominated debts as the peso's value fell. The government decreed that electricity and gas companies switch their contracts from dollars to less valuable pesos and then froze utility rates to protect consumers. But parent companies were not likely to rescue their ailing operations because many operations in Argentina were independent entities. AES Corp. (*www.aes.com*) of Arlington, VA, invested hundreds of millions of dollars in the Argentine electricity sector. It said in a statement that most of its Argentine businesses are in default on their project-financing arrangements but that AES "is not generally required to support the potential cash flow or debt service obligations of these businesses."

The government, trying to lighten its debt load and restore credibility with the International Monetary Fund (*www.imf.org*), ordered $50 billion in dollar-denominated government debt (mostly domestic) swapped into pesos. The swap was aimed at unlocking $10 billion in IMF loans that were frozen in December 2001 when Argentina failed to meet certain economic targets. U.S. and European investors owned another $46 billion in government bonds, which were to be restructured in a separate transaction. Argentina's government spent the previous decade amassing debts in dollars and other foreign currencies. But when the government cut loose the peso from the dollar in January 2002, the weak peso made the debt far more expensive to repay.

Previous crises in emerging-market nations seemed to infect other emerging economies. There was Mexico and its "tequila effect" on Latin America, Thailand's currency collapse caused the Asian "flu," and Russia's default was felt worldwide among industrialized nations. So why wasn't Argentina's default felt more widely? The only neighbor sharing the pain seemed to be Uruguay in tourism and banking. Some argue that it is due to improved information. Mohamed El-Erian, managing director at Pacific Investment Management Co. (*www.pimco.com*), says, "Now we have better information. We all went out and hired more analysts. Now, we have lot more understanding," he said. Others say that markets simply anticipated the crisis and money managers adjusted portfolios early on in the economic debacle. Regardless of any potential lack of contagion, the effect on Argentina's economy was real. Yet in late 2004, the economy had, in many respects, recovered from its 2001–02 collapse and had grown more than 12 percent for the year. Meanwhile, unemployment had fallen to around 14 percent from a high of 25 percent in 2002.

Thinking Globally

1. Update the economic situation in Argentina to reflect recent events. How is the value of the peso faring? Do you think it was wise to cut the ties between the peso and the dollar? Why did Argentina peg its currency to the dollar in the first place? Do you think that the peso–dollar link contributed to Argentina's problems? Explain your answers.

2. How did local and international companies adapt to the new business environment in Argentina? Did they pursue similar courses of action or design distinct strategies to deal with the effects of the crisis? Be specific in your answer by giving as many examples as you can.

3. What was the impact on ordinary citizens immediately after the default and later as the government tried to recover? What do the aftereffects of the crisis mean for ordinary citizens' spending power? What has it done to the value of their savings? In your opinion, has international aid helped or hurt the ordinary people of Argentina? Explain your answer.

learning objectives

After studying this chapter, you should be able to

1. Explain how *exchange rates* influence the activities of domestic and international companies.

2. Identify the *factors* that help determine exchange rates and their impact on business.

3. Describe the primary methods of *forecasting exchange rates.*

4. Discuss the evolution of the current *international monetary system,* and explain how it operates.

international
monetary system

10

a look *back*

CHAPTER 9 examined how the international capital market and foreign exchange market operate. We also explained how exchange rates are calculated and how different rates are used in international business.

a look *at this chapter*

This chapter extends our knowledge of exchange rates and international financial markets. We examine factors that help determine exchange rates and explore rate-forecasting techniques. We discuss international attempts to manage exchange rates and review recent currency problems in Russia, Argentina, and other emerging markets.

a look *ahead*

CHAPTER 11 introduces the topic of the last part of this book—international business management. We will explore the specific strategies and organizational structures that companies use in accomplishing their international business objectives.

The Point of No Return

BRUSSELS, Belgium—"Europe's Big Idea," "Ready, Set, Euros!," screamed headlines worldwide surrounding January 1, 2002. That was the day the euro began circulating in Europe. Pictured above with a giant euro coin, Romano Prodi, then President of the European Commission, proclaimed, "The euro is your money, it is our money. It's our future. It is a piece of Europe in our hands."

Not since the time of the Roman Empire has a currency circulated so widely in Europe. The Greeks gave up their drachma, a currency they had used for nearly 3,000 years. In Italy, multizeroed lire disappeared as billionaires became mere millionaires. Yet, the unprecedented changeover of national currencies went smoother than many thought possible. Within just two weeks nearly all cash transactions involved the receipt of euros for payment and the return of euros as change. After only two months, many of the so-called legacy currencies were no longer legal tender on the street.

Some companies were better suited than others to take advantage of the introduction of paper and coins. Security transport company, Securicor PLC (*www.securicor.com*), which shifts huge sums of money daily throughout Europe, was fully booked from September 2001 through March 2002. Some companies were even able to tie new products to the euro launch. For example, Italy's Gucci Group (*www.gucci.com*) saw the occasion as an opportunity to outfit Italians with new wallets that accommodate the euro notes, which are larger than the old lira.

But apart from such short-term benefits, the euro holds some very real, long-term benefits for Europe. For one thing, the euro eliminated exchange-rate risk for companies in the euro zone, making the financial aspects of business more predictable. Mergers and acquisitions soared as competition intensified and consolidation swept through one industry after another.

In late 2004, the euro was very strong against the dollar, buying around $1.28. But the relative weakness of the dollar was not all bad news for some—it supported exports and fueled growth in the United States. As you read this chapter, keep in mind how events in the international monetary system affect the decisions of managers and the performance of their companies.[1]

In Chapter 9, we explained the fundamentals of how exchange rates are calculated and how different types of exchange rates are used. This chapter extends our understanding of the international financial system by exploring factors that determine exchange rates and various international attempts to manage them. We begin by learning how exchange-rate movements affect a company's activities. We then examine the factors that help determine currency values and, in turn, exchange rates. Next, we learn about different methods of forecasting exchange rates. We conclude this chapter by exploring the international monetary system and its performance.

How Exchange Rates Influence Business Activities

Movement in a currency's exchange rate affects many activities of both domestic and international companies. For one thing, exchange rates affect the demand for a company's products in the global marketplace. When a country's currency is *weak* (valued low relative to other currencies), the price of its exports on world markets declines and the price of imports increases. Lower prices make the country's exports more appealing on world markets. They also give companies the opportunity to take market share away from companies whose products are priced high in comparison.

Furthermore, a company that is selling in a country with a *strong* currency (one that is valued high relative to other currencies) while paying workers in a country with a weak currency improves its profits. For example, Dell Computer (*www.dell.com*) makes nearly all of its products in Penang, Malaysia, and prices everything it exports in dollars. But at the same time, Dell pays its Malaysian workers and suppliers in the local currency, ringgits. In the late 1990s, Malaysia's currency lost a great deal of its value. The result for Dell was that revenue was being generated in a strong currency, whose value was climbing steadily, while expenses were being paid in a weak currency, whose value kept falling. On the downside, companies with such a price advantage might grow complacent about reducing production costs. Further, if managers view the temporary price advantage caused by exchange rates as permanent, long-term competitiveness could be impaired.[2]

devaluation
Intentional lowering of the value of a nation's currency.

The intentional lowering of the value of a currency by the nation's government is called **devaluation**. The reverse, the intentional raising of its value by the nation's government, is called **revaluation**. These concepts are not to be confused with the terms *weak currency* and *strong currency,* although their effects are similar.

Devaluation lowers the price of a country's exports on world markets and increases the price of imports because the country's currency is now worth less on world markets. Thus, a government might devalue its currency to give its domestic companies an edge over competition from other countries. However, devaluation reduces consumers' buying power. It might also allow inefficiencies to persist in domestic companies because there is now less pressure to be concerned with production costs. Revaluation has the opposite effects: It increases the price of exports and reduces the price of imports.

revaluation
Intentional raising of the value of a nation's currency.

FIGURE 10.1

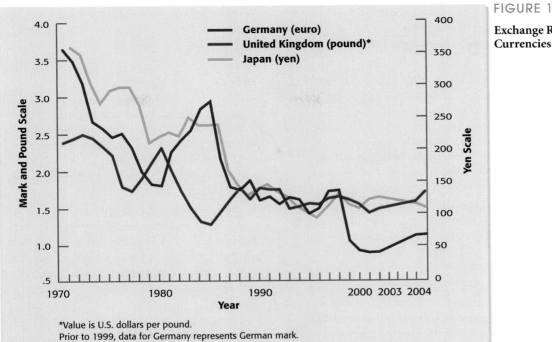

Figure 10.1 shows exchange rates between the U.S. dollar and several major world currencies. We can see that the Japanese yen fell steadily throughout the late 1980s. But in the early 1990s, a strong yen began to hurt Japan's automobile exports by adding about $3,300 to the cost of every Japanese auto sold in the United States. But the situation reversed in the middle to late 1990s, when the dollar rose against the yen. Japan's carmakers were once again able to price their exports attractively in the United States. U.S. carmakers were forced to reduce their own prices in order to stay competitive, thus hurting their profit margins. Even so, Japan's carmakers increased their U.S. market share by nearly 10 percent in 1997 alone. Meanwhile, U.S. domestic carmakers were trying to persuade U.S. policy makers that a weaker dollar was important for their short-term survival because it increased the price of imported autos.[3]

There are steps companies can take to counter the negative effects that too strong a currency can have on exports. For example, a strong dollar can cause U.S. companies to become more aggressive in boosting exports. For a look at some of these approaches, see the Global Manager's Toolbox titled, "Exporting Against the Odds: Key Strategies for Success."

Exchange rates also affect the amount of profit a company earns from its international subsidiaries. The earnings of international subsidiaries are typically integrated into the parent company's financial statements *in the home currency.* Translating subsidiary earnings from a weak *host* country currency into a strong *home* currency *reduces* the amount of these earnings when stated in the home currency. Likewise, translating earnings into a weak home currency increases stated earnings in the home currency. For instance, many companies saw their earnings badly hurt by the collapse of the Argentine peso in 2002. When firms translated profits into their home currencies, profits were far lower than they would have been without the peso's fall in value.

Desire for Stability and Predictability

As we have seen, unfavorable movements in exchange rates can be costly for both domestic and international companies. *Stable* exchange rates improve the accuracy of financial planning, including cash flow forecasts. Although methods do exist for insuring against potentially adverse movements in exchange rates, most of these are too expensive for small and medium-sized businesses. Moreover, as the unpredictability of exchange rates increases, so

Exporting Against the Odds: Key Strategies for Success

True or false: A nation's exports begin to fall after its currency has risen in value for 18 months.

Answer: Mostly true, but not necessarily so. Companies in the United States exported against the odds in the late 1990s when the U.S. dollar climbed up to 54 percent against major world currencies. Here's how:

○ **Getting Leaner and Meaner.** Companies cut costs by downsizing staff and reengineering factories for greater efficiency. According to the National Association of Manufacturers (*www.nam.org*), thousands of small manufacturers doubled or tripled sales within a few years by finding ways to shave production costs.

○ **Catering to the Customer.** European customers of Bison Gear & Engineering (*www.bisongear.com*), based in Chicago, stuck with the company despite its raising prices in local currencies. The reason: Bison was willing to custom-design the transmission gears for every factory machine in which its product was installed. Thus, despite the sticker shock, Bison's exports actually rose.

○ **Diversifying into Safer Sectors.** An increasing number of U.S.-based exporters are in industries such as software, services, and entertainment—industries less affected by currency fluctuations. Demand in these hot-growth categories is growing around the world. Software giant Microsoft (*www.microsoft.com*) draws some 55 percent of its sales from outside the United States.

○ **Going Where Demand Is Highest.** Today many U.S. companies export to developing nations, where demand is high. For instance, the share of total exports going to Latin America is nearly 20 percent. This is compared with a figure of just 11 percent a decade ago.

○ **Cutting or Freezing Prices.** A strong dollar means U.S. exports headed for Europe and Japan were more expensive than European- and Japanese-made goods. Some U.S. exporters froze prices of their goods in euros or yen even though it meant lower dollar revenues and lower profits. California-based Varian Associates froze prices on its chromatographs—industrial instruments that sell for upward of $40,000. To the company's surprise, it sold nearly 20 percent more units.

too does the cost of insuring against the accompanying risk. Figure 10.2 shows how the value of the U.S. dollar has changed over time. The figure reveals the instability of the dollar during the decade of the 1980s.

Managers also prefer that movements in exchange rates be *predictable*. Predictable exchange rates reduce the likelihood that companies will be caught off guard by sudden and unexpected rate changes. They also reduce the need for costly insurance (usually by currency

FIGURE 10.2

Value of the U.S. Dollar Over Time

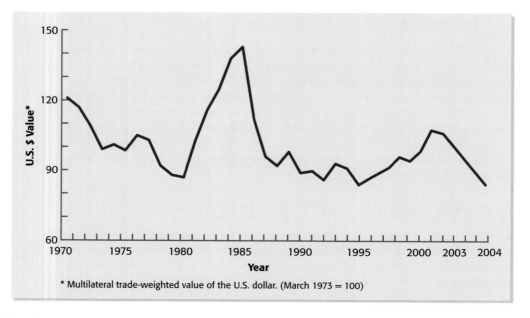

* Multilateral trade-weighted value of the U.S. dollar. (March 1973 = 100)

hedging) against possible adverse movements in exchange rates. Rather than purchasing insurance, companies would be better off spending their money on more productive activities, such as developing new products or designing more efficient production methods.

Quick Study

1. Why are exchange rates important to managers' decisions?
2. Explain the difference between *devaluation* and *revaluation*.
3. Why is it desirable for exchange rates to be stable and predictable?

What Factors Determine Exchange Rates?

To improve our knowledge of the factors that help determine exchange rates, we must first understand two important concepts: the law of one price and purchasing power parity. Each of these concepts tells us the level at which an exchange rate *should* be. While discussing these concepts, we will examine some of the many factors that affect the actual levels of exchange rates.

Law of One Price

An exchange rate tells us how much of one currency we must pay to receive a certain amount of another. But it does not tell us whether a specific product will actually cost us more or less in a particular country (as measured in our own currency). When we travel to another country, we discover that our own currency buys more or less than it does at home. In other words, we quickly learn that exchange rates do not guarantee or stabilize the buying power of our currency. Thus, we can lose purchasing power in some countries while gaining it in others. For example, a restaurant meal for you and a friend that costs 60 euros in France might cost you 11,000 yen (about 80 euros) in Japan and 22,000 bolivar (about 30 euros) in Venezuela. Thus, compared to your meal in France, you've suffered a loss of purchasing power in Japan but benefited from increased purchasing power in Venezuela.

The **law of one price** stipulates that an identical product must have an identical price in all countries when the price is expressed in a common currency. For this principle to apply, products must be identical in quality and content in all countries, and must be entirely produced within each particular country.

For example, suppose coal mined within the United States and Germany is of similar quality in each country. Suppose further that a kilogram of coal costs €1.5 in Germany and $1 in the United States. Therefore, the law of one price calculates the *expected* exchange rate between the euro and dollar to be €1.5/$. However, suppose the *actual* euro/dollar exchange rate as witnessed on currency markets is €1.2/$. A kilogram of coal still costs $1 in the United States and €1.5 in Germany. But in order to pay for German coal *with dollars denominated after the change in the exchange rate,* one must convert not just $1 into euros, but $1.25 (the expected exchange rate divided by the actual exchange rate, or €1.5 ÷ $1.2). Thus, the price of coal is higher in Germany than in the United States.

Moreover, because the law of one price is being violated in our example, an *arbitrage* opportunity arises—that is, an opportunity to buy a product in one country and sell it in a country where it has a higher value. For example, one could earn a profit by buying coal at $1 per kilogram in the United States and selling it at $1.25 (€1.5) per kilogram in Germany. However, note that as traders begin buying in the United States and selling in Germany, greater demand drives *up* the price of U.S. coal, whereas greater supply drives *down* the price of German coal. Eventually, the price of coal in both countries will settle somewhere between the previously low U.S. price and the previously high German price.

If it seems that the arbitrage opportunity would disappear for the same reason that it arose, that is essentially the case. According to William Louis Dreyfus, one of the world's leading commodities traders, companies like his are constantly seeking new opportunities

law of one price
Principle that an identical item must have an identical price in all countries when the price is expressed in a common currency.

as they themselves arbitrage old ones out of existence. In other words, it is the nature of arbitrage to even out excessive fluctuation by destroying its own profitability. An arbitrageur, says Dreyfus, is "like a microbe. While the microbe attacks your body, it has a wonderful time living, but it ends up killing your body and dies as a result. The arbitrageur is exactly the same. When he sees a market inefficiency, he goes to it and makes it efficient. As a consequence, his profit margin disappears."[4]

Big MacCurrencies   The usefulness of the law of one price is that it helps us determine whether a currency is overvalued or undervalued. Each year *The Economist* magazine publishes what it calls its "Big Mac index" of exchange rates (see Figure 10.3). This index uses the law of one price to determine the exchange rate that *should* exist between the U.S. dollar and other major currencies. It employs the McDonald's Big Mac as its single product to test the law of one price. Why the Big Mac? Because each one is fairly identical in quality and content across national markets and almost entirely produced within the nation in which it is sold. According to the most recent Big Mac index, the average price of a Big Mac was $2.80 in the United States. The cheapest Big Mac was found in China at a dollar-equivalent price of $1.23, the most expensive was found in Switzerland at $5.11. Therefore, according to the Big Mac index the Chinese yuan was undervalued by 56 percent ($\{[(2.80 - 1.23) / 2.80] \times -100\} = -56$ percent). On the other hand, the Swiss franc is over-valued by 83 percent ($\{[(2.80 - 5.11) / 2.80] \times -100\} = 83$ percent).

Such large discrepancies between a currency's exchange rate on currency markets and the rate predicted by the Big Mac index are not surprising, for several reasons. For one

FIGURE 10.3

Big Mac Index

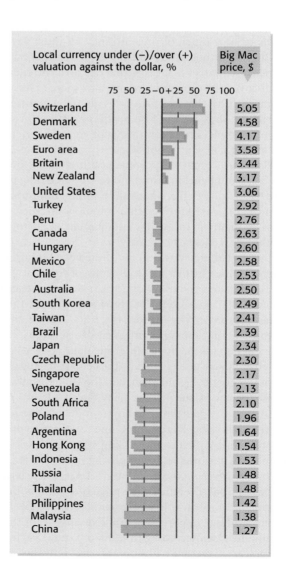

thing, the selling price of food is affected by subsidies for agricultural products in most countries. Also, a Big Mac is not a "traded" product in the sense that one can buy Big Macs in low-priced countries and sell them in high-priced countries. Prices can also be affected because Big Macs are subject to different marketing strategies in different countries. Finally, countries impose different levels of sales tax on restaurant meals.

The drawbacks of the Big Mac index reflect the fact that applying the law of one price to a single product is too simplistic a method for estimating exchange rates. Nonetheless, academic studies find that currency values tend to change in the direction suggested by the Big Mac index.[5]

Purchasing Power Parity

We were introduced to the concept of purchasing power parity in Chapter 4 when we discussed economic development. This concept is also useful in determining at what level an exchange rate should be. Recall that *purchasing power parity (PPP)* is the relative ability of two countries' currencies to buy the same "basket" of goods in those two countries. Thus, although the law of one price holds for single products, PPP is meaningful only when applied to a *basket* of goods. Let's look at an example to see why this is so.

Suppose 650 baht in Thailand will buy a bag of groceries that costs $30 in the United States. What do these two numbers tell us about the economic conditions of people in Thailand as compared with people in the United States? First, they help us compare the *purchasing power* of a Thai consumer with that of a consumer in the United States. But the question is: Are Thai consumers better off or worse off than their counterparts in the United States? In order to address this question, we first need to know the *GNP per capita* of both countries:

Thai GNP/capita = 122,277 baht

U.S. GNP/capita = 26,980 dollars

Suppose the *exchange rate* between the two currencies is 41.45 baht = 1 dollar. With this figure, we can translate 122,277 baht into dollars: 122,277/41.45 = $2,950. We can now restate our question: Do prices in Thailand enable a Thai consumer with $2,950 to buy more or less than a consumer in the United States with $26,980?

We already know that 650 baht will buy in Thailand what $30 will buy in the United States. Thus 650/30 = 21.67 baht per dollar. Note, then, that whereas the exchange rate on currency markets is 41.45 baht/$, the *purchasing power parity rate* of the baht is 21.67/$. Let's now use this figure to calculate a different comparative rate between the two currencies. We can now recalculate Thailand's GNP per capita at PPP as follows: 122,277/21.67 = $5,643. Clearly, Thai consumers, on average, are not nearly as affluent as their counterparts in the United States. But when we consider the *goods and services that they can purchase with their baht*—not the amount of U.S. dollars that they can buy—we see that a GNP per capita at PPP of $5,643 more accurately portrays the real purchasing power of Thai consumers.

Therefore, our new calculation considers *price levels* in adjusting the relative values of the two currencies. Thus, in the context of exchange rates, the principle of purchasing power parity can be interpreted as the exchange rate between two nations' currencies being equal to the ratio of their price levels (in our example, 21.67 instead of 41.45). In other words, in our example, PPP tells us how many units of Thai currency a consumer in Thailand needs in order to buy the same amount of products as a consumer in the United States can buy with 1 dollar.

As we can see in the above example, the exchange rate at PPP (21.67/$) is normally different from the actual exchange rate in financial markets (41.45/$). However, PPP states that economic forces will push the actual market exchange rate toward that determined by purchasing power parity. If not, arbitrage opportunities would arise. Purchasing power parity holds for internationally traded products that are not restricted by trade barriers and that entail few or no transportation costs. In order to earn a profit, arbitrageurs must be certain that the basket of goods purchased in the low-cost country would still be lower-priced in the high-cost country *after adding transportation costs, tariffs, taxes, and so forth*. Let's now see what impact inflation and interest rates have on exchange rates and purchasing power parity.

Role of Inflation

Inflation is the result of the supply and demand for a currency. If additional money is injected into an economy that is not producing greater output, people will have more money to spend on the same amount of products as before. As growing demand for products outstrips stagnant supply, prices will rise and devour any increase in the amount of money that consumers have to spend. Therefore, inflation erodes people's purchasing power.

Impact of Money-Supply Decisions   Because of the damaging effects of inflation, governments try to manage the supply of and demand for their currencies. They do this through the use of two types of policies designed to influence a nation's money supply. *Monetary policy* refers to activities that directly affect a nation's interest rates or money supply. Selling government securities reduces a nation's money supply because investors pay money to the government's treasury to acquire the securities. Conversely, when the government buys its own securities on the open market, cash is infused into the economy and the money supply increases.

Fiscal policy involves using taxes and government spending to influence the money supply indirectly. For instance, to reduce the amount of money in the hands of consumers, governments increase taxes—people are forced to pay money to the government coffers. Conversely, lowering taxes increases the amount of money in the hands of consumers. Governments can also step up their own spending activities to increase the amount of money circulating in the economy, or cut government spending to reduce it.

Impact of Unemployment and Interest Rates   Many industrialized countries are very effective at controlling inflation (see Figure 10.4). Some economists claim that international competition is responsible for keeping inflation under control. The logic (called "the new paradigm") runs as follows: Global competition and the mobility of companies to move anywhere that costs are lowest keeps a lid on wages. Because wages are kept under control, companies do not raise prices on their products, thus containing inflation. More research and time will be needed to see whether this is in fact the case.

Other key factors in the inflation equation are a country's unemployment and interest rates. When unemployment rates are low, there is a shortage of labor, and employers pay higher wages to attract employees. Then, in order to maintain reasonable profit margins with higher labor costs, they usually raise the prices of their products, passing off the cost of higher wages to the consumer—thus causing inflation.

Interest rates (discussed in detail later) affect inflation because they affect the cost of borrowing money. Low interest rates encourage people to take out loans to buy items such as new homes and cars and to run up debt on their credit cards. High interest rates prompt people to cut down on the amount of debt they carry because higher rates mean larger

FIGURE 10.4

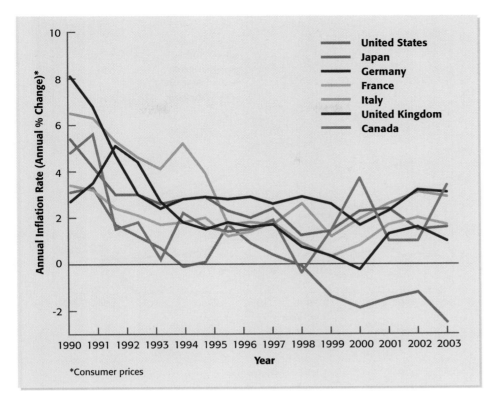

monthly payments on debt. Thus, one way to cool off an inflationary economy is to raise interest rates because raising the cost of debt reduces consumer spending and makes it more costly for businesses to expand.

How Exchange Rates Adjust to Inflation An important component of the concept of purchasing power parity is that exchange rates adjust to different rates of inflation in different countries. Such adjustment is necessary to maintain purchasing power parity between nations. For example, suppose that at the beginning of the year the exchange rate between the Mexican peso and the U.S. dollar is 8 pesos/$ (or $0.125/peso). Also suppose that inflation is pushing consumer prices higher in Mexico at an annual rate of 20 percent whereas prices are rising just 3 percent per year in the United States. To find the new exchange rate (E_e) at the end of the year, we use the following formula:

$$E_e = E_b(1 + i_1)/(1 + i_2),$$

where E_b is the exchange rate at the beginning of the period, i_1 is the inflation rate in country 1 and i_2 is the inflation rate in country 2. Plugging the numbers for this example into the formula, we get:

$$E_e = 8_{pesos/\$}[(1 + 0.20)/(1 + 0.03)] = 9.3_{pesos/\$}$$

It is important to remember that *because the numerator of the exchange rate is pesos, the inflation rate for Mexico must also be placed in the numerator for the ratio of inflation rates.* Thus, we see that the exchange rate adjusts from 8 pesos/$ to 9.3 pesos/$ because of the higher inflation rate in Mexico and the corresponding change in currency values. Higher inflation in Mexico reduces the number of U.S. dollars that a peso will buy and increases the number of pesos that a dollar will buy. In other words, whereas it had cost only 8 pesos to buy a dollar at the beginning of the year, it now costs 9.3 pesos.

In our example, tourists from the United States can now take less expensive vacations in Mexico, but Mexicans will find the cost of U.S. vacations more expensive. Whereas companies based in Mexico must pay more in pesos for any supplies bought from the United States, U.S. companies will pay less, in dollar terms, for supplies bought from Mexico.

This discussion illustrates at least one of the difficulties facing countries with high rates of inflation. Both consumers and companies in countries experiencing rapidly

FIGURE 10.5

The Curse of Inflation

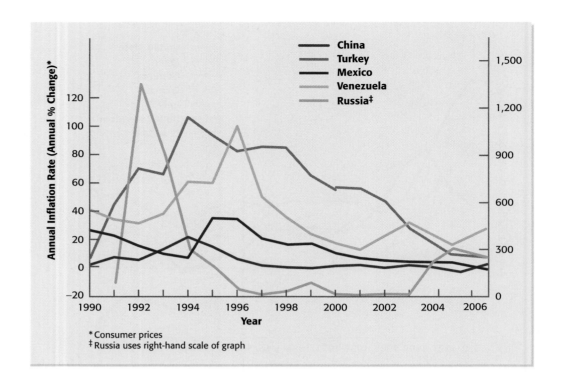

* Consumer prices
‡ Russia uses right-hand scale of graph

increasing prices see their purchasing power eroded. Figure 10.5 shows inflation rates in several developing countries and countries in transition—those most often plagued by rocketing prices. Notice the difference between these inflation rates and those we saw in Figure 10.4 for developed nations.

Role of Interest Rates

In order to see how interest rates affect exchange rates between two currencies, we must first review the connection between inflation and interest rates within a single economy. We distinguish between two types of interest rates: *real interest rates* and *nominal interest rates*. Let's say that your local banker quotes you an interest rate on a new-car loan. The quoted rate charged by the bank is the nominal interest rate, which consists of the real interest rate plus an additional charge for inflation. The reasoning behind this principle is simple. Recall from our earlier discussion that because inflation erodes the purchasing power of currencies, the lender must be compensated for this erosion during the loan period.

Fisher Effect   Now suppose instead that your bank lends you money to buy a delivery van for your home-based business. Let's say that, given your credit-risk rating, the bank would normally charge you 5 percent annual interest. But if inflation is expected to be 2 percent over the next year, your annual rate of interest will be 7 percent: 5 percent real interest plus 2 percent to cover inflation. This principle that relates inflation to interest rates is called the Fisher effect—the principle that the nominal interest rate is the sum of the real interest rate and the expected rate of inflation over a specific period. We write this relation between inflation and interest rates as:

Nominal Interest Rate = Real Interest Rate + Inflation Rate

If money were free from all controls when transferred internationally, the real rate of interest should be the same in all countries. To see why this is true, suppose that real interest rates are 4 percent in Canada and 6 percent in the United States. This situation creates an arbitrage opportunity: Investors could borrow money in Canada at 4 percent, lend it in the United States at 6 percent, and earn a profit on the 2 percent spread in interest rates. If enough people took advantage of this opportunity, interest rates would go up in Canada, where demand for money would become heavier, and down in the United States, where the money supply was growing. Again, the arbitrage opportunity would disappear because of

Fisher effect
Principle that the nominal interest rate is the sum of the real interest rate and the expected rate of inflation over a specific period.

the same activities that made it a reality. That is why, theoretically, real interest rates remain equal across countries.

We demonstrated earlier the relation between inflation and exchange rates. The Fisher effect clarifies the relation between inflation and interest rates. Now, let's investigate the relation between exchange rates and interest rates. To illustrate this relation, we refer to the **international Fisher effect**—the principle that a difference in nominal interest rates supported by two countries' currencies will cause an equal but opposite change in their *spot exchange rates*. Recall from Chapter 9 that the spot rate is the rate quoted for delivery of the traded currency within two business days.

Because real interest rates are theoretically equal across countries, any difference in interest rates in two countries must be due to different expected rates of inflation. A country that is experiencing inflation higher than that of another country should see the value of its currency fall. If so, the exchange rate must be adjusted to reflect this change in value. For example, suppose nominal interest rates are 5 percent in Australia and 3 percent in Canada. Expected inflation in Australia, then, is 2 percent higher than in Canada. The international Fisher effect predicts that the value of the Australian dollar will fall by 2 percent against the Canadian dollar.

Evaluating Purchasing Power Parity
Purchasing power parity is better at predicting long-term exchange rates (more than 10 years) than short-term rates. Unfortunately, accurate forecasts of short-term rates are most beneficial to international managers because most companies plan less than 5 years into the future. Even so, most short-term plans assume a great deal about future economic and political conditions in different countries. Among common considerations are added costs, trade barriers, and even investor psychology.

Impact of Added Costs There are many possible reasons for the failure of PPP to predict exchange rates accurately. For one thing, PPP assumes no transportation costs. Suppose that the same basket of goods costs $100 in the United States and 1,350 krone ($150) in Norway. Seemingly, one could make a profit through arbitrage by purchasing these goods in the United States and selling them in Norway. However, if it costs another $60 to transport the goods to Norway, the total cost of the goods once they arrive in Norway will be $160. Obviously, no shipment will occur. Because no arbitrage opportunity exists after transportation costs are added, there will be no leveling of prices between the two markets and the price discrepancy will persist. Thus, even if PPP predicts that the Norwegian krone is overvalued, the effect of transportation costs will keep the dollar/krone exchange rate from adjusting. In a world in which transportation costs exist, PPP does not always correctly predict shifts in exchange rates.

Impact of Trade Barriers PPP also assumes no barriers to international trade. However, such barriers certainly do exist. Governments establish trade barriers for many reasons, including helping domestic companies remain competitive and preserving jobs for their citizens. Suppose the Norwegian government in our earlier example imposes a 60 percent tariff on the $100 basket of imported goods or makes its importation illegal. Because no leveling of prices or exchange-rate adjustment will occur, PPP will fail to predict exchange rates accurately.

Impact of Business Confidence and Psychology Finally, PPP overlooks the human aspect of exchange rates—the role of people's confidence and beliefs about a nation's economy and its currency's value. Many countries gauge confidence in their economies by conducting a *business confidence survey*. The largest survey of its kind in Japan is called the tankan survey. It gauges business confidence four times each year among 10,000 companies.

Investor confidence in the value of a currency plays an important role in determining its exchange rate. Suppose several currency traders believe that the Indian rupee will increase in value. They will buy Indian rupees at the current price, sell them if the value increases, and earn a profit. However, suppose that all traders share the same belief and all follow the same course of action. The activity of the traders themselves will be sufficient to push the value of the Indian rupee higher. It does not matter why traders believed the price would increase. As long as enough people act on a similar belief regarding the future value of a currency, its value will change accordingly.

international Fisher effect
Principle that a difference in nominal interest rates supported by two countries' currencies will cause an equal but opposite change in their spot exchange rates.

That is why nations try to maintain the confidence of investors, businesspeople, and consumers in their economies. Lost confidence causes companies to put off investing in new products and technologies and to delay the hiring of additional employees. Consumers tend to increase their savings and not increase their debts if they have lost confidence in an economy. These kinds of behaviors act to weaken a nation's currency.

Quick Study

1. What is the *law of one price*? Explain its limitations.
2. What is *purchasing power parity* in the context of exchange rates?
3. Briefly explain how both inflation and interest rates influence exchange rates.
4. What are the limitations of purchasing power parity in predicting exchange rates?

Forecasting Exchange Rates

Before undertaking any international business activity, managers must consider the impact that currency values will have on financial results. Therefore, they must try to make the best possible guess at future exchange rates. This section explores two distinct views regarding how accurately future exchange rates can be predicted by forward exchange rates—the rate agreed upon for foreign exchange payment at a future date. We also take a brief look at different techniques for forecasting exchange rates.

Efficient Market View

efficient market view
View that prices of financial instruments reflect all publicly available information at any given time.

A great deal of debate revolves around the issue of whether markets themselves are efficient or inefficient in forecasting exchange rates. A market is *efficient* if prices of financial instruments quickly reflect new public information made available to traders. The **efficient market view** thus holds that prices of financial instruments reflect all publicly available information at any given time. As applied to exchange rates, this means that forward exchange rates are accurate forecasts of future exchange rates.

Recall from Chapter 9 that a *forward exchange rate* reflects a market's expectations about the future values of two currencies. In an efficient currency market, forward exchange rates reflect all relevant publicly available information at any given time. Therefore, they are considered the best possible predictors of exchange rates. Proponents of this view hold that there is no other publicly available information that could improve the forecast of exchange rates over that provided by forward rates. If one accepts this view, companies waste time and money collecting and examining information believed to affect future exchange rates. But there is always a certain amount of deviation between forward and actual exchange rates. The fact that forward exchange rates are less than perfect inspires companies to search for more accurate forecasting techniques.

Inefficient Market View

inefficient market view
View that prices of financial instruments do not reflect all publicly available information.

The **inefficient market view** holds that prices of financial instruments do not reflect all publicly available information. Proponents of this view believe that companies can search for new pieces of information to improve forecasting. However, the cost of searching for further information must not outweigh the benefits of its discovery.

Naturally, the inefficient market view is more compelling when the existence of *private* information is considered. Suppose a single currency trader holds privileged information regarding a future change in a nation's economic policy—information that she believes will affect its exchange rate. Because the market is unaware of this information, it is not reflected in forward exchange rates. Our trader will no doubt earn a profit by acting on her store of private information.

Now that we understand the two basic views related to market efficiency, let's look at the specific methods that companies use to forecast exchange rates.

Forecasting Techniques

The debate about whether markets are efficient or inefficient forecasters of exchange rates leads to the question of whether experts can improve on the forecasts of forward exchange rates in *either* an efficient or inefficient market. As we have already seen, some analysts believe that forecasts of exchange rates can be improved by uncovering information not reflected in forward exchange rates. In fact, companies exist to provide exactly this type of service. There are two main forecasting techniques based on this belief in the value of added information—fundamental analysis and technical analysis.

Fundamental Analysis **Fundamental analysis** uses statistical models based on fundamental economic indicators to forecast exchange rates. These models are often quite complex, with many variations reflecting different possible economic conditions. Economic variables used in these models include factors such as inflation, interest rates, money supply, tax rates, and government spending. Such analyses also often consider a country's balance-of-payments situation (see Chapter 7) and government intervention in foreign exchange markets to influence a currency's value.

fundamental analysis
Technique using statistical models based on fundamental economic indicators to forecast exchange rates.

Technical Analysis Another method of forecasting exchange rates is **technical analysis**—a technique that uses charts of past trends in currency prices and other factors to forecast exchange rates. Using highly statistical models and charts of past data trends, analysts estimate the conditions prevailing during changes in exchange rates and try to estimate the timing, magnitude, and direction of future changes. Many forecasters combine the techniques of both fundamental and technical analyses to arrive at potentially more accurate forecasts.

technical analysis
Technique using charts of past trends in currency prices and other factors to forecast exchange rates.

Difficulties of Forecasting

The business of forecasting exchange rates is a rapidly growing industry. This trend seems to provide evidence that a growing number of people believe it is possible to improve on the forecasts of exchange rates embodied in forward rates. However, difficulties remain. Despite highly sophisticated statistical techniques in the hands of well-trained analysts, forecasting is not a pure science. Few forecasts are ever 100 percent accurate because of unexpected events that occur throughout the forecast period.

Over and above the problems associated with the data used by these techniques, failings can be traced to the human element involved in forecasting. For example, people might miscalculate the importance of economic news becoming available to the market, placing too much emphasis on some elements and ignoring others.

Quick Study

1. What are the two market views regarding exchange-rate forecasting? Explain each briefly.
2. Describe the two primary methods of forecasting exchange rates. What are the difficulties of forecasting?

Evolution of the International Monetary System

So far in this chapter, we have discussed how companies are affected by changes in exchange rates and why managers prefer exchange rates to be stable and predictable. We saw how inflation and interest rates affect currency values, and in turn exchange rates, in different countries. We also learned that despite attempts to forecast exchange rates accurately, difficulties remain.

For all these reasons, governments develop systems designed to manage exchange rates between their currencies. Groups of nations have created both formal and informal agreements to control exchange rates between their currencies. The present-day **international monetary system** is the collection of agreements and institutions that govern exchange rates. In this section, we briefly trace the evolution of the current international monetary system and examine its performance.

international monetary system
Collection of agreements and institutions governing exchange rates.

Early Years: The Gold Standard

In the earliest days of international trade, gold was the internationally accepted currency for payment of goods and services. Using gold as a medium of exchange in international trade has several advantages. First, its limited supply made it a commodity in high demand. Second, because gold is highly resistant to corrosion, it can be traded and stored for hundreds of years. Third, because it can be melted into either small coins or large bars, gold is a good medium of exchange for both small and large purchases.

But gold also has its disadvantages. First, its weight made transporting it expensive. Second, when a transport ship sank at sea, the gold sank to the ocean floor and was lost. Thus, merchants wanted a new way to make their international payments without the need to haul large amounts of gold around the world. The solution was found in the **gold standard**—an international monetary system in which nations linked the value of their paper currencies to specific values of gold. Britain was the first nation to implement the gold standard in the early 1700s—it remained intact until the First World War.

gold standard
International monetary system in which nations linked the value of their paper currencies to specific values of gold.

Par Value   The gold standard required a nation to fix the value (price) of its currency to an ounce of gold. The value of a currency expressed in terms of gold is called its *par value*. Each nation must then guarantee to convert its paper currency into gold for anyone demanding it at its par value. The calculation of each currency's par value was based on the concept of purchasing power parity. This provision made the purchasing power of gold the same everywhere and maintained the purchasing power of currencies across nations.

All nations fixing their currencies to gold also indirectly linked their currencies to one another. Because the gold standard *fixed* nations' currencies to the value of gold, it is called a **fixed exchange-rate system**—one in which the exchange rate for converting one currency into another is fixed by international governmental agreement. This system and the use of par values made calculating exchange rates between any two currencies a very simple matter. For example, under the gold standard the U.S. dollar was originally fixed at $20.67/oz of gold and the British pound at £4.2474/oz. The exchange rate between the dollar and pound was $4.87/£ ($20.67 ÷ £4.2474).

fixed exchange-rate system
System in which the exchange rate for converting one currency into another is fixed by international agreement.

Advantages of the Gold Standard   The gold standard was quite successful in its early years of operation. In fact, this early record of success is causing some economists and policy makers to call for its rebirth today. Three main advantages of the gold standard underlie its early success.

First, the gold standard drastically *reduces the risk in exchange rates* because it maintains highly fixed exchange rates between currencies. Deviations that do arise are much smaller than they would be under a system of freely floating currencies. The more stable exchange rates are, the less companies are affected by actual or potential adverse changes in them. Because the gold standard significantly reduced the risk in exchange rates and, therefore, the risks and costs of trade, international trade grew rapidly following its introduction.

Second, the gold standard *imposes strict monetary policies* on all countries that participate in the system. Recall that the gold standard requires governments to convert paper currency into gold if demanded by holders of the currency. If all holders of a nation's paper currency decided to trade it for gold, the government must have an equal amount of gold reserves to pay them. That is why a government cannot allow the volume of its paper currency to grow faster than the growth in its reserves of gold. By limiting the growth of a nation's money supply, the gold standard also was effective in controlling inflation.

Third, the gold standard can *help correct a nation's trade imbalance.* Suppose Australia is importing more than it is exporting (experiencing a trade deficit). As gold flows out of Australia to pay for imports, its government must decrease the supply of paper currency in the domestic economy because it cannot have paper currency in excess of its gold reserves.

What's wrong with just printing more money when your country is in debt? It causes inflation. Germany learned that lesson the hard way in 1923 when it printed huge quantities of money to support workers in the Ruhr River valley. Prices spiraled 9,439 percent in just 1 year. At one point, the German mark had an exchange rate of DM 4.2 trillion to the dollar! Life savings were wiped out. A postage stamp cost billions of marks. Banks conducted transactions by the cartful and much daily business was done through barter.

As the money supply falls, so do prices of goods and services in Australia because demand is falling (consumers have less to spend) whereas the supply of goods is unchanged. Meanwhile, the falling prices of Australian-made goods causes Australian exports to become cheaper on world markets. Exports will rise until Australia's international trade is once again in balance. The exact opposite occurs in the case of a trade surplus: The inflow of gold supports an increase in the supply of paper currency, which increases demand for, and therefore the cost of, goods and services. Thus, exports will fall in reaction to their higher price until trade is once again in balance.

Collapse of the Gold Standard Nations involved in the First World War needed to finance their enormous war expenses, and they did so by printing more paper currency. This certainly violated the fundamental principle of the gold standard and forced nations to abandon the standard. The aggressive printing of paper currency caused rapid inflation for these nations. When the United States returned to the gold standard in 1934, it adjusted its par value from $20.67/oz of gold to $35.00/oz to reflect the lower value of the dollar that resulted from inflation. Thus the U.S. dollar had undergone devaluation. However, Britain returned to the gold standard several years earlier at its previous level, which did not reflect the effect inflation had on its currency.

Because the gold standard links currencies to one another, devaluation of one currency in terms of gold affects the exchange rates between currencies. The decision of the United States to devalue its currency and Britain's decision not to do so lowered the price of U.S. exports on world markets and increased the price of British goods imported into the United States. For example, whereas it had previously required $4.87 to purchase one British pound, it now required $8.24 ($35.00 ÷ £4.2474). This forced the cost of a £10 tea set exported from Britain to the United States to go from $48.70 before devaluation to $82.40 after devaluation. This drastically increased the price of imports from Britain (and other countries), lowering its export earnings. As countries devalued their currencies in retaliation, a period of "competitive devaluation" resulted. To improve their trade balances, nations chose arbitrary par values to which they devalued their currencies. People quickly lost faith in the gold standard because it was no longer an accurate indicator of a currency's true value. By 1939, the gold standard was effectively dead.

Bretton Woods Agreement

In 1944, representatives from 44 nations met in the New Hampshire resort town of Bretton Woods to lay the foundation for a new international monetary system. The resulting **Bretton Woods Agreement** was an accord among nations to create a new international

Bretton Woods Agreement Agreement (1944) among nations to create a new international monetary system based on the value of the U.S. dollar.

monetary system based on the value of the U.S. dollar. The new system was designed to balance the strict discipline of the gold standard with the flexibility that countries needed to deal with temporary domestic monetary difficulties. Let's now take a brief look at the most important features of that system.

Fixed Exchange Rates
The Bretton Woods Agreement incorporated fixed exchange rates by tying the value of the U.S. dollar directly to gold and the value of other currencies to the value of the dollar. The par value of the U.S. dollar was fixed at $35/oz of gold. Other currencies were then given par values against the U.S. dollar instead of gold. For example, the par value of the British pound was established as $2.40/£. Member nations were expected to keep their currencies from deviating more than one percent above or below their par values. The Bretton Woods Agreement also improved on the gold standard by extending the right to exchange gold for dollars only to national governments, rather than anyone who demanded it.

Built-In Flexibility
The new system also incorporated a degree of built-in flexibility. For example, although competitive currency devaluation was ruled out, large devaluation was allowed under the extreme set of circumstances called **fundamental disequilibrium**—an economic condition in which a trade deficit causes a permanent negative shift in a country's balance of payments. In this situation, a nation can devalue its currency more than 10 percent. Yet, devaluation under these circumstances should accurately reflect a permanent economic change for the country in question, not temporary misalignments.

fundamental disequilibrium
Economic condition in which a trade deficit causes a permanent negative shift in a country's balance of payments.

World Bank
To provide funding for countries' efforts toward economic development, the Bretton Woods Agreement created the *World Bank*—officially called the International Bank for Reconstruction and Development (IBRD). The immediate purpose of the World Bank (*www.worldbank.org*) was to finance European reconstruction following the Second World War. It later shifted its focus to the general financial needs of developing countries. The Bank finances many types of economic development projects in Africa, South America, and Southeast Asia. The World Bank also offers funds to countries that are unable to obtain capital from commercial sources for certain projects that are considered too risky. The Bank often undertakes projects to develop transportation networks, power facilities, and agricultural and educational programs.

International Monetary Fund
The Bretton Woods Agreement established the *International Monetary Fund (IMF)* as the agency to regulate the fixed exchange rates and enforce the rules of the international monetary system. At the time of its formation, the IMF (*www.imf.org*) had just 29 members—today 184 countries belong. Included among the main purposes of the IMF are:[6]

○ Promoting international monetary cooperation

○ Facilitating expansion and balanced growth of international trade

○ Promoting exchange stability, maintaining orderly exchange arrangements, and avoiding competitive exchange devaluation

○ Making the resources of the Fund temporarily available to members

○ Shortening the duration and lessening the degree of disequilibrium in the international balance of payments of member nations

Special Drawing Right (SDR)
World financial reserves of dollars and gold grew scarce in the 1960s, at a time when the activities of the IMF demanded greater amounts of dollars and gold. The IMF reacted by creating what is called a **special drawing right (SDR)**—an IMF asset whose value is based on a "basket" of its five biggest members' currencies (France, Germany, Japan, the United Kingdom, and the United States). Figure 10.6 shows the "weight" each currency contributes to the overall value of the SDR. The value of the SDR is set daily and changes with increases and declines in the values of its underlying currencies. Today there are more than 21 billion SDRs in existence worth about $29 billion (1SDR equals about $1.26).

special drawing right (SDR)
IMF asset whose value is based on a "weighted basket" of the currencies of five industrialized countries.

The significance of the SDR is that it is the unit of account for the IMF. Each nation is assigned a quota based on the size of its economy when it enters the IMF. Payment of this

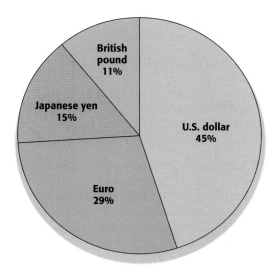

FIGURE 10.6

Valuation of the SDR

British
pound
11%

Japanese yen
15%

U.S. dollar
45%

Euro
29%

quota by each nation provides the IMF with the funds it needs to make short-term loans to members.

Collapse of the Bretton Woods Agreement

The system developed at Bretton Woods worked quite well for about 20 years—an era that boasted unparalleled stability in exchange rates. However, in the 1960s the Bretton Woods system began to falter. The main problem was that the United States was experiencing a trade deficit (imports were exceeding exports) and a budget deficit (expenses were outstripping revenues). Governments that were holding dollars began to doubt that the U.S. government had an adequate amount of gold reserves to redeem all its paper currency held outside the country. When they began demanding gold in exchange for dollars, a large sell-off of dollars on world financial markets followed.

Smithsonian Agreement In August 1971 the U.S. government held less than one-fourth of the amount of gold needed to redeem all U.S. dollars in circulation. In late 1971 the United States and other countries reached the so-called **Smithsonian Agreement** to restructure and strengthen the international monetary system. The three main accomplishments of the Smithsonian Agreement were: (1) the value of the dollar in terms of gold was lowered to $38/oz of gold, (2) other countries increased the values of their currencies against the dollar, and (3) the 1 percent band within which currencies were allowed to float was increased to 2.25 percent.

Final Days The success of the Bretton Woods system relied on the U.S. dollar remaining a strong reserve currency. However, high inflation and a persistent trade deficit had kept the dollar weak, and so demonstrated a fundamental flaw in the system. The weak U.S. dollar strained the abilities of central banks in Japan and most European countries to maintain exchange rates with the dollar. Because these nations' currencies were tied to the U.S. dollar, as the dollar continued to fall, so too did their currencies. Britain left the system in the middle of 1972 and allowed the pound to float freely against the dollar. The Swiss abandoned the system in early 1973. In January 1973 the dollar was again devalued, this time to around $42/oz of gold. But even this move was not enough. As nations began dumping their reserves of the dollar on a massive scale, currency markets were temporarily closed to prevent further selling of the dollar. When markets reopened, the values of most major currencies were floating against the U.S. dollar. The era of an international monetary system based on *fixed* exchange rates was over.

Smithsonian Agreement
Agreement (1971) among IMF members to restructure and strengthen the international monetary system created at Bretton Woods.

Quick Study

1. How did the *gold standard* function? Briefly describe its evolution and collapse.
2. Describe the most important features of the *Bretton Woods Agreement*.
3. What factors led to the demise of the monetary system created by Bretton Woods?

A Managed Float System Emerges

The Bretton Woods system collapsed because it depended so heavily on the stability of the dollar. As long as the dollar remained strong, it worked well. But when the dollar weakened, it failed to perform properly. Originally, the new system of *floating* exchange rates was viewed as a temporary solution to the shortcomings of the Bretton Woods and Smithsonian agreements. However, no new coordinated international monetary system was forthcoming. Rather, there emerged several independent efforts to manage exchange rates.

Jamaica Agreement

Jamaica Agreement
Agreement (1976) among IMF members to formalize the existing system of floating exchange rates as the new international monetary system.

By January 1976 returning to a system of fixed exchange rates seemed unlikely. Therefore, world leaders met to draft the so-called **Jamaica Agreement**—an accord among members of the IMF to formalize the existing system of floating exchange rates as the new international monetary system. The Jamaica Agreement contained several main provisions. First, it endorsed a **managed float system** of exchange rates—that is, a system in which currencies float against one another, with governments intervening to stabilize their currencies at particular target exchange rates. This is in contrast to a **free float system**—a system in which currencies float freely against one another without governments intervening in currency markets.

managed float system
Exchange-rate system in which currencies float against one another, with governments intervening to stabilize their currencies at particular target exchange rates.

Second, gold was no longer the primary reserve asset of the IMF. Member countries could retrieve their gold from the IMF if they so desired. Third, the mission of the IMF was augmented: Rather than being the manager of a fixed exchange-rate system only, it was now a "lender of last resort" for nations with balance-of-payment difficulties. Member contributions were increased to support the newly expanded activities of the IMF.

free float system
Exchange-rate system in which currencies float freely against one another, without governments intervening in currency markets.

Later Accords

Between 1980 and 1985 the U.S. dollar rose dramatically against other currencies, pushing up prices of U.S. exports and adding once again to a U.S. trade deficit. In September 1985 the world's five largest industrialized nations, known as the "G5" (Britain, France, Germany, Japan, and the United States), arrived at a solution. The *Plaza Accord* was a 1985 agreement among the G5 nations to act together in forcing down the value of the U.S. dollar. The Plaza Accord caused traders to sell the dollar, and its value fell.

By February 1987 the industrialized nations were concerned that the value of the U.S. dollar was now in danger of falling too low. Meeting in Paris, leaders of the "G7" nations (the G5 plus Italy and Canada) drew up another agreement. The *Louvre Accord* was a 1987 agreement among the G7 nations that affirmed that the U.S. dollar was appropriately valued and that they would intervene in currency markets to maintain its current market value. Once again, currency markets responded and the dollar stabilized.

Today's Exchange-Rate Arrangements

Today's international monetary system remains in large part a managed float system, whereby most nations' currencies float against one another and governments engage in limited intervention to realign exchange rates. However, within the larger monetary system certain countries try to maintain more stable exchange rates by tying their currencies to other currencies. Let's take a brief look at two ways nations attempt to do this.

Pegged Exchange-Rate Arrangement

Think of one country as a small lifeboat tethered to a giant cruise ship as it navigates choppy monetary waters. Many economists argue that rather than let their currencies face the tides of global currency markets alone, developing economies should tie them to other, more stable currencies. Pegged exchange-rate arrangements "peg" a country's currency to a more stable and widely used currency in international trade. Countries then allow the exchange rate to fluctuate within a specified margin (usually 1 percent) around a central rate.

Many small countries peg their currencies to the U.S. dollar, European Union euro, the special drawing right (SDR) of the IMF, or other individual currency. Belonging to this category are the Bahamas, El Salvador, Iran, Malaysia, Netherlands Antilles, and Saudi Arabia. Other nations peg their currencies to groups, or "baskets," of currencies. For example, Bangladesh and Burundi tie their currencies (the taka and Burundi franc, respectively) to those of their major trading partners. Other members of this group are Botswana, Fiji, Kuwait, Latvia, Malta, and Morocco.

Currency Board   A **currency board** is a monetary regime that is based on an explicit commitment to exchange domestic currency for a specified foreign currency at a fixed exchange rate. The government with a currency board is legally bound to hold an amount of foreign currency that is at least equal to the amount of domestic currency. Because a currency board restricts a government from issuing additional domestic currency unless it has the foreign reserves to back it, it helps cap inflation.

Thanks to a currency board, Bosnia and Herzegovina has built itself a strong and stable currency. However, observers remark that the currency board's survival depends on sound budget policies.[7] Argentina had a currency board from 1991 until it was abandoned in early 2002, when the peso was allowed to float freely on currency markets. Other nations with currency boards include Brunei Darussalam, Bulgaria, Hong Kong, Djibouti, Estonia, and Lithuania.

currency board
Monetary regime that is based on an explicit commitment to exchange domestic currency for a specified foreign currency at a fixed exchange rate.

European Monetary System

Following the collapse of the Bretton Woods system, leaders of many European Union (EU) nations did not give up hope for a system that could stabilize currencies and reduce exchange-rate risk. Their efforts became increasingly important as trade between EU nations continued to expand. In 1979, these nations created the *European monetary system (EMS)*. The EMS was established to stabilize exchange rates, promote trade among nations, and keep inflation low through monetary discipline. As planned, the system ceased to exist in 1999, when 12 EU member nations adopted a single currency.

How the System Worked   The mechanism that limited the fluctuations of European Union members' currencies within a specified trading range (or *target zone*) was called the *exchange rate mechanism (ERM)*. Members were required to keep their currencies within 2.25 percent of the highest- and lowest-valued currencies. To illustrate, suppose that a weakening French franc were about to reach the 2.25 percent variation in its exchange rate with the German mark. The central banks of both France and Germany were to drive the value of the French franc higher—forcing the exchange rate away from the 2.25 percent band limit. How did they do so? By buying up French francs on currency markets, thereby increasing demand for the franc and forcing its value higher.

The EMS was quite successful in its early years. Currency realignments were infrequent and inflation was fairly well controlled. But in late 1992, both the British pound and the Italian lira had been on the lower fringe of the allowable 2.25 percent fluctuation band with the mark for some time. Currency speculators began unloading their pounds and lira. The central banks of neither Britain nor Italy had enough money to buy their currencies on the open market. As their currencies' values plummeted, they were forced to leave the ERM. The EMS was revised in late 1993 to allow currencies to fluctuate 15 percent up or down from the midpoint of the target zone. Although the Italian lira returned to the ERM in November 1996, the British pound remained outside the ERM. Many European nations moved to the euro as their currency (see Chapter 8), which eliminated the need for the ERM.

Of the three nations (Britain, Denmark, and Sweden) opting out of the euro, Denmark is the only one participating in what is called the *exchange rate mechanism II (ERM II)*. The ERM II (in which membership is voluntary) was introduced January 1, 1999, and continues to function today. The aim of ERM II is to support nations that seek future membership in the European monetary union (see Chapter 8) by linking their currencies to the euro. The euro acts as an *anchor* of a *hub and spokes* model, to which a currency is linked on a bilateral basis. The currencies of participating countries have a central rate against the euro with acceptable fluctuation margins of 15 percent, although narrower margins can be arranged. Future accession countries to the EU will be obliged to join the single currency once they satisfy the criteria of the Maastricht Treaty.

Recent Financial Crises

Despite the best efforts of nations to head off financial crises within the international monetary system, the world has experienced several wrenching crises in recent years. Let's now take a look at the most prominent of these.

Developing Nations' Debt Crisis
By the early 1980s certain developing countries (especially in Latin America) had amassed huge debts payable not only to large international commercial banks but also to the IMF and the World Bank. In 1982 Mexico, Brazil, and Argentina announced that they would be unable to pay interest on their loans. At the same time, many of these countries were also experiencing runaway inflation. Many countries in Africa were facing similar problems.

To prevent a meltdown of the entire financial system, international agencies stepped in with a number of temporary solutions to the crisis. Repayment schedules were revised to put off repayment until further into the future. Then, in 1989, U.S. Treasury Secretary Nicholas Brady unveiled the Brady Plan. The Brady Plan called for large-scale reduction of the debt owed by poorer nations, the exchange of old loans for new low-interest loans, and the making of debt instruments (based on these loans) that would be tradable on world financial markets. This last feature allowed a debtor country to receive a loan from an institution and then use it to buy special securities (called "Brady Bonds") on financial markets. Funds for these new loans came from private commercial banks and were backed by the IMF and the World Bank.

Mexico's Peso Crisis
Armed rebellion in the poor Mexican state of Chiapas and assassination of a presidential candidate shook investors' faith in Mexico's financial system in 1993 and 1994. Capital flowing into Mexico was mostly in the form of stocks and bonds (portfolio investment) rather than factories and equipment (foreign direct investment). Portfolio investment fled Mexico for the United States as the Mexican peso grew weak and U.S. interest rates rose. A lending spree by Mexican banks, coupled with weak banking regulations, also played a role in delaying the government's response to the crisis. In late 1994 the Mexican peso was devalued, forcing a loss of purchasing power on the Mexican people.

In response to the crisis, the IMF and private commercial banks in the United States stepped in with about $50 billion in loans to shore up the Mexican economy. Thus, Mexico's peso crisis contributed to an additional boost in the level of IMF loans. Mexico repaid the loans ahead of schedule and once again has a sizable reserve of foreign exchange.

Southeast Asia's Currency Crisis
The roar of the "four tiger" economies and those of other high-growth Asian nations suddenly fell silent in the summer of 1997. For 25 years the economies of five Southeast Asian countries—Indonesia, Malaysia, the Philippines, Singapore, and Thailand—had wowed the world with growth rates twice those of most other countries. Even though many analysts projected continued growth for the region, and even though billions of dollars in investment flooded in from the West, savvy speculators were pessimistic.

On July 11, 1997, the speculators struck, selling off Thailand's baht on world currency markets. The selling forced an 18 percent drop in the value of the baht before speculators moved on to the Philippines and Malaysia. By November the baht had plunged another 22 percent and every other economy in the region was in a slump. The shock waves of Asia's crisis could be felt throughout the global economy.

Suddenly, countries thought to be strong emerging market economies—"tigers" to be emulated by other developing countries—were in need of billions of dollars to keep their economies from crumbling. When the dust settled, Indonesia, South Korea, and Thailand all needed IMF and World Bank funding. As incentives for these countries to begin the long process of economic restructuring, IMF loan packages came with a number of strings attached. For example, the Indonesian loan package involved three long-term goals to help put the Indonesian economy on a stronger footing: (1) to restore the confidence of international financial markets; (2) to restructure the domestic financial sector; and (3) to support domestic deregulation and trade reforms.

What caused the crisis in the first place? Well, it depends on whom you ask. Some believe it was caused by an Asian style of crony capitalism. They say that poor regulation, the practice of extending loans to friends and relatives who are poor credit risks, and a lack of transparency regarding the financial health of banks and companies are to blame. Others point to currency speculators and panicking investors as the main causes. Still others argue that persistent current account deficits in these countries are what caused the large dumping of these nations' currencies. What really caused the crisis is probably a combination of all these forces.[8]

Russia's Ruble Crisis   Russia had a whole host of problems throughout the 1990s—some were constant, others were intermittent. For starters, Russia was not immune to the events unfolding across Southeast Asia in the late 1990s. As investors became wary of potential problems in other emerging markets worldwide, stock market values in Russia plummeted. Another problem contributing to Russia's problems was depressed oil prices. Because Russia depends on oil production for a large portion of its GDP, the low price of oil on world markets cut into the government's reserves of hard currency. Also cutting into the government's coffers was an unworkable tax-collection system and a large underground economy—meaning that most taxes went uncollected.

Then there was the problem of inflation. We learned earlier in this chapter how an expanded amount of money chasing the same amount of goods forces prices higher. This is exactly what happened when Russia released prices in 1992. As prices skyrocketed, people dug beneath their mattresses where they had stashed their rubles during times when there were no goods to purchase. We also saw earlier how inflation eats away at the value of a nation's currency. Russia saw inflation take its exchange rate from less than 200 rubles to the dollar in early 1992 to more than 5,000 to the dollar in 1995.

Then in early 1996 as currency traders dumped the ruble, the Russian government found itself attempting to defend the ruble on currency markets. As its foreign exchange reserves dwindled in a hopeless effort, the government asked for, and received, a $10 billion aid package from the IMF. In return, Russia promised to reduce its debt (which was averaging about

7 percent of GDP), collect taxes owed it, cease printing inflation-stoking sums of currency, and peg its currency to the dollar.

Things seemed to improve for a while, but then in mid-1998 the government found itself once again trying to defend the ruble against speculative pressure on currency markets. In a single day the government spent $1 billion trying to prop up the ruble's value, forcing its hard currency reserves to shrivel to $14 billion. As it grew obvious that the government would soon be bankrupt, the IMF stepped in and promised Russia another $11 billion. But when it was alleged that some of the IMF loan had been funneled into off-shore bank accounts, the IMF held up distribution of the money. On August 17, 1998, badly strapped for cash, the government announced that it would allow the ruble to devalue by 34 percent by the end of the year. It also declared a 90-day foreign-debt moratorium and announced a de facto default on the government's domestic bond obligations. On August 26, the Russian Central Bank announced that it would no longer be able to support the ruble on currency markets. In less than one month, its value fell 300 percent. Inflation shot up to 15 percent a month in August from 0.2 percent in July and reached 30 percent in the first week of September.[9] By the time it was all over in late 1998, the IMF had lent Russia more than $22 billion.

Argentina's Peso Crisis
Argentina was the star of Latin America in the early and mid-1990s. Yet, by late 2001, Argentina had been in recession for nearly four years, mainly because of Brazil's devaluation of its own currency in 1999—making Brazil's exports cheaper on world markets. Meanwhile, Argentina's goods remained relatively expensive because its own currency was linked to a very strong U.S. dollar through a currency board. As a result, Argentina saw much of its export business dry up and the economy slowed significantly. By late 2001, the IMF had already promised $48 billion to rescue Argentina.

Things came to a head when the country began running out of money to service its debt obligations. The country finally defaulted on its $155 billion of public debt in early 2002, the largest default ever by any country. The government scrapped its currency board that linked the peso to the U.S. dollar and the peso quickly lost around 70 percent of its value on currency markets. The government, strapped for cash, seized the savings accounts of its citizens and restricted how much they could withdraw at a time. In April 2002, the IMF was reviewing the government's reforms before releasing more cash, and wanted greater reductions in government spending.

Later, critics blamed the IMF for giving in to Argentina, saying a September 2003 deal was more lax than that for either Brazil or Turkey. Yet IMF supporters respond that Argentina is carrying out radical pension reform, and is to receive no new money from the IMF or the World Bank. The IMF will lend Argentina only what it is due to repay to it over the next three years, a total of $12.5 billion. And, they say, Argentina's net repayments in 2002–03 to international financial institutions totaled $6.6 billion. Yet the IMF has much at stake. Because IMF lending to Argentina is 15 percent of its total loans, cutting the country off would mean acknowledging huge bad loans.

The debt talks are more complex than previous national restructurings—they involve 152 different bonds under eight different legal jurisdictions. The bondholders include Japanese pensioners, New York "vulture" funds, and Argentine institutions. But while talks drag on between the government and its creditors, the country's large firms cannot raise money and the government cannot implement tax reforms. So, Argentina has become a cash economy, with private sector debt at just 8 percent of GDP. But the banks are doing better, with bank deposits at 90 billion pesos in late 2004, compared with 80 billion before the collapse.[10]

Future of the International Monetary System

Recurring crises in the international monetary system are raising calls for a new system that is designed to meet the challenges of a global economy. Many believe that the vestiges of the IMF created by the Bretton Woods Agreement are no longer adequate to insulate the world's economies from disruptions in a single country or small group of countries.

Meanwhile, leaders of many developing and newly industrialized countries are bemoaning what global capital has done to their economies. Indian Prime Minister Bihari Vajpayee said the "world is paying the price for the dogma of the invisible hand of market forces."[11] Malaysian Prime Minister Mahathir Mohamad echoed these sentiments: "The only system allowed is that of capitalist free markets, of globalization. That the unfettered, unregulated free market has destroyed the economies of whole regions and of many countries in the world does not matter," he wrote.[12]

Although some call for the elimination of the IMF and its replacement by institutions not yet clearly defined, more likely is revision of the IMF and its policy prescriptions. Efforts have already been made to develop internationally accepted codes of good practice to allow comparisons of countries' fiscal and monetary practices. Countries have also been encouraged to be more open and clear regarding their financial policies. Transparency on the part of the IMF is also being increased to instill greater accountability on the part of its leadership. The IMF also is increasing its efforts at surveillance of member nations' macroeconomic policies and increasing its abilities in the area of financial-sector analysis.

Yet, orderly ways must still be found to integrate international financial markets so that risks are better managed. Moreover, the private sector must become involved in the prevention and resolution of financial crises. Policy makers are concerned with the way money floods into developing economies when growth is strong and then just as quickly heads for the exits at the first sign of trouble. Furthermore, some argue that because the IMF bails out debtor countries, private-sector banks do not exercise adequate caution when loaning money in risky situations: After all, the IMF will be there to pay off the loans of debtor countries. Greater cooperation and understanding between the IMF, private-sector banks, and debtor nations are needed.

Quick Study

1. Why did the world shift to a *managed float system* of exchange rates? Briefly describe the performance of this system.

2. What was the purpose of the European monetary system? Describe how it functioned and performed.

3. What role did the International Monetary Fund have in assisting nations during recent financial crises?

Bottom Line for Business

Recent financial crises, including those in Mexico, Southeast Asia, Russia, and Argentina, underscore the need for managers to fully understand the complexities of the international financial system. In Chapters 9 and 10, we've discussed the international financial markets and international monetary system in detail. Understanding this material improves managers' knowledge of financial risks in international business. But this knowledge must be paired with vigilance with regard to financial market conditions to manage businesses effectively in the global economy. Here we focus on only the main implications of this material for international businesses—business strategy and forecasting earnings and cash flows.

Impact on Business Strategy

Some industries (including software, services, and entertainment) are largely insulated from currency fluctuations in terms of their products' selling price. But changes in a currency's exchange rate influence all sorts of business activities for most domestic and international companies. First, exchange rates affect the demand for a company's products in the global marketplace. When a country's currency is *weak* (valued low relative to other currencies), the price of its exports on world markets declines and the price of imports increases. Lower prices make the country's exports more appealing on world markets. This gives companies the opportunity to take market share away from companies whose products are priced high in comparison.

A strong currency tends to hurt exporters because it increases their prices on world markets and can seriously jeopardize their future survival. Yet exporters affected by a rising currency can try to overcome its negative effects. First, companies can cut costs by downsizing and retooling factories for greater efficiency and find other ways to reduce production costs. Second, they can take the time to custom-design products for customers, thus increasing the value of their products and justifying a higher price. Third, firms might choose to absorb the currency rise by keeping prices where they are, then work harder to make additional sales and earn greater profit on volume. Fourth, companies may also try to persuade policy makers that a weaker currency is important for their survival, and by way of inference, good for the economy and the nation's people. Although a government might devalue its currency to give domestic companies an edge over competition from other countries, devaluation reduces consumers' buying power. It might also allow inefficiencies to persist in domestic companies because there is now less pressure to be concerned with production costs.

Finally, a company that is selling in a country with a strong currency (one that is valued high relative to other currencies) while paying workers in a country with a weak currency improves profits. Dell Computer produces much of its products in Malaysia (paying its Malaysian workers and suppliers in the local currency, ringgits) but prices its exports in dollars. When Malaysia's currency lost a great deal of its value several years ago, Dell was earning its revenue in a strong and climbing currency, while paying its expenses in a weak and falling currency. But companies finding themselves benefiting from a temporary price advantage caused by exchange rates must not grow complacent about their own long-term competitiveness.

Forecasting Earnings and Cash Flows

Exchange rates also affect the amount of profit a company earns from its international subsidiaries. The earnings of international subsidiaries are typically integrated into the parent company's financial statements in the home currency. Translating subsidiary earnings from a weak host country currency into a strong home currency reduces the amount of these earnings when stated in the home currency. Likewise, translating earnings into a weak home currency increases stated earnings in the home currency. For instance, many companies saw their earnings badly hurt by the recent collapse of the Argentine peso. When firms translated profits into their home currencies, profits were far lower than they would have been without the peso's fall in value.

Sudden, unfavorable movements in exchange rates can be costly for both domestic and international companies. On the other hand, stable exchange rates improve the accuracy of financial planning, including cash flow forecasts. Although companies can insure (usually by currency hedging) against potentially adverse movements in exchange rates, most available methods are too expensive for small and medium-sized businesses. Moreover, as the unpredictability of exchange rates increases, so too does the cost of insuring against the accompanying risk.

Managers also prefer movements in exchange rates be predictable. Predictable exchange rates reduce the likelihood that companies will be caught off guard by sudden and unexpected rate changes. They also reduce the need for costly insurance against possible adverse movements in exchange rates. Rather than purchasing insurance, companies would be better off spending their money on more productive activities, such as developing new products or designing more efficient production methods.

The next chapter begins our in-depth look at the main aspects of managing an international business. As we saw in this chapter, not only are a company's financial decisions affected by events in international financial markets, but so too are production and marketing decisions. Our understanding of national business environments, international trade and investment, and the international financial system will serve us well as we embark on our tour of the nuances of international business management.

SUMMARY

1. **Explain how *exchange rates* influence the activities of domestic and international companies.** Exchange rates influence many aspects of a firm's activities. For one thing, they affect demand for a company's products in the global marketplace. When a country's currency is *weak* (valued low relative to other currencies), the price of its exports on world markets declines and the price of imports increases. Lower prices make the country's exports more appealing on world markets. Furthermore, a company that sells in a country with a *strong* currency (one that is valued high relative to other currencies) while paying workers at home in its own weak currency improves its profits.

   The intentional lowering of the value of a currency by the nation's government is called *devaluation*. The reverse, the intentional raising of its value by the nation's government, is called *revaluation*. Devaluation lowers the price of a country's exports on world markets and increases the price of imports because the country's currency is now worth less on world markets. Revaluation has the opposite effects: It increases the price of exports and reduces the price of imports.

   Exchange rates also affect the amount of profit a company earns from its international subsidiaries. Translating subsidiary earnings from a weak *host* country currency into a strong *home* currency *reduces* the amount of these earnings when stated in the home currency.

2. **Identify the *factors* that help determine exchange rates and their impact on business.** Two concepts are used to determine the level at which an exchange rate *should* be. The *law of one price* stipulates that when price is expressed in a common-denominator currency, an identical product must have an identical price in all countries. For this principle to apply, products must be identical in quality and content in all countries and must be entirely produced within each particular country. The concept of *purchasing power parity (PPP)* helps determine the relative ability of two countries' currencies to buy the same "basket" of goods in those two countries. Thus, although the law of one price holds for *single* products, PPP is meaningful only when applied to a *basket* of goods.

   Two phenomena influence both exchange rates and PPP: inflation and interest rates. When additional money is injected into an economy that is not producing greater output, prices rise because more money is available to buy the same amount of products. When

unemployment is low, employers pay higher wages to attract or retain employees. Employers then typically raise prices to offset the additional labor costs to maintain profits.

   In turn, interest rates affect inflation because they affect the cost of borrowing money. Low rates encourage people and businesses to increase spending by taking on debt. On the other hand, high rates prompt them to reduce the debt because higher rates mean greater debt payments. Because real interest rates—rates that do not account for inflation—are theoretically equal across countries, any difference in the rates of two countries must be due to different expected rates of inflation. A country that is experiencing inflation higher than that of another country should see the relative value of its currency fall.

3. **Describe the primary methods of *forecasting exchange rates*.** There are two distinct views regarding how accurately future exchange rates can be predicted by *forward exchange rates*—that is, by the rate agreed upon for foreign exchange payment at a future date. The *efficient market view* holds that prices of financial instruments reflect all publicly available information at any given time. As applied to exchange rates, this means that forward exchange rates are accurate forecasts of future exchange rates. The *inefficient market view* holds that prices of financial instruments do not reflect all publicly available information. Proponents of this view believe that forecasts can be improved by information not reflected in forward exchange rates.

   Two main forecasting techniques are based on this belief in the value of added information. *Fundamental analysis* uses statistical models based on fundamental economic indicators to forecast exchange rates. *Technical analysis* employs a technique using charts of past trends in currency prices and other factors to forecast exchange rates. Many forecasters combine the techniques of fundamental and technical analyses to arrive at potentially more accurate forecasts.

4. **Discuss the evolution of the current *international monetary system* and explain how it operates.** The *Bretton Woods Agreement* (1944) was an accord among nations to create an international monetary system based on the value of the U.S. dollar. The system was designed to balance the strict discipline of the *gold standard*, which linked paper currencies to specific values of gold, with the

flexibility that countries needed to deal with temporary domestic monetary difficulties. The most important features of the system were fixed exchange rates, built-in flexibility, funds for economic development, and an enforcement mechanism.

Bretton Woods created the *World Bank,* which funds poor nations' economic development projects such as the development of transportation networks, power facilities, and agricultural and educational programs. It also established the *International Monetary Fund (IMF)* to regulate fixed exchange rates and enforce the rules of the international monetary system.

Ultimately, the Bretton Woods Agreement collapsed because it depended so heavily on the stability of the dollar. As long as the dollar remained strong, it worked well. But when the dollar weakened, it failed to perform properly. The *Jamaica Agreement* (1976) endorsed a *managed float system* of exchange rates—that is, a system in which currencies float against one another, with limited government intervention to stabilize currencies at a particular target exchange rate. This system differs from a *free float system* in which currencies float freely against one another without governments intervening in currency markets. But within the system, certain countries try to maintain more stable exchange rates by tying their currencies to another country's stronger currency. The *European monetary system (EMS)* was a complex system designed by the European Union (EU) to stabilize exchange rates, promote trade, and control inflation through monetary discipline.

TALK IT OVER

1. There are benefits of both floating and fixed exchange-rate systems. Describe briefly the advantages and disadvantages of each. Do you think the world will move toward an international monetary system more characteristic of floating or fixed exchange rates in the future? Explain your answer.

2. Do you think that an international monetary system with currencies valued on the basis of gold would work today? Why or why not? Do you think it would work to implement on a global scale a system similar to the old European monetary system? Why or why not?

3. The activities of the IMF and the World Bank largely overlap each other. Devise a plan to reduce the duplication of these institutions' services and to assign them responsibilities. Also, would you have them take a greater role on issues such as the environment and corruption? Describe your plan and justify your proposed solution.

TEAMING UP

1. Suppose you and several classmates are a team assigned with the decision of where to locate a new production facility for your firm based in Japan. Your team is forecasting the exchange rate between the Japanese yen and Indian rupee to decide whether to build a new factory in India. The current spot exchange rate is 0.32 rupee/¥. Inflation is 10 percent in India and 2 percent in Japan. What is your forecast of the rupee/yen exchange rate for 1 year from today?

2. In a small group, select a country that interests you. Is the nation a member of the IMF? Does it participate in a regional monetary system to manage exchange rates? How have inflation and interest rates affected the nation's exchange rate with other currencies? What impact has the country's exchange rate had on its imports and exports? How has the exchange rate recently affected the activities of companies operating in the country? What is the forecasted exchange rate for the coming weeks, months, and year?

Hint: Good sources to consult include various issues of *International Financial Statistics* (Washington, DC:

International Monetary Fund) and *Exchange Arrangements and Exchange Restrictions, Annual Reports* (Washington, DC: International Monetary Fund).

3. Suppose you and several classmates are a marketing team assembled by your Brazil-based firm to estimate demand in the U.S. market for its newly developed product. The market research firm your team hired requires $150,000 to perform a thorough study. However, you are informed that the total research budget for the year is 3 million Brazilian real and that no more than 20 percent of the budget can be spent on any one project.

a. If the current exchange rate is 5 real/$, will your group have the market study conducted? Why or why not?

b. If the exchange rate changes to 3 real/$, will your group have the study conducted? Why or why not?

c. At what exchange rate do you change your group's decision from rejecting the proposed research project to accepting the project?

Bretton Woods Agreement (p. 301)

fundamental analysis (p. 299)

law of one price (p. 291)

currency board (p. 305)

fundamental disequilibrium (p. 302)

managed float system (p. 304)

devaluation (p. 288)

gold standard (p. 300)

revaluation (p. 288)

efficient market view (p. 298)

inefficient market view (p. 298)

Smithsonian Agreement (p. 303)

Fisher effect (p. 296)

international Fisher effect (p. 297)

special drawing right (SDR) (p. 302)

fixed exchange-rate system (p. 300)

international monetary system (p. 300)

technical analysis (p. 299)

free float system (p. 304)

Jamaica Agreement (p. 304)

TAKE IT TO THE WEB

1. In this chapter, we examined factors that help determine exchange rates and explored rate-forecasting techniques. We also discussed international attempts to manage exchange rates and reviewed recent currency problems in Russia, Argentina, and other emerging markets.

   Use the Internet to research the economic crisis that struck Argentina in late 2001 and early 2002 and that continues to plague the nation today. Identify as many potential contributing factors to the crisis as you can. What are the current conditions in Argentina's exchange rate, inflation, and debt load? What effect has the crisis had on Brazil and other South American economies? Do you think Argentina's involvement in the trading bloc MERCOSUR had anything to do with its problems?

   Update how Argentina's companies, investors, and citizens are faring. How were companies' earnings and future projects affected? Are investors having renewed confidence in Argentina and returning? Are Argentines seeing the rebound of their currency's purchasing power? What is the IMF currently doing to aid Argentina's economy?

   Hint: Good sources of information to answer these questions include publications by international agencies such as the International Monetary Fund (*www.imf.org*), the World Bank (*www.worldbank.org*), and the Organization for Economic Cooperation and Development (*www.oecd.org*). Also good to consult are business publications, including *The Economist* (*www.economist.com*), the *Financial Times* (*www.ft.com*), and *The Wall Street Journal* (*www.wsj.com*).

ETHICAL CHALLENGES

1. You are the senior economic advisor in currency analysis with the United Nations (UN). The President of Malaysia has accused currency speculators with conspiring to devalue the Malaysian ringgit and wants the UN to create a formal policy designed to prevent similar financial crises in the future. Some years ago, when currency speculators turned their backs on Malaysia and forced a devaluation of the ringgit, Prime Minister Mahathir Mohamad denounced currency speculators as "immoral" and argued that currency trading should take place only to facilitate deals between countries. Although most observers dismissed these comments as coming from a man known for his outspoken tirades against Western investors, others contend that the prime minister's rhetoric voices a genuine concern. Do you think an international policy that restricts currency trading can prevent future problems? What other implications might stem from such a policy? Is it ethical for global currency speculators to bet against national currencies, perhaps sending whole economies into a tailspin while they profit? Or, do you think that currency speculators perform a valuable service by correcting overvalued or undervalued currencies?

2. You are the chair of an International Monetary Fund (IMF) task force reevaluating the policy of bailing out national governments that suffer major losses in the private sector. Current policy is to enlist the help of industrialized countries in bailing out emerging nations

in the midst of financial crises. Taxpayers in industrial countries typically foot the bill for IMF activities, with total loans running into the many billions of dollars. Recent examples are the bailouts of Mexico, Indonesia, and Thailand. Some critics call this system a kind of "remnant socialism" that rescues financial institutions and investors from their own mistakes with money from taxpayers. For instance, the financial crisis in Thailand was largely a private-sector affair. Thai banks and insurance companies were heavily in debt, and the central bank had recklessly pledged its foreign exchange reserves to shore up the currency. As chair of the task force, on which side of this dilemma do you come down? Do you agree that in the current system losses are *socialized* (that is, subsidized through government-sponsored bailouts) while profits are *privatized*? Explain exactly who benefits from such bailouts. What is an alternative to an IMF bailout?

PRACTICING INTERNATIONAL MANAGEMENT CASE

Banking On Forgiveness

When James Wolfensohn became head of the World Bank in 1996, he bluntly admitted that the Bank had "screwed up" in Africa. Decades of loans had erected a vast modern infrastructure—dams, roads, and power plants—for Africa's poor, but the gap between rich and poor did not narrow. In fact, the policies of the Bank and global financial regulators had created a new crisis in sub-Saharan Africa: These nations were now mired in debt they could not possibly repay. Africa's total debt at the time almost equaled the annual gross national product of the entire continent. For instance, in Mozambique, where 25 percent of all children die from infectious disease before the age of five, the government was spending twice as much paying off debt as it was spending on health care and education.

For years, nongovernmental organizations (NGOs), such as the advocacy group Oxfam International, had lobbied the Bank and the International Monetary Fund (IMF) to write off loans to their poorest borrowers, calling for "debt forgiveness" or "debt relief." Fortunately for the African people and their advocates, the new head of the Bank put debt forgiveness at the top of his agenda. In the fall of 1996 the World Bank and IMF announced a plan to reduce the external debt of the world's poorest, most heavily indebted countries. The purpose of the plan, called the Heavily Indebted Poor Countries (HIPC) Debt Initiative, is to slash overall debt stocks by 50 percent, lower poor nations' debt service, and boost social spending in poor nations. The HIPC identified 42 countries (34 in Africa, four in Latin America, three in Asia, and one in the Middle East) that may qualify for debt reduction. But debt relief is not automatic. The international banking community is using debt as both a carrot and a stick: Whereas nations with good reform records will get relief, those who can point to little reform will not.

For instance, Uganda was the first country declared eligible for assistance in 1997 and was the first to receive debt relief under the HIPC Initiative in 1998. The decision to begin the program with Uganda was not an arbitrary one. While under the brutal dictatorship of Idi Amin, Uganda was treated as a pariah by creditors. But when Amin and his regime were toppled, new president Yoweri Musevini led the country through a decade-long process of economic reform. Uganda is now considered a model country, boasting a steady growth rate of around five percent, with coffee as its main export. By offering debt relief to Uganda, the World Bank and IMF are rewarding Uganda's exemplary track record by reducing its debt to the lowest possible level—about twice the value of its exports. Savings from the debt-relief program are pledged to improve health care and to make primary education available to all Ugandan families. In addition to Uganda, Bolivia, Burkina Faso, Guyana, Ivory Coast, and Mozambique also qualified for early assistance.

But just when many countries were receiving debt relief under the HIPC Initiative, the debate over aid versus loans arose once again. In early 2002, 171 nations, the IMF, the World Bank, business leaders, and nongovernmental organizations met at Monterrey, Mexico to attend the UN Conference on Financing for Development. The group was discussing how to prevent economic collapses and debt problems in the developing world, and how to use dwindling aid more efficiently. A week prior to the conference, U.S. President George W. Bush pledged $5 billion more in foreign aid, but wanted the money given away in the form of grants to financially and politically stable nations. "Many have rallied to the idea of dropping the debt. I say let's rally to the idea of stopping the debt," he said, with U2 singer Bono at his side. Bush wanted 40 percent of all World Bank funds for poor nations to be distributed in the form of grants instead of loans they won't be able to repay.

Meanwhile, European Union (EU) leaders pledged to increase aid levels by $20 billion by 2006. But they feared that giving the money away as grants would drain the World Bank's coffers, as well as their own. EU Development Commissioner Poul Nielson said, "We may not be able to do as much for the least-developed countries. The role of the bank is a bank." For support, the EU pointed to World Bank data that showed more than 95 percent of all loans are repaid, and argued that poor nations are more careful with loans than handouts.

Thinking Globally

1. In negotiating the HIPC Debt Initiative, the World Bank and the IMF worked closely together. However, at one point the plan came to a standstill when the two organizations produced different figures for Uganda's coffee exports, with the IMF giving a more optimistic forecast and so arguing against the need for debt relief. In your opinion, is there any benefit to these organizations working together? Explain. Which organization do you think should play a greater role in aiding economic development? Why?

2. The World Bank and the IMF had once argued that the leniency of debt forgiveness would make it more difficult for the lenders themselves to borrow cheaply on the world's capital markets. If you were a World Bank donor, would you support the HIPC Debt Initiative or argue against it? Explain your answer.

3. At the time the HIPC Initiative was being developed, some critics contended that it fell short. For example, Harvard economist Jeffrey Sachs argued that the need for debt relief was obvious 10 years earlier. The carrot, said Sachs, is simply too little, too late, and he added that for some countries, the situation was so grim that entire external indebtedness, not just half, should be written off. Do you think the World Bank and the IMF should write off the entire debt of countries? What are the pros and cons of this approach for debt relief?

After studying this chapter, you should be able to

1. Explain the stages of *identification* and *analysis* that precede strategy selection.

2. Identify the two *international strategies* and the *corporate-level strategies* that companies use.

3. Identify the *business-level strategies* of companies and the role of *department-level strategies.*

4. Discuss the important issues that influence the choice of *organizational structure.*

5. Describe each type of *international organizational structure*, and explain the importance of *work teams.*

international strategy 11

Part 5   International Business Management

and organization

a look **back**

CHAPTER 10 explored the international monetary system. We examined the factors that affect the determination of exchange rates and discussed international attempts to create a system of stable and predictable exchange rates.

a look **at this chapter**

This chapter introduces us to the strategies used by international companies. We explore the different types of strategies available to international companies and important factors in their selection. We also examine the organizational structures that companies devise to suit their international operations.

a look **ahead**

CHAPTER 12 explains how managers screen and research potential markets and sites for operations. We also identify the information required in the screening process and explain where managers can go to obtain such information.

Ryanair Is Flying High

DUBLIN, Ireland—"There's no one in Europe doing what Ryanair is doing," says Martin Borghetto, European transport analyst at Morgan Stanley in London. What exactly is Ryanair (*www.ryanair.com*) doing? It offers low-fare, no-frills flying to about 15 million passengers a year. Ryanair's fares are an average of 50 percent lower than Europe's big national carriers and sometimes one-tenth as much. Growing from one flight daily between Ireland and London in 1985, Ryanair now has 149 routes between 16 European nations.

Ryanair has successfully carved out a niche among the flying public. Describing his company's approach, CEO Michael O'Leary (pictured above) said, "It's very simple. We're like Wal-Mart in the U.S.—we pile it high and sell it cheap." The cornerstone of Ryanair's strategy is to use less-congested, secondary airports just outside Europe's biggest cities. For instance, instead of serving London's Heathrow or Gatwick airport, Ryanair flies into Stansted. Instead of using Frankfurt Main, Ryanair services Hahn, a former U.S. fighter base 60 miles west of Frankfurt. This strategy allows Ryanair to negotiate airport fees as low as $1.50 per passenger as opposed to the $15 to $22 per passenger charged by Europe's major airports. No expense stands in the way of Ryanair's achieving its mission. When its caterer could no longer provide free ice, Ryanair stopped serving it, a move that should save about $50,000 a year. Even water costs a few dollars, so bring your own.

Big national carriers such as British Airways and Lufthansa are facing their own D-day invasions—D as in discount. Ryanair is hot on their heels and chipping away at their profits. In fact, Ryanair is the only European airline to make a profit every year since 1990. O'Leary is confident that his strategy is going to be a success. "Ryanair is going to be a monster in Europe within the next 10 to 12 years," he says. As you read this chapter, think of all the strategies that firms use to serve their customers.[1]

planning
Process of identifying and selecting an organization's objectives and deciding how the organization will achieve those objectives.

strategy
Set of planned actions taken by managers to help a company meet its objectives.

Planning is the process of identifying and selecting an organization's objectives and deciding how the organization will achieve those objectives. In turn, **strategy** is the set of planned actions taken by managers to help a company meet its objectives. The key to developing an effective strategy, then, is to define a company's objectives (or goals) clearly and to plan carefully how it will achieve those goals. This requires a company to undertake an analysis of its own capabilities and strengths to identify what it can do better than the competition. It also means that a company must carefully assess the competitive environment and the national and international business environments in which it operates.

A well-defined strategy helps a company to compete effectively in increasingly competitive international markets. It serves to coordinate a company's various divisions and departments so that it reaches its company-wide goals in the most effective and efficient manner possible. A clear, appropriate strategy focuses a company on the activities that it performs best and on the industries for which it is best suited and keeps it away from a future of mediocre performance or total failure. An inappropriate strategy can lead managers to take actions that cause internal tensions and pull a company in opposite directions, or take the firm into industries about which they know very little.

We begin this chapter by exploring important factors that managers consider when analyzing their companies' strengths and weaknesses. We examine the different international strategies and the corporate-, business-, and department-level strategies that companies use. Finally, we explore the different types of organizational structures that companies use to coordinate their international activities.

International Strategy

Many of the concerns facing managers when formulating a strategy are the same for both domestic and international companies. Firms must determine what products to produce, where to produce them, and where and how to market them. The biggest difference lies in complexity. Companies considering international production need to select from perhaps many potential countries, each likely having more than one possible location. Depending on its product line, a company that wants to market internationally might have an equally large number of markets to consider. Whether it is being considered as a site for operations or as a potential market, each international location has a rich mixture of cultural, political, legal, and economic traditions and processes. All these factors add to the complexity of planning and strategy for international managers.

Strategy Formulation

The strategy-formulation process involves both planning and strategy. Strategy formulation permits managers to step back from day-to-day activities and get a fresh perspective on the current and future direction of the company and its industry. As shown in Figure 11.1, this procedure can be regarded as a three-stage process. Let's now examine several important factors to consider in each stage of this process.

Identify Company Mission and Goals

mission statement
Written statement of why a company exists and what it plans to accomplish.

Most companies have a general purpose for why they exist that they express in a **mission statement**—a written statement of why a company exists and what it plans to

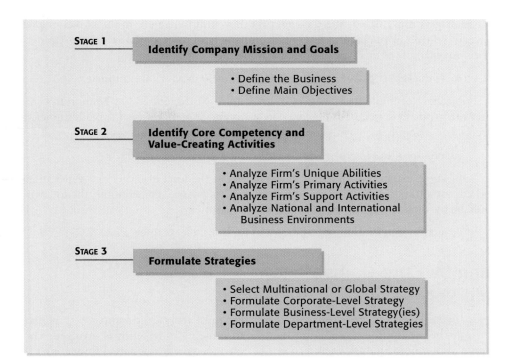

FIGURE 11.1

Strategy-Formulation Process

accomplish. For example, one company might set out to supply the highest level of service in a *market segment*—a clearly identifiable group of potential buyers. Another might be determined to be the lowest-cost supplier in its segment worldwide. The mission statement often guides decisions such as which industries to enter or exit and how to compete in chosen segments.

Types of Mission Statements

Mission statements often spell out how a company's operations affect its **stakeholders**—all parties, ranging from suppliers and employees to stockholders and consumers, who are affected by a company's activities. For instance, some statements focus on the interests of consumers. Thus global eye-care company Bausch & Lomb (*www.bausch.com*) includes the customer in its statement of its goals and activities:

> As a global eye care company, we will help consumers see, look and feel better through innovative technology and design.[2]

stakeholders
All parties, ranging from suppliers and employees to stockholders and consumers, who are affected by a company's activities.

Other companies issue very broad mission statements that recognize all their stakeholders. Britain's Cadbury Schweppes (*www.cadburyschweppes.com*) is a global company whose businesses in over 200 countries are beverages and confectionery (candies). Although most products in the confectionery group carry the Cadbury name, its beverage group includes well-known brands such as 7-Up, Dr. Pepper, Crush, and Mott's. The firm's mission statement reads as follows:

> Our task is to build on our traditions of quality and value to provide brands, products, financial results and management performance that meet the interests of our shareholders, consumers, employees, customers, suppliers and the communities in which we operate.[3]

Thus, the mission statement of an international business depends on (among other things) the type of business it is in, the stakeholders it is trying most to satisfy, and the aspect of the business that is most important to achieving its goals. However, companies must be sensitive to the needs of its different stakeholders in different nations. For instance, the need of a company's stockholders in one nation for financial returns must be balanced against the needs of buyers in another country or the public at large where it has production facilities. That is why a company cannot be irresponsible in its duties for proper waste disposal activities or excessive noise levels near residential areas, for example.

Managers must also define the *objectives* they wish to achieve in the global marketplace. Objectives at the highest level in a company tend to be stated in the most general terms. An example of this type of objective would be:

> To be the largest global company in each industry in which we compete.

Objectives of individual business units in an organization tend to be more specific. They are normally stated in more concrete terms and sometimes even contain numerical targets. For example, such a mission statement could be stated as follows:

> To mass-produce a zero-pollution emissions automobile by 2008.

Objectives usually become even more precise at the level of individual departments and almost always contain numerical targets of performance. For example, the following could be the objective of a marketing and sales department:

> To increase market share by 5 percent in each of the next three years.

Identify Core Competency and Value-Creating Activities

Before managers formulate effective strategies, they must analyze the company, its industry (or industries), and the national business environments in which it is involved. They should also examine industries and countries being targeted for potential future entry. In this section we address the company and its industries. We examine the business environment in the next section.

Unique Abilities of Companies

core competency
Special ability of a company that competitors find extremely difficult or impossible to equal.

Although large multinational companies are often involved in multiple industries, most perform one activity (or a few activities) better than any competitor does. A **core competency** is a special ability of a company that competitors find extremely difficult or impossible to equal. It is not a skill; individuals possess skills. An architect's ability to design an office building in the Victorian style is a skill. A core competency refers to multiple skills that are coordinated to form a single technological outcome.

Although skills can be learned through on-the-job training and personal experience, core competencies develop over longer periods of time and are difficult to teach. For example, at one point Canon of Japan (*www.canon.com*) purchased expertise in optic technology. However, only later did Canon succeed in developing a variety of products based on optic technology—cameras, copiers, and semiconductor lithographic equipment. Canon needed to possess the ability to create such products itself, before it could claim a legitimate core competency.[4] Likewise, Sony's (*www.sony.com*) core competency in miniaturizing electronic components fortifies its global leadership position in consumer electronics.

How do managers actually go about analyzing and identifying their firms' unique abilities? Let's take a look at a tool commonly used by managers to analyze their companies—*value-chain analysis*.

Value-Chain Analysis

value-chain analysis
Process of dividing a company's activities into primary and support activities and identifying those that create value for customers.

Managers must select strategies consistent with both their company's particular strengths and the market conditions faced by their firm. Managers should also select company strategies based on what the company does that customers find valuable. This is why managers conduct a **value-chain analysis**—the process of dividing a company's activities into primary and support activities and identifying those that create value for customers.[5] As you can see from Figure 11.2, value-chain analysis divides a company's activities into primary activities and support activities that are central to creating customer value. *Primary activities* include inbound and outbound logistics, manufacturing (or operations), marketing and sales, and customer service. Primary activities involve the physical creation of the product, its marketing and delivery to buyers, and its after-sales support and service. *Support activities* include firm infrastructure, human resource management, technology development, and procurement. Each of these activities provides the inputs and infrastructure required by the primary activities.

FIGURE 11.2

Components of a Company's Value Chain

Each primary and support activity is a source of strength or weakness for a company. Managers determine whether each activity enhances or detracts from customer value and incorporate this knowledge into the strategy-formulation process. Analysis of primary and support activities often involves finding activities in which improvements can be made with large benefits. Let's take a look at how managers determine whether an activity enhances customer value.

Primary Activities   When analyzing primary activities, managers often look for areas in which the company can increase the value provided to its customers. For instance, managers might examine production processes and discover new, more efficient manufacturing methods to reduce production costs and improve quality. Customer satisfaction might be increased by improving logistics management that shortens the time it takes to get a product to the buyer or by providing better customer service.

Companies might also lower costs by introducing greater automation into the production process. For example, computer maker Acer (*www.acer.com*) applied a fast-food production model to personal computer manufacturing. Rather than manufacture complete computers in Asia and ship them around the world, Acer first builds components at plants scattered throughout the world. Those components are then shipped to assembly plants, where computers are built according to customer specifications. Acer followed this approach because there was no longer any value added in simply assembling computers. So, by altering its production and logistics processes, Acer created a business model that created value for customers.

Support Activities   Support activities assist companies in performing their primary activities. For example, the actions of any company's employees are crucial to its success. Manufacturing, logistics, marketing and sales, and customer service all benefit when employees are qualified and well trained. International companies can often improve the quality of their product by investing in worker training and management development. In turn, ensuring quality can increase the efficiency of a firm's manufacturing, marketing and sales, and customer service activities. Effective procurement can locate low-cost, high-quality raw materials or intermediate products and ensure on-time delivery to production facilities. Finally, a sophisticated infrastructure not only improves internal communication but also supports organizational culture and each primary activity.

Thus, the in-depth analysis of a company inherent in the strategy-formulation process helps managers to discover their company's unique core competency and abilities and the activities that create customer value. For some guidelines on how small companies can perform a self-analysis, see the Entrepreneur's Survival Kit titled, "Know Yourself, Know Your Product."

Going international is the most popular blueprint today for company growth. But if the blueprint is flawed, if the foundation isn't stable, if the materials aren't first class, international expansion could prove to be the tremor that takes down the temple. Here are some factors any small business should consider to be successful abroad.

⟳ **Are you ready to go international?** Consider how long your company has been in business and whether it is stable enough to brave the rough international seas. Assess whether your product must be adapted for international markets and whether you can adapt successfully. Determine whether the expected sales volume abroad is worth the effort. Are you a success at home? Potential international partners will be more eager to partner with a company that is doing very well in its domestic market.

⟳ **Have a thorough understanding of your product.** You must know how to capitalize on your product's strengths, minimize its weaknesses, correct its flaws, and modify it for other markets—or not modify it as the case may be. Beverly Hills Polo Club (BHPC) (*www.bhpc.com*) licenses its trademark in more than 75 countries. "We export the concept of America," says Don Garrison, vice president of international marketing for BHPC. "That's difficult to define sometimes, but there's a certain identification with Beverly Hills and Southern California that people around the world find very appealing." The company understands that to modify its product or what it represents would gut it of its essence.

⟳ **Examine your company's internal activities.** Does your company have the infrastructure to take the com-

pany international? The effort will require a great deal of managerial and financial resources to tackle the job. Check that each department—procurement, production, marketing and sales, credit and collections, and so on—can devote the resources needed to the new international activities. The financial investment will be great, but early profits will be slim to none. Be certain that international activities will not overly burden the company's domestic business in the near- to mid-term. Also, make sure that everyone—from the CEO to the shipping room clerk—appreciates the commitment needed and the role each will play.

⟳ **Ask important questions about strategy.** Does your company have an overall strategy into which your international business will fit? Have you developed a separate international strategy? Is it one that can successfully complement your domestic strategy? The answers to these questions reflect what you want to gain from going international, how quickly you want to achieve profits, and how long-term your commitment is. The question of strategy development is also vital to building on your success.

⟳ **Finally, create the strategic plan.** Create a written strategic plan for your international ambitions. Include the commitment in time and money that you are willing to make and the resources you have available. Be certain of what resources you *can* devote to your international effort and what resources you *should* devote to it. They may well not be the same. Determine what kind of international partners you *want* to attract and what kind of international partners you *will* attract. These also may not be the same.

A company cannot identify its unique abilities in a vacuum, separate from the environment in which it operates. The external business environment consists of all the elements outside a company that can affect its performance, such as cultural, political, legal, and economic forces; workers' unions; consumers; and financial institutions. Let's now explore some of the main environmental forces that have an impact on strategy formulation.

National and International Business Environments National differences in language, religious beliefs, customs, traditions, and climate complicate strategy formulation. For example, language differences can increase the cost of operations and administration. Manufacturing processes must sometimes be adapted to the supply of local workers and to local customs, traditions, and practices. Marketing activities sometimes can result in costly mistakes if they do not incorporate cultural differences. For instance, a company once decided to sell its laundry detergent in Japan but did not adjust the size of the box in which it was sold. The company spent millions of dollars developing a detailed marketing campaign and was shocked when it experienced disappointing sales. It turns out that the company should have packaged the detergent in smaller containers for the Japanese market.

Japanese shoppers prefer smaller quantities because they tend to walk home from the store and have smaller storage areas in tight living quarters.[6]

Differences in political and legal systems also complicate international strategies. Legal and political processes often differ in target countries to such an extent that firms must hire outside consultants to teach them about the local system. Such knowledge is important to international companies because the approval of the host government is almost always necessary for making direct investments. Companies need to know which ministry or department has the authority to grant approval for a big business deal—a process that can become extremely cumbersome. For example, non-Chinese companies in China must often get approval from several agencies, and the process is further complicated by the tendency of local government officials to interpret laws differently than do bureaucrats in Beijing (the nation's capital).

Different national economic systems further complicate strategy formulation. Negative attitudes of local people toward the impact of direct investment can generate political unrest. Economic philosophy affects the tax rates that governments impose. Whereas socialist economic systems normally levy high taxes on business profits, free-market economies tend to levy lighter taxes. The need to work in more than one currency also complicates international strategy. To minimize losses from currency fluctuations, companies must develop strategies to deal with exchange-rate risk.

Finally, apart from complicating strategy, the national business environment can affect the location in which a company chooses to perform an activity. For instance, a nation that spends a high portion of its GDP on research and development attracts high-tech industries and high-wage jobs and, as a result, prospers. In contrast, countries that spend relatively little in the way of R&D tend to have lower levels of prosperity.

Quick Study

1. What are the three stages of the strategy-formulation process? Describe what is involved at each stage.

2. Define what is meant by the term *core competency*. How does it differ from a skill?

3. What is *value-chain analysis*? Explain the difference between primary and secondary activities.

4. How do national and international business environments influence strategy formulation?

Formulate Strategies

As we've already seen, the strengths and special capabilities of international companies, along with the environmental forces they face, play a large role in the type of strategy that managers choose. Let's now examine this final stage in the planning and strategy-formulation process—formulating strategies.

Two International Strategies   Companies engaged in international business activities can approach the market using either a *multinational* or a *global* strategy. It is important to note that these two strategies do not include companies that export. Exporters do not have foreign direct investments in other national markets and should instead devise an appropriate export strategy (see Chapter 13). Let's now examine what it means for a company to follow a multinational or a global strategy.

Multinational Strategy   Some international companies choose to follow a **multinational (multidomestic) strategy**—a strategy of adapting products and their marketing strategies in each national market to suit local preferences. In other words, a multinational strategy is just what its name implies—a separate strategy for each of the multiple nations in which a company markets its products. To implement a multinational strategy, companies often establish largely independent, self-contained units (or subsidiaries) in each national market. Typically, each subsidiary undertakes its own product research and development, production, and marketing. In many ways, each unit functions largely as an independent company.

multinational (multidomestic) strategy
Adapting products and their marketing strategies in each national market to suit local preferences.

Multinational strategies are often appropriate for companies in industries in which buyer preferences do not converge across national borders, such as certain food products and some print media.

The main benefit of a multinational strategy is that it allows companies to monitor buyer preferences closely in each local market and to respond quickly and effectively as new buyer preferences emerge. The result that companies hope for when offering a tailored product is that customers will perceive it as delivering greater value than do competitors' products, allowing a company using a multinational strategy to charge higher prices and/or gain market share.

The main drawback of a multinational strategy is that it does not allow companies to exploit scale economies in product development, manufacturing, or marketing. Thus, a multinational strategy typically increases the cost structure for international companies and forces them to charge higher prices to recover such costs. As such, a multinational strategy is usually poorly suited to industries in which price competitiveness is a key success factor. Furthermore, the high degree of independence with which each unit operates can reduce opportunities for sharing knowledge between units within a company.

global strategy
Offering the same products using the same marketing strategy in all national markets.

Global Strategy   Other companies decide that what suits their operations is a **global strategy**—a strategy of offering the same products using the same marketing strategy in all national markets. Companies that follow a global strategy often take advantage of scale and location economies by producing entire inventories of products or components in a few optimal locations. They also tend to perform product research and development in one or a few locations and typically design promotional campaigns and advertising strategies at headquarters. So-called global products are most common in industries characterized by price competition and, therefore, pressure to contain costs. They include certain electronic components, a wide variety of industrial goods such as steel, and some consumer goods such as paper and writing instruments.

The main benefit of a global strategy is its cost savings due to product and marketing standardization. These cost savings can then be passed on to consumers to help the company gain market share in its market segment. A global strategy also allows managers to share lessons learned in one market with managers at other locations.

The main problem with a global strategy is that it may cause a company to overlook important differences in buyer preferences from one market to another. A global strategy does not allow a company to modify its products except for the most superficial features, such as the color of paint applied to a finished product or small add-on features. This can present an opportunity for a competitor to step in and satisfy unmet needs that local buyers might have, thereby creating a niche market.

In addition to deciding whether the company will follow a multinational or a global strategy, managers must formulate strategies for the corporation, each business unit, and each department. Let's now explore the three different levels of company strategy shown in Figure 11.3: *corporate-, business-,* and *department-level* strategies.

Corporate-Level Strategies

Companies involved in more than one line of business must first formulate a *corporate-level strategy*. In part, this means identifying the national markets and industries in which the company will operate. It also involves developing overall objectives for the company's different business units and specifying the role that each unit will play in reaching those objectives. The four key approaches to corporate strategy are *growth, retrenchment, stability,* and *combination.*

growth strategy
Strategy designed to increase the scale (size of activities) or scope (kinds of activities) of a corporation's operations.

Growth Strategy   A **growth strategy** is designed to increase the scale or scope of a corporation's operations. *Scale* refers to the *size* of a corporation's activities, *scope* to the *kinds* of activities it performs. Yardsticks commonly used to measure growth include geographic coverage, number of business units, market share, sales revenue, and number of employees. *Organic growth* refers to a corporate strategy of relying on internally generated growth. For example, management at 3M (*www.3m.com*) strongly encourages entrepreneurial activity, often spinning off business units to nurture the best ideas and carry them to completion. Microsoft (*www.microsoft.com*), too, generates much of its growth organically, especially through the effective use of work teams.

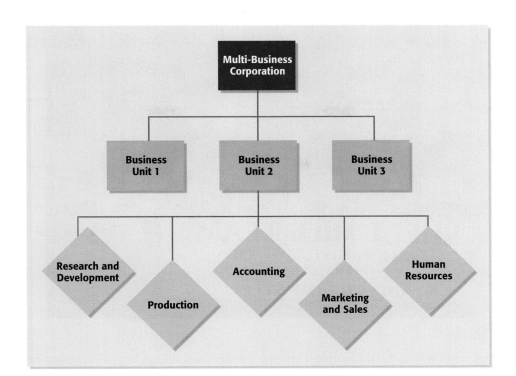

FIGURE 11.3

Three Levels of Company Strategy

Other methods of growth include mergers and acquisitions, joint ventures, and strategic alliances (see Chapter 13). These tactics are used when companies do not wish to invest in developing certain skills internally or when other companies already do what managers are trying to achieve. Common partners in implementing these strategies include competitors, suppliers, and buyers. Corporations typically join forces with competitors to reduce competition, expand product lines, or expand geographically. A common motivation for joining forces with suppliers is to increase control over the quality, cost, and timing of inputs.

One corporation undertaking an aggressive global growth strategy is Intel (*www.intel.com*). Intel's goal is "to be the preeminent building block supplier to the worldwide Internet economy." Intel manufactures computer components (the "building blocks" of computing systems), including microprocessors, chipsets, motherboards, memory units, and software. It provides these components to manufacturers in the computer, automobile, and mobile-phone industries. Intel's growth strategy focuses not only on delivering "the high-performance processors that drive today's connected PCs and related products," but working "with other industry leaders to expand the PC's role as a consumer and business communications device, driving future PC sales."[7] Central to Intel's accomplishing its growth strategy are the huge potential in large emerging markets such as China and Brazil, and the increasing penetration of the World Wide Web there.

Retrenchment Strategy   The exact opposite of a growth strategy is a **retrenchment strategy**—a strategy designed to reduce the scale or scope of a corporation's businesses. Corporations often cut back the *scale* of their operations when economic conditions worsen or competition increases. They may do so by closing factories with unused capacity and laying off workers. Corporations can also reduce the scale of their operations by laying off managers and salespeople in national markets that are not generating adequate sales revenue. Corporations reduce the *scope* of their activities by selling unprofitable business units or those no longer directly related to their overall aims. Weaker competitors often resort to retrenchment when national business environments grow more competitive.

retrenchment strategy
Strategy designed to reduce the scale or scope of a corporation's businesses.

Stability Strategy   A **stability strategy** is designed to guard against change. Corporations often use a stability strategy when trying to avoid either growth or retrenchment. Typically such corporations have met their stated objectives or are satisfied with what they have already accomplished. They believe that their strengths are being fully exploited and their

stability strategy
Strategy designed to guard against change and used by corporations to avoid either growth or retrenchment.

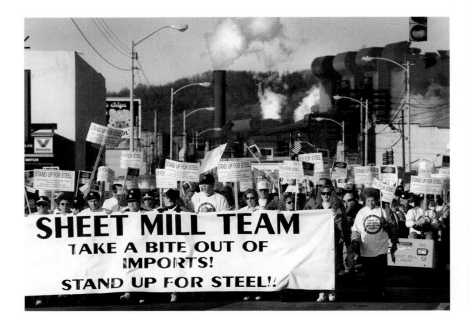

Retrenchment is often a painful strategy. Here workers protest at the Weirton Steel mill in Weirton, West Virginia. In the late 1990s, a rising tide of imported steel depressed U.S. steel prices by as much as 20 percent. Then, in 2002, the United States imposed up to 30 percent tariffs on imported steel to give the industry time to restructure. But Weirton Steel filed for bankruptcy in 2003 and was purchased by International Steel Group (www.intlsteel.com) in 2004. Can you think of other companies and industries that have undergone similar retrenchments and consolidations?

weaknesses fully protected against. They also see the business environment as posing neither profitable opportunities nor threats. They have no interest in expanding sales, increasing profits, increasing market share, or expanding the customer base; at present, they want simply to maintain their present positions.

combination strategy
Strategy designed to mix growth, retrenchment, and stability strategies across a corporation's business units.

Combination Strategy The purpose of a **combination strategy** is to mix growth, retrenchment, and stability strategies across a corporation's business units. For example, a corporation can invest in units that show promise, retrench in those for which less exposure is desired, and stabilize others. In fact, corporate combination strategies are quite common because international corporations rarely follow identical strategies in each of their business units.

Business-Level Strategies In addition to stipulating the overall corporate strategy, managers must also formulate separate *business-level strategies* for each business unit. For some companies, this means creating just one strategy. This is the case when the business-level strategy and the corporate-level strategy are one and the same because the corporation is involved in just one line of business.

For other companies, this means creating anywhere from two to dozens of strategies. For example, as we saw earlier in this chapter, Cadbury Schweppes (*www.cadburyschweppes. com*) of Britain has two main business units—beverages and confectionery—each with its own strategy. The strategy of the beverages business unit is to "strengthen our soft drink's position worldwide and to be the largest and most successful non-cola brand owner." For the confectionery unit, strategy is "based on building viable positions in prioritised markets through organic growth and acquisitions."[8] Thus, the beverages unit is focused on strengthening the position of its existing soft drink products, but the confectionery unit is attempting to create new products in promising markets through internal growth and by acquiring other firms.

The key to developing an effective business-level strategy is deciding on a *general competitive strategy in the marketplace*. Each business unit must decide whether to sell the lowest-priced product in an industry or to integrate special attributes into its products. As you can see in Figure 11.4, a business unit can use one of three generic business-level strategies for competing in its industry—*low-cost leadership, differentiation*, or *focus*.[9] Let's now explore each of these strategies in detail.

low-cost leadership strategy
Strategy in which a company exploits economies of scale to have the lowest cost structure of any competitor in its industry.

Low-Cost Leadership Strategy A strategy in which a company exploits economies of scale to have the lowest cost structure of any competitor in its industry is called a **low-cost leadership strategy**. Companies that pursue the low-cost leadership position also try to contain administrative costs and the costs of their various primary activities, including marketing, advertising, and distribution. We saw in this chapter's opening company

FIGURE 11.4

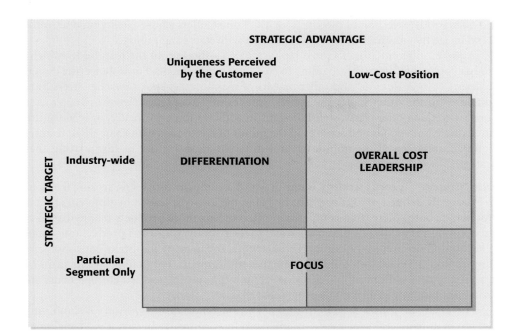

profile how Ryanair engages in aggressive cost cutting to be Europe's leading low-cost airline. Although cutting costs is the mantra for firms that pursue a low-cost leadership position, other important competitive factors such as product quality and customer service cannot be ignored. Factors underlying the low-cost leadership position (efficient production in large quantities) help guard against attack by competitors because of the large up-front cost of getting started. Also, because achieving low-cost leadership tends to rely on large-scale production to contain costs, the strategy typically requires the company to have a large market share. One negative aspect of the low-cost leadership strategy is low customer loyalty—all else equal, buyers will purchase from the low-cost leader regardless of who it is.

A low-cost leadership strategy works best with mass-marketed products aimed at price-sensitive buyers. This strategy is often well suited to companies with a standardized product and marketing promotions. Two global companies vying for the low-cost leadership position in their respective industries include Casio (*www.casio.com*) in sports watches and Texas Instruments (*www.ti.com*) in calculators and other electronic devices.

Differentiation Strategy A **differentiation strategy** is one in which a company designs its products to be perceived as unique by buyers throughout its industry. Because its buyers perceive the product as unique, a company that follows a differentiation strategy can charge a higher price and enjoys greater customer loyalty than does the low-cost leader. A differentiation strategy tends to force a company into a lower-market-share position because it generally involves the perception of exclusivity or as meeting the needs of only a certain group of buyers. Companies that use this strategy must develop loyal customer bases to offset smaller market shares and the higher costs of producing and marketing a unique product.

One way products can be differentiated is by improving their reputation for *quality*. Ceramic tableware for everyday use is found at department stores in almost every country. However, the ceramic tableware made by Japanese producer Noritake (*www.noritake.com*) differentiates itself from common tableware by emphasizing its superior quality. The perception of higher quality allows manufacturers to charge higher prices for their products worldwide.

Other products are differentiated by distinctive *brand images*. IZOD (*www.izod.com*) and Calvin Klein, for example, are relatively pricey global clothiers appealing to a young, fashionable clientele. Each is continually introducing new textures and colors that are at once stylish and functional. Another example is Italian carmaker Alfa Romeo (*www.alfaromeo.com*), which does not compete in the fiercely competitive mass-consumer segment of the global automobile industry. To do so, it would have to be price-competitive

differentiation strategy
Strategy in which a company designs its products to be perceived as unique by buyers throughout its industry.

and offer a wider selection of cars. Instead, Alfa Romeo offers a high-quality product with a brand image that rewards the Alfa Romeo owner with status and prestige.

Another differentiating factor is *product design*—the sum of the features by which a product looks and functions according to customer requirements. For instance, the designs of Casio (*www.casio.com*) and other makers of mass-market sports watches stress functionality. On the other hand, the sports watches of TAG Heuer (*www.tagheuer.com*) from Switzerland offer classy, stylish designs in addition to performance. Special features differentiate both goods and services in the minds of consumers who value those features. Manufacturers can also combine several differentiation factors in formulating their strategies.

focus strategy
Strategy in which a company focuses on serving the needs of a narrowly defined market segment by being the low-cost leader, by differentiating its product, or both.

Focus Strategy A **focus strategy** is one in which a company focuses on serving the needs of a narrowly defined market segment by being the low-cost leader, by differentiating its product, or both. Increasing competition often means more products distinguished by price or differentiated by quality, design, and so forth. In turn, a greater product range leads to the continuous refinement of market segments. Today many industries consist of large numbers of market segments and even smaller subsegments. For example, some firms try to serve the needs of one ethnic or racial group, whereas others, often entrepreneurs and small businesses, focus on a single geographic area.

For instance, Johnson & Johnson (*www.johnsonandjohnson.com*) is commonly thought of as being a single, large consumer-products company. In fact, it is a conglomerate consisting of more than 160 separately chartered companies that market an enormous variety of products to a wide array of market segments. Many of these individual J&J companies try to dominate their segments by producing specialty goods and services. In so doing, they focus on narrow segments using either low-cost leadership or differentiation techniques.

A focus strategy often means designing products and promotions aimed at consumers who are either dissatisfied with existing choices or who want something distinctive. Consider the highly fragmented gourmet coffee market. One brand of coffee called Luwak sells for around *$300 per pound!* Certainly the coffee is made from distinctive beans. Apparently, luwaks (weasels on the Indonesian island of Java) eat coffee berries containing coffee beans. The beans "naturally ferment" as they pass through the luwaks and are recovered from the animals' waste. The beans are then washed, roasted, and sold around the world as a specialty coffee (and they certainly have a "distinctive" taste).[10]

The strategies we've discussed here can be applied to practically all firms in all markets worldwide. However, companies in emerging markets often face special problems. See the Global Manager's Toolbox titled, "Competing with Giants" to see how domestic companies in emerging markets can survive the onslaught by the major multinational companies.

Department-Level Strategies

Achieving corporate- and business-level objectives depends on effective departmental strategies that focus on the specific activities that transform resources into products. Formulation of *department-level strategies* brings us back to where we began our analysis of a company's capabilities that support its strategy—to the primary and support activities that create value for customers. After managers analyze these activities, they must then develop strategies that exploit their firm's value-creating strengths.

Primary and Support Activities Each department is instrumental in creating customer value through lower costs or differentiated products. This is especially true of departments that conduct *primary activities*. Manufacturing strategies are obviously important in cutting the production costs of both standardized and differentiated products. They are also crucial to improving product quality. Effective marketing strategies allow companies to promote the differences in their products. A strong sales force and good customer service contribute to favorable images among consumers or industrial buyers and generate loyal customers of both kinds. Efficient logistics in bringing raw materials and components into the factory and getting the finished product out the factory door can result in substantial cost savings.

Support activities also create customer value. For example, research and development identifies market segments with unsatisfied needs and designs products to meet them.

Industries differ in the degree to which they are global—some, such as semiconductors or aircraft, are highly global, but others, such as retail banking, are not. However, most industries lie somewhere in between. Also, some emerging-market companies have a competitive edge that is germane to the local market, such as an extensive, strong distribution network. Others have a competitive advantage that is transferable to other markets, such as expertise in building efficient factories. By analyzing these two facets—industry globalization and asset transferability—emerging-market companies can choose one of four strategies to combat multinational giants.

○ **Defender.** If globalization pressures are weak, and a company's own assets are not transferable, the company needs to concentrate on defending its home turf. For instance, when India opened its automotive sector to international competitors in the mid-1980s, the country's largest domestic manufacturer of motor scooters, Bajaj Auto (*www.bajajauto.com*), was petrified. Honda (*www.honda.com*) soon burst onto the scene with superior technology, quality, and brand appeal. But Bajaj beefed up its distribution and service network and improved the design of its low-cost, rugged scooters. In the fall of 1998, Honda announced it was pulling out of its scooter-manufacturing venture in India.

○ **Extender.** If globalization pressures are weak, but a company's assets can be transferred abroad, the company may be able to extend its success to a limited number of other markets. For example, when McDonald's (*www.mcdonalds.com*) entered the Philippines, local fast-food company Jollibee Foods (*www.jollibee.com/ph*) upgraded its service and developed rival menus customized to local tastes. Using its battle-tested recipes from home, Jollibee established dozens of restaurants in markets with large Filipino populations, including Hong Kong, the Middle East, and California.

○ **Dodger.** If globalization pressures are strong, but a company's assets are not transferable, the company will need to dodge its larger rivals by restructuring itself around links in the value chain that buyers value. When Russia liberalized its economy, Russian personal-computer maker Vist (*www.vist.ru*) side-stepped oblivion by redefining its core business. When the big guns such as IBM (*www.ibm.com*) came in with superior PCs, Vist focused on its strengths—distribution, service, and warranties. Although Vist's computers are unremarkable, all its manuals are in Russian and the company provides lengthy warranties—unlike its multinational rivals, which charge a fee for an extended service contract. Vist is the leading brand of PCs in Russia, with 20 percent of the market.

○ **Contender.** If globalization pressures are strong, and a company's assets can be transferred abroad, the company may be able to compete head-to-head with its multinational rivals in world markets. For instance, when General Motors (*www.gm.com*) decided to purchase radiator caps for its North American autos rather than make them itself, Sundaram Fasteners (*www.sundaram.com*) of India bought an entire GM production line and shipped it home. One year later Sundaram was GM's sole North American supplier of five million radiator caps per year. What Sundaram learned as GM's supplier benefited its core fastener business and allowed the company to target markets in Japan and Europe. Sundaram is now capable of supplying markets worldwide.

Human resource managers can improve efficiency and cut costs by hiring well-trained employees and conducting worker training and management-development programs. Procurement tasks provide operations with quality resources at a reasonable cost. Accounting and finance (elements of a firm's infrastructure) must develop efficient information systems to assist managers in making decisions and maintaining financial control, thus having an impact on costs and quality in general.

There are important elements that drive the decisions of world-class companies with regard to strategy formulation. For example, the important *production* issues to consider are the number and dispersion of production facilities and whether to standardize production processes for all markets. The important *marketing* issue is whether to standardize either the physical features of products, or their marketing strategies, across markets. We will present the strategic considerations of production and marketing activities in later chapters.

1. Compare and contrast *multinational strategy* and *global strategy*. When is each strategy appropriate?

2. What are the four corporate-level strategies? Identify the main characteristics of each.

3. Identify the three business-level strategies. Describe how each strategy differs from the other two.

4. Explain the importance of department-level strategies. How do primary and support activities help a firm achieve its goals?

International Organizational Structure

organizational structure
Way in which a company divides its activities among separate units and coordinates activities between those units.

Organizational structure is the way in which a company divides its activities among separate units and coordinates activities between those units. If a company's organizational structure is appropriate for its strategic plans, it will be more effective in working toward its goals. In this section, we explore several important issues related to organizational structures and examine several alternative forms that an organization's structure can take.

Centralization Versus Decentralization

Managers must determine the degree to which decision making in the organization will be centralized or decentralized. *Centralized decision making* is when decision making is centralized at a high level in one location, such as headquarters. *Decentralized decision making* is when decisions are made at lower levels, such as in international subsidiaries.

Should managers at the parent company be actively involved in the decisions made by international subsidiaries? Or should they intervene relatively little, perhaps only in the most crucial decisions? Some decisions, of course, must be decentralized. If top managers involve themselves in the day-to-day decisions of every subsidiary, they are likely to be overwhelmed. For example, they cannot get directly involved in every hiring decision or assignment of people to specific tasks at each facility. On the other hand, overall corporate strategy cannot be delegated to subsidiary managers. Only top management has the appropriate perspective to formulate corporate strategy.

In our discussion of centralization versus decentralization of decision making, it is important to remember two points:

1. Companies rarely centralize or decentralize all decision making. Rather, they seek the approach that will result in the greatest efficiency and effectiveness.

2. International companies may centralize decision making in certain geographic markets while decentralizing it in others. Numerous factors influence this decision, including the need for product modification and the abilities of managers at each location.

With these points in mind, let's take a look at some of the specific factors that determine whether centralized or decentralized decision making is most appropriate.

When to Centralize   Centralized decision making helps to coordinate the operations of international subsidiaries. This fact is important for companies that operate in multiple lines of business or in many international markets. It is also important when one subsidiary's output is another's input. In such situations, coordinating operations from a single, high-level vantage point is more efficient. Purchasing is often centralized if all subsidiaries use the same inputs in production. For example, a company that manufactures steel filing cabinets and desks will need a great deal of sheet steel. A central purchasing department will get a better bulk price on sheet steel than would subsidiaries negotiating their own agreements. Each subsidiary then benefits by being able to purchase sheet steel from central purchasing at a lower cost than it would pay in the open market.

Some companies maintain strong central control over financial resources by channeling all subsidiary profits back to the parent for redistribution to subsidiaries based on their needs. This practice reduces the likelihood that certain subsidiaries will undertake investment projects when more promising projects go without funding at other locations. Other companies centrally design policies, procedures, and standards in order to stimulate a single global organizational culture. This policy makes it more likely that all subsidiaries will enforce company rules uniformly. It is also beneficial when companies transfer managers from one location to another. If policies are uniform, the transition proceeds more smoothly for both managers and subordinates.

When to Decentralize   Decentralized decision making is beneficial when fast-changing national business environments put a premium on local responsiveness. Because subsidiary managers are in closer contact with local culture, politics, laws, and economies, decentralized decisions can result in products that are better suited to the needs and preferences of local buyers. Local managers are more likely to perceive environmental changes that managers at headquarters would not notice. Even if central managers did perceive such changes, they are likely to get a secondhand account of local events. Delayed response and misinterpreted events can result in lost orders, stalled production, and weakened competitiveness. Similarly, decentralized decision making can save money because informed decisions can be made without flying executives around the world on fact-finding missions.

Participative Management and Accountability   Decentralization can also help to foster participative management practices. The morale of employees is likely to be higher if subsidiary managers and subordinates are involved in decision making. When delegated to subsidiaries, decisions related to national strategy—including production, promotion, distribution, and pricing decisions—can generate greater commitment from both managers and workers.

Decentralization often improves personal accountability for business decisions. When local managers are rewarded (or punished) for their decisions, they are likely to invest more effort in making and executing them. Conversely, if local managers must do nothing but implement policies dictated from above, they can attribute poor performance to decisions that were ill-suited to the local environment. When managers are held accountable for decision making and implementation, they typically delve more deeply into research and debate and consider all available options. The results are often better decisions and improved performance.

Coordination and Flexibility

When designing organizational structure, managers seek answers to certain key questions. What is the most efficient method of linking divisions to one another? Who should coordinate the activities of different divisions in order to achieve overall strategies? How should information be processed and delivered to managers when it is required? What sorts of monitoring mechanisms and reward structures should be established? How should the company introduce corrective measures, and whose responsibility should it be to execute them? To answer these types of questions, we must look at the issues of coordination and flexibility.

Structure and Coordination   As we have seen, some companies have a presence in several or more national business environments—they manufacture and market products practically everywhere. Others operate primarily in one country and export to, or import from, other markets. Each type of company must design an appropriate organizational structure. Each needs a structure that clearly defines areas of responsibility and **chains of command**—the lines of authority that run from top management to individual employees and specify internal reporting relationships. Finally, every firm needs a structure that

chains of command
Lines of authority that run from top management to individual employees and specify internal reporting relationships.

brings together areas that require close cooperation. For example, to avoid product designs that make manufacturing more difficult and costly than necessary, most firms ensure that R&D and manufacturing remain in close contact.

Structure and Flexibility   Organizational structure is not permanent—it is often modified to suit changes both within a company and in its external environment. Because companies usually base organizational structures on strategies, changes in strategy usually require adjustments in structure. Similarly, because changes in national business environments can force changes in strategy, the same changes will influence company structure. It is especially important to monitor closely the conditions in countries characterized by rapidly shifting cultural, political, and economic environments. Let's now explore four organizational structures that have been developed to improve the responsiveness and effectiveness of companies conducting international business activities.

Quick Study

1. Explain what is meant by *organizational structure*. What is the difference between centralized and decentralized decision making?
2. Why are coordination and flexibility important when designing organizational structure?
3. Describe what is meant by the term *chains of command*.

Types of Organizational Structure

There are many different ways in which a company can organize itself to carry out its international business activities. But four organizational structures tend to be most common for the vast majority of international companies—*division structure, area structure, product structure*, and *matrix structure*.

International Division Structure   An **international division structure** separates domestic from international business activities by creating a separate international division with its own manager (see Figure 11.5). In turn, the international division is typically divided into units corresponding to the countries in which a company is active—say, China, Indonesia, and Thailand. Within each country, a general manager controls the manufacture and marketing of the firm's products. Each country unit typically carries out

international division structure
Organizational structure that separates domestic from international business activities by creating a separate international division with its own manager.

FIGURE 11.5

International Division Structure

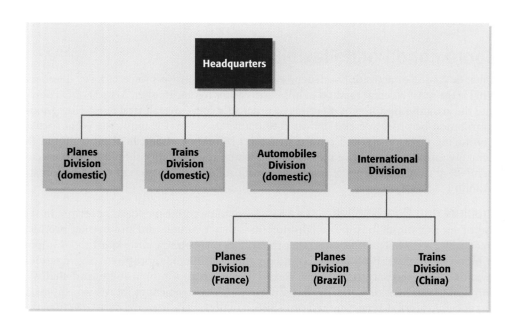

all of its own activities with its own departments such as marketing and sales, finance, and production.

Because the international division structure concentrates international expertise in one division, divisional managers become specialists in a wide variety of activities such as foreign exchange, export documentation, and host-government lobbying. By consigning international activities to a single division, a firm can reduce costs, increase efficiency, and prevent international activities from disrupting domestic operations. These are important criteria for firms that are new to international business and whose international operations account for a small percentage of their total business.

However, an international division structure can also create two problems for companies. First, international managers must often rely on home-country managers for the financial resources and technical know-how that give the company its international competitive edge. Poor coordination between managers can hurt the performance not only of the international division but also of the entire company. Second, the general manager of the international division typically is responsible for operations in all countries. Although this policy facilitates coordination across countries, it reduces the authority of each country manager. Rivalries and poor cooperation between the general manager and country managers can be damaging to the company's overall performance.

International Area Structure

An **international area structure** organizes a company's entire global operations into countries or geographic regions (see Figure 11.6). The greater the number of countries in which a company operates, the greater the likelihood it will organize into regions—say, Asia, Europe, and the Americas—instead of countries. Typically, a general manager is assigned to each country or region. Under this structure, each geographic division operates as a self-contained unit, with most decision making decentralized in the hands of the country or regional managers. Each unit has its own set of departments—purchasing, production, marketing and sales, R&D, and accounting. Each also tends to handle much of its own strategic planning. Management at the parent-company headquarters makes decisions regarding overall corporate strategy and coordinates the activities of various units.

The international area structure is best suited to companies that treat each national or regional market as unique. It is particularly useful when there are vast cultural, political, or economic differences between nations or regions. When they enjoy a great deal of control over activities in their own environments, general managers become experts on the unique needs of their buyers. On the other hand, because units act independently, allocated

international area structure
Organizational structure that organizes a company's entire global operations into countries or geographic regions.

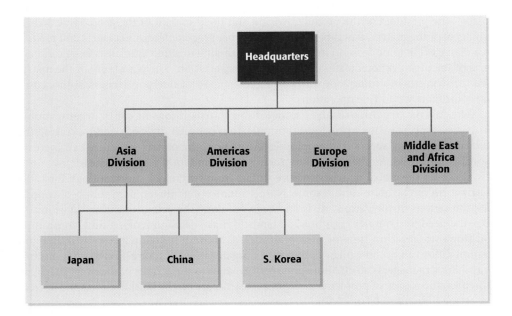

FIGURE 11.6

International Area Structure

FIGURE 11.7

Global Product Structure

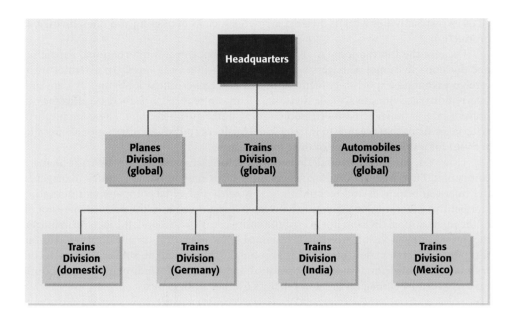

resources may overlap and cross-fertilization of knowledge from one unit to another may be less than desirable.

global product structure
Organizational structure that divides worldwide operations according to a company's product areas.

Global Product Structure

A **global product structure** divides worldwide operations according to a company's product areas (see Figure 11.7). For example, divisions in a computer company might be Internet and Communications, Software Development, and New Technologies. Each product division is then divided into domestic and international units. Each function—R&D, marketing, and so forth—is thus duplicated in both the domestic and international units of each product division.

Because it overcomes some of the coordination problems of the international division structure, the global product structure is suitable for companies that offer diverse sets of products or services. Because the primary focus is on the product, both domestic and international managers for each product division must coordinate their activities so that they do not conflict.

global matrix structure
Organizational structure that splits the chain of command between product and area divisions.

Global Matrix Structure

A **global matrix structure** splits the chain of command between product and area divisions (see Figure 11.8). Each manager reports to two bosses—the president of the product division and the president of the geographic area. A main goal of the matrix structure is to bring together *geographic* area managers and *product* area managers in joint decision making. In fact, bringing together specialists from different parts of the organization creates a sort of team organization. The popularity of the matrix structure has grown among companies trying to increase local responsiveness, reduce costs, and coordinate worldwide operations.

The matrix structure resolves some of the shortcomings of other organizational structures, especially by improving communication between divisions and increasing the efficiency of highly specialized employees. At its best, the matrix structure can increase coordination while simultaneously improving agility and local responsiveness.

However, the global matrix structure suffers from two major shortcomings. First, the matrix form can be quite cumbersome. Numerous meetings are required simply to coordinate the actions of the various division heads, let alone the activities within divisions. In turn, the need for complex coordination tends to make decision making time-consuming and slows the reaction time of the organization. Second, individual responsibility and accountability can become foggy in the matrix organization structure. Because responsibility is shared, managers can attribute poor performance to the actions of the other manager. Moreover, the source of problems in the matrix structure can be hard to detect and corrective action difficult to take.

FIGURE 11.8

There are other ways international companies can improve responsiveness and effectiveness. An increasingly popular method among international companies is the implementation of work teams to accomplish goals and solve problems. In the next section we explore in detail the use of work teams.

Work Teams

Forces of globalization demand that companies respond quickly to changes in all their business environments. The formation of teams can be highly useful in improving responsiveness by cutting across functional boundaries (such as that between production and marketing) that slow decision making in an organization. Although a matrix organization accomplishes this by establishing cross-functional cooperation, companies do not always want to change their entire organizational structure to reap the benefits that cross-functional cooperation provides. In such cases, companies can implement several different types of teams without changing the overall company structure.

Work teams are assigned the tasks of coordinating their efforts to arrive at solutions and implement corrective action. Today international companies are turning to work teams on an unprecedented scale to increase direct contact between different operating units. Apple Computer (*www.apple.com*), Federal Express (*www.fedex.com*), Motorola (*www.motorola.com*), and Volvo (*www.volvo.com*) are just some of the thousands of companies making extensive use of teams. Companies are even forming teams to design and implement their competitive strategies. Let's now take a look at several different types of teams—*self-managed teams, cross-functional teams*, and *global teams*.

Self-Managed Teams

A **self-managed team** is one in which the employees from a single department take on the responsibilities of their former supervisors. When used in production, such teams often reorganize the methods and flow of production processes. Because they are "self-managed," they reduce the need for managers to watch over their every activity. The benefits of self-managed teams typically include increased productivity, product quality, customer satisfaction, employee morale, and company loyalty. In fact, the most common self-managed teams in many manufacturing companies are

self-managed team
Team in which the employees from a single department take on the responsibilities of their former supervisors.

quality-improvement teams, which help reduce waste in the production process and, therefore, costs.

The global trend toward "downsizing" internal operations to make them more flexible and productive has increased the popularity of teams because they reduce the need for direct supervision. Companies around the world now employ self-managed teams in international operations. However, recent research indicates that cultural differences can affect resistance to the concept of self-management and the practice of using teams. Among other things, experts suggest that international managers follow some basic guidelines:[11]

○ Use selection tests to identify the employees most likely to perform well in a team environment.

○ Adapt the self-managed work-team concept to the national culture of each subsidiary.

○ Adapt the process of integrating self-managed work teams to the national culture of each subsidiary.

○ Train local managers at the parent company and allow them to introduce teams when resistance is expected to be great.

Similarly, the cultural differences discussed in Chapter 2 are important to managers who design teams in international operations. For example, certain cultures are less individualist and more collectivist. Some harbor greater respect for differences in status. In others, people tend to believe that the future is largely beyond their personal control, and other cultures reflect a so-called work-to-live mentality. Researchers say that in these cases conventional management should retain fairly tight authority over teams. But in cultures in which people are very hardworking, teams are likely to be productive if given greater autonomy.[12] However, researchers stress that much more study is needed into this aspect of work teams.

Cross-Functional Teams

cross-functional team
Team that is composed of employees who work at similar levels in different functional departments.

A **cross-functional team** is one composed of employees who work at similar levels in different functional departments. They work to develop changes in operations and are well suited to projects that require coordination across functions, such as reducing the time needed to get a product from the idea stage to the marketplace. International companies also use cross-functional teams to improve quality by having employees from purchasing, manufacturing, and distribution (among other functions) work together to address specific quality issues. For the same reason, cross-functional teams can help break down barriers between departments and reorganize operations around processes rather than by functional departments.

Global Teams

global team
Team of top managers from both headquarters and international subsidiaries who meet to develop solutions to company-wide problems.

Finally, some very large international corporations are moving toward so-called **global teams**—groups of top managers from both headquarters and international subsidiaries who meet to develop solutions to company-wide problems. For example, Nortel Networks (*www.nortel.com*) of Canada created a global team of top executives from Britain, Canada, France, and the United States that traveled to Asia, Europe, and North America looking for ways to improve product-development practices.

Depending on the issue at hand, team members can be drawn from a single business unit or assembled from several different units. While some teams are disbanded after resolving specific issues, others move on to new problems. The performance of global teams can be impaired by matters such as large distances between team members, lengthy travel times to meetings, and the inconvenience of working across time zones. Companies can sometimes overcome these difficulties, although doing so can be rather costly.

Quick Study

1. What are the four main types of organizational structure used in international business?
2. Explain how each type of organizational structure differs from the other three.
3. Identify the three different types of work teams. How does each improve responsiveness and effectiveness?

A Final Word

Managers have the important and complicated task of formulating international strategies at the levels of the corporation, business unit, and individual department. Managers often analyze their companies' operations by viewing them as a chain of activities that create customer value (value-chain analysis). It is through this process that managers can identify and implement strategies suited to their companies' unique capabilities. The strategies that managers select then determine the firm's organizational structure. National business environments also affect managers' strategy and structure decisions, including whether to alter their products (standardization versus adaptation), where to locate facilities (centralized versus decentralized production), and what type of decision making to implement (centralized versus decentralized decision making).

The role of managers in formulating strategies and creating the overall organizational structure cannot be overstated. The strategies they choose determine the market segments in which the firm competes and whether it pursues low-cost leadership in its industry or differentiates its product and charges a higher price. These decisions are crucial to all later activities of firms that are going international: they have an impact on how a company will 1) enter international markets, 2) employ its human resources, and 3) manage its day-to-day production, marketing, and other operations.

SUMMARY

1. **Explain the stages of *identification* and *analysis* that precede strategy selection.** The process of identifying and selecting an organization's objectives and deciding how the organization will achieve those objectives is called *planning*. In turn, *strategy* is the set of planned actions taken by managers to help a company meet its objectives.

   As part of the strategy-formulation process, managers must undertake two important steps—*identification* and *analysis*. First, they *identify the company's mission and goals*. A mission statement is a written statement of why a company exists and what it plans to accomplish. Second, they *identify the company's core competency and value-creating activities*. A *core competency* is a special ability of a company that competitors find extremely difficult or impossible to equal.

   Managers can analyze and identify their company's unique abilities that create value for customers by conducting a *value-chain analysis*—a procedure that divides a company's activities into primary activities and support activities that are central to creating value for customers. *Primary activities* include inbound and outbound logistics, manufacturing (or operations), marketing and sales, and customer service. *Support activities* include firm infrastructure, human resource management, technology development, and procurement. Finally, managers must analyze the cultural, political, legal, and economic environments.

2. **Identify the two *international strategies* and the *corporate-level strategies* that companies use.** Some companies choose to follow a *multinational (multidomestic) strategy*—adapting products and their marketing strategies in each national market to suit local preferences. Other companies decide that what suits their operations is a *global strategy*—offering the same products using the same marketing strategy in all national markets.

   Companies involved in more than one line of business must formulate a *corporate-level strategy* that encompasses all of the company's different business units. A *growth strategy* is designed to increase the *scale* (*size* of activities) or *scope* (*kinds* of activities) of a corporation's operations. The exact opposite of a growth strategy is a *retrenchment strategy*, which is designed to reduce the scale or scope of a corporation's businesses. A *stability strategy* is designed to guard against change and is often used by corporations that are trying to avoid either growth or retrenchment. The purpose of a *combination strategy* is to mix growth, retrenchment, and stability strategies across a corporation's business units.

3. **Identify the *business-level strategies* of companies and the role of *department-level strategies*.** Managers formulate separate *business-level strategies* for each business unit. Most companies use one of three generic business-level strategies for competing in an industry. A strategy in which a company exploits economies of scale to have the lowest cost structure of any competitor in its industry is called a *low-cost leadership strategy*. A *differentiation strategy* is one in which a company designs its products to be perceived as unique by buyers throughout its industry. A *focus strategy* is one in which a company focuses on serving the needs of a narrowly defined market segment by being the low-cost leader, by differentiating its product, or both. Achieving corporate- and business-level objectives depends on effective *department-level strategies* that focus on the specific activities that transform resources into products. Each

department is instrumental in creating customer value through lower costs or differentiated products. This is true of departments that conduct either *primary activities* or *support activities*.

4. **Discuss the important issues that influence the choice of *organizational structure*.** *Organizational structure* is the way in which a company divides its activities among separate units and coordinates activities between those units. Important to organizational structure is the degree to which decision making in an organization will be centralized (made at a high level) or decentralized (made at a low level such as international subsidiaries). *Centralized decision making* helps to coordinate the operations of international subsidiaries. *Decentralized decision making* is beneficial when fast-changing national business environments put a premium on local responsiveness.

When designing organizational structure, managers must consider the issues of *coordination* and *flexibility*. Every international company must design an organizational structure that clearly defines areas of responsibility and *chains of command*—the lines of authority that run from top management to individual employees and specify internal reporting relationships.

5. **Describe each type of *international organizational structure*, and explain the importance of *work teams*.** An *international division structure* separates domestic from international business activities by creating a separate division with its own manager. An *international area structure* organizes a company's entire global operations into countries or geographic regions, whereby each geographic division operates as a self-contained unit. A *global product structure* divides worldwide operations into product divisions, which are then divided into domestic and international units. A *global matrix structure* splits the chain of command between product and area divisions. Each manager and employee reports to two bosses—the general manager of the product division and the general manager of the geographic area.

Work teams are assigned the tasks of coordinating their efforts to arrive at solutions and implement corrective action. A *self-managed team* is one in which the employees from a single department take on the responsibilities of their former supervisors. A *cross-functional team* is composed of employees who work at similar levels in different functional departments. A *global team* is composed of top managers from both headquarters and international subsidiaries who meet to develop solutions to company-wide problems.

TALK IT OVER

1. The elements that affect strategy formulation are the same whether a company is domestic or international. Do you agree or disagree with this statement? Why? Support your argument with specific examples.

2. "Cultures around the world are becoming increasingly similar. Companies, therefore, should standardize both their products and global marketing efforts." Do you agree or disagree with this statement? Are there certain industries for which it might be more or less true? Provide specific examples.

3. Continuous advancements in technology are deeply affecting the way international businesses are managed. Do you think technology (the Internet, for example) should radically alter the fundamental strategies and organizational structures of international companies? Or do you think companies should simply graft new strategies and structures onto existing ones? Support your answers with specific examples.

TEAMING UP

1. In small groups, select one or more periodicals in the business press and identify several articles discussing changes taking place within a given industry over the past few months. What changes are occurring, and how are companies responding? Are firms altering strategies, relocating production, or leaving or entering certain markets and/or lines of business? Are they altering their organizational structures in some way? Write up a brief group report of your findings.

2. Select and research an international company that interests you and several classmates. Annual reports are

normally available from companies' investor relations departments or their Web sites. What is the company's mission statement or overriding objective? What are its corporate- and business-level strategies? In which nations does it produce and market its products? Are its production facilities centralized or decentralized? Does it standardize products or adapt them for different markets? What type of organizational structure does it have? Which of the two types of international strategy does it seem to follow? Does the company make use of work teams? Present your group's findings to the class.

3. As a team, list five products that you used or consumed within the past 24 hours. Your list might include such goods as your toothpaste or your CD player and such services as an express mailing service, a cable/satellite TV program, and so forth. What strategy does the company behind each good or service employ: low-cost, differentiation, or focus? For each company, explain in one or two paragraphs how you arrived at your answer.

KEY TERMS

chains of command (p. 331)

combination strategy (p. 326)

core competency (p. 320)

cross-functional team (p. 336)

differentiation strategy (p. 327)

focus strategy (p. 328)

global matrix structure (p. 334)

global product structure (p. 334)

global strategy (p. 324)

global team (p. 336)

growth strategy (p. 324)

international area structure (p. 333)

international division structure (p. 332)

low-cost leadership strategy (p. 326)

mission statement (p. 318)

multinational (multidomestic) strategy (p. 323)

organizational structure (p. 330)

planning (p. 318)

retrenchment strategy (p. 325)

self-managed team (p. 335)

stability strategy (p. 325)

stakeholders (p. 319)

strategy (p. 318)

value-chain analysis (p. 320)

TAKE IT TO THE WEB

1. This chapter explored different international strategies and the corporate-, business-, and department-level strategies that companies use. Altria Group is the parent company of global giants Kraft Foods and Philip Morris. Visit the Web site of Altria (*www.altria.com*). What corporate-level strategy(ies) do you think Altria is pursuing in its different businesses?

   Visit the Web sites of Kraft Foods (*www.kraft.com*) and Philip Morris (*www.philipmorris.com*)—both their domestic and international operations. What business-level strategy(ies) do you think is being pursued by: a) Kraft, and b) Philip Morris?

   In 2001, Kraft was spun off with an initial public offering of Kraft's stock. Why do you think this action was taken at the time? Do you think it had anything to do with the mix of businesses that then-parent Philip Morris was involved in? Why or why not? Identify as many stakeholders of Altria, Philip Morris, and Kraft Foods as you can. Aside from past smoking-related lawsuits, are there any trends that encouraged Kraft's independence?

ETHICAL CHALLENGES

1. You are the CEO of a multinational corporation that operates in more than 100 nations worldwide. Recent changes in the global economy (such as the expansion of the European Union in 2004 to include 10 new nations) are redrawing many geographical and political borders. The growing interdependence of socially, politically, economically, and legally diverse countries is causing firms to revise operating policies and strategies. You are personally involved in developing a code of ethics for your firm that reflects today's legal and moral atmosphere. You want your firm's code to be effective across all markets in which it operates. Given the complexity of the issues involved, what sort of policy do you think is appropriate for a firm involved in dissimilar nations? Do you think that it is possible to create a uniform code of ethics that is applicable to any business operating in any culture? What issues should such a code address?

2. You are a member of an international ethics commission assembled by the WTO that has been asked to assess the global tactics of Microsoft in recent years. A primary issue is whether Microsoft took unfair advantage of its powerful position in the computer industry by using "strong-arm tactics" on software customers throughout the

world, and by crushing weaker rivals. Regardless of whether or not Microsoft is guilty of anticompetitive acts in a legal sense, do you believe Microsoft has conducted itself in an ethical manner in its business dealings? Has it abused its power in the industry, or is Microsoft simply a tough competitor? Do you think the WTO should develop a policy to control such competitive tactics of global powerhouses like Microsoft?

3. You are the new president of Star Manufacturing, an international subsidiary of a large multinational firm that makes automotive parts. Since you arrived at Star three months ago, you are finding it difficult to get your firm's materials and finished products through customs quickly. Local legal counsel suggests a payment to local officials to eliminate your problem with customs, an apparently common local practice. The bribe would expedite the entire shipping process, which will help improve profits. What do you do? Is there a specific policy your firm could develop that all Star employees could follow? What other issues must you consider? If additional information would be helpful to you, what would it be?

PRACTICING INTERNATIONAL MANAGEMENT CASE

The Global Strategy of IKEA

IKEA (*www.ikea.com*) is a $10 billion global furniture power-house based in Sweden. With more than 150 stores in 29 countries, the company's success reflects founder Ingvar Kamprad's "social ambition" of selling a wide range of stylish, functional home furnishings at prices so low that the majority of people can afford to buy them. The story of Kamprad's success is detailed in a book titled *IKEA: The Entrepreneur, The Business Concept, The Culture.* The store exteriors are painted with Sweden's national colors, bright blue and yellow. Shoppers view furniture on the main floor in scores of realistic settings arranged throughout the cavernous showrooms.

In a departure from standard industry practice, IKEA's furniture bears names such as "Ivar" and "Sten" instead of model numbers. At IKEA, shopping is very much a self-service activity—after browsing and writing down the names of desired items in the showrooms, shoppers pick their furniture off shelves where they find boxes containing the furniture in kit form. In fact, one of the cornerstones of IKEA's strategy is having customers take their purchases home and assemble the furniture themselves. The typical IKEA store also contains a restaurant, a grocery store called the Swede Shop, a supervised play area for children, and a baby-care room.

IKEA's approach to the furniture business enables it to rack up impressive growth in an industry in which overall sales are flat. Sourcing furniture from more than 2,300 suppliers in 70 countries helps the company maintain its low-cost position. IKEA has also opened several stores in Central and Eastern Europe. Because many consumers in those regions have relatively low purchasing power, the stores offer a smaller selection of goods, and some of the furniture was designed specifically for the cramped living styles typical in former Soviet bloc countries. Throughout Europe, IKEA benefits from the perception that Sweden is the source of high-quality products. In fact, one of the company's key selling points is its "Swedishness." In Western Europe, the United Kingdom represents IKEA's fastest-growing market—its London store has achieved annual sales growth of 20 percent. The company recently decided to increase the size of all 11 of its U.K. stores by up to 25 percent to keep up with demand in the face of delays in getting permission to build new stores. And IKEA plans an aggressive expansion in Italy—over the next couple of years it will double to 14 the number of stores it has there.

Industry observers predict that the United States will eventually be IKEA's largest market. The company opened its first U.S. store in Philadelphia in 1985 and today has dozens of outlets that generate over a billion dollars in sales annually. And IKEA's competitors are taking it seriously. Jeff Young, chief operating officer of Lexington Furniture Industries, says, "IKEA is on the way to becoming the Wal-Mart Stores of the home-furnishing industry. If you're in this business, you'd better take a look." However, some U.S. customers are irked to find popular items sometimes out of stock. Another problem is the long lines resulting from the company's no-frills approach. Complained one shopper, "Great idea, poor execution. The quality of much of what they sell is good, but the hassles make you question whether it's worth it."

Goran Carstedt, president of IKEA North America, responds to such criticism by referring to the company's mission. "If we offered more services, our prices would go up," he explains. "Our customers understand our philosophy, which calls for each of us to do a little in order to save a lot. They value our low prices. And almost all of them say they will come back again." To keep them coming back, IKEA is spending between $25 million and $35 million on advertising to get its message across. Whereas common industry practice is to rely heavily on newspaper and radio advertising, two-thirds of IKEA's North American advertising budget is allocated for TV. John Sitnik, an executive at IKEA U.S. Inc., says, "We distanced ourselves from the other furniture stores. We decided TV is something we can own."

Thinking Globally

1. Has IKEA taken a standardization approach or an adaptation approach in its markets around the world? Do you think the company's approach is the right one? Explain your answers.

2. Which retailers do you think will be IKEA's biggest competitors in the United States? Why?

3. Company founder Kamprad recently decided to expand into China. Kamprad's decision was not based on market research but, rather, on his own intuition. Find a recent article or check IKEA's Web site to update the company's China strategy. Did Kamprad's decision pay off?

After studying this chapter, you should be able to

1. Explain each of the four steps in the *market- and site-screening process.*

2. Describe the three primary difficulties of conducting *international market research.*

3. Identify the main sources of *secondary international data,* and explain their usefulness.

4. Describe the main methods used to conduct *primary international research.*

analyzing international 12
opportunities

a look *back*

CHAPTER 11 showed us how companies plan and organize themselves for international operations. We explored the different types of strategies and organizational structures that international companies use to accomplish their strategic goals.

a look *at this chapter*

This chapter begins with an explanation of how managers screen potential new markets and new sites for operations. We then describe the main difficulties of conducting international market research. We also identify the information required in the screening process and where managers can go to obtain such information.

a look *ahead*

CHAPTER 13 describes the selection and management issues surrounding the different entry modes available to companies going international. We examine the importance of an export strategy for exporters and the pros and cons of each entry mode.

Starbucks Creates a Global Buzz

TOKYO, Japan—"New Starbucks Opens in Restroom of Existing Starbucks" read the alarming headline in humor publication, *The Onion*. Well, Starbucks' expansion strategy is not that desperate yet. Pictured above, Starbucks Coffee Chairman Howard Schultz and Yuji Tsunoda, president of Starbucks Japan, open *another* coffeehouse in Tokyo—bringing the number of stores in Japan to 500. Starbucks (*www.starbucks.com*) began its global journey in 1996 with its first coffeehouse in Tokyo, and today has more than 1500 coffeehouses in 31 markets outside North America.

Starbucks, which brought European-style coffee to the United States, is also opening its American-style coffeehouses in Europe. The coffee giant is betting paper-cupped lattes and non-smoking venues can take on Europe's traditional cafes. Although in Britain since the late 1990s, Starbucks waited until 2004 to steam into Paris, France. Starbucks is carefully approaching Europe by researching potential markets exhaustively—it first reached the continent in 2001 when it entered Zurich, Switzerland. With its multicultural and multilingual population, the Swiss market gave Starbucks a "tremendous opportunity to learn how to operate elsewhere in Europe," revealed Mark McKeon, president of Starbucks Europe, Middle East, and Africa.

At the same time, Starbucks is introducing a coffee culture to tea lovers in China. Starbucks is encouraged by the fact that one-third of all Chinese households keep a jar of instant coffee on hand. Starbucks does not expect to change the tea-drinking habits of the older generation. It is targeting China's newly rich, trying to establish its coffee as the drink of choice for the average 18- to 45-year-old Chinese consumer. "Per capita consumption of coffee in China is very small," admitted Howard Behar, president of Starbucks Coffee International. "But what you have is a tremendous amount of people, so the market will grow." As you read this chapter, consider how companies select markets to enter and the types of information they must acquire before entering new markets.[1]

Traditionally, companies become involved in international business by choosing to enter familiar, nearby countries first. Managers feel comfortable entering nearby markets because they likely have already interacted with the people of those cultures and have at least some understanding of them. That's why companies in Canada, Mexico, and the United States often gain their initial international experiences in one another's markets. Likewise, firms in Asian countries often seek out opportunities in one another's markets before pursuing investment opportunities outside the region.

But today companies find themselves bridging the gaps presented by space and culture far more often. For one thing, technological advances in communication and transportation continue to open national markets around the globe. Companies can realistically consider nearly every location on earth as either a potential market or as a site for business operations. In addition, the expansion of regional markets (such as the European Union) is causing companies to analyze opportunities farther from home. Companies are locating production facilities within regional markets because producing in one of a region's countries provides duty-free access to every consumer in the trade bloc.

Moreover, fast-paced change in the global marketplace is forcing companies to view business strategies from a global perspective. More than ever, they are formulating production, marketing, and other strategies as components of integrated plans. For instance, to provide a continuous flow of timely information into the production process, more and more firms are locating research and development (R&D) facilities near their production sites abroad. Managers also find themselves more often simultaneously screening and analyzing locations as potential markets *and* as potential sites for operations. When the M-class sport utility vehicle by Mercedes (*www.mercedes.com*) was introduced to the U.S. market, executives also decided to build the vehicle there. The company was obliged not merely to estimate the size of the potential market for the vehicle, but to decide at the same time on a suitable production site.

These realities of today's international marketplace lead many firms to a systematic approach regarding the decision of where to locate operations. This chapter presents just such a systematic screening process for both markets and sites. After coverage of important cultural, political, legal, and economic forces affecting the screening process, we describe the difficulties of conducting international research. The main sources of existing data and the main methods for conducting international research firsthand are then explored.

Screening Potential Markets and Sites

Two important issues concern managers during the market- and site-screening process. First, they want to keep the cost of the search as low as possible. Second, they want to examine every potential market and every possible location. To accomplish these two goals, managers typically approach the screening of markets and sites in a systematic way. We can break this *screening process* down into the following four steps:

1. Identify basic appeal.
2. Assess the national business environment.

FIGURE 12.1

Screening Process for Potential Markets and Sites

Step 4: Select the Market or Site
• Field trips
• Competitor analysis

Step 3: Measure Market or Site Potential
• Current sales, income elasticity, market potential indicator
• Quality of workforce, materials, infrastructure

Step 2: Assess the National Business Environment
• Language, attitudes, religious beliefs, traditions, work ethic
• Government regulation, government bureaucracy, political stability
• Fiscal and monetary policies, currency issues
• Cost of transporting goods, country image

Step 1: Identify Basic Appeal
• Suitability of climate, absolute bans
• Access to materials, labor, financing

3.   Measure market or site potential.

4.   Select the market or site.

Figure 12.1 shows that this screening process involves spending more time, money, and effort on the markets and sites that remain in the later stages of screening. Thus, expensive feasibility studies (conducted later in the process) are performed on a few markets and sites that hold the greatest promise. Therefore, this screening process is cost effective yet does not overlook potential locations. Let's now discuss each of these four steps in detail.

Step 1: Identify Basic Appeal

We have already seen that companies go international either to increase sales (and thus profits) or to access resources. Therefore, the first step in identifying potential markets is to assess the basic demand for a product. Similarly, the first step in selecting a site for a facility to undertake production, R&D, or some other activity is to explore the availability of the resources required.

Determining Basic Demand
The first step in searching for potential markets means finding out whether there is a basic demand for a company's product. Important in determining this basic appeal is a country's climate. For example, no company would try to market snowboards in Indonesia, Sri Lanka, or Central America because they receive no snowfall. The same product, on the other hand, is well suited for markets in the Canadian Rockies, northern Japan, and the Swiss Alps. Although this stage may seem quite simple, it cannot be taken too lightly as is illustrated by one classic example. During its initial forays into international business, Wal-Mart (*www.walmart.com*) found itself stocked with ice-fishing huts in Puerto Rico and out of snowshoes in Ontario, Canada.[2]

Certain countries also ban specific goods. Islamic countries, for instance, forbid the importation of alcoholic products, and the penalties for smuggling are stiff. Also, although alcohol is available on the planes of international airlines such as British Airways (*www.ba.com*) and KLM (*www.klm.com*), it cannot leave the airplane and consumption cannot take place until the plane has left the airspace of the country operating under Islamic law.

Determining Availability of Resources Companies that need particular resources to carry out local business activities must be sure that they are available. The raw materials needed for manufacturing must either be found in the national market or imported. However, imported inputs may encounter tariffs, quotas, or other government barriers. Therefore, managers must consider the additional costs of importing to ensure that total product cost does not rise to unacceptable levels.

The availability of labor is essential to production in any country. Many companies choose to relocate to countries where workers' wages are lower than they are in the home country. This practice is most common among makers of labor-intensive products—those for which labor accounts for a large portion of total cost. Companies that are considering local production must determine whether there is enough labor available locally for production operations.

Companies that hope to secure financing in a market abroad must determine the availability and cost of local capital. If local interest rates are too high, a company might be forced to obtain financing in its home country or in other markets in which it is active. On the other hand, access to low-cost financing may provide a powerful inducement to a company that is seeking to expand internationally. For example, British entrepreneur Richard Branson opened several of his Virgin (*www.virgin.com*) Megastores in Japan despite its reputation as a tough market to crack. One reason for Branson's initial attraction to Japan was a local cost of capital that was roughly one-third its cost in Britain. As the finance director for Virgin commented, "If resources are available locally, it would be silly for us not to utilize them."

Markets and sites that fail to meet a company's requirements for basic demand or resource availability in step 1 are removed from further consideration.

Step 2: Assess the National Business Environment

If the cultures, politics, laws, and economies of all countries were the same, deciding where to market or produce products would be rather straightforward. Managers could rely on data that report the performance of the local economy and analyze expected profits from proposed investments. But as we learned in Chapters 2, 3, and 4, national business environments differ greatly from one country to another. International managers must work to understand these differences and to incorporate that understanding into market- and site-selection decisions. Let's now examine how domestic forces in the business environment actually affect the location-selection process.

Cultural Forces Although some countries display cultural similarities, most differ in many ways, including language, attitudes toward business, religious beliefs, traditions, and customs. Some products can be sold in markets worldwide with little or no modification. Some of these products are industrial machinery such as packaging equipment and consumer products such as toothpaste and soft drinks. However, other products must undergo extensive adaptation to suit local preferences, including certain types of ready-to-eat meals and, sometimes, books and magazines.

Cultural elements can influence what kinds of products are sold and how they are sold. Managers must assess how local culture will affect the salability of its product if the location is a candidate as a market. For instance, consider the experience of Coca-Cola (*www.cocacola.com*) in China, where many people take a traditional medicine to fight off flu and cold symptoms. As it turns out, the taste of this traditional medicine—which most people do not find appealing—is similar to that of Coke. Because of Coca-Cola's global marketing policy of one taste worldwide, the company had to overcome the aversion to the taste of Coke among Chinese consumers. It did so by creating a marketing campaign that associated buying Coke with experiencing a piece of America. What initially looked like an unattractive market for Coke became very successful through a carefully tailored marketing campaign.

Cultural elements in the business environment can also affect site-selection decisions. When substantial product modifications are needed for cultural reasons, a company might choose to establish production facilities in the target market itself. However, better serving customers' special needs in a target market must be offset against any potential loss of economies of scale due to producing in several locations rather than just one. But today companies can minimize such losses through the use of flexible manufacturing methods. For example, although cellular phone manufacturer Nokia (*www.nokia.com*) produces in locations worldwide, it ensures that each one of its facilities can start producing any one of its mobile phones for its different markets within 24 hours.[3]

Having a qualified workforce is important for a company, whatever activity it is to undertake at a particular site. Also, a strong work ethic among the local workforce is essential to having productive operations. Managers must assess whether an appropriate work ethic exists in each potential country for the purposes of production, service, or any other business activity. An adequate level of educational attainment among the local workforce for the planned business activity is also very important. Although product-assembly operations may not require an advanced education, R&D, high-tech production, and certain services normally will require extensive higher education. If a potential site does not display an appropriate work ethic or educational attainment, it will be ruled out for further consideration.

Political and Legal Forces

Political and legal forces also influence the market and site-location decision. Important factors include government regulation, government bureaucracy, and political stability. Let's take a brief look at each of these.

Government Regulation   As we saw in earlier chapters, nations differ in their attitudes toward trade and investment, which is rooted in culture, history, and current events. Some governments take a strongly nationalistic stance, whereas others are quite receptive to international trade and investment. A government's attitude toward trade and investment is reflected in the quantity and types of restrictions it places on imports, exports, and investment in its country.

Government regulations can quickly eliminate a market or site from further consideration. First of all, they can create investment barriers to ensure domestic control of a company or industry. One way in which a government can accomplish this is by imposing investment rules on matters such as business ownership—for instance, forcing nondomestic companies into joint ventures. Although exercised by many governments (notably China and India) over the years, this technique is imposed less frequently today by large nations.

Governments also can extend investment rules to bar international companies entirely from competing in certain sectors of the domestic economy. The practice is usually defended as a matter of national security. Economic sectors commonly declared off-limits include television and radio broadcasting, automobile manufacturing, aircraft manufacturing, energy exploration, military-equipment manufacturing, and iron and steel production. Such industries are protected either because they are culturally important, are engines for economic growth, or are essential to any potential war effort. Host governments often fear (rightly or wrongly) that losing control in these economic sectors means placing their fate in the hands of international companies.

Second, governments can restrict international companies from freely removing profits earned in the nation. This policy can force a company either to hold cash in the host country or to reinvest it in new projects there. Such policies are normally rooted in the inability of the government in the host country to earn the foreign exchange needed to pay for badly needed imports. For example, Motorola's (*www.motorola.com*) Chinese subsidiary is required to convert the local currency (renminbi) to U.S. dollars before remitting profits back to the parent company in the United States. Motorola can satisfy this stipulation only as long as the Chinese government agrees to provide it with the needed U.S. dollars.

Third, governments can impose very strict environmental regulations. In most industrial countries, factories that produce industrial chemicals as their main output or as by-products must adhere to strict pollution standards. Regulations typically demand the installation of expensive pollution-control devices and the close monitoring of nearby air, water, and soil quality. While protecting the environment, such regulations also increase short-term production costs. Many developing and emerging markets have far less strict environmental regulations. Regrettably, some companies are alleged to have moved production of toxic materials to emerging markets to take advantage of lax environmental regulations and, in turn, lower production costs. Although such behavior is roundly criticized as highly unethical, it will occur less often as nations continue cooperating to formulate common environmental protection policies.

Finally, governments also can require that companies divulge certain information. Coca-Cola (*www.cocacola.com*) actually left India when the government demanded that it disclose its secret Coke formula as a requirement for doing business there. Coca-Cola returned only after the Indian government dropped its demand.

Government Bureaucracy A lean and smoothly operating government bureaucracy can make a market or site more attractive. But a bloated and cumbersome system of obtaining approvals and licenses from government agencies can make it less appealing. In many developing countries, the relatively simple matter of obtaining a license to establish a retail outlet often means acquiring numerous documents from several agencies. The bureaucrats in charge of these agencies generally are little concerned with high-quality service. Managers must be prepared to deal with administrative delays and a maze of rules. For instance, country managers for Millicom International Cellular (*www.millicom.com*) in Tanzania must wait 90 days to get customs clearance on the monthly import of roughly $1 million in cellular telephone equipment. But the size of the local market makes enduring such bureaucratic obstacles bearable: Several thousand cellular subscribers in Tanzania use their phones an average of 400 minutes per month.[4]

Thus, companies will endure a cumbersome bureaucracy if the opportunity is sufficient to offset any potential delays and expenses. Companies entering China cite the patience needed to navigate a maze of government regulations that often contradict one another and complain about the large number of permissions required from different agencies. The trouble stems from the fact that China is continually revising and developing its system of business law as its economy develops. But an unclear legal framework and inefficient bureaucracy are not deterring investment in China because the opportunities for both marketers and manufacturers are simply too great to ignore.

Political Stability Every nation's business environment is affected to some degree by political risk. As we saw in Chapter 3, political risk is the likelihood that a nation will undergo political changes that affect business activities negatively. Political risk can

By their actions, governments and nongovernmental organizations (NGOs) can attract or drive away international firms. These members of a student organization burn a poster at a 2003 protest in Bangalore, India. Activists were demanding a ban on Pepsi (www.pepsi.com) and Coke (www.cocacola.com) soft drinks, which an environmental group claimed contained pesticides. After an Indian court ordered the testing of the two soft-drink bottlers' products, sales of Pepsi and Coke plummeted as people quenched their thirst with coconut water and sugarcane juice.

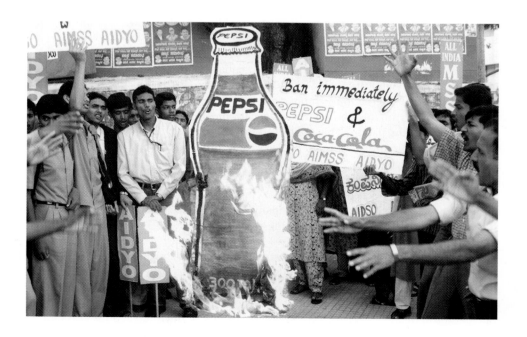

threaten the market of an exporter, the production facilities of a manufacturer, or the ability of a company to remove profits from the country in which they were earned.

The key element of political risk that concerns companies is *unforeseen political change.* If a company cannot estimate the future political environment with a fair degree of accuracy, political risk is increased. An event with a negative impact that is expected to occur in the future is not, in itself, bad for companies because the event can be planned for and necessary precautions taken. It is the unforeseen negative events that create political risk for companies.

The perception of a market's political risk is often affected by managers' memories of past political unrest in a nation. However, managers cannot let past events blind them to future opportunities. International companies must try to monitor and predict political events that threaten operations and future earnings' potential. By investigating the political environment proactively, managers can focus on political risk and develop action plans for dealing with it.

But where do managers get the information to answer such questions? They may assign company personnel to gather information on the level of political risk in a country, or they may obtain it from independent agencies that specialize in providing political-risk services. The advice of country and regional specialists who are knowledgeable about the current political climate of a market can be especially helpful. Such specialists can include international bankers, political consultants, reporters, country-risk specialists, international relations scholars, political leaders, union leaders, embassy officials, and other local businesspeople currently working and living in the country in question.

Economic and Financial Forces
Managers must carefully analyze a nation's economic policies before selecting it as a new market or site for operations. The poor fiscal and monetary policies of a nation's central bank can cause high rates of inflation, increasing budget deficits, a depreciating currency, falling productivity levels, and flagging innovation. Such consequences typically lower investor confidence and force international companies to scale back or cancel proposed investments. For example, restrictive trade and investment policies by the government of India finally gave way to more open policies in the early 1990s. Specifically, new investment policies encouraged investment in both production facilities and R&D centers, especially in the computer-software industry.

Currency and liquidity problems pose special challenges for international companies. Volatile currency values make it difficult for firms to predict future earnings accurately in terms of the home-country currency. Wildly fluctuating currency values also make it difficult to calculate how much capital a company needs for a planned investment. Unpredictable changes in currency values can also make liquidating assets more difficult because the greater uncertainty will likely reduce liquidity in capital markets—especially in countries with relatively small capital markets, such as Bangladesh and Slovakia.

In addition to their home government's resources, managers can obtain information about economic and financial conditions from institutions such as the World Bank, the International Monetary Fund, and the Asian Development Bank. Other information sources include business and economic publications such as the *Far Eastern Economic Review* (*www.feer.com*), the annual country-risk guide published by *Euromoney* (*www.euromoney.com*), and the series of reports called *Economic Outlook* published by *The Economist* (*www.economist.com*).

Other Forces
A country's image and the cost of transporting materials and goods also play important roles in the assessment of national business environments. Let's now take a brief look at each of these forces.

Cost of Transporting Materials and Goods
The cost of transporting materials and finished goods affects any decision about where to locate manufacturing facilities. Some products cost very little to transport through the production and distribution process and others cost a great deal. **Logistics** refers to the management of the physical flow of products

logistics
Management of the physical flow of products from the point of origin as raw materials to end users as finished products.

from the point of origin as raw materials to end users as finished products. Logistics weds production activities to the activities needed to deliver products to buyers. It includes all modes of transportation, storage, and distribution.

To realize the importance of efficient logistics, consider that global logistics is a $400 billion industry. We often think of the United States as an efficient logistics market because of its extensive interstate road system and rail lines that stretch from east to west. But because of overcrowded highways, 2 billion people-hours are lost to gridlock each year. That translates into $48 billion in lost productivity![5] Because of the financial cost to businesses of inefficient logistics, many transport companies and cargo ports strenuously advertise their services.

Country Image Because *country image* embodies every facet of a nation's business environment, it is highly relevant to the selection of sites for production, R&D, or any other activity. For example, country image affects the location of manufacturing or assembly operations because products must typically be stamped with labels identifying where they were made or assembled—such as "Made in China" or "Assembled in Brazil." Although such labels do not affect all products to the same degree, they can present important positive or negative images and boost or dampen sales.

Products made in relatively more developed countries tend to be evaluated more positively than those from less developed countries.[6] This relation can often be traced to the perception among consumers that the workforces of certain nations have superior skills in making particular products. For example, Procter & Gamble (*www.pg.com*) and Unilever (*www.unilever.com*), intense rivals in consumer products, both have manufacturing facilities in Vietnam. But Vietnamese consumers tend to shun locally made Close-Up toothpaste and Tide detergent and seek out the identical products produced in neighboring countries, such as Thailand. As one young Vietnamese shopper explained, "Tide from Thailand smells nicer." A general perception among Vietnamese consumers is that goods from Japan or Singapore are the best, followed by Thai goods. Unfortunately for Procter & Gamble and Unilever in Vietnam, many goods from these other countries are smuggled in and sold on the black market, thereby denying the companies of sales revenue.[7]

A country's image can be positive in one product class but negative in another. For example, consumers happily pay a premium for Corona (*www.corona.com*) beer imported from Mexico. Also, the fact that Volkswagen's (*www.volkswagen.com*) new Beetle is made in Mexico for the U.S. market has not hurt the Beetle's sales one bit. But would affluent consumers buy a hand-built Rolls-Royce (*www.rrmc.co.uk*) automobile if it were produced in Mexico? Because Rolls-Royce buyers pay for the image of a brilliantly crafted luxury car, the Rolls-Royce image probably would not survive intact if the company were to produce its cars in Mexico.

Finally, note that country image can and does change over time. For example, "Made in India" has traditionally been associated with low-technology products such as soccer balls and many types of textile products. But today world-class computer-software companies increasingly rely on the software-development skills of engineers located in and around Madras and Bangalore in southern India.

Throughout our discussion of step 2 of the screening process (assessing the national business environment), we have presented many factors central to traditional business activities. To read about other issues specific to entering international markets successfully over the Internet, read the Global Manager's Toolbox titled, "Global E-Commerce Issues."

Quick Study

1. What are the four steps in the screening process?
2. Identify the main factors to investigate when identifying the basic appeal of a market or site for operations.
3. What key forces should be examined when assessing a nation's business environment?
4. How do the cost of transport and country image affect the location decision?

Generating sales in new geographic markets over the Internet is an increasingly popular method of expansion for large multinationals and entrepreneurs alike. Managers around the globe who wish to learn more about entering new markets through the Internet can visit the e-commerce Web site of the U.S. Department of Commerce (*www.ecommerce.gov*). Here are some additional issues managers should consider when entering new markets over the Internet:

Infrastructure and Market Access Issues

⊃ **Telecommunications infrastructure and information technology.** Before investing heavily in e-commerce, be sure to investigate whether your potential customers have easy access to the Internet. It should also be determined whether their government's telecommunications policies hinder the development of advanced digital networks.

⊃ **Content.** Issues of content include topics such as truth in advertising, fraud prevention, and violent, seditious, or pornographic materials. Companies must be informed about the different policies of each country through which their information travels in order to avoid liability.

⊃ **Standards.** It is not yet clear which country has the power to establish standards of operations for e-commerce. Also, standards can be established to act as nontariff trade barriers to keep international companies out of a domestic market.

Legal Issues

⊃ **Privacy.** One of the strengths of e-commerce is that information on consumers can be easily collected and used to generate more sales. But consumer groups and others, particularly in the European Union, are concerned that collecting such data is an invasion of privacy. They are particularly vehement about this issue if consumers are not aware that this information is collected, how it is used, and if it is passed on to third parties.

⊃ **Security.** Companies must ensure that their data communications are safe from unauthorized access or modification. While the technology exists to provide security—encryption, password controls, and firewalls, for example—it needs to be supported by a global infrastructure.

⊃ **Intellectual property protection.** Protection of copyrights, databases, patents, and trademarks is governed by international agreements. But because a legal framework for the Internet has not yet been developed, these issues remain a global trade concern for managers of e-businesses.

Financial Issues

⊃ **Electronic payments.** Although secure encryption services in the credit card industry are well established, consumers remain concerned about security when it comes to their own credit card. Global electronic payment systems such as stored-value, smart cards, and other systems are still in various stages of development. Their increased use will alleviate many security issues for consumers.

⊃ **Tariffs and taxation.** International policies regarding who should pay taxes on international e-commerce and to what nation they should be paid are not yet fully developed. Countries have widely different views on how these matters should be treated.

Step 3: Measure Market or Site Potential

Markets and sites passing the first two steps in the screening process undergo further analysis to arrive at a more manageable number of potential locations. Despite the presence of a basic need for a product and an adequately stable national business environment, potential customers might not be ready or able to buy a product for a variety of reasons. Despite the availability of resources, certain sites may be unable to supply a given company with the *level* of resources it needs. Let's now explore the factors that further influence the potential suitability of markets and sites for operations.

Measuring Market Potential   As barriers to trade continue to fall around the world, companies are looking to increase sales in industrialized and emerging markets worldwide. But companies can seldom create one marketing plan for every market in which they sell their products. Nations enjoy different levels of economic development, which affect what kinds of goods are sold, the manner in which they are sold, and the features they have. Likewise, the different levels of economic development require varying approaches to researching market potential. But how do managers estimate potential demand for particular products? Let's take a look at the factors managers consider when analyzing industrialized markets and then examine a special tool for analyzing emerging markets.

Industrialized Markets   The information needed to estimate the market potential for a product in industrialized nations tends to be more readily available than in emerging markets. In fact, for the most developed markets, research agencies exist for the sole purpose of supplying market data to companies. Euromonitor (*www.euromonitor.com*) is one such company with an extensive global reach in consumer goods. The company sells reports and does company-specific studies for many international corporations and entrepreneurs. Some of the information in a typical industry analysis includes:

- Names, production volumes, and market shares of the largest competitors
- Volume of exports and imports of the product
- Structure of the wholesale and retail distribution networks
- Background on the market, including population figures, important social trends, and a description of the kinds of marketing approaches used
- Total expenditure on the product (and similar products) in the market
- Retail sales volume and market prices of the product
- Future outlook for the market and potential opportunities

The value of such information supplied by specialist agencies is readily apparent—these reports provide a quick overview of the size and structure of a nation's market for a product. Reports vary in their cost (depending on the market and product), but many can be had for around $750 to $1,500. The company also allows online purchase of reports in small segments for as little as $20 each. We discuss other sources for this type of market data later in this chapter.

Thus companies that enter the market in industrialized countries often have a great deal of data available on that particular market. What becomes important then is the forecast for the growth or contraction of a potential market. One way of forecasting market demand is determining a product's **income elasticity**—the sensitivity of demand for a product relative to changes in income. The income-elasticity *coefficient* for a product is calculated by dividing a percentage change in the quantity of a product demanded by a percentage change in income. A coefficient greater than 1.0 conveys an *income-elastic* product, or one for which demand increases more relative to an increase in income. These products tend to be discretionary purchases, such as computers, video games, jewelry, or expensive furniture—generally not considered essential items. A coefficient less than 1.0 conveys an *income-inelastic* product, or one for which demand increases less relative to an increase in income. These products are considered essential, and include food, utilities, and beverages. To illustrate, if the income-elasticity coefficient for carbonated beverages is 0.7, the demand for carbonated beverages will increase 0.7 percent for every 1.0 percent increase in income. Conversely, if the income-elasticity coefficient for DVD video players is 1.3, the demand for DVD players will increase 1.3 percent for every 1.0 percent increase in income.

Emerging Markets   Today, big emerging markets are more important than ever. Nearly every large company engaged in international business today is either already in or is considering entering the big emerging markets such as China and India. With their large consumer bases and rapid growth rates, they whet the appetite of marketers around the world. Although these markets are surely experiencing speed bumps along their paths of economic development, in the long term they cannot be ignored. Table 12.1 compares China and India on several key dimensions of their economies. We immediately notice that China attracted far more foreign investment than India. Despite this, India achieved respectable

income elasticity
Sensitivity of demand for a product relative to changes in income.

	Population (billions)	Population Growth (%)	Annual GDP Growth (%) (1990–2000)	Foreign Direct Investment (billions)	Labor Force (millions)
China	1.28	0.87	9.6	$ 44.2	706
India	1.05	1.51	5.5	$ 3.4	406

TABLE 12.1

Emerging Giants

economic growth during the 1990s and still is experiencing rapid growth, while China's economy is slowing somewhat.

Companies considering entering emerging markets often face special problems related to a lack of information. Data on market size or potential may not be available, for example, because of undeveloped methods for collecting such data in a country. But there are ways companies can assess potential in emerging markets. One way is for them to rank different locations by developing a so-called *market-potential indicator* for each. However, this method is useful only to companies considering exporting. Companies considering investing in an emerging market must look at other factors that we examine next in the discussion of measuring site potential. The main variables commonly included in market-potential analyses are:[8]

- ❍ *Market Size.* This variable provides a snapshot of the size of a market at any point in time. It does not estimate the size of a market for a particular product, but rather the size of the overall economy. Market-size data allow managers to rank countries from largest to smallest, regardless of a particular product. Market size is typically estimated from a nation's total population or the amount of energy it produces and consumes.

- ❍ *Market Growth Rate.* This variable reflects the fact that although the overall size of the market (economy) is important, so too is its rate of growth. It helps managers avoid markets that are large but shrinking and target those that are small but rapidly expanding. It is generally obtained through estimates of growth in gross domestic product (GDP) and energy consumption.

- ❍ *Market Intensity.* This variable estimates the wealth or buying power of a market from the expenditures of both individuals and businesses. It is estimated from per capita private consumption and/or per capita gross domestic product (GDP) at purchasing power parity (see Chapter 4).

- ❍ *Market Consumption Capacity.* The purpose of this variable is to estimate spending capacity. It is often estimated from the percentage of a market's population in the middle class, thereby concentrating on the core of an economy's buying power.

- ❍ *Commercial Infrastructure.* This factor attempts to assess channels of distribution and communication. Variables may include the number of telephones, televisions, fax machines, or personal computers per capita; the density of paved roads or number of vehicles per capita; and the population per retail outlet. An increasingly important variable for businesses relying on the Internet for sales is the number of Internet hosts per capita. But because these data become outdated quickly, care must be taken to ensure accurate information from the most current sources.

- ❍ *Economic Freedom.* This variable attempts to estimate the extent to which free-market principles predominate. It is typically a summary of government trade policies, government involvement in business, the enforcement of property rights, and the strength of the black market. An index of political freedom, such as the annual *Freedom in the World* report published by Freedom House (*www.freedomhouse.org*), can be a useful resource.

- ❍ *Market Receptivity.* This variable attempts to estimate market "openness." One way it can be estimated is by determining a nation's volume of international trade as a percent of gross domestic product (GDP). If a company wishes to see how receptive a market is to goods from its home country, it can ascertain the amount of per capita imports into the market from the home country. Managers can also examine the growth (or decline) in these imports.

- ○ *Country Risk.* This variable attempts to estimate the total risk of doing business, including political, economic, and financial risks. Some market-potential estimation techniques include this variable in the market-receptivity variable. This factor is typically obtained from one of the many services that rate the risk of different countries, such as Political Risk Services (*www.prsgroup.com*).

After each of these factors is analyzed, they are assigned values according to their importance to the demand for a particular product. Then potential locations are ranked (assigned a market-potential indicator value) according to their appeal as a new market. As you may recall, we discussed several of these variables earlier under the topics of national and international business environments. For example, *country-risk* levels are shown in Map 3.2 (pages 94–95); *economic freedom* is shown in Map 4.1 (pages 130–131), and *market receptivity* (or openness) in Map 5.1 (pages 152–153). Map 12.1 captures one other variable, *commercial infrastructure,* by showing the number of fixed-line and mobile phone subscribers per 1,000 people in each nation. This variable is an important indicator of a nation's overall economic development. Other variables that are also good proxies for this

MAP 12.1

Nations' Commercial Infrastructures

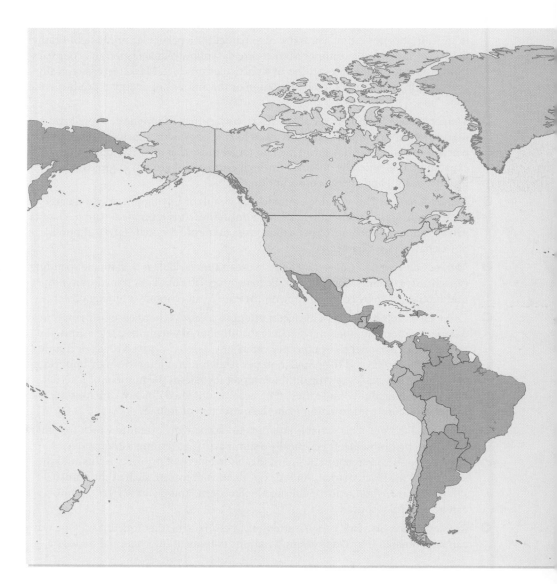

variable include the portion of a nation's roads that are paved or the number of personal computers, fax machines, and Internet hosts it has. However, one note of caution is important: Emerging markets often either lack such statistics, or in the case of paved roads, international comparison is difficult.

Measuring Site Potential   In this step of the site-screening process, managers must carefully assess the quality of the resources that they will use locally. For many companies, the most important of these will be human resources—both labor and management. Wages are lower in certain markets because labor is abundant, relatively less skilled (though perhaps well-educated), or both. Employees may or may not be adequately trained to manufacture a given product or to perform certain R&D activities. If workers are not adequately trained, the site-selection process must consider the additional money and time needed to train them.

Training local managers also requires a substantial investment of time and money. A lack of qualified local managers sometimes forces companies to send managers from the home market to the local market. This adds to costs because home-country managers must often receive significant bonuses for relocating to the local market. Companies must also assess the productivity of local labor and managers. After all, low wages may reflect low productivity levels among the workforce.

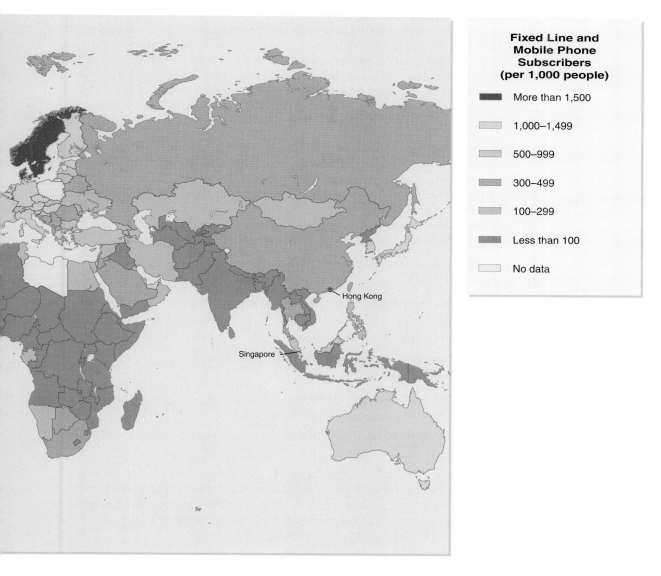

Managers should also examine the local infrastructure, including roads, bridges, airports, seaports, and telecommunications systems, when assessing site potential. Each of these systems can have a major impact on the efficiency with which a company transports materials and products. Of chief importance to many companies today is the state of a country's telecommunications infrastructure. Much business today is conducted through e-mail, and many businesses relay information electronically on matters such as sales orders, inventory levels, and production strategies, which must be coordinated among subsidiaries in different countries. Therefore, managers must examine each potential site to determine how well it is prepared for contemporary communications.

Step 4: Select the Market or Site

This final step in the screening process involves the most intensive efforts yet of assessing remaining potential markets and sites—typically less than a dozen, sometimes just one or two. At this stage, managers normally want to visit each remaining location to confirm earlier expectations and to perform a competitor analysis. In the final analysis, managers normally evaluate each potential location's contribution to cash flows by undertaking a financial evaluation of a proposed investment. The specialized and technical nature of this analysis can be found in most textbooks on corporate finance.

Field Trips   The importance of top managers making a personal visit to each remaining potential market or site cannot be overstated. Such trips typically involve attending strings of meetings and engaging in tough negotiations. The trip represents an opportunity for managers to see firsthand what they have so far seen only on paper. It gives them an opportunity to experience the culture, observe in action the workforce that they might soon employ, or make personal contact with potential new customers and distributors. Any issues remaining tend to be thoroughly investigated during field trips so that the terms of any agreement are known precisely in the event that a particular market or site is chosen. Managers can then usually return to the chosen location to put the terms of the final agreement in writing.

Competitor Analysis   Because competitor analysis was covered in detail in Chapter 11, we offer only a few comments here. Intensely competitive markets typically put downward pressure on the prices that firms can charge their customers. In addition, intensely competitive sites for production and R&D activities often increase the costs of doing business. Naturally, lower prices and higher costs due to competitive forces must be balanced against the potential benefits offered by each market and site under consideration. At the very least, then, competitor analysis should address the following issues:

- Number of competitors in each market (domestic and international)
- Market share of each competitor
- Whether each competitor's product appeals to a small market segment or has mass appeal
- Whether each competitor focuses on high quality or low price
- Whether competitors tightly control channels of distribution
- Customer loyalty commanded by competitors
- Potential threat from substitute products
- Potential entry of new competitors into the market
- Competitors' control of key production inputs (such as labor, capital, and raw materials)

So far we have examined a model that many companies follow when selecting new markets or sites for operations. We've seen what steps companies take in the screening process, but we have yet to learn how they undertake such a complex task. Let's now explore the types of situations companies encounter when conducting research in an international setting, and the specific tools used in their research.

1.   What is the significance of *income elasticity* in measuring market potential?

2.   Identify each component of a market-potential indicator. Why is it useful in assessing emerging markets?

3.   What are the most important factors to consider when measuring site potential?

4.   Explain why a field trip and competitor analysis are useful in the final stage of the screening process.

Conducting International Research

Today, increased global competition forces companies to engage in high-quality research and analysis before selecting new markets and sites for operations. Companies are finding that such research helps them to better understand both buyer behavior and business environments abroad. **Market research** is the collection and analysis of information in order to assist managers in making informed decisions. We define market research here to apply to the assessment of both potential markets and sites for operations. International market research provides information on national business environments, including cultural practices, politics, regulations, and the economy. It also informs managers about a market's potential size, buyer behavior, logistics, and distribution systems.

market research
Collection and analysis of information in order to assist managers in making informed decisions.

Conducting market research on new markets is helpful in designing all aspects of marketing strategy and understanding buyer preferences and attitudes. What works in France, for example, might not work in Singapore. Market research also lets managers learn about aspects of local business environments such as employment levels, wage rates, and the state of the local infrastructure before committing to the new location. It supplies managers with timely and relevant market information to anticipate market shifts, changes in current regulations, and the potential entry of new competitors.

In this section, we first learn about several common problems that confront companies when conducting international research. Then we explore some actual sources that managers use to assess potential new locations. We then examine some methods commonly used for conducting international research firsthand.

Difficulties of Conducting International Research

Market research serves essentially the same function in all nations. However, unique conditions and circumstances present certain difficulties that often force adjustments in the *way* research is performed in different nations. It is important for companies that are conducting market research themselves to be absolutely aware of potential obstacles so that their results are reliable. Companies that hire outside research agencies must also be aware of such difficulties. After all, they must evaluate the research results and assess their relevance to the location-selection decision. The three main difficulties associated with conducting international market research that we will now examine are:

1.   Availability of data

2.   Comparability of data

3.   Cultural differences

Availability of Data   When trying to target specific population segments, marketing managers require highly detailed information. Fortunately, companies are often spared the time, money, and effort of collecting firsthand data for the simple reason that it has already been gathered. This is particularly true in the highly industrialized countries, including Australia, Canada, Japan, those in Western Europe, and the United States, where both government agencies and private research firms supply information.

Information Resources Incorporated (*www.infores.com*), Survey Research Group (*www.surveyresearchgroup.com*), and ACNielsen (*www.acnielsen.com*) are just three of these types of information suppliers.

In many emerging and developing countries, however, previously gathered quality information is hard to obtain. Even when market data are available, their reliability is questionable. For example, analysts sometimes charge the governments of certain emerging markets (particularly China) with trying to lure investors by overstating estimates of gross income and consumption levels. In addition to deliberate misrepresentation, tainted information can also result from improper local collection methods and analysis techniques. But research agencies in emerging and developing markets that specialize in gathering data for clients in industrialized countries are developing higher-quality techniques of collection and analysis. For example, information supplier and pollster Gallup (*www.gallup.com*) is aggressively expanding its operations throughout Southeast Asia in response to the need among Western companies for more accurate market research.

Comparability of Data   Likewise, data obtained from other countries must be interpreted with great caution. Because terms such as *poverty, consumption,* and *literacy* differ greatly from one country to another, such data must be accompanied by precise definitions. In the United States, for example, a family of four is said to be below the poverty line if its annual income is less than around $18,800. The equivalent income for a Vietnamese family of four would place it in the high upper class.

The different ways in which countries measure data also affect comparability across borders. For instance, some countries state the total quantity of foreign direct investment in their nations in terms of its *monetary value.* Others specify it in terms of the number of *investment projects* implemented during the year. But a single foreign direct investment into an industrialized nation can be worth many times what several or more projects are worth in a developing nation. Thus, to gather a complete picture of a nation's investments, researchers will often need to obtain both figures. Moreover, reported statistics may not distinguish between foreign direct investment (accompanied by managerial control) and portfolio investment (which is not accompanied by managerial control). Misinterpreting data because one does not know how they are compiled or measured can sabotage even the best marketing plans and production strategies.

Cultural Problems   Marketers who conduct research in unfamiliar markets must pay attention to the ways in which cultural variables influence information. Perhaps the single most important variable is language. For example, if researchers are unfamiliar with a language in the market they are investigating, they might be forced to rely on interpreters. Interpreters might unintentionally misrepresent certain comments or be unable to convey the sentiment with which statements are made.

Researchers might also need to survey potential buyers through questionnaires written in the local language. To avoid any misstatement of questions or results, questionnaires must be translated into the language of the target market and the responses then translated back into the researcher's language. Written expressions must be highly accurate so that results do not become meaningless or, far worse, misleading. The potential to conduct written surveys is also affected by the illiteracy rates among the local population. A written survey is generally impossible to conduct in countries with high illiteracy rates such as Egypt (43 percent), Haiti (48 percent), and Pakistan (55 percent).[9] Researchers would probably need to choose a different information-gathering technique, such as personal interviews or observing retail purchases.

Companies that have little experience in an unfamiliar market often hire local agencies to perform some or all of their market research. Local researchers know the cultural terrain; they understand which practices are acceptable and which types of questions can be asked. They also typically know whom to approach for certain types of information. Perhaps most importantly, they realize how to interpret the information they gather and are likely to know its reliability. But a company that decides to conduct its own market research must, if necessary, adapt its research techniques to the local market. Many cultural elements that are taken for granted in the home market must be reassessed in the host business environment.

Sources of Secondary International Data

Companies can consult a variety of sources to obtain information on a nation's business environment and markets. The particular source that managers should consult depends on the company's industry, the national markets it is considering, and how far along it is in its location-screening process. The process of obtaining information that already exists within the company or that can be obtained from outside sources is called **secondary market research**. Managers often use information gathered from secondary research activities to broadly estimate market demand for a product or to form a general impression of a nation's business environment. Secondary data are relatively inexpensive because they have already been collected, analyzed, and summarized by another party. Let's now take a look at the main sources of secondary data that help managers make more informed location-selection decisions.

secondary market research
Process of obtaining information that already exists within the company or that can be obtained from outside sources.

International Organizations
A variety of international organizations are excellent sources of much free and inexpensive information about product demand in particular countries. For example, the *International Trade Statistics Yearbook* published by the United Nations (*www.un.org*) lists the export and import volumes of different products for each country. It also furnishes information on the value of exports and imports on an annual basis for the most recent 5-year period. The International Trade Center (*www.intracen.org*), based in Geneva, Switzerland, also provides current import and export figures for more than 100 countries.

International development agencies, such as the World Bank (*www.worldbank.org*), the International Monetary Fund (*www.imf.org*), and the Asian Development Bank (*www.adb.org*), also provide valuable secondary data. For example, the World Bank publishes annual data on each member nation's population and economic growth rate. Today, most secondary sources supply data on CD-ROM and through the Internet, in addition to traditional printed versions.

Government Agencies
The commerce departments and international trade agencies of most countries typically supply information about import and export regulations, quality standards, and the sizes of various markets. These data are normally available directly from these departments, from agencies within each nation, and from the commercial attaché in each country's embassy abroad. In fact, visiting embassies and attending their social functions while visiting a potential location are excellent ways of making contacts with potential future business partners.

Granted, the attractively packaged information supplied by host nations often ignores many potential hazards in a nation's commercial environment—governments typically try to present their country in the best possible light. By the same token, such sources are prone to paint incomplete or one-sided portraits of the home market. Thus, it is important for managers to seek additional sources that take a more objective view of a potential location.

One source that takes a fairly broad view of markets is the Central Intelligence Agency's *World Factbook* (*www.odci.gov/cia/publications/factbook*). This source can be a useful tool throughout the entire market- or site-screening process because of its wealth of facts on each nation's business environment. It identifies each nation's geography, climate, terrain, natural resources, land use, and important environmental issues in some detail. It also examines each nation's culture, system of government, and economic conditions, including government debt and exchange-rate conditions. It also provides an overview of the quality of each country's transportation and communications systems.

The Trade Information Center (TIC) (*www.trade.gov/td/tic*) operated by the U.S. Department of Commerce is a first stop for many importers and exporters. The TIC details product standards in other countries and offers advice on opportunities and best prospects for U.S. companies in individual markets. It also offers information on federal export-assistance programs that can be essential for first-time exporters. Other TIC information includes:

- National trade laws and other regulations
- Trade shows, trade missions, and special events

- Export counseling for specific countries
- Import tariffs and customs procedures
- The value of exports to other countries

The Chilean Trade Commission within Chile's Ministry of Foreign Affairs has been particularly aggressive in recent years in promoting Chile to the rest of the world. ProChile (*www.chileinfo.com*) has 35 commercial offices worldwide. The organization assists in developing the export process, establishing international business relationships, fostering international trade, attracting investment, and forging strategic alliances. It offers a wealth of information on all of Chile's key industries and provides business-environment information such as risk ratings. It also provides details on important trade regulations and standards of which exporters, importers, and investors must be aware.[10]

Commercial offices of the states and provinces of many countries also typically have offices in other countries to promote trade and investment. These offices usually encourage investment in the home market by companies from other countries and will sometimes even help companies in other countries export to the home market. For instance, the Lorraine Development Corporation (*www.lorrainedc.com*) in Atlanta is the investment-promotion office of the Lorraine region of France. This corporation helps U.S. companies evaluate location opportunities in the Lorraine region—a popular area for industrial investment. It supplies information on sites, buildings, financing options, and conditions in the French business environment and conducts 10 to 20 site-selection studies per year for specific companies. "We've been in the U.S.A. since 1988," says director Frederic Mot. "Our main goal is to identify potential U.S. investors, and we contact about 2,000 American companies each year."[11] Figure 12.2 shows the U.S. states that have the most investment-promotion and trade offices abroad and the most popular locations for such offices.

Finally, many governments open their research libraries to businesspeople from all countries. For example, the Japanese External Trade Organization (JETRO) (*www.jetro.go.jp*) in central Tokyo has a large library full of trade data available to international companies already in Japan. In addition, the JETRO Web site can be useful for companies screening the potential of the Japanese market for future business activities from any location. The organization is dedicated to serving companies interested in exporting to or investing in Japan in addition to assisting Japanese companies in going abroad.

Industry and Trade Associations Companies often join associations composed of firms within their own industry or trade. In particular, companies trying to break into new markets join such associations in order to make contact with others in their field.

FIGURE 12.2

U.S. States' Global Development Offices

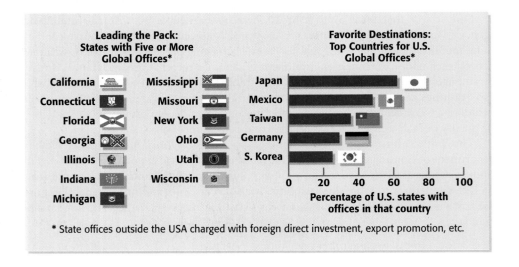

The publications of these organizations keep members informed about current events and help managers to keep abreast of important issues and opportunities. Many associations publish special volumes of import and export data for domestic markets. Frequently, they compile directories that list each member's top executives, geographic scope, and contact information such as phone numbers and addresses. Today, many associations also maintain informative Web sites. Two interesting examples are the sites of the National Pasta Association (*www.ilovepasta.org*) and the National Onion Association (*www.onions-usa.org*).

Sometimes industry and trade associations will commission specialized studies of their industries, the results of which are then offered to their members at subsidized prices. These types of studies typically address particularly important issues or explore new opportunities for international growth. The Chocolate Manufacturers Association (*www.nca-cma.org*) of the United States together with the state of Washington's Washington Apple Commission (*www.bestapples.com*) once hired a research firm to study the sweet tooth of Chinese consumers. The findings of the study were then made available to each organization's members to act on as they saw fit.

Service Organizations Many international service organizations in fields such as banking, insurance, management consulting, and accounting offer information to their clients on cultural, regulatory, and financial conditions in a market. For example, the accounting firm of Ernst & Young (*www.ey.com*) publishes a "Doing Business In" series for most countries. Each booklet contains information on a nation's business environment, regulations regarding foreign investment, legal forms of businesses, labor force, taxes, and culture.

Another service that provides information on world markets is MARKET: newsletters (see Figure 12.3). This company supplies specialized reports on market demographics, lifestyles, and consumer data and trends. Newsletters for each world region cover trends in areas such as population growth, consumer spending, purchase behavior, media, and advertising.

FIGURE 12.3

MARKET: Newsletters

Internet and World Wide Web Companies engaged in international business are quickly realizing the wealth of secondary research information available on the Internet and the World Wide Web. These electronic resources are usually user-friendly and have vast amounts of information.

LEXIS-NEXIS (*www.lexis-nexis.com*) is a leading online provider of market information. The LEXIS-NEXIS database of full-text news reports from around the world is updated continuously. It also offers special services such as profiles of executives and products and information on the financial conditions, marketing strategies, and public relations of many international companies. Knight-Ridder (*www.knightridder.com*), CompuServe (*www.compuserve.com*) DIALOG (*www.dialog.com*), and Dow Jones (*www.dj.com*) are other popular online providers of global information. Internet search engines such as Google (*www.google.com*), and Yahoo! (*www.yahoo.com*) are quite helpful in narrowing down the plethora of information available electronically.

The Internet can be especially useful in seeking information about potential production sites. Because field trips to most likely candidates are expensive, online information can be enormously helpful in saving both time and money. For instance, you can begin a search for information on a particular country or region with most large online information providers. Narrowing your search to a more manageable list of subjects—say, culture, economic conditions, or perhaps a specific industry—can yield clues about sites that are promising and those that are not.

Quick Study

1. Identify the benefits associated with conducting international *secondary market research*.
2. What are the three main difficulties of conducting research in international markets? Explain each briefly.
3. Identify some of the main sources of *secondary market research* data.

Methods of Conducting Primary International Research

primary market research
Process of collecting and analyzing original data and applying the results to current research needs.

Although secondary information is very informative and useful in the early stages of the screening process, sometimes more tailored data on a location are needed. Under such circumstances, it might be necessary to conduct **primary market research**—the process of collecting and analyzing original data and applying the results to current research needs. This type of research is very helpful in filling in the blanks left by secondary research. However, it is often more expensive to obtain than secondary research data because studies must be conducted in their entirety. Let's now explore some of the more common methods of primary research used by companies in the location-screening process.

trade show
Exhibition at which members of an industry or group of industries showcase their latest products, see what rivals are doing, and learn about recent trends and opportunities.

Trade Shows and Trade Missions An exhibition at which members of an industry or group of industries showcase their latest products, see what rivals are doing, and learn about recent trends and opportunities is called a **trade show**. They are held on a continuing basis in virtually all markets and normally attract companies from around the globe. They are typically held by national or global industry trade associations or by government agencies. An excellent source of trade shows and exhibitions worldwide is EXPOguide, Inc. (*www.expoguide.com*).

Not surprisingly, the format and scope of trade shows differ from country to country. For example, because of its large domestic market, shows in the United States tend to be oriented toward business opportunities within the U.S. market. In line with U.S. culture, the atmosphere tends to be fairly informal, and business cards are handed out to all the contacts one meets—no matter how briefly. Conversely, because of the relatively smaller market of Germany and its participation in the European Union, trade shows there are

SURVIVAL KIT

Is the World Your Oyster?

How can an entrepreneur or small business succeed in international markets? How can they compete with the more competitive pricing and sales efforts of large multinationals? It isn't easy, but it can be done. First, small companies must do lots of homework before jumping into the global marketplace. Going international is a long-term investment and preparedness is a critical success factor. They also must plan on investing a good deal of cash. A typical small business can expect to pay anywhere from $10,000 to $20,000 to perform some basic market research, to attend a trade show, and to visit one or two countries. Here are the tales of how two small companies are exploiting international opportunities at different stages of going international.

○ Lucille Farms, Inc. of Montville, New Jersey, produces and markets cheese products. Alfonso Falivene, Lucille's chief executive, is taking a cautious approach to going international. He recently joined the U.S. Dairy Export Council, which offers members, among other things, international trips to study new business opportunities and the competition. The Council also offers its members a great deal of free information on international markets. Notes Falivene, "I have stacks of information in my office. If I had to go out and get the information on my own, it would cost me thousands and thousands of dollars."

○ Meter-Man, Inc. of Winnebago, Minnesota, manufactures agricultural measuring devices. When Meter-Man decided to go international, it saw trade shows as a great way to gain market intelligence and establish contacts. At a 5-day agricultural fair in Paris, company executives held 21 meetings with potential customers and sealed an agreement with a major distributor that covers the Parisian market for Meter-Man's products. James Neff, Meter-Man's sales and marketing director, was on a flight to a trade show in Barcelona, Spain, and struck up a conversation with the man next to him. The man wound up ordering $200,000 of Meter-Man's products and is today a major South American distributor for the company.

more international in focus, showcasing business opportunities in markets all across Europe. They also tend be quite formal, and business cards are given to a contact only when a business relationship is highly desirable. To see how small companies can use trade shows and other tools to be successful abroad, read this chapter's Entrepreneur's Survival Kit titled, "Is the World Your Oyster?"

On the other hand, a **trade mission** is an international trip by government officials and businesspeople that is organized by agencies of national or provincial governments for the purpose of exploring international business opportunities. Businesspeople who attend trade missions are typically introduced both to important business contacts and well-placed government officials.

Small and medium-sized companies often find trade missions very appealing for two reasons. First, the support of government officials gives them additional clout in the target country as well as access to officials and executives whom they would otherwise have little opportunity to meet. Second, although such trips can sometimes be expensive for the smallest of businesses, they are generally worth the money because they almost always reap cost-effective rewards. Trade missions to faraway places sometimes involve visits to several countries to maximize the return for the time and money invested. For instance, a trade mission for European businesspeople to Latin America may include stops in Argentina, Brazil, Chile, and Mexico. A trade mission to Asia for North American or European companies might include stops in China, Hong Kong, Japan, South Korea, and Thailand.

trade mission
International trip by government officials and businesspeople that is organized by agencies of national or provincial governments for the purpose of exploring international business opportunities.

Interviews and Focus Groups Although industry data are very useful to companies early in the screening process for potential markets, subsequent steps must assess buyers' emotions, attitudes, and cultural beliefs. Industry data cannot tell us how individuals feel about a company or its product. Deciding whether to enter a market and the subsequent development of an effective marketing plan require this type of buyer information.

Therefore, many companies supplement the large-scale collection of country data with other types of research, such as interviews with prospective customers. Interviews, of course, must be conducted carefully if they are to yield reliable and unbiased information. Respondents in some cultures might be unwilling to answer certain questions or may intentionally give vague or misleading answers to avoid getting too personal. For example, although individuals in the United States are renowned for their willingness to divulge all sorts of information about their shopping habits and even their personal lives, this is very much the exception as one goes around the world.

An unstructured but in-depth interview of a small group of individuals (8 to 12 people) by a moderator to learn the group's attitudes about a company or its product is called a **focus group**. Moderators guide a discussion on a topic but interfere as little as possible with the free flow of ideas. The interview is recorded for later evaluation to identify recurring or prominent themes among the participants. This type of research helps marketers to uncover negative perceptions among buyers and to design corrective marketing strategies. Because subtle differences in verbal and body language could go unnoticed, focus group interviews tend to work best when moderators are natives of the countries in which the interview is held. Ironically, it is sometimes difficult to conduct focus groups in collectivist cultures (see Chapter 2) because people have a tendency to agree with others in the group. In such instances, it might be advisable to use a **consumer panel**—research in which people record in personal diaries, information on their attitudes, behaviors, or purchasing habits.

Surveys
Research in which an interviewer asks current or potential buyers to answer written or verbal questions to obtain facts, opinions, or attitudes is called a **survey**. For example, if Reebok (*www.reebok.com*) wants to learn about consumer attitudes toward its latest women's aerobics shoe in Britain, it could ask a sample of British women about their attitudes toward the shoe. Verbal questioning could be done in person or over the telephone, whereas written questioning could be done in person, through the mail, or through forms completed at Reebok's Web site. The results would then be tabulated, analyzed, and applied to the development of a marketing plan.

The single greatest advantage of survey research is the ability to collect vast amounts of data in a single sweep. But as a rule, survey methods must be adapted to local markets. For example, survey research can be conducted by any technological means in industrialized markets, such as over the telephone or the Internet. But telephone interviewing would yield poor results in Bangladesh because only a small percentage of the general population has telephones. Also, although a survey at a Web site is an easy way to gather data, it must be remembered that even in industrialized nations users still tend to represent only the middle- to upper-income households.

Written surveys can also be hampered by other problems. Some countries' postal services are unreliable to the point that parcels are delivered weeks or months after arriving at post offices, or never arrive at all because they are stolen or simply lost. Naturally, written surveys are impractical to conduct in countries with high rates of illiteracy, although this problem can perhaps be overcome by obtaining verbal responses to spoken questions.

Environmental Scanning
An ongoing process of gathering, analyzing, and dispensing information for tactical or strategic purposes is called **environmental scanning**. The environmental scanning process entails obtaining both factual and subjective information on the business environments in which a company is operating or considering entering. The continuous monitoring of events in other locations keeps managers aware of potential opportunities and threats to minimize financial losses and maximize returns. Environmental scanning contributes to making well-informed decisions and the development of effective strategies. It also helps companies develop contingency plans for a particularly volatile environment.

---

focus group
Unstructured but in-depth interview of a small group of individuals (8 to 12 people) by a moderator to learn the group's attitudes about a company or its product.

consumer panel
Research in which people record in personal diaries, information on their attitudes, behaviors, or purchasing habits.

survey
Research in which an interviewer asks current or potential buyers to answer written or verbal questions to obtain facts, opinions, or attitudes.

environmental scanning
Ongoing process of gathering, analyzing, and dispensing information for tactical or strategic purposes.

1. How does *primary market research* differ from secondary market research?

2. Describe each main method used to conduct primary market research.

3. What are some of the difficulties of conducting international market research?

A Final Word

In order to keep pace with an increasingly hectic and competitive global business environment, companies should follow a systematic screening process that incorporates high-quality research methods. This chapter provided a systematic way to screen potential locations as new markets or sites for business operations. However, these issues constitute only the *first step* in the process of "going international." The next step involves actually accomplishing the task of entering selected markets and establishing operations abroad. In the following chapters, we survey the types of entry modes available to companies, how they acquire the resources needed to carry out their activities, and how they manage their sometimes far-flung international business operations.

SUMMARY

1. **Explain each of the four steps in the *market- and site-screening process.*** The *screening process* can be approached in a systematic four-step manner. Step 1 involves identifying basic appeal for potential markets (e.g., basic product demand) and/or assessing availability of resources for production (e.g., raw materials, labor, capital).

Step 2 of the screening process is to assess the national business environment of the market or site. This involves examining the local culture, political and legal forces (e.g., government bureaucracy, political stability), and economic variables (e.g., fiscal and monetary policies).

Step 3 of the screening process is to measure the potential of each market (e.g., market size and growth, *market-potential indicator*) and/or suitability of a site for operations (e.g., availability of workers, managers, raw materials, infrastructure).

In Step 4 of the screening process, managers normally visit each remaining location to make a final decision (e.g., competitor analysis, financial evaluation).

2. **Describe the three primary difficulties of conducting *international market research.*** The collection and analysis of information in order to assist managers in making informed decisions is called *market research*. Unique conditions and circumstances present three main difficulties that often force adjustments in the *way* research is performed in different nations.

First, managers can face problems with regard to the availability of data. It can be difficult to obtain high-quality, reliable information. In addition to deliberate misrepresentation, tainted information can also result from improper local collection methods and analysis techniques.

Second, the comparability of data across markets can be difficult because terms such as *poverty, consumption,* and *literacy* can differ from nation to nation. Different ways of measuring statistics also affect the comparability of data.

Third, managers can face problems rooted in cultural differences. Companies entering unfamiliar markets often hire local agencies to perform their market research for them. Local researchers know the cultural terrain: they understand which practices are acceptable; which types of questions can be asked; and how to interpret information gathered and its reliability.

3. **Identify the main sources of *secondary international data,* and explain their usefulness.** The process of obtaining information that already exists within the company or that can be obtained from outside sources is called *secondary market research*.

International organizations are excellent sources of free and inexpensive information about demand for a product in a particular country. International development agencies, such as the World Bank and the International Monetary Fund, also provide valuable secondary data. *Government agencies*—commerce departments and international trade agencies of most countries—often have information on import-export regulations, quality standards, and the sizes of markets. Commercial agencies of many states and provinces often have offices in other countries to promote trade and investment.

Companies often join *industry and trade associations* composed of firms within their own industries or trades. The publications of these organizations help managers to keep abreast of important issues and opportunities. Many international *service organizations* in fields such as banking, insurance, management consulting, and accounting offer information to their clients on cultural, regulatory, and financial conditions in a market.

4. **Describe the main methods used to conduct *primary international research.*** The process of collecting and analyzing original data and applying the results to current research needs is called *primary market research.* However, primary research data are often more expensive to obtain than secondary research data because studies must be conducted in their entirety. Exhibitions at which members of an industry or group of industries showcase their latest products, see what rivals are doing, and learn about recent trends and opportunities are called *trade shows.* A *trade mission* is an international trip by government officials and businesspeople that is organized by agencies of national or provincial governments for the purpose of exploring international business opportunities.

Companies can use *interviews* to assess potential buyers' emotions, attitudes, and cultural beliefs. An unstructured but in-depth interview of a small group of individuals by a moderator to learn the group's attitudes about a company or its product is called a *focus group.* In *surveys*, interviewers obtain facts, opinions, or attitudes by asking current or potential buyers to answer written or verbal questions. An ongoing process of gathering, analyzing, and dispensing information for tactical or strategic purposes is called *environmental scanning.*

TALK IT OVER

1. For many global companies, China represents a very attractive market in terms of size and growth rate. However, because China has a communist government, it ranks lower in terms of economic freedom and higher in political risk than some other countries. But in spite of these risks, hundreds of companies have established manufacturing operations in China. In large part, this is because the Chinese government makes selling in China contingent on a company's willingness to locate production there. The government wants Chinese companies to learn modern management skills from non-Chinese companies and to acquire technology. Some observers believe that when Western companies agree to such conditions, they are bargaining away important industry know-how in exchange for sales today. Should companies go along with China's terms, or should they risk losing sales by refusing to transfer technology?

2. When Sony (*www.sony.com*) mounted its third official attempt to launch its MiniDisc recorder/player in the United States, it thought it finally had the right formula. Although the product was a success in Japan, response to the MiniDisc in the U.S. market was lukewarm. A Sony executive noted, "This time around, we've done our homework, and we've found out what's in consumers' heads." What type of research do you think Sony used to "get inside the heads" of its target market? Do you think different cultures rely on different types of market research? Explain.

3. What are some of the benefits of "soft" market research data gathered using techniques such as focus groups and observation. What are the benefits of using "hard" data such as statistics on consumers' buying habits and figures on market size? As a manager, explain when each kind of data would be preferred and tell why.

TEAMING UP

1. As a group, visit your college's library and consult the *Encyclopedia of Associations* or similar organization on the Web. Select one or two industry associations of interest to your group. Write or call the association(s) and request an information packet, and compile a summary of the information received from them. Compare the information your group receives with information sent by trade associations fellow groups of students researched. Rank the trade associations in terms of the usefulness of their available information.

2. Select an emerging market that your team would like to learn more about. Start by compiling fundamental country data. Then do additional research to flesh out the

nature of the market opportunity offered by this country or its suitability as a manufacturing site (*Hint*: Follow the steps identified in this chapter). Make a list of the international companies pursuing market opportunities in the country, and identify the products or brands that the companies are marketing. Are their reasons for doing business in the country consistent with the market opportunity as you have researched it? Determine whether these companies have established facilities for manufacturing, sales, or both.

3. A great deal of market information can be found in business-oriented magazines and journals. However, depending on where the magazine is published, the

editorial point of view or emphasis may vary. Have each member of your team find a recent feature article on a different country market. Some places to start include *The Economist* (www.economist.com), *Far Eastern Economic Review* (www.feer.com), and *Business Week* (www.businessweek.com). Each member should write a brief summary of each article, which compares and contrasts issues such as content coverage, point of view, and editorial tone in the different magazines. How might a manager's opinion of a market be shaped by the views expressed?

KEY TERMS

consumer panel (p. 364)

environmental scanning (p. 364)

focus group (p. 364)

income elasticity (p. 352)

logistics (p. 349)

market research (p. 357)

primary market research (p. 362)

secondary market research (p. 359)

survey (p. 364)

trade mission (p. 363)

trade show (p. 362)

TAKE IT TO THE WEB

1. We learned in this chapter how managers might screen potential new markets and new sites for operations in a systematic manner. Because the U.S. market absorbs the vast majority of Mexico's exports, it is no surprise that the fates of the two economies are closely related. Yet the relative high cost of Mexico's economy means that some Western companies are heading east, not south.

   Research the recent performance of Mexico's economy on the Internet (both Mexican and U.S. publications if possible). Update the performance of Mexico's economy using resources such as the business press and statistical databases. (*Hint*: You may begin your Internet research by visiting some of the many Web sites listed in this chapter.) If wages are rising, why are companies still investing in Mexico? If wages are rising, is it across the board or just in specific sectors? From what sectors are investments flowing in to Mexico, and from where are they coming?

   Select a country that competes with Mexico for foreign direct investment. What characteristics make Mexico a better production base? What makes it a worse production base? Compare the two countries in terms of their long-term market potential. List as many direct and relevant comparisons as you can. (*Hint*: You may want to use this chapter's screening process as a guide.)

ETHICAL CHALLENGES

1. You are a member of the Council of Economic Advisors to the U.S. President asked to assess the moral basis for outsourcing to low-wage countries. Many globalization protesters argue that multinational corporations from wealthy countries endanger the global economic system by investing capital in developing countries and laying-off workers at home. They say globalization pits the interests of more prosperous workers in wealthy countries against the interests of lower-paid workers in developing countries. It is also claimed that the practice pits nations against one another as companies move from one developing country to another in search of lower wages or bigger market opportunities. Do multinationals have an ethical obligation to try to preserve jobs for workers in their home-country markets? How would you advise the President on this issue? Justify your advice with concrete information.

2. You are the CEO of a large multinational company that has become highly profitable by investing in a Latin American country. As a catalyst in mobilizing the nation's low-cost labor force, your company has helped the nation achieve double-digit economic growth. Following a political upheaval, however, a military government takes control. Workers' rights are being violated, as are those of individual citizens. As CEO, it is up to you to decide on a course of action. Should you pull out of the country, effectively abandoning your employees? Should you publicly and directly confront the leaders of the new government and insist that they respect workers' rights? Should you proceed more discreetly and pursue diplomacy out of the public's eye? Or, would another course of action be advisable? Can you make an ethical decision that is also a good business decision?

3. You are executive director of Qualitative Research Consultants Association (QRCA), an organization designed to assist market research practitioners. As part of their membership agreement, QRCA members agree to abide by a nine-point code of ethics that forbids practices such as discriminating in respondent recruitment and offering kickbacks or other favors in exchange for business. The code also calls for research to be conducted for legitimate research purposes, and not as a front for product promotion. Why do you think the QRCA and other market research organizations create such codes? Do you believe they are helpful in reducing unethical research practices? As QRCA director, what other areas of marketing research do you believe should be covered by ethical codes of conduct?

PRACTICING INTERNATION

Vietnam's Emerging Market Potential

learning objec...

After studying this chapter, yo...

1. Explain why and how comp... importing, and countertr...

2. Explain the various m... and import activities

3. Describe the diff... that are availab...

4. Explain the... modes.

5. Discus... sele...

In 1990, Vietnam's communist government announced that non-Vietnamese manufacturers were welcome to set up shop in the Southeast Asian country. South Korea's Daewoo (*www.dm.co.kr*) quickly established itself as the number-o... investor in Vietnam. Other well-known companies, includ... Toshiba (*www.toshiba.co.jp*), Peugeot (*www.peugeot.com*), British Petroleum (*www.bp.com*), also took Hanoi up on its tation. However, the absence of trade and diplomatic rela... between the United States and Vietnam meant that U.S. com... had to sit on the sidelines. Nearly 4 years later, the U.S. gove... lifted the trade embargo with Vietnam, paving the way for U.S. companies to pursue opportunities in Vietnam. Vietn... tion in the heart of Asia and the presence of a literate... workforce are powerful magnets for international compa...

Today there are many challenges for investors in V... population of around 83 million is very poor, with an annua... capita income (at purchasing power parity) of only about $2,500. The infrastructure is undeveloped: Only 25 percent of roads are paved; electricity sources are somewhat unreliable; there is roughly one telephone per 100 people (though mobile phone use is growing rapidly); and the banking system is undeveloped. And although Vietnam holds tremendous long-term potential, it may be two decades before Vietnam reaches the level of economic development found even in Thailand today.

In addition, the Communist Party of Vietnam is struggling to adapt to the principles of a market economy, and the layers of bureaucracy built up over decades of communist rule slow the pace of change. Despite the efforts of the State Committee for Cooperation and Investment, the government sometimes still conducts itself in a way that leaves international investors scratching their heads. In one incident Hanoi embarked on a "social evils crackdown" that included pulling down or painting over any sign or billboard printed in a language other than Vietnamese. And laws concerning taxes and foreign exchange are in constant flux.

Yet an emerging entrepreneurial class in Vietnam has developed a taste for expensive products such as Nikon (*www.nikon.co.jp*) cameras and Ray Ban (*www.rayban.com*) sunglasses—both of which are available in stores. Says Do Duc Dinh of the Institute on the World Economy, "There is a huge unofficial economy. For most people, we can live only 5 days or 10 days a month on our salary. But people build houses. Where does the money come from? Even in government ministries, there are two sets of books—one for the official money and one for unofficial."

u... price of an...

Aside from Chi... economy. For a decade to 2005, ... shows no sign of slowing down. In fact, ... crisis that gripped Southeast Asia in the late 1990... nomic growth rate never dipped below 4.8 percent. The ... trade-driven economic boom has lifted many Vietnamese out of poverty. Whereas the World Bank labeled as much as 58 percent of the population poor in 1993, that number had fallen to 29 percent by 2003.

Thinking Globally

1. Update the political, legal, and economic situation in Vietnam. Then, select a product of your choosing and evaluate Vietnam's potential both as a market and as a manufacturing site.

2. What, if anything, can Western countries do to help improve the political climate for doing business in Vietnam? Give specific examples.

3. What problems might a company encounter while conducting market research in Vietnam? Explain your answer.

4. What would be your perception of a product with the label "Made in Vietnam"? Do you think the type of product would play a role in forming your perception? If so, why?

...should be able to

...anies use *exporting*,
...de.

...ans of *financing* export

...erent *contractual entry modes*
...le to companies.

...various types of *investment entry*

...the important *strategic factors* in
...cting an entry mode.

selecting and managing 13

entry modes

a look **back**

CHAPTER 12 explained how companies analyze international business opportunities. We learned how managers screen and research both potential markets and sites for operations.

a look **at this chapter**

This chapter introduces the different entry modes companies use to "go international." We discuss the important issues surrounding the selection and management of: (1) exporting, importing, and countertrade; (2) contractual entry modes; and (3) investment entry modes.

a look **ahead**

CHAPTER 14 explains the international marketing efforts of companies. We identify the key elements that influence how companies promote, price, and distribute their products.

License to Thrill

LONDON, England—Marvel Enterprises (*www.marvel.com*) is a global character-based entertainment licensing company that spent the past 60 years developing a library of over 4,700 characters. Pictured above and center, Marvel CEO, Allen Lipson is joined by Marvel Comics characters as he rings the opening bell on the first day Marvel is listed on the New York Stock Exchange.

Marvel has come a long way since its days of bankruptcy proceedings in 1996. It was back then Marvel discovered licensing and turned itself into more than just a comics and toys company. To date, Marvel has brought 5 comic-book characters—Spider-Man, Blade, X-Men, Daredevil, and Hulk—to the big screen, and more are on the way. Yet the films generate little of Marvel's revenue, operating instead as vehicles for popularizing the firm's comic-book characters.

Driving much of Marvel's earnings in recent years are its character-based licensing agreements for products such as lunch boxes, toys, and video games. Marvel's licensing activity includes a deal with Toy Biz Worldwide (*www.toybiz.com*) of Hong Kong to distribute action figures based on Marvel's characters. In return, Marvel earns a royalty on all toys sold through Toy Biz. Marvel also has a 50/50 joint venture with Sony (*www.sony.com*) that oversees all licensing and merchandising for *Spider-Man*, as well as Sony's animated TV series titled, *Spider-Man*.

But the company is not resting easy, marveling at its past success. Newly created Marvel International, based in London, England, is charged with developing the firm's licensing in key international markets. Commenting on the new entity, CEO Lipson said, "This is a major strategic initiative for the company. Marvel's international growth is largely untapped." As you read this chapter, think about why companies go international, the different market entry modes available to them, and when each mode is appropriate.[1]

entry mode
Institutional arrangement by which a firm gets its products, technologies, human skills, or other resources into a market.

The decision of how to enter a new market abroad is influenced by many factors, including the local business environment and a company's own core competency. An **entry mode** is the institutional arrangement by which a firm gets its products, technologies, human skills, or other resources into a market.[2] Thus companies seek entry to new markets for the purposes of manufacturing and/or selling products within them. Firms going international have many potential entry modes at their disposal. The specific mode chosen depends on many factors, including experience in a market, amount of control managers desire, and potential size of the market. Let's now explore each of the three categories of entry modes that are available to companies:

1. Exporting, importing, and countertrade
2. Contractual entry
3. Investment entry

Exporting, Importing, and Countertrade

The most common method of buying and selling goods internationally is exporting and importing. Companies often import products in order to obtain less expensive goods or those that are simply unavailable in the domestic market. Companies export products when the international marketplace offers opportunities to increase sales and, in turn, profits. Companies worldwide (from both developed and developing countries) often see the United States as a great export opportunity because of the size of the market and the strong buying power of its citizens. Figure 13.1 showcases the top 10 exporters to the United States in terms of the value of goods sold.

Because this chapter focuses on how companies take their goods and services to the global marketplace, the following discussion concentrates on exporting. Because the other side of the transaction—importing—is a sourcing decision for most firms, it is covered in

FIGURE 13.1

Land of Opportunity

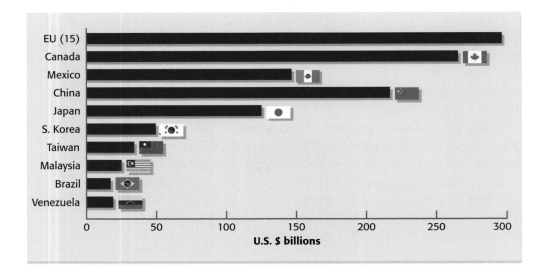

Chapter 15. Following the presentation of exporting, we explain how companies use *countertrade* to conduct product exchanges across borders when cash transactions are not possible.

Why Companies Export

In the global economy, companies increasingly sell goods and services to wholesalers, retailers, industrial buyers, and consumers in other nations. Generally speaking, there are three main reasons why companies begin exporting:

1. *Expand Sales.* Most large companies use exporting as a means of expanding total sales when the domestic market has become saturated. Greater sales volume allows them to spread the fixed costs of production over a greater number of manufactured products, thereby lowering the cost of producing each unit of output. In short, going international is one way to achieve economies of scale.

2. *Diversify Sales.* Exporting permits companies to diversify their sales. In other words, they can offset slow sales in one national market (perhaps due to a recession) with increased sales in another. Diversified sales can level off a company's cash flow—making it easier to coordinate payments to creditors with receipts from customers.

3. *Gain Experience.* Companies often use exporting as a low-cost, low-risk way of getting started in international business. For example, owners and managers of small companies, which typically have little or no knowledge of how to conduct business in other cultures, use exporting to gain valuable international experience.

Developing an Export Strategy: A Four-Step Model

Companies are often drawn into exporting when customers in other countries solicit their goods. This is a fairly natural way for companies to become aware of their product's international potential. In the process, companies get their first taste of how international business differs from that in the domestic market. Unfortunately, it is also during these initial tentative steps outside the domestic market that companies commit their first international blunders.

Firms should not fall into the habit of simply responding to random international requests for their products. A more logical approach is to research and analyze international opportunities and to develop a coherent export strategy. A firm with such a strategy actively pursues export markets rather than sitting back and waiting for international orders to come in by fax or e-mail. Let's now take a look at each of the four steps in developing a successful export strategy.

Step 1: Identify a Potential Market
In order to identify clearly whether demand exists in a particular target market, market research should be performed and the results interpreted (see Chapter 12). Novice exporters should focus on one or only a few markets. For example, a first-time Brazilian exporter might not want to export simultaneously to Argentina, Britain, and Greece. A better strategy would probably be to focus on Argentina because of its cultural similarities with Brazil (despite different, although related, languages). The company could then expand into more diverse markets after it gains some international experience in a nearby country. Also, the would-be exporter should seek the advice of experts on the regulations and the process of exporting in general, and exporting to the selected target market in particular.

Step 2: Match Needs to Abilities
The next step is to assess carefully whether the company has the ability to satisfy the needs of the market. For instance, suppose a market located in a region with a warm, humid climate for much of the year displays the need for home air-conditioning equipment. If a company recognizes this need but makes only industrial-size air-conditioning equipment, it might not be able to satisfy demand with its current product.

However, if the company is able to use its smallest industrial air-conditioning unit to satisfy the needs of several homes, it might have a market opportunity. If there are no other options or if consumers want their own individual units, the company will probably need to design a smaller air-conditioning unit or rule out entry into that market.

Step 3: Initiate Meetings

Having meetings early with potential local distributors, buyers, and others is a must. Initial contact should focus on building trust and developing a cooperative climate among all parties. The cultural differences between the parties will come into play already at this stage. Beyond building trust, successive meetings are designed to estimate the potential success of any agreement if interest is shown on both sides. At the most advanced stage, negotiations take place and details of agreements are finalized.

A group of companies from Arizona called the Environmental Technology Industry Cluster was searching for a market for its environmental products in Taiwan. When a delegation from Taiwan arrived in the Arizona desert to survey the group's products, it was not all formal meetings and negotiations. Although the schedule during the day was busy with company visits, evenings were designed to build relationships, which are important to businesspeople from Taiwan. There were outdoor barbecues, hayrides, line dancing, and visits to Mexican restaurants and frontier towns to give the visitors from Taiwan a feel for local culture and history. To create the type of environment in which their counterparts from Taiwan prefer getting to know business associates, nighttime schedules also included visits to karaoke spots and Chinese restaurants, where a good deal of singing took place. Follow-up meetings resulted in several successful deals.[3]

Step 4: Commit Resources

After all the meetings, negotiations, and contract signings, it is time to put the company's human, financial, and physical resources to work. First, the objectives of the export program must be clearly stated and should extend out at least 3 to 5 years. For small firms, it may be sufficient to assign one individual the responsibility for drawing up objectives and estimating resources. However, as companies expand their activities to include more products and/or markets, many firms discover the need for an export department or division. The head of this department usually has the responsibility (and authority) to formulate, implement, and evaluate the company's export strategy. See Chapter 11 for a detailed discussion of important organizational design issues to be considered at this stage.

Degree of Export Involvement

Entrepreneurs, small and medium-sized companies, and large multinational firms all engage in exporting. However, not all companies get involved in exporting activities to the same extent. Some companies (usually entrepreneurs and small and medium-sized firms) perform few or none of the activities necessary to get their products in a market abroad. Instead they use intermediaries that specialize in getting products from one market into another. Other companies (usually only the largest of companies) perform all of their export activities themselves, with an infrastructure that bridges the gap between the two markets. Let's take a closer look at the two basic forms of export involvement—*direct exporting* and *indirect exporting*.

Direct Exporting

Some companies become deeply involved in the export of their products. **Direct exporting** occurs when a company sells its products directly to buyers in a target market. Direct exporters operate in industries such as aircraft (Boeing) (*www.boeing.com*), industrial equipment (John Deere) (*www.deere.com*), apparel (Lands' End) (*www.landsend.com*), and bottled beverages (Evian) (*www.evian.com*). Bear in mind that "direct exporters" need not sell directly to *end users*. Rather, they take full responsibility for getting their goods into the target market by selling directly to local buyers and not going through intermediary companies. Typically, they rely on either local *sales representatives* or *distributors*.

Sales Representatives A *sales representative* (whether an individual or an organization) represents only its own company's products, not those of other companies. They promote those products in many ways, such as by attending trade fairs and making personal visits to

direct exporting
Practice by which a company sells its products directly to buyers in a target market.

local retailers and wholesalers. They do not take title to the merchandise. Rather, they are hired by a company and normally are compensated with a fixed salary plus commissions based on the value of their sales.

Distributors Alternatively, a direct exporter can sell in the target market through *distributors*, who take ownership of the merchandise when it enters their country. As owners of the products, they accept all the risks associated with generating local sales. They sell either to retailers and wholesalers or to end users through their own channels of distribution. Typically, they earn a profit equal to the difference between the price they pay and the price they receive for the exporter's goods. Although using a distributor reduces the exporter's risk, it also weakens the exporter's control over the prices actually charged to buyers. A distributor who charges unwarranted prices can stunt the growth of an exporter's market share. Therefore, it is important that exporters select reliable distributors. They should choose distributors who are willing to invest in the promotion of their products and who do not sell directly competing products. Despite the benefits of direct exporting, some companies implement a policy of *indirect exporting*.

Indirect Exporting

Some companies have few resources available to commit to exporting activities. Others simply find exporting a daunting experience because of a lack of contacts and experience. Fortunately, there is an option for such firms. **Indirect exporting** occurs when a company sells its products to intermediaries who then resell to buyers in a target market. The choice of intermediary depends on many factors, including the ratio of the exporter's international sales to its total sales, the company's available resources, and the growth rate of the target market. Let's take a closer look at several different types of intermediaries: *agents*, *export management companies*, and *export trading companies*.

indirect exporting
Practice by which a company sells its products to intermediaries who resell to buyers in a target market.

Agents Individuals or organizations that represent one or more indirect exporters in a target market are called **agents**. Agents typically receive compensation in the form of commissions on the value of sales. Because establishing a relationship with an agent is relatively easy and inexpensive, it is a fairly common approach to indirect exporting. However, agents should be chosen very carefully because it can be costly and difficult to terminate an agency relationship if problems arise. Careful selection is also necessary because agents often represent several indirect exporters simultaneously. They might focus their promotional efforts on the products of the company paying the highest commission rather than on the company with the better products.

agents
Individuals or organizations that represent one or more indirect exporters in a target market.

Export Management Companies A company that exports products on behalf of an indirect exporter is called an **export management company (EMC)**. An EMC operates contractually, either as an agent (being paid through commissions based on the value of sales) or as a distributor (taking ownership of the merchandise and earning a profit from its resale).

An EMC will usually provide additional services on a retainer basis, charging set fees against funds deposited on account. Typical EMC services include gathering market information, formulating promotional strategies, performing specific promotional duties (such as attending trade fairs), researching customer credit, making shipping arrangements, and coordinating export documents. It is common for an EMC to exploit contacts predominantly in one industry (say, agricultural goods or consumer products) or in one geographic area (such as Latin America or the Middle East). Indeed, the biggest advantage of an EMC is usually a deep understanding of the cultural, political, legal, and economic conditions of the target market. Its staff works comfortably and effectively in the cultures of both the exporting and the target nation. The average EMC tends to deploy a wide array of commercial and political contacts to facilitate business activities on behalf of its clients.

Perhaps the only disadvantage of hiring an EMC is that the breadth and depth of its service can potentially hinder the development of the exporter's own international expertise. But an exporter and its EMC typically have such a close relationship that an exporter often considers its EMC as a virtual exporting division. When this is the case, exporters learn a great deal about the intricacies of exporting from their EMC. Then, after the EMC contract expires, it is common for a company to go it alone in exporting its products.

export management company (EMC)
Company that exports products on behalf of indirect exporters.

export trading company (ETC)
Company that provides services to indirect exporters in addition to activities related directly to clients' exporting activities.

Export Trading Companies   A company that provides services to indirect exporters in addition to activities directly related to clients' exporting activities is called an **export trading company (ETC)**. Whereas an EMC is restricted to export-related activities, an ETC assists its clients by providing import, export, and countertrade services, developing and expanding distribution channels, providing storage facilities, financing trading and investment projects, and even manufacturing products.

European trading nations first developed the ETC concept centuries ago. More recently, the Japanese have refined the concept, which they call *sogo shosha*. The Japanese ETC can range in size from small, family-run businesses to enormous conglomerates such as C. Itoh (*www.itochuele.co.jp*), Mitsubishi (*www.mitsubishi.com*), and Mitsui (*www.mitsui.com*). An ETC in South Korea is called a *chaebol* and includes well-known companies such as Hyundai (*www.hyundai.com*) and Samsung (*www.samsung.com*).

Because of their enormous success in gaining market share in global markets, Japanese and South Korean ETCs became formidable competitors. These Asian companies quickly came to rival the dominance of large multinationals based in the United States. The U.S. multinationals lobbied lawmakers in their home country for assistance in challenging the large Asian ETCs in global markets. The result was the Export Trading Company Act, passed in 1982. Despite this effort, the ETC concept never really caught on in the United States. Operations of the typical ETC in the United States remain small and are dwarfed by those of their Asian counterparts. One reason for the lack of interest in the ETC concept in the United States relative to Asia is that governments, financial institutions, and companies have much closer working relationships in Asia. Thus, the formation of huge conglomerates that engage in activities ranging from providing financing to manufacturing to distribution is easier to accomplish. In contrast, the regulatory environment in the United States is wary of such cozy business arrangements, and the lines between companies and industries are more clearly drawn.

Avoiding Export and Import Blunders

There are several errors common to companies that are new to exporting. First, many fail to conduct adequate market research before exporting. In fact, many companies begin exporting by responding to unsolicited requests for their products. If a company enters a market in this manner, it should quickly devise an export strategy to manage its export activities effectively and not strain its resources.

Second, many companies fail to obtain adequate export advice. National and regional governments are often willing to assist firms that are new to exporting. Such sources can help managers and small-business owners understand and cope with the vast amounts of paperwork required by each country's exporting and importing laws. Naturally, more experienced exporters can be extremely helpful as well. They can help novice exporters avoid embarrassing mistakes by guiding them through unfamiliar cultural, political, and economic environments.

freight forwarder
Specialist in export-related activities such as customs clearing, tariff schedules, and shipping and insurance fees.

To better ensure that it will not make embarrassing blunders, an inexperienced exporter might also wish to engage the services of a **freight forwarder**—a specialist in export-related activities such as customs clearing, tariff schedules, and shipping and insurance fees. Freight forwarders also can pack shipments for export and take responsibility for getting a shipment from the port of export to the port of import.

Quick Study

1. Briefly describe each of the four steps involved in building an export strategy.
2. How does *direct exporting* differ from *indirect exporting*?
3. Compare and contrast *export management companies* and *export trading companies*.

Countertrade

Companies are sometimes unable to import merchandise in exchange for financial payment. The two common reasons for this are that the government of the importer's nation lacks the hard currency to pay for imports or it restricts the convertibility of its currency.

Fortunately, there is a way for firms to trade by using either a small amount of hard currency or even none at all. Selling goods or services that are paid for, in whole or part, with other goods or services is called **countertrade**. Although the effective use of countertrade often requires an extensive network of international contacts, even smaller companies can take advantage of its benefits.

Since the 1960s the formerly communist countries in Eastern and Central Europe have used countertrade extensively. The governments of some nations in Africa, Asia, and the Middle East also use countertrade. A lack of adequate hard currency has often forced those nations to use countertrade to exchange oil for passenger aircraft and military equipment. Today, because of insufficient hard currency, developing and emerging markets frequently rely on countertrade to import goods. The greater involvement of firms from industrialized nations in those markets is causing the use of countertrade to increase.

Types of Countertrade

There are several different types of countertrade: *barter*, *counterpurchase*, *offset*, *switch trading*, and *buyback*. Let's take a brief look at each of these.

- **Barter** is the exchange of goods or services directly for other goods or services without the use of money. It is the oldest known form of countertrade.

- **Counterpurchase** is the sale of goods or services to a country by a company that promises to make a future purchase of a specific product from that country. The purpose of this type of agreement is to allow the country to earn back some of the currency that it paid out for the original imports.

- **Offset** is an agreement that a company will offset a hard-currency sale to a nation by making a hard-currency purchase of an unspecified product from that nation in the future. It differs from a counterpurchase in that this type of agreement does not specify the type of product that must be purchased, just the amount that will be spent. Such an arrangement gives a firm greater freedom in fulfilling its end of a countertrade deal.

- **Switch trading** is countertrade whereby one company sells to another its obligation to make a purchase in a given country. For example, in return for market access, a firm that wishes to enter a target market might promise to buy a product for which it has no use. The company then sells this purchase obligation to a large trading company that may make the purchase itself because it has a use for the merchandise. Alternatively, if the trading company has no use for the merchandise, it can arrange for yet another buyer, which has a use for the product, to make the purchase.

- **Buyback** is the export of industrial equipment in return for products produced by that equipment. This practice usually typifies long-term relationships between the companies involved.

countertrade
Practice of selling goods or services that are paid for, in whole or part, with other goods or services.

barter
Exchange of goods or services directly for other goods or services without the use of money.

counterpurchase
Sale of goods or services to a country by a company that promises to make a future purchase of a specific product from the country.

offset
Agreement that a company will offset a hard-currency sale to a nation by making a hard-currency purchase of an unspecified product from that nation in the future.

switch trading
Practice in which one company sells to another its obligation to make a purchase in a given country.

buyback
Export of industrial equipment in return for products produced by that equipment.

With Argentina's economy mired in seemingly endless recession, barter is a way of life. Barter, or trueque, is a $400 million-a-year business nationwide. With unemployment on the rise and people strapped for cash, the use of trueque could grow further. In this market near Buenos Aires, you can swap audio CDs, clothing, fruit, pizzas, plumbing supplies, soup, and vegetables. Even local newspapers run ads for such things as apartments, cars, and washing machines, all offered on a barter basis. In your opinion, what are some of the positive and negative aspects of barter?

Thus, countertrade can provide access to markets that are otherwise off-limits because of a lack of hard currency. But it can also cause a company a headache. The root cause is that much countertrade involves commodity and agricultural products such as oil, wheat, or corn—products whose prices on world markets tend to fluctuate a good deal. A problem arises when the price of a bartered product falls on world markets between the time that a deal is arranged and the time at which one party tries to sell the product. Thus, fluctuating prices generate the same type of risk that is encountered in currency markets. Managers might be able to hedge some of this risk on commodity futures markets in much the same way as they hedge against currency fluctuations in currency markets (see Chapter 9).

Export/Import Financing

International trade poses risks for both exporters and importers. Exporters run the risk of not receiving payment after their products are delivered. Importers fear that delivery might not occur once payment is made for a shipment. Accordingly, a number of export/import financing methods are designed to reduce the risk to which exporters and importers are exposed. These include *advance payment, documentary collection, letter of credit,* and *open account*. Let's take a closer look at each of these methods and the risk each holds for exporters and importers.

Advance Payment

advance payment
Export/import financing in which an importer pays an exporter for merchandise before it is shipped.

Export/import financing in which an importer pays an exporter for merchandise before it is shipped is called **advance payment**. This method of payment is common when two parties are unfamiliar with each other, the transaction is relatively small, or the buyer is unable to obtain credit because of a poor credit rating at banks. Payment normally takes the form of a wire transfer of money from the bank account of the importer directly to that of the exporter. Although prior payment eliminates the risk of nonpayment for exporters, it creates the complementary risk of nonshipment for importers—importers might pay for goods but never receive them. Thus, advance payment is the most favorable method for exporters but the least favorable for importers (see Figure 13.2).

Documentary Collection

documentary collection
Export/import financing in which a bank acts as an intermediary without accepting financial risk.

Export/import financing in which a bank acts as an intermediary without accepting financial risk is called **documentary collection**. This payment method is commonly used when there is an ongoing business relationship between two parties. The documentary-collection process can be broken into three main stages and nine smaller steps (see Figure 13.3).

FIGURE 13.2

Risk of Alternative Export/Import Financing Methods

FIGURE 13.3

Documentary Collection Process

Exporter

Importer

Exporter's Bank

Importer's Bank

① **Exporter/Importer contract to sell/buy goods**

② **Exporter's bank gives draft to exporter**

③ **Exporter ships goods to importer**

④ **Exporter delivers documents to its bank**

⑤ **Exporter's bank sends documents to importer's bank**

⑥ **Importer delivers payment to its bank**

⑦ **Importer's bank gives bill of lading to importer**

⑧ **Importer's bank pays exporter's bank**

⑨ **Exporter's bank pays exporter for goods**

1. Before shipping merchandise, the exporter (with its banker's assistance) draws up a **draft (bill of exchange)**—a document ordering the importer to pay the exporter a specified sum of money at a specified time. A *sight draft* requires the importer to pay when goods are delivered. A *time draft* extends the period of time (typically 30, 60, or 90 days) following delivery by which the importer must pay for the goods. (When inscribed "accepted" by an importer, a time draft becomes a negotiable instrument that can be traded among financial institutions.)

2. Following the creation of the draft, the exporter delivers the merchandise to a transportation company for shipment to the importer. The exporter then delivers to its banker a set of documents that includes the draft, a *packing list* of items shipped, and a **bill of lading**—a contract between the exporter and shipper that specifies destination and shipping costs of the merchandise. The bill of lading is proof that the exporter has shipped the merchandise. An international ocean shipment requires an *inland bill of lading* to get the shipment to the exporter's border, and an *ocean bill of lading* for water transport to the importer nation. An international air shipment requires an *air way bill* that covers the entire international journey.

3. After receiving appropriate documents from the exporter, the exporter's bank sends the documents to the importer's bank. After the importer fulfills the terms stated on the draft and pays its own bank, the bank issues the bill of lading (which becomes title to the merchandise) to the importer.

Documentary collection reduces the importer's risk of nonshipment, because the packing list details the contents of the shipment and the bill of lading is proof that the merchandise was shipped. The exporter's risk of nonpayment is increased because although the exporter retains title to the goods until the merchandise is accepted, the importer does not pay until all necessary documents have been received. Although importers have the option of refusing the draft (and, therefore, the merchandise), this

draft (bill of exchange)
Document ordering an importer to pay an exporter a specified sum of money at a specified time.

bill of lading
Contract between an exporter and a shipper that specifies merchandise destination and shipping costs.

action is unlikely. Refusing the draft—despite all terms of the agreement being fulfilled—would cause the importer's bank to be leery of doing business with the importer in the future.

Letter of Credit Export/import financing in which the importer's bank issues a document stating that the bank will pay the exporter when the exporter fulfills the terms of the document is called **letter of credit**. A letter of credit is typically used when an importer's credit rating is questionable, when the exporter needs a letter of credit to obtain financing, and when a market's regulations require it.

Before a bank issues a letter of credit, it checks on the importer's financial condition. Banks normally issue letters of credit only after an importer has deposited on account a sum equal in value to that of the imported merchandise. The bank is still required to pay the exporter, but the deposit protects the bank if the importer fails to pay for the merchandise. Banks will sometimes waive this requirement for their most reputable clients.

There are several types of letters of credit:

- An *irrevocable letter of credit* allows the bank issuing the letter to modify its terms only after obtaining the approval of both exporter and importer.

- A *revocable letter of credit* can be modified by the issuing bank without obtaining approval from either the exporter or the importer.

- A *confirmed letter of credit* is guaranteed by both the exporter's bank in the country of export and the importer's bank in the country of import.

The letter of credit process for the payment of exports is shown in Figure 13.4. After the issuance of a letter of credit, the importer's bank informs the exporter (through the exporter's bank) that a letter of credit exists and that it may now ship the merchandise. The exporter then delivers a set of documents (according to the terms of the letter) to its

letter of credit
Export/import financing in which the importer's bank issues a document stating that the bank will pay the exporter when the exporter fulfills the terms of the document.

FIGURE 13.4

Letter of Credit Process

1. Exporter/Importer contract to sell/buy goods
2. Importer applies for letter of credit
3. Importer's bank issues letter of credit to exporter's bank on importer's behalf
4. Exporter's bank informs exporter of letter of credit
5. Exporter ships goods to importer
6. Exporter delivers documents to its bank
7. Exporter's bank checks documents and pays exporter
8. Exporter's bank delivers documents to importer's bank
9. Importer pays its bank for value of goods
10. Importer's bank sends payment to exporter's bank
11. Importer's bank delivers documents to importer

own bank. These documents typically include an invoice, customs forms, a packing list, and a bill of lading. The exporter's bank ensures that the documents are in order and pays the exporter.

When the importer's bank is satisfied that the terms of the letter have been met, it pays the exporter's bank. At that point, the importer's bank is responsible for collecting payment from the importer. Letters of credit are popular among traders because banks assume most of the risks. The letter of credit reduces the importer's risk of nonshipment (as compared with advance payment) because the importer receives proof of shipment before making payment. Although the exporter's risk of nonpayment is slightly increased, it is a more secure form of payment for exporters because the nonpayment risk is accepted by the importer's bank when it issues payment to the exporter's bank.

Open Account Export/import financing in which an exporter ships merchandise and later bills the importer for its value is called **open account**. Because some receivables may not be collected, exporters should reserve shipping on open account only for their most trusted customers. This payment method is often used when the parties are very familiar with each other or for sales between two subsidiaries within an international company. The exporter simply invoices the importer (as in many domestic transactions), stating the amount and date due. This method reduces the risk of nonshipment faced by the importer under the advance payment method.

By the same token, the open account method increases the risk of nonpayment for the exporter. Thus, open account is the least favorable for exporters but the most favorable for importers. The Entrepreneur's Survival Kit titled, "Global Collection Guidelines" provides some insight on how small exporters can increase the probability of getting paid for a shipment.

open account
Export/import financing in which an exporter ships merchandise and later bills the importer for its value.

Quick Study

1. Why do companies engage in *countertrade*? List each of its five types.
2. What are the four main methods of export/import financing?
3. Describe the various risks that each financing method poses for exporters and importers.

---

entrepreneur's SURVIVAL KIT

Global Collection Guidelines

As Robbie Evans, president of Con-Tech International, says, "It doesn't do any good to make a sale if you don't get paid." Exporters should perform their due diligence in export deals and should always consider worst-case scenarios. They should also make sure that collection terms are clearly understood as an integral part of the sale. Below are several more pointers on how entrepreneurs can arrange export deals to reduce the likelihood of not being paid.

- Know your market, its customary payment times for business debts, and its laws governing debt collections.

- Know which courts in a nation handle business debts. In some countries debt collections may take place in several different courts, depending on the amounts involved.

- Have a clear understanding of the payment terms built into your export sales agreements.

- Don't wait too long after shipment to begin collection efforts. Collection experts say they often see exporters wait a year or more to seek payment. Waiting too long may cause you to lose the opportunity to collect.

- If you find yourself with a bad debt on your hands, contact an international trade attorney, a global collection agency, or a collection agency in the debtor's country. If an arbitration process is available, be open to the idea. It could save time and money.

- If your customer wants to be cooperative but is having financial problems, consider stretching out the payment terms.

- Keep tabs on which parts of the globe are problem areas. Review journals, newsletters, and other news sources regularly so you can try to work around external events that may prevent a debtor from paying.

Contractual Entry Modes

The products of some companies simply cannot be traded in open markets because they are *intangible*. Thus, a company cannot use importing, exporting, or countertrade to exploit opportunities in a target market. Fortunately, there are other options for this type of company. A company can use a variety of contracts—*licensing, franchising, management contracts,* and *turnkey projects*—to market highly specialized assets and skills in markets beyond its nations' borders. Let's examine each of these entry modes in detail.

Licensing

licensing
Practice by which one company owning intangible property (the licensor) grants another firm (the licensee) the right to use that property for a specified period of time.

Companies sometimes grant other firms the right to use an asset that is essential to the production of a finished product. **Licensing** is a contractual entry mode in which a company that owns intangible property (the *licensor*) grants another firm (the *licensee*) the right to use that property for a specified period of time. Licensors typically receive royalty payments based on a percentage of the licensee's sales revenue generated by the licensed property. The licensors might also receive a one-time fee to cover the cost of transferring the property to the licensee. Commonly licensed intangible property includes patents, copyrights, special formulas and designs, trademarks, and brand names. Thus, licensing often involves granting companies the right to use *process technologies* inherent to the production of a particular good.

Here are a few examples of successful licensing agreements:

- Novell (United States) licensed its software to three Hong Kong universities that installed it as the campus-wide standard.

- Hitachi (Japan) licensed from Duales System Deutschland (Germany) technology to be used in the recycling of plastics in Japan.

- Hewlett-Packard (United States) licensed from Canon (Japan) a printer engine for use in its monochrome laser printers.

An *exclusive license* grants a company exclusive rights to produce and market a property, or products made from that property, in a specific geographic region. The region can be the licensee's home country or may extend to worldwide markets. A *nonexclusive license* grants a company the right to use a property but does not grant it sole access to a market. Thus, a licensor can grant several or more companies the right to use a property in the same region.

cross licensing
Practice by which companies use licensing agreements to exchange intangible property with one another.

Cross licensing occurs when companies use licensing agreements to swap intangible property with one another. For example, Fujitsu (*www.fujitsu.com*) of Japan signed a 5-year cross-licensing agreement with Texas Instruments (*www.ti.com*) of the United States. The agreement allowed each company to use the other's technology in the production of its own goods—thus lowering R&D costs. It was a very extensive arrangement, covering all but a few semiconductor patents owned by each company.[4] Because asset values are seldom exactly equal, cross licensing also typically involves royalty payments from one party to the other.

Advantages of Licensing   There are several advantages to using licensing as an entry mode into new markets. First, licensors can use licensing to finance their international expansion. Most licensing agreements require licensees to contribute equipment and investment financing, whether by building special production facilities or by using existing excess capacity. Access to such resources can be a great advantage to a licensor who wants to expand but lacks the capital and managerial resources to do so. Moreover, because it need not spend time constructing and starting up its own new facilities, the licensor earns revenues sooner than it would otherwise.

Second, licensing can be a less risky method of international expansion for a licensor than other entry modes. For instance, whereas some markets are risky because of social or political unrest, others defy accurate market research for a variety of reasons. Licensing helps shield the licensor from the increased risk of operating its own local production facilities in markets that are unstable or hard to assess accurately.

Third, licensing can help reduce the likelihood that a licensor's product will appear on the black market. The side streets of large cities in many emerging markets are dotted with tabletop vendors eager to sell bootleg versions of computer software, Hollywood films, and recordings of internationally popular musicians. Producers can, to some extent, foil bootleggers by licensing local companies to market their products at locally competitive prices. Granted, the royalties will be lower than the profits generated by sales at higher international prices, but lower profits are better than no profits at all—which is what owners get from bootleg versions of their products.

Finally, licensees can benefit from licensing by using it as a method of upgrading existing production technologies. For example, manufacturers of plastics and other synthetic materials in the Philippines are working to meet the high standards demanded by the local subsidiaries of Japanese electronics and office-equipment producers. Thus, D&L Industries of the Philippines upgraded its manufacturing process by licensing materials technology from Nippon Pigment of Japan.[5]

Disadvantages of Licensing   There also are some important disadvantages to using licensing. First, it can restrict a licensor's future activities. For example, suppose that a licensee is granted the exclusive right to use an asset but fails to produce the sort of results that a licensor expected. Because the license agreement is exclusive, the licensor cannot simply begin selling directly in that particular market to meet demand itself or contract with another licensee. Thus, a good product and lucrative market do not, in themselves, guarantee success for a producer trying to enter a market through the use of licensing.

Second, licensing might reduce the global consistency of the quality and marketing of a licensor's product in different national markets. A licensor might find the development of a coherent global brand image an elusive goal if each of its national licensees is allowed to operate in any manner it chooses. Promoting a global image might later require considerable amounts of time and money to change the misconceptions of buyers in the various licensed markets.

Third, licensing might amount to a company "lending" strategically important property to its future competitors. This is an especially dangerous situation when a company licenses assets on which its competitive advantage is based. Licensing agreements are often made for several years or more (perhaps even a decade or more). During this time, licensees often become highly competent at producing and marketing the licensor's product. When the agreement expires, the licensor might find that its former licensee is capable of producing and marketing a better version of the product. Licensing contracts can (and should) restrict licensees from competing in the future with products based strictly on licensed property. However, enforcement of such provisions works only for identical or nearly identical products, not when substantial improvements are made.

Franchising

Franchising is a contractual entry mode in which one company (the *franchiser*) supplies another (the *franchisee*) with intangible property and other assistance over an extended period. Franchisers typically receive compensation as flat fees, royalty payments, or both. The most popular franchises are those with widely recognized brand names, such as Mercedes (*www.mercedes.com*), McDonald's (*www.mcdonalds.com*), and Holiday Inn (*www.holiday-inn.com*). In fact, the brand name or trademark of a company is normally the single most important item desired by the franchisee. For this reason, smaller companies with lesser known brand names and trademarks have greater difficulty locating interested franchisees.

Franchising differs from licensing in several important ways. First, franchising gives a company greater control over the sale of its product in a target market. Franchisees must often meet strict guidelines on product quality, day-to-day management duties, and marketing promotions. Second, although licensing is fairly common in manufacturing industries, franchising is primarily used in service industries such as auto dealerships, entertainment, lodging, restaurants, and business services. Third, although licensing normally involves a one-time transfer of property, franchising requires ongoing assistance from the franchiser. In addition to the initial transfer of property, franchisers typically offer start-up capital, management training, location advice, and advertising assistance to their franchisees.

franchising
Practice by which one company (the franchiser) supplies another (the franchisee) with intangible property and other assistance over an extended period.

Like this restaurant at the Ramada Hotel in Guayaquil, Ecuador, the lodging industry typically relies on franchising to exploit international opportunities. Franchising allows Ramada (www.ramada.com) and others to maintain strict control over hotels carrying their names. In this way, they can ensure that guests experience a stay that meets the company's guidelines regarding such things as cleanliness, service, and meal preparation. Can you think of any other industries that employ franchising?

Some examples of the kinds of companies involved in international franchising include:

- Ozemail (Australia) awarded Magictel (Hong Kong) a franchise to operate its Internet phone and fax service in Hong Kong.
- Jean-Louis David (France) awarded franchises to more than 200 hairdressing salons in Italy.
- Brooks Brothers (U.S.) awarded Dickson Concepts (Hong Kong) a franchise to operate Brooks Brothers stores across Southeast Asia.

Companies based in the United States dominate the world of international franchising. While U.S. companies were perfecting the practice of franchising (due to a large, homogeneous domestic market and low barriers to interstate trade and investment), most other markets remained small and dissimilar to one another. However, franchising is growing in the European Union, with the advent of a single currency and, since 1999, a unified set of franchise laws. Many European managers with comfortable early-retirement packages have discovered franchising to be an appealing second career. Franchising across much of Europe is expected to grow at between 10 and 15 percent per year through 2007.[6]

Despite projections for such robust growth, obstacles remain. For one thing, local European managers often misunderstand the franchising concept. For instance, Holiday Inn's Spanish franchise expansion is going more slowly than expected. According to the company's development director in Spain, Holiday Inn finds that it must convince local managers that the franchiser does not want to "take control" of their hotels.[7] In some eastern European countries, local managers do not understand why they must continue to pay royalties to brand and trademark owners. Franchise expansion in eastern European markets also suffers from a lack of local capital, high interest rates, high taxes, bureaucratic obstacles, restrictive laws, and corruption.[8]

Advantages of Franchising   There are several important advantages of franchising. First, franchisers can use franchising as a low-cost, low-risk entry mode into new markets. In particular, companies following global strategies rely on consistent products and common themes in worldwide markets. Franchising allows them to maintain consistency by replicating the processes for standardized products in each target market. However, many franchisers make small modifications in products and promotional messages when marketing specifically to local buyers. But because franchisers exercise a high degree of control over operations, they do maintain consistency across national markets.

Second, franchising is an entry mode that allows for rapid geographic expansion. Firms often gain a competitive advantage by being first in seizing a market opportunity. For instance, Microtel Inns & Suites (*www.microtelinn.com*) of Atlanta, Georgia, is using franchising to fuel its international expansion. Although it operates only 42 locations in the United States, Microtel is boldly entering Argentina and Uruguay and eyeing opportunities in Brazil and Western Europe. Rooms cost $50 to $60 per night and target business travelers who cannot afford $200 per night.[9]

Finally, franchisers can profit from the cultural knowledge and know-how of local managers. This aspect of franchising is helpful both in lowering the risk of business failure in unfamiliar markets and in creating a competitive advantage.

Disadvantages of Franchising
Franchising can also pose problems for both franchisers and franchisees. First, franchisers may find it cumbersome to manage a large number of franchisees in a variety of national markets. A major concern is that product quality and promotional messages among franchisees will not be consistent from one market to another. One way to ensure greater control is by establishing in each market a so-called *master franchisee*, which is responsible for monitoring the operations of individual franchisees.

Second, franchisees can experience a loss of organizational flexibility in franchising agreements. Franchise contracts can restrict their strategic and tactical options, and they may even be forced to promote products owned by the franchiser's other divisions. For example, for years PepsiCo (*www.pepsico.com*) owned the well-known restaurant chains Pizza Hut, Taco Bell, and KFC. As part of their franchise agreements with PepsiCo, restaurant owners were required to sell only PepsiCo beverages to their customers. Many franchisees worldwide were displeased with such restrictions on their product offerings and were relieved when PepsiCo spun off the restaurant chains.[10]

Management Contracts

Under the stipulations of a **management contract**, one company supplies another with managerial expertise for a specific period of time. The supplier of expertise is normally compensated with either a lump-sum payment or a continuing fee based on sales volume. Such contracts are commonly found in the public utilities sectors of both developed and emerging markets.

Two types of knowledge can be transferred through management contracts—the specialized knowledge of technical managers and the business-management skills of general managers. BAA (*www.baa.co.uk*) of Britain, for example, possesses general airport-management skills. In the United States, BAA operates the Indianapolis Airport under a 10-year management contract and provides retail management at the Air Mall in the Pittsburgh Airport.[11]

Other examples of management contracts include:

- ⊙ DBS Asia (Thailand) awarded a management contract to Favorlangh Communication (Taiwan) to set up and run a company supplying digital television programming in Taiwan.
- ⊙ Lyonnaise de Eaux (France) and RWE Aqua (Germany) agreed to manage drinking-water quality and client billing and to maintain the water infrastructure for the city of Budapest, Hungary, for 25 years.

Advantages of Management Contracts
Management contracts can benefit both organizations and countries. First, a firm can award a management contract to another company and thereby exploit an international business opportunity without having to place a great deal of its own physical assets at risk. Financial capital can then be reserved for other promising investment projects that would otherwise not be funded.

Second, governments can award companies management contracts to operate and upgrade public utilities, particularly when a nation is short of investment financing. That is why the government of Kazakhstan contracted with a group of international companies called ABB Power Grid Consortium to manage its national electricity-grid system for 25 years. Under the terms of the contract, the consortium paid past wages owed to workers by the government and is to invest more than $200 million during the first 3 years of the agreement. The Kazakhstan government had neither the cash flow to pay the workers nor the funds to make badly needed improvements.[12]

management contract
Practice by which one company supplies another with managerial expertise for a specific period of time.

Third, governments use management contracts to develop the skills of local workers and managers. For example, ESB International (*www.esb.ie*) of Ireland signed a 3-year contract not only to manage and operate a power plant in Ghana, Africa, but also to train local personnel in the skills needed to manage it at some point in the future.[13]

Disadvantages of Management Contracts Unfortunately, management contracts also pose two important disadvantages for suppliers of expertise. For one thing, although management contracts reduce the exposure of physical assets in another country, the same is not true for the supplier's personnel. International management in countries that are undergoing political or social turmoil can place managers' lives in significant danger.

Second, suppliers of expertise may end up nurturing a formidable new competitor in the local market. After learning how to conduct certain operations, the party that had originally needed assistance may be in a position to compete on its own. Obviously, firms must weigh the financial returns from a management contract against the potential future problems caused by a newly launched competitor.

Turnkey Projects

turnkey (build–operate–transfer) project
Practice by which one company designs, constructs, and tests a production facility for a client firm.

When one company designs, constructs, and tests a production facility for a client, the agreement is called a **turnkey (build–operate–transfer) project**. The term *turnkey project* derives from the understanding that the client, who normally pays a flat fee for the project, is expected to do nothing more than simply "turn a key" to get the facility operating. The expression conveys the fact that the company awarded a turnkey project leaves absolutely nothing undone when preparing the facility for the client.

Like management contracts, turnkey projects tend to be large-scale and often involve government agencies. However, unlike management contracts, turnkey projects transfer special process technologies or production-facility designs to the client. They typically involve the construction of power plants, airports, seaports, telecommunication systems, and petrochemical facilities that are then turned over to the client. Under a management contract, the supplier of a service retains the asset—the managerial expertise.

Here are two examples of international turnkey projects:

- Telecommunications Consultants India constructed telecom networks in both Madagascar and Ghana—two turnkey projects worth a combined total of $28 million.

- Lubei Group (China) agreed with the government of Belarus to join in the construction of a facility for processing a fertilizer by-product into cement.

A turnkey project is a venture in which one organization designs, builds, and tests a facility for another, which then merely "turns the key" to get things underway. This arrangement characterizes the building of four hydroelectric dams on Turkey's Coruh River, one of which is pictured here. The Turkish government benefited from the expertise of two international consortiums it hired for the project. What other types of operations do you think would be appropriate for a turnkey project?

Advantages of Turnkey Projects

Turnkey projects provide benefits to both providers and recipients. First, turnkey projects permit firms to specialize in their core competencies and to exploit opportunities that they could not undertake alone. Mobil Exploration (now ExxonMobil, *www.exxonmobil.com*), for example, awarded a turnkey project to PT McDermott Indonesia (*www.mcdermott.com*) and Toyo Engineering (*toyo-eng.co.jp*) of Japan to build a liquid natural gas plant on the Indonesian island of Sumatra. The providers are responsible for constructing an offshore production platform, laying a 100-kilometer underwater pipeline, and building an on-land liquid natural gas refinery. The $316 million project is feasible only because each company will contribute unique expertise to the design, construction, and testing of the facilities.[14]

Second, turnkey projects allow governments to obtain designs for infrastructure projects from the world's leading companies. For instance, Turkey's government enlisted two separate consortiums of international firms to build four hydroelectric dams on its Coruh River. The dams combine the design and technological expertise of each company in the two consortiums.[15] The Turkish government also awarded a turnkey project to Ericsson (*www.ericsson.com*) of Sweden to expand the country's mobile telecommunication system.[16]

Disadvantages of Turnkey Projects

Among the disadvantages of turnkey projects is the fact that a company may be awarded a project for political reasons rather than for technological know-how. Because turnkey projects are often of high monetary value and awarded by government agencies, the process of awarding them can be highly politicized. When the selection process is not entirely open, companies with the best political connections often win contracts, usually at inflated prices—the costs of which are typically passed on to local taxpayers.

Second, like management contracts, turnkey projects can create future competitors. A newly created local competitor could become a major supplier in its own domestic market and perhaps even in other markets in which the supplier operates. Therefore, companies try to avoid projects in which there is danger of transferring their core competencies to others.

Quick Study

1. Identify the advantages and disadvantages of *licensing* for both the licensor and the licensee.

2. Describe how *franchising* differs from licensing. What are its main benefits and drawbacks?

3. When is a *management contract* useful? Identify two types of knowledge it is used to transfer.

4. What is a *turnkey project*? Describe its main advantages and disadvantages.

Investment Entry Modes

The final category of entry modes is investment entry. Investment entry modes entail direct investment in plant and equipment in a country coupled with ongoing involvement in the local operation. Entry modes in this category take a company's commitment to a market to the next level. Let's now explore three common forms of investment entry: *wholly owned subsidiaries*, *joint ventures*, and *strategic alliances*.

Wholly Owned Subsidiaries

As the term suggests, a **wholly owned subsidiary** is a facility entirely owned and controlled by a single parent company. Companies can establish a wholly owned subsidiary either by forming a new company from the ground up and constructing entirely new facilities (such as factories, offices, and equipment) or by purchasing an existing company and internalizing its facilities. Whether an international subsidiary is purchased or newly created depends to a large extent on its proposed operations. For example, when a parent company designs

wholly owned subsidiary
Facility entirely owned and controlled by a single parent company.

a subsidiary to manufacture the latest high-tech products, it typically must build new facilities because state-of-the-art operations are hard to locate. In other words, it is easier to find companies in most target markets that make pots and pans rather than produce the most advanced computer chips. The major drawback of creation from the ground up is the time it takes to construct new facilities, hire and train employees, and launch production.

Conversely, finding an existing local company capable of performing marketing and sales will be easier because special technologies are typically not needed. By purchasing the existing marketing and sales operations of an existing firm in the target market, the parent can have the subsidiary operating relatively quickly. Buying an existing company's operations in the target market is a particularly good strategy when the company to be acquired has a valuable trademark, brand name, or process technology.

Advantages of Wholly Owned Subsidiaries

There are two main advantages to entering a market using a wholly owned subsidiary. First, managers have complete control over day-to-day operations in the target market and over access to valuable technologies, processes, and other intangible properties within the subsidiary. Complete control also decreases the chance that competitors will gain access to a company's competitive advantage, which is particularly important if it is technology-based. Managers also retain complete control over the subsidiary's output and prices. Unlike licensors and franchisers, the parent company also receives all profits generated by the subsidiary.

Second, a wholly owned subsidiary is a good mode of entry when a company wants to coordinate the activities of all its national subsidiaries. Companies using global strategies (see Chapter 11) view each of their national markets as one part of an interconnected global market. Thus, the ability to exercise complete control over a wholly owned subsidiary makes this entry mode attractive to companies that are pursuing global strategies.

Disadvantages of Wholly Owned Subsidiaries

Wholly owned subsidiaries also present two primary disadvantages. First, they can be expensive undertakings. Companies must finance investments internally or raise funds in financial markets. Therefore, obtaining the needed funding can be difficult for small and medium-sized companies. As a rule, only large companies are equipped to establish international wholly owned subsidiaries. However, citizens of one country living abroad in another country can find their unique knowledge and abilities an advantage.

Second, risk exposure is high because a wholly owned subsidiary requires substantial company resources. One source of risk is political or social uncertainty or outright instability in the target market. Such risks can place both physical assets and personnel in serious jeopardy. The sole owner of a wholly owned subsidiary also accepts all the risk that buyers will reject the company's product. Parent companies can reduce this risk by gaining a better understanding of target-market consumers prior to entry into the market.

Joint Ventures

joint venture
Separate company that is created and jointly owned by two or more independent entities to achieve a common business objective.

Under certain circumstances, companies prefer to share ownership of an operation rather than take complete ownership. A separate company that is created and jointly owned by two or more independent entities to achieve a common business objective is called a **joint venture**. Joint venture partners can be privately owned companies, government agencies, or government-owned companies. Each party may contribute anything valued by its partners, including managerial talent, marketing expertise, market access, production technologies, financial capital, and superior knowledge or techniques of research and development.

Examples of joint ventures include:

○ A joint venture between Suzuki Motor Corporation (Japan) and the government of India to manufacture a small-engine car specifically for the Indian market

○ A joint venture between a group of Indian companies and a Russian partner to produce television sets in Russia for the local market

○ Biltrite Corporation (United States) and Shenzhen Petrochemical (China) created a shoe-soling factory as a joint venture in China to supply international shoe manufacturers located in China

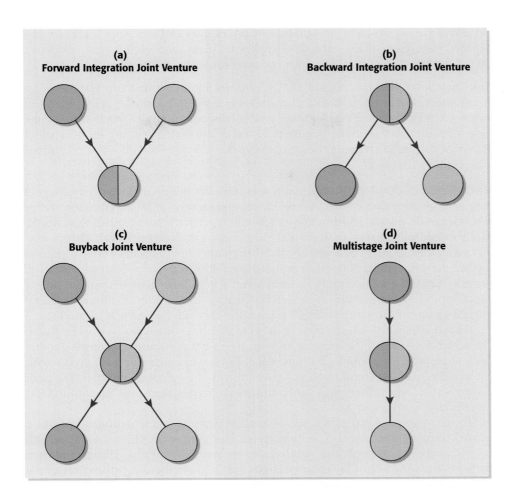

FIGURE 13.5

Alternative Joint Venture Configurations

(a)
Forward Integration Joint Venture

(b)
Backward Integration Joint Venture

(c)
Buyback Joint Venture

(d)
Multistage Joint Venture

Joint Venture Configurations   As you can see from Figure 13.5, there are four main joint venture configurations.[17] Although we illustrate each of these as consisting of just two partners, each configuration can also apply to ventures of several or more partners.

Forward Integration Joint Venture   Figure 13.5(a) outlines a joint venture characterized by *forward integration*. In this type of joint venture, the parties choose to invest together in *downstream* business activities—activities farther along in the "value system" that are normally performed by others. For instance, Hewlett-Packard (*www.hp.com*) and Apple Computer (*www.apple.com*) opening a retail outlet in a developing country would be a joint venture characterized by forward integration. The two companies now perform activities normally performed by retailers farther along in the product's journey to buyers.

Backward Integration Joint Venture   Figure 13.5(b) outlines a joint venture characterized by *backward integration*. In other words, the joint venture signals a move by each company into *upstream* business activities—activities earlier in the value system that are normally performed by others. Such a configuration would result if two steel manufacturers formed a joint venture to mine iron ore. The companies now engage in an activity that is normally performed by mining companies.

Buyback Joint Venture   Figure 13.5(c) outlines a joint venture whose input is provided by, and whose output is absorbed by, each of its partners. A *buyback joint venture* is formed when each partner requires the same component in its production process. It might be formed when a production facility of a certain minimum size is needed to achieve economies of scale, but neither partner alone enjoys enough demand to warrant building it. However, by combining resources the partners can construct a facility that serves their needs while achieving savings from economies of scale production. For instance, this was one reason behind the $500 million joint venture between Chrysler (*www.chrysler.com*)

and BMW (*www.bmw.com*) to build small-car engines in Latin America. Each party benefited from the economies of scale offered by the plant's annual production capacity of 400,000 engines—a volume that neither company could absorb alone.

Multistage Joint Venture   Figure 13.5(d) outlines a joint venture that features downstream integration by one partner and upstream integration by another. A *multistage joint venture* often results when one company produces a good or service required by another. For example, a sporting goods manufacturer might join with a sporting goods retailer to establish a distribution company designed to bypass inefficient local distributors in a developing country.

Advantages of Joint Ventures
Joint ventures offer several important advantages to companies going international. Above all, companies rely on joint ventures to reduce risk.[18] Generally, a joint venture exposes fewer of a partner's assets to risk than would a wholly owned subsidiary—each partner risks only its own contribution. That is why a joint venture entry might be a wise choice when market entry requires a large investment or when there is significant political or social instability in the target market. Similarly, a company can use a joint venture to learn about a local business environment prior to launching a wholly owned subsidiary.[19] In fact, many joint ventures are ultimately bought outright by one of the partners after it gains sufficient expertise in the local market.

Second, companies can use joint ventures to penetrate international markets that are otherwise off-limits. For instance, some governments either require nondomestic companies to share ownership with local companies or provide incentives for them to do so. Such requirements are most common among governments of developing countries. The goal is to improve the competitiveness of local companies by having them team up with and learn from international partner(s).

Third, a company can gain access to another company's international distribution network through the use of a joint venture. The joint venture between Caterpillar (*www.caterpillar.com*) of the United States and Mitsubishi Heavy Industries (*www.mitsubishi.com*) of Japan was designed to improve the competitiveness of each against a common rival, Komatsu (*www.komatsu.com*) of Japan. While Caterpillar gained access to Mitsubishi's distribution system in Japan, Mitsubishi got access to Caterpillar's global distribution network—helping it to compete more effectively internationally.[20]

Finally, companies form international joint ventures for defensive reasons. Entering a joint venture with a local government or government-controlled company gives the government a direct stake in the venture's success. In turn, the local government will be less likely to interfere if it means that the venture's performance will suffer. This same strategy can also be used to create a more "local" image when feelings of nationalism are running strong in a target country.

Disadvantages of Joint Ventures
Among its disadvantages, joint venture ownership can result in conflict between partners. Conflict is perhaps most common when management is shared equally—that is, when each partner supplies top managers in what is commonly known as a "50–50 joint venture." Because neither partner's managers have the final say on decisions, managerial paralysis can result, causing problems such as delays in responding to changing market conditions. Conflict can also arise from disagreements over how future investments and profits are to be shared. Parties can reduce the likelihood of conflict and indecision by establishing unequal ownership, whereby one partner maintains 51 percent ownership of the voting stock and has the final say on decisions. A multiparty joint venture (commonly referred to as a *consortium*) can also feature unequal ownership. For example, ownership of a four-party joint venture could be distributed 20–20–20–40, with the 40 percent owner having the final say on decisions.

Second, loss of control over a joint venture's operations can also result when the local government is a partner in the joint venture. This situation occurs most often in industries considered culturally sensitive or important to national security, such as broadcasting, infrastructure, and defense. Thus, the profitability of a joint venture could suffer because the local government would have motives that are based on cultural preservation or security.

Strategic Alliances

Sometimes companies willing to cooperate with one another do not wish to go so far as to create a separate jointly owned company. A relationship whereby two or more entities cooperate (but do not form a separate company) to achieve the strategic goals of each is called a **strategic alliance.** Like joint ventures, strategic alliances can be formed for relatively short periods or for many years, depending on the goals of the participants. Strategic alliances can be established between a company and its suppliers, its buyers, and even its competitors. In forming such alliances, sometimes each partner purchases a portion of the other's stock. In this way, each company has a direct stake in its partner's future performance. In turn, this stake decreases the likelihood that one partner will try to take advantage of the other.

Examples of strategic alliances include:

strategic alliance
Relationship whereby two or more entities cooperate (but do not form a separate company) to achieve the strategic goals of each.

- ❍ An alliance between Siemens (Germany) and Hewlett-Packard (United States) to create and market devices used to control telecommunications systems
- ❍ A strategic alliance between Nippon Life Group (Japan) and Putnam Investments (United States) to permit Putnam to develop investment products and manage assets for Nippon

Advantages of Strategic Alliances

Strategic alliances offer several important advantages to companies. First, companies use strategic alliances to share the cost of an international investment project. For example, many firms are developing new products that not only integrate the latest technologies but also shorten the life spans of existing products. In turn, the shorter life span is reducing the number of years during which a company can recoup its investment. Thus, many companies are cooperating to share the costs of developing new products. For example, Toshiba (*www.toshiba.com*) of Japan, Siemens (*www.siemens.com*) of Germany, and IBM (*www.ibm.com*) of the United States shared the $1 billion cost of developing a facility near Nagoya, Japan, to manufacture small, efficient computer memory chips.

Second, companies use strategic alliances to tap into competitors' specific strengths. Some alliances formed between Internet portals and technology companies are designed to do just that. For example, an Internet portal provides access to a large, global audience through its Web site, while the technology company supplies its know-how in delivering, say, music over the Internet. Meeting the goal of the alliance—marketing music over the Web—requires the competencies of both partners.

Finally, companies turn to strategic alliances for many of the same reasons that they turn to joint ventures. Some use strategic alliances to gain access to a partner's channels of distribution in a target market. Others use them to reduce exposure to the same kinds of risks from which joint ventures provide protection.

Disadvantages of Strategic Alliances

Perhaps the most important disadvantage of a strategic alliance is that it can create a future local or even global competitor. For example, one partner might be using the alliance to test a market and prepare the launch of a wholly owned subsidiary. By declining to cooperate with others in the area of its core competency, a company can reduce the likelihood of creating a competitor that would threaten its main area of business. Likewise, a company can insist on contractual clauses that constrain partners from competing against it with certain products or in certain geographic regions. Firms are also careful to protect special research programs, production techniques, and marketing practices that are not committed to the alliance. Naturally, managers must weigh the potential for encouraging new competition against the benefits of international cooperation.

As in the case of joint ventures, conflict can arise and eventually undermine cooperation. As a rule, then, alliance contracts are drawn up to cover as many such contingencies as possible. Even so, communication and cultural differences can arise. As Tsuyoski Kawanishi, Toshiba director and senior executive vice president for partnerships and alliances, explains, "Each pact includes the equivalent of a prenuptial agreement, so both sides know who gets what if the partnership doesn't work out. During the honeymoon time, everything is great. But as you know, divorce is always a possibility, and that's when things can get bitter."[21]

Selecting Partners for Cooperation

Every company's goals and strategies are influenced by both its competitive strengths and the challenges it faces in the marketplace. Because the goals and strategies of any two companies are never exactly alike, cooperation can be difficult. Moreover, ventures and alliances often last many years, perhaps even indefinitely. Therefore, partner selection is a crucial ingredient for success. The following discussion focuses on partner selection in joint ventures and strategic alliances. However, many of the same points also apply to contractual entry modes such as licensing and franchising, for which choosing the right partner is also important.

Every partner must be firmly committed to the goals of the cooperative arrangement. Many companies engage in cooperative forms of business, but the reasons behind each party's participation are never identical. Sometimes, a company stops contributing to a cooperative arrangement once it achieves its own objectives. Therefore, detailing the precise duties and contributions of each party to an international cooperative arrangement through prior negotiations can go a long way toward ensuring continued cooperation. See the Global Manager's Toolbox titled, "Negotiating the Terms of Market Entry" for some important considerations in negotiating international agreements.

Although the importance of locating a trustworthy partner seems obvious, cooperation should be approached with caution. Companies can have hidden reasons for cooperating. Sometimes they try to acquire more from cooperation than their partners realize. If a hidden agenda is discovered during the course of cooperation, trust can break down—in

global manager's TOOLBOX

Negotiating the Terms of Market Entry

The participants in any international business arrangement must negotiate the terms of their deals. A cooperative atmosphere between partners to a deal depends on both parties viewing contract negotiations as a success. Managers should be aware of the negotiation process and influential factors. The process normally occurs in four stages.

Stage 1: Preparation. Negotiators must develop a clear vision of what the company wants to achieve. For instance, is the proposed business arrangement a one-time technology transfer to a local company or the first phase of a long-term relationship?

Stage 2: Launch of Discussions. Discussions begin with each side stating its opening position—the most favorable terms for itself. Parties might state their positions immediately or make them known gradually so as to leave themselves room to modify them.

Stage 3: Bargaining and Persuasion. The bargaining power of each party plays an important role in the final outcome of negotiations. Although this is the stage at which direct conflict is most likely, cultures differ in their attitudes toward conflict. For instance, Chinese negotiators try to avoid conflict more than Canadians do. But if conflict erupts, the Chinese are more likely to pursue negative strategies, including calling off talks.

Stage 4: Agreement. Negotiations reaching this stage are a success. Negotiators from Western cultures view the

signing of contracts as the end of negotiations. Yet in most Asian cultures it signals the beginning of a long-term working relationship; terms can be modified as the relationship matures and circumstances change.

Two key elements influence international business negotiations:

Cultural Elements. Negotiating styles differ from one culture to another. Negotiating in Asian cultures revolves around protecting the other party from losing face (being embarrassed or shamed). Thus, "victory" normally means that each party gives equal ground and meets the other halfway. In most Western cultures negotiators typically hope to gain as many concessions as possible with little concern for whether the other party appears to have "lost" the negotiations.

Political and Legal Elements. Negotiators must be aware of any political motives underlying their counterparts' strategy. For example, an inflexible public posture might simply be a ploy to show company or government officials back home that they are working first and foremost in the company's or nation's interest. Also, consumer groups, labor unions, and even stockholders can influence the outcome of a firm's negotiations. If consumer groups feel that a proposed arrangement will increase prices or restrict product choice, they might lobby government officials to kill the deal.

which case the cooperative arrangement is virtually destroyed. Because trust is so important, firms naturally prefer partners with whom they have had a favorable working relationship in the past. However, such arrangements are much easier for large multinationals than for small and medium-sized companies with little international experience and few international contacts.

Each party's managers must be comfortable working with people of other cultures and traveling to (even perhaps living in) other cultures. As a result, cooperation will go more smoothly and the transition—both in work life and personal life—will be easier for managers who are sent to work for a joint venture. Each partner's managers should also be comfortable working with, and within, one another's corporate culture. For example, although some companies encourage the participation of subordinates in decision making, others do not. Such differences often reflect differences in national culture, and when managers possess cultural understanding, adjustment and cooperation are likely to run more smoothly.[22]

Above all, a suitable partner must have something valuable to offer. Firms should avoid cooperation simply because they are approached by another company. Rather, managers must be certain that they are getting a fair return on their cooperative efforts. In short, they must evaluate the benefits of a potential international cooperative arrangement just as they would any other investment opportunity.

Strategic Factors in Selecting an Entry Mode

The choice of entry mode has many important strategic implications for a company's future operations.[23] Because enormous investments in time and money can go into determining an entry mode, the choice must be made carefully. Several key factors that influence a company's international entry mode selection are the *cultural environment*, *political and legal environments*, *market size*, *production and shipping costs*, and *international experience*. Let's now explore each of these factors in-depth.

Cultural Environment

As we saw in Chapter 2, the dimensions of culture—values, beliefs, customs, languages, religions—can differ greatly from one nation to another. In such cases, managers can be less confident in their ability to manage operations in the host country. They can be concerned about the potential not only for communication problems but also for interpersonal difficulties. As a result, they may avoid investment entry modes in favor of exporting or a contractual mode. On the other hand, cultural similarity encourages manager confidence and thus the likelihood of investment. Likewise, the importance of cultural differences diminishes when managers are knowledgeable about the culture of the target market.[24]

Political and Legal Environments

As mentioned earlier in this chapter, political instability in a target market increases the risk exposure of investments. That is why significant political differences and levels of instability cause companies to avoid large investments and to favor entry modes that shelter assets.

A target market's legal system also influences the choice of entry mode. For example, certain import regulations, such as high tariffs or low quota limits, can encourage investment: A company that produces locally avoids tariffs that increase product cost and does not have to worry about making it into the market below the quota (if there is one). But low tariffs and high quota limits discourage investment. Also, governments may enact laws that ban certain types of investment outright. For many years (but no longer), China banned wholly owned subsidiaries by non-Chinese companies and required that they form joint ventures with local partners. Finally, because investment entry often gives a company greater control over assets and marketing, firms tend to prefer investment when a market is lax in enforcing copyright and patent laws.

Market Size

The size of a potential market also influences the choice of entry mode. For example, rising incomes in a market encourage investment entry modes because investment allows a firm to prepare for expanding market demand and to increase its understanding of the target market. Thus, high domestic demand in China is attracting investment in joint ventures, strategic alliances, and wholly owned subsidiaries. On the other hand, if investors believe that a market is likely to remain relatively small, better options might include exporting or contractual entry.

Production and Shipping Costs

By helping to control total costs, low-cost production and shipping can give a company an advantage. Accordingly, setting up production in a market is desirable when the total cost of production there is lower than in the home market. Low-cost local production might also encourage contractual entry through licensing or franchising. If production costs are sufficiently low, the international production site might even begin supplying other markets, including the home country. An additional potential benefit of local production might be that managers observe buyer behavior and modify products to be better suited to the needs of the local market. Lower production costs at home make it more appealing to export to international markets.

Naturally, companies that turn out products with high shipping costs typically prefer local production. Contractual and investment entry modes are viable options in this case. Alternatively, exporting is feasible when products have relatively lower shipping costs. Finally, because they are subject to less price competition, products for which there are fewer substitutes or those that are discretionary items can more easily absorb higher shipping and production costs. In this case exporting is a likely selection.

International Experience

By way of summary, Figure 13.6 illustrates the control, risk, and experience relationships of each entry mode. Most companies enter the international marketplace through exporting. As companies gain international experience, they will tend to select entry modes that require deeper involvement. But this means that they must accept greater risk in return for

FIGURE 13.6

Evolution of the Entry Mode Decision

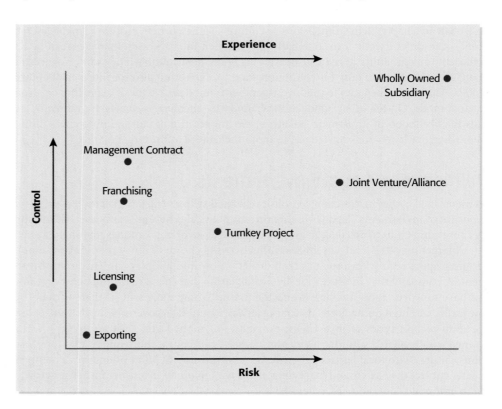

greater control over operations and strategy. Eventually, they may explore the advantages of licensing, franchising, management contracts, and turnkey projects. Once they become comfortable in a particular market, joint ventures, strategic alliances, and wholly owned subsidiaries become viable options.

Bear in mind that this evolutionary path of accepting greater risk and control with experience does not hold for every company. Whereas some firms remain fixed at one point, others skip several entry modes altogether. In particular, advances in technology and transportation are allowing more and more small companies to leapfrog several stages at once. These relationships will also vary for each company depending on its product and the relevant characteristics of the home and target markets.

Quick Study

1. What is a *wholly owned subsidiary*? Identify its advantages and disadvantages.

2. Define what is meant by the term *joint venture.* Identify the four main joint venture configurations.

3. How does a *strategic alliance* differ from a joint venture? Explain the pluses and minuses of such alliances.

4. What strategic factors should be considered when selecting an entry mode? Discuss each briefly.

A Final Word

This chapter explained the important factors in selecting entry modes and key aspects in their management. We studied the circumstances under which each entry mode is most appropriate and the advantages and disadvantages that each provides. The choice of which entry mode(s) to use in entering international markets matches a company's international strategy. Some companies will want entry modes that give them tight control over international activities because they are pursuing a global strategy, for example. Meanwhile, another company might not require an entry mode with central control because it is pursuing a multinational strategy. The entry mode must also be chosen to align well with an organization's structure.

SUMMARY

1. **Explain why and how companies use *exporting, importing,* and *countertrade.*** Companies begin exporting to *expand sales, diversify sales,* or *gain experience.* Companies often use exporting as a low-cost, low-risk way of getting started in international business. A successful export strategy involves four steps: (1) *Identify a potential market*; (2) *Match needs to abilities*; (3) *Initiate meetings*; and (4) *Commit resources.*

There are two basic forms of export involvement. *Direct exporting* occurs when a company sells its products directly to buyers in a target market. Typically, the company relies on either local *sales representatives* (who represent only their own company's products, not those of other companies) or *distributors* (who take ownership of merchandise when it enters their countries). *Indirect exporting* occurs when a company sells its products to intermediaries who then resell to buyers in a target market. There are three general types of intermediaries: *agents* (individuals or organizations that represent one or more indirect exporters in a target market); *export management companies* (firms that export products on behalf of indi-

rect exporters); and *export trading companies* (firms that provide services to indirect exporters in addition to the activities directly related to clients' exporting activities).

Selling goods or services that are paid for, in whole or part, with other goods or services is called *countertrade.* There are several different types of countertrade: (a) *barter*; (b) *counterpurchase*; (c) *offset*; (d) *switch trading*; and (e) *buyback.*

2. **Explain the various *means of financing* export and import activities.** With *advance payment,* an importer pays an exporter for merchandise before it is shipped. *Documentary collection* calls for a bank to act as an intermediary without accepting financial risk. A *draft (bill of exchange)* is a document ordering the importer to pay the exporter a specified sum of money at a specified time. A *bill of lading* is a contract between an exporter and a shipper that specifies destination and shipping costs of the merchandise.

Under a *letter of credit,* the importer's bank issues a document stating that the bank will pay the exporter when the exporter fulfills the terms of the document. There are several types of letters of credit. An *irrevocable letter of credit* allows the bank issuing the letter to modify the terms of the letter only after obtaining the approval of both exporter and importer. A *revocable letter of credit* can be modified by the issuing bank without obtaining approval from either the exporter or the importer. A *confirmed letter of credit* is guaranteed by both the exporter's bank in the country of export and the importer's bank in the country of import.

Finally, under *open account*, an exporter ships merchandise and later bills the importer for its value.

3. **Describe the different *contractual entry modes* that are available to companies.** The products of some companies simply cannot be traded in open markets because they are intangible. *Licensing* is a contractual entry mode in which a company that owns intangible property (the *licensor*) grants another firm (the *licensee*) the right to use that property for a specified period of time. An *exclusive license* grants a company exclusive rights to produce and market a property, or products made from that property, in a specific geographic region. A *nonexclusive license* grants a company the right to use a property but does not grant it sole access to a market. *Cross licensing* occurs when companies use licensing agreements to swap intangible property with one another.

Franchising is a contractual entry mode in which one company (the *franchiser*) supplies another (the *franchisee*) with intangible property and other assistance over an extended period. Under the stipulations of a *management contract*, one company supplies another with managerial expertise for a specific period of time. Two types of knowledge can be transferred through management contracts—the specialized knowledge of technical managers and the business-management skills of general managers.

When one company designs, constructs, and tests a production facility for a client, the agreement is called a *turnkey (build–operate–transfer) project*. Turnkey projects permit firms to specialize in their core competencies and to exploit opportunities that they could not undertake alone.

4. **Explain the various types of *investment entry modes*.** *Investment entry modes* entail the direct investment in plant and equipment in a country coupled with ongoing involvement in the local operation. A *wholly owned subsidiary* is a facility entirely owned and controlled by a single parent company.

A separate company that is created and jointly owned by two or more independent entities to achieve a common business objective is called a *joint venture*. In a joint venture characterized by *forward integration*, the parties choose to invest together in downstream business activities. A joint venture characterized by *backward integration* signals a move by each company into upstream business activities. A *buyback joint venture* is one whose input is provided by, and whose output is absorbed by, each of its partners. A *multistage joint venture* features downstream integration by one partner and upstream integration by another.

A relationship in which two or more entities cooperate (but do not form a separate company) to achieve the strategic goals of each is called a *strategic alliance*. Companies use strategic alliances to share the cost of an international investment project, tap into competitors' strengths, and gain access to distribution channels.

5. **Discuss the important *strategic factors* in selecting an entry mode.** The key factors that influence a company's international entry mode selection are the *cultural, political,* and *legal environments, market size, production and shipping costs,* and *international experience.*

Managers are typically less confident in their ability to manage operations in unfamiliar cultures and may avoid investment entry modes in favor of exporting or a contractual mode. On the other hand, cultural similarity increases the likelihood of investment. Likewise, political differences and levels of instability cause companies to avoid large investments and favor entry modes that shelter assets.

The size of a potential market also influences the choice of entry mode. For example, rising incomes in a market encourage investment entry modes because investment allows a firm to prepare for expanding market demand and to increase its understanding of the target market.

Setting up production in a market is desirable when the total cost of production in that market is lower than in the home market. Naturally, companies that turn out products with high shipping costs typically prefer local production. Contractual and investment entry modes are viable options in this case. Alternatively, exporting is feasible when products have relatively lower shipping costs.

Finally, most companies make their initial foray into the international marketplace through exporting. As companies gain international experience, they will tend to select entry modes that require deeper involvement.

TALK IT OVER

1. Not all companies "go international" by exporting, then using contracts, and then investing in other markets. How does a company's product influence the process of going international? How (if at all) is technology, like the Internet, affecting the process of going international?

2. "Companies should use investment entry modes whenever possible because they offer the greatest control over business operations." Do you agree or disagree with this statement? Are there times when other types of market entry offer greater control? When is investment entry a poor option?

3. In earlier chapters, we learned how governments get involved in the international flow of trade and foreign direct investment. We also learned how regional economic integration is influencing international business. Identify two market entry modes and describe how each might be affected both by the actions of governments and by increasing regional integration.

TEAMING UP

1. With several of your classmates, have each person list five goods or services that they've consumed within the past week (this list might include food products, Internet services, television programs, etc.). For the company that produces each of these, which entry modes are possible options for entering new markets? Provide a one-paragraph explanation of your group's answer for each good or service.

2. As a team, interview a manager of a company involved in international business. What method did the company use initially to go international? Which entry mode is the company currently using? Does the company export? If so, is it a direct or an indirect exporter? How does the company receive payment for its goods? Does the company use different entry modes in different markets? What factors influenced its choice of entry mode in each case? How do managers deal with cultural differences when negotiating across cultures? Provide any other information on the company that your group believes is relevant to the discussion of market entry.

3. The following project is designed to introduce you to the complexity of negotiations and to help develop your negotiating skills.

   Background: A western European automobile manufacturer is considering entering markets in Southeast Asia. The company wants to construct an assembly plant outside Bangkok, Thailand, to assemble its lower-priced cars. Major components would come in from manufacturing plants in Brazil, Poland, and China. The cars would then be sold in emerging markets throughout Southeast Asia and the Indian subcontinent. Managers are hoping to strike a $100 million joint venture deal with the Thai government. The company would supply technology and management for the venture, and the government would contribute a minority share of financing to the venture. The company considers the government's main contributions to be providing tax breaks (and other financial incentives) and a stable business environment in which to operate.

   Financial capital is flowing into Thailand at a fair pace, although not in the volume it did in the mid-1990s. The currency is strong, and inflation remains low. Unlike some other nations in the region, there is general political and social stability. The new auto assembly plant would boost the local economy, reduce unemployment, and increase local wages. But some local politicians fear the company might be interested only in exploiting the country's relatively low cost labor.

   Activity: Break into an equal number of negotiating teams of three or four persons. Half the teams are to represent the company and the other half, the government. As a team, meet for 15 minutes to develop your opening position and negotiating strategy. Meet with a team from the other side and undertake 20 minutes of negotiations. After the negotiating session, spend 15 minutes comparing the progress of your negotiations with that of the other pairs of teams.

KEY TERMS

advance payment (p. 378)

agents (p. 375)

barter (p. 377)

bill of lading (p. 379)

buyback (p. 377)

counterpurchase (p. 377)

countertrade (p. 377)

cross licensing (p. 382)

direct exporting (p. 374)

documentary collection (p. 378)

draft (bill of exchange) (p. 379)

entry mode (p. 372)

export management company (EMC) (p. 375)

export trading company (ETC) (p. 376)

franchising (p. 383)

freight forwarder (p. 376)

indirect exporting (p. 375)

joint venture (p. 388)

letter of credit (p. 380)

licensing (p. 382)

management contract (p. 385)

offset (p. 377)

open account (p. 381)

strategic alliance (p. 391)

switch trading (p. 377)

turnkey (build–operate–transfer) project (p. 386)

wholly owned subsidiary (p. 387)

1. This chapter presented various entry modes companies use in international markets. We also learned about issues surrounding the selection of partners when cooperation is desirable, and the kinds of things that can go wrong in alliances.

   In this chapter's opening company profile, we read about Marvel's 50/50 joint venture with Sony that oversees all licensing and merchandising for *Spider-Man*, as well as Sony's animated TV series titled, *Spider-Man*. But we did not mention in the opener that Marvel and Sony became embroiled in a series of lawsuits and counter-lawsuits between themselves. Perform an Internet search for the name of the joint venture, "Spider-Man Merchandising L. P.," and locate several or more stories that discuss the various lawsuits and their settlement in mid-2004.

   What reasons did Marvel give for its initial lawsuit against Sony over its activities? Do you think Marvel was justified in filing suit against Sony? Was it a ruse for Marvel to exact something out of Sony, as some believe? Do you think Sony was right to counter-sue as it did? What do you think was the main motivation to form the venture from the perspective of each partner? List as many reasons as you can.

   Do you think the 50/50 split had anything to do with the joint venture's difficulties? Why or why not? Do you think differences in organizational culture (perhaps rooted in national culture) played any role in the conflict? Do you think anything could have been done during the formation of the joint venture that would have reduced the chances of this dispute arising? Explain your answer.

ETHICAL CHALLENGES

1. You are director of international operations for a leading clothing designer based in New York. Your firm has recently formed a joint venture with a top Latin American manufacturer—with each firm being an equal partner. On a recent trip to the joint venture's factory in Latin America, you discovered major discrepancies between the financial results sent to the U.S. parent's headquarters and those sent to the local parent firm. On further investigation, you are convinced that the local venture's top management is keeping two sets of accounting records to facilitate the diversion of funds to personal bank accounts. This scenario is not surprising to you, however, because it is rather common in the local country. What do you do? Do you confront your local joint venture partner directly or find another solution? Might you devise a policy that encourages the local partner to be honest in its financial reporting?

2. You own a small manufacturing firm in California and are considering entering the market of either Australia or Hong Kong. You are unsure which country you should target and unclear about which entry mode is most appropriate. A recent study investigated the differences between ethical perceptions of business managers from Australia and Hong Kong. The researchers determined that two factors had an impact on the perception of ethical problems: (a) culture and (b) the particular mode of market entry (e.g., exporting, contractual, investment in subsidiaries, or joint ventures). What ethical issues do you think might arise in conjunction with the various market entry modes discussed in this chapter? How might these issues influence your entry-mode selection?

3. You are chief operating officer of a German-based telecommunications firm considering a joint venture inside China with a Chinese firm. The consultant you've hired to help you through the negotiations has just informed you that ethical concerns can arise when international companies consider a cooperative form of market entry (such as a joint venture) with a local partner. This is especially true when each partner contributes personnel to the venture because cultural perspectives cause people to see ethical decisions differently. This is of special concern to you because the venture plans to employ people from both China and Germany—which have very different cultural backgrounds. Is there anything that your two companies can do to establish ethical principles in such a situation—either before or after formation of the cooperative arrangement? Can you think of a company that succeeded in the face of such difficulties?

PRACTICING INTERNATIONAL MANAGEMENT CASE
Telecom Ventures Unite the World

The world of telecommunications is changing. The era of global e-commerce is here, driven by new technologies such as broadband and wireless Internet access that make possible video telephone connections and high-speed data transmission. Annual worldwide revenues for telecommunications services total $600 billion, with international companies accounting for 20 percent of the business.

Market opportunities are opening around the world as post, telephone, and telegraph (PTT) monopolies are undergoing privatization. Since 1998 telecom deregulation has been taking place in earnest in Europe. Meanwhile, governments in developing countries are boosting investments in infrastructure improvements to increase the number of available telephone lines. The demand for telephone service is growing at a sharp pace—international telephone call volume more than doubled over a recent 6-year period. The net result of these changes is the globalization of the telecommunications industry. As William Donovan, a vice president at Sea-Land Service, said recently, "I don't want to have to talk to a bunch of different PTTs around the world. I don't want to have to go to one carrier in one country and a second in another just because it doesn't have a presence there."

Several alliances and joint venture partnerships formed between companies hoped to capitalize on the changed market and business environment. France Telecom, Deutsche Telekom, and Sprint created Global One to bring international telecommunications services to Multinational companies. As part of the deal, Sprint sold 10 percent of its stock to each of its French and German partners. One hurdle for the company was how to integrate the three partners' communication networks into a unified whole. Yet start-up costs were high, and the need to communicate in three different languages created some friction among personnel. Early on, lengthy negotiations were required to reach agreement about the value each partner brought to the venture. A former Global One executive noted, "There is no trust among the partners." Other problems included equipment and billing incompatibilities resulting from distribution agreements with telephone monopolies in individual countries. And then there were the financial losses that prompted Sprint chairman William T. Esrey to install Sprint executive Gary Forsee as CEO and president of Global One.

AT&T also depends on various partnership strategies as entry modes. WorldPartners began as an alliance of AT&T, Kokusai Denshin Denwa (KDD) of Japan, and Telecom of Singapore. The goal was to provide improved telecommunications services for companies conducting business globally. Guaranteeing that virtually any call can be completed required better wiring as well as improved network transmission systems. Today WorldPartners is comprised of 10 companies, including Telecom New Zealand, Telestra (Australia), Hong Kong Telecom, and Unisource.

Unisource is itself a joint venture that originally included Sweden's Telia AB, Swiss Telecom PTT, and PTT Telecom Netherlands. Later, Telefonica de España became an equal equity partner in Unisource. Unisource and AT&T then agreed to form a 60–40 joint venture known as AT&T–Unisource Communications to offer voice, data, and messaging services to businesses with European operations. AT&T would have preferred to form a joint venture with the French or German telephone companies. However, European regulators, concerned about AT&T's strong brand name and enormous size, refused to approve such a deal.

There was strong logic for the deal. As AT&T–Unisource CEO James Cosgrove explained from headquarters near Amsterdam in Hoofddorp, "You have to be European to play in Europe and yet you have to offer global solutions." Despite the fact that there are five corporate parents, a sense of equality and congeniality has developed. Notes CEO Cosgrove, "Working practices of 2 years have ironed out remarkably well. We have learned that you have to see this thing as a common operation. Otherwise too many bad compromises can be made." The presence of Telefonica de España in the alliance was especially significant for AT&T because of the Spanish company's strong influence in Latin America. Unfortunately, the alliance was weakened when Telefonica decided to ally itself with Concert Communications. To fill the void, AT&T and Italy's Stet announced a new alliance that would expand communication services to Latin America as well as Europe.

The third major telecommunications alliance, Concert Communications, was formed when British Telecommunications PLC bought a 20 percent stake in MCI Communications. Again, the goal of the alliance was to offer global voice and data network services to global corporations.

Thinking Globally

1. What strengths did AT&T bring to its joint venture with Unisource?

2. Can you think of any potential complications that could arise in the AT&T–Unisource joint venture?

3. Assess the formation of Global One, Unisource, and other partnerships discussed in this case in terms of the strategic factors for selecting entry modes identified in the chapter.

learning objectives

After studying this chapter, you should be able to

1. Explain the impact *globalization* is having on international marketing activities.

2. Describe the types of things that managers must consider when developing international *product strategies*.

3. Discuss the factors that influence international *promotional strategies* and the blending of product and promotional strategies.

4. Explain the elements that managers must take into account when designing international *distribution strategies*.

5. Discuss the elements that influence international *pricing strategies*.

developing and

marketing products

14

a look **back**

CHAPTER 13 explained the pros and cons of international entry modes and when each one is most appropriately used. We also described management issues with regard to each entry mode and the important strategic factors in their selection.

a look **at this chapter**

This chapter explores how globalization and differences in national business environments have an impact on the development and marketing of products internationally. We examine the many variables that must be considered when creating product, promotional, distribution, and pricing strategies.

a look **ahead**

CHAPTER 15 explains how companies launch and manage their international production efforts. Again, an emphasis is placed on how environmental variables affect production strategies.

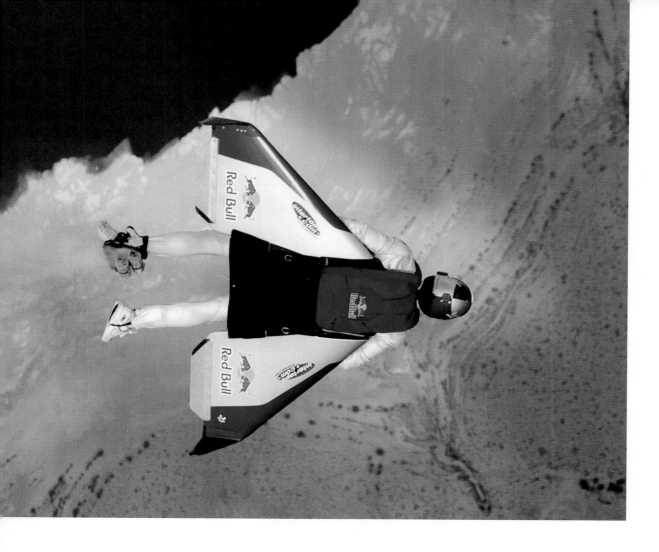

Learning to Fly

VIENNA, Austria—When Dietrich Mateschitz traveled to Asia on business, he got a taste of some popular energy drinks. Sensing opportunity, he brought a sample of the drinks back to Austria and started Red Bull, GmbH (*www.redbull.com*) in 1987. Red Bull Energy Drink is now available in more than 100 countries, selling over 1 billion cans of the raging stuff each year.

Red Bull is identical in every market in which it's sold. The slender red, blue, and silver can packs 8.3 ounces of caffeine, carbohydrates, vitamins, and taurine—an amino acid. That's music to the ears of club-goers, who swear by the drink's ability to keep them going till dawn. In fact, sales are soaring partly due to the word-of-mouth advertising the company gets from loyal customers. And around the world, Red Bull recruits young people to be "brand ambassadors" to hand out free samples at events and hires "student managers" who spread the word and drink on campuses.

Red Bull is also racking up double-digit revenue growth with creative TV ads in some markets. The ads display the company's "Red Bull Gives You Wings" tag line after cartoon characters float into the air after downing a can of the sweet drink. The company also sponsors top athletes and sporting events, including snowboarding, hang-gliding, skateboarding, and daredevil stunts. Pictured above is Felix Baumgartner, the first man to glide the 22 miles across the English Channel, reaching speeds of up to 220 miles per hour.

And although some people complain about the extreme sweetness of the drink, the company doesn't seem to mind. "It's not meant to be a taste drink, you either love us or you hate us," says the spokesperson. So far, it seems that many people are running with the bulls. As you read this chapter, think about the many ways in which products are marketed around the world.[1]

In earlier chapters, we continually emphasized the greater complexity of managing an international business as compared with a purely domestic one. Myriad differences in all aspects of a nation's business environment complicate management. Managing marketing activities that span time zones and cultures can test the most seasoned marketing managers.

We first introduced the concept of globalization and how it affects international business activities in Chapter 1 and returned continuously to this theme in subsequent chapters. We have seen that globalization's impact is not uniform. It affects different industries and products in different ways and to varying degrees. Some companies can take advantage of globalization's effects and create a single product that is marketed identically around the world. As we saw in this chapter's opening company profile, Red Bull (*www.redbull.com*) markets an identical energy drink in the same manner in more than 100 countries around the world. Others realize that differences in national business environments are too great to ignore. This group then must create new products, modify promotional campaigns, or adjust their marketing strategies in some other way.

We begin this chapter by taking a brief look at the debate over the extent to which globalization *should* affect marketing strategies. We then describe how marketing internationally differs in terms of how companies create their product strategies, promote and advertise a product, decide on a pricing strategy, and design distribution channels. Throughout the chapter, we examine how globalization on one hand and national differences on the other are having an impact on international marketing activities.

Globalization and Marketing

Globalization is transforming the way in which some products are marketed internationally, but not all. Some companies implement a global strategy that uses similar promotional messages and themes to market the same product around the world. Others find that their products require physical changes so that they suit the tastes of consumers in markets abroad. Other firms' products need different marketing campaigns to reflect the unique circumstances of local markets. How do managers decide when their marketing strategies need modifying? In this section, we explain the impact of globalization on the standardization versus adaptation decision.

Standardization Versus Adaptation

In a well-known article, U.S. researcher Theodore Levitt argued that because the world is becoming standardized and homogeneous, companies should market the same products in the same way in all countries.[2] Technology, claimed Levitt, was already causing people's needs and preferences to converge throughout the world. He urged companies to reduce production and marketing costs by standardizing both the physical features of their products and their strategies for marketing them.

Since that article appeared, some researchers have countered that standardization is just one of a number of strategies with which firms have successfully entered the international marketplace.[3] Still others argue that standardization is not always the best strategy, and they advise smaller companies to adapt to local cultures while exploiting their unique international images to gain local market share.[4]

Influence of National Business Environments
Consumers in different national markets often demand products that reflect their unique tastes and preferences. Cultural,

Swedish furniture retailer IKEA (www.ikea.com) sells many of the same products worldwide without modification, adapting only the language used in its lighthearted ads. Here, in a Dutch print ad, a young man makes creative use of an "Alång" standing lamp that he received as a Huwelijkscadeaus ("Wedding Gift" in Dutch). Another young man invents a new use for a "Mållen" opbergbakje ("storage bin").

political, legal, and economic environments have a great deal to do with the preferences of both consumers and industrial buyers worldwide. Recall from Chapter 2 that a culture's aesthetics involves, among other things, preferences for certain colors. Ohio-based Rubbermaid (*www.rubbermaid.com*) discovered the role of aesthetics as it attempted to increase its international sales. Consumers in the United States prefer household products in neutral blues or almond; in southern Europe, red is the preferred color. The Dutch want white. In addition, many European cultures perceive plastic products as inferior and want tight lids on metal wastebaskets as opposed to U.S.-style plastic versions with open tops.[5]

But certain products do appeal to practically all cultures. Although it is not a traditional Asian drink, a passion for red wine is currently sweeping Asian markets such as Hong Kong, Singapore, Taiwan, and Thailand. Driving this demand are medical studies reporting the health benefits of red wine (the king of Thailand has publicly proclaimed its healthy properties). But other factors—including the fact that red is considered good luck in many Asian cultures—are also at work. Many Asians choose red wine at restaurants because of its image as the beverage of choice for people who are sophisticated and successful. (The same is not true of white wine, because from a distance it may resemble water.) Today in Beijing, fashionable young people often give red wine as a housewarming present instead of the traditional favorites of their parents and grandparents.[6]

Product standardization is more likely when nations share the same level of economic development. In the 1980s, consumers in India faced limited options when it came to purchasing automobiles. Most were made in India, expensive, and not fuel-efficient. Thanks to a fairly good record of economic progress over the past two decades, Indian consumers have a better standard of living and more discretionary income. Affording an imported brand-name automobile with a global reputation, such as Suzuki (*www.suzuki.co.jp*) or Ford (*www.ford.com*), is more commonplace in Indian cities than it was years ago.

With this brief introduction to some of the issues relevant to international marketing strategy, let's take an in-depth look at the elements that influence a company's *product*, *promotional*, *distribution*, and *pricing strategies*.

Developing Product Strategies

Companies can standardize or adapt their products in many alternative ways when they decide to "go international." Let's take a look at some of the factors that influence the standardize-versus-adapt decision as well as several other international product strategy issues.

Laws and Regulations

Companies often must adapt their products to satisfy the laws and regulations in a target market. Consider the dilemma facing chocolate makers in a unified European Union (EU). People's tastes, of course, vary across markets, and taste in chocolate is no exception to the rule. A so-called Chocolate War has erupted in the EU as it tries to standardize member countries' product content regulations. On one side stand the so-called cocoa purists, including Belgium, France, Germany, Spain, Italy, the Netherlands, Luxembourg, and Greece. Opposite stand Britain, Denmark, Portugal, Austria, Finland, and Sweden—nations who permit manufacturers to add vegetable fats to chocolate products. The purists argue not only that European advertising should restrict the word "chocolate" to 100 percent cocoa products, but also that the term "milk chocolate" be outlawed altogether. They want nonpure products labeled something like "chocolate with milk and noncocoa vegetable fats."[7]

The fact that many developing countries have fewer consumer-protection laws creates an ethical issue for some companies. Ironically, lower levels of education and less buying experience mean that consumers in developing countries are more likely to need protection. However, many governments impose fewer regulations in order to hold down production costs and consumer prices. Unfortunately, this can be an invitation for international distributors to withhold full information about products and their potential dangers.

Cultural Differences

Companies also adapt their products to suit local buyers' product preferences that are rooted in culture. Häagen-Dazs (*www.haagendazs.com*) is an international company that prides itself on its ability to identify the taste preferences of consumers in target markets. It then modifies its base product with just the right flavor to make a product that satisfies consumers' needs. Following years of trial and error developing secret formulas and conducting taste tests, Häagen-Dazs finally launched its green-tea flavor ice cream throughout Japan. The taste is that of *macha* tea—an elite strain of green tea that's been used in elaborate Japanese ceremonies for centuries. Green-tea ice cream was a hit instantly and one day may even surpass Häagen-Dazs' perennial flavor champion in Japan—vanilla.[8]

Not all companies need to modify their product to the culture; instead they may need to identify a different cultural need that it satisfies. Altoids (*www.altoids.com*), for example, is a British product that has been used for 200 years to soothe upset stomachs. But the company identified a different use for its product in the United States. Because of its strong flavor, Altoids also acts as a breath mint. Altoids breath mints have pushed aside weaker-flavored candies, including Certs (*www.certs.com*), to command 17 percent of the $281 million U.S. market.[9]

Brand and Product Names

brand name
Name of one or more items in a
product line that identifies the source
or character of the items.

Several issues related to a company's brand name are important concerns for the day-to-day activities of international managers. A **brand name** is the name of one or more items in a product line that identifies the source or character of the items. When we see a product labeled with a particular brand name, we assign to that product a certain value based on our past experiences with that brand. That is why a brand name is central to a product's personality and the image that it presents to buyers. It informs buyers about a product's source and protects both customer and producer from copycat products. Brand names help consumers to select, recommend, or reject products; they also function as legal property that owners can protect from trespass by competitors.

Indeed, a strong brand can become a company's most valuable asset and primary source of competitive advantage. A consistent worldwide brand image is increasingly important as more consumers and businesspeople travel internationally than ever before. Any inconsistency in brand name can confuse existing and potential customers. Although

A brand name is central to a product's personality and to how buyers perceive it. Shown in this photo illustration are some of the most powerful global brands that exist today. As you can see, they span all sorts of industries, including photographic film, delivery services, mobile phones, financial services, computer software, and aerospace. Take a moment to think about some of the brands shown here. What is your perception of each?

companies keep their brand names consistent across markets, they often do create new product names or modify existing ones to suit local preferences.

Companies also need to review the image of their brand from time to time and update it if it seems old fashioned. For instance, Lipton (*www.lipton.com*) is trying to get people to think of Lipton tea as an alternative to colas and other soft drinks. Since the 1890s Lipton had as its mascot Sir Thomas J. Lipton, the tea maker's founder. But in a major overhaul of the brand all references to Mr. Lipton were removed. "The guy had to go," admits vice president John Caron. "The Lipton brand is known all over the world, but people told us, 'My mother drinks that stuff.' In the world of branding, that isn't a good thing." Lipton booted the founder in favor of "Tom," a sassy young Briton.[10]

Selecting International Brand and Product Names Whether they are standardized or adapted locally, products in international markets need carefully selected names. All company and product brand names (like all nouns) are made up of *morphemes*—semantic elements, or language building blocks, such as the *van* in *advantage*. NameLab (*www.namelab.com*) is an identity-consultant firm that uses over 6,000 morphemes to develop new product names. NameLab points out that because most Western languages stem from the same linguistic source—Indo-European—companies can create brand names having similar meanings in these nations. *Accu*, for example, connotes *accuracy* in both Western and Japanese cultures. Thus, Honda (*www.honda.com*) created the upscale car division Acura. Other names that are constructed to have similar connotations in many languages or to embody no cultural bias include Compaq (*www.compaq.com*), Kodak (*www.kodak.com*), and Sony (*www.sony.co.jp*).[11] Once a name is chosen, companies can survey local native speakers about their reactions to it. These techniques help companies reduce the likelihood of committing potential marketing blunders.

Brand names seldom offend people in international markets, but product names can be highly offensive if they are not carefully researched and selected. Clarks Shoes (*www.clarks.com*), a British shoe company, once gave a name to a line of shoes that was offensive to the Hindu religious community in Britain. Consequently, the company had to issue the following apology in the British press:[12]

> Clarks Shoes are concerned that the naming of some of their products with the names of Hindu Gods Vishnu and Krishna has caused hurt and offence to the British Hindu Community. The Company apologises for this mistake and is withholding the products before resuming sales with new names. In the future the company will carry out more detailed research before naming products.

Other times, product names must be changed not because they're offensive, but because they mislead consumers. Consider the problem faced by the British beverage and chocolate producer Cadbury Schweppes (*www.cadburyschweppes.com*). When Swiss chocolate manufacturers sued on the grounds that the public was being misled into thinking that Cadbury's Swiss Chalet bar was genuine Swiss chocolate, the company was forced to withdraw the product from the marketplace. A British court confirmed that the name and packaging of the product—the "Swiss" part of the name and the image of a snow-capped Swiss Alp—were likely to mislead consumers.[13]

National Image

The value that customers obtain from a product is heavily influenced by the image of the country in which it is designed, manufactured, or assembled. We consider the influence of a country's name when thinking of Italian shoes, German luxury cars, and Japanese electronics. This image can be positive for some products but negative for others. For example, the best Russian caviar and vodkas have reputations of quality around the world. But how do you feel about Russian automobiles or computers? Attaching "Russia" to certain products is beneficial, whereas attaching it to others could be detrimental.

Because it affects buyers' perceptions of quality and reliability, national image is an important element of product policy. However, national image can and does change over time—although slowly. Decades ago, Japanese products were considered to be of poor quality and rather unreliable. But a national effort toward quality improvement and the installation of quality-control procedures by companies earned Japan a national image for precision and quality products.[14] Japanese cars, which were once vehicles for the budget-conscious consumer, now have luxury models that rival the quality and technological advancement of German autos.

Likewise, years ago Taiwan was known for basic, no-frills items such as toys and industrial products of all sorts. But today many of Taiwan's industries possess a reputation for innovation—designing products that reflect decades of investing in people's research and engineering skills. One company that benefited from an intense devotion to R&D is Giant Manufacturing (*www.giant-bicycles.com*), Taiwan's leading bicycle manufacturer. The company began in Taichung, Taiwan, nearly three decades ago producing bikes under the brand names of other companies. But in 1980 the company began to manufacture under its own brand name, and today it has a solid niche in the mountain bike market. Giant's innovation in using lightweight materials and creating groundbreaking designs even earned it sponsorship of Spain's world-champion racing team. Today, high-tech products, and even those not traditionally thought of as high tech (such as bikes), stamped "Made in Taiwan" command respect in global markets.[15]

Counterfeit Goods and Black Markets

In Chapter 3 we discussed how companies are trying to protect their intellectual property and trademarks from counterfeit goods. Recall that *counterfeit goods* are imitation products passed off as legitimate trademarks, patents, or copyrighted works—products that normally enjoy legal protection. Because developing nations often are weakest in enforcing such legal protections, they normally have the most active counterfeiting markets. Countries that top the list for the portion of their markets comprised of counterfeits include China, India, Russia, Thailand, and Turkey. Currently representing between 5 and 10 percent of international trade, counterfeiting is worth as much as $50 billion to $80 billion worldwide.[16]

Counterfeiting is common among highly visible brand-name consumer goods, including watches, perfumes, clothing, movies, music, and computer software. Counterfeit products are typically sold to consumers on what is called the **black market**—a marketplace of underground transactions that typically appears because a product is either illegal (such as counterfeits) or tightly regulated. Tabletop vendors working the back streets of the world's largest cities represent the retail side of the black market. For instance, in Sofia, the capital of Bulgaria, you can buy one CD-ROM that contains 50 software applications for $10; buying all the official versions of these products would cost about $5,000.[17] In Estonia's Kadaka flea market you can find the full Microsoft Office (*www.microsoft.com*) software bundle for around $18—about one-fiftieth of its official selling price.[18] Increasingly, engineered industrial components such as aircraft parts, medicines, and other pharmaceutical products are also becoming targets of counterfeiters.

Counterfeit goods can damage buyers' image of a brand when the counterfeits are of inferior quality—which is nearly always the case. Buyers who purchase an item bearing a company's brand name expect a certain level of craftsmanship and, therefore, satisfaction. But when the product fails to deliver on the expectations, the buyer is dissatisfied and the company's reputation is tarnished. Japanese motorcycle manufacturers recently saw their sales in China fall sharply, as people are buying near-replicas of their products at discounts of up to 40 percent of the originals. But the counterfeiting problem is more serious today because the Chinese producers are now exporting their cycles to other Asian nations. Yamaha (*www.yamaha.co.jp*), Japan's second-largest motorcycle producer, is considering legal action against one Chinese company. Yamaha officials say the Chinese firm's products resemble its own models right down to the Yamaha name stamped on the side.[19]

Shortened Product Life Cycles

Companies traditionally managed to extend a product's life by introducing it into different markets consecutively. Firms accomplished this by introducing products in industrialized countries and only later marketing them in developing and emerging markets. Thus, while a product's sales are declining in one market, they might be growing in another.

However, advances in telecommunications have alerted consumers around the world to the latest product introductions. Consequently, consumers in developing and emerging markets also demand the latest products and are not happy with receiving what is yesterday's fad in the highly developed nations. Also, the rapid pace with which technological innovation occurs today is shortening the life cycles of products. The actions of international companies themselves actually helped to create this situation. Companies are undertaking new-product development at an increasingly rapid pace and thus shortening the life cycles of their products.

> **Quick Study**
>
> 1. How is globalization affecting international marketing activities?
> 2. List elements of the national business environment that influence the standardization-versus-adaptation decision.
> 3. What is the link between *brand names* and competitive advantage?
> 4. Explain the potential impact of national image and counterfeit products on international product strategy.

Creating Promotional Strategies

promotion mix
Efforts by a company to reach distribution channels and target customers through communications such as personal selling, advertising, public relations, and direct marketing.

Efforts by a company to reach distribution channels and target customers through communications such as personal selling, advertising, public relations, and direct marketing are called its **promotion mix**. Not surprisingly, promotional activities often receive the greatest attention among marketers because many people, even professionals, tend to equate "marketing" with "promotion." After we examine two general promotional strategies, we discuss the complications that can arise in international advertising and communications.

Push and Pull Strategies

pull strategy
Promotional strategy designed to create buyer demand that will encourage channel members to stock a company's product.

push strategy
Promotional strategy designed to pressure channel members to carry a product and promote it to final users of the product.

There are two general promotional strategies that companies can use to get their marketing message across to buyers. They can rely completely on just one of these or use them in combination. A promotional strategy designed to create buyer demand that will encourage channel members to stock a company's product is called a **pull strategy**. In other words, buyer demand is generated in order to "pull" products through distribution channels to end users. Creating consumer demand through direct marketing techniques is a common example of a pull strategy. For instance, when Procter & Gamble (*www.pg.com*) encountered distribution difficulties in trying to introduce Rejoice hair-care products into Asia, the company opted to generate grassroots consumer demand. The company hired a fleet of trucks to drive through village squares and hand out free trial packages to potential end users.

In contrast, a **push strategy** is a promotional strategy designed to pressure channel members to carry a product and promote it to final users. Manufacturers of products that are commonly sold through department and grocery stores often use a push strategy. For example, manufacturer's sales representatives are constantly calling on Wal-Mart (*www.walmart.com*) to encourage it to stock the manufacturer's product and give it good visibility. Push strategies are also used for office products, including computers and office furniture. A company's international sales force is the key to successfully implementing a push strategy abroad. For insights into how companies can better manage their salespeople in other cultures, see the Global Manager's Toolbox titled, "Managing an International Sales Force."

Whether the push or pull strategy is most appropriate in a given marketing environment depends on several factors:

- *Distribution System.* Implementing a push strategy can be difficult when channel members (such as distributors) wield a great deal of power relative to that of producers. It can also be ineffective when distribution channels are lengthy: the more levels of intermediaries there are, the more channel members there are who must be convinced to carry a product. In such cases, it might be easier to create buyer demand using a pull strategy than to persuade distributors to stock a particular product.

global manager's TOOLBOX

Managing an International Sales Force

Today, companies are reaping a greater portion of their revenues from international sales. How can you become a better global manager of your company's international sales force? Here are some helpful hints on improving the effectiveness of your company's representatives abroad.

⊙ **Know the sales scene.** Your company should conduct research before hiring and managing an international sales force. Then formulate a targeted sales strategy and empower your sales force to meet their performance targets. The amount of compensation as well as the way in which it is delivered varies from country to country. For instance, in the United States a greater portion of salary is based on commission than it is in Europe. Know the salary structure and incentive plans that salespeople with similar jobs have at local companies.

⊙ **Research the customer.** Do not assume that customers abroad have the same needs and preferences as customers at home. Investigate what potential buyers want and how much they are willing to pay. When ECA International (a market information provider) expanded into Asia it was unsuccessful time and again. The company found out through its sales force that potential customers wanted to buy research piece-by-piece rather than buy a membership in the company. ECA was able to sell its memberships in Asia only after it adapted its methods to suit local buyers. The sales force is a valuable source of information on the local market.

⊙ **Work with the culture.** "In order to motivate individuals, you need to set realistic objectives for salespeople, and much of that is culturally bound," says John Wada, sales and marketing director for IOR, a cross-cultural management company. Your company should seek answers to a host of questions. Do people in the local culture feel differently about work teams and competition than your sales force at home? How about schedules and deadlines? Are you moving into a culture where "time is of the essence" or one where time is far less important? Make sure your company and the local sales force fully understand what is expected of one another.

⊙ **Learn from your representatives.** If your salespeople believe they are pushing products that bear no relationship to the local market, their performance will suffer. "I'd do a great job," so the story goes, "but the product just won't sell here." Salespeople may begin focusing on critiquing products rather than selling them. Involve your sales reps in the R&D process so that they have a better sense of what's going on with the product. You might also bring your sales force to the home office each year to learn about your business so that they understand their vital link in your company's chain of business activities. Finally, top managers should visit the local office to better comprehend the needs of local customers.

⊙ *Access to Mass Media.* Developing and emerging markets typically have fewer available forms of mass media for use in implementing a pull strategy. Accordingly, it is difficult to increase consumer awareness of a product and generate product demand. Many consumers in these markets cannot afford cable or satellite television, or perhaps even glossy magazines. In such cases, advertisers might turn to billboards and radio. At other times, gaining wide exposure can be difficult because existing media have only local, as opposed to national, reach. For example, Indonesia did not launch its first nationwide television station until 1994. In yet other situations, advertising certain products on certain media is unlawful. For example, companies that enter Canada or the United States cannot use television or radio to advertise tobacco products.

⊙ *Type of Product.* A pull strategy is most appropriate when buyers display a great deal of brand loyalty toward one particular brand name. In other words, brand-loyal buyers know what brand of a product they want before they go out to buy it. On the other hand, push strategies tend to be appropriate for inexpensive consumer goods characterized by buyers who are not brand loyal. Low brand loyalty means that a buyer will go shopping for a product, not knowing which brand is best, and simply will buy one of those carried by the retailer or wholesaler. A push strategy is also suited to industrial products because potential buyers usually need to be informed about a product's special features and benefits.

International Advertising

International advertising differs a great deal from advertising in domestic markets. Managers must rely on their knowledge of a market to decide whether an ad is suitable for the company's international promotional efforts. For instance, cultural similarities can mean that ads must be modified only slightly for use in different nations. Cultural differences may mean that entirely new ads must be created.

Coca-Cola's (*www.cocacola.com*) experience in creating an ad to appeal to Chinese people both in China and throughout the world illustrates the problems that can arise when developing highly specialized ads. Coca-Cola's desire to create a Coke ad that looked authentically Chinese drew it to Harbin, a city in northeast China. But along the way, the bus in which the crew that was to shoot the commercial was traveling stalled. When the driver lit a fire under the gas tank to thaw the fuel, the horrified crew scrambled off the bus thinking it might explode. The crew stood in biting, subzero temperatures until the bus was once again running—the director's frostbitten nose bears the scars of the adventure. Then when a local older man hired to be in the ad had trouble following the director's instructions, local villagers pointed out why—he was deaf. Finally, the crew had to trudge around in knee-deep snow first to get a field of frozen red pinwheels to spin and then to reorient the whole set so that the wind (which was blowing in an unfavorable direction) could spin the pinwheels. But it appears that Coke's efforts at creating an ad depicting people celebrating Chinese New Year in the traditional manner in a picturesque village paid off—"It made me feel very emotional," said Fang Chuanbao, an office worker in Shanghai who saw the ad. The localized ads exemplify Coke's "think local, act local" mantra, which was pioneered by Chairman Douglas Daft as part of an effort to remake Coke into the nimble marketer it once was.[20]

Let's now explore some of the factors involved in the decision of whether to standardize or adapt advertisements.

Standardizing or Adapting Advertisements

The vast majority of advertising that occurs in any one nation is produced solely for that domestic audience. But companies that advertise in multiple markets must determine the aspects of the advertising campaign that can be standardized across markets and those that cannot. Companies that do market their products across national boundaries try to contain costs by standardizing as many aspects of their campaigns as possible. However, companies seldom standardize all aspects of their international promotions, for a variety of reasons, including differences in culture and laws.[21]

Firms that standardize advertising usually control campaigns from the home office.[22] This policy helps them to project consistent brand images and promotional messages across all markets—the aim of a global strategy (see Chapter 11). Companies can achieve consistency by standardizing their basic promotional message, creative concepts, graphics, and information content. Once a company decides to pursue a global marketing strategy, it naturally tries to get the most for its advertising expenditure. Despite hurdles and mixed results with Web ads, companies continue to try to reach a global audience by marketing on the World Wide Web.

Another way in which companies can reach a global audience is to sponsor global sporting events, such as the Olympics, World Cup Soccer, and Formula One automobile racing. These types of events receive heavy media coverage and are often telecast simultaneously in multiple nations. Even posting banners around the venues of such events can boost recognition of a company's brand name by exposing it to perhaps millions of viewers around the world. In fact, viewers in 102 countries see the banners of companies that sponsor Formula One auto racing.[23]

Case: The Elusive Euro-Consumer

The continuing integration of nations belonging to the European Union is causing many marketers to dream of a day when they can standardize their advertising to appeal to a so-called Euro-consumer. But the Euro-consumer remains a rare, almost mythical, beast that is eluding even the world's most clever advertisers.

Some well-known international advertising agencies have tried a pan-European advertising approach only to fail because of national differences. Consider the experience of the acclaimed Leo Burnett Company (*www.leoburnett.com*) when it took on the goal of creating a single European campaign for United Distillers' Johnnie Walker (*www.johnniewalker.com*) whiskey. It took many painful tests and revisions before the ad could be rolled out. In the original ad, the tag line read "The Water of Life" and showed a man attending "the running of the bulls" in Pamplona, Spain. After narrowly escaping being trampled by the bull, the man celebrates with a glass of Johnnie Walker Red Label. But in many countries, the Pamplona setting raised hackles because people said, "The Spanish don't know anything about making good whiskey." Tests of the ad in Germany showed it would not work because to Germans it seemed simply reckless—not a widely admired trait there. Says Jenny Vaughn, worldwide brand director for Johnnie Walker, "Also, because of the German animal rights campaigners, you can't show a goldfish in a goldfish bowl on German television, so a bull run was just not [acceptable]." The tag line "The Water of Life" was baffling in many languages. "People thought it meant watered-down whiskey," said Vaughn, so the line was changed to "Taste Life." Then a voice-over in the ad was incorrectly translated in one language as "when your life flashes in front of you, make sure it's worth watching." In every market the words didn't make sense or the meaning was lost. In Italy the line was totally discarded. In Germany attempts at translation proved so maddening that the line was replaced with "Live every day as if it were your last."

Europe's many languages certainly create thorny translation issues for marketers. Thus, the most successful pan-European ads are those that contain a great deal of visuals, have few written or spoken words, and focus on the product and consumer. One such ad is that for TAG Heuer (*www.tagheuer.com*) watches, which positions the company's product as competitive and a winner. In the ad, a swimmer is shown racing a shark and a hurdler is shown leaping an oversize razor blade. The highly visual ad gets across the company's message that it is a winner.[24]

Blending Product and Promotional Strategies

When companies extend their marketing efforts internationally, they develop communication strategies that blend product and promotional strategies.[25] A company's communication strategy for a particular market takes into account the nature of the product being marketed and the promotion mix to market it. After we discuss the marketing communication process, we examine five product/promotional methods that companies use and the appropriate situation for using each.

Communicating Promotional Messages
The process of sending promotional messages about products to target markets is called **marketing communication**.[26] Communicating the benefits of a product can be more difficult in international business than in domestic business for several reasons. Marketing internationally usually means translating promotional messages from one language into another. Marketers must also be knowledgeable of the many cultural nuances that can affect how buyers interpret a promotional message. A nation's laws that govern the promotion of products in another country can also force changes in marketing communication.

Marketing communication is typically considered a circular process, as shown in Figure 14.1. The company that has an idea it wishes to communicate is the source of the communication. The idea is *encoded* (translated into images, words, and symbols) into a *promotional message* that the company is trying to get across. The promotional message is then sent to the *audience* (potential buyers) through various *media*. Media commonly used by companies to communicate their promotional messages include radio, television, newspapers, magazines, billboards, and direct mailings. Once the audience receives the message, they decode the message and interpret its meaning. Information in the form of *feedback* (purchase or nonpurchase) then flows back to the source of the message. The decoding process by the audience can be disrupted by the presence of *noise*—anything that disrupts the audience's ability to receive and interpret the promotional message. By ignoring important cultural nuances, companies can inadvertently increase the potential for noise that can cloud the audience's understanding of their promotional message. For instance, language barriers between the company and potential buyers can create noise if a company's promotional message is translated incorrectly into the local language.

Product/Communications Extension (Dual Extension)
This method extends the same home-market product and marketing promotion into target markets. Under certain conditions, it can be the simplest and most profitable strategy. For example, because of a common language and other cultural similarities, companies based in English-speaking Canadian provinces can sell the same product with packaging and advertising identical to that in the U.S. market—provided the product is not required by the U.S. government to carry any special statements or warnings. Thus, the Canadian companies contain costs by developing a single product and one promotional campaign for both markets. However, it is important for Canadian companies not to ignore any

marketing communication
Process of sending promotional messages about products to target markets.

FIGURE 14.1

Marketing Communications Process

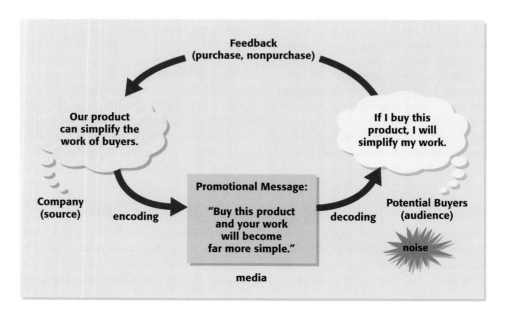

subtle cultural differences that could cause confusion in interpreting the promotional message.

As the information age continues to knit the world more tightly together, this method will probably grow more popular. Today, consumers in seemingly remote parts of the world are rapidly becoming aware of the latest worldwide fads and fashions. But it appears that this strategy is better suited for certain groups of buyers, including brand-conscious teenagers, business executives, and wealthy individuals. The strategy also tends to be better suited for companies that use a global strategy with their products, such as upscale personal items with global brand names—examples include Rolex (*www.rolex.com*) watches, Hermes (*www.hermes.com*) scarves and ties, and Coco Chanel (*www.chanel.com*) perfumes. It can also be appropriate for global brands that have mass appeal and cut across all age groups and social classes—such as Canon (*www.canon.com*), Mars (*www.mars.com*), and Nokia (*www.nokia.com*). The strategy also is useful to companies that are the low-cost leaders in their industries. One product and one promotional message keep costs down.

Product Extension/Communications Adaptation   Under this method, a company extends the same product into target markets but alters its promotion. Communications require adaptation because the product satisfies a different need, serves a different function, or appeals to a different type of buyer. Companies adjust their marketing communication to inform potential buyers that the product either satisfies their needs or serves a distinct function. This approach helps companies contain costs because the good itself does not need to undergo any alteration. However, altering communications can be expensive—especially if there are significant cultural differences among target markets. Filming altered ads with local actors and on location can add significantly to promotional costs.

One company that changes its promotional message for international markets is the Japanese retailer Muji (*www.muji.co.jp*). Muji offers a wide variety of goods, including writing materials, clothing, and home furnishings. However, everything is inspired by a central theme rooted in centuries of Japanese culture—the simplicity of everyday life. Muji's philosophy is one of selling unbranded quality goods, and company promotions boast the motto "Functional Japanese minimalism for everyone." Its target market in Japan is the average school-aged child and young adult. However, Muji's European stores use a different promotional message. Muji's European customers tend to be older and see themselves as sophisticated and stylish buyers of the company's products. In Europe, Muji's promotional message is "shop at a business that has a very respectable brand name"—clearly different from its message in Japan. Also, the company's European customers are not buying simply a product (as do its Japanese customers); they are buying into the traditional Japanese concept of simplicity.[27]

Low economic development also can demand that communications be adapted to suit local conditions. For instance, companies in Europe and North America and certain Asian countries can rely on a modern telecommunications system to reach millions of consumers through television, radio, and even the World Wide Web. But in developing countries (such as rural parts of India and China), television and radio coverage are limited, and development of the Web is years behind developed nations. Marketers in those countries must use alternative techniques, including door-to-door personal selling and regional product shows or fairs.

Product Adaptation/Communications Extension   Using this method, a company adapts its product to the requirements of the international market while retaining the product's original marketing communication. There are many reasons why companies need to adapt their products. One might be to meet legal requirements in the local market. Moreover, governments can require that firms use a certain amount of local materials, labor, or some other resource in their local production process. If the exact same materials or components are not available locally, the result can be a modified product.

This method can be costly because appropriately modifying a product to suit the needs of local buyers often means that the company must invest in production facilities in the local market. If each national market requires its own production facility, cost savings provided by economies of scale in production can be elusive. However, a company can implement this strategy successfully if it sells a differentiated product for which it can charge a higher price to offset the greater production costs.[28]

Product/Communications Adaptation (Dual Adaptation)
This method adapts both the product and its marketing communication to suit the target market. The product itself is adapted to match the needs or preferences of local buyers. The promotional message is adapted to explain how the product meets those needs and preferences. Because both production and marketing efforts must be altered, this strategy can be expensive; therefore, it is not very common. However, it can be implemented successfully if a sufficiently large and profitable market segment exists.

Product Invention
This method requires that an entirely new product be developed for the target market. Product invention is often necessary when many important differences exist between the home and target markets. One reason for product invention is that local buyers cannot afford a company's current product because of low purchasing power. For example, Honda (*www.honda.com*) developed a car called the "City" that is designed for budget-conscious buyers in Southeast Asian and European markets.

Product inventions can also arise because of a lack of adequate infrastructure needed to operate certain products. One day, London inventor Trevor Baylis was watching a television documentary on the difficulty of educating Africans about AIDS because much of the continent did not have the electricity infrastructure or batteries to operate radios. Baylis set to work and developed the Freeplay windup radio—30 seconds of cranking keeps it going for 40 minutes. Baylis and several South African businessmen then formed a company called Bay-Gen Power Corporation in Cape Town, South Africa. The radio was first sold only to relief agencies working in developing nations. However, due mostly to word of mouth, it is now popular worldwide among hikers, environmentalists, and even hip shoppers looking for "retro" appliances.[29]

Quick Study

1. Identify several factors that influence the choice between a *push strategy* and a *pull strategy*.
2. What issues affect the decision of whether to standardize or adapt international advertising?
3. Identify each element in the *marketing communications* process and describe how they interact.
4. What five generic methods are used to blend product and promotional strategies for international markets? Describe each briefly.

Designing Distribution Strategies

distribution
Planning, implementing, and controlling the physical flow of a product from its point of origin to its point of consumption.

Planning, implementing, and controlling the physical flow of a product from its point of origin to its point of consumption is called **distribution**. The physical path that a product follows on its way to customers is called a *distribution channel*. Companies along this channel that work together in delivering products to customers are called *channel members* or *intermediaries*. Bear in mind that manufacturers of goods are not the only producers who need distribution channels. Service providers such as consulting companies, health-care organizations, and news services also need distribution (or delivery) systems to reach their customers. Consider the business of delivering news services over the World Wide Web. Channel members involved in getting news from the newsroom to the Web surfer can include, among others, Internet service providers such as America Online (*www.aol.com*) and search engine providers such as Excite (*www.excite.com*).

Companies develop their international distribution strategies based on two related decisions: (1) how to get the goods *into* a country and (2) how to distribute goods *within* a country. We presented the different ways companies get their products into countries in Chapter 13. Thus, here we focus on distribution strategies within countries.

Designing Distribution Channels

Managers consider two overriding concerns when establishing channels of distribution: (1) the amount of *market exposure* that a product needs and (2) the *cost* of distributing a product. Let's now take a look at each of these concerns.

Degree of Exposure   In promoting its product to the greatest number of potential customers, a marketer must determine the amount of exposure needed. An **exclusive channel** is one in which a manufacturer grants the right to sell its product to only one or a limited number of resellers. Thus, an exclusive channel gives producers a great deal of control over the sale of their product by channel members such as wholesalers and retailers. It also helps a producer to constrain distributors from selling competing brands. In this way, an exclusive channel creates a barrier that makes it difficult or impossible for outsiders to penetrate the channel. For example, in most countries new car dealerships reflect exclusive distribution—normally, Mitsubishi (*www.mitsubishi.com*) dealerships cannot sell Toyotas (*www.toyota.com*) and General Motors (*www.gm.com*) dealers cannot sell Fords (*www.ford.com*).

An interesting story comes to us from the Himalayan kingdom nation of Nepal. Although Nepal's per capita gross domestic product is just $150 to $200, people today can more easily afford the personal-care products of companies such as Colgate-Palmolive (*www.colgate.com*). As a result, competition for shelf space in stores is heating up. In a small spice shop in Katmandu, for example, the shopkeeper says his distributor pays him about $4.20 each month for carrying only Colgate dental-care products. He says this doubles his monthly profit from toothpaste and toothbrush sales.[30]

When a producer wants its product to be made available through as many distribution outlets as possible, it prefers to use an **intensive channel**—one in which a producer grants the right to sell its product to many resellers. An intensive channel provides buyers with location convenience because of the large number of outlets through which a product is sold. However, it does not create strong barriers to channel entry for other producers, nor does it provide much control over reseller decisions such as what competing brands to sell. Large companies whose products are sold through grocery stores and department stores typically take an intensive channel approach to distribution. The obstacle faced by small companies that choose an intensive channel approach is gaining shelf space—especially small companies with lesser-known brands. This problem is exacerbated by the increasing global trend toward retailers developing their own *private-label brands*—brands created by retailers themselves. Manufacturers produce the good for the retailer and label it with the retailer's brand name instead of their own. Thus, retailers give their own products shelf space close to the best brands, and small, lesser-known brands end up getting the poorest shelf location—up high or near the floor.

Channel Length and Cost   *Channel length* refers to the number of intermediaries between the producer and the buyer. In a *zero-level channel*—which is also called direct marketing—producers sell directly to final buyers. A *one-level channel* places only one intermediary between the producer and the buyer. Two intermediaries make up a *two-level channel*, and so forth. Generally, the more intermediaries in a channel, the more costly it becomes because each additional player tacks on to the product a charge for its services. This is an important consideration for companies that sell price-sensitive consumer

exclusive channel
Distribution channel in which a manufacturer grants the right to sell its product to only one or a limited number of resellers.

intensive channel
Distribution channel in which a producer grants the right to sell its product to many resellers.

products such as candy, food, and small household items that usually compete on the basis of price. As we saw in Chapter 11, companies that sell highly differentiated products can charge higher prices because of their products' distinctiveness; therefore, they have fewer problems using a channel of several levels.

Influence of Product Characteristics

value density
Value of a product relative to its weight and volume.

The value of a product relative to its weight and volume is called its **value density**. Value density is an important variable in formulating distribution strategies. As a rule, *the lower a product's value density, the more localized the distribution system.* Most commodities, including cement, iron ore, and crude oil, have low value-density ratios—they're heavy but not particularly "valuable" if gauged in, say, shipping weight per cubic meter. Therefore, relative to their values the cost of transporting them is high. Consequently, such products are processed or integrated into the manufacturing process at points close to their original locations. Products with high value-density ratios include emeralds, semiconductors, and premium perfumes. Because the cost of transporting these products is small relative to their values, they can be processed or manufactured in the optimal location then shipped to market. For instance, because Johnson & Johnson's (*www.jnj.com*) Vistakon contact lenses have high value density, the company produces and inventories its products in one U.S. location and serves the world market from there.

When products need to be modified for local markets, companies can design their distribution systems accordingly. Caterpillar (*www.caterpillar.com*) redesigned its distribution system so that it doubles as the final component in the company's production system. Each national market carries a range of optional product components for Caterpillar's lift trucks. The company ships partially completed lift trucks, along with optional parts, to distribution warehouses in each target market. After a buyer decides what options it desires, final assembly takes place. Thus, Caterpillar's distribution warehouses now extend the company's assembly line—allowing the company to maintain or improve service at little cost.

Special Distribution Problems

A nation's distribution system develops over time and reflects its unique cultural, political, legal, and economic traditions. Thus, the distribution system of each nation has its own unique pros and cons. However, it is the negative aspects of distribution that pose the greatest threat to the business activities of international companies. In some countries risks arise mostly from the potential for theft and property damage. In others it is simply the lack of understanding that creates uncertainty and risk. Let's take a look at two special problems that can affect a company's international distribution activities.

Lack of Market Understanding

Companies can experience a great deal of frustration and financial loss simply by not fully understanding the local market in which they operate. Amway Asia Pacific Ltd., the Asian arm of U.S.-based Amway (*www.amway.com*), learned the hard way the pitfalls of overestimating the knowledge of distributors in emerging markets. The company has a worldwide policy of giving distributors a full refund on its soaps and cosmetics if the distributor's customers are dissatisfied—even if the returned containers are empty. But the policy had some bizarre results shortly after Amway entered China. Word of the guarantee spread quickly. Some distributors repackaged the products in other containers, sold them, and took the original containers back to Amway for a refund. Others scoured garbage bins, gathering bags full of discarded bottles. In Shanghai returns were beginning to total $100,000 a day. Amway's Shanghai chief Percy Chin admitted, "Perhaps we were too lenient." Amway changed its refund policy to allow a refund only for bottles at least half full. Amway's distributors were furious. Grumbled one unhappy distributor, "Don't open a company if you can't afford losses."[31]

Theft and Corruption

A high incidence of theft and corruption can present obstacles to distribution. For instance, the distribution system in Russia reflects its roughly

75-year experiment with communism. When Acer Computers (*www.acer.com*) decided to sell its computers in Russia, it built production facilities in Russia's stable neighbor Finland—the company was leery of investing directly in Russia. Acer also considered it too risky to navigate Russia's archaic distribution system on its own. In three years' time, a highway that serves as a main route to get goods overland from Finland to Russia saw 50 Finnish truckers hijacked, two drivers killed, and another two missing. Acer solved its distribution problem by selling its computers to Russian distributors outside its factory in Finland. The Russian distributors, who understood how to negotiate their way through Russia's distribution system, would deal with headaches in Russia.[32]

Quick Study

1. How do *exclusive* and *intensive* channels of distribution differ? Give an example of each.
2. Explain the importance of *value density* to distribution strategy.
3. How might a lack of market understanding, theft, and corruption affect international distribution?

Developing Pricing Strategies

The pricing strategy that a company adopts must match its overall international strategy. For instance, the product of a company that is the low-cost leader in its industry usually cannot be sold at a premium price because it likely has few special features and stresses functionality rather than uniqueness. On the other hand, a company that follows a differentiation strategy usually can charge a premium price for its product because buyers value the product's uniqueness. Let's now examine two pricing policies (*worldwide pricing* and *dual pricing*) that companies use in international markets and then explore the important factors that influence managers' pricing decisions.

Worldwide Pricing

A pricing policy in which one selling price is established for all international markets is called **worldwide pricing**. In practice, a worldwide pricing policy is very difficult to achieve. First, production costs differ from one nation to another. Keeping production costs the same is not possible for a company that has production bases within each market it serves. Thus, selling prices often reflect these different costs of production.

worldwide pricing
Policy in which one selling price is established for all international markets.

   Second, a company that produces in just one location (to maintain an equivalent cost of production for every product) cannot guarantee that selling prices will be the same in every target market. The cost of exporting to certain markets will likely be higher than the cost of exporting to other markets. In addition, distribution costs differ across markets. Where distribution is efficient, selling prices might well be lower than in locations where distribution systems are archaic and inefficient. Third, the purchasing power of local buyers must be taken into account. Managers might decide to lower the sales price in a market so that buyers can afford the product and the company can gain market share. Finally, fluctuating currency values also must be taken into account. When the value of the currency in a country where production takes place rises against a target market's currency, the product will become more expensive in the target market.

Dual Pricing

Because of the problems associated with worldwide pricing, another pricing policy is often used in international markets. A pricing policy in which a product has a different

dual pricing
Policy in which a product has a different selling price (typically higher) in export markets than it has in the home market.

selling price in export markets than it has in the home market is called **dual pricing**. When a product has a higher selling price in the target market than it does in the home market (or the country where production takes place), it is called *price escalation*. It is commonly the result of the reasons just discussed—exporting costs and currency fluctuations.

But sometimes a product's export price is lower than the price in the home market. Under what circumstances does this occur? Some companies determine that domestic market sales are to cover all product costs (such as expenses related to R&D, administration, and overhead). Thus, exports must cover only the *additional* costs associated with exporting and selling in a target market (such as tariffs). In this sense, exports are considered a sort of "bonus."

To apply dual pricing in international marketing successfully, a company must be able to keep its domestic buyers and international buyers separate. Buyers in one market might cancel orders if they discover that they are paying a higher price than are buyers in another market. If a company cannot keep its buyers separate when using dual pricing, buyers could potentially undermine the policy through *arbitrage*—buying products where they are sold at lower prices and reselling them where they command higher prices. However, as is often the case, the higher selling price of a product in an export market often reflects the additional costs of transportation to the local market and any trade barriers of the target market, such as tariffs. For arbitrageurs to be successful, the profits they earn must be enough to outweigh these additional costs.

Factors That Affect Pricing Decisions

Many factors have an important influence on managers' pricing decisions. We devote the following discussion to four of the most important—*transfer prices, arm's length pricing, price controls*, and *dumping*.

transfer price
Price charged for a good or service transferred among a company and its subsidiaries.

Transfer Prices
Prices charged for goods or services transferred among a company and its subsidiaries are called **transfer prices**. It is common for parent companies and their subsidiaries to buy from one another. For example, the parent company often licenses technologies to its subsidiaries in return for royalties or licensing fees. Subsidiaries prefer this route to buying on the open market because they typically enjoy lower prices. Parent companies then buy finished products from subsidiaries at the stated transfer price.

At one time, companies enjoyed a great deal of freedom in setting their transfer prices. Subsidiaries in countries with high corporate tax rates would reduce their tax burdens by charging a low price for their output to other subsidiaries. The subsidiary lowered the taxes that the parent company must pay by reducing its profits in the high-tax country. Likewise, subsidiaries in countries with low tax rates would charge relatively high prices for their output.

Transfer prices followed a similar pattern based on the tariffs of different nations. Subsidiaries in countries that charged relatively high tariffs were charged lower prices to lower the cost of the goods in the local market. This pattern of transfer prices helped large corporations with many subsidiaries to better manage their global tax burden and become more price-competitive in certain markets.

arm's length price
Free-market price that unrelated parties charge one another for a specific product.

Arm's Length Pricing
Today, increasing regulation of transfer pricing practices is causing reduced freedom in manipulating transfer prices. In fact, many governments now regulate internal company pricing practices by assigning products approximate transfer prices based on their free-market price. Thus, most international transfers between subsidiaries now occur at a so-called **arm's length price**—the free-market price that unrelated parties charge one another for a specific product.

Another factor that is increasing the use of arm's length pricing is pressure on companies to be good corporate citizens in each of their target markets. Developing and emerging markets are hurt most by lost revenue when international companies manipulate prices to reduce tariffs and corporate taxes. They depend on the revenue for building things such as schools, hospitals, and infrastructure, including telecommunications systems and shipping ports. These items in turn benefit international companies by improving the productivity and efficiency of the local business environment. Indeed, some international companies have even developed codes of conduct specifying that transfer prices will follow the principle of arm's length pricing.

Price Controls Pricing strategies must also consider the potential for government **price controls**—upper or lower limits placed on the prices of products sold within a country. Upper-limit price controls are designed to provide price stability in an inflationary economy (one in which prices are rising). Companies that want to raise prices in a price-controlled economy must often apply to government authorities to request permission to do so. Companies with good contacts in the government of the target market might be more likely to get a price-control exemption. Those unable to obtain an exemption will typically try to lessen the impact of upper-limit price controls by reducing production costs.

In contrast, lower-limit price controls prohibit the lowering of prices below a certain level. Governments sometimes impose lower-limit prices to help local companies compete against the less expensive imports of international companies. Other times, lower-limit price controls are designed to ward off price wars that could eliminate the competition and thereby give one company a monopoly in the domestic market.

price controls
Upper or lower limits placed on the prices of products sold within a country.

Dumping We detailed the practice of dumping in Chapter 6 when discussing government involvement in international trade. Recall that *dumping* occurs when the price of a good is lower in export markets than it is in the domestic market. Accusations of dumping are often made against competitors from other countries when inexpensive imports flood a nation's domestic market. Although charges of dumping normally result from deliberate efforts to undercut the prices of competitors in the domestic market, changes in exchange rates can cause unintentional dumping. When a country's government charges another nation's producers of dumping a good on its market, antidumping tariffs are typically imposed. Such tariffs are designed to punish producers in the offending nation by increasing the price of their products to a fairer level.

Quick Study

1. What is the difference between *worldwide pricing* and *dual pricing*?
2. Explain what is meant by the terms *transfer pricing* and *arm's length pricing*.
3. How might price controls and dumping affect the pricing decisions of international companies?

A Final Word

Despite the academic debate over globalization and the extent to which companies should standardize their international marketing activities, many companies continue to adapt to local conditions. Sometimes this takes the form of only slightly modifying promotional campaigns and at other times it can require the creation of an entirely new product. The causes of alterations in promotional aspects of marketing strategy can be cultural, such as language differences. They can also be legal, such as requirements to produce locally so as to help ease local unemployment or to spur local industry around the production facility. Other companies are able to reap the rewards of standardization and centralized production that can result from the ability to sell one product worldwide. In the next chapter, we take an in-depth look at the factors that influence the development of production strategies and the types of decisions managers must make along the way.

1. **Explain the impact** *globalization* **is having on international marketing activities.** Some experts argue that because the world is becoming standardized and homogeneous, companies should market the same products in the same way in all countries. They claim that technology has already caused people's needs and preferences to converge throughout the world and urge companies to reduce production and marketing costs by standardizing both the physical features of their products and their strategies for marketing them. However, others counter that standardization is just one of a number of strategies or that it is not always the best strategy to use.

   Consumers worldwide appear content with a standardized product in *certain* product categories. However, in others they demand products that reflect their unique tastes and preferences. Cultural, political, legal, and economic environments have a great deal to do with the preferences of both consumers and industrial buyers worldwide. Product standardization is more likely when producer and buyer nations share the same level of economic development.

2. **Describe the types of things that managers must consider when developing international** *product strategies.* Many elements influence a company's decision about whether to standardize or adapt its product. First, companies undertake mandatory product adaptation in response to a target market's *laws and regulations*. Companies also adapt their products to suit *cultural differences*. Sometimes companies do not need to modify their product if they can identify a different need that the product serves in the culture.

   Although companies keep their *brand names* consistent across markets, they often create new *product names* or modify existing ones to suit local preferences. The *image of a nation* in which a company designs, manufactures, or assembles a product influences buyers' perceptions of quality and reliability. *Counterfeit goods* can damage buyers' image of a brand when the counterfeits are of inferior quality—which is nearly always the case. Buyers expect a certain level of craftsmanship from any given brand but are disappointed with the counterfeited product's performance, which tarnishes the company's reputation. Finally, *shortened product life cycles* are affecting the timing of when to market internationally.

3. **Discuss the factors that influence international** *promotional strategies* **and the blending of product and promotional strategies.** Efforts by a company to reach distribution channels and target customers through communications such as personal selling, advertising, public relations, and direct marketing are called its *promotion mix*. A promotional strategy designed to create buyer demand that will encourage channel members to stock a company's product is called a *pull strategy*. In contrast, a promotional strategy designed to pressure channel members to carry a product and promote it to final users of the product is called a *push strategy*.

   Companies blend their international product and promotional policies to create five generic promotional methods. *Product/communications extension (dual extension)* extends the same home-market product and marketing promotion into target markets. *Product extension/communications adaptation* extends the same product into new target markets but alters its promotion. *Product adaptation/communications extension* adapts a product to the requirements of the international market while retaining the product's original marketing communication. *Product/communications adaptation (dual adaptation)* adapts both the product and its marketing communication to suit the target market. *Product invention* requires that an entirely new product be developed for the target market.

4. **Explain the elements that managers must take into account when designing international** *distribution strategies.* Planning, implementing, and controlling the physical flow of a product from its point of origin to its point of consumption is called *distribution*. The physical path that a product follows on its way to customers is called a *distribution channel*. An exclusive channel is one in which a manufacturer grants the right to sell its product to only one or a limited number of resellers. An *exclusive channel* provides a great deal of control over their products' sale by wholesalers and retailers. An *intensive channel* is one in which a producer grants the right to sell its product to many resellers. This type of channel offers less control over reseller decisions.

   Channel length refers to the number of intermediaries between the producer and the buyer. In a *zero-level channel* producers sell directly to final buyers. A *one-level channel* places only one intermediary between producer and buyer, two intermediaries make up a *two-level channel*, and so forth. The value of a product relative to its weight and volume is called its *value density*. As a rule, the lower a product's value density, the more localized the distribution system.

   A nation's distribution system develops over time and reflects its unique cultural, political, legal, and economic traditions. Special distribution problems that pose the biggest threat for international marketing efforts include a lack of market understanding and theft and corruption.

5. **Discuss the elements that influence international** *pricing strategies.* *Worldwide pricing* is a pricing policy in which one selling price is established for all international markets—a difficult task to achieve in practice. A pricing policy in which a product has a different selling price in export markets than it has in the home market is called *dual pricing*. When a product has a higher selling price in the target market than it does in the home market (or the country where production takes place) it is called *price escalation*.

   Several factors have an important influence on managers' pricing decisions. A *transfer price* is the price charged for products sold between a company's divisions or subsidiaries. Today, many governments regulate internal company pricing practices by assigning products approximate transfer prices based on a so-called *arm's length price*—the free-market price that unrelated parties charge one another for a specific product.

Price controls are upper or lower limits placed on the prices of products sold within a country. Upper-limit price controls are designed to provide price stability in an inflationary economy. When a country's government charges another nation's producers of *dumping* a good on its market, antidumping tariffs are typically imposed to punish producers in the offending nation.

TALK IT OVER

1. Suppose that the product preferences of cultures and people around the world continue to converge. Identify two products that will likely be affected and two products that will likely not be affected by such a convergence. For each product that is affected, how will the changes influence the marketing manager's job?

2. Price escalation can present serious problems for companies wishing to export their products to other markets under a worldwide pricing policy. How might companies combat the effects of price escalation? List as many possibilities as you can.

TEAMING UP

1. With several of your classmates, choose a company in which you are interested. Consult recent annual reports and Internet sources to find out what new products that company has brought to market in the past year or two. Are those products truly new innovations, or are they simply extensions of existing products? What considerations guided the company in its product development efforts?

2. For this team project, ask each member of your group to select a magazine publication from a nation other than their own. Look through each of them for ads from a single international firm or for advertisements featuring a particular product or brand. After you have identified three or four such ads, determine which of the five types of product and promotion policies is being used: dual extension, product extension/communications adaptation, product adaptation/communications extension, dual adaptation, or product invention. What explanation do you have for the particular method being used?

KEY TERMS

arm's length price (p. 418)	exclusive channel (p. 415)	pull strategy (p. 408)
black market (p. 406)	intensive channel (p. 415)	push strategy (p. 408)
brand name (p. 404)	marketing communication (p. 412)	transfer price (p. 418)
distribution (p. 414)	price controls (p. 419)	value density (p. 416)
dual pricing (p. 418)	promotion mix (p. 408)	worldwide pricing (p. 417)

TAKE IT TO THE WEB

1. In this chapter, we've seen how globalization and nuances in nations' business environments influence decisions regarding the marketing of products internationally. Firms must carefully consider every facet of marketing, including product, promotional, distribution, and pricing strategies.

The Web sites of both Adobe (*www.adobe.com*) and Amazon (*www.amazon.com*) have reputations as being excellent examples of marketing. Partner with another student and visit the Web site of one of these companies while your partner visits the other firm's Web site. For the site you chose, what features do you think account for the favorable reputation? Note the different ads on the site and rate their effectiveness. Compare your findings with those of your partner.

Now select another international company of your choosing and visit as many of its national Web sites as you can locate. How much freedom do you think the company allows in each nation's Web site design? Why? If you were the CEO of the company, would you follow a similar approach or centralize/decentralize authority over Web site design? How do Adobe and Amazon compare to the apparent freedom (or lack of freedom) that this company allows? Explain your answer.

ETHICAL CHALLENGES

1. You are a lawyer working with the International Court of Justice in The Hague, Netherlands. You have been asked to review a recent decision regarding extraterritoriality. The case: French survivors of the Holocaust sued Yahoo U.S.A. because French citizens were purchasing Nazi memorabilia on Yahoo's U.S. Web site. The lawsuit also charged Yahoo U.S.A. with hosting the Web sites of anti-Semitic groups. Although both these actions are illegal according to French law, they are permitted in the United States because of U.S. legislation protecting free speech. Because Yahoo's French Web site did not violate French law, the U.S. federal judge hearing the case threw it out. The judge ruled that French law does not have the right to dictate the behavior of U.S. firms operating inside the United States. Today, the Internet sometimes makes it difficult to determine where jurisdictions begin and end. If you had been the judge in this case, how would you have ruled? Can you think of any Internet controls that could be used to stop incidents such as this from happening in the future?

2. You are an independent consultant currently working for Philip Morris. Competitors are alleging that in important developing markets such as Turkey, Philip Morris created special blends containing additives that give brands such as Marlboro an extra "kick." If true, practices such as this by tobacco companies put the "standardization versus adaptation" issue in an unusual perspective. If Philip Morris does adapt its products in this way, can it argue such policies are ethical? If summoned before the firm's board of directors, what advice would you give regarding the company's policy on this issue?

PRACTICING INTERNATIONAL MANAGEMENT CASE

Fair Game or Out-of-Bounds? You Decide

It's no secret that marketers use a good dose of psychology in both designing and implementing their promotional campaigns—or at least it shouldn't be. But some people, including Gary Rushkin of Washington, D.C.–based Commercial Alert (*www.commercialalert.org*), argue that parents are being duped. "I don't think people understand the extent of psychological tools employed against their kids to whip up their desire to buy products," says Rushkin. "When they find out, they're horrified." Rushkin's organization was behind a recent letter signed by 60 U.S. psychologists that was sent to the American Psychological Association (*www.apa.org*) that complained of "the use of psychology to exploit and influence children for commercial purposes."

What was the cause of their fury? Apparently, it was an article by Dr. James McNeal appearing in *Marketing Tools* magazine that described what is called a projective completion test. Suppose a children's TV program is a hit and boys are buying the company's toy that is tied to the program but girls aren't. To find out why, a company assembles a group of girls. They are given a picture of a boy and girl watching the program in which the boy is asking the girl, "Why do you like watching this program?" The girls' answers help provide clues to how the company can modify its marketing strategy to appeal to girls. Dr. McNeal refers to the method as "good sense and good science." Rushkin counters, "Psychologists are going to have to decide whether psychology is a tool for healing or for exploitation." the American Psychological Association admits that there are currently no guidelines for psychologists working in advertising.

Advertising executives are not just busy creating TV ads. Over a 1-year period from 2000 to 2001, the number of children's Web sites with no advertising dropped from 10 percent down to 2 percent. In what forms do the promotions appear? One tool is *games*. Roughly 55 percent of all children's and teens' Web sites feature games. Ellen Neuborne told her 6-year-old that he could choose a candy at the supermarket checkout. With a pack of Sweet Tarts in hand, he broke into a little song-and-dance about the sweets. When asked if that was from the TV commercial, he replied, "No. It's from the Sweet Tarts Internet game." With the use of such games, companies get to spend an extended period of time with kids—far more than they get from a TV ad.

Another tool is *e-mail*. The U.S. Children's Online Privacy Act forbids companies from using e-mail to sell to kids under 13 without parental permission. But companies get around the problem by having kids e-mail each other. For instance, children can go to the Web site (*www.sesameworkshop.org*) and e-mail a greeting card to a friend that features a *Sesame Street* character. And then there are the *chat rooms*. Brian Rubash is manager for technical marketing at Tiger electronics (*www.tigertoys.com*), a division of toy-maker Hasbro (*www.hasbro.com*). He says he regularly signed on to a newsgroup he found on Yahoo! (*www.yahoo.com*) to offer product news and answer questions about the i-Cybie robotic dog the company was launching.

European nations have some of the strictest regulations covering marketing to children. However, nations belonging to the European Union (EU) have widely varying rules. For example, Greece bans all TV ads for war toys and bans ads for all other toys between 7 A.M. and 10 P.M. The Dutch-speaking part of Belgium bans TV advertising within 5 minutes of the start and end of children's programs. But Sweden bans all ads aimed at children under age 12. This means that when kids in Sweden watch the Pokemon cartoon series, they don't hear the closing jingle "Gotta catch'em all" that plays elsewhere.

But the problem for the Swedes (and others with more restrictive bans) is that they can only enforce their laws on programs originating from within the country. They have no power of enforcement over programs broadcast from other nations or from satellite transmissions. That is why the Swedes are pushing for a common restrictive policy toward advertising aimed at children. Says Stephan Loerke, a lobbyist for the World Federation of Advertisers (*www.wfanet.org*) in Brussels, "They're gradually trying to forge a consensus among the member states." Although an outright ban like Sweden's is unlikely, partial bans such as that in place in Belgium could be implemented. To forestall stricter EU-wide legislation, advertisers could initiate "voluntary" limits themselves.

Yet some marketers are defending their actions. Advertising executive Geoffrey Roche of Toronto, Canada, dismissed the influence of psychologists, saying that, "They don't have mind-altering powers and kids are a lot smarter than we give them credit for. I don't think there is any way that we, as advertisers, can convince children of anything." But Dr. Allen Kanner asks, "If advertising is so ineffective, then why do they spend billions of dollars on it each year?" Dr. Curtis Haugtvedt, president of the Society for Consumer Psychology, says that although evidence of the negative aspects of advertising does exist, ads can also benefit kids. "Even Barbie has pluses and minuses," says Haugtvedt. "Barbie helps kids imagine and play with one another, but Barbie also portrays the image of a certain body shape." Haugtvedt also stresses the role of guidance in helping kids become responsible consumers, saying, "The child hopefully is not making choices about purchasing things in a vacuum."

Thinking Globally

1. Put yourself in the position of Stephan Loerke of the World Federation of Advertisers. First, make an argument for why the EU should not enact more strict advertising laws. Second, make a case for why advertisers operating in the EU should initiate "voluntary" limits. Third, make a case for why current laws need no modification whatsoever. Which case do you agree with? Which case do you think is the strongest?

2. Certain organizations regularly attack advertisers for their promotional methods. What do you think the advertising industry could do to make themselves a smaller target for such criticisms? Be specific.

3. Some critics charge advertisers with creating wants among consumers rather than helping them satisfy needs. Select a product and describe how, if it were marketed in a developing economy, it can create wants and not satisfy needs. Explain the ethical issues surrounding the decision of whether to market the product in developing nations.

learning objectives

After studying this chapter, you should be able to

1. Identify the elements that are important to consider when formulating *production strategies.*

2. Identify key considerations when *acquiring physical resources.*

3. Identify several production matters that are of special concern to managers.

4. Describe the three potential *sources of financing* and the main financial instruments of each.

managing international **15**
operations

a look **back**

CHAPTER 14 explored the influence of globalization on international marketing activities. We also examined how differences in national business environments have an impact on the development of marketing strategies.

a look **at this chapter**

This chapter examines how companies launch and manage their international production efforts. We analyze how companies acquire the materials and products they need and how aspects of the business environment affect production strategies. We also look briefly at how companies finance their activities.

a look **ahead**

CHAPTER 16 examines how international companies manage their human resources. Topics include international staffing policies, recruitment, training, compensation, labor relations, and culture shock.

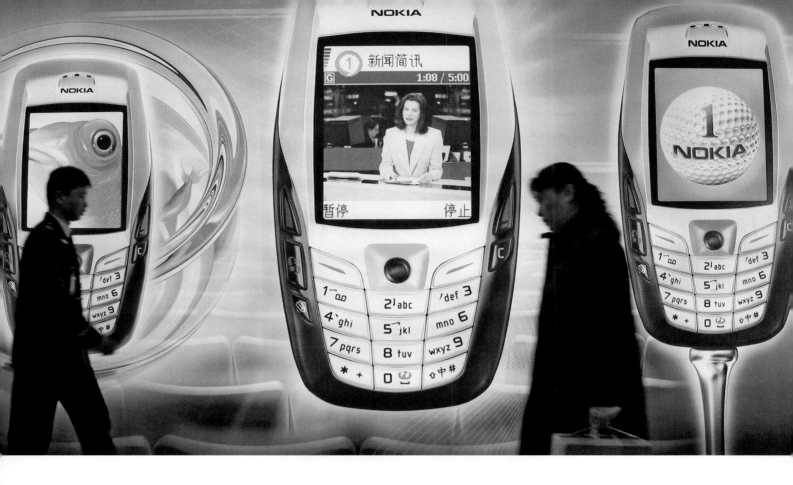

Connecting People

HELSINKI, Finland — Is it the end of the line for mobile phones? A maturing market is causing some to say that mobile phones are going the way of the personal computer. But Nokia Corporation (*www.nokia.com*), for one, is not buying it. The firm controls about one-third of the total worldwide market for mobile phones and is a leading supplier of the networks that comprise the infrastructure for voice and data communications. Nokia is betting that its market power will help it to extend the life of the mobile handset.

Nokia's activities are spread across the globe. In fact, it has sales in over 130 countries, manufactures at 16 facilities in 10 countries, and conducts research and development in 11 nations. The company employs 51,000 people and has annual sales of more than $33 billion. It is one of the few remaining companies that designs and makes its own chips, software, and phones. Nokia's size makes this strategy economically viable. Smaller players such as Philips (*www.philips.com*) and Alcatel (*www.alcatel.com*) outsource their phone production. Naturally, a firm like Nokia must undertake a great deal of planning for things such as production capacity, where to locate facilities, the technology used in production, and the layout of the facilities.

As you can imagine, building production facilities and a communications infrastructure requires a great deal of money. For part of its funding, Nokia looks to capital markets in Finland and abroad. In order to access the large pool of investors in the U.S. capital market, Nokia does what many non–U.S. companies do and issues what are called *American Depository Receipts (ADRs)*. These ADRs are certificates that trade in the United States and represent a specific number of shares of Nokia's stock.

Nokia also finances its activities with internal funding. For example, the Nokia Research Center is divided into six "strategic focus areas." Each area is profit-driven and obtains about 70 percent of its funding from the business groups it serves within the company. As you read this chapter, consider all the ways that companies structure their global production activities and how they finance their production (and other) activities.[1]

Whether an international company's production activity involves manufacturing a product or providing a service, it must acquire many resources before beginning operations. Where will it get the raw materials or components it needs to perform its production activities? How much production capacity is needed? Will the company construct or buy new facilities? How large must its service centers be? Where will it get the financial capital it needs? The answers to these questions are complex and interrelated.

This chapter begins by examining important considerations when formulating international production strategies. The topics covered include the decision about whether to centralize or decentralize production and whether production will be standardized or adapted to national markets. In the process, we draw linkages to earlier discussions, including overall corporate strategy and marketing strategy. We then describe how companies acquire the resources they need to accomplish their production goals. Specifically, we explain how firms acquire fixed (or tangible) assets such as production facilities, offices, equipment, and materials. We also consider several key production concerns, such as international logistics and total quality management. We then explain the important factors influencing managers' decisions of whether to expand or reduce operations abroad. We close by taking a brief look at how companies finance their international production operations and other activities.

Production Strategy

Production operations are important to achieving a company's strategy. Careful planning of all aspects of production helps companies cut costs (to become low-cost leaders) or design new products and product features necessary for a differentiation strategy. Among the important strategic issues that managers must consider are planning for production capacity, the location of facilities, production processes to be used, and the layout of facilities.

Capacity Planning

capacity planning
Process of assessing a company's ability to produce enough output to satisfy market demand.

The process of assessing a company's ability to produce enough output to satisfy market demand is called **capacity planning**. Companies must estimate global demand for their products as accurately as possible. If capacity now used is greater than the expected market demand, production must be scaled back. For example, the number of employees or work shifts can be reduced at certain locations. However, countries have different laws regulating the ability of employers to eliminate jobs. Depending on the country, a firm may or may not need to give advance notice of layoffs or plant closings. On the other hand, if market demand is growing, managers must determine in which facilities to expand production or whether additional facilities are needed to expand capacity. In fact, rather than miss out on potential sales, a company might contract with other producers to meet the excess demand until new facilities are up and running.

Capacity planning is also extremely important for service companies. For example, a hotel chain that is moving into a new geographic market must estimate the number of rooms that its facilities should contain. It must also determine whether a facility will be used for conventions and the like and the number of meeting rooms that it must build. Videoconferencing facilities might be added if local firms require them to keep in touch with geographically dispersed operations.

Facilities Location Planning

Selecting the location for production facilities is called **facilities location planning.** Companies often have many potential locations around the world from which to choose a site for production, research and development, or some other activity. Aspects of the business environment that are important for facilities location planning include the cost and availability of labor and management, raw materials, component parts, and energy. Other key factors include political stability, the extent of regulation and bureaucracy, economic development, and the local culture, including beliefs about work and important traditions.

facilities location planning
Selecting the location for production facilities.

Reducing production costs by taking advantage of lower wages in another country is often essential to keeping a company's products competitive in terms of pricing. This is especially important when labor accounts for a large portion of total production costs. However, the lower wages of a nation's workforce must be balanced against its potentially lower productivity. Worker productivity tends to be lower in most developing nations and some emerging markets as compared with developed nations. Figure 15.1 shows how nations differ in their statutory minimum wage rates. As you see, there is a large gap in statutory minimum wages between countries. Even within the European Union there are wide differences, with Spain's minimum wage being about one-fifth that of Luxembourg's.

Although most service companies must locate near their customers, they must still consider a wide variety of customers' needs when locating facilities. Are convenience and being located in a high-traffic area important to customers? Such a location is clearly important for some companies, including restaurants, banks, and cinemas. For other service businesses, such as consulting companies or public utilities, a convenient location is less important.

Supply issues are also important in location planning. For any one mode of transportation, the greater the distance between production facilities and target markets, the longer it takes for customers to receive shipments. In turn, companies must compensate for delays by maintaining larger inventories in target markets—adding to storage and

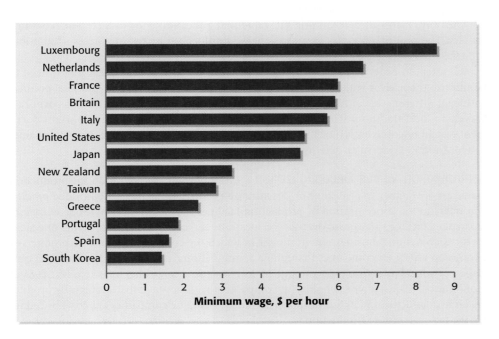

FIGURE 15.1

The Gap in Minimum Wages

insurance costs. Shipping costs themselves are also greater when production is conducted away from target markets. Transportation costs are one of the driving forces behind the globalization of the steel industry. Shipping costs for steel can run $40 to $50 per ton—a significant amount when steel sells for $400 to $500 per ton. By building steel mills in countries where their customers are located, steel producers significantly reduce their transportation costs.

Automobile makers from Japan and Germany invested in production facilities inside the United States for some of the reasons just identified. For example, Toyota (*www.toyota.com*) and other Japanese auto companies manufacture cars in the United States to offset the risks from currency fluctuations, to defuse political concerns about the United States' trade deficit with Japan, and to be closer to their customers. BMW (*www.bmw.com*) of Germany assembles automobiles in the United States for similar reasons. For one thing, the strength of Germany's currency in the 1990s made German products more expensive on world export markets. Another reason is that Germany is home to the world's highest paid workers—the average hourly income is approximately $32. Finally, German companies are attracted by the lower cost of land, along with concessions, such as tax breaks, offered by state governments eager to attract industry.

Location Economies

Selecting highly favorable locations often allows a company to achieve **location economies**—economic benefits derived from locating production activities in optimal locations. Location economies result from the right mix of the kinds of elements just described. To take advantage of location economies, companies either undertake business activities themselves in a particular location or obtain products and services from other companies located there. Location economies can involve practically any business activity that companies in a particular location do very well, including performing research and development or providing financial or advertising services.

The following examples illustrate the extent to which service and manufacturing companies exploit location economies. One company designed its precision ice hockey equipment in Sweden, obtained financing from Canada, assembled it in Cleveland and Denmark, and marketed it in North America and Europe. This equipment incorporated alloys whose molecular structure was researched and patented in Delaware and fabricated in Japan. Airplane manufacturer Boeing (*www.boeing.com*) designed aircraft in the state of Washington and Japan, which was assembled in Seattle with tail cones made in Canada, special tail sections made in China and Italy, and engines from Britain. Finally, one company's advertising campaign was conceived in Britain, shot in Canada, dubbed in Britain, and edited in New York.[2]

The key fact to remember here is that *each production activity generates more value in a particular location than it could generate elsewhere.* Productivity is a very important (though not the only) factor in determining the value that a location adds to a certain economic activity. The productivity of a location is heavily influenced by two resources—labor and capital.

Granted, in order to take advantage of location economies, managers might need to familiarize themselves with vastly different customs and traditions. For example, political and legal differences can force firms to retain outside consultants or to train corporate lawyers in local traditions. Language differences might mean translating important documents on an ongoing basis. For these reasons, companies sometimes hire other companies in a location to perform an activity for them.

Centralization Versus Decentralization

An important consideration for production managers is whether to centralize or decentralize production facilities. *Centralized production* refers to the concentration of production facilities in one location. With *decentralized production*, facilities are spread over several locations and could even mean having one facility for each national business environment in which the company markets its products—a common policy for companies that follow a multinational strategy. Companies often centralize production facilities in pursuit of low-cost strategies and to take advantage of economies of scale—a typical policy for companies that follow a global strategy. By producing large quantities of identical products in one location, the companies cut costs by reducing the per-unit cost of production.

Transportation costs and the physical landscape also affect the centralization-versus-decentralization decision. For example, because they usually sell undifferentiated products in all their markets, low-cost competitors generally do not need to locate near their markets in order to stay on top of changes in buyer preferences. That is why low-cost producers often choose locations with the lowest combined production and transportation costs. But even these firms must balance the cost of getting inputs into the production process and the cost of getting products to markets. Key factors in the physical environment that affect the transport of goods are the availability of seaports, airports, or other transportation hubs.

Conversely, companies that sell differentiated products may find decentralized production the better option. By locating separate facilities near different markets, they remain in close contact with customers and can respond quickly to changing buyer preferences. Closer contact with customers also helps firms develop a deeper understanding of buyer behavior in local cultures.

When close cooperation between research and development and manufacturing is essential for effective differentiation, both activities are usually conducted in the same place. However, new technologies are giving companies more freedom to separate these activities. The speed with which information travels today allows the rapid relaying of information between subsidiaries and the home office.

Process Planning

Deciding on the process that a company will use to create its product is called **process planning**. The particular process to be used is typically determined by a firm's business-level strategy. For instance, low-cost strategies normally require large-scale production because producers want the cost savings generated by economies of scale. A company that mass-produces snowboards for average skiers will typically use a highly automated production process that integrates advanced computer technology. However, differentiation strategies demand that producers provide extra value by offering customers something unique, such as superior quality, added features, or special brand images. Companies that handcraft snowboards for professionals will rely not on automated production but on skilled craftspeople. The company will design and produce each snowboard to suit the habits and special needs of each individual snowboarder. For such a company, service is a major component of the production process.

process planning
Deciding the process that a company will use to create its product.

Availability and cost of labor in the local market is crucial to process planning. If labor in the host country is relatively cheap, an international company will likely opt for less technology and more labor-intensive methods in the production process—depending on its particular product and strategy. But again, the availability of labor and the level of wages in the local market must be balanced against the productivity of the local workforce.

Standardization Versus Adaptation
Another important issue in production strategy is deciding whether the production process will be standardized for all markets or adapted to manufacture products modified for different markets. For example, low-cost leadership often dictates automated, standardized production in large batches. Large production batches reduce the cost of producing each unit, thus offsetting the higher initial investment in automation. Costs are further reduced as employees improve performance through repetition and a continual learning process that minimizes errors and waste.

But differentiation often demands decentralized facilities designed to improve local responsiveness. Because decentralized production facilities produce for one national market or for a regional market, they tend to be smaller. This tends to eliminate the potential to take advantage of economies of scale, and therefore increases per-unit production costs. Similarly, the smaller market share at which a differentiation strategy aims normally calls for relatively smaller scale production. Differentiating a product by incorporating certain features desired by customers requires more costly manufacturing processes. Research and development costs also tend to be higher for products with special product designs, styles, and features.

Facilities Layout Planning

facilities layout planning
Deciding the spatial arrangement of production processes within production facilities.

Deciding the spatial arrangement of production processes within production facilities is called **facilities layout planning**. Consider the fact that in Japan, Singapore, and Hong Kong, the supply of land is limited and its cost is high. Companies that locate in these markets must use the available space wisely by designing compact facilities. Conversely, in countries such as Canada, China, and the United States, an abundance of space reduces the cost of building facilities in many locations. Because land is cheaper, companies have more flexibility in designing facilities.

More importantly, facility layout depends on the type of production process a company uses, which in turn depends on a company's business-level strategy. For instance, rather than produce mass quantities of computers to be stored in inventory, Compaq (*www.compaq.com*) competes by manufacturing computers as it receives orders from individual customers. To implement this business strategy, Compaq executives decided to replace mass-assembly lines with three-person work cells. In production trials at a plant in Scotland, output increased 23 percent as compared with the best assembly line. In addition, output per square foot went up 16 percent—a significant increase in the efficiency within the facility.

Quick Study

1. Explain why *capacity planning* is important when formulating production strategy.
2. How is *facilities location planning* affected by: a) *location economies,* and b) centralized versus decentralized production?
3. Explain how *process planning* is affected by the standardization-versus-adaptation decision.
4. How is *facilities layout planning* relevant to the formulation of production strategies?

Acquiring Physical Resources

Before an international company begins operations, it must acquire a number of physical resources. For example, managers must answer questions including, will the company make or buy the components it needs in the production process? What will be the sources of any required raw materials? Will the company acquire facilities and production equipment or build its own? In this section, we present the main elements that managers need to consider when answering these types of questions.

Make-or-Buy Decision

make-or-buy decision
Deciding whether to make a component or to buy it from another company.

The typical manufacturing company requires a wide range of inputs into its production process. These inputs typically enter the production line either as raw materials that require processing or as components needing only assembly. Bear in mind, too, that a component may require minor adjustments or other minor processing before it goes into production. Deciding whether to make a component or to buy it from another company is called the **make-or-buy decision**. Each option has its own set of advantages and disadvantages.

vertical integration
Extension of company activities into stages of production that provide a firm's inputs (backward integration) or absorb its output (forward integration).

Reasons to Make   The process by which a company extends its control over additional stages of production—either inputs or outputs—is called **vertical integration**. When a company decides to make a product rather than buy it, it engages in "upstream" activities: production activities that come before a company's current business operations. For example, a carmaker that decides to manufacture its own window glass is engaging in a new upstream activity.

Lower Costs   Above all, companies make products rather than buy them in order to reduce total costs. Generally speaking, the manufacturer's profit is the difference between the product's selling price and its production cost. When a company buys a product, it rewards the manufacturer by contributing to the latter's profit margin. Therefore, companies often undertake in-house production when they can manufacture a product for less than they must pay someone else to produce it. Thus, in-house production allows a company to reduce its own production costs.

For example, a computer motherboard is the physical foundation of a personal computer to which the microprocessor, memory chips, and other components are attached. This critical component accounts for about 40 percent of a personal computer's total cost. Compaq (*www.compaq.com*) discovered that it could produce motherboards itself for $25 less than its Asian suppliers and save 2 weeks' shipping time in the process.

Small companies are less likely than large ones to make rather than buy, especially when a product requires a large financial investment in equipment and facilities. However, this rule of thumb might not necessarily hold if the company possesses a proprietary technology or some other competitive advantage that is not easily copied.

Greater Control   Companies that depend on others for key ingredients or components give up a degree of control. Making rather than buying can give managers greater control over raw materials, product design, and the production process itself—all of which are important factors in product quality. In turn, quality control is especially important when customers are highly sensitive to even slight declines in quality. For the same reason, greater quality control also gives a company greater control over its reputation among customers.

In addition, persuading an outside supplier to make significant modifications to quality or features can be difficult. This is especially true if modifications entail investment in costly equipment or if they promise to be time-consuming. If just one buyer requests costly product adaptations, or if there is reason to suspect that a buyer will eventually take its business elsewhere, a supplier may be reluctant to undertake a costly investment. Unless that buyer purchases in large volumes, the cost of the modifications may be too great for the supplier to absorb. In such a case, the buyer simply may be unable to obtain the product it wants without manufacturing it in-house. Thus, companies maintain greater control over product design and product features if they manufacture components themselves.

Finally, making a product can be a good idea when buying from a supplier means providing the supplier with a firm's key technology. Through licensing agreements (see Chapter 13), companies often provide suppliers in low-wage countries with the technologies needed to make their products. However, if a company's competitive advantage depends on that technology, the licensor could inadvertently be creating a future competitor. When controlling a key technology is paramount, it is often better to manufacture in-house.

Reasons to Buy

The practice of buying from another company a good or service that is not central to a company's competitive advantage is called **outsourcing**. Outsourcing results from continuous specialization and technological advancement. For each successive specialization of its operations process, a manufacturer requires greater skill and knowledge than it did before. By outsourcing, a company can reduce the degree to which it is vertically integrated and the overall amount of specialized skills and knowledge that it must possess.

Outsourcing has become extremely popular in the business of computer manufacturing. Component makers, including Intel (*www.intel.com*) in microprocessors, Seagate (*www.seagate.com*) in hard drives, U.S. Robotics (*www.usr.com*) in modems, and Mitsumi (*www.mitsumi.com*) in CD-ROM drives, supply big and small manufacturers worldwide. Computer companies buy components from these manufacturers, assemble them in their own facilities, and sell completed systems to consumers and businesses. A related practice in the computer industry is known as "stealth manufacturing," which calls for outsourcing the actual assembly of the computers themselves, plus the job of shipping them to distributors and other intermediaries.[3]

A new and interesting type of outsourcing seems to be catching on in the pharmaceutical industry. Eli Lilly & Company (*www.lilly.com*) and other drug companies sometimes run into chemistry problems that their internal scientists need help solving. So, Lilly established a subsidiary company called Innocentive (*www.innocentive.com*). The subsidiary's

outsourcing
Practice of buying from another company a good or service that is not central to a company's competitive advantage.

Dell Computer Corporation (www.dell.com) has perfected the art of outsourcing. The company designs and builds computing systems for both consumers and companies, but it does not build the components themselves. The production strategy has made Dell a model of efficiency in the PC industry. Dell can deliver custom-made PCs in just three days while most of its rivals measure their delivery times in weeks. Do you think outsourcing will (will not) gain wider acceptance in the future?

Web site lists chemistry problems that need solving and the amount that Lilly will pay for the solution. Lilly offers cash awards of as much as $100,000 to the solution finder. In this way, Lilly goes beyond its own 600 scientists and taps a global pool of scientists from countries such as India and China.[4]

Many companies buy when buying is the lower-cost option. When a firm cannot integrate vertically by manufacturing a product for less than a supplier can, it will typically outsource. Let's explore some other reasons why companies prefer to buy rather than make.

Lower Risk In earlier chapters, we described the many types of risks faced by companies that construct and staff facilities in other countries. For example, recall that political risk is quite high in certain markets. Social unrest or open conflict can threaten physical facilities, equipment, and employee safety.

One way a company can eliminate the exposure of assets to political risk in other countries is simply by refusing to invest in plants and equipment abroad. It can instead purchase products from international suppliers. This policy also eliminates the need to purchase the expensive insurance coverage that is needed when a company undertakes production in an unstable country. However, this policy will not completely shield the buyer from all potential disruptions—political instability can cause delays in the timely receipt of needed parts. Indeed, even under normal circumstances, the longer delivery times involved in international outsourcing can increase the risk that the buyer will not meet its own production schedule.

Greater Flexibility Maintaining sufficient flexibility to respond to market conditions is increasingly important for companies everywhere. Making an in-house product that requires large investments in equipment and buildings often reduces flexibility. In contrast, companies that buy products from one or more outside suppliers gain flexibility. In fact, added flexibility is the key factor in a fundamental change in attitude toward outsourcing, which many managers now regard as a full-fledged strategy for change rather than a limited tactical tool for solving immediate problems.

Maintaining flexibility is important when the national business environments of suppliers are volatile. By buying from several suppliers, or by establishing production facilities in more than one country, a company can outsource products from one location if instability erupts in another. The same is true during periods of great volatility in exchange rates. Exchange-rate movements can increase or decrease the cost of importing a product from a given country. By buying from multiple suppliers located in several countries, a company can maintain the flexibility needed to change sources and reduce the risk associated with sudden swings in exchange rates.

Companies also maintain operational flexibility simply by not having to invest in production facilities. Unencumbered by investment in costly production equipment and facilities, a firm can alter its product line very quickly. This capability is especially important for products with small production runs or those with highly uncertain potential. Furthermore, a company can obtain financial flexibility if its capital is not locked up in plants and equipment. It can then use excess financial capital to pursue other domestic or international opportunities. Outsourcing can also free a company from having to recoup large investments in research and development.

Market Power   Companies can gain a great deal of power in their relationships with suppliers simply by becoming important customers. In fact, sometimes a supplier can become a sort of hostage to one particular customer. This situation occurs when a supplier becomes heavily dependent on a company that it serves with nearly all of its production capacity. If the main buyer suddenly begins outsourcing elsewhere, the supplier will have few other customers to whom it can turn. This situation gives the buyer significant control in dictating quality improvements, forcing cost reductions, and making special modifications.

Barriers to Buying   For various reasons, companies sometimes face obstacles when buying products from international suppliers. First, the government of the buyer's country may impose import tariffs designed to improve the nation's balance of trade. Tariffs can add anywhere from 15 to 50 percent to the cost of a component that a manufacturer needs from abroad.

Second, the services provided by intermediaries increase the cost of buying abroad. Obtaining letters of credit, arranging physical transportation, and obtaining insurance all add to the final cost that a manufacturer pays for a product supplied from abroad. Although these expenses are currently lower than they have ever been, they can significantly increase total product cost. If high enough, they can negate any advantage of buying from an international supplier.

Raw Materials

Decisions about the selection and acquisition of raw materials are important to many different types of manufacturers. The twin issues of quantity and quality drive many of these decisions. First, some industries and companies rely almost exclusively on the quantity of locally available raw materials. This is most true for companies involved in mining, forestry, and fishing. There must be an adequate supply of iron ore, oil, lumber, or fish to justify the large financial investment required to build processing facilities.

Second, the quality of raw material has a huge influence on the quality of a company's end product. For instance, food-processing companies must examine the quality of the locally grown fruit, vegetables, grains, and any other ingredients. Beverage companies must assess the quality of the local water supply. Some markets may require large financial investments to build water-purifying facilities. Elsewhere (such as much of the Middle East), the only local water source may be seawater, which must be desalinized.

Fixed Assets

Most companies must acquire **fixed (tangible) assets**—such as production facilities, inventory warehouses, computer storage capacity, retail outlets, and production and office equipment—in the host country. Many companies have the option of either (1) acquiring or modifying existing factories or (2) building entirely new facilities—called a *greenfield* investment. Considering either option involves many individuals within the company. For example, production managers must verify that an existing facility (or an empty lot) is large enough and will suit the company's facility layout needs. Site-acquisition experts and legal staff must guarantee that the proposed business activity abides by local laws. Public relations staff must work with community leaders to ensure that the company does not jeopardize the rights, values, and customs of the local population.

Finally, managers must make sure that the local infrastructure can support the firm's proposed on-site business operations. Also, factory and office equipment is likely to be available locally in most newly industrialized and developed markets. However, little, if any,

fixed (tangible) assets
Company assets such as production facilities, inventory warehouses, retail outlets, and production and office equipment.

equipment is likely to be available in developing markets. Thus, managers must assess both the cost in tariffs that will be imposed on imported equipment and the cost in time and effort that will be required to import it.

Quick Study

1. List the main reasons why a company might decide to either *make or buy* a component.
2. Explain the roles of *vertical integration* and *outsourcing* in the make-or-buy decision.
3. What are the main factors involved in acquiring: a) raw materials, and b) *fixed assets*?

Key Production Concerns

In Chapter 11 we covered the issues surrounding the number and location of manufacturing facilities because of their important influence on company strategy and organizational structure. At this point, there remain just several issues to discuss related to manufacturing operations. In this section, we first examine how companies maximize quality and minimize shipping and inventory costs. Then we take a brief look at the important reinvestment-versus-divestment decision.

Quality-Improvement Efforts

Companies strive toward quality improvement for two reasons: costs and customer value. First, quality products help keep production costs low because they reduce waste in valuable inputs, reduce the cost of retrieving defective products from buyers, and reduce the disposal costs that result from defective products. Second, some minimum level of acceptable quality is an aspect of nearly every product today. Even companies that produce low-cost products try to maintain or improve quality, as long as it does not erode their position in what is typically a price-competitive market or market segment. A company that succeeds in combining a low-cost position with a high-quality product can gain a tremendous competitive advantage in its market.

Improving quality is also important for a company that provides services—whether as its only product or in conjunction with the goods it manufactures and markets. Managing quality in services is complicated by the fact that a service is created and consumed at the same time. For this reason, the human interaction between an employee who delivers a service and the buyer is important to service quality. However, activities that must be conducted prior to the actual delivery of a service are also important. For example, it is important that a restaurant be clean and have an inventory of the ingredients it needs to prepare the meals on its menu. Likewise, a bank can provide high-quality service only if employees arrive for work on time and interact professionally with customers.

Let's now take a brief look at two movements that inspire the drive toward quality—total quality management and International Standards Organization (ISO) 9000 certification.

total quality management (TQM)
Emphasis on continuous quality improvement to meet or exceed customer expectations involving a company-wide commitment to quality-enhancing processes.

Total Quality Management
An emphasis on continuous quality improvement to meet or exceed customer expectations is called **total quality management (TQM)**. TQM stresses a company-wide commitment to quality-enhancing processes. It also places a great deal of responsibility on each individual to be focused on the quality of his or her own output—regardless of whether the employee's activities are based in the factory, in administration, or in management.

By continuously improving the quality of its products, a company can differentiate itself from rivals and attract loyal customers. The TQM philosophy initially took hold in the 1960s and 1970s in Japan, where electronics and automobile firms applied TQM techniques to reduce costs and thereby gain significant market share around the world through price competitiveness and a reputation for quality. It was not until U.S. and European companies lost a great deal of market share to their Japanese rivals that they embraced TQM principles.

ISO 9000 The International Standards Organization (ISO) 9000 is an international certification that companies get when they meet the highest quality standards in their industries. Firms in the European Union are leading the way in quality certification. But both European and non-European companies alike are working toward certification in order to ensure access to the European marketplace. To become certified, companies must demonstrate the reliability and soundness of all business processes that affect the quality of their products. Many companies also seek ISO 9000 certification because of the message of quality that certification sends to prospective customers. To see how companies can blend together TQM principles and the drive toward ISO 9000 certification, see the Global Manager's Toolbox titled, "Linking TQM and ISO 9000 Standards."

Shipping and Inventory Costs

Shipping costs can have a dramatic effect on the cost of getting materials and components to the location of production facilities. When the cost of getting inputs into the production process is a large portion of the product's total cost, producers tend to locate close to the source of those inputs. Shipping costs are affected by many elements of a nation's business environment, such as its general level of economic development, including the condition of seaports, airports, roads, and rail networks.

It used to be the practice that producers bought large quantities of materials or components and stored them in large warehouses until they were needed in the production process. However, storing great amounts of inventory for production is costly in terms of insuring them against damage or theft and the rent or purchase price of the warehouse needed to store them.

Because companies have far better uses for the money tied up in such inventory, they developed better inventory-management techniques. A production technique in which

global manager's TOOLBOX

Linking TQM and ISO 9000 Standards

In today's competitive environment many companies are applying TQM principles. When doing business internationally, ISO 9000 certification is becoming increasingly important. However, the ISO 9000 standards do not specify how a company should develop its quality processes. Rather, ISO requires each company to define and document its own quality processes and show evidence of implementing them. The following is a framework describing how TQM and ISO 9000 principles can be linked to enhance a company's capability for delivering quality products or services.

The main principles of TQM include:

- **Delight the customer.** Companies must strive to be the best at what customers consider most important. This can change over time, so business owners must be in close touch with customers.

- **Use people-based management.** Systems, standards, and technology cannot, in and of themselves, guarantee quality. The key is to provide employees with the knowledge of what to do and how to do it and to provide feedback on performance.

- **Continuous improvement.** TQM is not a short-term quick fix. Major breakthroughs are less important than incremental improvement.

- **Management by fact.** Quality management and improvement requires that managers clearly understand how consumers perceive the performance of a company's goods and services. Rather than trusting "gut feelings," obtain factual information and share it with employees.

Companies can link these TQM principles to ISO 9000 standards in three ways:

- **Process definition.** The existing business process must be defined. Once defined, it must be satisfying to key stakeholders and it must "delight the customer."

- **Process improvement.** Everyone within the organization must use the defined process properly. If this is not the case, then a company must improve the management of its human resources.

- **Process management.** Management and employees must possess factual knowledge about process details in order to manage them properly.

just-in-time (JIT) manufacturing
Production technique in which inventory is kept to a minimum and inputs to the production process arrive exactly when they are needed (or just in time).

inventory is kept to a minimum and inputs to the production process arrive exactly when they are needed (or *just in time*) is called **just-in-time (JIT) manufacturing**. Although the technique was originally developed in Japan, it quickly spread throughout manufacturing operations worldwide. JIT drastically reduces the costs associated with large inventories. It also helps reduce wasteful expenses because defective materials and components are spotted quickly during production. Under traditional systems, defective materials or components were sometimes discovered only after being built into finished products.

Reinvestment Versus Divestment

Companies maintain the current level of operations when no new opportunities are foreseen. Yet, changing conditions in the competitive global marketplace often force managers to choose between *reinvesting* in operations and *divesting* them.

Companies often continue to reinvest profits in markets that require long payback periods as long as the long-term outlook is good. This is often the case in developing countries and large emerging markets. For example, corruption, red tape, distribution problems, and a vague legal system present challenges for non-Chinese companies. Yet, because long-term returns on their investments are expected, Western companies reinvested heavily in China despite uncertain short-term profits.[5] Most of these companies invested in production facilities to take advantage of a low-cost labor pool and low-cost energy.

Companies scale back their international operations when it becomes apparent that making operations profitable will take longer than expected. Again, China serves as a good example. Some companies were lured to China by the possibilities for growth offered by 1.2 billion consumers. However, some had to scale back ambitions based on overly optimistic marketing plans.

Companies usually decide to reinvest when a market is experiencing rapid growth. Reinvestment can mean either expanding in the market itself or expanding in a location that serves the growing market. Investing in expanding markets is often an attractive option because potential new customers usually have not yet become loyal to the products of any one company or brand. It can be easier and less costly to attract customers in such markets than it is to gain a share of markets that are stagnant or contracting.

Yet, problems in the political, social, or economic sphere can force a company either to reduce or eliminate operations altogether. Such problems are usually intertwined with one another. For example, in recent years some Western companies pulled their personnel out of Indonesia because of intense social unrest stemming directly from a combination of political problems (discontent with the nation's political leadership) and economic upheaval (the collapse of the Indonesian economy), and because of terrorist attacks.

Finally, companies invest in the operations that offer the best return on their investments. That policy often means reducing or divesting operations in some markets, even though they may be profitable, in order to invest in more profitable opportunities elsewhere.

Quick Study

1. How do *TQM* and ISO 9000 help companies to improve quality and control costs?
2. Explain how shipping and inventory costs influence a firm's international logistics decisions. What is *just-in-time manufacturing*?
3. What are several considerations that underlie the reinvest-versus-divest decision?

Financing Business Operations

Companies need financial resources to pay for a variety of operating expenses and new projects. They must buy raw materials and component products for manufacturing and assembly activities. At certain times, they need large sums of capital, whether for expanding production capacity or entering new geographic markets. But companies also need financing to pay for all sorts of activities in addition to those related to production. They must pay for training and development programs and compensate workers and managers. They must pay advertising agencies for helping the company promote its goods and services. They also must make periodic interest payments to lenders and perhaps reward stockholders with dividends.

But all companies have a limited supply of resources at their disposal to invest in current operations or new endeavors. So, where do companies obtain needed funds? Generally speaking, organizations obtain financial resources through one of three sources:

1. Borrowing (debt)
2. Issuing equity (stock ownership)
3. Internal funding

Borrowing

International companies (like domestic companies) try to get the lowest interest rates possible on borrowed funds. However, this objective is more complex on a global scale. Difficulties include exchange-rate risk, restrictions on currency convertibility, and restrictions on the international flow of capital.

Borrowing locally can be advantageous, especially when the value of the local currency has fallen against that of the home country. Suppose a Japanese company borrows from U.S. banks for investment in the United States. Let's say that one year later, the U.S. dollar has fallen against the Japanese yen; in other words, fewer yen are now needed to buy one dollar. In that case, the Japanese company can repay the loan with fewer yen than would have been required if the value of the dollar had not fallen.

But companies are not always able to borrow funds locally. Often they are forced to seek international sources of capital. This is sometimes the case when a subsidiary is new to the market and has not yet built a reputation with local lenders. In such cases, a parent firm can help a subsidiary acquire financing through a so-called **back-to-back loan**—a loan in which a parent company deposits money with a host-country bank, which then lends the money to a subsidiary located in the host country.

For instance, suppose that a Mexican company forms a new subsidiary in the United States but that this subsidiary cannot obtain a U.S. bank loan. The Mexican parent company can deposit Mexican pesos in the branch of a U.S. bank in Mexico (see Figure 15.2). The U.S. bank's home office then lends dollars to the subsidiary in the United States. The amount of money lent in dollars will be equivalent to the amount of pesos on deposit with the U.S. bank's Mexican branch. When the U.S. subsidiary repays the loan in full, the parent company withdraws its deposit (plus any interest earned) from the U.S. bank's Mexican branch.

back-to-back loan
Loan in which a parent company deposits money with a host-country bank, which then lends the money to a subsidiary located in the host country.

Issuing Equity

Recall from Chapter 9 that the *international equity market* consists of all stocks bought and sold outside the home country of the issuing company. Companies issue such stock primarily to access pools of investors with funds that are unavailable domestically. However, getting shares listed on another country's stock exchange can be a complex process. For one thing, complying with all the rules and regulations governing the operation of a particular stock exchange costs a great deal of time and money. Therefore, only large companies tend to list shares on multiple exchanges.

Issuing American Depository Receipts
To maximize international exposure (and access to funds), non-U.S. companies often list themselves on U.S. stock exchanges. Non-U.S. companies can list shares directly in the United States by issuing **American Depository Receipts (ADRs)**—certificates that trade in the United States and represent a specific number of shares in a non-U.S. company. Large U.S. banks, such as Citibank (*www.citibank.com*), issue ADRs that then trade on the New York Stock Exchange

American Depository Receipt (ADR)
Certificate that trades in the United States and represents a specific number of shares in a non-U.S. company.

FIGURE 15.2

Mexico–United States Back-to-Back Loan

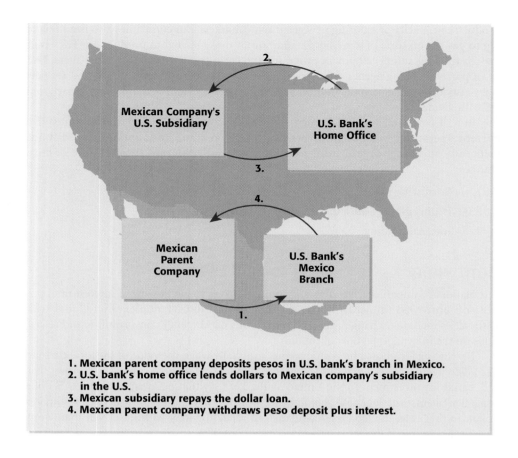

1. Mexican parent company deposits pesos in U.S. bank's branch in Mexico.
2. U.S. bank's home office lends dollars to Mexican company's subsidiary in the U.S.
3. Mexican subsidiary repays the dollar loan.
4. Mexican parent company withdraws peso deposit plus interest.

(*www.nyse.com*), the computerized National Association of Securities Dealers Automated Quotation system (*www.nasdaq.com*), and the over-the-counter (OTC) market. As we saw in the company profile at the start of this chapter, Finland-based Nokia (*www.nokia.com*) accesses U.S. investors by issuing ADRs.

International companies also make use of Global Depository Receipts (GDRs). These are similar in principle to ADRs but are listed and traded in London and Luxembourg. Companies from India aggressively issue GDRs to circumvent stringent listing requirements in their home market.[6]

Advantages of ADRs Companies gain several important advantages through ADRs. First, investors who buy ADRs pay no currency-conversion fees. In contrast, if a U.S. investor were to purchase the shares of a non-U.S. company on another country's stock exchange, he or she would incur the expense of converting currencies. Avoiding such expenses, plus the added convenience of paying in dollars, encourages U.S. investors to buy ADRs. Second, there are no minimum purchase requirements for ADRs, as there sometimes are for shares of a company's stock.

Third, companies offer ADRs in the United States to appeal to mutual funds. Investment laws in the United States limit the amount of money that a mutual fund can invest in the shares of companies not registered on U.S. exchanges. U.S. mutual fund managers were forced to sell shares of German software producer SAP (*www.sap.com*) when they appreciated in price. Says Kevin McKay, chief operating officer of SAP America: "Some of these guys were telling us, 'We hate to sell, but we have to. Please get some ADRs.' " SAP complied. Listing ADRs in the United States also allowed the company to reward employees with discounted shares of company stock—something that it could not have done otherwise because companies are barred from awarding shares in unregistered companies to employees in the United States.[7]

Venture Capital Another source of equity financing for entrepreneurial start-ups and small businesses is **venture capital**—financing obtained from investors who believe that the

venture capital
Financing obtained from investors who believe that the borrower will experience rapid growth and who receive equity (part ownership) in return.

borrower will experience rapid growth and who receive equity (part ownership) in return. Those who supply the venture with the capital it needs are called *venture capitalists*. Although there is often substantial risk associated with new, rapidly expanding enterprises, venture capitalists invest in them because they can also generate very large returns on investment.

In recent years, the venture capital industry has become global. For some key strategies that savvy entrepreneurs use to find international investors, see the Entrepreneur's Survival Kit titled, "Get Global Cash: Overseas Investors Await You."

Emerging Stock Markets   Naturally, companies from countries with emerging stock markets face certain problems. First, emerging stock markets commonly experience extreme volatility. An important contributing factor is that investments into emerging stock markets are often so-called *hot money*—money that can be quickly withdrawn in times of crisis. In contrast, *patient money*—foreign direct investment in factories, equipment, and land—cannot be pulled out as readily. Large and sudden sell-offs of equity are signs of market volatility that characterize many emerging stock markets. Such large sell-offs occur because of uncertainty regarding the nation's future economic growth.

Second, companies that issue equity on their countries' emerging stock markets are often plagued by poor market regulation. This can allow large local companies to wield a great deal of influence over their domestic stock markets. As long as powerful domestic shareholders dominate such exchanges, international investors will likely hesitate to enter. The root of the problem often lies in regulation that favors insiders over international investors.

Internal Funding

Ongoing international business activities and new investments can also be financed internally, whether with funds supplied by the parent company or by its international subsidiaries.

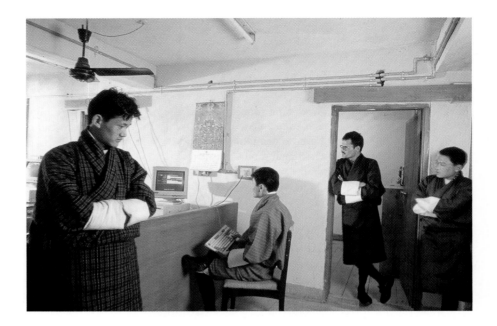

Internal Equity, Debt, and Fees   Spin-off companies and new subsidiaries typically require a period of time before they become financially independent. During this period, they often obtain internal financing from parent companies.

Many international subsidiaries obtain financial capital by issuing equity, which as a rule is not publicly traded. In fact, equity is often purchased solely by the parent company, which obviously enjoys great influence over the subsidiary's decisions. If the subsidiary performs well, the parent earns a return from the appreciating share price, which reflects the increasing valuation of the company. If the subsidiary decides to pay stock dividends, the parent company can also earn a return in this way. Parent companies commonly lend money to international subsidiaries during the start-up phase and when subsidiaries undertake large new investments. Conversely, subsidiaries with excess cash often lend money to parent or sister companies when they need capital.

Revenue from Operations   Money earned from the sale of goods and services is called **revenue**. This source of capital is the lifeblood of international companies and their subsidiaries. If a company is to succeed in the long term, it must at some point generate sufficient internal revenue to sustain day-to-day operations. At that point, outside financing is required only to expand operations or to survive lean periods—say, during seasonal sales fluctuations.

As we saw in earlier chapters, international companies and their subsidiaries also generate revenues internally through so-called *transfer prices*—prices charged for goods or services transferred among a company and its subsidiaries. Companies set subsidiaries' transfer prices high or low, according to their own goals. For instance, often they pursue transfer pricing aggressively when they wish to minimize taxes in a high-taxation country. Transfer pricing can be used if there are no national restrictions on the use of foreign exchange or on the repatriation of profits to home countries. Figure 15.3 summarizes the internal sources of capital for international companies and their subsidiaries.

revenue
Monies earned from the sale of goods and services.

Capital Structure

The **capital structure** of a company is the mix of equity, debt, and internally generated funds that it uses to finance its activities. Firms try to strike the right balance among financing methods in order to minimize risk and the cost of capital.

Debt requires periodic interest payments to creditors such as banks and bondholders. If the company defaults on interest payments, creditors can take the company to court to force it to pay—even forcing it into bankruptcy. On the other hand, in the case of equity, only holders of certain types of preferred stock (which companies issue sparingly) can

capital structure
Mix of equity, debt, and internally generated funds used to finance a company's activities.

FIGURE 15.3

Internal Sources of Capital for International Companies

force bankruptcy because of default. As a rule, then, companies do not want to carry so much debt in relation to equity that it increases its risk of insolvency. However, debt appeals to companies in many countries because interest payments can be deducted from taxable earnings—thus lowering the amount of taxes the firm must pay.

The basic principles of capital structure do not vary from domestic to international companies. However, research indicates that multinational firms have lower ratios of debt to equity than domestic firms. Why is this so? Some observers cite increased political risk, exchange-rate risk, and the number of opportunities available to multinationals as possible explanations for the difference. Others suggest that the debt-versus-equity option depends on a company's national culture. However, this suggestion has come under fire because companies from all cultures want to reduce their cost of capital. Moreover, many large international companies generate revenue from a large number of countries. How does one determine the "national culture" of these companies?

National restrictions can influence the choice of capital structure. These restrictions include limits on the international flows of capital, the cost of local financing versus the cost of international financing, access to international financial markets, and controls imposed on the exchange of currencies. The choice of capital structure for each of a company's international subsidiaries—and, therefore, its own capital structure—is a highly complex decision.

Quick Study

1. Explain when a *back-to-back loan* might be useful to a company.
2. Why might a firm list its stock in the international capital market? Explain the advantages of an *American Depository Receipt*.
3. Identify several difficulties facing companies that issue equity on emerging stock markets.
4. What is meant by the term *capital structure*? Explain its significance.

A Final Word

Whether an international company's production activity involves manufacturing a product or providing a service, it must acquire many resources before beginning operations. It needs to resolve issues such as where it will get raw materials or components, how much production capacity it needs, whether to construct or buy new facilities, the size of service centers, and where it will get financing. The answers to these questions are complex and interrelated.

This chapter discussed important considerations when formulating international production strategies, including planning for production capacity, the location of facilities, production processes to be used, and the layout of facilities. We also presented the decision of when companies prefer to centralize or decentralize production and whether production will be standardized or adapted to national markets. In the process, we saw how production issues are linked to earlier discussions of overall corporate strategy and marketing strategy. We closed the chapter with a discussion of how companies finance their international production operations and other activities.

SUMMARY

1. **Identify the elements that are important to consider when formulating *production strategies*.** The process of assessing a company's ability to produce enough output to satisfy market demand is called *capacity planning*. If capacity is greater than the expected market demand, production must be scaled back, and vice versa.

   Selecting the location for production facilities is called *facilities location planning*. Selecting highly favorable locations often allows a company to achieve *location economies*—economic benefits derived from locating production activities in optimal locations. Another important consideration is whether to centralize or decentralize production facilities. *Centralized production* refers to the concentration of production facilities in one location. With *decentralized production*, facilities are spread over several locations.

   Deciding on the process that a company will use to create its product is called *process planning*. Another important production issue is deciding whether the production process will be *standardized* for all markets or *adapted* to manufacture products modified for different markets.

   Deciding the spatial arrangement of production processes within production facilities is called *facilities layout planning*. Facility layout depends on the type of production process a company employs.

2. **Identify key considerations when *acquiring physical resources*.** In essence, the *make-or-buy* decision represents the decision for or against greater *vertical integration*—the process whereby a company extends control over additional stages of production. A firm that chooses to *make* a particular product or component often does so to take advantage of lower costs or to achieve greater control. On the other hand, *outsourcing*—buying from another company a good or service that is not central to a firm's competitive advantage—can provide greater flexibility while reducing the exposure to exchange-rate fluctuations and other forms of risk.

   Decisions about the selection and acquisition of raw materials are also important. First, some companies must rely exclusively on the *quantity* of locally available raw materials such as iron ore, oil, lumber, or fish. Second, the *quality* of raw material has a huge influence on the quality of a company's end product such as fruit, vegetables, grains, and water.

   Finally, most companies must acquire *fixed (tangible) assets* in a host country. Many companies have the option of either (1) acquiring or modifying existing factories, or (2) building entirely new facilities. Managers also must make sure that the local infrastructure can support the firm's proposed on-site business operations.

3. **Identify several production matters that are of special concern to managers.** Companies strive toward quality improvement for two reasons: costs and customer value. An emphasis on continuous quality improvement to meet or exceed customer expectations is called *total quality management (TQM)*. TQM stresses a company-wide commitment to quality-enhancing processes. The *International Standards Organization (ISO) 9000* is an international certification that companies get when they meet the highest quality standards in their industries. Many companies seek ISO 9000 certification because of the message of quality that certification sends to prospective customers.

   Shipping costs can have a dramatic effect on the cost of getting materials and components to production facilities. A production technique in which *inventory* is kept to a minimum and inputs to the production process arrive exactly when they are needed is called *just-in-time (JIT) manufacturing*. JIT drastically reduces the costs associated with large inventories.

   Managers also monitor events and might *reinvest* in operations or *divest* them. Companies often reinvest when (1) managers believe a market will provide a large return over time or (2) a market is experiencing rapid growth. Companies often divest (reduce investments) when (1) profitability is further off than expected, (2) problems in the political, social, or economic sphere arise, or (3) more profitable opportunities arise in other markets.

4. **Describe the three potential *sources of financing* and the main financial instruments of each.** One source of financing is borrowing. Because interest rates vary around the world, cross-border borrowing can be attractive. In *back-to-back loans*, parent firms loan money to subsidiaries by depositing money in host-country banks.

   Another source of funds is *equity financing*, wherein a company sells stock to raise capital. Companies outside the United States can still access its capital market by issuing what are called *American Depository Receipts (ADRs)*—certificates that trade in the United States and represent a specific number of shares in a non-U.S. company. *Venture capital* is a source of equity for entrepreneurial start-ups and small businesses.

A third source of financing is *internal funding*. Parent companies and their subsidiaries can obtain internal funding through (1) a swapping of debt or equity and (2) charging one another royalties and licensing fees. *Revenue* from ongoing operations can be used to finance company growth and expansion. International companies and their subsidiaries can also obtain funds from *transfer prices*—prices charged one another for goods and services purchased internally.

TALK IT OVER

1. Companies around the world are increasingly committing themselves to attaining International Standards Organization (ISO) certification in a variety of areas, including quality and pollution minimization. Do you think this is just the beginning of a trend toward worldwide homogenization of product and process standards? Do you think that someday all companies and their products will need certification in order to conduct international business? Explain your answers.

2. Despite the difficulties many technology companies experienced in the early 2000s, electronic business (e-commerce) is here to stay. What resources does an Internet retailer need other than merely a storefront on the Internet? Does it require fewer physical, financial, and human resources than a traditional retailer or just as many? Explain your answer.

TEAMING UP

1. The United States is home to some of the world's leading computer software companies, most of which commonly outsource software development to other countries, including Egypt, India, Ireland, Israel, Malaysia, Hungary, and the Philippines. As a group, select one of these countries and explain why it has become a supplier to the computer software industry. Do you think that development of the industry in your chosen country is a threat to companies in the United States? Why or why not?

2. With several classmates, contact a manager at a local company that does business internationally. Talk to the manager about total quality management and ISO standards. Find out whether the company has a formal TQM program and whether it has obtained any type of ISO certification. Compile your findings and present them to the class in a short talk. Compare and contrast the findings obtained for each company the class studied.

3. Suppose that you and several classmates are a team assembled by the chief financial officer of a consumer-goods company based in Mexico. Your company wishes to expand internationally but lacks the necessary financial capital. Describe all the financing options that are available to your company. Explain why each option is feasible, taking into account the prevailing situation in the Mexican and international capital markets. Develop a short presentation to be delivered to your board of directors (the rest of your classmates).

KEY TERMS

American Depository Receipt (ADR) (p. 437)

back-to-back loan (p. 437)

capacity planning (p. 426)

capital structure (p. 440)

facilities layout planning (p. 430)

facilities location planning (p. 427)

fixed (tangible) assets (p. 433)

just-in-time (JIT) manufacturing (p. 436)

location economies (p. 428)

make-or-buy decision (p. 430)

outsourcing (p. 431)

process planning (p. 429)

revenue (p. 440)

total quality management (TQM) (p. 434)

venture capital (p. 438)

vertical integration (p. 430)

TAKE IT TO THE WEB

1. In this chapter, we learned how international companies manage their international production efforts. We saw how firms acquire the materials and products they need and how aspects of the business environment and competitors' actions affect production strategies.

    Visit the Web site of Netherlands-based firm Philips NV (*www.philips.com*), and research the company on the Internet. As best you can, identify Philips' production and assembly locations. What types of products does Philips, one of the world's top three consumer-electronics companies, produce? Do you think Philips is following a centralized or decentralized production strategy? Explain your answer. Where does Philips conduct much of its R&D, and why is it performed there?

    Visit the Web site of LG.Philips LCD (*www.lgphilips-lcd.com*), Philips' joint venture with South Korean firm LG (*www.lg.co.kr*). What do you think Philips had to gain by cooperating with LG? Why do you think Philips did not simply build its own facilities in South Korea to produce LCD displays? How can the LG and Philips joint venture be explained using the criteria of a make-or-buy decision? Explain your answers.

ETHICAL CHALLENGES

1. You are senior vice president of human resources for a major multinational company. Your firm recently "reengineered" and fired a number of long-time workers. As the economy began to pick up again your firm rehired many of the same workers but this time as consultants, with no benefits paid by your firm. Critics charge that your firm's practice of reengineering is synonymous with "downsizing"—laying off employees or reducing employment ranks through early retirement and other means. Is it ethical for your company to behave in this manner? As the head of human resources, is there an alternative to the current practice of your firm?

2. You are special assistant to the governor of a southeastern U.S. state in which unemployment (especially rural areas) is well above the national average. After nearly three years in office and elected on a pledge to attract industry and create jobs, the governor is concerned. Because he respects your moral stance on issues, the governor has come seeking your insights. A European automobile maker has just told the governor that your state is on its short list of potential sites for a new manufacturing facility. The facility is expected to employ about 1,500 people, with plenty of spillover effects on the wider economy. The governor informs you the European automaker expects significant incentives and concessions. The governor would like to offer some $300 million in tax breaks and subsidies in an effort to bring the new plant to the state. How do you advise the governor? Would the outlay be proper use of taxpayer money? Why or why not? Would you feel comfortable defending your advice if it were to become public?

Toyota's Strategy for Production Efficiency

Toyota Motor Corporation (*www.toyota.com*) commonly appears in most rankings of the world's most respected companies. One reason for Toyota's strong showing in such rankings is that the company seems always to manage to maintain profitability in the face of economic downturns and slack demand. Another reason is that leaders in a wide range of industries have high regard for Toyota's management and production practices.

Toyota first began producing cars in 1937. In the mid-1950s, a machinist named Taiichi Ohno began developing a new concept of automobile production. Today, the approach known as the Toyota Production System (TPS) has been intently studied and widely copied throughout the automobile industry. Ohno, who was addressed by fellow employees as *sensei* ("teacher and master"), followed the lead of the family that founded Toyota (spelled Toyoda) by exhibiting high regard for workers. Ohno also believed that mass production of automobiles was obsolete and that a flexible production system that produced cars according to specific customer requests would be superior.

It was at Toyota that the well-known just-in-time approach to inventory management was developed and perfected. Implementing just-in-time required *kanban*, a simple system of colored paper cards that accompanied the parts as they progressed down the assembly line. *Kanban* eliminates inventory buildup by quickly telling the production personnel which parts are being used and which are not. The third pillar of the Toyota Production System was quality circles, groups of workers that discuss ways of improving the work process and making better cars. Finally, the entire system was based on *jidoka*, which literally means "automation." However, as used at Toyota, the word expresses management's faith in the worker as a human being and a thinker.

A simple example illustrates the benefits of Toyota's system. Toyota dealerships found that customers kept returning their vehicles with leaking radiator hoses. When a team of workers at the U.S. plant where the vehicle was made was asked to help find a solution, they found the problem was the clamp on the radiator hose. In assembly, the clamp is put over the hose, a pin on the side is pulled out, and the hose is secured. But sometimes the operator would forget to pull the pin. The hose would remain loose and would leak. So the team installed a device next to the line that contains a funnel and electric eye. If a pin is not tossed into the funnel (passing the electric eye) every 60 seconds, the device senses that the operator must have forgotten to pull the pin and stops the line. As a result, a warranty problem at the dealerships was eliminated, customer dissatisfaction was reduced, and productivity increased.

Nearly 50 years after the groundwork for the Toyota Production System was first laid, the results speak for themselves. Toyota's superior approach to manufacturing has been estimated to yield a cost advantage of $600 to $700 per car due to more efficient production, plus another $300 savings per car because fewer defects mean less warranty repair work. Ohno's belief in flexible production can also be seen in the fact that Toyota's Sienna minivan is produced on the same assembly line in Georgetown, Kentucky, as the company's Camry models. The Sienna and Camry share the same basic chassis and 50 percent of their parts. Out of 300 different stations on the assembly line, Sienna models require different parts at only 26 stations. Toyota expects to build one Sienna for every three Camrys that come off the assembly line.

Thinking Globally

1. Chrysler (*www.chrysler.com*) engineers helped Toyota develop its Sienna minivan. In return, Toyota provided input on automobile production techniques to Chrysler. Why do you think Chrysler was willing to share its minivan know-how with a key competitor?

2. Many companies seek to cut costs and improve quality by introducing techniques such as just-in-time and quality circles. However, the results often fall short of those achieved at Toyota. Why do you think this is the case?

3. What other benefits do you think Toyota obtains from its production system? Think in broader terms than just production, and consider financial, marketing, and human resource management issues.

1. Explain the three different types of *staffing policies* used by international companies.

2. Describe the *recruitment* and *selection* issues facing international companies.

3. Discuss the importance of *training* and *development programs*, especially cultural training.

4. Explain how companies *compensate managers* and *workers* in international markets.

5. Describe the importance of *labor–management relations* and how they differ around the world.

hiring and managing 16

employees

a look *back*

CHAPTER 15 examined how companies launch and manage their international production efforts. We also explored briefly how companies finance their various international business operations.

a look *at this chapter*

This final chapter examines how a company acquires and manages its most important resource—its employees. The topics we explore include international staffing policies, recruitment and selection, training and development, compensation, and labor–management relations. We also learn about culture shock and how employees can deal with its effects.

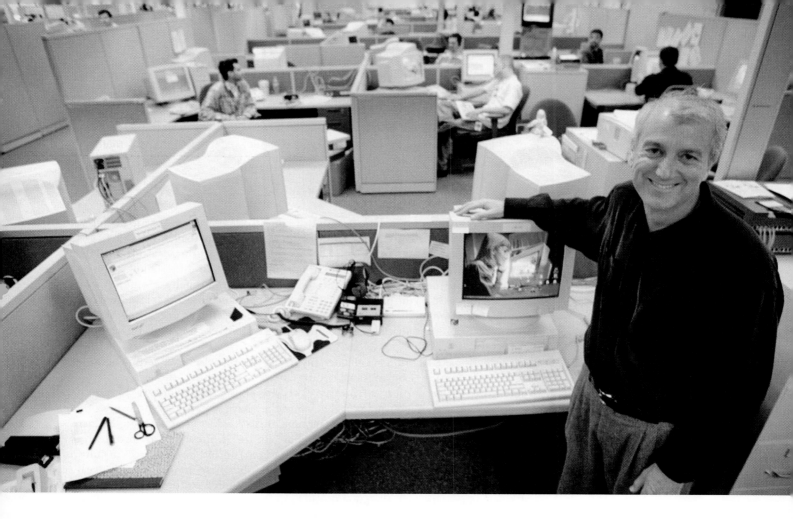

Culture Inside

SANTA CLARA, California—Intel (*www.intel.com*) created the world's first micro-processor in 1971. Today, annual revenue is $30 billion, around 75 percent of which is earned outside the United States. Intel is the world's largest maker of computer chips and a leading manufacturer of computer, networking, and communications products.

A global company such as Intel, which has 78,000 employees worldwide, must deal with many issues when managing its people. Naturally, with offices in 45 countries Intel must select people who will manage each local office by answering several key questions. Can a qualified manager be found locally? What will it pay a manager hired locally? Or, will it send in a manager from the United States or from an office in another nation? If it sends someone in, what will be his or her pay? Because of different practices around the world, Intel's compensation and benefits packages vary greatly from one country to another.

Then there is the issue of culture. A manager hired locally understands the culture, but what if a manager is brought into the local market? Although the depth of knowledge required differs, Intel wants all of its employees to be knowledgeable about other cultures. That is why Intel created culture-specific training courses that teach how business is conducted internationally and how business differs across cultures. The firm says its training is designed "to develop the knowledge, awareness, and skills to ensure effectiveness and productivity and to identify strategies for successfully doing business in other countries and with people from other countries."

So, whether a globetrotting manager or a tech-support rep dealing with customers in other nations by telephone or e-mail, Intel believes that all of its employees need an ability to communicate across cultures. As you read this final chapter, think of all the human resource issues that arise when international companies manage their employees around the world.[1]

human resource management (HRM)
Process of staffing a company and ensuring that employees are as productive as possible.

expatriates
Citizens of one country who are living and working in another.

Perhaps the most important resource of any successful business is the people who comprise it. If a company gives its human resource management practices the importance they deserve, it can have a profound impact on performance. Highly trained and productive employees who are proficient in their duties allow a company to achieve its business goals both domestically and internationally. **Human resource management (HRM)** is the process of staffing a company and ensuring that employees are as productive as possible. It requires managers to be effective in recruiting, selecting, training, developing, evaluating, and compensating employees and in forming good relationships with them.

International HRM differs considerably from HRM in a domestic setting because of differences in national business environments. For one thing, there is the issue of expatriates—citizens of one country who are living and working in another. Companies must deal with many issues when they have expatriate employees on job assignments that could last several years. Some of these issues are related to the inconvenience and stress of living in an unfamiliar culture. In the company profile at the start of this chapter, we saw how Intel (*www.intel.com*) enrolls its employees in culture-specific training courses to prepare them for doing business internationally. Because culture is so important to international business, we studied culture early (Chapter 2) and returned repeatedly to the topic throughout this book. For these reasons, culture is central to this final chapter's discussion of how international companies manage their employees.

Likewise, training and development programs must often be tailored to local practices. Some countries, such as Germany and Japan, have extensive vocational-training schools that turn out graduates who are quite well prepared to perform their jobs proficiently. Finding well-qualified nonmanagerial workers in those markets is relatively easy. In contrast, developing a production facility in many emerging markets requires far more basic training of workers. For example, workers in China work hard and tend to be well educated. But because China lacks a vocational training system like those in Germany and Japan, Chinese workers tend to require more intensive on-the-job training. Also, recruitment and selection practices must often be adapted to the host nation's hiring laws. Hiring practices regarding nondiscrimination among job candidates must be carefully monitored so that the company does not violate such laws.

Many companies go abroad in the first place to take advantage of a lower pay scale in another country. Then they adjust their pay scales and advancement criteria to suit local customs. Union Bank of Switzerland in Zurich publishes an annual survey of earnings around the world. The bank's survey of Big Mac buying power (see Figure 16.1) has an interesting twist: It ranks earnings in terms of how long the average wage earner must work to be able to afford a Big Mac at McDonald's (*www.mcdonalds.com*). According to the survey, if you live in Nairobi it takes three hours to afford a Big Mac; in Tokyo it takes just 10 minutes.

We begin this chapter by discussing the different types of human resource staffing policies that international companies use. We then learn about the important factors that have an effect on recruitment and selection practices internationally. Later, we explore the many different types of training and development programs companies can use to improve the effectiveness of their employees. We also examine the compensation policies of international companies. Finally, we close the chapter with a discussion of the importance of labor–management relations around the world.

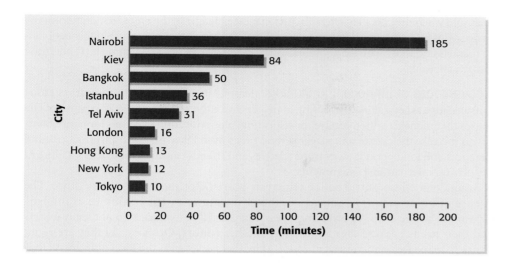

FIGURE 16.1

Amount of Time Needed to Earn a Big Mac

International Staffing Policy

The customary means by which a company staffs its offices is called its **staffing policy**. Staffing policy is greatly influenced by the extent of a firm's international involvement. There are three main approaches to the staffing of international business operations—*ethnocentric, polycentric,* and *geocentric.* Although we discuss each of these approaches as being distinct from one another, companies often blend different aspects of each staffing policy in practice. The result is an almost infinite variety of international staffing policies among international companies.

staffing policy
The customary means by which a company staffs its offices.

Ethnocentric Staffing

In **ethnocentric staffing**, individuals from the *home* country manage operations abroad. This policy tends to appeal to companies that want to maintain tight control over decision making in branch offices abroad. Accordingly, those companies work to formulate policies designed to work in every country in which they operate. However, note that firms generally pursue this policy in their international operations for top managerial posts—implementing it at lower levels is often impractical.

ethnocentric staffing
Staffing policy in which individuals from the home country manage operations abroad.

Advantages of Ethnocentric Staffing
Firms pursue this policy for several reasons. First, locally qualified people are not always available. In developing and newly industrialized countries, there is often a shortage of qualified personnel—resulting in a highly competitive local labor market.

Second, companies use ethnocentric staffing to re-create local operations in the image of home-country operations. Especially if they have climbed the corporate ladder in the home office, expatriate managers tend to infuse branch offices with the corporate culture. Naturally, this policy is important for companies that need a strong set of shared values among the people in each international office—such as firms implementing global strategies. For example, Mihir Doshi was born in Bombay but his family moved to the United States in 1978. Doshi graduated from New York University and became a naturalized U.S. citizen in 1988. In 1995 he became executive director of Morgan Stanley's (*www.ms.com*) operations in India. "Mentally," he reports, "I'm very American. Here, I can be Indian. What the firm gets is somebody to indoctrinate Morgan Stanley culture. I provide the link."[2]

By the same token, a system of shared values is important when a company's international units are highly interdependent. For instance, fashioning branch operations in the image of home-office operations can also ease the transfer of special know-how. This advantage is particularly valuable when that know-how is rooted in the expertise and experience of home-country managers.

Finally, some companies feel that managers sent from the home country will look out for the company's interests more earnestly than will host-country natives. Japanese companies are notorious for their reluctance to place non-Japanese managers at the helm of international offices, and when they do, they often place a Japanese manager in the office to monitor important decisions and report back to the home office. Companies that operate in highly nationalistic markets and those worried about industrial espionage also typically find an ethnocentric approach appealing.

Disadvantages of Ethnocentric Staffing
Despite its advantages, ethnocentric staffing has its negative aspects. First, relocating managers from the home country is expensive. The bonuses that managers often receive for relocating, plus relocation expenses for entire families, can increase the cost of a manager several times over. Likewise, the pressure of cultural differences and long periods away from relatives and friends can contribute to the failure of managers on international assignments.

Second, an ethnocentric policy can create barriers for the host-country office. The presence of home-country managers in the host country might encourage a "foreign" image of the business. Lower-level employees might feel that managers do not really understand their needs because they come from another culture. Occasionally they are right: Expatriate managers sometimes fail to integrate themselves into the local culture. As they fail to overcome cultural barriers, they fail to understand the needs not only of their local employees but those of their local customers.

Polycentric Staffing

polycentric staffing
Staffing policy in which individuals from the host country manage operations abroad.

In **polycentric staffing,** individuals from the *host* country manage operations abroad. Companies can implement a polycentric approach for top and mid-level managers, for lower-level staff, or for nonmanagerial workers. It is well suited to companies who want to give national units a degree of autonomy in decision making. This policy does not mean that host-country managers are left to run operations in any way they see fit. Large international companies usually conduct extensive training programs in which host-country managers visit home offices for extended periods. In this way they are exposed to the company's culture and specific business practices. Small and medium-sized companies can find this policy expensive, but being able to depend on local managers who fully understand what is expected of them can far outweigh any costs.

Advantages and Disadvantages of Polycentric Staffing
Polycentric staffing places managerial responsibility in the hands of people intimately familiar with the local business environment. Managers with deep cultural understanding of the local market can be an enormous advantage. They are familiar with local business practices and can read the subtle cues of both verbal and nonverbal language. They need not overcome any cultural

According to Microsoft
*(**www.microsoft.com**) CEO Bill Gates, when opening an international office, "it sends the wrong message to have a foreigner come in to run things." So, when Microsoft opened a branch in India, it hired native Indian Rajiv Nair to see that legitimate copies of Microsoft software went into the hundreds of thousands of PCs built in India each year. Five years later, Indian operations were promoted to a full-fledged subsidiary, with Nair as general manager.*

Growing Global

For an entrepreneur or small business, going global can put a strain on resources, including time, money, and people. Here is some advice on important human resource issues to consider when expanding internationally:

◯ **Don't entrust the local operations solely to U.S. expatriates.** "While they understand the company and the product, they don't understand the local practices and culture and don't have the relationships," said Joseph Monti, a partner at Grant Thornton LLP (*www.gt.com*). "The best strategy is to have a local general manager with a support staff that could be seeded with U.S. expatriates."

◯ **Contacts don't guarantee contracts.** "Relationships matter more than mere contacts," said Virginia Kamsky, CEO of Kamsky Associates Inc. (*www.kamsky.com*). "Don't assume that hiring the son of a government official will automatically get you business. It's more important to hire a person with a good attitude and strong relationship-building skills," she added.

◯ **Treat your employees abroad as you want to be treated.** "People are basically the same worldwide; it doesn't matter where you are," notes Jeff Dzuira, director of international sales at Ferris Manufacturing Corp. (*www.ferrispolymem.com*). "Awareness and respect of cultural protocol demonstrates honesty and goodwill, and this leads to trust, which in turn leads to mutually profitable relationships."

◯ **Employ the Web in your search.** One of the largest employment Web sites is Monster (*www.monster.com*). It has branches in 22 countries and literally millions of resumes. Another popular Web site for international job seekers is at (*www.hotjobs.com*). Employers can also post job announcements on the Web site at (*www.overseasjobs.com*). Of course, there are many more Web sites out there, and undertaking an aggressive job search or recruitment drive on the Internet is becoming increasingly common.

barriers created by an image of being an outsider, and they tend to have a better feel for the needs of employees, customers, and suppliers.

Another important advantage of polycentric staffing is elimination of the high cost of relocating expatriate managers and families. This advantage can be extremely helpful for small and midsize businesses that cannot afford the expenses associated with expatriate employees. See the Entrepreneur's Survival Kit titled, "Growing Global" for additional issues that small companies should consider when staffing internationally.

The major drawback of polycentric staffing is the potential for losing control of the host-country operation. When a company employs natives of each country to manage local operations, it runs the risk of becoming a collection of discrete national businesses. This situation might not be a problem when a firm's strategy calls for treating each national market differently. It is not a good policy, however, for companies that are following global strategies. If these companies lack integration, knowledge sharing, and a common image, performance will surely suffer.

Geocentric Staffing

In **geocentric staffing,** the best-qualified individuals, regardless of nationality, manage operations abroad. The local operation may choose managers from the host country, from the home country, or from a third country. The choice depends on the operation's specific needs. This policy is typically reserved for top-level managers.

geocentric staffing
Staffing policy in which the best-qualified individuals, regardless of nationality, manage operations abroad.

Advantages and Disadvantages of Geocentric Staffing
Geocentric staffing helps a company develop global managers who can adjust easily to any business environment—particularly to cultural differences. This advantage is especially useful for global companies trying to break down nationalistic barriers, whether between managers in a single office or between different offices. One hope of companies using this policy is that a global perspective among its managers will help them seize opportunities that may otherwise be overlooked.

The downside of geocentric staffing is the expense. Understandably, top managers who are capable both of fitting into different cultures and being effective at their jobs are highly prized among international companies. The combination of high demand for their skills and their short supply inflates their salaries. Moreover, there is the expense of relocating managers and their families—sometimes every year or two.

> ### Quick Study
>
> 1. List several ways in which *HRM* differs in the international versus domestic environment.
> 2. What are the three different types of international *staffing policies* that companies can implement?
> 3. Identify the advantages and disadvantages of each type of international staffing policy.

Recruiting and Selecting Human Resources

Naturally, companies try to recruit and select qualified managers and nonmanagerial workers who are well suited to their tasks and responsibilities. But how does a company know the number of managers and workers it needs? How does it recruit the best available individuals? How does it select from the pool of available candidates? In this section, we explore some answers to these and other important questions about recruiting and selecting employees.

Human Resource Planning

human resource planning
Process of forecasting both a company's human resource needs and supply.

Recruiting and selecting managers and workers requires **human resource planning**—the process of forecasting both a company's human resource needs and supply. The first phase of HR planning involves taking an inventory of a company's current human resources—that is, collecting data on every employee, including educational background, special job skills, previous jobs, language skills, and experience living abroad.

The second phase of HR planning is estimating the company's future HR needs. For example, consider a firm that plans to sell its products directly to buyers in a new market abroad. Will it create a new operation abroad and staff it with managers from the home office, or will it train local managers? Will it hire its own local sales force, or will it hire a distributor? Likewise, manufacturing or assembling products in an international market requires factory workers. A company must decide whether to hire these people itself or to subcontract production to other producers—thus eliminating the need for it to hire factory workers.

As we have noted in previous chapters, this decision frequently raises ethical questions. The general public is becoming increasingly well informed about the fact that global companies make extensive use of subcontractors in low-wage nations. Of particular concern is the question of whether subcontractors are taking advantage of "sweatshop labor." But publicity generated by allegations of workplace abuse cause many firms to establish codes of conduct and step up efforts to ensure compliance. For example, in the late 1990s Nike (*www.nike.com*) severed ties with subcontractors in Indonesia that paid wages below the minimum levels set by the government.

In the third phase of HR planning, managers develop a plan for recruiting and selecting people to fill vacant and anticipated new positions, both managerial and nonmanagerial. Sometimes, a firm must also make plans for reducing its workforce—a process called *decruitment*—when current HR levels are greater than anticipated needs. Planning for decruitment normally occurs when a company decides to discontinue manufacturing or selling in a market. Unfortunately, the decision by global companies to shift the location of manufacturing from one country to another can also result in lost jobs. Let's now take a closer look at the recruitment and selection processes.

Recruiting Human Resources

recruitment
Process of identifying and attracting a qualified pool of applicants for vacant positions.

The process of identifying and attracting a qualified pool of applicants for vacant positions is called **recruitment**. Companies can recruit internally from among their current employees or look to external sources.

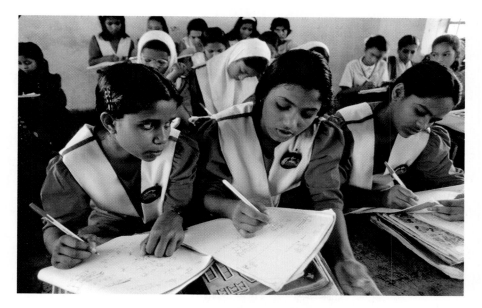

Current Employees   Finding an international manager among current employees is easiest for a large company with an abundance of internal managers. Likely candidates within the company are managers who were involved in previous stages of an international project—say, in *identifying* the new production site or potential market. It is likely that these individuals have already made important contacts inside the host country and they have already been exposed to its culture.

Recent College Graduates   Companies also recruit from among recent college graduates who have come from other countries to attend college in the firm's home country. This is a particularly common practice among companies in the United States. Over a 1-year period, these new hires receive general and specialized training and then are given positions in their native countries. As a rule, they learn about the organization's culture and the way in which it conducts business. Most important, perhaps, is their familiarity with the culture of the target market, including its customs, traditions, and language.

Local Managerial Talent   Companies can also recruit local managerial talent. Hiring local managers is common when cultural understanding is a key job requirement. Hiring local managers with government contacts can speed the process of getting approvals for local operations. In some cases, governments force companies to recruit local managers so that they can develop their own internal pools of managerial talent. Also, governments sometimes restrict the number of international managers that can work in the host country.

Nonmanagerial Workers   Companies typically recruit locally for nonmanagerial positions because there is often little need for highly specialized skills or training. However, a specialist from the home country is typically brought in to train people chosen for more demanding positions.

Firms also turn to the local labor market when governments restrict the number of people allowed into the host country for work purposes. Such efforts are usually designed to reduce unemployment among the local population. On the other hand, countries sometimes permit the importation of nonmanagerial workers. Kuwait, a wealthy oil-producing country in the Middle East, has brought in large numbers of nonmanagerial workers for its blue-collar and technical jobs. Many of these workers come from Egypt, India, Lebanon, Pakistan, Palestinian territories, and the Philippines in search of jobs or higher wages.

Selecting Human Resources

The process of screening and hiring the best-qualified applicants with the greatest performance potential is called **selection**. The process for international assignments includes measuring a person's ability to bridge cultural differences. Expatriate managers must be able to adapt to a new way of life in the host country. Conversely, native host-country managers must be able to work effectively with superiors who have different cultural backgrounds.

selection
Process of screening and hiring the best-qualified applicants with the greatest performance potential.

"WHEN YOU CAME TO WORK WITH US, WALSH, YOU STRESSED THAT YOU HOPED TO GO FAR WITH THE COMPANY. WELL, WE'VE DECIDED TO OPEN AN OFFICE IN TIBET, AND..."

In the case of expatriate managers, cultural differences between home country and host country are important factors in their potential success. Culturally sensitive managers increase the likelihood that a company will achieve its international business goals. Recruiters can assess cultural sensitivity by asking candidates questions about their receptiveness to new ways of doing things and questions about racial and ethnic issues. They can also use global aptitude tests such as the one mentioned in the Take It to the Web exercise at the end of this chapter.

It is also important to examine the cultural sensitivity of each family member who will be going to the host country. The inability of a family member (particularly a spouse) to adapt to a new culture is the most common reason for the failure of expatriate managers. In fact, in one recent survey of Canadian and U.S. companies, nearly 20 percent cited "lack of adaptability by the employee's spouse" as the number-one cause of failed relocation.[3]

Culture Shock

Successful international managers typically do not mind, and often enjoy, living and working outside their native lands. In extreme cases, they might even be required to relocate every year or so. These individuals are capable of adapting quickly to local conditions and business practices. Such managers are becoming increasingly valuable with the emergence of markets in Asia, Central and Eastern Europe, and Latin America. They are also helping to create a global pool of managers who are ready and willing to go practically anywhere on short notice. However, the size of this pool remains limited because of the difficulties that many people experience in relocating to unfamiliar cultures.

Living in another culture can be a stressful experience. Therefore, selecting managers who are comfortable traveling to and living in unfamiliar cultures is an extremely important factor in recruitment for international posts. Set down in the midst of new cultures, many expatriates experience culture shock—a psychological process affecting people living abroad that is characterized by homesickness, irritability, confusion, aggravation, and depression. In other words, they have trouble adjusting to the new environment in which they find themselves. *Expatriate failure*—the early return by an employee from an international assignment because of inadequate job performance—often results from cultural stress. The higher cost of expatriate failure is convincing many companies to invest in cultural-training programs for employees sent abroad. For a detailed look at the culture-shock process and how to reduce its effects, see the Global Manager's Toolbox titled, "A Shocking Ordeal."

culture shock
Psychological process affecting people living abroad that is characterized by homesickness, irritability, confusion, aggravation, and depression.

Reverse Culture Shock

Ironically, expatriates who successfully adapt to new cultures often undergo an experience called **reverse culture shock**—the psychological process of readapting to one's home culture. Because values and behavior that once seemed so natural now seem so strange, reverse culture shock may be even more disturbing than culture shock. In addition, returning managers often find that either no position or merely a "standby" position awaits them in the home office. Often, companies do not know how to take full advantage of the cross-cultural abilities developed by managers who have spent several potentially valuable years abroad. In fact, expatriates commonly leave their companies within a year of returning home because of difficulty blending back into the company culture.

Moreover, spouses and children often have difficulty leaving the adopted culture and returning home. For many Japanese employees and their families, reentry into Japanese culture after a work assignment in the United States can be particularly difficult. The fast pace of business and social life in the United States, plus the relatively high degree of freedom and independence for women, contrasts sharply with conditions in Japan. Returning Japanese expatriates can find it difficult to adjust back to life in Japan after years of living in the United States.

reverse culture shock
Psychological process of readapting to one's home culture.

global manager's **TOOLBOX**

A Shocking Ordeal

Culture shock typically occurs during stays of a few months or longer in an unfamiliar culture. It begins on arrival and normally occurs in four stages (although not all people go through every stage):

⊙ **Stage 1,** the "honeymoon," typically lasts from a few days to a few weeks. New arrivals are fascinated by local sights, pleasant hospitality, and interesting habits. They are thrilled about their opportunity and optimistic about prospects for success. However, this sense of security is often false because, so far, interactions with locals are similar to those of a tourist.

⊙ **Stage 2** lasts from a few weeks to a few months; in fact, some people never move on to stage 3. Unpredictable quirks of the culture become annoying, even maddening. Visitors begin mocking the locals and regarding the ways of their native cultures as superior. Relationships with spouses and children suffer, and depression, perhaps even despair, sets in.

⊙ In **Stage 3**, emotions hit bottom—and recovery begins. As visitors begin to learn more about the local culture, interact more with locals, and form friendships, cynical remarks cease.

⊙ In **Stage 4**, visitors not only better understand local customs and behavior but actually appreciate many of them. They now treat differences as "unique" solutions to familiar problems in different cultural contexts. Reaching Stage 4 is a sign that the expatriate has adapted well and that success in his or her international assignment is likely.

Here are some steps that prospective expatriates can take to reduce the burden of culture shock during an international assignment:

⊙ Undergo extensive psychological assessment to ensure that both you and your family members are emotionally able to handle the assignment.

⊙ Obtain knowledge of the local culture (especially the language) and critically examine your own culture biases before leaving home.

⊙ If possible, visit the assigned country, mingling with local people and getting a feel for your future assignment. Ask about local educational, financial, and health-care services.

⊙ Once you are inside a culture, meet with others—both natives and expatriates—to discuss your negative and positive experiences.

⊙ Most important: Relax, be adventurous, take a worldly perspective, and keep your sense of humor.

Dealing with Reverse Culture Shock The effects of reverse culture shock can be reduced. Home-culture reorientation programs and career-counseling sessions for returning managers and their families can be highly effective. For example, the employer might bring the entire family home for a short stay several weeks before the official return. This kind of trip allows returnees to prepare for at least some of the reverse culture shock that may await them.

Likewise, good career development programs can help companies retain valuable managers. Ideally, the career development plan was worked out before the employee went abroad and revised before his or her return. Some companies work with employees before they go abroad to plan career paths of up to 20 years within the company. Mentors who have previously gone abroad and had to adjust on returning home can also be assigned to returning managers. The mentor becomes a confidant with whom the expatriate manager can discuss particular problems related to work, family, and readjusting to the home culture.

Quick Study

1. Why is *human resources planning* important? Identify its three phases.
2. What are the main sources from which companies *recruit* their international managers?
3. What is meant by the term *culture shock*? Describe its four stages and how its effects can be reduced.
4. Under what circumstances might someone experience *reverse culture shock*?

Training and Development

After a company recruits and selects its managers and other employees, it normally identifies the skills and knowledge that employees have and those that they need to perform their duties. Employees who lack the necessary skills or knowledge can then be directed into specific training or development programs.

According to the National Foreign Trade Council (*www.nftc.org*), 250,000 U.S. citizens live outside the United States on international assignments—in addition to hundreds of thousands more who travel abroad on business for stays of up to several weeks. Some of the many costs of relocating an employee for a long-term international assignment include moving expenses and ongoing costs for things such as housing, education, and cost-of-living adjustments. That is why many companies realize the need for in-depth training and development programs if they are to get the maximum productivity from managers posted abroad.

Methods of Cultural Training

Ideally, everyone involved in business should be culturally literate and prepared to go anywhere in the world at a moment's notice. Realistically, many employees and many companies do not need or cannot afford to be entirely literate in another culture. The extent of a company's international involvement demands a corresponding level of cultural knowledge from its employees. Companies whose activities are highly international need employees with language fluency and in-depth experience in other countries. Meanwhile, small companies or those new to international business can begin with some basic cultural training. As a company increases its international involvement and cross-cultural contact, employees' cultural knowledge must keep pace.

As you can see from Figure 16.2, companies use many methods to prepare managers for an international assignment. These methods tend to reflect a manager's level of international involvement. The goal is to create informed, open-minded, flexible managers with a level of cultural training appropriate to the duties required of them.

FIGURE 16.2

**International Assignment
Preparation Methods**

The pyramid, from bottom to top, reads:
- Environmental Briefings
- Cultural Orientations
- Cultural Assimilation
- Sensitivity Training
- Language Training
- Field Experience

The arrow along the left side reads: Extent of Manager's International Involvement

Environmental Briefings and Cultural Orientations

Environmental (area) briefings constitute the most basic level of training—often the starting point for studying other cultures. Briefings include information on local housing, health care, transportation, schools, and climate. Such knowledge is normally obtained from books, films, and lectures. *Cultural orientations* offer insight into social, political, legal, and economic institutions. Their purpose is to add depth and substance to environmental briefings.

Cultural Assimilation and Sensitivity Training

Cultural assimilation teaches the culture's values, attitudes, manners, and customs. So-called guerrilla linguistics, which involves learning some phrases in the local language, is often used at this stage. It also typically includes role playing: The trainee responds to a specific situation in order to be evaluated by a team of judges. This method is often used when someone is given little notice of a short stay abroad and wishes to take a crash course in social and business etiquette and communication. *Sensitivity training* teaches people to be considerate and understanding of other people's feelings and emotions; it gets the trainee "under the skin" of the local people.

Language Training

The need for more thorough cultural preparedness brings us to intensive *language training*. This level of training entails more than memorizing phrases for ordering dinner or asking directions. It gets a trainee "into the mind" of local people. The trainee learns more about why local people behave as they do. This is perhaps the most critical part of cultural training for long-term assignments.

A survey of top executives found that foreign-language skills topped the list of skills needed to maintain a competitive edge. According to the survey, 31 percent of male employees and 27 percent of female employees lacked foreign-language skills. To remedy this situation, many companies either employ outside agencies that specialize in language training or develop their own programs. Employees at 3M Corporation (*www.3m.com*) developed a third way. They created an all-volunteer "Language Society" comprised of current and retired employees and family members. About 1,000 people are members, and the group offers classes in 17 languages taught by 70 volunteer employee teachers. The society meets 45 minutes per week and charges a nominal membership fee of $5. Officials at 3M say that the society nicely complements the company's formal language education program.[4]

Field Experience

Field experience means visiting the culture, walking the streets of its cities and villages, and becoming absorbed by it for a short time. The trainee gets to enjoy some of the unique cultural traits and feel some of the stresses inherent in living in the culture.

Finally, remember that spouses and children also need cultural training. Training for them is a good investment because the alternatives—an international "commuter marriage" or expatriate failure—are both psychologically and financially expensive options.[5]

Compiling a Cultural Profile

Cultural profiles can be quite helpful in deciding whether to accept an international assignment. The following are some excellent sources for constructing a cultural profile:

- *CultureGrams.* Published by ProQuest, this guide can be found in the reference section of many libraries. Frequent updates make *CultureGrams* (*www.culturegrams.com*) a timely source of information. Individual sections profile each culture's background and its people, customs and courtesies, lifestyle, and society. A section entitled "For the Traveler" covers details such as required entry visas and vaccinations.

- *Country Studies Area Handbooks.* This series explains how politics, economics, society, and national security issues are related to one another and shaped by culture in more than 70 countries. Handbooks tend to be politically oriented because they are designed for U.S. military personnel. The Country Studies Area Handbooks are available on the Web at (*http://lcweb2.loc.gov/frd/cs/cshome.html*).

- *Background Notes.* These notes contain much relevant factual information on human rights and related issues in various countries. However, because they are published by the U.S. Department of State (*www.state.gov*), they take a U.S. political perspective.

Information can also be obtained by contacting the embassies of other countries in your home nation. People with firsthand knowledge and specific books and films are also good sources of information. Once you're inside a country, you'll find your home country's embassy a good source of further cultural advice. Embassies maintain networks of home-nation professionals who work in the local culture, some with many years of experience on which you can draw.

Nonmanagerial Worker Training

Nonmanagerial workers also have training and development needs. This is especially true in some developing and newly industrialized countries where people have not even completed primary school. Even if the workforce is fairly well educated, workers may lack experience working in industry. In such cases, companies that do business abroad can train local workers in how to work on an assembly line or cultivate business leads to make sales. The need for such basic-skills training continues to grow as companies increasingly explore opportunities in emerging markets.

In many countries, national governments cooperate with businesses to train nonmanagerial workers. Japan and Germany lead the world in vocational training and apprenticeship programs for nonmanagerial workers. Students who are unable or unwilling to enter college can enter programs paid for by the government and private industry. They undergo extensive practical training that exposes them to the cutting-edge technologies used by the country's leading companies. For example, Germany's Mittelstand is a network of 3 million small and midsized companies that account for about two-thirds of the country's jobs. Mittelstand companies provide 80 percent of Germany's apprenticeships. Although they typically employ fewer than 100 people, many Mittelstand companies are export powerhouses.

Employee Compensation

Essential to good international HRM is a fair and effective compensation (reward) system. Such a system is designed to attract and retain the best and brightest employees and to reward them for their performance. Because a country's compensation practices are rooted in its culture and legal and economic systems, determining compensation can be complicated. For example, base pay accounts for nearly all employee compensation in some countries. In others, bonuses and fringe benefits account for more than half.

Managerial Employees

Naturally, compensation packages for managers differ from company to company and from country to country. Good packages are fairly complicated to design, for several reasons. First, consider the effect of *cost of living,* which includes factors such as the cost of groceries, dining out, clothing, housing, schooling, health care, transportation, and utilities. Quite simply, it costs more to live in some countries than in others. Moreover, within a given country the cost of living typically varies from large cities to rural towns and villages. Most companies add a certain amount to an expatriate manager's pay to cover greater cost-of-living expenses. On the other hand, managers who are relocating to lower cost-of-living countries are typically paid the same amount that they were receiving at the home office. Otherwise, they would be financially penalized for accepting an international job assignment.

Even when the cost of living abroad is lower than at home, companies must cover other costs incurred by expatriate managers. One important concern for relocating managers is the quality of local education. In many cases, children cannot immediately enter local classes because they do not speak the local language. In such instances, most companies pay for private-school education.

Bonus and Tax Incentives Companies commonly offer managers inducements to accept international postings. The most common is a financial bonus. This bonus can be in the form of a one-time payment or an add-on to regular pay—generally 15 to 20 percent. Bonuses for managers who are asked to go into a particularly unstable country or one with a very low standard of living often receive *hardship or "combat" pay.*

Managers can also be attracted by another income-related factor. For example, the U.S. government permits citizens working abroad to exclude "foreign-earned income" from their taxable income in the United States—even if it was earned in a country with no income tax.

Cultural and Social Contributors to Cost Culture also plays an important role in the compensation of expatriate managers. Some nations offer more paid holidays than others. Many offer free medical care to everyone living and working there. Granted, the quality of locally available medical care is not always good. Therefore, many companies have plans for taking seriously ill expatriates and family members home or to nearby countries where medical care is equal to that available in the home country.

Companies that hire managers in the local market might encounter additional costs engendered by social attitudes. For instance, in some countries employers are expected to provide free or subsidized housing. In others, the government obliges employers to provide paid maternity leaves of up to one and a half years. Government-mandated maternity leaves vary significantly across European countries. Although companies need not absorb all such costs, they tend to be reflected in a generally higher cost of doing business in a given country.

Managers recruited from within the host country generally receive the same pay as managers who work for local companies. However, they often receive perks not offered by local firms. For example, some are required to visit the home office two or three times per year. If time allows, many managers will make these into short vacations by taking along their families and adding a few extra days onto the length of the trip.

Nonmanagerial Workers

Two main factors influence the wages of nonmanagerial workers. First, their compensation is strongly influenced by increased cross-border business investment. Employers can relocate fairly easily to nations where wages are lower. Meanwhile, in the home country workers must often accept lower wages when an employer gives them a choice of accepting the reduction or watching their jobs move abroad. One result of this situation is a trend toward greater equality in workers' pay around the world. In turn, this equalizing effect encourages economic development and improvement in workers' lives in some countries at the expense of those in others.

However, the freedom with which an employer can relocate differs from country to country. Although firms in some countries are allowed to move with little notice, in others they are highly restricted. In fact, some countries force companies to compensate workers

FIGURE 16.3

Long Time, No Work

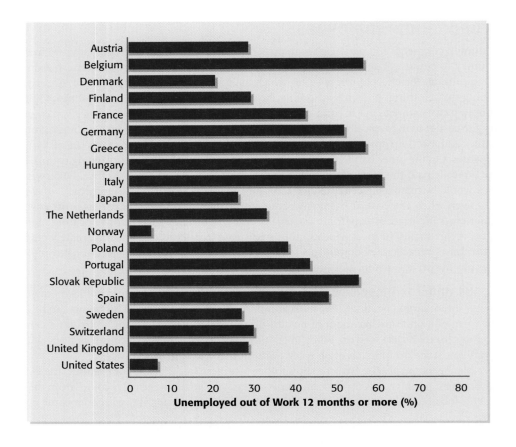

who lose their jobs because of relocation. This policy is common in European countries that have erected extensive social safety nets for unemployed workers.

Second, the fact that labor is more mobile today than ever before also affects wages. Although labor laws in Europe are still more stringent than in the United States, the countries of the European Union are abolishing the requirement that workers from one EU nation must obtain visas to work in another. If workers in Spain cannot find work at home, or if they feel that their current pay is inadequate, they are free to move to another EU country where unemployment is lower (say, Britain). A problem that plagues some European countries today is that they seem to be creating a group of people who are permanently unemployed. Examine Figure 16.3 to see how a group of countries compare on this point.

Quick Study

1. Identify the types of training and development used for: a) international managers, and b) nonmanagerial workers.

2. Describe each type of cultural training used to prepare managers for international assignments.

3. What variables are involved in decisions regarding employee compensation for: a) managers, and b) nonmanagerial workers?

Labor–Management Relations

labor–management relations
Positive or negative condition of relations between a company's management and its workers.

The positive or negative condition of relations between a company's management and its workers (labor) is referred to as **labor–management relations**. Cooperative relations between labor and management can give a firm a tremendous competitive advantage. When management and workers realize they depend on one another, the company is often better prepared to meet its goals and surmount unexpected obstacles that may crop up. Giving workers a greater stake in the company—say, through profit-sharing plans—is one way to increase morale and generate commitment to improved quality and customer service.

Because relations between laborers and managers are human relations, they are rooted in culture and are often affected by political movements in a market. Large international companies tend to make high-level labor decisions at the home office because it gives them greater control over their network of production operations around the world. However, lower-level decisions are often left to managers in each country. In effect, this policy places decisions that have a direct impact on workers' lives in the hands of experts in the local market. Such decisions might include the number of annual paid holidays, the length of maternity leave, and the provision of day-care facilities. Localizing such management decisions tends to contribute to better labor–management relations because managers familiar with local practices are better equipped to handle matters that affect workers personally.

Importance of Labor Unions

The strength of labor unions in a country where a company has operations is important to its performance and can even affect the selection of a location. Developing and emerging markets in Asia are a popular location for international companies. Some Asian governments appeal to international companies to locate facilities in their nations by promising to keep labor unions in check. But companies also find developed nations attractive if, for whatever reason, a cooperative atmosphere exists between company management and labor unions. In some Asian countries, especially Japan, a cultural emphasis on harmony and balanced interests discourages confrontation between labor and management.

Meanwhile, Britain and Ireland are becoming favorite locations for toeholds in the European Union (EU). The main attractions are productive labor, lower wages, and a reduced likelihood of disruptive strikes. Labor unions are not as strong in these countries as they are on the continent, particularly in France and Germany. Nevertheless, Germany has not been immune to the trend of falling union membership. Union membership has dropped off in Germany over the past decade from about 12 million to about 8 million workers. The main reason for the decline is the lack of interest in union membership in the former East German territories. By contrast, labor unions comprise only about 9 percent of the labor force in the United States today, compared with 36 percent 50 years ago.[6]

Despite declines in union membership, labor in Germany exercises a good deal of power in management decisions. In fact, under a plan called *codetermination*, German workers enjoy a direct say in the strategies and policies of their employers. This plan allows labor representatives to participate in high-level company meetings by actually voting on proposed actions.

Workers in Germany and France are typically protected by very powerful labor unions. In fact, German workers have a direct influence on company decisions through a plan called codetermination. Here German autoworkers take to the streets to demand action on their request for a pay hike. Why do you think countries around the world differ in the amount of influence that they give labor unions?

International Labor Movements The global activities of unions are making progress in areas such as improving the treatment of workers and reducing incidents involving child labor. However, the efforts of separate national unions to increase their cooperation are somewhat less successful. Although unions in one nation might wish to support their counterparts in another country, generating grassroots support is difficult for two reasons. First, events taking place in another country are difficult for many people to comprehend. Distance and cultural difference make it hard for people to understand others who live and work elsewhere.

Second, whether they realize it or not, workers in different countries sometimes compete against one another. For example, today firms can relocate internationally rather easily. Thus, labor unions in one country might offer concessions in order to attract the jobs that will be created by a new production facility. In this way, unions in different nations can wind up competing against one another. Some observers argue that this phenomenon creates downward pressure on both wages and union power worldwide.[7]

Quick Study

1. What is meant by the term *labor–management relations*?
2. Explain how labor–management relations differ around the world.

A Final Word

This chapter concluded our survey of international business. We did so by studying how firms, ranging from small and medium-sized businesses to large global companies, hire and manage their most important resource—their employees. We covered a great deal of territory in our "tour" of international business. We hope we piqued your interest in the goings-on of the global marketplace and in the activities of international companies of all types and sizes. Nevertheless, our learning does not end here. Each of us will continue to be exposed to international business in our daily lives—whether as consumers or as current or future business managers. As a result, we will continue to expand our knowledge of other national cultures, the international business environment, and how companies manage their international operations. We wish you well on your continued journey through this fascinating and dynamic subject.

SUMMARY

1. **Explain the three different types of *staffing policies* used by international companies.** In a company with an *ethnocentric staffing policy,* operations outside the home country are staffed and managed by home-country nationals. To provide headquarters with tight controls over the decision making of branch offices in other countries, policies are designed to work in each market in which the company operates. A *polycentric staffing policy* accomplishes just the opposite: International operations are staffed and managed by host-country natives, who usually have participated in extensive training programs. Such policies are generally designed to give national units a certain level of autonomy in decision making. *Geocentric staffing* means staffing operations outside the home country with the best-qualified individuals, regardless of nationality. This policy is typically reserved for top-level managers, who may be chosen from the home country, from the host country, or from a third country.

2. **Describe the *recruitment* and *selection* issues facing international companies.** Large companies often recruit international managers from within the ranks of existing employees. Because small and midsized companies may not have qualified managers, managers for international assignments may have to be hired from other companies. Sometimes international students who have graduated from local colleges are hired, trained locally, and then posted in their home countries. Local managerial talent can also be recruited in the host country; such persons bring special capabilities, such as an understanding of the local culture and political system. In addition, local hires are often required when a company sets up manufacturing abroad or engages in extensive marketing activities. When selecting employees for international positions, companies look for an ability to adapt to cultural differences. When hiring in-country personnel, the employer's home-country bias may make it difficult to determine technical competence or leadership ability.

3. **Discuss the importance of *training* and *development programs,* especially cultural training.** *Culture shock* refers to the psychological difficulties experienced when living in an unfamiliar culture—it is often characterized by homesickness, irritability, confusion, aggravation, and depression. Ironically, returning managers often experience *reverse culture shock:* the psychological process of readapting to one's home culture. For these reasons, cultural training is becoming increasingly important.

   Cultural training is often effective in reducing the effects of both culture shock and reverse culture shock. Training ranges from reading books and seeing films about a culture to visiting it on a field trip, and there are various methods for preparing people for international assignment. *Environmental briefings* and *cultural orientations* provide insight on matters such as local housing and health care and describe political, economic, and social institutions. *Cultural assimilation* and *sensitivity training* explain the local values, attitudes, and customs and stress the importance of understanding local feelings and emotions. *Language training* provides specific, practical skills that allow employees to communicate in the local language. *Field experience* means visiting the culture for a brief period to begin growing accustomed to it.

4. **Explain how companies *compensate managers* and *workers* in international markets.** An effective compensa-tion policy takes into account local cultures, laws, and practices. Issues include base pay as a percentage of total compensation, bonuses, and fringe benefits. Managerial compensation packages may have to be adjusted to reflect the cost of living; the cost of education for family members may also be a consideration. *Bonus payments* or hardship pay may be required as an incentive for managers to accept international assignments. Nonmanagerial compensation levels can be influenced by wage rates in other countries. Investment capital tends to flow to nations with low-cost labor, resulting in increased equality in workers' pay from country to country.

5. **Describe the importance of *labor–management relations* and how they differ around the world.** The positive or negative condition of relations between company management and its workers is referred to as *labor–management relations.* When management and workers realize they depend on one another, the company is often better prepared to meet its goals and to surmount unexpected obstacles that may crop up. Because relations between labor and managers are human relations, they are rooted in culture and are often affected by political movements in the local market. Finally, the strength of labor unions in a country where a company has operations is important to its performance and can even affect the selection of a location.

TALK IT OVER

1. Many Japanese companies use *ethnocentric* staffing policies in international operations. Why do you think Japanese companies prefer to have Japanese in top management positions? Would you recommend a change in this policy?

2. Have you ever experienced culture shock? If so, in which country did it occur? What, if anything, did you do to overcome it? Did your methods work? Did you experience reverse culture shock on returning home?

TEAMING UP

1. Suppose you and several of your classmates are the senior management team for a major automobile manufacturer. Among your company's worldwide operations are plants in Spain and Germany. Your company is considering closing these two plants and moving production to Poland in order to take advantage of lower wages. As a group, write a short report explaining how easy (or difficult) it will be for your company to close the plant and lay off workers in both Spain and Germany.

2. Small and medium-sized businesses sometimes face significant obstacles when expanding operations abroad. Write a group report on the obstacles they face in the area of recruiting and selecting employees when first venturing internationally. Address specific issues such as financial constraints, a lack of contacts, cultural differences, legal issues, geographical distance, and so on.

culture shock (p. 454)

ethnocentric staffing (p. 449)

expatriates (p. 448)

geocentric staffing (p. 451)

human resource management (HRM) (p. 448)

human resource planning (p. 452)

labor–management relations (p. 460)

polycentric staffing (p. 450)

recruitment (p. 452)

reverse culture shock (p. 455)

selection (p. 453)

staffing policy (p. 449)

1. Intercultural Business Center (IBC) is a top-ranked global and multicultural business training company specializing in cross-cultural training. Visit the Intercultural Business Center Web site (*www.ib-c.com*) and read about its services. One evaluative technique the firm offers is called the Global Mentality Test, which measures a person's aptitude of doing business globally.

   A British company recently found that the top-three reasons people quit or under-perform are rooted in personality, rather than skill, knowledge, or qualification. What do you think are the aspects of a person's personality that cause this to occur? Explain your answer. What advantages do you think global aptitude tests might offer companies doing business internationally?

   Personality testing in the workplace is widespread in Australia, Europe, and the United States. However, it is just beginning to catch on in Asia. Why do you think this is? Do you think the reason could be rooted in Asian societies and culture? Explain your answer.

   What personal characteristics do you think make someone better suited to doing business globally? Be specific. Do you think these characteristics are innate or can they be learned?

1. You are an expatriate manager at a manufacturing facility in Asia on your first assignment abroad. You are aware of increasing concern among your employees (mostly young women) about wages that barely permit them to live at subsistence level. The plant is not unionized, and you know that your superiors in your home country are not particularly supportive of efforts to organize workers. You also know that if workers vote to form a union and then demand higher wages, headquarters is likely to shift production elsewhere. If the plant were shut down, your employees would lose their jobs, and you would be transferred. Should you encourage or discourage your workers in their efforts to unionize? Explain your decision.

2. You are an assistant marketing manager for a financial-services firm expanding operations in Latin America. You were sent to Mexico City, Mexico, in part because you double-majored in Spanish and marketing and spent a semester abroad there. Your company's policy is to provide you and your expatriate colleagues with hardship pay, a generous housing allowance, a company car, and a fund of several thousand dollars to be used at your discretion. You are quite comfortable living abroad, but you have some expatriate friends who have not adjusted so well. Every two months or so, they fly back home to visit friends and get a change of scenery. You are not homesick at all, but your friends want you to go with them on an upcoming holiday. What would you do? Would you dip into your discretionary funds and go along? Or, would you remain in the community and do volunteer work with a local charity?

PRACTICING INTERNATIONAL MANAGEMENT CASE

Expatriation or Discrimination? You Make The Call

One issue faced by companies with international operations is determining the right time to bring expatriate managers home, or "repatriate" them. Promoting host-country personnel into key managerial positions can boost morale and provide a sense of equal opportunity. Also, local managers often have keen insights into local business conditions and, therefore, a potential advantage when it comes to decision making. Moreover, by bringing expatriate managers home, firms can often save considerable amounts of money. In China, for example, compensation for an expatriate can cost between $200,000 and $300,000 per year; the total package includes both cost-of-living and hardship allowances of 15 to 20 percent each. By comparison, total compensation for a top-notch Chinese manager would be only about $50,000 per year.

Despite the benefits to be gained from turning over control to local managers, some industry experts warn that "localizing" too quickly can be a mistake. For example, as one expatriate manager in China put it, "Doing business the Chinese way is much less well-documented and can be dangerous. There is a serious risk when you give up financial control." Another problem is the fact that many expatriate managers are evaluated according to operating results rather than according to their efforts to train local managers.

The issue of expatriate assignments is not limited to emerging markets such as China. In developed countries, laying off employees or replacing local managers with persons from the home country can be controversial moves. For example, Japanese-owned Ricoh Corporation (*www.ricoh.com*) replaced a U.S. manager with a Japanese manager in charge of optical computer-disk sales at its California File Products Division (FPD). After being laid off as a result of the move, Chet Mackentire sued his former employer for

discrimination under Title VII of the Civil Rights Act of 1964. But Ricoh argued that Mackentire was laid off for business reasons, not because he was a Caucasian-American.

Mackentire lost his case. The court said that it found "no evidence to support Mackentire's theory that the layoff was discriminatory" and ruled that there was "substantial evidence that it was due to business necessity." Mackentire appealed the ruling, but lost again. The appellate court wrote that Ricoh "offered affidavits stating that FPD was losing money, running into the millions of dollars annually. It also offered evidence that it reorganized the division to de-emphasize the product for which Mackentire was most responsible."

Thinking Globally

1. What are some key reasons for keeping expatriate managers in top positions?

2. Suppose a company decides that it has made a mistake by hiring local personnel in a key Asian country. What are some potential problems that it will face if it decides to install or reinstate expatriate managers in these positions?

3. In addition to those mentioned in the case, what are some other advantages associated with the hiring of local managers in emerging markets?

4. What steps should a company take to ensure that, if taken to court, it can demonstrate that staffing cuts have not been discriminatory?

Notes, Sources and Credits

Notes

Chapter 1

1. Marc Gunther, "MTV's Passage To India," *Fortune* (**www.fortune.com**), August 9, 2004; Kenny Santana, "MTV Goes to Asia," *Yale Center for the Study of Globalization* (**www.yaleglobal.yale.edu**), August 12, 2003; Kerry Capell et al., "MTV's World," *Business Week*, February 18, 2002, pp. 81–84.

2. Timothy Mullaney, "The E-Biz Surprise," *Business Week*, European edition, May 12, 2003, pp. 40–48.

3. *International Trade Statistics 2003* (Geneva, Switzerland: World Trade Organization, November 2003) (**www.wto.org**), Tables A4–A7; "The 2003 Global 500," *Fortune*, (**www.fortune.com**), July 21, 2003 issue.

4. Kevin Maney, "Companies Cast Worldwide Net: Technology Is "Demolishing" Time, Distance," *USA Today*, April 24, 1997, p. B1.

5. Rebecca Buckman, "H-P Outsourcing: Beyond China," *Wall Street Journal* (**www.wsj.com**), February 23, 2004.

6. Moisés Naím, "Post-Terror Surprises," *Foreign Policy* (**www.foreignpolicy.com**).

7. Heather Green, "China's Great March Online," *Business Week*, July 12, 2004, p. 14.

8. Catherine Taylor, "U.K. Insurance Industry to Cut 70,000 Jobs by 2010–Accenture," *Wall Street Journal* (**www.wsj.com**), February 18, 2002.

9. "The Simpsons Goes Global," *Associated Press* (**www.cartoons.com**), August 5, 2001; Fox's Simpsons Web site (**www.thesimpsons.com**).

10. "Globalization: Is It at Risk?" *The Economist*, February 2, 2002, pp. 61–63.

11. Stephan Kueffner, "Chile's Lagos sees Doha Round as Key to FTAA Agreement," *Wall Street Journal* (**www.wsj.com**), July 15, 2004; "A Step Forward," *The Economist*, August 7, 2004, pp. 11–12.

12. "The Case for International Videoconferencing," *World Trade Magazine*, Global Online Supplement (**www.worldtrademag.com**), June 14, 2001.

13. William Gurley, "The Soaring Cost of E-Commerce," *Fortune*, August 3, 1998, pp. 226–228.

14. Don Phillips, "Globalization Helps to Keep Old Economy's Shippers Afloat," *International Herald Tribune*, August 28, 2001, p. 11.

15. This discussion is drawn from "Measuring Globalization," *Foreign Policy*, March/April 2004, pp. 54–69.

16. This comparison between the first and second ages of globalization is drawn from Thomas L. Friedman, *The Lexus and the Olive Tree* (New York: Anchor Books, 2000), pp. xvi–xix.

17. "Economics A-Z," *The Economist* Web site (**www.economist.com**).

18. Alexander Stille, "Globalization Now, a Sequel of Sorts," *New York Times*, August 11, 2001, p. B7.

19. Globalization and Human Rights, PBS Program transcripts (**www.pbs.org**).

20. Michael Kelly, "Ghost Towns Mark Globalization's Path," *International Herald Tribune*, April 26, 2001, p. 9.

21. For an example of these and other criticisms leveled at Wal-Mart, see Jane Birnbaum, "Corporate Greed vs. Public Good, Where America Shops," AFL-CIO Web site (**www.aflcio.org**).

22. Anthony Bianco and Wendy Zellner, "Is Wal-Mart Too Powerful?," *Business Week*, October 6, 2003, pp. 100–110.

23. Lori G. Kletzer and Robert E. Litan, *A Prescription to Relieve Worker Anxiety* (Washington, D.C.: Institute for International Economics, 2001) (**www.iie.com**).

24. Naomi Klein, "Outsourcing the Friedman," *The Nation* (**www.thenation.com**), March 22, 2004.

25. As reported in Gary Clyde Hufbauer, *Globalization Facts and Consequences* (Washington, D.C.: Institute for International Economics, 2001) (**www.iie.com**).

26. Anthony Bianco and Wendy Zellner, "Is Wal-Mart Too Powerful?," *Business Week*, October 6, 2003, pp. 100–110.

27. Craig Karmin, " 'Offshoring' Can Generate Jobs in the U.S.," *Wall Street Journal*, March 16, 2004, p. B1.

28. Salil Tripathi, "Outsourcing: the Myths and the Facts," *Wall Street Journal* (**www.wsj.com**), March 1, 2004.

29. Martin Khor, "How the South Is Getting a Raw Deal," in Robin Broad, ed., *Global Backlash* (Lanham, MD: Rowman & Littlefield, 2002), pp.154–157.

30. As reported in Daniel W. Drezner, "Bottom Feeders," *Foreign Policy* (**www.foreignpolicy. com**), November/December 2000.

31. See, for example, David C. Korten, *When Corporations Rule the World* (San Francisco, CA: Berrett-Koehler, 2001).

32. As reported in Drezner, "Bottom Feeders."

33. As reported in Drezner, "Bottom Feeders."

34. M. Lundberg and L. Squire, *The Simultaneous Evolution of Growth and Inequality* (Washington, D.C.: World Bank, 1999).

35. David Dollar and Aart Kraay, *Growth Is Good for The Poor* (Washington, D.C.: World Bank, 2001) (**www.worldbank.org**).

36. Studies cited in *Poverty in an Age of Globalization* (Washington, D.C.: World Bank, 2000) (**www.worldbank.org**).

37. Christian Weller, Robert Scott, and Adam Hersh, *The Unremarkable Record of Liberalized Trade* (Washington, D.C.: Economic Policy Institute, October 2001).

38. "The WTO and The Developing World: Do as We Say, Not as We Did," Press Release, Public Citizen Global Trade Watch (**www.citizen.org/trade**), September 11, 2003.

39. As reported in Gary Clyde Hufbauer, *Globalization Facts and Consequences* (Washington, D.C.: Institute for International Economics, 2001) (**www.iie.com**).

40. *Globalization, Growth and Poverty: Building an Inclusive World Economy* (Washington, D.C.: World Bank, 2002).

41. "Liberty's Great Advance," A Survey of Capitalism and Democracy, *The Economist*, June 28, 2003, pp. 4–7.

42. Xavier Sala-i-Martin, "The World Distribution of Income," NBER Working Paper w8933 (Cambridge, MA: National Bureau of Economic Research, 2002).

43. Shaohua Chen and Martin Ravallion, "How Well Did the World's Poorest Fare in the 1990s?" *Review of Income and Wealth*, September 2003, 47(3), pp. 283–300.

44. For an analysis of why these studies' results differ, see "Global Economic Inequality," *The Economist*, March 13, 2004, pp. 73–75; and "Pessimistic on Poverty?," *The Economist*, April 10, 2004, p. 70.

45. *Globalization, Growth and Poverty: Building an Inclusive World Economy* (Washington, D.C.: World Bank, 2002).

46. Stephen Krasner, "Sovereignty," *Foreign Policy*, January/February 2001, pp. 20–29.

47. Marc Thiessen, "Out with the New," *Foreign Policy*, March/April 2001, pp. 64–66.

48. "Undermining Sovereignty and Democracy," *The Ten Year Track Record of the North American Free Trade Agreement* (Washington, D.C.: Public Citizen's Global Trade Watch, 2004).

49. Mark Leonard, "Soybeans and Security," *Foreign Policy*, March/April 2001, pp. 66–68.

50. Stephen Krasner, "Sovereignty," *Foreign Policy*, January/February 2001, pp. 20–29.

51. Michael Elliott, "A Not-So-New World Order," *Time*, European edition, April 2, 2001, p. 69.

52. Tyler Cowen and Eric Crampton, "Uncommon Culture," *Foreign Policy*, July/August, 2001, p. 28.

53. "Economic Globalization and Culture: A Discussion with Dr. Francis Fukuyama," Merrill Lynch Forum Web site (**www.ml.com/woml/forum**), 1998.

54. "Cross-Border M&As," *The Economist*, July 7, 2001, p. 107.

55. Data for this discussion was obtained from "The 2003 Global 500," *Fortune,* (**www.fortune.com**), July 21, 2003 issue.

56. Gary A. Knight and S. Tamer Cavusgil, "Innovation, Organizational Capabilities, and The Born-Global Firm," *Journal of International Business Studies* (2004) 35: 124–141.

57. Efraim Turban, et al., "Online Weekend in Florence: A Customer Service Success Story," in *Electronic Commerce: A Managerial Perspective* (Upper Saddle River, NJ: Pearson Education, 2004) p. 150; Weekend a Firenze Web Site (**www.wif.it**), selected articles.

58. "Measuring Globalization," *Foreign Policy,* March/April 2004, pp. 54–69.

59. Louis Uchitelle, "Globalization Marches on As U.S. Eases up on the Reins," *New York Times,* December 17, 2001, p. C12.

60. Moisés Naim, "Post-Terror Surprises," *Foreign Policy* (**www.foreignpolicy.com**).

61. "Measuring Globalization," *Foreign Policy,* March/April 2004, pp. 54–69.

62. "Managing Risk: An Assessment of CEO Preparedness," *Seventh Annual Global CEO Survey* (New York: PriceWaterhouseCoopers, 2004), pp. 11–12.

63. Guy Matthews, "Globalization Creates Logistics Jobs in U.S.," *Wall Street Journal* (**www.wsj.com**), March 1, 2004.

64. *Globalization, Growth and Poverty: Building an Inclusive World Economy* (Washington, D.C.: World Bank, 2002).

65. Kimberly A. Elliott, *Dealing with Labor and Environment Issues* (Washington, D.C.: Institute for International Economics, July 2002), (**www.iie.com**).

Chapter 2

1. Hans Greimel, "Gummi Bears Solve a Sticky Problem," *International Herald Tribune,* April 17, 2001, p. 14; Haribo Web site (**www.haribo.com**).

2. For a more detailed definition of culture, see Geert Hofstede, *Culture and Organizations: Software of the Mind* (New York: McGraw-Hill, 1997), pp. 3–19.

3. Suzanne Daley, "In Europe Many Try to Protect Local Languages," *International Herald Tribune,* April 17, 2001, p. 1.

4. Jeffrey E. Garten, "Cities: Investing in Culture Is Simply Good Business," *Business Week,* European edition, March 5, 2001, p. 13.

5. Diane Brady, "A Thousand and One Noshes," *Business Week,* June 14, 2004, pp. 54–56.

6. Information obtained from the Web of Culture Web site (**www.webofculture.com**).

7. Melik Kaylan, "Reality Check on Arabic TV," *Wall street Journal* (**www.wsj.com**), March 4, 2004.

8. Alessandra Galloni, "European Attitudes Toward Technology Vary Widely, Ad Agency's Survey Finds," *Wall Street Journal* (**www.wsj.com**), July 9, 2001.

9. Jane Black, "In Britain, "Entrepreneur' Is No Longer an Insult," *Business Week,* (**www.businessweek.com**), February 6, 2001.

10. Larry Levy, "Second Chances," *Business 2.0,* U.K. edition, May 2001, p. 121.

11. Patti Waldmeir, "The Long Arm of The U.S. Workplace," *Financial Times,* February 8, 2004, as published by Yale Center for The Study of Globalization (**www.yaleglobal.yale.edu**).

12. Mei Fong, "Chinese Charm School," *Wall Street Journal* (**www.wsj.com**), January 13, 2004.

13. Beth Rasmussen, "Despite Gains, Female Workers Struggle in Spain," *Wall Street Journal Europe,* June 12, 2001, p. 2.

14. Kerry Capell with Carlos Tromben, William Echikson, and Wendy Zellner, "Renegade Ryanair," *Business Week,* European edition, May 14, 2001, pp. 38–43.

15. Marlise Simons, "Did VW Mock the Gospel? French Bishops Sue," *New York Times,* February 7, 1998, p. A4.

16. Elaine Sciolino, "Explain It Again, Please: Who Says I Can't Wear a Hat?" *New York Times,* February 8, 1998, p. WK7.

17. "McAtlas Shrugged," *Foreign Policy,* May/June 2001, pp. 26–37.

18. Serge Schmemann, "If It's a Hard Sell, Let's Try Beards and Yarmulkes," *New York Times,* February 4, 1998, p. A4.

19. Nicholas Ostler, "A Loss for Words," *Foreign Policy,* November/December 2003, pp. 30–31.

20. "Beyond Multilingualism," *World Trade Magazine,* (**www.worldtrademag.com**), June 14, 2001; Jennifer L. Schenker, "The Gist of Translation," *Time Europe,* July 16, 2001, p. 42.

21. "Avoid My Party," *Business 2.0* (**www.business2.com**), February 2000; James Daly, "Going Global Gets More Complicated," *Business 2.0* (**www.business2.com**), November 27, 2000.

22. Caixia Lu, "Chinese, or Just Chinglish?" *Far Eastern Economic Review* (**www.feer.com**), April 19, 2001, p. 39.

23. Kitty McKinsey, "The Mother of All Tongues," *Far Eastern Economic Review* (**www.feer.com**), April 19, 2001, p. 38.

24. Suzanne Daley, "In Europe Many Try to Protect Local Languages," *International Herald Tribune,* April 17, 2001, p. 1.

25. Kate Hazelwood, "Yanks Wanted," *Business Week,* April 26, 2004, p. 118

26. Tatiana D. Helenius, "Body Language Savvy," CNN Web site (**www.cnnfn.com**), May 3, 2000.

27. For a detailed discussion of the connection between education and "brainpower" industries, see Paul Krugman, *Pop Internationalism* (Cambridge, MA: MIT Press, 1996); Michael E. Porter, *The Competitive Advantage of Nations* (New York: Free Press, 1990); Robert B. Reich, *The Work of Nations* (New York: Vintage Books, 1992); and Lester Thurow, *The Future of Capitalism* (New York: William Morrow, 1996).

28. Christina Passariello, "Why Italians Are Saying 'Arrivederci'," *Business Week,* December 15, 2003, p. 16.

29. Iain McDonald, "Australian Study Finds Worker Brain Gain, Not Drain," *Wall Street Journal* (**www.wsj.com**), July 17, 2001.

30. "Serbian Government Officials See Inflation at 40% in 2001," *Wall Street Journal* (**www.wsj.com**), July 2, 2001.

31. Raymond Scupin, *Cultural Anthropology: A Global Perspective,* 3rd ed. (Upper Saddle River, NJ: Prentice Hall, 1998), p. 47.

32. Florence Kluckhohn and F. L. Strodtbeck, *Variations in Value Orientations* (Evanston, IL: Harper & Row, 1961).

33. Geert Hofstede, "The Cultural Relativity of Organizational Practices and Theories," *Journal of International Business Studies,* Fall 1983, pp. 75–89.

34. Hofstede's study, from which his four dimensions were developed, has been criticized on a number of grounds. First, it suffers from a "Western" bias in design and analysis, querying employees in just one firm in one industry. Second, it treats culture as "national" only and, therefore, ignores subcultures. Finally, it now appears old—it was conducted in the 1960s and 1970s. See R. Mead, *International Management: Cross-Cultural Dimensions* (Oxford: Basil Blackwell, 1994), pp. 73–75.

35. Manjeet Kripalani, "A Corporate Pilgrimage to the Taj," *Business Week,* European edition, June 11, 2001, p. 62.

36. Gerry Khermouch, "An Almost-Invisible $1 Trillion Market," *Business Week,* European edition, June 18, 2001, p. 80.

37. As reported in "Why Americans Work So Hard," *Business Week,* European edition, June 11, 2001, p. 14.

Chapter 3

1. "Yahoo China Launches Chinese Search Engine," *Wall Street Journal* (**www.wsj.com**), June 22, 2004; "Geography and the Net," *The Economist,* August 11, 2001, pp. 18–20; Chen May Yee, "Big Internet Companies Often Censor Their Asian Sites to Please Local Officials," *Wall Street Journal* (**www.wsj.com**), July 9, 2001; Tim Phillips, "Law & Disorder," *Business 2.0,* U.K. edition, May 2001, pp. 90–95; Yahoo!, Inc. Web site (**www.yahoo.com**), select reports.

2. Chen May Yee, "Big Internet Companies Often Censor Their Asian Sites to Please Local Officials," *Wall Street Journal* (**www.wsj.com**), July 9, 2001.

3. Tim Phillips, "Law & Disorder," *Business 2.0,* U.K. edition, May 2001, pp. 90–95.

4. Jeff Fischer, "The Global Ballot Box," *Foreign Policy,* May–June, 2001, p. 24; Richard S. Dunham, et al., "Does Your Vote Matter?," *Business Week,* Special Report, June 14, 2004, pp. 60–75.

5. Geri Smith, "Democracy on the Ropes," *Business Week,* May 17, 2004, p. 54; "The Stubborn Survival of Frustrated Democrats," *The Economist,* November 1, 2003, pp. 53–54.

6. John Pomfret, "Rewriting Marx: China Allows Capitalists in on the Party," *International Herald Tribune,* July 2, 2001, p. 1.

7. Dexter Roberts, "In Rural China, Baby Steps toward Democracy," *Business Week,* European edition, March 19, 2001, p. 32.

8. "S. Korea to Slap Antidumping Duties on Japan Steel," *Wall Street Journal* (**www.wsj. com**), July 1, 2004.

9. Anthony Bianco, "Exxon Unleashed," *Business Week,* European edition, April 9, 2001, pp. 86–94.

10. "Indonesia's Island Fever," *Newsweek,* International edition, March 12, 2001, pp. 20–22.

11. Pete Engardio, "A New World," *Business Week,* European edition, October 8, 2001, pp. 18–19.

12. Suzanne Timmons, "Doing Business among the Body Snatchers," *Business Week* (**www.businessweek.com**), July 31, 2000.

13. "Taiwan Business Welcomes China Shift," *International Herald Tribune,* August 28, 2001, p. 13; Dexter Roberts, Bruce Einhorn, and Alysha Webb, "Taiwan & China," *Business Week,* European edition, June 11, 2001, pp. 46–50.

14. Shell company Web site (**www.shell.com**).

15. Ray August, *International Business Law: Text, Cases, and Readings* (Upper Saddle River, NJ: Prentice Hall, 1993), p. 51.

16. *First Annual BSA and IDC Global Software Piracy Study* (International Planning and Research Corporation, July 2004), Business Software Alliance Web site (**www.bsa.org**).

17. "BSA Initiates Legal Proceedings against 7 Irish Companies," Business Software Alliance Web site (**www.bsa.org**), August 2, 2001.

18. "Recording Companies Urge Vietnam Government to Fight Piracy," *Wall Street Journal* (**www.wsj.com**), July 18, 2001.

19. "China Plans Anti-Piracy Seals to Combat Counterfeiting," *Wall Street Journal* (**www.wsj.com**), February 10, 2004.

20. "The Patent Debate," *Business 2.0,* U.K. edition, May 2001, pp. 96–99.

21. Theodore Hong, "Birthday Song Blues," *International Commentary, Wall Street Journal* (**www.wsj.com**), August 21, 2001.

22. Tom Spring "Napster Fans Find Lively Alternative," CNN Web site (**www.cnn.com**), July 16, 2001; "Report: Napster Users Lose That Sharing Feeling," CNN Web site (**www.cnn.com**), June 28, 2001.

23. Michael Elliott, "How Jack Fell Down," *Time,* International edition, July 16, 2001, pp. 16–20.

24. "Abuse in Nike Factories in Vietnam," *Reuters* (**www.reuters.com**), March 28, 1997.

25. John R. Emshwiller and Rebecca Smith, "Minutes from a 1997 Meeting Reveal Enron Brass Were in Partnership Loop," *Wall Street Journal* (**www.wsj.com**), February 1, 2002.

26. David Fairlamb, "Aftershocks in Europe," *Business Week,* European edition, December 17, 2001, pp. 38–39.

27. Peter Elkind and Bethany McLean, "Ken Lay Flunks Ignorance Test," *Fortune,* July 26, 2004, p. 28.

28. Levi-Strauss Web site (**www.levistrauss.com**).

29. Starbucks Web site (**www.starbucks.com**); TransFair USA Web site (**www.transfair.org**).

30. "Rockin' All Over the World: Economic Potential of Music for LDCs," United Nations Conference on Trade and Development Web site (**www.unctad.org**), May 16, 2001.

31. Heather Green, "The Underground Internet," *Business Week,* (**www.businessweek.com**), September 15, 2003.

Chapter 4

1. Manjeet Kripalani and Pete Engardio, "The Rise of India," *Business Week,* December 8, 2003, pp. 66–76; Manjeet Kripalani and Bruce Einhorn, "Global Designs for India's Tech King," *Business Week,* October 13, 2003, pp. 56–58; Yasheng Huang and Tarun Khanna, "Can India Overtake China?," *Foreign Policy,* July/August 2003, pp. 74–81.

2. Amabelle Layug, "N. Korean Harvest Cannot Avert Food Crisis: UN," CNN Web site (**www.cnn.com**), October 29, 2001.

3. Moon Ihlwan, "North Korea: Open for Business—A bit," *Business Week* (**www.businessweek.com**), July 26, 2004.

4. "Ideological Gymnastics," *The Economist* (**www.economist.com**), March 11, 2004.

5. "Taiwan Drops China Trade Ban," CNN Web site (**www.cnn.com**), November 17, 2001.

6. "Taiwan Joins China in WTO," CNN Web site (**www.cnn.com**), November 11, 2001.

7. Panos Mourdoukoutas, "China's Challenge," *Wall Street Journal* (**www.wsj.com**), February 16, 2004.

8. "Economic and Financial Indicators," *The Economist,* July 17, 2004, p. 96.

9. Craig R. Whitney, "French Jobless Find the World Is Harsher," *New York Times,* March 19, 1998, pp. A1, A6.

10. Carol Matlack, "Time to Tame This Electrical Storm," *Business Week* (**www.businessweek.com**), June 21, 2004.

11. "FTC Settlement Preserves Competition in Global Markets for Rock Processing Equipment," Press Release, Federal Trade Commission (**www.ftc.gov**), September 7, 2001.

12. Gerald P. O'Driscoll, Kim R. Holmes, and Melanie Kirkpatrick, "Executive Summary," *2001 Index of Economic Freedom* (Washington, DC: The Heritage Foundation, 2001) (**www.heritage.org**).

13. "In The Shadows," *The Economist* (**www.economist.com**), June 17, 2004.

14. *World Development Indicators 2001* (Washington, DC: World Bank, 2001) (**www.worldbank.org**).

15. Daniel S. Levine, "Got a Spare Destroyer Lying Around? Make a Trade: Embracing Countertrade as a Viable Option," *World Trade,* June 1997, pp. 34–35.

16. "Central Russian Teachers to Get Paid in Vodka." CNN Web site (**www.cnn.com**).

17. Clay Chandler, "China Deluxe," *Fortune,* July 26, 2004, pp. 148–156.

18. Stephen Parker, Gavin Tritt, and Wing Thye Woo, "Some Lessons Learned from the Comparison of Transitions in Asia and Eastern Europe," in: Wing Thye Woo, Stephen Parker, and Jeffrey D. Sachs, eds., *Economies in Transition: Comparing Asia and Europe* (Cambridge, MA: MIT Press, 1997), pp. 3–5; *World Development Report 1996,* (Washington, DC: World Bank, 1996), p. 2.

19. Monika Mudranincová, and Klára Smolová, "Czech Managers Go Global," *The Prague Tribune* (**www.prague-tribune.cz**), November 2001.

20. Monika Mudranincová, and Klára Smolová, "Vanda Wolfová: Right Place, Right Time," *The Prague Tribune* (**www.prague-tribune.cz**), November 2001.

21. Joe Cook, "Worlds Apart?" *Business Central Europe,* May 1997, p. 48.

22. "Watch Your Back," *The Economist: A Survey of Russia,* May 22, 2004, pp. 11–12.

23. Jason Bush, Ben Aris, and Vitaly Sych, "Resurrection," *A Survey of Russia and the CIS, Business Central Europe,* April 2001, pp. 53–61.

24. "Taming The Robber Barons," *A Survey of Russia, The Economist,* May 22, 2004, pp. 5–6.

25. Manjeet Kripalani and Bruce Einhorn, "Global Designs for India's Tech King," *Business Week,* October 13, 2003, pp. 56–58.

26. Yasheng Huang and Tarun Khanna, "Can India Overtake China?," *Foreign Policy,* July/August 2003, pp. 74–81.

27. Manjeet Kripalani and Pete Engardio, "The Rise of India," *Business Week,* December 8, 2003, pp. 66–76.

28. David Fairlamb and Andy Reinhardt, "Productivity Paralysis," *Business Week,* August 2, 2004, pp. 54–56.

Chapter 5

1. *International Trade Statistics 2003* (Geneva, Switzerland: World Trade Organization, November 2003) (**www.wto.org**), Overview, pp. 1–2; Rich Miller and Pete Engardio, "Is The Job Drain China's Fault?," *Business Week* (**www.businessweek.com**), October 13, 2003; Anthony Bianco and Wendy Zellner, "Is Wal-Mart Too Powerful?," *Business Week,* October 6, 2003, pp. 100–110.

2. "Getting on the Fast Track: Small Business and International Trade," Small Business Survival Committee Web site (**www.sbsc.org**).

3. Karen Kerrigan, "Presidential 'Trade Promotion Authority' Good for Small Business," Small Business Survival Committee Web site (**www.sbsc.org**), June 11, 2001.

4. "Merchant Fleets," *The Economist,* February 10, 2001, p. 120.

5. Geri Smith, "Is the Magic Fading?" *Business Week,* August 6, 2001, pp. 30–32.

6. Adam Smith, *The Wealth of Nations* (Chicago: University of Chicago Press, 1976).

7. David Ricardo, *The Principles of Political Economy and Taxation,* first published in 1817.

8. Paul R. Krugman and Maurice Obstfeld, *International Economics: Theory and Policy* (Reading, MA: Addison-Wesley, 1997), pp. 32–34.

9. Bertil Ohlin, *Interregional and International Trade* (Cambridge, MA: Harvard University Press, 1933).

10. Wassily Leontief, "Domestic Production and Foreign Trade: The American Capital Position Re-Examined," *Economia Internationale,* February, 1954, pp. 3–32.

11. Raymond Vernon and Louis T. Wells, Jr., *Economic Environment of International Business,* 7th ed. (Upper Saddle River, NJ: Prentice Hall, 1991).

12. William Greider, *One World, Ready or Not: The Manic Logic of Global Capitalism* (New York: Simon & Schuster, 1997), p. 15.

13. Gary A. Knight and S. Tamer Cavusgil, "The Global Firm: A Challenge to Traditional Internationalization Theory." *Advances in International Marketing 8*, pp. 11–26.

14. "Ingenico and Palm Plan to Develop Secure Infrastructure for Virtual Card Payment," Palm Press Release at Palm Web site (**www.palmos.com**), January 6, 2001; David Carnoy, "Teaming Up: Prospering from Alliances with Other Entrepreneurs," *Success,* April 1997, p. 20.

15. Elhanan Helpman and Paul Krugman, *Market Structure and Foreign Trade* (Cambridge, MA: MIT Press, 1985).

16. For a detailed discussion of the first-mover advantage and its process, see Alfred D. Chandler, *Scale and Scope* (New York: Free Press, 1990).

17. Michael E. Porter, *The Competitive Advantage of Nations* (New York: Free Press, 1990).

18. Michael E. Porter, "Clusters and the New Economics of Competition," *Harvard Business Review* (November–December 1998), pp. 77–90.

19. As reported in "India's Sluggish Privatization: Unproductive," *The Economist,* September 8, 2001, pp. 73–74.

Chapter 6

1. "Who's Afraid of AOL Time Warner?" *The Economist,* January 26, 2002, pp. 57–58; Tom Lowry, Catherine Yang, and Ronald Grover, "What the Shocker Means," *Business Week,* December 17, 2001, pp. 40–41; Time Warner Web site (**www.timewarner.com**), select reports.

2. "Guyanans Urged to Be 'Patriotic' and Spurn Imports," *World Trade,* January 1999, p. 20.

3. Dexter Roberts, "Will Kodak Get Lucky in Japan?" *Business Week,* July 28, 1997, p. 48.

4. "Technology Deals with China Harmed U.S. Security, House Committee Says," CNN Web site (**www.cnn.com**), December 30, 1998.

5. Brian Bremner, "Two Japans," *Business Week,* January 27, 1997, pp. 24–28.

6. "U.S. Congress Considers Stiff Restraints against Korea's Firms," *Business Korea,* December 1995–January 1996, p. 79.

7. Steven V. Brull and Catherine Keumhyun Lee, "Why Seoul Is Seething," *Business Week,* January 27, 1997, pp. 44–46.

8. Deborah Baldwin, "The Proof Will Be in the 'Europudding,'" *Los Angeles Times,* April 24, 1997, p. D4.

9. Gareth Porter, "Natural Resource Substitutes and International Policy: A Role for APEC," *Journal of Environment and Development,* September 1997, pp. 276–291.

10. Daniel S. Levine, "Ex-Im Bank Year in Review," *World Trade,* January 1999, p. 30.

11. Kenneth E. Grubbs, Jr., "The Opening of Japan," *World Trade,* June 1997, pp. 28–32.

12. Lily Tung, "Behind-the-Scenes Obstacles for Film-Makers," *Asian Business,* February 1996, p. 11.

13. Emily Thornton, "The Japan That Can Say No to Cold Pills," *Business Week,* May 19, 1997, p. 54.

14. "Saudi Arabia Simplifies Import Clearance," *World Trade,* January 1999, p. 24.

15. The facts in this discussion of the GATT and the WTO are drawn from the WTO Web site (**www.wto.org**).

16. "Unfair Protection," *The Economist,* November 7, 1998, p. 75–76.

17. "Globalization: Is It at Risk?" *The Economist,* February 2, 2002, pp. 61–63.

Chapter 7

1. William Boston and Paul Hofheinz, "Germany's Protection of VW May Hinder EU Takeover Law," *Wall Street Journal* (**www.wsj.com**), February 27, 2002; Volkswagen Web site (**www.vw.com**), select reports.

2. United Nations Conference on Trade and Development, *World Investment Report 2003* (New York: United Nations, 2003).

3. United Nations Conference on Trade and Development, *World Investment Report 2004* (New York: United Nations, 2004); United Nations Conference on Trade and Development, *World Investment Report 2003* (New York: United Nations, 2003).

4. "How to Merge: After the Deal," *The Economist,* January 9, 1999, pp. 21–23.

5. Janet Guyon, "Cellular Start-Up: Some Good Old Boys Make Lots of Money Phoning Up Tashkent," *Wall Street Journal,* June 21, 1996, p. A1.

6. This section draws heavily upon the data and analysis contained in: United Nations Conference on Trade and Development, *World Investment Report 2003* (New York: United Nations, 2003).

7. Raymond Vernon and Louis T. Wells, Jr., *Economic Environment of International Business,* 7th ed. (Upper Saddle River, NJ: Prentice Hall, 1991).

8. John H. Dunning, "Toward an Eclectic Theory of International Production," *Journal of International Business Studies,* Spring–Summer, 1980, pp. 9–31.

9. For an excellent discussion of the economic benefits particular geographic locations can provide, see Paul Krugman, "Increasing Returns and Economic Geography," *Journal of Political Economy,* June 1991, pp. 483–499.

10. Naomi Freundlich, "Finding a Cure in DNA?" *Business Week,* March 10, 1997, pp. 90–91.

11. Richard Florida, "The Globalization of R&D: Results of a Survey of Foreign-Affiliated R&D Laboratories in the USA," *Research Policy,* March 1997, pp. 85–103.

12. "China's Growing Pains," *The Economist,* August 21, 2004, pp. 11–12.

Chapter 8

1. "The Taskmaster of Nestle," *Business Week* (**www.businessweek.com**), June 11, 2001; Julie Forster and Becky Gaylord, "Can Kraft Be a Big Cheese Abroad?" *Business Week,* European edition, June 4, 2001, pp. 54–55; Nestle Web site (**www.nestle.com**), select reports.

2. Geri Smith et al., "Betting on Free Trade," *Business Week,* European edition, April 23, 2001, pp. 32–35.

3. Judith Warner, John Parry, and Stefan Theil, "A Race Won by the Swift and the Strong," *Newsweek,* Euroland Special Issue, Winter 1998, pp. 42–46.

4. Emeric Lepoutre, "Europe's Challenge to the U.S. in South America's Biggest Market," *Christian Science Monitor,* April 8, 1997, p. 19.

5. "NAFTA after Five: The Impact of The North American Free Trade Agreement on Australia's Trade and Investment," Australian Department of Foreign Affairs and Trade (**www.dfat.gov.au/geo/americas/nafta**), March 2000.

6. "USTR Documents Benefits of Trade for American Families," Office of the United States Trade Representative (**www.ustr.gov**), September 19, 2001.

7. "Doing Business in NAFTA Country," *Industrial Distribution* (Supplement), May 1995, pp. S10–S12.

8. Data obtained from United States–Mexico Chamber of Commerce Web site (**www.usmcoc.org**).

9. Data obtained from Industry of Canada Strategis Web site (**www.strategis.ic.gc.ca**).

10. "USTR Documents Benefits of Trade for American Families," Office of the United States Trade Representative (**www.ustr.gov**), September 19, 2001.

11. "NAFTA's Seven-Year Itch," Published by the AFL-CIO (**www.aflcio.org**).

12. Richard Bruner, "Delphi Gets into Gear Now for the Year 2000," *El Financiero,* International Edition, June 30–July 6, 1997, p. 16.

13. Geri Smith et al., "Betting on Free Trade."

14. Amy Guthrie, "IMF Advisor Fischer Sees One NAFTA Currency Eventually," *Wall Street Journal* (**www.wsj.com**), October 18, 2001.

15. Stephen Wisnefski, "Free Trade Push Offers Latin America a Glimmer of Hope," *Wall Street Journal* (**www.wsj.com**), October 9, 2001.

16. Ian Katz, "Is Europe Elbowing the U.S. Out of South America?" *Business Week,* August 4, 1997, p. 56.

17. "CARICOM Braves the New World," *Business Week,* Advertising Supplement, March 5, 2001.

18. "Small, Vulnerable—and Disunited," *The Economist,* August 11, 2001, pp. 44–45.

19. "Leaders Sign All-Americas Free Trade Agreement," *International Herald Tribune,* April 23, 2001, p. 3.

20. Campion Walsh, "USTR Zoellick: Free Trade More Important Than Ever," *Wall Street Journal* (**www.wsj.com**), September 24, 2001.

21. Geri Smith et al., "Betting on Free Trade."

22. "The Roots of Music Piracy," *World Trade,* December 1998, p. 12.

23. The European Union and the World (Brussels, Belgium: European Commission, December 2000), p. 7.

24. "Burma and Laos Admitted to ASEAN," *Wall Street Journal,* July 24, 1997, p. A1.

25. Don Kirk, "Next WTO Chief Sees Speedup on Asia Free-Trade Zone," *International Herald Tribune,* October 19, 2001, p. 15.

26. Julius Caesar Parrenas, "Theme for Shanghai: Stay on Track to Free and Open Trade,"

International Herald Tribune, October 19, 2001, p. 8.

Chapter 9

1. Leslie P. Norton, "Playing Games," *Wall Street Journal* (**www.wsj.com**), February 25, 2002; Nintendo Co., Ltd. 2003 Annual Report, Nintendo Web site (**www.nintendo.com**); Nintendo Web site (**www.nintendo.com**), select reports.
2. See Frank J. Fabozzi, Franco Modigliani, and Michael G. Ferri, *Foundations of Financial Markets and Institutions,* 2nd ed. (Upper Saddle River, NJ: Prentice Hall, 1998), p. 18.
3. See Alan C. Shapiro, *Foundations of Multinational Financial Management,* 3rd ed. (Upper Saddle River, NJ: Prentice Hall, 1998), pp. 424–425.
4. Paula Dwyer, Andrew Osterland, Kerry Capell, and Sharon Reier, "The 21st Century Stock Market," *Business Week,* August 10, 1998, pp. 66–72.
5. "Assessing the Damage," *Euromoney* (**www. euromoney.com**).
6. *Central Bank Survey of Foreign Exchange and Derivatives Market Activity,* 2001 (Basel, Switzerland: Bank for International Settlements, March 2002).
7. Chicago Board of Trade Web site (**www.cbt.com**).
8. Chicago Mercantile Exchange Web site (**www.cme.com**).
9. Philadelphia Stock Exchange Web site (**www.phlx.com**).

Chapter 10

1. "Saying Goodbye to the National Currencies," European Union Web site (**www.europa. eu.int**), February 28, 2002; "Europe's Big Idea," *The Economist,* January 5, 2002, p. 11; "Ring In the New," *The Economist,* January 5, 2002, pp. 22–24; David Fairlamb, "Ready, Set, Euros!," *Business Week,* July 2, 2001, pp. 48–50; Christopher Rhoads and Geoff Winestock, "The Euro: Cash in Hand," *Wall Street Journal* (**www.wsj.com**), September 10, 2001.
2. "Exporters in Germany: The Subtle Curse of a Cheap Mark," *The Economist,* August 16, 1997, pp. 50–51.
3. Keith Naughton, "Who's Afraid of the Dollar?" *Business Week,* February 24, 1997, pp. 34–36.
4. Joshua Levine and Graham Button, " 'A' Is for Arbitrage," *Forbes,* July 15, 1996, pp. 116–121.
5. "Food for Thought," *The Economist,* May 29, 2004, pp. 71–72; "The Big Mac Index," *The Economist* (**www.economist.com**), January 15, 2004; Big Mac Currencies," *The Economist,* April 21, 2001, p. 82.
6. Stanley Fischer, "The Asian Crisis and the Changing Role of the IMF," *Finance & Development,* June 1998, pp. 2–5.
7. Elizabeth Price, "IMF Says Bosnia Must Foster Private Sector as Aid Falls," *Wall Street Journal* (**www.wsj.com**), March 22, 2002.
8. "The Asian Crisis: Causes and Cures," Finance & Development, June 1998, pp. 18–21; "The Perils of Global Capital," *The Economist,* April 11, 1998, pp. 52–54.

9. Ariel Cohen, "Russia's Meltdown: An Anatomy of the IMF Failure," The Heritage Foundation (**www.heritage.org**), October 23, 1998.
10. "The Long Road Back," *The Economist,* Survey of Argentina, June 5, 2004; Pamela Druckerman, "IMF Returns to an Argentina with Economy Under Pressure," *Wall Street Journal* (**www.wsj.com**), April 2, 2002.
11. Pete Engardio, "Crisis of Faith for the Free Market," *Business Week,* October 19, 1998, pp. 38–39.
12. Steve Barth, "The New Asia?" *World Trade,* November 1998, pp. 38–42.

Chapter 11

1. Kerry Capell, "Don't Clip Ryanair's Wings," *Business Week* (**www.businessweek.com**), December 15, 2003; "The Ryanair Story," Ryanair Web site at (**www.ryanair.com**); Kerry Capell, et al., "Renegade Ryanair," *Business Week,* European edition, May 14, 2001, pp. 38–43; "Ryanair Takes on Lufthansa," CNN Web site (**www.cnn.com**), November 22, 2001; Kerry Capell, Carol Matlack, and Christine Tierney, "Day of the Discount Airlines," *Business Week* (**www.businessweek. com**), February 11, 2002.
2. Bausch & Lomb Web site (**www.bausch.com**).
3. Cadbury Schweppes 1996 Annual Report, London, England, p. 1.
4. Helen Deresky, *International Management: Managing Across Borders and Cultures* (New York: HarperCollins, 1997), p. 156.
5. Michael E. Porter, *On Competition* (Boston: Harvard Business School Press, 1998).
6. Sherrie E. Zhan, "Marketing Across Cultures: To Minimize Faux Pas, Don't Assume Anything," *World Trade,* February 1999, pp. 80–81.
7. Intel Web site (**www.intel.com**).
8. Cadbury Schweppes 1996 Annual Report, pp. 11, 19.
9. The discussion of these strategies is based on Michael E. Porter, *Competitive Strategy* (New York: Free Press, 1980), pp. 34–46.
10. Dave Barry, "Poopacino Pick-Me-Up Not So Swell after All," *Wisconsin State Journal,* November 9, 1997, p. 3G.
11. Bradley L. Kirkman and Debra L. Shapiro, "The Impact of Cultural Values on Employee Resistance to Teams," *Academy of Management Review,* 22, no. 3 (1997): 730–757.
12. Kirkman and Shapiro, "The Impact of Cultural Values on Employee Resistance to Teams."

Chapter 12

1. "Seeing The World on Ten Coffees A Day," *Fortune,* July 12, 2004, pp. 46–48; Cristine Whitehouse, "Whole Latte Skakin'," *Time,* European edition, April 9, 2001, p. 47; "Starbucks Sets Sights on Converting China to Coffee," CNN Web site (**www.cnn.com**); Starbucks Web site (**www.starbucks.com**), select reports.
2. Wendy Zellner, Louisa Shepard, Ian Katz, and David Lindorff, "Wal-Mart Spoken Here,"

Business Week (**www.businessweek.com**), June 23, 1997.
3. Jack Lyne, "Nokia Wirelessly Takes On the World," *Site Selection,* December 1997– January 1998, pp. 1124–1128.
4. Robert S. Greenberger, "Africa Ascendant: New Leaders Replace Yesteryears' 'Big Men,' and Tanzania Benefits," *Wall Street Journal,* December 10, 1996, pp. A1, A6.
5. Laurie Joan Aron, "Global Logistics Boosts Competitive Advantage," *Site Selection,* August 1997.
6. Johny K. Johansson, Ilkka A. Ronkainen, and Michael R. Czinkota, "Negative Country-of-Origin Effects: The Case of the New Russia," *Journal of International Business Studies,* 25:1, pp. 157–176.
7. Samantha Marshall, "Soap Smugglers Cleaning Up in Vietnam," *Wall Street Journal,* April 1, 1998, pp. B1, B15.
8. This discussion is based on S. Tamer Cavusgil, "Measuring the Potential of Emerging Markets: An Indexing Approach," *Business Horizons,* January–February 1997, pp. 87–91; "Market Potential Indicators for Emerging Markets," Michigan State University CIBER (**www.ciber.bus.msu.edu**).
9. *World Development Indicators 2004* (Washington, D.C.: World Bank, April 2004) (**www.worldbank.org**).
10. Information obtained from the ProChile Web site (**www.chileinfo.com**).
11. Tim Venable, "Searching the World for Facility Investments: U.S. States' Global Development Offices," *Site Selection,* December 1997–January 1998, p. 1122.

Chapter 13

1. Jacqueline Doherty, "Heroic Expectations," *Barron's Online* (**www.wsj.com**), December 1, 2003; Gene Marcial, "A Tinseltown Marvel," *Business Week* (**www.businessweek.com**), May 5, 2003; Marvel Web site (**www.marvel.com**), select press releases.
2. Franklin R. Root, *Entry Strategies for International Markets* (Lexington, MA: Lexington Books, 1987), p. 5.
3. Arthur Jones, "The 10 Steps of Global Trade," *World Trade,* Supplement, 1997.
4. Martyn Williams, "Fujitsu Wins Texas Instruments Japan Lawsuit," *Newsbytes News Network,* September 10, 1997.
5. "Philippines: Nippon Pigment Provides Compounding Technology," *Japan Chemical Week,* September 11, 1997.
6. Julie Bennett, "Europe Finally Right for U.S. Franchises," *Franchise Times,* 3, no. 9, p. 13.
7. David Ing, "Spain Proves Tough to Crack," *Hotel & Motel Management,* 212, no. 15, p. 8.
8. Laura Gatland, "Eastern Europe Eagerly Accepts U.S. Franchisors," *Franchise Times,* 3, no. 9, p. 17.
9. Frank H. Andorka, Jr., "Microtel Introduces New-Construction Plan," *Hotel & Motel Management,* 212, no. 13, p. 1.
10. Ian Jones, "She's Leaving Home . . . Bye-Bye," *World Trade,* May 1997, pp. 90–92.
11. "BAA Takes Majority Stake in Naples," *Airports International,* March 1997, p. 3.

12. "ABB Snatches Grid Management Contract from National Grid," *Modern Power Systems,* June 1997, p. 7.

13. "Power Plant Management Contract," *Power in Europe,* June 6, 1997, p. 30.

14. "$316m LNG Refining Deal," *Power in Asia,* April 7, 1997, p. 21.

15. "Projects," *Power in Europe,* August 29, 1997, pp. 25–26.

16. "Telecom Roundup—Ericsson Inks Turkish Contract," *Newsbytes News Network,* July 28, 1997.

17. This classification is made in Peter Buckley and Mark Casson, "A Theory of Cooperation in International Business," in Farok J. Contractor and Peter Lorange (eds.), *Cooperative Strategies in International Business* (Lexington, MA: Lexington Books, 1988) pp. 31–53.

18. Kathryn R. Harrigan, "Joint Ventures and Competitive Strategy," *Strategic Management Journal,* 9 (1988), pp. 141–158.

19. See, for example, Sanjeev Agarwal, "Socio-Cultural Distance and the Choice of Joint Ventures: A Contingency Perspective," *Journal of International Marketing,* 2, no. 2, 1994, pp. 63–80.

20. Brian Bremner et al., "Cozying Up to Keiretsu," *Business Week* (**www.businessweek. com**), July 22, 1996.

21. Brenton R. Schlender, "How Toshiba Makes Alliances Work," *Fortune,* October 4, 1993, pp. 116–118.

22. Geert Hofstede, *Cultures and Organizations: Software of the Mind* (New York: McGraw-Hill, 1997), p. 228.

23. This section is based in part on Franklin R. Root, *Entry Strategies for International Markets* (Lexington, MA: Lexington Books, 1987), pp. 8–21.

24. See, for example, Sanjit Sengupta and Monica Perry, "Some Antecedents of Global Strategic Alliances," *Journal of International Marketing,* 5, no. 1, 1997, pp. 31–50.

Chapter 14

1. "Skydiver in Record Channel Flight," BBC News (**www.bbc.co.uk**), July 31, 2003; Darek Klimczak, "As Ski Jumper Leaps to Stardom, Sponsors Win, Too," *Wall Street Journal Europe,* February 23–24, 2001, p. 23; Nicole St. Pierre, "Red Bulls' Energy Drink Claims May Be Hype—But Not Its Sales," *Business Week* (**www.businessweek.com**), June 30, 2000; Red Bull Web site (**www.redbull.com**), select reports.

2. Theodore Levitt, "The Globalization of Markets," *Harvard Business Review,* May–June 1983, pp. 92–102.

3. Susan Douglas and Yoram Wind, "The Myth of Globalization," *Columbia Journal of World Business,* Winter 1987, pp. 19–29.

4. Vern Terpstra, *International Dimensions of Marketing,* 3rd ed. (Belmont, CA: Wadsworth, 1993), p. 9.

5. Raju Narisetti, "Can Rubbermaid Crack Foreign Markets?" *Wall Street Journal,* June 20, 1996, p. B1.

6. Antony Thorncroft, "Do You Drink Lots?," *Financial Times* ('How To Spend It' Magazine Issue), October 18, 1997, pp. 24–32; Janis Robinson, *Financial Times,* September 27–28, 1997, p. 1.

7. Charles Bremner, "All Because the Belgians Do Not Like Milk Tray," *London Times,* October 24, 1997, p. 5.

8. Bill Spindle, "Are Sushi Sundaes Next? Tokyo Screams for Green-Tea Ice Cream," *Wall Street Journal,* August 27, 1997, p. B1.

9. David Leonhardt, "It Was a Hit in Buenos Aires—So Why Not Boise?" *Business Week,* September 7, 1998, pp. 56, 58.

10. Vanessa O'Connell, "Sir Thomas Takes His Leave as Lipton's Marketing Icon," *Wall Street Journal Europe,* May 22, 2001, p. 31.

11. NameLab, Inc. Web site (**www.namelab.com**).

12. This one-quarter-page apology appeared in *The Independent* (London), November 8, 1997.

13. Robin Young, "Cadbury Loses Swiss Chocolate Bar Wars," *Time,* October 30, 1997, p. 11.

14. Johny K. Johansson, Ilkka A. Ronkainen, and Michael R. Czinkota, "Negative Country-of-Origin Effects: The Case of the New Russia," *Journal of International Business Studies,* 25, no. 1 (1994): 157–176.

15. Julian Baum, "Riding High: A Taiwanese Bicycle Maker Races to Success in the West," *Far Eastern Economic Review* (**www.feer.com**), May 7, 1998.

16. Dan Atkinson, "Fakes the Real Thing on Hooky Street," *The Guardian* (London), Jobs and Money Supplement, October 25, 1997, p. 2.

17. Harry Maurer and Justin Keay, ". . . 'We Have Nowhere to Go but Up' . . . CD Pirates Are Raking It In," *Business Week* (**www.businessweek.com**), April 28, 1997.

18. William Echikson, "Finnish Cash Helps a Baltic Tiger . . . and Buys Some Useful Lessons, Too," *Business Week* (**www.business-week.com**), March 23, 1998.

19. Todd Zaun and Peter Wonacott, "Japan Motorcycle Firms Ask China to Stop Fakes," *Wall Street Journal Europe,* February 22, 2001, p. 28.

20. Pamela Yatsko, "Coke on Ice," *Far Eastern Economic Review,* February 27, 1997, p. 54; Alessandra Galloni, "Coca-Cola Tests the Waters with Localized Ads in Europe," *Wall Street Journal* (**www.wsj.com**), July 18, 2001.

21. See for example, Robert Hite and Cynthia Fraser, "International Advertising Strategies of Multinational Corporations," in Michael Czinkota and Ilkka Ronkainen, eds., *Readings in Global Marketing* (Fort Worth, TX: Dryden Press, 1995), pp. 206–218.

22. Ursula Gruber, "The Role of Multilingual Copy Adaptation in International Advertising," in Stanley Paliwoda and John Ryans, eds., *International Marketing Reader* (London: Routledge, 1995), pp. 202–213.

23. Alan Henry and Ewen MacAskill, "Analysis: Tobacco Sponsorship," *The Guardian* (London), November 6, 1997, p. 21.

24. John Helemann, "All Europeans Are Not Alike," *The New Yorker,* April 28–May 5, 1997, pp. 174–181.

25. This section draws on Warren J. Keegan, *Global Marketing Management,* 5th ed. (Upper Saddle River, NJ: Prentice Hall, 1995), pp. 489–494.

26. John Burnett and Sandra Moriarty, *Introduction to Marketing Communication: An Integrated Approach* (Upper Saddle River, NJ: Prentice Hall, 1998), p. 3.

27. Michael Horsham, "Is High Tech Making Way for an Earthy Orientalism in Japan? Or Is It Just a Case of Smart Marketing?" *The Guardian* (London), October 21, 1994, pp. 4–5.

28. This comparison is made in Tatsuo Ohbora, Andrew Parsons, and Hajo Riesenbeck, "Alternative Routes to Global Marketing," *McKinsey Quarterly,* 3 (1992): 52–74.

29. Kimberely A. Strassel, "Low-Tech, Windup Radio Makes Waves," *Wall Street Journal,* July 15, 1997, p. B1.

30. Jesse Pesta, "Soap Makers Battle It Out for Market Share in Nepal," *Wall Street Journal* (**www.wsj.com**), June 28, 2001.

31. Craig S. Smith, "In China, Some Distributors Have Really Cleaned Up with Amway," *Wall Street Journal,* August 4, 1997, p. B1.

32. "Laptops from Lapland," *The Economist,* September 6, 1997, pp. 67–68.

Chapter 15

1. "The 2004 Global 500," *Fortune,* July 26, 2004, pp. 159–186; Andy Reinhardt, "Eavesdropping at Europe's Wireless Bash," *Business Week* (**www.businessweek.com**), March 6, 2002; Jane Black, "Here Come the Souped-Up Cell Phones," *Business Week* (**www.businessweek. com**), February 15, 2002; Nokia Web site (**www.nokia.com**), various reports.

2. Robert B. Reich, *The Work of Nations* (New York: Vintage Books, 1992), p. 112.

3. Saul Hansell, "Is This the Factory of the Future?," *New York Times,* July 26, 1998, Sec. 3, pp. 1, 12. See also, Scott Thurm, "Solectron Becomes a Force in 'Stealth Manufacturing,' " *Wall Street Journal,* August 18, 1998, p. B4.

4. "Eli Lilly Prescribes the Cure for Its Chemical Imbalances," *Wall Street Journal Europe,* December 28–29, 2001, p. 23.

5. Richard Tomlinson, "Why So Many Western Companies Are Coming Down with China Fatigue," *Fortune,* May 25, 1998, pp. 60–64.

6. Kenneth M. Morris, Alan M. Siegel, and Beverly Larson, *Guide to Understanding Money and Investing in Asia* (New York: Lightbulb Press, 1998), p. 37.

7. Sandy Serwer, "It's Big. It's German. It's SAP," *Fortune,* September 7, 1998, p. 191.

Chapter 16

1. "The 2004 Global 500," *Fortune,* July 26, 2004, pp. 159–186; Intel Web site (**www.intel.com**), select reports.

2. Barry Newman, "Expat Archipelago: The New Yank Abroad Is the 'Can-Do' Player in the Global Village," *Wall Street Journal,* December 12, 1995, p. A12.

‏3. Valeria Frazee, "An Unhappy Spouse Is the #1 Deal Breaker," *Global Workforce,* July 1998, p. 8.
4. Stephen Dolainski, "Are Expats Getting Lost in the Translation?" *Workforce,* February 1997, pp. 32–39.

5. Valeria Frazee, "Special Preparation When Relocating with Children," *Global Workforce,* January 1997, p. 10.
6. "Unhappy German Peace," *The Economist,* February 20, 1999, p. 62.

7. William Greider, *One World, Ready or Not: The Manic Logic of Global Capitalism* (New York: Simon & Schuster, 1997).‎

Sources

‏## Chapter 1

Breaking Views: *The E-Biz Surprise* Andy Reinhardt, "Europe Heads for The E-Mall," *Business Week,* July 12, 2004, p. 51; "E-commerce Takes Off," *The Economist* (www.economist.com), May 13, 2004; "Unlimited Opportunities?," *The Economist* (www.economist.com), May 13, 2004; Timothy Mullaney, "The E-Biz Surprise," *Business Week,* European edition, May 12, 2003, pp. 40–48.
Figure 1.1 Rebecca Buckman, "H-P Outsourcing: Beyond China," *Wall Street Journal,* (www.wsj. com), February 23, 2004.
Cartoon 1.1 Dave Carpenter cartoon in "Strategic Humor" section, *Harvard Business Review,* August 2003, p. 68.
Global Manager's Toolbox: *The Keys to Success* "The LRMing Curve," *World Trade,* (www. worldtrademag.com), June 28, 2001; John Davies, "That Elusive Success," *International Business,* October 1996, p. 35.
Figure 1.2 "Liberty's Great Advance," A Survey of Capitalism and Democracy, *The Economist,* June 28, 2003, pp. 4–7.
Figure 1.3 "Globalization's Top 20," *Foreign Policy,* March/April 2004, pp. 54–69.
Global Challenges: *Investing In Security Pays Dividends* "Be Prepared," *The Economist,* (www.economist.com), January 22, 2004; "Living Dangerously," *The Economist,* (www.economist. com), January 22, 2004; "Your Jitters Are Their Lifeblood," *Business Week,* (www.businessweek. com), April 14, 2003.
Figure 1.4 "Engineering on the Cheap," *Business Week,* October 6, 2003, p.13.
Figure 1.5 UNICEF (United Nations International Children's Emergency Fund).
Figure 1.6 "Liberty's Great Advance," A Survey of Capitalism and Democracy, *The Economist,* June 28, 2003, pp. 4–7.
Figure 1.7 "The Overall Picture," *Foreign Policy,* July/August 2001, p. 28.
Figure 1.8 Data obtained from "The 2003 Global 500," *Fortune,* (www.fortune.com), July 21, 2003 issue; *World Development Indicators 2004* (Washington, D.C.: World Bank, April 2004), (www.worldbank.org).
Table 1.1 Data obtained from "The 2003 Global 500," *Fortune,* (www.fortune.com), July 21, 2003 issue.
Entrepreneur's Survival Kit: *Four Myths Keeping Small Businesses from Export Success* "Is Business Really Going International?," *Inc.,* The State of Small Business, 1997, p. 121.
Practicing International Management Case: *MTV: Going Global with a Local Beat* Marc Gunther, "MTV's Passage To India," *Fortune* (www.fortune.com), August 9, 2004; Kenny‎ ‏Santana, "MTV Goes to Asia," *Yale Center for the Study of Globalization,* (www.yaleglobal.yale.edu), August 12, 2003; Kerry Capell et al., "MTV's World," *Business Week,* February 18, 2002, pp. 81–84; "MTV: 20 Years of Entertainment Innovation," *CNN,* (www.cnn.com), August 2, 2001; "Doug Herzog, Dan Cortese on MTV's 20th," *CNN,* (www.cnn.com), August 2, 2001.

Chapter 2

Entrepreneur's Survival Kit: *Give Your Web Site A Local Feel* Theresa Forsman, "Patience Is an e-Virtue," *Business Week,* (www.businessweek. com), July 31, 2001; "Adapting Products and Services for Global e-Commerce," *World Trade,* (www.worldtrademag.com), December 20, 2000; Moira Allen, "Net the World," *Entrepreneur Magazine,* (www.entrepreneur.com), June 2000.
Global Manager's Toolbox: *A Globetrotter's Guide to Manners* Moira Allen "Talking Heads," *Entrepreneur Magazine,* (www.entrepreneur. com), January 2001; Moira Allen "Touchy-Feely," *Entrepreneur Magazine,* (www.entrepreneur. com), September 2000; Moira Allen "Czech List," *Entrepreneur Magazine,* (www.entrepreneur. com), July 2000; Tatiana D. Helenius, "Body Language Savvy," *CNN Web site,* (www.cnnfn. com), May 3, 2000.
Map 2.1 Mapping © Bartholomew, 1990. Extract taken from Plate 5 of *The Comprehensive Atlas of the World,* 8th ed. Reprinted with permission.
Global Challenges: *Speaking in Fewer Tongues* Clyde Haberman, "Watch Your Languages. They're Ancient," *New York Times,* (www.nytimes. com), February 24, 2004; Mauro E. Mujica, "English: Not America's Language?," *The Globalist,* (www.theglobalist.com), June 19, 2003; Steve Connor, "Speaking in Fewer Tongues," *The World in 2001* (London, The Economist Newspaper Limited, 2000), pp. 142–143; Anthony C. Woodbury, "What Is An Endangered Language?," Linguistic Society of America, (www.lsadc.org).
Figure 2.1 Louis E. Boone, David L. Kurtz, and Judy R. Block, *Contemporary Business Communication,* 2nd ed. (Upper Saddle River, NJ: Prentice Hall, 1997), p. 71.
Table 2.1 Adapted from *World Development Indicators 2004* (Washington, D.C.: World Bank, April 2004), (www.worldbank.org).
Breaking Views: *Crossing the Digital Divide* Manjeet Kripalani, "India: Bridging The Digital Divide," *Business Week,* June 28, 2004, pp. 60–62; "Beyond the Digital Divide," *The Economist Technology Quarterly,* March 13, 2004, p. 7; Jane Black, "Technology with Social Skills," *Business Week,* (www.businessweek.com), August 19,‎ ‏2003; Olga Kharif, "Plotting the War on Terror and Disease," *Business Week,* (www.businessweek. com), August 19, 2003; Amey Stone, "The Digital Divide That Wasn't," *Business Week,* (www. businessweek.com), August 19, 2003.
Figures 2.2 and 2.3 Geert Hofstede, "The Cultural Relativity of Organizational Practices and Theories," *Journal of International Business Studies,* Fall 1983, p. 82, 84.
Practicing International Management Case: *Modernization or Westernization? You Make The Call* Saritha Rai, "U.S. Payrolls Change Lives in Bangalore," *New York Times,* (www.nytimes. com), February 22, 2004; Joanna Slater, "For India's Youth, New Money Fuels A Revolution," *Wall Street Journal,* (www.wsj.com), January 27, 2004; Lara Sowinski, "Southeast Asia Reeling from a One-Two Punch," *World Trade,* (www.worldtrademag.com), July 3, 2001.

Chapter 3

Map 3.1 Data obtained from *Freedom in The World,* 2004 (New York: Freedom House, 2004), (www.freedomhouse.org).
Global Challenges: *From Civil War to Civil Society* "Putting the World to Rights," *The Economist,* (www.economist.com), June 3, 2004; "The Price of Peace," *The Economist,* (www. economist.com), April 22, 2004; "The Global Menace of Local Strife," *The Economist,* (www.economist.com), May 22, 2003; Paul Collier and Anke Hoeffler, *The Challenge of Reducing the Global Incidence of Civil War* (Oxford: Copenhagen Consensus, March 2004); "Coping with Conflict," *The Economist,* (www.economist.com), January 15, 2004.
Map 3.2 Data obtained from *International Country Risk Guide* (East Syracuse, NY: PRS Group, 2004), (www.countrydata.com), March 2004.
Table 3.1 Adapted from *Corruption Perceptions Index 2003* (Paris: Transparency International, October 2003), Transparency International Web site, (www.transparency.org).
Breaking Views: *Governments Take The 'E-nitiative'* Efraim Turban, et al, *Electronic Commerce: A Managerial Perspective* (Upper Saddle River, NJ: Pearson Education, 2004), pp. 349–351; "No Thanks, We Prefer Shopping," *The Economist* (www.economist.com), January 2, 2003; Michael Shari, "Cutting Red Tape in Singapore," *Business Week* (www.businessweek. com), September 18, 2000.
Figure 3.1 Adapted from: *First Annual BSA and IDC Global Software Piracy Study* (International Planning and Research Corporation, July 2004), p. 3, Business Software Alliance Web site (www.bsa.org).‎

‏‎

Entrepreneur's Survival Kit: *The Long Arm of The Law* Federal Trade Commission Web site, (**www.ftc.gov**); U.S. Consumer Product Safety Commission Web site, (**www.cpsc.gov**); U.S. Patent and Trademark Office Web site, (**www.uspto.gov**); U.S. International Trade Commission Web site, (**www.usitc.gov**).
Figure 3.2 United Nations Department of Public Information, (**www.un.org**).
Practicing International Management Case: *Caveat Emptor—Who Said Latin Was Dead?* "Psst, Wanna Buy a Cheap Bracelet?," *The Economist* (**www.economist.com**), July 1, 2004; Nick Wingfield, "Tiffany Sues eBay for Allowing Counterfeit Merchandise on Site," *Wall Street Journal* (**www.wsj.com**), June 22, 2004; Frederik Balfour, "Armani Is Starting His Long March to China," *Wall Street Journal* (**www.wsj.com**), May 3, 2004; Cliff Edwards, "Why China Is Making The Valley Fret," *Business Week* (**www.businessweek.com**), March 29, 2004; Murray Hiebert, "Car-Parts Piracy Has Auto Makers Spinning Their Wheels," *Wall Street Journal* (**www.wsj. com**), February 26, 2004.

Chapter 4

Global Manager's Toolbox: *Guidelines for Good Guanxi* Steve Barth, "Bridge over Troubled (Cultural) Water," *World Trade*, August 1997, pp. 32–33; Michele Marchetti, "Selling in China? Go Slowly," *Sales & Marketing Management*, January 1997, pp. 35–36; Charlene Marmer Solomon, "The Big Question," *Global Workforce*, July 1997, pp. 10–16.
Map 4.1 Data obtained from *2004 Index of Economic Freedom*, The Heritage Foundation Web site at (**www.heritage.org**).
Figure 4.2 Gerald P. O'Driscoll, Kim R. Holmes, and Melanie Kirkpatrick, "Executive Summary," *2001 Index of Economic Freedom*, (Washington, DC: The Heritage Foundation, 2001), The Heritage Foundation Web site at (**www.heritage.org**).
Breaking Views: *IT Matters to Productivity* Robert D. Hof, *Business Week*, May 24, 2004, p. 24; Diana Farrell, "The Real New Economy," *Harvard Business Review*, October 2003, pp. 104–112; "Paradox Lost," *The Economist* (**www.economist. com**), September 11, 2003; "The New 'New Economy,'" *The Economist* (**www.economist. com**), September 11, 2003; "On The Shop Floor," *The Economist* (**www.economist.com**), September 11, 2003.
Map 4.2 Data obtained from World Bank, Country Classification section, (**www. worldbank.org**), July 2003.
Table 4.1 Data obtained from Organisation for Cooperation and Development (OECD), "Statistics" section, (**www.oecd.org**), February 7, 2004.
Table 4.2 Data obtained from *Human Development Report 2003*, (New Nork, NY: United Nations Development Programme, 2003), (**www.undp.org**), Table 1, pp. 237–240.
Global Challenges: *Public Health Goes Global* Donald G. McNeil Jr., "Herbal Drug Is Embraced in Treating Malaria," *New York Times* (**www.**

nytimes.com), May 10, 2004; "The Cost of AIDS," *The Economist*, May 22, 2004, pp. 68 & 71; Gavin Yamey, "Roll Back Malaria: A Failing Global Health Campaign," *British Medical Journal* (**www.bmj.com**), May 8, 2004, pp. 1086-1087; Anne Mills and Sam Shillcutt, *The Challenges of Communicable Disease* (Oxford: Copenhagen Consensus, February 2004); "Mothers Could Slash Malaria Deaths," BBC News (**www.bbc.co.uk**), August 10, 2000; Malaria Foundation International (**www.malaria.org**), various reports.
Practicing International Management Case: *Talkin' Bout A Revolution* "Cuba's Gulag," *The Economist* (**www.economist.com**), April 1, 2004; "Nickel, but No Dimes," *The Economist* (**www.economist.com**), September 18, 2003; "The Disaster Is Now 'Irrevocable,'" *The Economist* (**www.economist.com**), July 4, 2002; Sheridan Prasso, "Think Twice About Havana Holidays," *Business Week*, September 10, 2001; *Wall Street Journal Report* #701; Gail DeGeorge, "A Touch of Capitalism," *Business Week*, March 17, 1997, pp. 50, 52; William C. Symonds and Gail DeGeorge, "Castro's Capitalist," *Business Week*, March 17, 1997, pp. 48–49.

Chapter 5

Map 5.1 *World Development Indicators 2004* (Washington, D.C.: World Bank, April 2004), (**www.worldbank.org**).
Table 5.1 *International Trade Statistics 2003* (Geneva: World Trade Organization, November 2002), Tables I.5 & I.7, (**www.wto.org**).
Figure 5.1 Adapted from "Merchant Fleets," *The Economist*, February 10, 2001, p. 120.
Table 5.2 *International Trade Statistics 2003*, (Geneva: World Trade Organization, November 2002), (**www.wto.org**), Table III.3.
Global Manager's Toolbox: *Building Good Relations in the Pacific Rim* Bradford W. Ketchum, Jr., "Five Rules for Building Good Relations in the 'Rim' and Beyond," *Inc.*, [Advertising Supplement], May 20, 1997.
Figure 5.5 Raymond Vernon and Louis T. Wells, Jr., *The Economic Environment of International Business*, 5e (Upper Saddle River, NJ: Prentice Hall, 1991), p. 85.
Entrepreneur's Survival Kit: *Five Common Fulfillment Mistakes* Adapted from "Five Common Fulfillment Mistakes," *World Trade*, Global Online supplement, (**www. worldtrademag.com**), February 27, 2001.
Figure 5.6 Michael E. Porter, "The Competitive Advantage of Nations," *Harvard Business Review* (March-April 1990), p. 77.
Map 5.2 *Harvard Business Review* (November-December 1998), p. 82.
Practicing International Management Case: *DHL Worldwide Express: First in Asia and the World* "The New DHL Makes U.S. Debut," DHL Web site, (**www.dhl.com**), Press release, February 16, 2004; "DHL Earns Gold Medal as Third Party Logistics Provider for Second Year in Quest for Quality Survey," DHL Web site, (**www.dhl.com**), Press release, October 2, 2001; Josephine Bow, "The Fast-Paced World of

Asian Express," *Distribution* (February 1996), pp. 44–47.

Chapter 6

Entrepreneur's Survival Kit: *Ex-Im Bank: Experts in Export Financing* Export-Import Bank of the United States Web site (**www.exim.gov**).
Global Manager's Toolbox: *Surfing the Regulatory Seas* Eric J. Adams, "More Web Galore: There's No End to Trade-Dedicated Web Sites," *World Trade*, August 1997, pp. 40–42; Adams, "Navigating the Regulatory Seas," *World Trade*, September 1996, pp. 44–46.
Figure 6.1 World Trade Organization Web site (**www.wto.org**).
Table 6.2 "About the WTO," World Trade Organization Web site (**www.wto.org**).
Practicing International Management Case: *Unfair Protection or Valid Defense?* "Shrimp Wars," *The Economist* (**www.economist.com**), July 8, 2004; "China to Begin Probe of Synthetic Rubber Imports," *Wall Street Journal Online* (**www.wsj. com**), March 19, 2002; Neil King, Jr. and Geoff Winestock, "Plan to Rescue U.S. Steel Industry Draws the Ire of Critics Abroad," *Wall Street Journal Online* (**www.wsj.com**), March 7, 2002.

Chapter 7

Figure 7.1 *World Investment Report 2003, FDI Policies for Development: National and International Perspectives* (Geneva, Switzerland: UNCTAD, 2003), Chapter 1, Box figure I.2.1, p. 16.
Figure 7.2 *World Investment Report 2003, FDI Policies for Development: National and International Perspectives* (Geneva, Switzerland: UNCTAD, 2003), Chapter 1, Box figure I.2.2, p. 16.
Entrepreneur's Survival Kit: *Cowboy Candy Rides into Manchuria* Adapted from Marcus W. Brauchli, "Global Investing: Pick An Instrument: Sweet Dreams," *Wall Street Journal*, June 27, 1996, R, 10:1.
Global Manager's Toolbox: *Investing Abroad? Be Prepared for Surprises* Adapted from Jim Schriner, "Be Prepared for Surprises," *Industry Week*, December 2, 1996, p. 22.
Table 7.1 *World Investment Report 2003, FDI Policies for Development: National and International Perspectives* (Geneva, Switzerland: UNCTAD, 2003), Overview, Table 5, p. 13.
Table 7.2 *Survey of Current Business, July 2001*, (Washington, D.C.: U.S. Department of Commerce, 2001), p. 47.
Practicing International Management Case: *Mercedes-Benz: Footloose in Tuscaloosa* Based in part on "Real People, Real Choices," #2, *Custom Videos for Marketing*, Part II. Robert Baxter, Mercedes-Benz of North America; Justin Martin, "Mercedes: Made in Alabama," *Fortune*, July 7, 1997, pp. 150–158; Bill Vlasic, "In Alabama, the Soul of a New Mercedes?," *Business Week*, March 31, 1997, pp. 70–71.

Chapter 8

Entrepreneur's Survival Kit: *Czech List* Adapted from Moira Allen, "Czech List: Doing Business with Eastern Europe," *Entrepreneur Magazine*, (**www.entrepreneur.com**), July 2000.

Business Case 8: *Tainted Trade: Increasing Imports Brings Increase in Illness* Janet Ginsburg, "Bio Invasion," *Business Week,* September 11, 2000, 70–78; Jeff Gerth and Tom Weiner, "Imports Swamp U.S. Food-Safety Efforts," *New York Times,* September 29, 1997, p. A1; Richard A. Ryan, "Mom Says NAFTA Is A Safety Issue," *Detroit News,* September 10, 1997, p. B3; Lawrence K. Altman, "153 Hepatitis Cases Are Traced to Frozen Imported Strawberries," *New York Times,* April 3, 1997, p. A1.

Chapter 9

Entrepreneur's Survival Kit: *Where Microcredit Is Due* Adapted from Skip Kaltenheuser, "Spearing Loan Sharks," *World Trade,* May 1997, pp. 32–34.
Tables 9.1 and 9.2 *Wall Street Journal,* (**www.wsj.com**), May 13, 2004.
Global Manager's Toolbox: *Five Strategies for More Effective Foreign Exchange Management* Adapted from David Spiselman, *Five Strategies for Saving Money and Improving Control over Foreign Exchange* (San Mateo, CA: Sonnet Financial Inc., 1995), pp. 8–10.
Practicing International Management Case: *Argentina: Back From The Abyss?* "Pickets and Police," *The Economist* (**www.economist.com**), July 1, 2004; Sonja Ryst, "Argentine Utilities Squeezed Amid Rate Fix, Peso Slide," *Wall Street Journal* (**www.wsj.com**), March 26, 2002; Pamela Druckerman, "Argentine Crisis Deepens As Peso Falls to New Lows," *Wall Street Journal* (**www.wsj.com**), March 26, 2002; Pamela Druckerman and Matt Moffett, "With IMF in Mind, Argentina Switches Dollar Debt to Pesos," *Wall Street Journal* (**www.wsj.com**), March 15, 2002; Bernard Wysocki Jr., "Like a Virus, Contagion Comes in Many Forms," *Wall Street Journal* (**www.wsj.com**), March 4, 2002; "A Decline Without Parallel," *The Economist,* March 2, 2002, pp. 27–29.

Chapter 10

Figure 10.1 "Exchange Rates of Major World Currencies," and **Figure 10.2** "Value of the U.S. Dollar over Time," *Economic Report of the President,* Table B110, multiple years.
Global Manager's Toolbox: *Exporting Against the Odds: Key Strategies for Success* Louis Uchitelle, "Reconsidering a Trade Equation," *New York Times,* October 31, 1997, pp. D1, D2.
Figure 10.3 "Big Mac Index," *The Economist* (**www.economist.com**), January 15, 2004.
Figure 10.4 "How Low Can They Go?," *World Economic Outlook* (Washington, DC: International Monetary Fund, multiple years).
Figure 10.5 "The Curse of Inflation," *World Economic Outlook* (Washington, DC: International Monetary Fund, multiple years).
Figure 10.6 Data obtained from *IMF Annual Report, 2001* (Washington, DC: International Monetary Fund, 2001), Table 6.5, p. 68.
Practicing International Management Case: *Banking On Forgiveness* "US, Europe Debating Grants Vs. Loans For Debt Relief," *Wall Street Journal* (**www.wsj.com**), March 19, 2002; Richard

W. Stevenson, "Global Banks Offer a First: Forgiveness on Some Debt," *New York Times,* March 12, 1997, p A5; "Debt Relief for Model Countries," *New York Times,* May 1, 1997, p. A26; World Bank, (**www.worldbank.org**), various reports on the HIPC Debt Initiative.

Chapter 11

Figure 11.2 Michael E. Porter, *On Competition* (Boston: Harvard Business School Press, 1998), p. 77.
Entrepreneur's Survival Kit: *Know Yourself, Know Your Product* Adapted from Davis P. Goodman, "The First Pillar: Assess Your Capabilities," *World Trade,* March 1999, pp. 48–53.
Figure 11.4 Michael E. Porter, *Competitive Strategy* (New York: Free Press, 1980), p. 39.
Global Manager's Toolbox: *Competing with Giants* Adapted from Niraj Dawar and Tony Frost, "Competing with Giants: Survival Strategies for Local Companies in Emerging Markets," *Harvard Business Review,* March–April 1999, pp. 119–129.
Practicing International Management Case: *The Global Strategy of IKEA* "IKEA To Spend GBP50M Extending UK Stores," *Wall Street Journal Online* (**www.wsj.com**), January 11, 2002; "IKEA To Expand In Southern Europe," *Wall Street Journal Online,* (**www.wsj.com**), December 18, 2001; Julia Flynn and Lori Bongiorno, "IKEA's New Game Plan," *Business Week,* October 6, 1997, pp. 99, 102; IKEA Web site (**www.ikea.com**), selected reports.

Chapter 12

Table 12.1 Adapted from Yasheng Huang and Tarun Khanna, "Can India Overtake China?" *Foreign Policy,* July/August 2003, pp. 74–81.
Map 12.1 *World Development Indicators 2004* (Washington, DC: World Bank, April 2004), (**www.worldbank.org**).
Figure 12.2 *Site Selection,* December 1997/ January 1998, p. 1122.
Figure 12.3 Graphic obtained from Market: Newsletters Company.
Practicing International Management Case: *Vietnam's Emerging Market Potential* "The Good Pupil," *The Economist* (**www.economist. com**), May 6, 2004; "Vietnam Buys Boeing As It Inks U.S. Trade Deal," *CNN* (**www.cnn.com**), December 11, 2001; Samantha Marshall, "Vietnam Pullout: This Time, Investors Pack Up Gear, Stymied by Bureaucracy, Lack of Reforms," *The Wall Street Journal,* June 30, 1998, p. A18.

Chapter 13

Figure 13.1 *International Trade Statistics 2003* (Geneva, Switzerland: World Trade Organization, November 2003), Table III.16, p. 50.
Entrepreneur's Survival Kit: *Global Collection Guidelines* Adapted from James Welsh, "Covering Your Bets on Credit and Collections," *World Trade,* February 1999, pp. 28–29.
Figure 13.5 Peter Buckley and Mark Casson, "A Theory of Cooperation in International Business," in Farok J. Contractor and Peter

Lorange (eds.), *Cooperative Strategies in International Business* (Lexington, MA: Lexington Books, 1988) pp. 31–53.
Global Manager's Toolbox: *Negotiating the Terms of Market Entry* Andrew C. Inkpen and Paul W. Beamish, "Knowledge, Bargaining Power, and the Instability of International Joint Ventures," *Academy of Management Review,* vol. 22, no. 1, pp. 177–202; Arvind V. Phatak and Mohammed M. Habib, "The Dynamics of International Business Negotiations," *Business Horizons,* May–June 1996, pp. 30–38; David K. Tse, June Francis, and Jan Walls, "Cultural Differences in Conducting Intra- and Inter-Cultural Negotiations: A Sino-Canadian Comparison," *Journal of International Business Studies,* vol. 25, no. 3, pp. 537–555.
Figure 13.6 Franklin R. Root, *Entry Strategies for International Markets* (Lexington, MA: Lexington Books, 1987), pp. 8–21.
Practicing International Management Case: *Telecom Ventures Unite the World* Barbara Martinez, "Sprint Names Its Long-distance Chief to Run Loss-Beset Global One Venture," *Wall Street Journal,* February 17, 1998, p. B20; Jennifer L. Schenker and James Pressley, "European Telecom Venture with Sprint Hasn't Become the Bully Some Feared," *Wall Street Journal,* December 23, 1997, p. A11; Alan Cane, "Unisource Partners to Strengthen Ties," *Financial Times,* June 4, 1997, p. 13; Gautam Naik, "Unisource Expected to Merge Operations," *Wall Street Journal,* June 4, 1997, p. B6.

Chapter 14

Global Manager's Toolbox: *Managing an International Sales Force* Adapted from Charlene Marmer Solomon, "Managing An Overseas Sales Force," *World Trade,* Global Sales and Technology Special Section, pp. S4–S6.
Figure 14.1 Adapted from Courtland L. Bovee, John V. Thill, George P. Dovel, and Marian Burk Wood, *Advertising Excellence* (New York, NY: McGraw-Hill, 1995), p. 14.
Practicing International Management Case: *Fair Game or Out-of-Bounds? You Decide* Ellen Neuborne, "For Kids on the Web, It's an Ad, Ad, Ad, Ad World," *Business Week,* (**www.businessweek.com**), August 13, 2001; Brandon Mitchener, "Banning Ads on Kids' TV," *Wall Street Journal Europe,* May 22, 2001, p. 25; James MacKinnon, "Psychologists Act against Ad Doctors," *Adbusters* Web site, (**www.adbusters.org**).

Chapter 15

Figure 15.1 Adapted from "Wages," *The Economist,* December 8, 2001, p. 106.
Global Manager's Toolbox: *Linking TQM and ISO 9000 Standards* Adapted from G.K. Kanji, *An Innovative Approach to Make ISO 9000 Standards More Effective.* *Total Quality Management,* February 1998, pp. 67–79.
Entrepreneur's Survival Kit: *Get Global Cash: Overseas Investors Await You* Adapted from Jenny C. McCune, "Get Global Cash," *Success,* December 1995, p. 16.

Practicing International Management Case:
Toyota's Strategy for Production Efficiency
"Q&A: Pushing Carmakers to Rev Up Factories,"
Business Week, (**www.businessweek.com**),
February 18, 2002; William Greider, *One World,
Ready or Not: The Manic Logic of Global
Capitalism,* (New York, NY: Simon & Schuster,
1997), Chapter 6 *"Jikoda"*; Micheline Maynard,
"Camry Assembly Line Delivers New Minivan,"
USA Today, August 11, 1997, p. 3B.

Chapter 16
Figure 16.1 Union Bank of Switzerland.
Entrepreneur's Survival Kit: *Growing Global*
Laurel Delaney, "Is It Time To Go Global?,"
Entrepreneur Magazine (**www.entrepreneur.com**),
April 04, 2001; Ysabel de la Rosa, "In Country,"
Entrepreneur Magazine (**www.entrepreneur.
com**), March 2001; Charlotte Mulhern, "Going
The Distance," *Entrepreneur Magazine* (**www.
entrepreneur.com**), May 1998.
Global Manager's Toolbox: *A Shocking Ordeal*
Adrian Furnham and Stephen Bochner, *Culture
Shock* (London: Methuen, 1986); Kalvero Oberg,
"Culture Shock: Adjustments to New Cultural
Environments," *Practical Anthropology,* July–August
1960, pp. 177–182; J.T. Gullahorn and J.E.
Gullahorn, "An Extension of the U-Curve
Hypothesis," *Journal of Social Sciences,* January
1963, pp. 34–47; David Stamps, "Welcome to
America: Watch out for Culture Shock," *Training,*
November 1996, pp. 22–30; John R. Engen,
"Coming Home," *Training,* March 1995, pp. 37–40;
Gary P. Ferraro, *The Cultural Dimensions of
International Business* (Upper Saddle River, NJ:
Prentice Hall, 1994), pp. 145–156. Box Figure from
Stephen P. Robbins, *Organizational Behavior:
Concept, Controversies, Applications,* 7th ed. (Upper
Saddle River, NJ: Prentice Hall, 1996), p. 60.
Figure 16.3 "Long Time No Work," *Wall Street
Journal Europe,* August 28, 2001, p. 15.
Practicing International Management Case:
*Expatriation or Discrimination? You Make The
Call* James Harding, "When Expats Should Pack
Their Bags," *Financial Times,* September 1, 1998,
p. 10; C.K. Prahalad and Kenneth Lieberthal, "The
End of Corporate Imperialism," *Harvard Business
Review,* July–August 1998 pp. 68–79.

Photo Credits

Chapter 1
Page 3 Brad Trent Photography
Page 10 Douglas Kirkland/Corbis/Bettmann
Page 19 Antoine Serra/In Visu/Corbis/Bettmann

Chapter 2
Page 49 AP Wide World Photos
Page 52 David Samuel Robbins/Corbis/
Bettmann
Page 57 Corbis/Bettmann/Getty Images, Inc.—
Agence France Presse
Page 65 Emmanuel Dunand/AFP/Getty Images,
Inc.—Agence France Presse

Chapter 3
Page 85 AP Wide World Photos
Page 91 Kaveh Kazemi
Page 100 AP Wide World Photos
Page 111 Paulo Fridman

Chapter 4
Page 121 AP Wide World Photos
Page 124 Yann Layma/Stone/Getty Images Inc.—
Stone Allstock
Page 128 Suzanne & Nick Geary/Stone/Getty
Images Inc.—Stone Allstock

Chapter 5
Page 151 Keith Dannemiller/ Corbis/Bettmann
Page 157 Keith Dannemiller/ Corbis/SABA Press
Photos, Inc.

Chapter 6
Page 177 Corbis/Bettmann
Page 179 Shaun Best/ Reuters/Corbis/Bettmann
Page 181 AP Wide World Photos
Page 189 Jeffrey Aaronson/Network Aspen

Chapter 7
Page 203 Susana Gonzalez/Getty Images, Inc—
Liaison
Page 211 Museum of Flight/Corbis/Bettmann

Chapter 8
Page 229 Barry Iverson/Getty Images
Page 240 Chamussy/SIPA Press

Chapter 9
Page 259 AP Wide World Photos
Page 261 AP Wide World Photos
Page 263 Tom Wagner/Corbis/SABA Press
Photos, Inc.
Page 269 AP Wide World Photos

Chapter 10
Page 287 AFP/Getty Images, Inc.—Agence
France Presse
Page 294 Tarik Tinazay/Getty Images, Inc.—
Agence France Presse
Page 301 AP Wide World Photos
Page 307 Youn-Kong/Getty Images, Inc.—
Agence France Presse

Chapter 11
Page 317 Steve Pyke Studio
Page 326 AP Wide World Photos

Chapter 12
Page 342 AP Wide World Photos
Page 348 Jagadeesh Nv/Reuters/Landov LLC

Chapter 13
Page 371 AP Wide World Photos
Page 377 AP Wide World Photos
Page 384 Pablo Corral/Corbis—NY
Page 386 Aral/ SIPA Press

Chapter 14
Page 401 Red Bull/Getty Images
Page 405 Aaron Goodman
Page 407 Pornchai Kittiwongsakul/Getty Images
Page 411 AP Wide World Photos

Chapter 15
Page 425 AP Wide World Photos
Page 432 Dan Cohen
Page 440 Dilip Mehta/Contact Press Images Inc.

Chapter 16
Page 447 AP Wide World Photos
Page 450 Dilip Mehta/Contact Press Images Inc.
Page 453 Pablo Bartholomew/Getty Images,
Inc—Liaison
Page 461 AP Wide World Photos

Glossary

absolute advantage Ability of a nation to produce a good more efficiently than any other nation.

ad valorem tariff Tariff levied as a percentage of the stated price of an imported product.

administrative delays Regulatory controls or bureaucratic rules designed to impair the rapid flow of imports into a country.

advance payment Export/import financing in which an importer pays an exporter for merchandise before it is shipped.

aesthetics What a culture considers to be in "good taste" in the arts, the imagery evoked by certain expressions, and the symbolism of certain colors.

agents Individuals or organizations that represent one or more indirect exporters in a target market.

American Depository Receipt (ADR) Certificate that trades in the United States and represents a specific number of shares in a non-U.S. company.

antidumping duty Additional tariff placed on an imported product that a nation believes is being dumped on its market.

antitrust (antimonopoly) laws Laws designed to prevent companies from fixing prices, sharing markets, and gaining unfair monopoly advantages.

arm's length price Free-market price that unrelated parties charge one another for a specific product.

attitudes Positive or negative evaluations, feelings, and tendencies that individuals harbor toward objects or concepts.

back-to-back loan Loan in which a parent company deposits money with a host-country bank, which then lends the money to a subsidiary located in the host country.

balance of payments A national accounting system that records all payments to entities in other countries and all receipts coming into the nation.

barter Exchange of goods or services directly for other goods or services without the use of money.

base currency In a quoted exchange rate, the currency that is to be purchased with another currency.

Berne Convention International treaty that protects copyrights.

bill of lading Contract between an exporter and a shipper that specifies merchandise destination and shipping costs.

body language Language communicated through unspoken cues, including hand gestures, facial expressions, physical greetings, eye contact, and the manipulation of personal space.

bond Debt instrument that specifies the timing of principal and interest payments.

born-global firm Company that takes a global perspective on its market and engages in international business from or near its inception.

brain drain Departure of highly educated people from one profession, geographic region, or nation to another.

brand name Name of one or more items in a product line that identifies the source or character of the items.

Bretton Woods Agreement Agreement (1944) among nations to create a new international monetary system based on the value of the U.S. dollar.

buyback Export of industrial equipment in return for products produced by that equipment.

capacity planning Process of assessing a company's ability to produce enough output to satisfy market demand.

capital account A national account that records transactions involving the purchase or sale of assets.

capital market System that allocates financial resources in the form of debt and equity according to their most efficient uses.

capital structure Mix of equity, debt, and internally generated funds used to finance a company's activities.

capitalism The belief that ownership of the means of production belongs in the hands of individuals and private businesses.

caste system System of social stratification in which people are born into a social ranking, or caste, with no opportunity for social mobility.

centrally planned economy Economic system in which a nation's land, factories, and other economic resources are owned by the government, which plans nearly all economic activity.

chains of command Lines of authority that run from top management to individual employees and specify internal reporting relationships.

civil law Legal system based on a detailed set of written rules and statutes that constitute a legal code.

class system System of social stratification in which personal ability and actions determine social status and mobility.

clearing Process of aggregating the currencies that one bank owes another and then carrying out the transaction.

climate Weather conditions of a geographic region.

combination strategy Strategy designed to mix growth, retrenchment, and stability strategies across a corporation's business units.

common law Legal system based on a country's legal history (tradition), past cases that have come before its courts (precedent), and the ways in which laws are applied in specific situations (usage).

common market Economic integration whereby countries remove all barriers to trade and the movement of labor and capital between themselves but erect a common trade policy against nonmembers.

communication System of conveying thoughts, feelings, knowledge, and information through speech, actions, and writing.

communism The belief that social and economic equality can be obtained only by establishing an all-powerful Communist Party and by granting the government ownership and control over all types of economic activity.

comparative advantage Inability of a nation to produce a good more efficiently than other nations, but an ability to produce that good more efficiently than it does any other good.

compound tariff Tariff levied on an imported product and calculated partly as a percentage of its stated price and partly as a specific fee for each unit.

confiscation Forced transfer of assets from a company to the government without compensation.

consumer panel Research in which people record in personal diaries, information on their attitudes, behaviors, or purchasing habits.

convertible (hard) currency Currency that trades freely in the foreign exchange market, with its price determined by the forces of supply and demand.

copyright Property right giving creators of original works the freedom to publish or dispose of them as they choose.

core competency Special ability of a company that competitors find extremely difficult or impossible to equal.

counterpurchase Sale of goods or services to a country by a company that promises to make a future purchase of a specific product from the country.

countertrade Practice of selling goods or services that are paid for, in whole or part, with other goods or services.

countervailing duty Additional tariff placed on an imported product that a nation believes is receiving an unfair subsidy.

cross licensing Practice by which companies use licensing agreements to exchange intangible property with one another.

cross rate Exchange rate calculated using two other exchange rates.

cross-functional team Team that is composed of employees who work at similar levels in different functional departments.

cultural diffusion Process whereby cultural traits spread from one culture to another.

cultural imperialism Replacement of one culture's traditions, folk heroes, and artifacts with substitutes from another.

cultural literacy Detailed knowledge about a culture that enables a person to function effectively within it.

cultural trait Anything that represents a culture's way of life, including gestures, material objects, traditions, and concepts.

culture Set of values, beliefs, rules, and institutions held by a specific group of people.

culture shock Psychological process affecting people living abroad that is characterized by homesickness, irritability, confusion, aggravation, and depression.

currency arbitrage Instantaneous purchase and sale of a currency in different markets for profit.

currency board Monetary regime that is based on an explicit commitment to exchange domestic currency for a specified foreign currency at a fixed exchange rate.

currency controls Restrictions on the convertibility of a currency into other currencies.

currency futures contract Contract requiring the exchange of a specific amount of currency on a specific date at a specific exchange rate, with all conditions fixed and not adjustable.

currency hedging Practice of insuring against potential losses that result from adverse changes in exchange rates.

currency option Right, or option, to exchange a specific amount of a currency on a specific date at a specific rate.

currency speculation Purchase or sale of a currency with the expectation that its value will change and generate a profit.

currency swap Simultaneous purchase and sale of foreign exchange for two different dates.

current account A national account that records transactions involving the import and export of goods and services, income receipts on assets abroad, and income payments on foreign assets inside the country.

current account deficit When a country imports more goods and services and pays more abroad than it exports and receives from abroad.

current account surplus When a country exports more goods and services and receives more income from abroad than it imports and pays abroad.

customs Habits or ways of behaving in specific circumstances that are passed down through generations in a culture.

customs union Economic integration whereby countries remove all barriers to trade between themselves but erect a common trade policy against nonmembers.

debt Loans in which the borrower promises to repay the borrowed amount (the principal) plus a predetermined rate of interest.

demand Quantity of a good or service that buyers are willing to purchase at a specific selling price.

democracy Political system in which government leaders are elected directly by the wide participation of the people or by their representatives.

derivative Financial instrument whose value derives from other commodities or financial instruments.

devaluation Intentional lowering of the value of a nation's currency.

developed country Country that is highly industrialized, highly efficient, and whose people enjoy a high quality of life.

developing country (also called *less-developed country*) Nation that has a poor infrastructure and extremely low personal incomes.

differentiation strategy Strategy in which a company designs its products to be perceived as unique by buyers throughout its industry.

direct exporting Practice by which a company sells its products directly to buyers in a target market.

distribution Planning, implementing, and controlling the physical flow of a product from its point of origin to its point of consumption.

documentary collection Export/import financing in which a bank acts as an intermediary without accepting financial risk.

draft (bill of exchange) Document ordering an importer to pay an exporter a specified sum of money at a specified time.

dual pricing Policy in which a product has a different selling price (typically higher) in export markets than it has in the home market.

dumping Practice of exporting a product at a price either lower than the price that the product normally commands in its domestic market or lower than the cost of production.

e-business (e-commerce) Purchase, sale, or exchange of goods and services, as well as servicing customers, collaboration with business partners, and transactions within a company via computer networks.

eclectic theory Theory stating that firms undertake foreign direct investment when the features of a particular location combine with ownership and internalization advantages to make a location appealing for investment.

economic development Measure for gauging the economic well-being of one nation's people as compared with that of another nation's people.

economic system Structure and processes that a country uses to allocate its resources and conduct its commercial activities.

economic transition Process by which a nation changes its fundamental economic organization and creates new free-market institutions.

economic union Economic integration whereby countries remove barriers to trade and the movement of labor and capital, erect a common trade policy against nonmembers, and coordinate their economic policies.

efficient market view View that prices of financial instruments reflect all publicly available information at any given time.

e-government Use of information technology and e-commerce techniques that allow citizens and businesses to access government information and obtain public services.

embargo Complete ban on trade (imports and exports) in one or more products with a particular country.

emerging markets Newly industrialized countries plus those with the potential to become newly industrialized.

entry mode Institutional arrangement by which a firm gets its products, technologies, human skills, or other resources into a market.

environmental scanning Ongoing process of gathering, analyzing, and dispensing information for tactical or strategic purposes.

equity Part ownership of a company in which the equity holder participates with other part owners in the company's financial gains and losses.

ethical behavior Personal behavior that is in accordance with rules or standards for right conduct or morality.

ethnocentric staffing Staffing policy in which individuals from the home country manage operations abroad.

ethnocentricity Belief that one's own ethnic group or culture is superior to that of others.

Eurobond Bond issued outside the country in whose currency it is denominated.

Eurocurrency market Market consisting of all the world's currencies (referred to as "Eurocurrency") that are banked outside their countries of origin.

European monetary union The European Union plan that established its own central bank and currency.

exchange rate Rate at which one currency is exchanged for another.

exchange-rate risk (foreign exchange risk) Risk of adverse changes in exchange rates.

exclusive channel Distribution channel in which a manufacturer grants the right to sell its product to only one or a limited number of resellers.

expatriates Citizens of one country who are living and working in another.

export management company (EMC) Company that exports products on behalf of indirect exporters.

export trading company (ETC) Company that provides services to indirect exporters in addition to activities related directly to clients' exporting activities.

exports All goods and services produced or based in one country that are sold abroad.

expropriation Forced transfer of assets from a company to the government with compensation.

facilities layout planning Deciding the spatial arrangement of production processes within production facilities.

facilities location planning Selecting the location for production facilities.

factor proportions theory Trade theory holding that countries produce and export goods that require resources (factors) that are abundant and import goods that require resources in short supply.

first-mover advantage Economic and strategic advantage gained by being the first company to enter an industry.

Fisher effect Principle that the nominal interest rate is the sum of the real interest rate and the expected rate of inflation over a specific period.

fixed (tangible) assets Company assets such as production facilities, inventory warehouses, retail outlets, and production and office equipment.

fixed exchange-rate system System in which the exchange rate for converting one currency into another is fixed by international agreement.

focus group Unstructured but in-depth interview of a small group of individuals (8 to 12 people) by a moderator to learn the group's attitudes about a company or its product.

focus strategy Strategy in which a company focuses on serving the needs of a narrowly defined market segment by being the low-cost leader, by differentiating its product, or both.

folk custom Behavior, often dating back several generations, that is practiced by a homogeneous group of people.

foreign bond Bond sold outside the borrower's country and denominated in the currency of the country in which it is sold.

Foreign Corrupt Practices Act 1977 statute forbidding U.S. companies from bribing government officials or political candidates in other nations.

foreign direct investment The purchase of physical assets or a significant amount of the ownership (stock) of a company in another country to gain a measure of management control.

foreign exchange market Market in which currencies are bought and sold and their prices determined.

foreign trade zone (FTZ) Designated geographic region in which merchandise is allowed to pass through with lower customs duties (taxes) and/or fewer customs procedures.

forward contract Contract that requires the exchange of an agreed-upon amount of a currency on an agreed-upon date at a specific exchange rate.

forward market Market for currency transactions at forward rates.

forward rate Exchange rate at which two parties agree to exchange currencies on a specified future date.

franchising Practice by which one company (the franchiser) supplies another (the franchisee) with intangible property and other assistance over an extended period.

free float system Exchange-rate system in which currencies float freely against one another, without governments intervening in currency markets.

free trade Pattern of imports and exports that would result in the absence of trade barriers.

free-trade area Economic integration whereby countries seek to remove all barriers to trade between themselves, but each country determines its own barriers against nonmembers.

freight forwarder Specialist in export-related activities such as customs clearing, tariff schedules, and shipping and insurance fees.

fundamental analysis Technique using statistical models based on fundamental economic indicators to forecast exchange rates.

fundamental disequilibrium Economic condition in which a trade deficit causes a permanent negative shift in a country's balance of payments.

GDP or GNP per capita Nation's GDP or GNP divided by its population.

General Agreement on Tariffs and Trade (GATT) Treaty designed to promote free trade by reducing both tariffs and nontariff barriers to international trade.

geocentric staffing Staffing policy in which the best-qualified individuals, regardless of nationality, manage operations abroad.

global matrix structure Organizational structure that splits the chain of command between product and area divisions.

global product structure Organizational structure that divides worldwide operations according to a company's product areas.

global strategy Offering the same products using the same marketing strategy in all national markets.

global team Team of top managers from both headquarters and international subsidiaries who meet to develop solutions to companywide problems.

globalization Trend toward greater economic, cultural, political, and technological interdependence among national institutions and economies.

gold standard International monetary system in which nations linked the value of their paper currencies to specific values of gold.

gross domestic product (GDP) Value of all goods and services produced by a country's domestic economy over a 1-year period.

gross national product (GNP) Value of all goods and services produced by a country during a 1-year period, including income generated by both domestic and international activities.

growth strategy Strategy designed to increase the scale (size of activities) or scope (kinds of activities) of a corporation's operations.

Hofstede framework Framework for studying cultural differences along four dimensions, such as individualism versus collectivism and equality versus inequality.

human development index (HDI) Measure of the extent to which a people's needs are satisfied and the degree to which these needs are addressed equally across a nation's entire population.

human resource management (HRM) Process of staffing a company and ensuring that employees are as productive as possible.

human resource planning Process of forecasting both a company's human resource needs and supply.

imports All goods and services brought into a country that are acquired from organizations located abroad.

income elasticity Sensitivity of demand for a product relative to changes in income.

indirect exporting Practice by which a company sells its products to intermediaries who resell to buyers in a target market.

industrial property Patents and trademarks.

inefficient market view View that prices of financial instruments do not reflect all publicly available information.

intellectual property Property that results from people's intellectual talent and abilities.

intensive channel Distribution channel in which a producer grants the right to sell its product to many resellers.

interbank interest rates Interest rates that the world's largest banks charge one another for loans.

interbank market Market in which the world's largest banks exchange currencies at spot and forward rates.

interest arbitrage Profit-motivated purchase and sale of interest-paying securities denominated in different currencies.

international area structure Organizational structure that organizes a company's entire global operations into countries or geographic regions.

international bond market Market consisting of all bonds sold by issuing companies, governments, or other organizations outside their own countries.

international business Any commercial transaction that crosses the borders of two or more nations.

international capital market Network of individuals, companies, financial institutions, and governments that invest and borrow across national boundaries.

international division structure Organizational structure that separates domestic from international business activities by creating a separate international division with its own manager.

international equity market Market consisting of all stocks bought and sold outside the issuer's home country.

international Fisher effect Principle that a difference in nominal interest rates supported by two countries' currencies will cause an equal but opposite change in their spot exchange rates.

International Monetary Fund (IMF) Agency created to regulate fixed exchange rates and enforce the rules of the international monetary system.

international monetary system Collection of agreements and institutions governing exchange rates.

international product life cycle theory Theory stating that a company will begin by exporting its product and later undertake foreign direct investment as a product moves through its life cycle.

international trade Purchase, sale, or exchange of goods and services across national borders.

Jamaica Agreement Agreement (1976) among IMF members to formalize the existing system of floating exchange rates as the new international monetary system.

joint venture Separate company that is created and jointly owned by two or more independent entities to achieve a common business objective.

just-in-time (JIT) manufacturing Production technique in which inventory is kept to a minimum and inputs to the production process arrive exactly when they are needed (or just in time).

Kluckhohn–Strodtbeck framework Framework for studying cultural differences along six dimensions, such as focus on past or future events and belief in individual or group responsibility for personal well-being.

labor–management relations Positive or negative condition of relations between a company's management and its workers.

law of one price Principle that an identical item must have an identical price in all countries when the price is expressed in a common currency.

legal system Set of laws and regulations, including the processes by which a country's laws are enacted and enforced and the ways in which its courts hold parties accountable for their actions.

letter of credit Export/import financing in which the importer's bank issues a document stating that the bank will pay the exporter when the exporter fulfills the terms of the document.

licensing Practice by which one company owning intangible property (the licensor) grants another firm (the licensee) the right to use that property for a specified period of time.

lingua franca Third or "link" language that is understood by two parties who speak different native languages.

liquidity Ease with which bondholders and shareholders may convert their investments into cash.

lobbying Policy of hiring people to represent a company's views on political matters.

local content requirements Laws stipulating that a specified amount of a good or service be supplied by producers in the domestic market.

location economies Economic benefits derived from locating production activities in optimal locations.

logistics Management of the physical flow of products from the point of origin as raw materials to end users as finished products.

low-cost leadership strategy Strategy in which a company exploits economies of scale to have the lowest cost structure of any competitor in its industry.

make-or-buy decision Deciding whether to make a component or to buy it from another company.

managed float system Exchange-rate system in which currencies float against one another, with governments intervening to stabilize their currencies at particular target exchange rates.

management contract Practice by which one company supplies another with managerial expertise for a specific period of time.

manners Appropriate ways of behaving, speaking, and dressing in a culture.

market economy Economic system in which the majority of a nation's land, factories, and other economic resources are privately owned, either by individuals or businesses.

market imperfections Theory stating that when an imperfection in the market makes a transaction less efficient than it could be, a company will undertake foreign direct investment to internalize the transaction and thereby remove the imperfection.

market power Theory stating that a firm tries to establish a dominant market presence in an industry by undertaking foreign direct investment.

market research Collection and analysis of information in order to assist managers in making informed decisions.

marketing communication Process of sending promotional messages about products to target markets.

material culture All the technology used in a culture to manufacture goods and provide services.

mercantilism Trade theory that nations should accumulate financial wealth, usually in the form of gold, by encouraging exports and discouraging imports.

mission statement Written statement of why a company exists and what it plans to accomplish.

mixed economy Economic system in which land, factories, and other economic resources are rather equally split between private and government ownership.

multinational (multidomestic) strategy Adapting products and their marketing strategies in each national market to suit local preferences.

multinational corporation (MNC) Business that has direct investments abroad in multiple countries.

national competitive advantage theory Trade theory holding that a nation's competitiveness in an industry depends on the capacity of the industry to innovate and upgrade.

nationalism Devotion of a people to their nation's interests and advancement.

nationalization Government takeover of an entire industry.

new trade theory Trade theory holding that (1) there are gains to be made from specialization and increasing economies of scale, (2) the companies first to market can create barriers to entry, and (3) government may play a role in assisting its home companies.

newly industrialized country (NIC) Country that has recently increased the portion of its national production and exports derived from industrial operations.

normal trade relations (formerly "most favored nation status") Requirement that WTO members extend the same favorable terms of trade to all members that they extend to any single member.

offset Agreement that a company will offset a hard-currency sale to a nation by making a hard-currency purchase of an unspecified product from that nation in the future.

offshore financial center Country or territory whose financial sector features very few regulations and few, if any, taxes.

open account Export/import financing in which an exporter ships merchandise and later bills the importer for its value.

organizational structure Way in which a company divides its activities among separate units and coordinates activities between those units.

outsourcing Practice of buying from another company a good or service that is not central to a company's competitive advantage.

over-the-counter (OTC) market Exchange consisting of a global computer network of foreign exchange traders and other market participants.

patent Property right granted to the inventor of a product or process that excludes others from making, using, or selling the invention.

planning Process of identifying and selecting an organization's objectives and deciding how the organization will achieve those objectives.

political risk Likelihood that a government or society will undergo political changes that negatively affect local business activity.

political system Structures, processes, and activities by which a nation governs itself.

political union Economic and political integration whereby countries coordinate aspects of their economic and political systems.

polycentric staffing Staffing policy in which individuals from the host country manage operations abroad.

popular custom Behavior shared by a heterogeneous group or by several groups.

portfolio investment Investment that does not involve obtaining a degree of control in a company.

price controls Upper or lower limits placed on the prices of products sold within a country.

primary market research Process of collecting and analyzing original data and applying the results to current research needs.

private sector Segment of the economic environment comprised of independently owned firms that exist to make a profit.

privatization Policy of selling government-owned economic resources to private companies and individuals.

process planning Deciding the process that a company will use to create its product.

product liability Responsibility of manufacturers, sellers, and others for damage, injury, or death caused by defective products.

promotion mix Efforts by a company to reach distribution channels and target customers through communications such as personal selling, advertising, public relations, and direct marketing.

property rights Legal rights to resources and any income they generate.

pull strategy Promotional strategy designed to create buyer demand that will encourage channel members to stock a company's product.

purchasing power Value of goods and services that can be purchased with one unit of a country's currency.

purchasing power parity (PPP) Relative ability of two countries' currencies to buy the same "basket" of goods in those two countries.

push strategy Promotional strategy designed to pressure channel members to carry a product and promote it to final users of the product.

quota Restriction on the amount (measured in units or weight) of a good that can enter or leave a country during a certain period of time.

quoted currency In a quoted exchange rate, the currency with which another currency is to be purchased.

rationalized production System of production in which each of a product's components are produced where the cost of producing that component is lowest.

recruitment Process of identifying and attracting a qualified pool of applicants for vacant positions.

regional economic integration (regionalism) Process whereby countries in a geographic region cooperate with one another to reduce or eliminate barriers to the international flow of products, people, or capital.

representative democracy Democracy in which citizens elect individuals from their groups to represent their political needs and views.

retrenchment strategy Strategy designed to reduce the scale or scope of a corporation's businesses.

revaluation Intentional raising of the value of a nation's currency.

revenue Monies earned from the sale of goods and services.

reverse culture shock Psychological process of readapting to one's home culture.

secondary market research Process of obtaining information that already exists within the company or that can be obtained from outside sources.

secular totalitarianism Political system in which leaders rely on military and bureaucratic power.

securities exchange Exchange specializing in currency futures and options transactions.

securitization Unbundling and repackaging of hard-to-trade financial assets into more liquid, negotiable, and marketable financial instruments (or securities).

selection Process of screening and hiring the best-qualified applicants with the greatest performance potential.

self-managed team Team in which the employees from a single department take on the responsibilities of their former supervisors.

Smithsonian Agreement Agreement (1971) among IMF members to restructure and strengthen the international monetary system created at Bretton Woods.

social group Collection of two or more people who identify and interact with one another.

social mobility Ease with which individuals can move up or down a culture's "social ladder."

social responsibility Practice of companies going beyond legal obligations to actively balance commitments to investors, customers, other companies, and communities.

social stratification Process of ranking people into social layers or classes.

social structure A culture's fundamental organization, including its groups and institutions, its system of social positions and their relationships, and the process by which its resources are distributed.

socialism The belief that social and economic equality is obtained through government ownership and regulation of the means of production.

special drawing right (SDR) IMF asset whose value is based on a "weighted basket" of the currencies of five industrialized countries.

specific tariff Tariff levied as a specific fee for each unit (measured by number, weight, etc.) of an imported product.

spot market Market for currency transactions at spot rates.

spot rate Exchange rate requiring delivery of the traded currency within 2 business days.

stability strategy Strategy designed to guard against change and used by corporations to avoid either growth or retrenchment.

staffing policy The customary means by which a company staffs its offices.

stakeholders All parties, ranging from suppliers and employees to stockholders and consumers, who are affected by a company's activities.

stock Shares of ownership in a company's assets that give shareholders a claim on the company's future cash flows.

strategic alliance Relationship whereby two or more entities cooperate (but do not form a separate company) to achieve the strategic goals of each.

strategy Set of planned actions taken by managers to help a company meet its objectives.

subculture A group of people who share a unique way of life within a larger, dominant culture.

subsidy Financial assistance to domestic producers in the form of cash payments, low-interest loans, tax breaks, product price supports, or some other form.

supply Quantity of a good or service that producers are willing to provide at a specific selling price.

survey Research in which an interviewer asks current or potential buyers to answer written or verbal questions to obtain facts, opinions, or attitudes.

switch trading Practice in which one company sells to another its obligation to make a purchase in a given country.

tariff Government tax levied on a product as it enters or leaves a country.

tariff-quota Lower tariff rate for a certain quantity of imports and a higher rate for quantities that exceed the quota.

technical analysis Technique using charts of past trends in currency prices and other factors to forecast exchange rates.

technological dualism Use of the latest technologies in some sectors of the economy coupled with the use of outdated technologies in other sectors.

theocracy Political system in which a country's political leaders are religious leaders who enforce laws and regulations based on religious beliefs.

theocratic law Legal system based on religious teachings.

theocratic totalitarianism Political system in which religious leaders govern without the support of the people and do not tolerate opposing viewpoints.

topography All the physical features that characterize the surface of a geographic region.

total quality management (TQM) Emphasis on continuous quality improvement to meet or exceed customer expectations involving a company-wide commitment to quality-enhancing processes.

totalitarian system Political system in which individuals govern without the support of the people, government maintains control over many aspects of people's lives, and leaders do not tolerate opposing viewpoints.

trade creation Increase in the level of trade between nations that results from regional economic integration.

trade deficit Condition that results when the value of a country's imports is greater than the value of its exports.

trade diversion Diversion of trade away from nations not belonging to a trading bloc and toward member nations.

trade mission International trip by government officials and businesspeople that is organized by agencies of national or provincial governments for the purpose of exploring international business opportunities.

trade show Exhibition at which members of an industry or group of industries showcase their latest products, see what rivals are doing, and learn about recent trends and opportunities.

trade surplus Condition that results when the value of a nation's exports is greater than the value of its imports.

trademark Property right in the form of words or symbols that distinguish a product and its manufacturer.

transfer price Price charged for a good or service transferred among a company and its subsidiaries.

turnkey (build–operate–transfer) project Practice by which one company designs, constructs, and tests a production facility for a client firm.

United Nations (UN) International organization formed after World War II to provide leadership in fostering peace and stability around the world.

value added tax (VAT) Tax levied on each party that adds value to a product throughout its production and distribution.

value density Value of a product relative to its weight and volume.

value-chain analysis Process of dividing a company's activities into primary and support activities and identifying those that create value for customers.

values Ideas, beliefs, and customs to which people are emotionally attached.

vehicle currency Currency used as an intermediary to convert funds between two other currencies.

venture capital Financing obtained from investors who believe that the borrower will experience rapid growth and who receive equity (part ownership) in return.

vertical integration Extension of company activities into stages of production that provide a firm's inputs (backward integration) or absorb its output (forward integration).

voluntary export restraint (VER) Unique version of export quota that a nation imposes on its exports, usually at the request of an importing nation.

wholly owned subsidiary Facility entirely owned and controlled by a single parent company.

World Bank Agency created to provide financing for national economic development efforts.

World Trade Organization (WTO) International organization that regulates trade between nations.

worldwide pricing Policy in which one selling price is established for all international markets.

Name/Company Index

Subject Index

Consensus, regional integration and, 233
Consortium (multiparty joint venture), 390
Constitutional guarantees, lack of, and totalitarian governments, 90
Consumer panel, 364
Consumers
in centrally planned economies, 124
euro-consumer, 410–11
Consumption abroad, GATS, 193
Consumption taxes, 108
Contacts
in China, 126
for finding international capital, 439
personal, 14, 126, 213
political, 213
third-party, in Pacific Rim, 156
vs. contracts, 126
Contender strategy, competition with multinational corporations, 329
Content
e-commerce, 351
local content requirements, 98
Contracts
business, in common law, 103
entrepreneurial globalization, 451
forward, 274
management, 385–86
in Pacific Rim, 156
vs. contacts, 126
Contractual entry modes
franchising, 383–85
licensing, 382–83
management contracts, 385–86
turnkey projects, 386–87
Controls. *See also* Regulations and regulatory controls
of currency, 191–92, 197
foreign direct investment (FDI) management, 210–11
physical resources of production, 431
price controls, 419
Convention on International Trade in Endangered Species, 195
Convertible (hard) currency, 279
Cooperation
foreign direct investment (FDI) management and, 211
partner selection, for investment entry modes, 392
political, regional integration and, 233
Coordination, in international organization, 331–32
Copenhagen Criteria, for EU membership, 238
Copyright, defined, 107
Core competence identification, 320–23
Corporate-level strategies, 324–26
Corruption
Foreign Corrupt Practices Act, 1977, 101
Free Trade Area of the Americas (FTAA), 247
to gain political influence, 100–101
piracy of intellectual property, 105, 106
theft and, 416–17
Cost issues
counterfeit goods, 119
employees compensation and, 459

facilities and, 429
as fulfillment mistake by entrepreneurs, 167
impact of added, in purchasing power parity (PPP), 297
labor, investing abroad and, 213
low-cost leadership strategy in international operations, 326–27
of marketing and globalization of markets, 8
physical resources of production, 430–31
of production, 212–14, 394
quality and, 434
of research and development, 214
of shipping and inventory, 435–36
transportation, and location planning, 429
of workers and globalization of production, 8–9
Council of the European Union, in EU, 239
Counterfeit goods, 406–7
Counterfeiting, trademark, 119
Counterpurchase, 377
Countertrade
advantages and disadvantages of, 378
barter, 377
buyback, 377
counterpurchase, 377
defined, 280, 377
offset, 377
switch trading, 377
Countervailing duty, 195
Country(ies)
corrupt, least and most, 101
image, 350
poor, 23
rich, 23
risk, **94–95**, 354
statutory minimum wage rates, 427
totalitarian, doing business in, 93
Country Studies Area Handbooks, 458
Court of Auditors, in European Union (EU), 240
Court of Justice, in European Union (EU), 239–40
Credit information services, Ex-Im bank, 185
Criminal lawsuits, for product safety and lawsuit, 107
Cross border supply, GATS, 193
Cross-functional teams, 336
Cross licensing, 382
Cross rates, currency exchange, 272–73
Cuba
countertrade in, 280
economic system, 122, 123, 149
Cultural assimilation, 457
Cultural change, attitude toward, 56–57
Cultural diffusion, 56
Cultural imperialism, defined, 56, 182
Cultural literacy
defined, 51, 78
developing, 51
expatriates and, 79
gender and, 79
marketing and, 78–79
work attitudes and, 79
Cultural orientations, 457
Cultural profile, 458
Cultural training, 456–57

Cultural traits, 56
Culture. *See also* Culture, components of; Culture, in international business
accommodation, 50–51
assessing national business environment, 346–47
attitudes toward change, 56–57
classification of, 74–78
compiling profile, 458
and cultural literacy, 51
defined, 50
economic transition and, 141–42
employee management and, 459
entry mode selection, 393
globalization's influence on, 26–27, 57
government trade relation motivation, 182–83
management of international sales force, 409
market entry negotiation, 392
national culture and subcultures, 51–53
physical and material environment and, 72–74
politics and, 86
product strategies, 404
Culture, components of. *See also* Culture; Culture, in international business
aesthetics, 53
body language, 69–70
education, 70–72
manners and customs, 58–59
material environment, 73–74
personal communication, 66–70
physical environment, 72–74
religion, 62–66
social structure, 60–61
values and attitudes, 54–57
Culture, in international business. *See also* Culture; Culture, components of
about, 50–53
case studies, 49–50, 83
classification of cultures, 74–78
components of. *See* Culture, components of
global products, 7–8
national business environment, 30
national culture and subculture, 51–53
CultureGrams, 458
Culture shock, 454–55
reverse, 455–56
Currency
convertibility of, 279–80
cross rates of exchange, 272–73
foreign exchange market, 267–69
forward rates, 274–75, 298
international companies and, 348
Maastricht Treaty, 237
options, 275
quoting, 270–73
special drawing right (SDR), 302–3
spot rates, 273
swaps, 275
v. barter, 143
value of U.S. dollar, 290
vehicle, 276–77
Currency board, 305
Currency controls, 191–92, 197
Currency futures, 275
Current account, 217
Current account deficit, 217

Current account surplus, 217
Customer issues
Asians and, 156
international success and, 9
knowledge of, 214
linking TQM and ISO 9000 standards of production, 435
management of international sales force, 409
returns as fulfillment mistakes by entrepreneurs, 167
Customs
climate and, 72–73
defined, 58
and manners, 58–59
union, and regional economic integration, 231
Cybermarkets, advent of, 266
Czech Republic
checklist for working in, 238
estimates of GDP per capita at PPP, 137
level of globalization in, 14

D

Data, in international research
availability of, 357
comparability of, 358
cultural problems and, 358
secondary, 359–62
Data sources, political risk and, 100
Davos, Switzerland, World Economic Forum meeting in, 16
Debt. *See also* Financial issues
Argentina and, 308
crisis in developing nations, 306–8
defined, 261
forgiveness by World Bank and IMF, 315
international business activities and, 440
local, as adaptation to political risk, 99
as national capital market purpose, 260–61
role of, 261
Decentralization
of decision making, 330
in international organizational structure, 331
in production, 428–29
Decoding process, in marketing communication, 412
Decruitment, 452
Defender strategy, competition with multinational corporations, 329
Deficit, current account, 217
Demand conditions, in national competitive advantage theory, 169
Demand for products, potential markets and, 345–46
Demand issues, in market economy, 128
Democracy, as political ideology
defined, 87
doing business in, 114
globalization and, 25–26
in Latin American nations, 93
parliamentary, 89
as political ideology, 87–90
representative, 87
totalitarianism vs., 90

Environmental regulation, globalization and, 21–22
Environment scanning, for primary market research, 364
EPZs. *See* Export processing zones (EPZs)
Equity
  defined, 261
  internal, 440
  international equity market, 266
  issuing, 437–38
  local, debt as adaptation to political risk and, 99
  stockholders, and role of equity, 261
  venture capital, 438–39
ERM (Exchange rate mechanism), 305
ERM II (Exchange rate mechanism II), 305
ETC (Export trading company), 376
Ethical behavior
  defined, 110
  Enron and, 110–11
  in global business environment, 110–12
  globalization and, 17
Ethnic issues, and political risk, 96
Ethnocentricity
  avoiding, 50–51
  defined, 50, 78
Ethnocentric staffing, 449–50
EU. *See* European Union (EU)
Euro
  Maastricht Treaty, 237
  management implications of, 237–38
Eurobonds, 265
Euro-consumer, 410–11
Eurocurrency market, 267
Eurodollars, 267
Europe. *See also* Eastern Europe; European Union (EU)
  customer service in, 9
  economic development, 132
  foreign direct investment (FDI) in, 222
  intra and inter-regional merchandise trade, 156
  level of globalization in, 14
  map of, **44**
  mixed economy, 127–28
  monetary system, 305–6
  regional economic integration in, 235–40
  vs. United States, productivity in, 145–46
European Coal and Steel Community, 236
European Commission
  in EU, 239
  president of, 287
European Community, 236
European Economic Area (EEA), 240
European Economic Community (EEC), 236
European Free Trade Association (EFTA), 235, **236**, 240
European monetary system (EMS), 305–6
European monetary union, 237–38
European Parliament, in EU, 239
European terms, 270
European Union (EU). *See also* Europe
  antitrust regulations, 108
  Council of, 239

enlargement of, 238
European monetary union, 237–38
foreign direct investment (FDI) and, 207
franchising in, 384
Germany trade dependencies, 157
labor unions, 461
Maastricht treaty, 237
membership, **236**
Néstlé and Coca-Cola and, 229–30, 232
number of countries in, 11
origins of, 235–37, 240
Single European Act (SEA), 237
structure of, 239–40
summit in Gothenburg, Sweden (2001), 16
trademark infringement, 106
Europounds, 267
Euroyen, 267
Events, global mindset and, 13
Exchange rate mechanism (ERM), 305
Exchange rate mechanism II (ERM II), 305
Exchange-rate risk, 271
Exchange rates
  Big Mac index, 292–93
  business activities and, 288–91
  currency board, 305
  currency controls and, 191–92
  defined, 267
  forecasting, 298–99
  gold standard and, 300
  inflation rate role in, 294–96
  interest rate role in, 296–97
  international monetary system, 304–5
  key country rates, 273, 289
  law of one price, 291–93
  in May 13, 2004, 271
  multiple, 279
  pegged exchange-rate arrangement, 304–5
  purchasing power parity (PPP), 293
  stable, 289
Exclusive channel, 415
Exclusive license, 383
Ex-Im Bank (Export-Import Bank of the United States), 30, 184–85
Expansion of sales, 373
Expatriates
  and cultural literacy, 79
  defined, 448
Experience
  export and, 373
  field, 457
  international, 373, 394–95
Export credit insurance, Ex-Im bank, 185
Export financing programs, Ex-Im Bank and, 184–85
Export-Import Bank of the United States (Ex-Im Bank), 30, 184–85
Export management company (EMC), 375
Export processing zones (EPZs), 21
Exports and exporting. *See also* International trade
  blunder avoidance, 376
  clusters in, 169, **170**
  of cultural goods, 26
  defined, 5, 372
  direct exporting, 374–75
  financing of, 184–85, 378–81

gross domestic product (GDP), **152–53**
  indirect, 375–76
  intraregional, Western Europe and, 155
  in Mexico, 157–58
  national security and, 180
  quotas, 189–90
  reasons for, 373
  small business and, 30
  strategy development, 373–74
  top exporters to the United States, 372
  top service and merchandise exporters, 154
Export tariff, 187
Export trading company (ETC), for indirect exporting, 376
Exposure, market, 415
Expressions, freedom of, in representative democracies, 88
Expropriation
  defined, 97
  of property, political risk and, 97
Extended family, in social structure, 60
Extender strategy, competition with multinational corporations, 329
Extension, in marketing communication, 412–13
Extranet, as technological innovation, 13

F

Facilities and production
  layout planning, 430
  location planning, 427–29
Facility security management, 17
Factor conditions, in national competitive advantage theory, 169
Factor proportions theory, of international trade
  defined, 164
  labor *vs.* land and capital equipment, 164
  Leontief paradox, 164–65
Fair Trade Commission (Japan), 108
Fair trade products, 111
Family
  importance in China, 126
  in social structure, 60
Far Eastern Review, 349
Fast track authority, 243
FDI. *See* Foreign direct investment (FDI)
Federal Trade Commission (FTC), 109, 130
FedWorld Web site, 187
Feedback, in marketing communication, 412
Fees, international business activities and, 440
Field experience, 457
Field trips, for market or site selection, 356
Filmmaking industry, import quota in, 189
Financial instruments, 263
Financial issues. *See also* Capital; Debt; Financial markets, international

business operations and production, 436–41
developing nations debt crisis, 306
export financing, 184–85, 378–81
global e-commerce, 351
import financing, 378–81
incentives, governments and, 220
in national business environment assessment, 349–50
Financial markets, international
  case studies, 259–60, 285
  crisis in international monetary system, 306–8
  currency convertibility, 279–80
  foreign exchange market, 267–78
  international business environment, 29–31, 322–23
  international capital market, 260–67
  local business as adaptation to political risk, 99
  trading centers for foreign exchange markets, 276, **276**
Finland
  international trade in, 153
  level of globalization in, 14
  Web sites in, 55
Firm strategy, structure, and rivalry, in national competitive advantage theory, 170
First age of globalization, 15
First mover advantage, 167–68
Fiscal policy, 130–31
Fisher effect, 296–97
Fixed exchange-rate system, 300
Fixed line subscribers, **354–55**
Fixed (tangible) assets, 433–34
Flexibility
  in international organization structure, 331–32
  in make-or-buy decisions, 432
  of price in market economy, 129
Focus groups
  defined, 364
  for primary market research, 363–64
Focus strategy, 328
Folk custom, defined, 58
Following client, FDI management and, 214
Following rivals, FDI management and, 215
Food
  contamination of, case study, 257
  physical environment and, 73
Forecasting
  difficulties of, 299
  exchange rates, 299
  political risk, 100
Foreign bond, 265
Foreign Corrupt Practices Act, 1977, 101
Foreign direct investment (FDI)
  in Asia, 222–23
  case studies, 203–4, 227
  defined, 204
  in Europe, 222
  explanations for, 208–10
  government intervention in, 215–19
  government policy instruments and, 219–21
  growth and downturn of, 204–5
  management issues in, 210–15
  national governments and, 221–22

geocentric staffing, 451–52
reverse cultural shock, 456
Hong Kong
foreign direct investment (FDI),
208
in Four Tigers, 90, 114
human development index (HDI),
138
national culture in, 51
Host country
foreign direct investment (FDI),
217–18, 219–21
geocentric staffing, 451–52
polycentric staffing, 450–51
Hot money, 439
HRM (Human resources
management), 448
Hub and spokes model, of European
monetary system, 305
Human development index (HDI)
defined, 137
overview of, 137–38
Human resources. See also Employees
cultural shock, 454–55
human resource management
(HRM), 448
planning, 452
policy, investing abroad and, 213
recruitment, 452–54
selection, 454
Human rights, 110, 111
Hungary, GDP per capita at PPP in,
137

I

IBRD (International Bank for
Reconstruction and
Development), 302
Identity crisis, in Asia, 83
Image
brand issues in differentiation
strategy, 327–28
country, 350
national, 406
Imagery, in international marketing,
53
IMF. See International Monetary Fund
(IMF)
Import deposit requirements, 279–80
Imports and importing. See also
International trade
blunder avoidance, 376
of cultural goods, 26
defined, 5, 372
financing of, 378–81
national security and, 179
restriction of, 188–89
Imports quotas, 188–89, 196
Import tariff, 188, 196
Imposed authority, and totalitarian
governments, 90
Impressions of culture, 52
Improvement, continuous, linking
TQM and ISO 9000 standards
of production, 435
Incentives
centrally planned economy and,
123
economic-development, 213
tax, employee compensation and,
459
Income
global products and, 8
human development index and, 137
per capita, 134, **134–35**

Income elasticity, 352
Income elasticity coefficient, 352
Income elastic product, 352
Income inelastic product, 352
Income payments, current account,
217
Income receipts, current account, 217
Independencies of international trade,
157–58
India
caste system, 61
China's economy vs., 353
economic system, 121–22
English as lingua franca, 69
industrialized market potential,
352–55
intellectual property issues in, 119
legal system, 102–3
as a location to outsource
engineering, 20–21
McDonald's in, 8, 64
nationalism and legal system in,
102
vs. China, economic development
in, 144–45
Indices, for measuring globalization,
13–14
Indirect exporting, 375
Indirect quotes, 270, 272
Individualism, vs. collectivism, 76–77
Individualist cultures, 129
Indonesia, brain drain in, 71
Industrialized countries, 165
Industrialized markets, assessing
national business environment
and, 352
Industrial property
defined, 106
patents, 106
trademarks, 106
Industry and trade associations, for
secondary international data,
360–61
Inefficient market views, 298–99
Inequality
global, 24–25
between nations, 23–24
within nations, 22–23
Infant industry argument, 180–81
Inflation
exchange rates and, 294–95
interest and, 294
purchasing power parity (PPP) and,
294
Influence over other nations,
governments and, 180
Information, investing abroad and,
213
Information gathering, and political
risk, 100
Information technology (IT)
capital market expansion and, 262
economic systems and, 121–22
global e-commerce and, 351
governments embrace of, 102
productivity and, 133
United States and Europe spending
on, 145
Infrastructure
commercial, emerging market and,
353, **354–55**
improvements, and government
policy instruments, 220
telecommunications, information
technology and, 351
Infringement, trademark, 119

Inland bill of lading, in export/import
financing, 379379
Institute for International Economics,
policy agenda for rich nations,
34
Institute of Computer Science, 6
Insurance
as adaptation to political risk, 99
encouraging foreign direct
investment, 221
as home country promotion, 221
Intellectual property
copyrights, 107
counterfeit goods and black
markets, 406–7
defined, 104
GATT and, 193
global e-commerce and protection
of, 351
industrial property, 106
licensing of, 382
piracy of, 119
property rights, 105–6
rights, GATT treaty definition of,
11
Intensive channel, 415
Interbank interest rates, 267
Interbank market, 277
Interdependencies, of international
trade, 158
Interest
arbitrage, 268–69
inflation impact, 294–95
interbank, 267
in international bond market,
265–66
low, loans and, 220
rates in driving force, 265
role of, 296–97
and role of debt, 261
Intermediaries
capital-market, 261, 266
channel, 414
for finding international capital,
439
Internal equity, 440
Internal funding, production and,
439–40
Internalization (market
imperfections) theory, 209
International advertising. See
advertising
International area structure, 333–34
International Bank for Reconstruction
and Development (IBRD), 302
International bond market,
definitions and types of, 265
International business. See also
Planning of international
business
about, 4–5
advertising and language blunders
in, 68
antitrust laws and, 109
combating multinational
corporations, 329
cultural change and, 56–57
development assistance and,
99–100
environment of, 29–31, 322–23
and foreign direct investment
(FDI), 205
globalization. See Globalization
hedging and, 268
implications of legal issues for, 115
key players in, 27–29
keys to success, 9

levels of strategy in, 325
number by country, 28
reasons for export, 373
International capital markets. See
Capital markets, international
International Court of Justice, United
Nations, 114
International division structure,
332–33
International equity market
defined, 266
factors responsible for, 266
International experience, 373, 394–95
International financial market. See
Financial markets,
international
International firm management, 31
International Fisher effect, 297
International Forum of Globalization,
16
International Institute for the
Unification of Private Law, 104
Internationalization, defined, 7
International labor movements,
461–62
International Labor Organization, 21
International marketing, Nike and, 53
International Monetary Fund (IMF)
creation and purposes of, 302
debt crisis in developing nations,
306
debt forgiveness, 315
defined, 17
NAFTA and, 243
as source of international data, 359
special drawing right (SDR), 302–3
violence at meeting, 16
International monetary system
Bretton Woods Agreement, 301–3
case studies, 287–88, 315
defined, 300
European monetary system, 305–6
and exchange rates, 304–5
financial crises, 306–8
future of, 308–9
gold standard, 300–301
managed float system, 304
International opportunities, analysis
of
case studies, 343–44, 369
conducting international business,
357–64
screening potential markets and
sites. See Screening process
International organizations, for
secondary international data,
359
International outsourcing, 20
International product life cycle theory
defined, 165, 208
limitations of, 166–67, 208
stages of, 165–67, 208
International relations, and United
Nations, 112–15
International Standards Organization
(ISO) 9000, certification, 435
International strategy and
organization
case studies, 317–18, 341
centralization vs. decentralization,
330–31
company mission and goals, 318–20
coordination and flexibility, 331–32
identifying core competency and
value-creating activities,
320–23
strategy formulation, 318, 323–29

types of organizational structures, 332–35
work teams, 335–36
International trade. *See also* Trade
absolute advantage theory of, 160–62
benefits of, 153–54
case studies, 151, 175
comparative advantage theory of, 162–64
defined, 152
dependencies of, 157–58
factor proportions theory of, 164–65
independencies of, 157–58
interdependencies of, 158
international product life cycle theory of, 165–67
mercantilism, 158–60
national competitive advantage theory of, 168–71
new trade theory of, 167–68
overview of, 152–53
patterns, 154–57
volume of, 154
International Trade Administration (ITA), 187
International Trade Center, as source of international data, 359
International Trade Statistics Yearbook (UN), 359
Internet and World Wide Web, as source of international data, 362
Intervention
of government and mercantilism, 159
of government in foreign direct investment (FDI), 215–19
home country, 218–19
host country, 217–18
Interviews, for primary market research, 363–64
Intranets, as technological innovation, 13
Invention, product, 414
Inventory costs, as production concern, 435–36
Investment, barriers to, 10–11
Investment banks
activity of, 266
defined, 261
Investment entry modes, selection and management of
joint ventures, 388–90
partner selection for cooperation, 392
strategic alliances, 391
wholly owned subsidiaries, 387–88
Iran, theocratic totalitarianism, 91
Ireland
intellectual property issues, 105
level of globalization in, 14
Irrevocable letter of credit, in export/import financing, 380
Islam
and business culture, 49, 52
climate and pork consumption, 73
customs of, 58
gender and, 60
product aesthetics, 53
religion of, 64
theocratic law, 103–4
theocratic totalitarianism, 91
values in, 54

ISO (International Standards Organization) 9000, certification, 435
ITA. *See* International Trade Administration (ITA)
Italy, brain drain in, 71

J

Jamaica Agreement, 304
Japan
administrative delays, 191
antitrust regulations, 108–9
Asia, map of, **45**
attitude toward time, 55
automobile production facilities, 428
currency cross rates, 273
customs of, 58–59
estimates of GDP per capita at PPP, 137
exports to the United States, 372
foreign bonds in, 265
gender and cultural literacy, 79
globalization of production in, 9
green-tea ice cream, 404
human development index (HDI), 138
influence over other nations, 180
Kluckhohn-Strodtbeck framework, 74–75
number of companies in, 28
political power, 89–90
political system, 86
religion of, 66
trade barriers and, 191
values in, 54
Japan External Trade Organization (JETRO), 186, 360
JETRO. *See* Japan External Trade Organization (JETRO)
Jobs. *See also* Unemployment
exporting and, 153
globalization impact on, 18–21, 33
home country and foreign direct investment, 218–19
protection, government trade relations and, 178–79
statistics on exports and, 153
Joint ventures
advantages of, 390
backward integration, 389
buyback, 389–90
configurations, 389–90
consortium (multiparty), 390
defined, 388
disadvantages of, 390
examples of, 388
trade dependency and, 157
Juche policy, in North Korea, 123
Judaism
and business culture, 49, 52
climate and pork consumption, 73
religion, 66
in the world, **63**
Just-in-time (JIT) manufacturing, 436

K

Key players in International business, 27–29
Kidnapping and political risk, 96
Kluckohn-Strodtbeck framework, 74

Knowledge
in competitive advantage, 209
cultural, 55
customer, 214
Kuwait, 87

L

Labor
costs, globalization of production and, 8–9
costs, investing abroad and, 213
costs, process planning and, 429
factors proportions theory of international trade, 164
globalization and labor markets, 20
international labor movements, 461–62
productivity, 133
standards, 21
vs. land and capital equipment, 164
Labor management relations, 460–61
LAFTA (Latin American Free trade Association), 243–44
Laissez-faire economics, 129
Lamaist Buddhism, **62–63**
Land, factor proportions theory of international trade, 164
Language
blunders, 68
body, 59, 69
business operations and, 322
gap, 74
globalization and, 67
lingua franca, 61
spoken, 66–68
training in, 457
of Web, 67
Latin America
culture of, 55
and foreign direct investment (FDI), 208
intra- and inter-regional merchandise trade, 156
political systems in time of change, 93
Latin American Free trade Association (LAFTA), 243–44
Latin American Integration Association (ALADI), 235, **244**, 245
Law of one price, 291
Left-wing totalitarianism, 92
Legal behavior, globalization and, 17
Legal issues. *See also* Global legal issues; Law; Legal systems; Political risk; Politics
case study, 85–86
contractual entry modes, 382–87
e-commerce, 351
entry mode selection, 393
implications for companies, 115
intellectual property right in Asia, 00
market entry negotiation, 392
in national business environment, 30
national business environment assessment, 327–28
negotiations and, 392
Legal systems. *See also* Law; Regulations and regulatory controls
defined, 101

international strategies and, 323
types of, 103–4
Lenders, international capital markets and, 262
Leontief paradox, factor proportions theory, 164–65
Less-developed countries/nations. *See* Developing countries/nations (less-developed countries/nations)
Letter of credit, definition and types of, 380
Liability, products, 107–8
LIBID (London Interbank Bid Rate), 267
LIBOR (London Interbank offer Rate), 267
Licensing
advantages of, 382–83
defined, 382
disadvantages of, 383
examples of agreements, 382
franchising *vs.*, 383
nonexclusive, 382
requirements, export and, 30
Life cycle theory of international product, 165–67
Life expectancy, human development index and, 137
Lifestyle, climate, and work, 72
Lingua franca, defined, 68
The Lion King (film), 189
Liquidity, defined, 261
Literacy rates, 71
Loan guarantee, 184
Loans
Ex-Im bank program, 185
as home countries promotion, 221
as host countries promotion, 220
Lobbying, 100, 105
Local content requirements, 98, 191, 196, 241
Local equity and debt, as adaptation to political risk, 99
Localization, as adaptation to political risk, 99
Local managerial talent, for recruitment of human resources, 454
Local needs, globalization of markets and, 8
Local presence, in international web sites, 54
Location, facilities selection and, 427–29
Location advantage, 209
Location economies, 428
Logistics
assessing national business environment, 349–50
defined, 349
as fulfillment mistakes by entrepreneurs, 167167
global business and, 9
London Interbank Bid Rate (LIBID), 267
London Interbank offer Rate (LIBOR), 267
The Lord of the Rings: The Return of the king (film), 177, 178
Louvre Accord, 304
Low-cost leadership strategy, 326–27
Low human development, 138
Low-interest loans, 220

Natural persons present, GATS, 193
Negotiations, management and, 392
Neo-mercantilism, 159
Nepal, 415
Nepotism, 60
Netherlands
level of globalization in, 14
mixed economy, 127
number of companies in, 28
Newly industrialized country (NIC), defined, 138
New product stage, in international product life cycle theory, 165, 208
New trade theory, in international trade, 167–68
New Zealand, level of globalization in, 14
NGOs (Non government organizations), 315, 348
NIC (Newly industrialized country), 138
Noise, in marketing communication, 412
Nominal interest rates, 296
Nonexclusive license, 382
Nongrovernment organizations (NGOs), 315, 348
Nonmanagerial workers
compensation of, 459–60
for recruitment of human resources, 454
training of, 458
Nonpolitical bureaucracies, in representative democracies, 88–89
Nontariff barriers, 10–11
Normal trade relations, defined, 194
North America. *See also* Canada; United States
intra-and inter-regional merchandise trade, 156
map of, **42**
regional economic integration, 241–43
North American Free Trade Agreement (NAFTA)
effects of, 241–43
expansion of, 243
and globalization, 11, 25
impact on Australia, 234
local content requirements and rules of origin, 241
map, **242**
market imperfections (internalization) theory, 209
spoken language, 67–68
trade dependency, 157
North Korea
economic growth, 123–24
Juche policy, 123
Norway, 14, 138, 297
Nuclear family, in social structure, 60
Numerator, 270
Nurturing, achievement *vs.*, 77–78

O

Objectives, in mission statement, 320
Ocean bill of lading, in export/import financing, 379
Oceania, map of, **47**
OECD (Organization for Economic Cooperation and Development), 104
Offset, 377

Offshore financial centers, 264
On Air Together, "Hawa Sawa," 54
One-level channel, 415
Online security, 17
OPEC. *See* Organization of Petroleum Exporting Countries (OPEC)
Open account, export/import financing, 381
Operational centers, as offshore financial centers, 264
OPIC. *See* Overseas Private Investment Corporation (OPIC)
Opportunity analysis. *See* International opportunities, analysis of
Options, currency, 275
Organic growth, 324, 326
Organizational structure
defined, 330
forms of, 330–32
types of, 332–35
work teams, 335–36
Organization for Economic Cooperation and Development (OECD), 104
Organization of Petroleum Exporting Countries (OPEC), 189
OTC market. *See* Over-the-counter (OTC) market
Outsourcing, 171, 431–32
Overpromising, as fulfillment mistake by entrepreneurs, 167
Overseas Private Investment Corporation (OPIC), 184
Over-the-counter (OTC) market, 277, 278
Ownership advantage, 209
Ownership restrictions, government policy instruments and, 220

P

"Pacific century," 156
Pacific Rim, doing business in, 156
Packing list, in export/import financing, 379
Pakistan, 138
Paraguay, 92, 93
Paris Convention for the Protection of Industrial Property, 106, 194
Parliamentary democracy, 89
Participation
in political systems, 87
by public referendum, 86
restricted, in totalitarianism, 90
Participative management practices, decentralization and, 331
Partnership, as adaptation to political risk, 99
Partnerships, foreign direct investment (FDI) management, 210–11
Par value, 300
of gold standard, 300
Passion of Christ (film), 67
Patents, 106
Patient money, 439
Patterns, in international trade, 154–57
Pegged exchange-rate arrangement, 304–5
Pentagon terrorism, September 11 (2001), 96
People-based management, 435
Percent change, calculating, 271–72

Performance demands, government policy instruments and, 220
Personal accountability, decentralization and, 331
Personal communication. *See* Communication
Personal contacts
in China, 126
globalization and, 14
and political, global management and, 213
Personal relationship. *See* Communication
Persuasion, negotiations and, 392
Physical environment, and culture, 72–74
Physical gestures, 70
Physical resources acquisition, production and, 430–34
Piracy of intellectual property, 105, 106, 119
Planning of international business
capacity, 426–27
defined, 318
facilities layout, 430
human resource, 452
process, 429
Plaza Accord, 304
Pluralism, 87
Policy agenda, globalization and, 33–34
Policy changes, and political risk, 98
Policy instruments, foreign direct investments (FDI) and, 219–21
Political cooperation, regional integration and, 233
Political engagement, 13
Political ideologies
democracy, 87–90
overview, 87
totalitarianism, 90–93
types of, 87–93
Political instability, economic transition and, 142
Political participation, 87
Political risk
agencies specializing in, 100
around the world, **94–95**
defined, 94
management of, 99–101
national business environment assessment, 347–48
sources of, 94
types of, 95–98
Political Risk Services, 354
Political stability, market economy and, 131
Political systems. *See also* Politics
defined, 86
international strategies and, 323
in Japan, 86
political and civil liberties around world, **88–89**
political ideologies, 87–93
political participation, 87
politics and culture, 86
in Switzerland, 86
in times of change, 93
Political union, regional integration and, 232
Politicized bureaucracies, 88–89
Politics. *See also* Political systems
ASEAN nations, diverse cultures and, 250
in China, 125

and culture, 86
entry mode selection, 393
ideologies, 87–93
influencing local, and political risk, 100–101
market entry negotiation, 392
motives in government trade relations, 178–80
in national business environment, 30
negotiations and, 392
participation in, 87
political cooperation and regional integration, 233
political stability and market economy, 131
pressure as home country promotion, 221
Polycentric staffing, 450–51
Poor countries, 23
Popular custom, defined, 58
Porter diamond, 168
Portfolio investment, defined, 204
Portugal, level of globalization in, 14
Positive-sum game, in absolute advantage theory, 162
Post, telephone, and telegraph (PTT), 399
Power distance, in Hofstede framework, 76
PPP. *See* Purchasing power parity (PPP)
Prague, World Bank meeting in, 16
Precedent, in common law, 103
Predictability, of exchange rates, 289–90
Premium, currency exchange rate, 274–75
Price/pricing
controls, 419
dual pricing, 417–18
escalation, 418
factors affecting pricing decisions, 418–19
flexibility, in market economy, 129
of imported products from China, 18
mechanism, 128
transfer, 440
worldwide, 417
Primary activities
in department-level strategies, 328–29
in value chain analysis, 320, 321
Primary international research, 362–64
Primary market research, 362
Principal, and role of debt, 261
Privacy, e-commerce and, 351
Private label brands, 415
Private sector, defined, 90
Privatization
defined, 128
international equity market and, 266
move toward, 127–28
Process management, linking TQM and ISO 9000 standards of production, 435
Process planning, 429
Process technologies, licensing, 0
ProChile (Chile's Ministry of Foreign Affairs), 360
Product development and marketing. *See also* Products
blending promotional and, 411–14

case studies, 401–2, 423
country image and, 350
designing distribution strategies, 414–17
developing product strategies, 403–8
differentiation strategy, 327–28
distribution strategies, 408, 414–19
globalization and, 402–3
internationalization, 322
pricing strategies, 417–19
product safety and liability, 107–8
promotional strategies, 408–14
Production. *See also* Production strategy; Productivity
centralized, 428–29
costs and foreign direct investment (FDI), 212–14
decentralized, 428–29
globalization of, 8–10, 17
of goods, 8
information technology and, 133
innovative, 6
key concerns, 434–36
national, 133–36
rationalized, 212
strategy for efficiency, 445
strategy formulation and, 329
Production of services, 8
Production strategy
capacity planning, 426–27
facilities layout planning, 430
facilities location planning, 427–28
importance of, 426
process planning, 429
Productivity. *See also* Production
defined, 132
information technology and, 133
levers, 133
location economies and, 428
in United States *vs.* Europe, 145–46
Product liability, defined, 107
Products. *See also* Product development and marketing
global, 7–8
high-quality, developing, 9
invention, 414
life cycle, 165–67, 407–8
promotional strategies and, 411–12
safety and liability, 107–8
small business and understanding of, 322
value density, 416
Product strategies
brand and product names, 404–6
counterfeit goods and black markets, 406–7
cultural differences, 404
distribution, 415–17
internationalization, 322
laws and regulations, 404
life cycles, shortened, 407–8
national image, 406
pricing, 417–19
promotional, 411–16
Product type, promotional strategies and, 409
Profit, currency and, 268–69, 310
Pro-globalization, 19, 20
Progress, in economic transition, 141
Promotional message, in marketing communication, 412
Promotional strategies, product development and marketing
blending product and, 411–14
international advertising, 410–12

promotion mix, 408
push and pull strategies, 408–9
Promotion mix, 408
Promotion of trade by governments
export financing, 184–85
foreign trade zones, 185–86
special government agencies, 186–87
subsidies, 184
Property rights. *See also* intellectual property
defined, 105
preservation, market economy and, 130
in representative democracies, 88
Property seizure, political risk and, 97
Proximity, in body language, 70
PTT (Post, telephone, and telegraph), 399
Public referendum voting, 86
Pull strategy, 408–9
Purchase-or-build decision, 212
Purchasing power, defined, 136
Purchasing power parity (PPP)
comparative economics, 136–37
defined, 136, 293
evaluating, 297–98
inflation rate role, 294
interest rate role, 294–98
trade importance, **152–53**
Pure democracy, 87
Push strategy, 408–9

Q

Quality-improvement teams, 336
Quality issues
in differentiation strategy, 327
in franchising, 385
improvement in production, 434–35
licensing and, 383
quality-improvement teams, 336
raw materials, 433
Quotas, for trade restriction
defined, 188
import, 188–89, 196
reasons for, 188–90
tariff, 190
Quoted currency, 270

R

Racial issues, and political risk, 96
Rationalized production, 212
Raw materials, as resource, 433
Real interest rates, 296
Recruitment, of human resources, 452–54
Red wine, 403
Regional economic integration (regionalism)
in Americas, 241–47
in Asia, 248–50
benefits of, 232–33
business operations and, 252–53
case studies, 230–31, 257
defined, 230
drawbacks of, 233–34
effects of, 232–33
and employment, 234, 253
in Europe, 235–40
levels of, 230–32
in Middle East and Africa, 250–52

regional trading blocs, 229, 230, 231, 235
Regional trade agreements, 11
Regional trading blocs, 229, 230, 231, 235
Regulations and regulatory controls. *See also* Global legal issues; Law; Legal issues
administrative delays, 191, 196
antimonopoly regulations and laws, 104, 108–9
deregulation and capital market expansion, 262
national, foreign direct investment (FDI) and, 216
national business environment assessment, 347–48
of product liability, 108
product strategies, 404
Reinvestment *vs.* divestment, in production, 436
Religion
ad campaign and, 63–64
around world, **62–63**
Buddhism, 65
Christianity, 62–64
Confucianism, 65–66
Hinduism, 64
Islam, 64
Judaism, 66
respecting values of, 59
Shinto, 66
values and, 54
Relocation of services, 171
Representative democracy
defined, 87
freedoms, 88–89
Reputational risk, 17
Research and development, international
conducting primary research, 362–64
cost of, 214
difficulties in conducting, 357–58
market research, 357
nations and, 323
sources of secondary data, 359–62
Resources
commitment in export strategy, 374
in Czech Republic, 238
globalization of products and, 9–10
human. *See* Human resources
physical, acquisition of, 430–34
screening potential markets and sites, 346
technology, and host country intervention, 218
Restriction of trade by governments
administrative delays, 191, 196
currency controls, 191–92, 197
embargoes, 190–91
home countries, 221
host countries, 219–20
local content requirements, 98
market imperfections (internalization) theory, 209
quotas, 188–90
tariffs, 187–88
Retrenchment strategy, 325
Returns, as fulfillment mistakes by entrepreneurs, 167
Reunification, in China, 125–26
Revaluation, of currency, 288
Revenue, 440
Revenue, tariff and, 188
Reverse brain drain, 72

Reverse culture shock, 455–56
Revocable letter of credit, in export/import financing, 380
"Riceland," as example of international trade, 160–61, 162–63
Rich countries, 23
Right-wing totalitarianism, 92
Risk
country, **94–95**, 354
eurocurrency, 267
exchange-rate risk, 271
exchange rates and gold standard, 300
export/import financing, 378, 379, 381
lenders, reduction of, 262
macro, 95
in make-or-buy decisions, 432
micro, 95
political. *See* Political risk
Rivalry, of firm, in national competitive advantage theory, 170
Rivals, following, in FDI management, 215
Russia
economic transition in, 142–44
human development index (HDI), 138
pointers for doing business, 143
ruble crisis, 307–8
in Security Council of United Nations (UN), 114

S

Safety products, 107–8
Sales
diversified, exports and, 373
expansion of, 373
management of international sales force, 409
representatives in direct export, 374–75
Samurai bonds, 265
Sanctions, as home country restriction, 221
Sarbanes-Oxley Act, 111
Saudi Arabia, 191
SBA (Small Business Administration), 30
Scale of corporations, retrenchment strategy and, 325
Scope of corporations, retrenchment strategy and, 325
Screening process, potential markets and sites
about, 344–45
assessing national business environment, 326–50
identifying basis appeal, 345–46
measuring market or site potential, 351–56
selecting the market or site, 356
SDR (Special drawing right), 302–3
SEA (Single European Act), 237
Seattle, Washington, World Trade Organization (WTO) 1999 meeting in, 16
Second age of globalization, drivers of, 16
Secondary market research, 359
Secretariat of United Nations (UN), **113**, 114

tax incentives, 220, 459
"Tealand," as example of international trade, 160–61, 162–63
Teams, work, 335–36
Technical analysis, 299
Technical expertise, globalization of products and, 9
Technological connectivity, 13–14
Technological dualism, 139
Technological innovation. See also Technology
global business environment and, 30
globalization and, 12–13
Technology. See also Information technology (IT)
attitudes toward technology, 55
as facilitator of globalization, 4
in foreign direct investment (FDI), 214
innovation and globalization, 12–13
material culture and, 73–74
nations with low levels of, 14
resources and host country intervention, 218
Telecommunications, 351, **354–55**
TEP (Transatlantic Economic Partnership), 235, 247
Terms of Engagement, 111
Terrorism and political risk, 96
Thai baht, 269
Thailand, 22, 74, 293
Theft, product distribution and, 416–17
"The Long Arm of the Law," 109
Theocracy, 90
Theocratic law, defined, 103
Theocratic totalitarianism, defined, 90
TIC (Trade Information Center), 359
Time, attitude toward, 55
Time draft, in export/import financing, 379
Tobacco liability, 108
Topography
and communication, 72
defined, 72
Totalitarianism, as political ideology about, 90
and centrally planned economy, 123
communist, 91–92
defined, 87
doing business with, 93
legal system and, 101
right-wing, 92
tribal, 92
types of, 90–93
vs. democracy, 90
Totalitarian nations, doing business in, 114–15
Totalitarian system, 90
Total quality management (TQM), 434, 435
Township and village enterprises (TVEs), 125
TQM (Total quality management), 434, 435
Trade. See also International trade
agreements and growth, 11–12
barriers to, 10–11, 30, 209
countertrade, 280
creation, 232–33
deficit, 159, 279
domestic, 152
globalization and, 171
intra- and inter-regional merchandise trade, 156

methods of promoting, 183–87
methods of restricting, 187–92
regional agreements, 11
specialization and, 161–62
surplus, 159
unions, 21
volume of, international maps, **152–53,** 154
Trade and Development Agency, 30
Trade associations, as secondary international research, 361
Trade barriers. See also Restriction of trade by governments
and purchasing power parity (PPP), 297
Uruguay Round of negotiations and, 192–93
and World Trade Organization (WTO), 195
Trade diversion, regional integration and, 233–34
Trade imbalance, gold standard and, 300–301
Trade Information Center (TIC), 359
Trademarks, 106
Trade mission, 363
for primary market research, 362–63
Trade promotion. See Promotion of trade by governments
Trade-Related Aspects of Intellectual Property (TRIPS), 193–94
Trade shows, for primary market research, 362–63
Trading bloc, regional, 230, 233
Trading centers, 276, **276**
Tradition in common law, 103
Training
cultural, 456–57
cultural assimilation and sensitivity training, 457
language, 457
nonmanagerial worker, 458
Transactions, uncounted, national production and, 134–35
Transatlantic Economic Partnership (TEP), 235, 247
Transfer price, 418, 440
Transition nations, trade dependence and independence, 157
Transit tariff, 188
Transportation and shipping
assessing national business environment, 349–50
capacity of merchant ships, 155
costs, and location planning, 429
documentary financing and shipping, 379
entry mode selection, 394
and inventory costs, 435–36
top ten countries share of shipping capacity, 155
Transportation technologies, globalization and, 13
Treaty of Paris (1951), 236
Treaty of Rome (1957), 236
Trends, globalization and, 6
Tribal totalitarianism, 92
TRIPS. See Trade-Related Aspects of Intellectual Property (TRIPS)
Trusteeship Council, of United Nations (UN), 114
Tuberculosis, global challenges, 139
Turkey, 137, 294
Turnkey (build-operate-transfer) projects, as contractual entry mode

advantages of, 387
defined, 386
disadvantages of, 387
international, examples of, 386
TVEs. See Township and village enterprises (TVEs)
Two-level channel, 415

U

Uganda, debt relief for, 315
UK. See United Kingdom (UK)
UN. See United Nations (UN)
Uncertainty avoidance, in Hoftsted framework, 77
UNCTAD (United Nations Conference on Trade and Development), 114
Underground economies (black markets), 124, 155
Unemployment. See also Jobs
in China, 125
economy and, 130
in former Soviet Union, 140
in a group of countries, 460
inflation impact, 294
political motive for trade, 178–79
Uneven material culture, 74
Unfair trade practices, government and, 178
Unions, investing abroad and, 213
United Kingdom (UK)
attitude toward entrepreneurs, 55
currency cross rates, 273
estimates of GDP per capita at PPP, 137
foreign bonds in, 265
gestures in, 70
labor unions in, 461
level of globalization in, 14
national culture, 51
number of companies in, 28
in Security Council of United Nations (UN), 114
spoken language in, 67
values in, 54
United Nations Conference on Trade and Development (UNCTAD), 114
United Nations (UN)
defined, 112
standardization of rules of conduct, 104
system, 113
United States Trade Representative, 187
United States (U.S.)
antitrust, 108
attitude toward time, 55
balance of payments account (2000), 216
clusters in, **170**
conducting business in, 58
cultural influence of, 182–83
customer service in, 9
estimates of GDP per capita at PPP, 137
foreign bonds in, 265
foreign direct investment (FDI), 207
human development index (HDI), 138
level of globalization in, 14
merchandise and commercial service exports, 154
North America, map of, **42**

North American Free Trade Agreement (NAFTA) and, 241–43
number of companies in, 28
in Security Council of United Nations (UN), 114
subcultures in, 52
top exporters to, 372
uncertainty avoidance and power distance, 77
values in, 54
vs. Europe, productivity in, 145–46
work attitude, 55, 79
Universal Copyright Convention, 1954, 107
Upstream business activities, 389, 430
Uruguay Round, GATT, 192–93, 205
U.S. See United States (U.S.)
U.S.-Canada Free Trade Agreement, 241, **242**
U.S. Chamber of Commerce, 187
U.S. Children's Online Privacy Act and, 423
U.S. Department of Commerce
Bureau of Export Administration, license requirements, 30
developing future markets study, 22
foreign direct investment (FDI) threshold, 204
foreign trade zones, 186
as informative Web site for managers, 187, 351
statistics on exports and jobs, 153
U.S. Department of State, 458
U.S. Federal Patent Statute, 106
U.S. International Trade Commission (USITC), 109
U.S. Patent and Trademark Office (USPTO), 109, 119
U.S. Trade Representative, 187
Usage, in common law, 103
USITC (U.S. International Trade Commission), 109
USPTO (U.S. Patent and Trademark Office), 109, 119

V

Value added tax (VAT), 108, 109
Value-chain analysis, defined, 320–21
Value density, 416
Value(s)
in culture, 54
defined, 54
of Dollar over time, 290
of e-business activity, 4
identity crisis in Asia, 83
of imports and exports, 5
religion and, 62
VAT (Value added tax), 108, 109
Vehicle currency, 276–77
Venezuela, exports to the United States, 372
Venture capital, 438–39
VER. See Voluntary export restraint (VER)
Vertical integration, 210, 430
Videoconferencing, globalization and, 12
Vietnam
annual income in, 358
Asia, map of, **45**
attitude toward time, 57
consumers in, 350
emerging market potential, 369
globalization of production and, 10

intellectual property issues, 105
Violation, trademark, 106
Violence
  globalization backlash, 16
  terrorism and kidnapping, 96
Volume
  of international business, 5
  mergers and acquisitions (M&A), 205–6
  trade volume in gross domestic product
    (GDP), **152–53**
Voluntary export restraint (VER), 188
Voter turnaround, 87

W

Wages
  globalization impact on, 18–21, 33
  of nonmanagerial workers, 459
  statutory minimum wage rates, 427
Wall Street Journal, 270
"Wal-Mart effect," 20
Weak currency, 288
Wealth
  economic freedom and, 131
  globalization and, 20
Web. *See* World Wide Web (WWW) and
    Internet
Web sites
  of government agencies, 187
  international, pointers for launching, 54
  as a source of technological information,
    55
  as technological innovation, 13
Western Europe, intra and inter-regional
    merchandise trade, 156
Wholly owned subsidiaries
  advantages of, 388
  defined, 387
  disadvantages of, 388
Wide participation, politics, 87

Women
  in Islamic culture, 64
  in Japan, 79
  microcredit and, 263
  and social structure, 60
Work
  attitude and cultural literacy, 79
  attitude toward, 55–56
  climate, lifestyle, and, 72
Workers
  dislocation of, 20
  globalization and, 19
Working Capital Guarantee Program, Ex-Im
    bank, 185
Work teams, 335–36
World
  intra and inter-regional merchandise trade,
    156
  output and trade, 154
  political and civil liberties around, **88–89**
World atlas, 39, **41–47**
World Bank
  Bretton Woods Agreement and, 302
  country classification by Gross National
    Income per capita, 133–34, **134–35**
  defined, 17
  global challenge and, 92
  meeting in Prague, 16
  MERCOSUR report, 233, 235, **244,** 245
  policy agenda for developing countries,
    33–34
  as source of secondary data, 359
  sources of capital and, 141
  support for poverty-reduction, 73
World Economic Forum, meeting in Davos,
    Switzerland, 16
World Factbook (Central Intelligence Agency),
    359
World financial centers, in capital markets,
    264
World map (2005), **41**

World Trade Center, September 11, 2001
    terrorism and, 96
World Trade Organization (WTO)
  China's entry, 126
  creation at Uruguay Round of GATT, 194
  dispute settlement, 194
  Doha, Qatar, round of negotiations (2001),
    11, 195
  dumping and, 194–95
  and environment, 195–96
  global trading system and, 194–96
  goals of, 11, 194
  meeting in Seattle, Washington (1999), 16
  patents, 106
  subsidies, 195
Worldwide pricing, 417
World Wide Web (WWW) and Internet
  access in Eastern Europe, 74
  aesthetics and international business in
    using, 53
  cybermarkets, 266
  Eastern Europe and, 74
  e-commerce, 351
  as source of international data, 362
  as technological innovation, 12–13
  use in e-business, 4, 5
  use in getting products, 5–6
WTO. *See* World Trade Organization (WTO)
WWW. *See* World Wide Web (WWW) and
    Internet

Y

Yankee bonds, 265

Z

Zero-level channel, 415
Zero-sum game, in mercantilism, 160